THE
HUMAN RIGHTS
READER

Revised Edition

EDITED BY

Walter Laqueur
and
Barry Rubin

A MERIDIAN BOOK

MERIDIAN
Published by the Penguin Group
Penguin Books USA Inc., 375 Hudson Street, New York, New York 10014, U.S.A.
Penguin Books Ltd, 27 Wrights Lane, London W8 5TZ, England
Penguin Books Australia Ltd, Ringwood, Victoria, Australia
Penguin Books Canada Ltd, 10 Alcorn Avenue, Toronto, Ontario, Canada
M4V 3B2
Penguin Books (N.Z.) Ltd, 182–190 Wairau Road, Auckland 10, New Zealand
Penguin Books Ltd, Registered Offices: Harmondsworth, Middlesex, England

Published by Meridian, an imprint of Dutton Signet, a division of Penguin Books
USA Inc.

First Meridian Printing, October, 1979
First Meridian Printing (Revised Edition), January, 1990
13 12 11 10 9 8 7 6 5

"The Politics of Human Rights" reprinted by permission of *Commentary
Magazine* and Senator Daniel P. Moynihan © 1977 American Jewish
Committee.

The Philosophical Background
Immanuel Kant's "On the Relationship of Theory to Practice in Political
Right" from *Kant's Political Writings*, Hans Reiss, ed. © 1970
Cambridge University Press. Reprinted by permission of Cambridge
University Press.

The Standpoint of International Law
"International Law" from *International Law: A Treatise*, 2d Edition, by L.
Oppenheim. © 1912 by L. Oppenheim. Reprinted by permission of
Longman Group Limited. "Revision of Oppenheim" from *International
Law: A Treatise*, 8th Edition, by L. Oppenheim, edited by H.
Lauterpacht. © 1955 H. Lauterpacht. Reprinted by permission of
Longman Group Limited.

The Marxist Critique
"The New Class" from *The New Class: An Analysis of the Communist System*
by Milovan Djilas. © 1957 Frederick A. Praeger Inc. Reprinted by
permission of Holt, Rinehart and Winston.

The Contemporary Debate
"Statement of the Chilean Bishops" reprinted from *World Parish Newsletter*
with permission of Orbis Books.

HUMAN RIGHTS IN THE MODERN ERA

In recent years the definition of human rights has been expanded to include additional groups and areas of life. This completely updated edition of a basic sourcebook covers over eight centuries of human rights issues, fully chronicling the events, trends, and documents of the modern era—including new detailed definitions of the rights of women, children, and the handicapped, documented rights to peace and economic development, and protection against torture and religious discrimination. But amid these encouraging signs, human rights abuse continues— brutal dictatorships in Central America, political prisoners in South Africa, and the rampant spread of terrorism all over the world. This important work adresses the events, the agreements, the speeches, the conferences, and the thinkers that define human rights around the world and help shape our common future.

THE HUMAN RIGHTS READER

WALTER LAQUEUR is Chairman of the International Research Council of the Center for Strategic and International Studies, Washington, D.C., and Director of the Institute of Contemporary History and Wiener Library, London. He is the editor of two previous Meridian anthologies, THE TERRORISM READER and THE GUERRILLA READER, and author of many widely praised studies on international politics.

BARRY RUBIN is a fellow and teaches at the Johns Hopkins University School of Advanced International Studies and its Foreign Policy Institute in Washington, D.C. He is the author of INTERNATIONAL NEWS AND THE AMERICAN MEDIA and MODERN DICTATORS: THIRD WORLD COUP MAKERS, STRONGMEN, AND POPULIST TYRANTS (available in a Meridian editon).

Contents

DOCUMENTS ON HUMAN RIGHTS

Part VII: Speeches, Policy Statements and Other Documents 307

Preface

Human rights as an idea, as an issue in religious, political, and moral philosophy, have an ancient and illustrious pedigree. The differences between empirical and normative foundations of human rights, between moral rights and legal rights, between groups rights and individual rights—each of these topics has been the object of substantial intellectual disquisition. The English Bill of Rights, and more emphatically the American Declaration of Independence and the French Declaration of the Rights of Man and Citizen, were all based on the idea of inalienable, universal, and absolute rights. Nor is it true that the idea of human rights is an invention alien to most non-Western cultures and that it has been foisted on a more or less unwilling world. Even if there were no explicit covenants to that effect in traditional societies in Asia, Africa, and Latin America, the idea of freedom was hardly alien to those civilizations.

Throughout the last century it was commonly argued that international law concerned states alone, but this interpretation is no longer widely held. Though the Covenant of the League of Nations did not address itself specifically to the issue of human rights (other than the protection of certain minorities), but rather to the pacific settlement of disputes, a new approach manifested itself in the Atlantic Charter of 1941, the Declaration of the United Nations the year after, and in countless speeches of wartime leaders. This new approach found expression in the United Nations Charter and, more specifically, in the Universal Declaration of Human Rights, approved without a dissenting voice in December 1948. The President of the General Assembly, Dr. H.V. Evatt of Australia, said at the time that this was the first occasion on which the organized world community had recognized the existence of human rights and fundamental freedoms transcending the laws of sovereign states, and "millions of men, women, and children all over the world, many miles from Paris and New York, will turn for help, guidance, and inspiration to this document."

Three decades have passed since these words were spoken, but while millions of men and women have indeed turned to the Universal Declaration of Human Rights, they have received very little guidance and no help from the organization that propagated it. The failure of the United Nations to live up to early expectations and to become an effective instrument for the promotion of human rights has induced individual governments and nongovernmental bodies to take fresh initiatives in this area. In 1947 the Organization of American States

passed a declaration on the rights and duties of man; in 1950 the Council of Europe agreed on a covenant for the protection of human rights and fundamental freedoms and established a European Commission for Human Rights as well as a European Court in Strasbourg that has heard many cases since it first met in 1960. Various private bodies such as the International League for Human Rights, Freedom House, and Amnesty International have published reports about the condition of oppression in various parts of the world, drawing attention to particularly flagrant violations and on occasion mobilizing public support to bring pressure on the governments concerned. The scope of these activities and their impact were of necessity limited. But public opinion in many countries has become increasingly preoccupied in recent years with human rights, and they received fresh impetus when a new Democratic administration in the United States entered office in 1977. In his inaugural address, President Carter mentioned his commitment to human rights no less than three times.

Human rights have become a major issue in international affairs, even though it was clear from the very beginning that the walls of oppression would not crumble at the first clarion call. To speak or write on human rights is, of course, to accept that the same standards cannot be applied all over the globe. The cultural and social context, the level of development of each country, are factors that have to be taken into account. What has especially to be considered is the general trend in a country: Has there been a movement *toward* greater human rights or *away* from them? And however backward a country, there is no convincing argument in favor of torture, of arbitrary execution, of keeping sections of a population or a whole people in a state of slavery. Seen in this light, the case for human rights is unassailable.

The present volume provides a general overview of the subject. It is at the same time a work of reference and a guide to further study. It opens with essays by several distinguished students of the human rights issue, discussing the historical background as well as the philosophical and legal implications. This is followed by a documentary history of the development of the concept of human rights, and lastly a detailed bibliography.

This volume was sponsored by the Institute of Contemporary History and Wiener Library in London, an institution devoted to the study of human rights since its foundation in 1933. Our thanks are due to our contributors, and to the generous help provided by the American Bar Association through a committee which encourages the study of comparative ideologies and values.

W.L.
B.R.

London—Washington, March 1978

Preface to the Second Edition

The place taken by human rights issues on the international agenda has been in flux but has never disappeared in recent years. The debate has become more varied and complex, particularly about the issue's proper role in U.S. foreign policy. The 1980s saw a trend away from dictatorship in certain countries and more hope for an increase in human rights within the Soviet bloc than at any time since those Communist regimes came to power.

The scope of rights was broadened—both in the literature and through international agreements—but rationalizations for dictatorial regimes became more sophisticated as well. There was increasing interest in what is sure to remain a central question for humanity's future: whether the existence of an open, free society may be a precondition for economic progress beyond a certain point. The study of how different cultures define and respect rights, in often clashing ways, is also both intellectually intriguing and politically important.

Another practical and theoretical issue was the paradox of revolution. In many parts of the world, major political changes—often including violence—seemed necessary to improve the rights of the vast majority of citizens. This had been the lesson of the democratic revolutions of eighteenth and nineteenth century Europe and the United States. Yet revolution in the twentieth century, with all its ideology for improving the lot of the common people and removing roadblocks to economic and social progress, often produced worse conditions and some of history's most terrible atrocities.

As at the time of this Reader's first edition, the salient question is whether there has been a movement *toward* greater human rights or *away* from them. The matter has been further confused by the growing use of public relations' techniques both by governments—including their opponents as well as their supporters—in developing the images of regimes. An examination of actual practice is necessary.

We wish to thank Mr. F. Joseph Spieler for his assistance on this project and Hugh Rawson of New American Library for his involvement. Cecilia Alban made a valued and creative contribution by doing research for revising Parts Six and Seven.

W.L.
B.R.

Washington, April 1989

Kenneth Minogue

The History of the Idea of Human Rights

The idea of human rights is as modern as the internal combustion engine, and from one point of view, it is no less a technological device for achieving a common human purpose. The internal combustion engine moves us around swiftly, while human rights are protective devices designed to shield us from random violence and neglect. If the idea is widespread that men have a *right* to life, it may help to discourage careless aggression. Human beings badly need some sort of protection, since they are extremely vulnerable creatures. Snails have houses, chameleons can hide, and lions are strong and swift, but man is slow and soft. This point was made by political thinkers in the early modern period whenever the distinction between human and animal association was discussed. "Of all the animals with which this globe is peopled," wrote David Hume, "there is none towards whom nature seems, at first sight, to have exercised more cruelty than towards man, in the numberless wants and necessities with which she has loaded him, and in the slender means which she affords to the relieving of these necessities."[1]

The solution to the problem Hume describes is society itself. Men can cooperate more effectively and intelligently than the animals. But society in its turn brings a new threat, for unlike most other species, men need protection also against other men. The protection can never be complete, but from early modern times the idea began to develop that, in addition to eyes and ears and all the other normal equipment, human beings also possess invisible things called "rights" that morally protect them from the aggression of their fellow men, and especially from the power of the governments under which they live. The idea grew very popular and prospered, in spite of the fact that it presents many intellectual difficulties. To say that each person ought not to be killed is an easily comprehensible moral statement, however much it may in practice be violated. By contrast, the idea that each person has a "right" to life is, on the face of it, much more puzzling. The puzzling element has usually been concealed because of the fact that the idea usually comes to us accompanied by the beating of rhetorical drums,

Kenneth Minogue is Reader in Political Science at the London School of Economics, University of London.

as in the Declaration of Independence of the United States in 1776: "We hold these truths to be self-evident, that all men are created equal, that they are endowed by their Creator with certain unalienable Rights, that among these are Life, Liberty and the Pursuit of Happiness." But is the idea of rights a "truth" at all? And in what sense can an idea developed so late in human history be described as "self-evident"? The idea of rights is indispensable to modern moral discussion, but it is also a thicket of problems. The history of the idea throws some light upon these problems.

The conceptual difficulties presented by the idea result from attributing rights to a universal class such as "man." For if a right means, as it always has, the legitimate powers that may be exercised by someone holding a special position, then it is as old as the institution of human society. Every officeholder has the rights belonging to his office. Kings and consuls in the ancient world enjoyed appropriate rights, and fathers in Rome possessed a bundle of rights described as *patria potestas*. Much of the political debate of the Middle Ages revolved around the question of just how extensive were the rights of pope, king, or baron. But the point of a "right" in this familiar sense was that it distinguished one person from his fellows.

The idea of a "right" that belonged to "man" as such is clearly a major extension of this idea. The status a man enjoyed—whether it was as officeholder or noble, as citizen or clerk—had previously been legal and customary, and its value resided in its exclusiveness. Everyone had some status or other, and those of low status enjoyed relatively less protection—though even slaves could seldom be killed with impunity. The new idea of natural rights involved appropriating ideas current in philosophy and religion in order to create, by philosophical fiat, a kind of universal status from which all other forms of status were thought ultimately to derive. The problem of doing so was to provide convincing arguments to show that a right was not merely a demand dogmatically asserted in moral language; the solution in the early modern period was to derive rights from a comprehensive idea of nature which had been philosophically current for many centuries. "Nature" described the proper ordering of the universe, and knowledge of its structure was believed to be accessible to all men by virtue of the faculty of reason they all possessed. A claim to a universal status couched in terms of "rights" by itself would have been vulnerable to the charge of dogmatism; but rights derived from a conception of nature could draw upon a long and splendid tradition of thought. Hence, the word "rights" has usually been partnered by an adjective that indicates the supposed source of the rights. In the early modern period, we find ourselves dealing with "natural" rights, and in more recent times it has become the practice to talk of "human" rights. The force of the word "human" here is to indicate that the rights in question are those we believe to be an essential part of a properly human life.

It is easy enough to give a date to inventions like the steam engine, but to say when an idea first became current is much more difficult. In trying to detect this moment, we must use the familiar distinction between the medieval and the modern world. It is an elastic distinction, but historians generally agree that the modern world superseded the medieval in the course of the sixteenth century. In the medieval world, men were regarded as dangerous brutes likely to do a great deal of damage unless they were carefully circumscribed within the roles appropriate to their station in life. The moral concept appropriate to this vivid sense of the sinfulness of man is that of duty. Duties set limits to the empire of desire, and it is extremely useful to know one's duty because such knowledge removes moral perplexities. A duty is something that must be performed; it is by definition morally obligatory, while a right may or may not be exercised, according as we choose. A common and useful way of describing the change from the medieval to the modern world is to say that the idea of *duty* gave way to the idea of *right*. It was certainly not the case, of course, that the idea of duty disappeared; it merely happened that instead of beginning with the structure of the creation and deducing the duties of man, thinkers took their initial bearings from man and derived the structure of the creation.

This reversal of philosophical priorities reflected far-reaching changes in the way the more active Europeans behaved. Kings grew restless under the tutelage of the Pope, and eventually rejected his authority—no less in Catholic than in Protestant lands. Ordinary men asserted the primacy of their consciences over the traditional authority of the church. Merchants broke free of the constraints forbidding usury. Society began to swarm with adventurers seeking to make their fortunes. Generation by generation, it often seemed as if the orderly conceptions of the Middle Ages had broken down, but in time it became clear that what was happening was the painful emergence of a new type of civilization.

One of the marks of this new civilization was the assertive vocabulary of rights. Kings claimed divine right in throwing off the shackles of the Pope, and they were led on to claim ever more grandiose powers over the subjects whom they now came to dominate. But the temper of the epoch was such that subjects as well as kings were growing more willful. In England, king and subjects fell out in 1642, and a long contest took place which was not finally settled until 1688, when James II (son of the Charles I, who had been executed in 1649) fled to France, still babbling about divine right. And in that year it was clear that, so far as England was concerned, natural rights had defeated divine right.

Philosophy in the form of John Locke legitimized the victory and carried the message to other lands.

The idea of natural rights found its base in England, but its victory there was doubly ironic. Although the idea had been a commonplace of political discussion during the civil war of the 1640s, most political discussion in England tended to be conducted in historical and legal terms rather than philosophical. Although the second of Locke's *Two Treatises on Civil Government* (published anonymously in 1690) became the most famous and influential of seventeenth-century Whig utterances, it was not typical in its time, nor did it set the tone for English political discussion in the century that followed. Edmund Burke, for example, was in many respects a good Lockean—he was certainly a defender of the Settlement of 1688—but he was profoundly hostile to the idea of natural rights. They were strictly a commodity for export, particularly to France, and to the American colonies.

The second irony is that such philosophical plausibility as the idea of natural rights could claim resulted from its association with the idea of natural law—yet that tradition had seldom found England a hospitable shore. Natural law had been first elaborated by the Stoics, who based their thinking upon Aristotelian ideas of nature. It had later been taken up by the Christian Scholastics and had found its classic expression in the *Summa Theologica* of St. Thomas Aquinas. In the sixteenth century, this tradition of thought had been particularly vital in Spain and Germany, though it also found an exponent in the Englishman Richard Hooker, whose *Laws of Ecclesiastical Polity*, first published in 1593, had strongly influenced John Locke. In the seventeenth century, this tradition had been invaded by the dominant intellectual current of rationalism, leading some of its exponents to dream that natural law might become an absolutely certain and deductive system of ethics, such that men faced with a moral or political problem would merely have to calculate in order to arrive at a solution. Such had been the dream of Leibniz, and even Locke had let drop some teasing remarks about the possibility of ethics becoming no less certain a science than mathematics. He did not follow them up.

No one familiar with the civil strife that ravaged Europe from the Reformation to the end of the Thirty Years War in 1648 could fail to sympathize with any intellectual project for bringing peace. Both natural law and natural rights had this character; the difficulty, however, was that any abstract body of ideas can function in diametrically opposite ways. It might be that such ideas represented the rational solution to all human conflict, the discovery at last of the proper basis of social and political life. In that case, all that competing and quarreling parties needed to do would be to consult a competent philosopher in order to discover the correct solution to their disputes. But, as Rousseau was later to observe, for all its supposed source in man's natural and unaided reason, the idea of nature was the subject of many learned disputes and disagreements among the philosophers. If it was self-evident, it was clearly not self-evident enough. It might thus be that the idea of nature, far from being the solution to civil strife, was in fact the problem itself. For one of its implications was that ordinary men might claim the right to pronounce upon the correct ordering of society; and since ordinary men did not agree in what they pronounced, they soon fell to killing each other.

Such was certainly the view of Thomas Hobbes, whose *Leviathan*, published in 1651, transposed the idea of natural law into individualist terms.

Hobbes was the first to produce a genuinely philosophical account of something called "natural right," but it was very different from the natural rights of later time. He was also the first philosopher (by contrast with the publicists of his time) to locate the source of political authority in the people below, rather than in God above. It is easy to misunderstand the character of this change. The medieval currency of the idea of *vox populi, vox dei* reminds us that something very like this idea has its roots in early medieval thought. But in the Middle Ages, the authority was unquestionably given by God, even though the end or *telos* of the authority was the good of the people; the famous slogan uniting the voice of the people with that of God amounted to an identification of the *source* of authority with the *end* for which authority was entrusted to rulers. The consent of the ruled was often thought necessary to authority, but it was not sufficient. In the Hobbesian argument, men who live in the perilous and insecure state of nature *authorize* a sovereign to declare and enforce the rules by which they will live. The authority thus given to the ruler is virtually without limit, and the subject's duty is to obey whatever laws the sovereign may make, for that is what justice *means*. No subject may appeal against the sovereign's decision to any natural rights he imagines to be declared by his faculty of reason. Hence, in a story full of twists and paradoxes, it is notable that Thomas Hobbes, generally regarded as a supporter of Stuart absolutism, should have produced the first full-dress philosophy of government by consent. It was partly because of this element of consent that his philosophy was not popular in Stuart circles, and some of his works were publicly burned in 1685 at the University of Oxford. Nevertheless, he must be counted as an ancestor of the idea of natural rights.

But he is certainly a somewhat remote ancestor. His right of nature is not some limited right to life, or property, or happiness. It is a right to everything, "even to one another's body." It is because men have this right in the state of nature that their situation is one of war and insecurity; the first thing a rational man does with this right of nature is to get rid of it. It is renounced in favor of the sovereign, who thereafter makes the laws and protects the persons of his subjects. The right of nature is nothing more than the moral capital with which men enter into civil society and invest its ruler with authority. And once in that civil society, men lose all right except that of self-defense. One of the strongest drives in Hobbes's thought is to destroy any possible plausibility that might attach to the idea that man may rationally appeal to an external standard of rights and thereby criticize the positive laws under which he lives. It is just this capacity to appeal to one's individual conscience that Hobbes thought had plunged his country into civil war. There can be no doubt that he was an inveterate foe of the idea that (as his contemporary, the pamphleteer Richard Overton, puts it) "To every Individuall in nature, is given an individual property by nature, not to be invaded or usurped by any [man]. . . .² Yet Hobbes did shift the center of gravity in political philosophy by deriving civil authority, however remotely, from the consent of the subjects.

It was John Locke who pushed this movement very much further, and with whom we rightly associate the idea not only that the subjects authorize a government, but that they also require that it should be responsive to their wishes. Locke's *Second Treatise* has become a great classic of the liberal tradition, and any modern reader will find in it many familiar ideas. But the familiarity is in some ways misleading. The background of Locke's thought is profoundly theological: Men are God's property and may not dispose of each other, or even of themselves, entirely as they wish. The strong element of constitutionality in Locke's writings should be understood not in terms of the later practices of liberal and democratic states, but in terms of the medieval tradition from which it actually comes. And as we have seen, it is a gross error to imagine that the idea of government by consent is a modern invention. If anything, that idea was more strongly held in medieval times than it has been in modern. Nevertheless, Locke did take the existing materials of natural right and social contract and cast them in a form which later generations have found definitive. Just as the makers of the Settlement of 1688 in England were careful to conceal the novelty of their work beneath layers of traditional legalism, so also did Locke conceal the novelty and radical logic of his thought by placing it squarely in the natural law tradition represented by Richard Hooker. He did it all so plausibly as to conceal from later generations the main difficulty facing any doctrine of natural rights: namely, how to rescue it from hopeless dogmatism.

The real center of Locke's argument is in the last chapter of the *Second Treatise*, where he discusses the circumstances in which a people may legitimately overthrow a government that has breached its trust, but many later readers have looked with more attention to the arguments he presents for a natural right to property. The importance of property in Locke has provided a warrant for many interpreters[3] to see in Locke a spokesman for a class of people usually known in history textbooks as "the rising bourgeoisie." The main problem that actually concerned Locke, however, was theological rather than political. God had given the fruits of the earth in common to all men. How, then, could any particular man ever acquire the right of individual appropriation? This problem did not weigh so heavily upon medieval writers in the same tradition because they could interpret the holding of property as a trust: Those who own property have duties of charity toward the needier of their fellow men, and the property is given to them because only personal possession will impel men to keep property in good order. Such is the argument of Aquinas, living in times when property had a fixity and stability in comparison with which the men of each generation who passed over the earth looked like little more than (as Burke would say) the butterflies of a season. But Locke is concerned with individuals who own property and dispose of it at their pleasure, and he justifies their original title to property in terms of the labor they invest in developing it. This is the famous labor theory of value advanced in Chapter V of the *Second Treatise*. In the state of nature, men may pluck acorns from trees and take water from rivers for their own personal use, just so long as they only take what they need and do not prevent others from doing the like. The invention of money and the convenience of the division of labor justify the supersession of these somewhat quaint provisions, and the principle of equality is maintained by the suggestion that everyone has a property in his own person. Property and personhood are conceptually yoked together, and government is a trust whose duty it is to regulate and protect the enjoyment of these rights.

Locke's *Two Treatises of Government* was a Whig document designed to justify resistance to the pretensions of a divine-right monarchy threatening to abuse the prerogative powers attached to the English crown. And we may perhaps summarize the significance of the situation by saying that a claim to absolute right on the part of the sovereign had provoked a counterclaim to equally absolute rights on the part of the subjects. The ordinary business of government had been conspicuously incompatible with the idea of divine right under the Stuarts; it would no doubt have proved equally incompatible with a rigid doctrine of natural rights in later times. But England was saved from experiencing the latter kind of incompatibility because the idiom of natural rights did not take root in the center of British political thinking in the eighteenth century. Locke's writing was, compared with the flood of British political writing in his time, uncommonly abstract and philosophical;

it justified a highly contingent historical settlement in terms of supremely abstract principles that, had they been taken seriously, might well have been extremely disruptive. As it happens, they were taken very seriously abroad, especially in France and in the American colonies, and they did in fact turn out to be highly disruptive.

That the idea of natural rights might be politically disruptive was clear, a century after Locke, to both Edmund Burke (whose *Reflections on the Revolution in France* of 1790 attacked the idea) and to Tom Paine (whose *Rights of Man*, written in reply to Burke, restated the idea and welcomed the element of disruption). But the explosive effect of the idea of natural rights was not merely a result of its logical implications becoming more evident. It was the result of a growing sense of the progress of the human race, in which progress the discovery of natural rights and the idea of government by consent played a major part. Educated men contemplated the Newtonian account of the cosmos with wonder and pride. They looked back with dismay at the sectarian passions of the earlier modern period. They often embraced a supposedly rational religion, Deism, in preference to many of the superstitious and archaic elements of Christianity to be found especially in the Old Testament. Science even came to be applied to the operations of the mind, as Locke's epistemology was converted by Frenchmen like Condillac into a reforming psychology. As has often been observed, the era of the Enlightenment was paradoxical in that, despising the very word "enthusiasm," it yet managed to become hopelessly intoxicated with its own brand of tolerance and moderation. The men of that time were irrationally rational, immoderately moderate, and very proud of themselves. "The age we live in is a busy age," as Bentham wrote in the preface to his *Fragment on Government*, "in which knowledge is rapidly advancing to perfection." It was the destiny of the doctrine of rights to take its place in the muted millenarianism of that optimistic period of European history. Natural rights emerged fully onto the grand stage of politics toward the end of the eighteenth century, and it was associated with two revolutions. In the end, logic triumphed over Locke's own cautious temperament. The apostle of order became the prophet of revolution itself.

It would be an exaggeration, though a pardonable one, to say that at the height of its vogue the idea of natural rights toppled two powerful governments—that of George III over the American colonies, and that of Louis XVI over France. Abstract ideas have no power to act alone. Nevertheless, the idea of natural rights was the vocabulary in which these revolutions were conducted, and the idea soon came to shine with all the luster of the events and the documents with which it was associated. The American Declaration of Independence and the French Declaration of the Rights of Man and Citizen have become statements of universal significance, testaments of the highest standards in politics to which, for example, colonial peoples might appeal against their European masters. At the very moment when Europeans were preparing to spread their domination all over the globe, their philosophers were devising the instrument of recoil. Indeed, it was sometimes the case, as in British India, that the very Europeans who came to rule were in the forefront of nationalist movements.

Natural rights were the cutting edge of the ax of rationalism that toppled many of the inherited medieval traditions of eighteenth-century Europe. They were part of that general aspiration toward bringing peace and order to the world that led Immanuel Kant to think that royal dynasties were the cause of war, and that a world of republics would bring a peaceful era to mankind. Tom Paine looked forward not only to peace but to a happy anarchy marked by little taxation and minimal government regulation of the lives of men.

Yet, although the idea of rights in one form or another has proved extremely durable, the heyday of natural rights was relatively short. By the end of the nineteenth century, the philosopher David Ritchie felt impelled to defend his criticism of the doctrine by denying that he was taking a sword to an already dead dragon. "Recent experience," he wrote, ". . . has convinced me that the theory is still, in a sense, alive, or at least capable of mischief."⁴ Ritchie's argument was that the doctrine was excessively abstract and thus impeded mankind's capacity to learn from the experience of the human race. This criticism merely elaborated, in terms of evolutionary thought, much that had been said about the idea by Bentham and by Burke.

The more influential attack on the idea of natural rights, however, was voiced by Karl Marx. His interest for us is twofold. Firstly, he was a powerful critic of the received opinions on the subject; secondly, he represented a new direction of those millenarian strivings that had appeared in the course of the eighteenth-century Enlightenment.

Marx's criticism of the doctrine of natural rights was to issue in an altogether different conception of a right. The point can perhaps best be made if we say that having a right is like having an admission ticket to a club, or like having a supply of gambling chips. There is no guarantee that the club will be entertaining, or that the gambler will win anything. The slave has no right to property, though he may possibly enjoy the use of his owner's property. A free man, on the other hand, has a right to property, though he may possess little or nothing at all. Natural rights, then, are entirely formal, and all they describe is a status.

Now the actual world in which these rights were asserted was one in which some people were rich and powerful, and others were poor and powerless. Since this is a very common condition of things, it would be perilous to conclude that the doctrine of natural rights had actually brought this situation about. But opponents of the idea could, with rather more plausibility, suggest that the doctrine was designed to legitimize the inequalities that were universal in modern societies. Marx thought that the *meaning* of natural rights could be discovered if one looked to what he thought were their *consequences*. The whole idea seemed to him to be an ideological statement of the conditions necessary for the accumulation of wealth by the people who had done well out of modern industry, people whom he called "the bourgeoisie."

Marx himself thought of membership of a human community not in terms of formal rights, but in terms of what was actually enjoyed by the citizens. He thought, for example, that the right to a paid employment meant something more than merely that no man should be barred from taking employment by virtue of some irrelevant circumstance such as race or sex, and that the holder of such a right could (unlike a slave) change his employer if it should suit him. Marx considered that a right to employment meant that a job should actually be available to any bearer of the right. It is easy to see why he thought that a right to property was a meaningless mockery to the propertyless industrial workers of Europe; it is also easy to see that such an opinion quite transforms the meaning of the idea of a right. A right, construed in these terms, becomes a straightforward demand, rather than the assertion of a rule in terms of which something else might be demanded. For a natural (i.e., formal) right to work merely means that I may demand a specific job (if circumstances should make such a thing available) against any attempt to bar my claim in terms of characteristics which the right assumes to be irrelevant. Similarly, my right to property is not in itself a demand, though it may become the basis of a demand if some other citizen, or the government under which I live, should try to take my property away in some illegitimate manner. It was, of course, this right to private property which Marx thought to reveal most clearly the bourgeois provenance of the whole idea of natural rights, and he might seem to gain some support from Locke's deliberately dramatic juxtaposition of the rights of life and property: ". . . the Sergeant," Locke tells us, "that could command a Soldier to march up to the mouth of a Cannon, or stand in a Breach, where he is almost sure to perish, [cannot] command that Soldier to give him one penny of his Money. . . ."[5] This does not mean, of course, that Locke values money more than life; it merely means that the end or purpose of entering a State and the end or purpose of running an army require different things.

Marx criticizes the idea of natural rights on a variety of grounds which have since become the familiar currency of the discussion. He agrees with Burke that they are abstract and unhistorical. He regards the idea as expressing what the bourgeoisie thinks is the essence of human nature. ". . . man as he actually is," Marx tells us, "is only recognized in the form of the egoistic individual, and the true man only in the form of the abstract citizen." This particular point may confidently be regarded as a mistake. We have already observed that the modern world came into existence when individualist modes of action came to replace the communal sense of the Middle Ages, and everyone is familiar with the moral distinction between egoism and altruism. Like many other writers, Marx simply identified individualism with egoism, and a tendency to think in communal terms with altruism. An individualist, however, may well be altruistic to the point of self-ab-negation; he merely wishes to choose his own way of acting. Similarly, egoism and selfishness can appear in the most communally minded people. That I should claim the right to own property might mean that I am greedy and wish to do in my fellow men; but it might also mean many other things—such as that I enjoy taking risks, investing, saving money, and so on. And if I should acquire a great deal of property, I may spend it on my own pleasure, or I may set up charitable founda-tions for art and science, or even (as some millionaires have done) spend it financing socialist revolutions, because such is my pleasure. There is, in other words, no logical relationship whatever between a right on the one hand, and a motive (such as egoism) on the other.

The crux of Marx's criticism appears when he writes:

> But the right of man to liberty is based not on the association of man with man, but on the separation of man from man. It is the *right* of this separation, the right of the *restricted* individual, withdrawn into himself.[6]

Superficially considered, this statement falsely describes modern life, since modern men and women associate together in a great variety of ways, in families, churches, conferences, unions, and all the rest. But it is certainly true that all of these communal activities are volun-tary, and that the idea of natural rights operates to prevent the invasion of one man's right by another man, or by such institutions as govern-ment. This is the element of individuality in modern life; it is also the basis of the fundamental political distinction between the private and the public spheres of life. Such an idea is fundamental to the modern state. But Marx, it is well known, believed that the modern state should, and would, wither away. It would be replaced by a form of society in which men's communal qualities, supposedly frustrated by the alienation of capitalist life, would flow freely into a rich and supe-rior common life. Whether such a condition of things would be pref-erable is perhaps a matter of choice; but it would certainly be very different from anything we know now. It would also be a good deal less plural than the modern world. For one thing, the variety of religious beliefs would have disappeared, discarded as incomplete stages in man's realization of his full social being.[7] For another, men would be understood as producers, and as satisfiers of needs, and these are the respects in which men are least differentiated one from another. Men would be equal, and equally satisfied.

A society conceived in this way has no place for the idea of rights in the strict sense; hence, it is a tribute to the strength of the idea that the ideological tradition to which Marx belonged did choose to appropriate —indeed to extend—at least the rhetoric, if not the reality, of rights. In this way, the tradition of rights has spread to new areas, at the price of becoming much more diffuse. The social and economic rights that have been added to the traditional canon of rights are in effect statements of desirable conditions of life for every human being. In the U.N. *Universal Declaration of Human Rights*, for example, the provision of appropriate holidays with pay is included as a right, and this is admitted to be something entirely dependent upon the level of industrial development a country has reached. It would certainly be entirely meaningless in the case, for example, of the nomadic tribes of sub-Saharan Africa. In this minimal sense, at least, the new rights are undeniably historical, if by the word "historical" is meant the fact that they cannot be asserted abstractly of the entity "man," but must be related to the economic development of the country in which particular men live.

Further, we now tend to talk of "human" rather than of "natural" rights, and this is because their derivation has changed. Rights are no longer derived from the operations of natural reason, but rather from our ideas of what it is to be human. We think that a person who is malnourished, tortured, wrongly imprisoned, illiterate, and perhaps lacking in regular paid holidays is not living in a manner appropriate to a human being. Again, natural rights, being abstract and eternal, were in principle available to any thoughtful caveman who considered the matter, but we tend today to regard the idea of rights as one that evolves from generation to generation. Marx talked sarcastically of the French and North Americans as being the people who "*discovered*" natural rights, but it is not uncommon these days to believe that modern society concerned itself over the centuries with political, then with social, and then with economic rights in turn. It is in this sense that, for example, Sir Leslie Scarman, a Lord Chief Justice of Appeal, talked of "the great strides that have been made by mankind generally in the identification of rights since 1948."[8] Human rights of this kind require much more positive action on the part of whoever is charged with the running of society. The natural rights to life, liberty, and property required little more of governments and other citizens than forebearance, but the right to be provided with an actual job requires that governments shall manage the economy, and it may also require that governments shall manage the lives of their citizens in very considerable detail. To have the right to be provided with an actual job is in some ways a great practical advance upon the old natural right to work, but it has an obverse side. It is the right—which may also become a duty—to do a socially necessary job. But such a job may not at all be the kind of job the bearer of the right had in mind. The evolution of the idea of rights to a point where they may become oppressive duties is a fascinating object lesson on the relation between rhetoric and reality.

Meanwhile, however, the rhetoric of rights, as it became increasingly sundered from any very sophisticated view of reason and the nature of man, spread in two directions. One of these is the elaboration of the rights of those who were thought to have been wrongly denied the full status of "man." This class of person includes racial minorities, homosexuals, children, and, above all, women.[9] In 1792, Mary Wollstonecraft published her *Vindication of the Rights of Women*. In her dedication to Talleyrand (who had until recently been Bishop of Autun), she wrote: "If the abstract rights of man will bear discussion and explanation, those of woman, by a parity of reasoning, will not shrink from the same test. . . . if women are not permitted to enjoy legitimate rights, they will render both men and themselves vicious to obtain illicit privileges."[10] Here, then, is the idea of rights setting off on a new adventure as the argument of those seeking equal treatment. In such remarks is also to be found the classic, if slightly disingenuous, argument that the inequality is fundamentally as harmful to those who appear to benefit from it as it is to those who feel themselves oppressed. Both men and women will benefit from a liberation, Mary Wollstonecraft explains, since the time that women "choose to spend at their glass . . . is only an instinct of nature to enable them to obtain indirectly a little of that power of which they are unjustly denied a share. . . ."[11] And women's liberation has been partnered by a variety of other demands for liberation, down to and including the British National Council for Civil Liberties' call for "the right of children to determine their personal appearance."[12]

The other direction in which the idea of rights began to extend its sway was the expression of communal claims. When the individualism of the seventeenth and eighteenth centuries came to seem abstract and unhistorical, many Europeans believed that social reality was to be found in cultural groups, such as nations. Some of these people asserted that each nation should be a self-governing unity, and this political idea was advanced in the form of a "right to self-determination." In this form, it was no less disruptive of established patterns of rule than natural rights had been a few generations earlier, and in the Revolution of 1848, Europe was filled with the sounds of a new kind of turbulence. Nationalism was, by and large, hostile to the rationalism of the Enlightenment, and the basis of the right was a theory to the effect that a nation could not properly be a nation unless it was free to govern itself. National rights and human rights thus rest alike upon the abstract idea found in the adjective that partners the word "rights." In 1919, the map of Europe was redrawn in accordance with this theory, and since 1945 the modern world has seen a series of "liberations" which has increased the number of United Nations from the original 51 to over 150. As with the earlier theory of natural rights, the fundamental belief was that a moral imbalance was causing the majority of human discontents, and that once this imbalance had been removed, human beings would be happy, or at least less aggressive.

Such is the story of the idea of rights from its beginnings to its resurgence in the latter half of the twentieth century. Under U.S. President Carter, the idea became an instrument of foreign policy, and pressure was brought to bear upon America's allies and dependents to discourage them from expedients like arbitrary arrest and the torture of political opponents. In the elaborate package of agreements negotiated between the United States and the Soviet Union collectively referred to as *détente*, human rights played a pivotal role, even though skeptics suggest that the Russian government barely understands what the idea means. A glance at any newspaper will reveal the great variety of ways in which both ordinary people and professional politicians talk of rights. Were the word to be stricken from their vocabulary, they would be briefly dumb, though they would certainly find new words before long in which to state their moral convictions. And it is in that uneasy borderland between people's demands on the one hand and their moral convictions on the other that the idea of rights has always belonged.

NOTES

1. David Hume, *Treatise of Human Nature*, vol. III, Part 2, Chap. 2, (Dents, London, 1911 [1951]), p. 191.

2. *An Arrow Against All Tyrants* (London, 1646); (Exeter: The Rota Press, 1976), p. 1.

3. See, for example, C. B. MacPherson, *The Political Theory of Possessive Individualism* (Oxford: Oxford University Press, 1962).

4. *Natural Rights: A Criticism of Some Political and Ethical Conceptions*, (London, 1894), p. ix.

5. *Second Treatise*, Section 139.

6. Karl Marx, "On the Jewish Question," Karl Marx and Friedrich Engels, *Collected Works*, vol. 3 (Moscow: International Publishers, 1974), pp. 162–163.

7. Marx regards a right to choose one's religious belief as incompatible with the very idea of the rights of man as it will be fully realized. ". . . the religious spirit cannot be *really* secularised, for what is it in itself but the non-secular form of a stage in the development of the human mind? . . . Not Christianity, but the *human praxis* of Christianity is the basis of this state." Ibid., pp. 158–9.

8. "Human Rights" (Centenary Celebrity Lecture delivered at Senate House, University of London, October 13th, 1976; Subsequently published in the *University Bulletin* 39, February 1977).

9. It could even be extended to include animals, on the ground that they can certainly suffer, and may perhaps be conscious.

10. *The Rights of Women*, Mary Wollstonecraft (Everyman Edition, Dents, London, 1929) pp. 11–12.

11. Ibid.

12. See the letter to the *London Times* of May 26th, 1972, from Mr. Tony Smythe.

Maurice Cranston

What Are Human Rights?

What are nowadays called "human rights" or the "rights of man" were once called "natural rights," and men's understanding of them was linked to their understanding of natural law. Indeed, it would once have been said that just as men's positive rights derive from positive law, so do men's natural rights derive from natural law. This is a reasonable enough assertion, but it is, in some ways, a perplexing one and needs some explanation.

What is characteristic of a positive right is that someone actually has it. Positive rights are those rights conferred (or confirmed) and enforced by the system of municipal law that prevails in any country. If a man is uncertain as to whether he has a positive right, he can consult legal documents or a lawyer; if two men dispute a positive right, a court will determine which of them has the right and which of them has not. In this way, questions about positive rights can be resolved into questions about positive law, which are questions about fact. Questions of fairness are subsidiary. For example, the positive law of the United Kingdom confers on citizens of the Republic of Ireland the right to vote in English elections, whether they pay English taxes or not, and denies that right to certain British Commonwealth citizens, even if they do pay English taxes.[1] Some people feel that this law is unjust, and they may be able to argue a strong case, but such moral considerations have nothing whatever to do with the validity of the positive right that Irish citizens do have to vote in England. Positive rights are facts. They are what men actually have. What men *ought* to have is another question.

Human rights, or natural rights, plainly belong to a different logical category from positive rights. The second clause of Article 13 of the Universal Declaration of Human Rights, proclaimed by the United

Maurice Cranston is Professor of Political Science at the London School of Economics, University of London.

Nations in 1948, states: "Everyone has the right to leave any country, including his own, and return to his country." This sounds true enough. It is another way of saying what the Greeks said when they spoke of freedom as the right "to go wherever I wish and from whence I wish."[2] But it is clearly not a statement of fact. Millions of people in the world of 1948 were not, and still more millions today are not, allowed by their rulers to leave their own country and return to it. Far from this right being upheld and enforced by all the systems of municipal law in the modern world, there are numerous such systems that deny the right which is named in Article 13 of the Universal Declaration.

In what sense, then, are we entitled to call the right to leave and return to one's country a universal right? Some philosophers would reply: in no sense at all. Jeremy Bentham, for example, said: "Right is the child of law; from real laws come real rights, but from imaginary laws, from 'laws of nature' come imaginary rights. . . . Natural rights is simple nonsense. . . ."[3] Edmund Burke was of much the same opinion; he once protested that he could understand what was meant by the rights of Englishmen but not what was meant by the Rights of Man. Bentham's remark is shocking, and one hopes false, but it was worth saying because it obliges those of us who believe that talk about natural rights is *not* nonsense to say what kind of sense it is. For Bentham— and for Burke—the test of a right was "Is it actually enjoyed?" or "Is it really enforced?"—in other words, "Is it a positive right?" From this perspective—which is that of what has come to be known as legal positivism—only those rights that are positive rights are granted the name of rights at all. Burke saw the Rights of Man as mere "abstractions" while the rights of Englishmen were realities—a "positive recorded hereditary title to all that can be dear to the man and the citizen."[4]

Both Burke and Bentham had a political as well as a philosophical interest in this question. Both regarded talk about the Rights of Man as mischievous as well as meaningless. Burke, the conservative, objected to such talk because it stimulated revolutionary sentiments in the common people and introjected "false ideas and vain expectations into men destined to travel the obscure walk of laborious life."[5] Bentham, the radical, objected to talk about the Rights of Man because it produced manifestos that had no real significance in positive law, declarations that took the place of substantive legislation. Burke disliked the rhetoric that led to public unrest, and Bentham disliked the rhetoric that enabled politicians to fob off the public with words instead of deeds. Being thus attacked from Right and Left, it is not surprising that the idea of natural rights became unfashionable in the nineteenth century.

The past forty years have witnessed a marked revival of the idea of natural rights, or human rights. One reason for this revival is perhaps to be found in the great twentieth-century evils—Nazism, fascism, and other totalitarian ideologies, regimes, and wars, which all present a fierce challenge to human rights. Another reason is perhaps to be found in an increased demand for equality among men. One of the main tasks assigned to the United Nations after the Second World War was to secure what Winston Churchill called "the enthronement of human rights," and the Council of Europe has made notable efforts since the war to promote this same objective.

What Winston Churchill's word "enthronement" was intended to mean was the translation of human rights into positive rights. Since a positive right, by definition, needs a system of positive-law interpretation and positive-law enforcement to become a reality, the European-wide, or world-wide, enjoyment of human rights as positive rights depends on the establishment of European-wide, or world-wide institutions with the necessary powers. Some such institutions have already been designed and brought, on a limited scale, into existence. But for the great mass of mankind in the world, there is as yet no supranational institution that can uphold and enforce the human rights for anyone who does not have these rights already recognized by the system of municipal law under which he lives.

Are we then to agree with Bentham, and to say that for many millions of the people in the world today, the rights named in the Universal Declaration are nonsense? A man who is refused permission to leave his country may well be the first to agree with Bentham that it is nonsense to assert (as does Article 13) that "everyone has the right to leave any country." But on further reflection he might begin to admit that there is some sense in such assertions, after all. For when we speak of a right we are not simply talking about the facts of a positive legal system, and it is a distortion of language to pretend that is so. The word "right," by definition, means not only a "*lawful* entitlement," it also means a "*just* entitlement." We all of us speak of our moral rights as well as legal or positive rights. Indeed, the most common use of the word "right" is both to make a claim and to assert, in making that claim, that one is morally entitled to do so. To say, for example, "I have a right to a decent salary" is not to say "It is a fact that I am receiving a decent salary." On the contrary, the man who says he has a right to a decent salary is most likely to be the man who is *not* getting one. Kant once said we are most aware of the nature of our duty when it conflicts with our inclination; similarly, we tend to be most aware of our rights when they are *not* being recognized.

Just as a positive right belongs, by definition, to the realm of fact, of what *is*, so a moral right belongs, by definition, to the category of what *ought to be*. If Bentham's dictum is accepted, we should never be allowed to use the word "right" in this second sense of a just entitlement. And why should we allow Bentham to rob us of a very important concept, to deny the ambiguity of a word and permit only one of its traditional and accepted uses? Surely Bentham's demand is intolerably high-handed and unacceptable.

Even so, once the distinction is admitted between the logical categories of positive rights and moral rights, we confront another problem. How are we to explain and vindicate the "just entitlement" that constitutes a moral right? We have seen that the validity of a positive right can be confirmed by reference to the institutions of positive law. But how do we establish the validity of a moral right?

The kind of moral right that is the easiest to understand is the right of one person only. I, for example, claim a series of moral rights, and if called upon to justify these claims, I may put forward one of the following arguments:

(1) I may say that I have *earned* the right. If I have composed a song, I claim the moral right to impose conditions on the publication of it. I have acquired that right by the creative labor of composition: I have earned it.

(2) I may say that I have *bought* the right. If I am a publisher and have acquired, in a fair bargain, your authority to publish your song, then I have the moral right to publish it on the terms stipulated in the bargain. Buying, of course, is an exercise that depends on the existence of money. But even in a society where money was unknown, it would still be possible to acquire moral rights by barter or some other form of contract analogous to buying. Promises, or contracts, create moral rights at the same time as they institute duties.

(3) I may say I have *inherited* the right. This is a form of right that depends on the existence of a type of society where inheritance is a customary institution. But in all societies where fathers are expected to be breadwinners, a widow and a young child could reasonably claim a just entitlement to inherit a certain share of the estate of a dead man, on the grounds that in a marriage a man acquires a contractual duty toward his wife to nourish her and her children, and this gives the wife the right to expect, with her children, to be nourished from his estate if he dies before she does.

In short, we justify the moral rights of an individual by arguing that those rights have either been earned or been acquired by a binding contractual undertaking.

Besides the moral rights of one particular individual, we also speak of the moral rights of a given class of persons, such as parents, doctors, teachers, and priests. Many of the special rights of these classes of persons are set out in positive law, and are therefore positive rights, but I am concerned here with their moral rights (which may or may not be positive rights), and the justification of these moral rights. This is sometimes expressed in the language of roles. If a man enacts a certain role, he acquires certain rights. For example, if a man becomes Archbishop of Canterbury, he acquires certain moral rights that derive from the role. He may claim, for example, the moral right to be consulted by the King of England about the matrimonial arrangements of the royal family. No other person, except the person who enacts the role of Prime Minister, has this same moral right. So here we have three people with moral rights and moral duties that flow from the roles they perform. Performing the role of King of England obliges— or establishes the duty—for one man to tell the Archbishop of Canterbury and the Prime Minister about his matrimonial plans; performing the roles of Archbishop and Prime Minister gives these two men the moral right to inquire into the King's intentions.

It is worth noticing that performing a role is largely a matter of doing a set of duties, and that a man acquires the moral rights largely to the extent that he does the duties that the role imposes. A negligent or lazy Archbishop of Canterbury might well be said to forgo some (though scarcely all) of his moral rights. In this way, it would seem that the rights that derive from roles are for the most part earned rights, or closely analogous to earned rights, as well as being exclusive rights, or rights that not everybody has.

One great difficulty in the justification of natural rights or human rights is that, while they clearly belong to the category of moral rights, they cannot be justified by the kind of arguments we commonly use to justify the moral rights of the kinds I have so far considered. A human right is something that pertains to all men at all times. Therefore, it cannot be justified in the way we justify rights that are earned or are acquired by the enactment of special roles; human rights are not bought, nor are they created by any other specific contractual undertaking. They are not exclusive, they do not "go with the job." They belong to a man simply because he is a man. In the words of Jacques Maritain: "The human person possesses rights because of the very fact that it is a person, a whole, a master of itself and its acts, and which consequently is not merely a means to an end, but an end, which must be treated as such."[6]

This brings us back once more to the word "nature." In speaking of human rights, we are claiming that there is something about man's nature that entitles him to a particular respect. Natural rights can be seen in their origin as claims that everyone naturally makes. No one wants to die a violent death or be injured or bound. These aversions are so universally felt that we speak of them as natural. Furthermore, man is a being who is exceedingly vulnerable. Unlike lobsters and porcupines, *homo sapiens* has no physical defenses in his own body. The strongest man on earth can, while he is asleep, easily be killed or be injured or captured. This vulnerability gives a special urgency to his desire to avoid such fates.

It is sometimes suggested further that this vulnerability is what makes man a social animal. For his own preservation, a man must live peaceably with his neighbors, and this means he must live under some form of rules. Man is without the instincts that make ants and bees each perform a certain social role. Men have independent impulses and critical minds, so that even though man has to live in society, he can only do so if there are rules. "Natural law" is an attempt to explain the basic principles that all societies should observe in devising their rules if their system of positive law is to conform to man's natural needs and reasonable claims.

Rousseau once suggested that morality begins with human society. At any rate, man's understanding of morality is something he must owe to the experience of living in society. In society, a man can not only make a claim, he can *justify* a claim: He can speak of being morally entitled; he can use the language of moral rights. He can say not only that he does not want to be injured, but that in society, which springs from man's desire and willingness to live and let live, every man has the right not to be injured so long as he does not injure anyone else. Society creates at the same time the duty not to injure one's neighbor and the moral right not to be injured by one's neighbor.

It is, however, a fact of history that not all the civil institutions that have been set up in the world conform to these principles. Systems of positive law are often established by force or conquest, and while they do generally maintain peace and order, their edicts are sometimes more concerned with the satisfaction of some ambition than the protection of each individual's moral rights. Yet one is tempted to say, however paradoxically, that a system of law that violates the natural rights of the people does not deserve the name of law—for law, by definition, is "a system of justice," and the exigencies of justice are different only in terminology from the demands of natural law. To violate natural law is to relapse from the rule of law into the rule of arbitrary despotism. One of the things that is meant by saying that men have a natural right to freedom is to assert that the desire to be free is a natural, universal, and reasonable one; hence, it is not so much a man's desire for freedom that needs to be justified as any attempt to frustrate the satisfaction of that desire.

There is a very ancient Western tradition of belief both in the reality of natural law—a law higher than the edicts of princes—and of the universal rights that this law confers on all rational, sentient beings. Greeks, Stoics, Romans, medieval Christians, and modern rationalists have sustained much the same conception of basic moral rights that every human being possesses simply by virtue of being human. They are not rights that are conferred exclusively on its members by a particular society. They are universal. And they are inherited, so to speak, with men's humanity itself. Their very generality, however, makes it hard for us to discern these rights at all clearly.

Hence the various attempts that have been made to set down lists of human rights. John Locke, the philosopher most often quoted as an authority on the subject, wrote of the rights to life, liberty, and property. The Bill of Rights enacted by the English Parliament after the "Glorious Revolution" in 1689 named also the right to trial by jury and prescribed that there should be neither excessive bail nor excessive fines, and outlawed cruel and unusual punishments. Locke's reasoning and the example of the English Bill of Rights had a great influence throughout the world. When the American states gained their independence, several issued declarations of rights, adding to those the English had named the right to happiness (or, in more cautiously worded documents, the right to the *pursuit* of happiness).

The United States Constitution of 1789, along with the concurrent amendments known as the Bill of Rights, defined these rights in somewhat greater detail, and understandably so, since the purpose of the document was to translate moral rights into positive rights by making them enforceable in American positive law. The famous French Declaration of the Rights of Man and Citizen, which came out at much the same moment in history, named more or less the same civil and political rights, in language that was inspired more by English and American theory than by anything that belonged to French experience. It was a stirring document, but it had one great defect. It was abstract, idealistic, and had no real force in positive law, as the English Bill of Rights and the American Constitution had. It was a "Declaration," and no more than a declaration.

The U.N. Universal Declaration of Human Rights of 1948 resembled the French Declaration in that it provided no machinery whatever for passing from the abstract exercise of naming human rights to the concrete exercise of upholding human rights. It should be said in the defense of the United Nations that it did at least pass from the Universal Declaration of 1948 to the establishment of treaties and institutions for the enforcement of human rights. Not one, but *two* Covenants of Human Rights were approved by the General Assembly in 1966. It remains to be seen whether these Covenants will prove effective.

The Council of Europe has achieved more. The European Convention for the Protection of Human Rights, drawn up in Rome in 1950, was followed by the institution at Strasbourg of a Commission and a Court of Human Rights, bodies to which the individual has access as a petitioner if he believes that his rights, as set out in the European Convention, have been violated. It is perhaps ironical that access to the Strasbourg institutions is limited to the inhabitants of countries where political and civil human rights—that is, human rights as understood in the Western tradition—are already generally well respected by the governments concerned.

But even if the Western understanding of human rights is to some extent culture-bound, the rights set forth in the European Convention are not meant to be the rights of Europeans only, but to be the rights of all men. The European Convention is just as much a universal document, in this sense, as are the Universal Declaration and the Covenants of the United Nations. The European Convention confers certain positive rights on inhabitants of member states. But it claims moral rights for everyone as well—and indeed it would make no sense as a statement of *human rights* if it did not do so. Indeed, a large part of the justification of a claim to a positive right must be that it is a universally compelling claim. To establish that a thing is a right is to distinguish it from a privilege. To say, for example, that all men have a right to freedom of movement is to dispute the justice of any government which refuses to allow people to move. And this is not to make anything so vague and utopian as a statement of aspirations and ideals; it is to indict, from the perspective of justice and morality, all governments that restrain men's freedom.

It is inevitable that the rights of one individual collide, from time to time, with those of another, and there may occasionally be a conflict also between the rights of the individual and the security of the nation. But security in general is not something that is at odds with human rights, because it is itself a human right; it is a part of the right to life. The security of the individual is bound up with the security of the community; the private enjoyment of the right depends on the common enjoyment of the right. The demand for liberty and security is *not* the demand for two things that can only with difficulty be balanced or reconciled: It is a demand for two things that naturally belong together. Part of the Western understanding of human rights is the belief that a free country is safer than an unfree country. History gives us good grounds for continuing to think this is true.

NOTES

1. And some holders of British passports are not even allowed to enter the United Kingdom; for example, the "Kenya Asians" who were excluded by an act of the Labor Government in 1968.
2. Epictetus IV. I, 34.

3. *Anarchical Fallacies.*

4. Quoted in Louis I. Bredvold and Ralph G. Ross, *The Philosophy of Edmund Burke* (Ann Arbor: University of Michigan, 1960), p. 205. It would be a mistake to consider Burke a legal positivist, however, for he believed in natural law, if not in what was understood in his time as natural rights. For him, the importance of natural law was that it imposed duties rather than entitlement.

5. Edmund Burke, *Works* (London, 1832) vol. V, pp. 180-181.

6. *The Rights of Man* (London, 1944) p. 37.

Daniel P. Moynihan

The Politics of Human Rights

> There's an ideological struggle that has been in progress for decades between the Communist nations on the one hand and the democratic nations on the other. Mr. Brezhnev and his predecessors have never refrained from expressing their view when they disagreed with some aspect of social or political life in the free world. And I think we have a right to speak out openly when we have a concern about human rights wherever those abuses occur.
>
> —Jimmy Carter
> March 25, 1977

It is as simple as that. What needs to be explained is not why the United States has raised this standard, but why it has taken so long. Anthony Lewis remarks of the President:

> He is giving not just Americans but people in the West generally a sense that their values are being asserted again, after years of silence in the face of tyranny and brutality.

But again, what needs to be explained is how those "years of silence" came about, and what they signify. For there *were* reasons, and deep ones, and they could reassert themselves far more readily than any— perhaps especially the President—might suppose.

Human rights as an issue in foreign policy was by no means central to Jimmy Carter's campaign for the Presidency. It was raised in the Democratic platform drafting committee, and at the Democratic convention, but in each instance the Carter representatives were at best neutral, giving the impression of not having heard very much of the matter before and not having any particular views.

Daniel P. Moynihan, former U.S. Ambassador to India, and to the United Nations, is now a United States Senator from New York.

This is understandable enough, for by 1976 those "years of silence" had done their work. As a tactical or strategic concern of foreign policy, human rights had disappeared so completely from the councils of the West that a newcomer to the field might well never have heard the issue even discussed. Given our celebrated penchant for promptly forgetting even the most recent history, it may serve to record just how nearly total this blackout on human rights had become.

On November 12, 1975, as Permanent Representative at the United Nations, I introduced to the Third Committee of the General Assembly a United States proposal for a worldwide amnesty for political prisoners. The General Assembly, our delegation argued, had already that year taken two important steps in such a direction. A resolution had been adopted calling for unconditional amnesty for all political prisoners in South Africa. The United States had supported that resolution. Further, a resolution had been adopted calling for amnesty for all political prisoners in Chile. The United States had supported that resolution as well. But, we now asked, was there any reason to stop there? There were 142 members of the UN. Were we not all bound by the same standards that bound Chile and South Africa? There were grounds for a concern with universality in this matter which struck us with special force:

> The first is that the selective morality of the United Nations in matters of human rights threatens the integrity not merely of the United Nations, but of human rights themselves. There is no mystery in this matter. Unless standards of human rights are seen to be applied uniformly and neutrally to all nations, regardless of the nature of their regimes or the size of their armaments, unless this is done, it will quickly be seen that it is not human rights at all which are invoked when selective applications are called for, but simply arbitrary political standards dressed up in the guise of human rights. From this perception it is no great distance to the conclusion that in truth there are no human rights recognized by the international community.

This concern was not allayed by examining the list of sponsors of the resolutions already adopted on South Africa and Chile. According to the Freedom House Comparative Survey of Freedom, no fewer than 23 of the sponsors of the South African resolution and 16 of the sponsors of the Chilean resolution were countries which held political prisoners themselves.

Moreover, at the other end of the spectrum, but in a discernibly consistent pattern, that same General Assembly had adopted resolutions denouncing our own democracy for violation of human rights, and denouncing the Israeli democracy on the same score. Thus we came to the second of our concerns:

This is the concern not only that the language of human rights is being distorted and perverted; it is that the language of human rights is increasingly being turned in United Nations forums against precisely those regimes which acknowledge some or all of its validity and they are not, I fear, a majority of the regimes in this United Nations. More and more the United Nations seems only to know of violations of human rights in countries where it is still possible to protest such violations.

Let us be direct. If this language can be turned against one democracy, why not all democracies? Are democracies not singular in the degree to which at all times voices will be heard protesting this injustice or that injustice? If the propensity to protest injustice is taken as equivalent to the probability that injustice does occur, then the democracies will fare poorly indeed.

Now it might be supposed that the totalitarian nations would have gone to great lengths to suppress this American initiative. Not at all. There was no need. The other democratic nations did it for them.

There is a "Western" caucus of sorts at the UN. Somnolent in most matters, it was roused to decisive action by the threat which the American resolution presented to the peace of the UN. A meeting was called. We were asked to explain ourselves. We said we were worried about the perversion of the language of human rights and its transformation into a weapon against democracy. We also said that we thought it a good idea for the democratic world to regain the ideological initiative after the defeat we had just suffered over the Zionism-racism resolution. The explanation was greeted with a cold dismay that on the edges verged into anger. It was quickly agreed that if the resolution were somehow to pick up sponsors and to pass, the caucus would immediately insist on a formal undertaking to define the term "political prisoner." I asked: would this be carried out along the lines of the recently completed exercise to define "aggression"? Yes. But that, I said, had taken from 1951 to 1974, nearly a quarter-century. Yes. But our resolution called for amnesty, a voluntary act of governments. Inasmuch as no one would be telling governments who their political prisoners were, no formal definition was necessary. The response remained cold: the other democracies would not join in sponsoring our resolution. And there the matter ended.

Two points essential to an understanding of the issue of human rights and its political meaning are to be seen in this episode. The first is that the issue of human rights is nothing new to international politics in this age. To the contrary, *as defined by the totalitarian nations*—led in this as in so much else by the Soviet Union, no matter what other issues may divide them at one time or another—the issue of human rights has long been at the center of international politics. In fact, from the time the Soviets commenced to be so hugely armed that their "peace" campaigns lost credibility, and Khrushchev opted for Russian involvement in "liberation" struggles, this issue has been acquiring greater and greater salience. Which is to say that in human-rights terms the Western democracies have been attacked without letup. The second point is that the Western democracies, having allowed themselves to be placed on the defensive, finally ceased almost wholly to resist. In the language of diplomatic instructions, this lack of resistance was known as "danger limitation." In truth it was something very like capitulation, a species of what Jean-François Revel has called "Finlandization from within."

If anything is now to come of our initiative in human rights, these points will have to be far better understood. It needs to be understood, for example, that it was a British Labor government which was primarily behind the move in the Western caucus to disown the United States amnesty proposal. Earlier Labor governments would not in all probability have acted in this way. It was said of Ernest Bevin, Britain's first postwar Foreign Secretary, that he regarded Communism as a dissident faction of the Transport and General Workers Union—the point being that such familiarity bred contempt. By the mid-70's, a different kind of familiarity was at work. The Labor party in October 1976, for example, could invite the likes of Boris Ponomarev—head of the international department of the Soviet Communist party and a notorious vintage Stalinist—to London on a "fraternal" visit and arrange to have him received by the Prime Minister and the Foreign Secretary of a Labor government.

What was true of Britain was true of the West in general. Democratic regimes and values were under totalitarian assault in every region of the world, and resistance was everywhere weakening. The great exception was Israel, where Dr. Johnson's adage that the prospect of hanging wonderfully concentrates the mind still seemed to apply. In the West, however, the preferred contrivance for dealing with the prospect of hanging was denial. A stunning instance of just such denial was the Western response to the 1975 resolution of the UN General Assembly equating Zionism with racism. In this case, denial took the form of a refusal to recognize the extent to which Soviet inspiration lay behind the resolution.

A long-established propaganda technique of the Soviet government has been to identify those it would destroy with Naziism, especially with the racial doctrines of the Nazis. Following World War II, for example, pan-Turkish, Iranian, and Islamic movements appeared in the southern regions of the Soviet Union. They were promptly accused of Nazi connections and branded as *racist*. Jews escaped this treatment until the Six-Day War of 1967. That event, however, aroused sufficient pro-Israel, pro-Jewish sentiment within the Soviet Union to evoke the by now almost bureaucratic response. Bernard Lewis writes:

> The results were immediately visible in the vehement campaign of abuse, particularly in the attempt to equate the Israelis with the Nazis as aggressors, invaders, occupiers, racists, oppressors, and murderers.

Within a short period of time, and coincidentally with the introduction of "racist" into currency as a general term of abuse, Soviet propagandists began to equate Zionism *per se* with racism. In a statement released to the press on March 4, 1979, a "group of Soviet citizens of Jewish nationality"—making use of the facilities of the Soviet foreign ministry—attacked "the aggression of the Israeli ruling circles," and said that "Zionism has always expressed the chauvinistic views and *racist* [my emphasis] ravings of the Jewish bourgeoisie." This may well be the first official Soviet reference to Zionism as racism in the fashionable connotation of the term.

Steadily and predictably, these charges moved into international forums. In 1973 Israel was excluded from the regional bodies of UNESCO. In 1974 the International Labor Conference adopted a "Resolution Concerning the Policy of Discrimination, Racism, and Violation of Trade Union Freedoms and Rights Practiced by the Israeli Authorities in Palestine and Other Occupied Arab Territories." The charge of racism was now pressed. In June 1975 it appeared at the Mexico City Conference of the International Women's Year.

One must be present on those occasions to sense their intensity and their implications. It happens that the British critic Goronwy Rees was present at the moment the Third Committee of the General Assembly adopted the Zionism resolution. This is how it struck him:

> There were ghosts haunting the Third Committee that day; the ghosts of Hitler and Goebbels and Julius Streicher, grinning with delight to hear, not only Israel, but Jews as such denounced in language which would have provoked hysterical applause at any Nuremberg rally. . . . And there were other ghosts also at the debate: the ghosts of the 6,000,000 dead in Dachau and Sachsenhausen and other extermination camps, listening to the same voices which had cheered and jeered and abused them as they made their way to the gas chambers. For the fundamental thesis advanced by the supporters of the resolution, and approved by the majority of the Third Committee, was that to be a Jew, and to be proud of it, and to be determined to preserve the right to be a Jew, is to be an enemy of the human race.

Rees was right: evil was loose in that chamber on that day. And it is still abroad in the world. The Zionism resolution was adopted by the

General Assembly in November 1975. The following February, the United Nations Commission on Human Rights found Israel guilty of "war crimes" in the occupied Arab territories. The counts read as if they could have come from the Nuremberg verdicts:

> annexation of parts of the occupied territories
> destruction and demolition
> confiscation and expropriation
> evacuation, deportation, expulsion, displacement and transfer of inhabitants
> mass arrests, administrative detention, and ill-treatment
> pillaging of archaeological and cultural property
> interference with religious freedoms and affront to humanity.

In April 1976, in the Security Council, a representative of the Palestine Liberation Organization spoke of the "Pretoria-Tel Aviv Axis," making an explicit reference to the "axis" between Nazi Germany and Fascist Italy in the 1930's. In May, in the same body, the Soviet Union accused Israel of "racial genocide" in putting down unrest on the occupied West Bank of the Jordan River. The same month, in a General Assembly committee, a PLO document likened Israeli measures to Nazi atrocities during World War II:

> The sealing of a part of the city of Nablus is a violation of the basic human rights . . . reminiscent of the ghettos and concentration camps erected by the Hitlerites. . . .

That the purpose of all this was to delegitimize Israel in the interest of its Arab enemies was of course obvious to everyone. What should have been equally obvious was that the assault on Israel—the most vulnerable of the democracies—served a more generalized effort to deprive the democratic nations of their legitimacy as democracies. Salami tactics, as the Communists used to say—first one small unit of the democratic world, then the next. For in true Orwellian fashion, the free societies in the world were under attack precisely and paradoxically for *not* being free. *They were attacked for violating human rights.* The charge could range from genocide to unemployment, but it always followed the Orwellian principle: hit the democracies in the one area where they have the strongest case to make against the dictatorships.

Representatives of the Soviet Union and other Communist countries are not especially adept at this. But in a diplomatic maneuver which foreshadowed the military strategy of using Cuban troops as surrogates, they could sit back and allow most of the talking to be done by spokesmen from the Third World, some of whom were very good indeed at the Orwellian game. Of course, just as the Arabs had their own good reasons for attacking Israel, quite apart from any benefit to the Soviet Union, so these Third World regimes had their own good reasons for attacking democracy. With a handful of exceptions, the fourscore new nations which have come into the world in the last twenty-five years or so began their existence as constitutional democracies. By now the vast majority have succumbed to dictators and strongmen of one kind or another for whom the opportunity to attack any countries which *have* remained faithful to their constitutional vows is —to put it mildly—compelling.

Western policy has never seen the new nations in this light. For one thing, there was the tremendous investment of hope in what we saw as the small seedlings of our various great oaks and a corresponding reluctance to think, much less speak, ill of them. Then there was the trauma of Vietnam, which perhaps made it seem even more necessary that we should be approved by nations so very like the one we were despoiling. In consequence we were as thrown by these onslaughts from the Third World as we were when the Russians came up with the Cuban army as an extension of the same school of diplomacy. When in 1975 the Conference of the International Women's Year resolved that Zionism is a form of racism, the senior American diplomat present cabled Washington: "ALL ESSENTIAL AMERICAN OBJECTIVES HAVE BEEN ACHIEVED." If American diplomats could fail to recognize so egregious an attack on our own position, and were even unable to recognize that the attack had succeeded, is it any wonder that they were altogether incapable of understanding its general political significance?

Then, suddenly, everything changed. It would be hard to establish just why, but a useful axiom is that of Michael Polanyi: People change their minds. They wake up one day to find they no longer think as they did. Something like this happened in the case of human rights. One could see the evidence, for example, in the drafting committee for the 1976 Democratic platform. Sam Brown, representing what might be termed the McGovernite forces in the party, introduced a resolution demanding that all American military aid be cut off to regimes that did not respect human rights. Brown's resolution was directed against authoritarian regimes of the Right and was in the spirit of the Foreign Assistance Act of 1973 which called on the President to "request the government of Chile to protect the human rights of all individuals." I thereupon spoke for what might be called the Jackson forces in the party. The Jackson amendment to the Trade Act of 1974 was directed against certain policies of the same administration which in effect supported dictatorships of the Left. "To assure the continued dedication of the United States to the fundamental human rights," declared the amendment, no credits were to be extended to non-market economies which denied their citizens the right to emigrate on reasonable terms.

The Brown proposal, we suggested, was too much a convenience for those nations which get their hardware from Czechoslovakia, and want their soft loans from the United States. Why not oppose any form of aid? "We'll be against the dictators you don't like the most," I said across the table to Brown, "if you'll be against the dictators we don't like the most." The result was the strongest platform commitment to human rights in our history. Whether or not it was this commitment which directly influenced the new President to take the offensive on human rights, he began doing so from the very first, in his inaugural address.

The problem now is to sustain the initiative. For not everyone in America—or at any rate in the American government—has changed his mind. The President, unavoidably, is getting the same advice that led to the passivity of his immediate predecessors. The State Department is uneasy about Soviet anger. The cult of the Third World is, if anything, greater now than ever. It is entirely possible the whole initiative will come to nothing if we do not establish a sufficiently firm conceptual base to sustain the inevitable tremor and shock.

Four principles come to mind on which to construct such a base.

First principle: *International law and treaty obligations are wholly on our side*. That for so long a period we appear to have forgotten this gave an inestimable advantage to the totalitarians. The Soviet reaction to the signs that our memories are stirring has been angry. But this "surprising adverse reaction to our stand on human rights," as the President recently characterized it, will get worse, not better—they would be fools to respond in any other way. The more then should we know and understand that the law is on our side.

The United Nations Charter imposes two obligations on members. The first, which is well-known, is to be law-abiding in their relations with other nations: not to attack them, not to subvert them, and so on. But there is a second obligation, which very simply is to be law-abiding in the treatment of one's own citizens. The United Nations Charter requires that members govern themselves on liberal principles, as these principles have evolved and are understood in the Western democracies.

Improbable as this may sound, it happens nonetheless to be true. The Charter, in the main, was drafted by British and American constitutional lawyers. The Preamble speaks of "fundamental human rights," of "the dignity and worth of the human person," of "the equal rights of men and women." Article I enjoins the members to promote through the UN

respect for human rights and for fundamental freedoms for all without distinction as to race, sex, language, or religion.

The meaning of these words, as lawyers say, is entirely discoverable. They mean just what any of us in the Western democracies would assume they mean.

The Russians knew what they were signing. We do well to remember that they began World War II as allies of Nazi Germany, partners in the conquest and partition of Poland. They had a true pro-Nazi past to overcome. In the early days of the United Nations they sought to do this by taking the lead in asserting that members had to be—liberal states! In the first year of the new organization, the question arose as to whether Spain should be admitted to membership. Absolutely not, said Andrei Gromyko in the Security Council: to the contrary, punitive measures should be taken against Spain. Then in December 1946, on the initiative of Poland, the General Assembly adopted a resolution directed to Spain providing that

> . . . if within a reasonable time there is not established a government which derives its authority from the consent of the governed, committed to respect freedom of speech, religion, and assembly, and to the prompt holding of an election in which the Spanish people, free from force and intimidation and regardless of party, may express their will, the Security Council consider the adequate measures to be taken in order to remedy the situation.

Poland and all the Communist members voted in the affirmative. (Spain was not admitted until 1955.)

Today there is not one member of the United Nations in five which can meet the standard of the Polish resolution. And yet it is those very nations who go about attacking members who do maintain those standards. There is a term for this: the big lie. But clearly, as we have been seeing, a counterattack can be devastating.

This brings us to the second principle: *Human rights is a political component of American foreign policy, not a humanitarian program.* It is entirely correct to say (as was repeatedly said during all those "years of silence" in Washington) that quiet-diplomacy is much the more effective way to obtain near-term concessions from totalitarian regimes with respect to particular individuals who seek our help. But the large result of proceeding in this fashion is that the democracies accommodate to the dictators. Concepts of human rights should be as integral to American foreign policy as is Marxist-Leninism to Soviet or Chinese or Yugoslav operations and planning. Yet it seems clear that this is not what the career officers in the State Department who make up the permanent government wish to see, and the signs already suggest that the Secretary of State is not resisting the permanent government.

At Law Day ceremonies on April 30, Cyrus R. Vance delivered his first public address since becoming Secretary of State, and chose for his subject "Human Rights and Foreign Policy." "Our human-rights policy," he said, "must be understood in order to be effective." He would "set forth the substance of that policy, and the results we hope to achieve."

This effort was surely in order, for the policy was still singularly unformed. The President's single sentence in his inaugural address—"Because we are free we can never be indifferent to the fate of freedom elsewhere"—had led to press speculation, then queries, then to a sequence of presidential acts—e.g., the letter to Andrei Sakharov, the meeting with the Soviet dissident Vladimir Bukovsky, and partial statements such as those in the address at the United Nations on March 17—but still nothing that could be described as a policy. The impression was that of a President responding at successively higher levels of commitment to successively greater levels of approval, but with no very clear notions of where it would all come out. There is nothing much the matter with this in a democracy. But there comes a time when the agents of policy must be told *what to do*. This is a Secretary's task, and Vance undertook to perform it.

The result, it must be stated, bodes disaster. The Secretary's speech missed the whole point. For the entire thrust of his speech was to assert that human rights is not a political issue but rather a humanitarian aid program, a special kind of international social work. After rousing the rage of the Muscovite and the scorn of Latin American grandees, after stirring the timorousness of European allies and inducing something between anxiety and fear in smaller capitals around the world, it turned out that all we really intended was to be of help to individuals.

Freud's remark that anatomy is destiny has been used to suggest the importance of organization in government. The Ford administration established a "Coordinator for Human Rights and Humanitarian Affairs" in the office of the Secretary of State. The Coordinator had three deputies: "Refugee and Migration Affairs," "Prisoners of War and Missing-in-Action," and "Human Rights." To reflect the greater salience which these issues are now to have, the Carter administration has asked Congress to make the Coordinator an Assistant Secretary. However, in the past, when this kind of change has been made, it has in fact signaled that the Secretary of State was no longer that much interested in the issue involved, and was turning it over to the bureaucracy. Thus, only a few years ago, coordinators or special assistants for environmental affairs and population matters were to be found in the Secretary's office. But with the fading of those issues, they were turned over to the office of the Deputy Assistant Secretary for Environmental and Population Affairs, reporting to the Assistant Secretary for Oceans and International Environmental and Scientific Affairs. Secretary

Vance may not intend to relegate human rights to the destiny of departmental routine, but in organizational terms, this is what he has done.

Rounding out the pattern of a depoliticized conception of human rights, the Secretary in his speech announced:

> We are expanding the program of the Agency for International Development for "New Initiatives in Human Rights" as a complement to present efforts to get the benefits of our aid to those most in need abroad.

He added that the Department's Bureau of Educational and Cultural Affairs would also be involved. He declared our efforts would "range from quiet diplomacy . . . through public pronouncements, to withholding of assistance." We would meet at Belgrade in June to review the Helsinki accords and "to work for progress there on important human issues: family reunification, binational marriages. . . ." He mentioned "that many [*sic*] nations of the world are organized on authoritarian rather than democratic principles." He did not mention totalitarian governments. Nor might he, so long as the foreign service has its way. If the foreign service prevails, the Secretary of State will soothe the Soviet Union and only challenge Ecuador.

Can one already detect this influence not only in the Secretary's statements but even in the President's own more recent words? Only weeks ago, expressing his surprise at the "adverse reaction in the Soviet Union to our stand on human rights," Mr. Carter said: "We have never singled them out. I think I have been quite reticent in trying to publicly condemn the Soviets. I have never said anything except complimentary things about Mr. Brezhnev, for instance." But the Soviets are *necessarily* singled out by any serious human-rights offensive—and they know it. They are singled out by the force of their arms: they are the most powerful opponents of liberty on earth today. And they are singled out by the force of their ideology which, since the passing of Naziism and the eclipse of fascism as a school of political thought (Franco's Spain having been its last paltry bastion), remains the only major political doctrine that challenges human rights *in principle*. When the authoritarian regimes of the Right violate human rights nowadays, they generally do so not in the name of a different political creed but in the name of national security. They must torture, they say, to uproot guerrillas and terrorists; or they must keep political prisoners to protect themselves against armed subversion from without and within. Unlike the Soviets and their ideological progeny in other countries ruled by Marxist-Leninist regimes, these right-wing regimes do not deride liberty as a "bourgeois" illusion. They commit abominations in practice; the Communist countries commit abominations on principle. Anyone who cares about human rights will know what type of abomination is the more destructive of those rights.

According to a presidential aide quoted by the New York *Times*, the President's human-rights initiative, among other things, has alarmed the Soviet leadership. The Soviets had "viewed the United States under the Ford and Nixon administrations . . . as running a kind of defensive, rear-guard foreign policy of retreat. . . . Mr. Carter and his advisers feel the Soviet leaders have been dismayed by the thought that their concept of the decline of the West might no longer be valid."* If the human-rights initiative turns out to be serious, the Soviets will have good cause to be dismayed at the stirring of a new American will to resist the advance of totalitarianism.

But here again, the permanent government can be expected to push in exactly the opposite direction—toward a policy of reassurance and accommodation. Indeed it already has, and with some success, to judge by the President's commencement address at Notre Dame, the first and still most comprehensive statement of the foreign policy of his new administration. The President begins in this speech by reaffirming "America's commitment to human rights as a fundamental tenet of our foreign policy." But when he goes on to explain what this commitment requires of us, he suddenly changes the subject:

> Abraham Lincoln said that our nation could not exist half-slave and half-free. We know that a peaceful world cannot long exist one-third rich and two-thirds hungry.

This is a most startling and extraordinary transition. The first sentence reminds us, truly, that the world today *is* half-slave and half-free. Out of four billion persons, something approaching a billion-and-a-half live in totalitarian Marxist states. We have come to think of this opposition as the East-West conflict. But then, having thus reminded us of it, the President immediately directs our concern away from this conflict to quite a different matter, that of relations between the industrial North and the developing South. He even calls on the Soviets, as part of the former group, to join in "common aid efforts" to help the latter (although the Soviets accept no responsibility whatever for the plight of the developing world: in their unwavering view it is all our fault).

The implication seems clear: we are to divert our attention from the

---

* June 26, 1977. The *Times* may not have known it, but it was onto a government secret here of possibly more interest than the Pentagon Papers. In the first half of the 1970's the Democratic opposition generally attacked the foreign policy of the Nixon-Kissinger-Ford era as aggressive, risk-taking, and sometimes mindlessly anti-Communist. In truth, within the Republican administration itself, and at least within the more sophisticated circles of the Democratic opposition, it was understood that, to the contrary, what was going on was precisely a "kind of defensive, rear-guard foreign policy of retreat. . . ." Moreover, it was understood that the Russians understood it this way.

central political struggle of our time—that between liberal democracy and totalitarian Communism—and focus instead on something else. We can do this, says the President, because we are now "free" of the "inordinate fear of Communism" which led us at times to abandon our values for the values of the totalitarians. But was our fear of Communism "inordinate"? And is there nothing to fear from Communism today? Does the President mean to suggest that the military and ideological competition we face from the Soviet Union has declined? If so, why have the Soviets engaged in a massive military buildup? And why do they continue and even intensify their ideological offensive against the West?

Whatever his answer to these questions, the President does state explicitly that it was our "inordinate fear of Communism" which led us to the "intellectual and moral poverty" of the war in Vietnam. This causal connection can also be challenged. Some of us said at the time that the enterprise was doomed, because it was misconceived and mismanaged. Are we to say now—in this, echoing what our enemies say of us—that it was also wrong or immoral to wish to resist the advance of totalitarian Communism?

This brings us to the third principle; *Human rights has nothing to do with our innocence or guilt as a civilization. It has to do with our survival.* The President has staffed the Department of State and the Department of Defense with curiously opposite groups of persons who have attracted each other in a not wholly reassuring way. Put plainly, the leading foreign-policy and defense-policy officials of the administration are men who made their reputations running the war in Vietnam. The second echelon of officials made its reputation by opposing that war. There is something troubling in this cross-generational relationship. Put plainly once again, the top echelon seems to be seeking absolution from its juniors for what the President himself now calls the "moral and intellectual poverty" of its ideas in the past.

Of the Secretary of State, Hedrick Smith, chief of the New York *Times* Washington bureau, has reported:

> With the hindsight of history, Secretary of State Cyrus R. Vance, who as Deputy Secretary of Defense played a major role in the American buildup in Vietnam, has publicly said that he now feels that "it was a mistake to intervene in Vietnam." And those who know him well say that the Vietnam war is the single most important experience in shaping this current outlook.

One does not ask of the Secretary that he not be influenced by that experience: only that he be thoughtful about it. (At the University of Georgia Law School, where he spoke on Law Day, he shared the platform with Dean Rusk, a Secretary of State who came to office preoccupied with "the loss of China"—the opposite experience.) The Vietnam war was a mistake because we could not successfully halt a totalitarian advance there—not at costs acceptable to a liberal society. But it did not end the expansion of totalitarianism, nor yet the need to resist. If anything, it added enormously to the importance of ideological resistance, and this precisely is the role of "Human Rights in Foreign Policy."

Guilt as a political weapon is but little understood. Still, it should be evident that it is used quite effectively within the United States and against the United States. Some years back Nathan Glazer observed that the political rhetoric of our age was capable of depicting a prosperous and tolerant and reasonably creative society such as our own as utterly detestable—and could persuade many of those best off in this society that this is exactly the case. In 1977 an Associate Justice of the Supreme Court declared in an opinion handed down from that bench that it were better never to be born than to be born an American and go to "second-rate" schools.

The President—any President—will face particularly subtle variations on the theme of guilt, a worldly, ex-ambassadorial, Council-on-Foreign-Relations concern that we Americans are such inveterate moralizers. Washington is awash with former cold warriors (they were only *giving* orders) who, having failed so miserably in their monstrously misconceived adventure in Vietnam, have decided that the country really is hopeless, that it has no capacity to resist the advance of totalitarianism, and that the best thing to do is to accommodate and to appease.

There is no way to deal with this save to raise it to the level of awareness, and to repudiate it. Human rights is a weapon in the struggle for the survival of the nation—a nation partly right and partly wrong, as it ever has been and doubtless ever will be. That we have a right and a duty to survive ought to be too obvious to need saying explicitly. That it is not obvious to our political culture is a measure of how savagely our guilt is turned against us.

Guilt has among other things paralyzed us in our relations with the developing world—and this leads to the fourth principle of a sound human-rights policy: *The new nations must be made to understand that our commitment to them depends on their ceasing to be agents of the totalitarian attack on democracy.*

Only a handful of these nations are Soviet satellites. But a Marxist might well say that time and again they *objectively* support the Soviet cause. The concept of objective political behavior is, of course, a favorite debating device of Marxists. Thus, Lucio Lombardo Radice, a leading member of the Central Committee of the Italian Communist party, recently explained in an interview in *Encounter* how Stalin in the 1930's realized the dangers of Naziism and ceased attacking Western Social Democrats. "In the situation existing at the time, Stalin was, objectively speaking, supporting the struggle for freedom, democracy, and peace." The time has come to explain to the representatives of a great many nations for which on other grounds we have a good deal of sympathy that, "objectively speaking," they are supporting anti-Semitism, totalitarianism, and war.

An example was on display in June 1977 at the International Labor Conference in Geneva. The American labor movement is one of the few groups to have sensed early on the drift of world events and Soviet tactics. In 1974, after the International Labor Organization passed a resolution denouncing Israel for racism, the labor movement, supported by the business community, asked that the United States give notice that we would withdraw if such intrusions of anti-democratic politics into the proceedings of ILO did not stop.

The ILO charter requires a two-year notice of intent to withdraw, and this was given in the fall of 1975. The letter made clear that the United States did not want to withdraw. We, after all, had helped to found the ILO at the Paris Peace Conference in 1919. We had joined it when we never joined any other of the League organizations. We have provided the great share of its funds, and it was we who helped turn its attention to the problems of developing nations which now almost exclusively concern it. All we asked was that it stay out of international politics of the kind associated with foul-mouthed excoriations of Israel. This position was characterized by *Trud*, the Soviet labor paper, as a demand by "reactionary circles, and primarily the U.S. delegation . . . to exclude . . . political questions connected with the people's struggle against imperialism, neo-colonialism, and racism."

We got our answer on June 3. "Using a procedural device," the New York *Times* reported, "the Communist and Third World countries blocked action on an American-inspired proposal that the assembly's rules be amended to screen out politically motivated resolutions." With a handful of exceptions, the Third World sided with the Communist world against the democratic world.

On June 22, the Secretary of Labor, Ray Marshall, told a press conference that the United States will now likely leave the International Labor Organization. It is a little heartbreaking to those who have cared much about this organization which once seemed to hold such promise. But why did it happen? Because the Third World *objectively* chose to back Communism against democracy. *They* know this. And they will make a distinct judgment about which way the world is headed depending on whether we make clear to them that we know it.

Jean-François Revel puts the case at the most extreme in his new book, *The Totalitarian Temptation*. He describes a world struggle between a truly revolutionary democratic model of society (to give Secretary Vance his due, he did quote Archibald MacLeish: "The cause of human liberty is now the one great revolutionary cause") and a "Marxist-Leninist-Maoist model, with all its little brothers," implementing a brand of totalitarian socialism which Revel calls "unofficial Stalinism." These, Revel writes, are the real reactionaries, but in his view they are winning, because more and more the world finds such regimes to be more attractive:

> Therefore . . . the new American revolution, or the new world revolution that started in America, will probably fail—not because of the United States but because the world steadily rejects democracy.

This is the "worst case," and there are those who are resigned to it and appear already to have made their peace with it. Thus, George Kennan in his new book, *The Cloud of Danger: Current Realities of American Foreign Policy*, asserts that democracy is a North Atlantic phenomenon, and in no way a "natural form of rule for people outside those narrow perimeters." It were folly and worse, he maintains, to go about correcting and improving "the political habits of large parts of the world's population."

This is an arguable point—does it not display a lofty disdain for what is after all a well-documented and universal human aspiration, namely, the desire to be free? But my point is a different one. I believe that Mr. Kennan underestimates the impact *on the democracies* of the totalitarian attack (for example: in 1977 more than half a dozen *British* universities banned Jewish spokesmen from their campuses on the ground that Zionism was a form of racism). Most of the world is not free, and what we can do about that is problematic. But surely we can do something—surely we should do everything—to preserve that part of the world which *is* free. The point, Revel's point, in putting the case at its worst is not to become resigned to the present state of affairs but to elicit countermeasures that will prevent the worst case from coming true. And it is here that the issue of human rights becomes essential.

For the moment our first task is our own defense. An implacable, forceful, and unvarying counterattack—"castigating mercilessly the prevailing mendacity," as Walter Laqueur puts it—whenever the issue of human rights and the nature of our respective societies is raised by our adversaries or their objective allies could yet save the democratic world from "Finlandization from within." Human rights is the single greatest weapon we have left for the defense of liberty. It would be calamitous if we allowed ourselves to be robbed of it by the voices of fear and guilt, inside the government or out.

Dennis J. Driscoll

The Development of Human Rights in International Law

I

Over the last three decades, the international political system has undergone a number of changes which now distinguish our present system from any previous historical system. The most visible change, no doubt, is the geometric growth in the number of states in the system itself. One manifestation of this change is membership in the United Nations, which has grown from its original membership of 51 to its present membership of 149. But other changes are even more profound. The growth in the number of states in the system has been accompanied by a growing interdependence which has intimately wed the fate of one state with the domestic and international policies of others.[1] There has, moreover, been a phenomenal growth in the "rules" of the international system. Perhaps the most remarkable development in this regard has been the growth of rules with regard to human rights, the subject of this essay. It is difficult to capture in so brief an essay the phenomenon of the developing international protection of human rights; only the most salient institutional features will be outlined, and readers are referred to the literature cited in the footnotes for detailed discussion.[2]

In the past, international law was not concerned with events within a state's jurisdiction. The greater part of the law concerned matters of external conduct and problems of privileges and immunities. What went on *within* a state's jurisdiction was, for the most part, purely the state's own affair. Such matters were matters of "domestic jurisdiction" and were, by definition, outside the scope of international law. One of the most sacrosanct matters of domestic jurisdiction was a state's treatment of its own nationals. Hence, protests about a state's treatment of its nationals were legally unwarranted, and, in fact, such protests rarely occurred. This position has changed utterly since the establishment of the United Nations. Basic issues of human rights are now governed by

Dennis J. Driscoll is Senior Lecturer in Law at the National University of Ireland (Galway). One of his special interests is the international protection of human rights, and he has acted as a consultant to Amnesty International. He is the author of *International Law and International Terrorism* (forthcoming).

treaty and by customary international law, and it can now no longer be maintained that human rights are exclusively matters of domestic jurisdiction. It is fair to say that what has occurred is a revolution in international legal affairs.

It has just been seen that before the establishment of the United Nations, questions of human rights were matters of domestic jurisdiction. However, there were a number of exceptions to this general proposition.[3] Probably the most important exception concerned the duty of states to observe certain minimum standards in their treatment of aliens.[4] Failure to observe the appropriate standards resulted in the duty to compensate the state of which the alien was a national, because the wrong, in legal theory, was considered to have been done not to the alien, who was not a subject of international law, but to his state.

The second such exception concerned slavery and the slave trade.[5] The difficulty of abolishing slavery at a stroke was recognized. The first step, then, was to secure the abolition of the slave trade itself, and from 1814 onward, at Great Britain's initiative, a number of bilateral treaties dealt with its suppression.[6] In 1926, in the Slavery Convention, the states parties undertook in Article 2 to "bring about, progressively and as soon as possible, the complete abolition of slavery in all its forms."

The third exception concerned the rights of certain persons in times of armed conflict.[7] Treaties of 1864, 1906, and 1929 regulated the rights of the wounded in armies in the field; the wounded at sea and also the civilian population were regulated by treaties in 1907; and prisoners of war were dealt with by treaty in 1929.

The last principal exception concerned the rights of minorities.[8] The first system-wide guarantees for minorities occurred at the end of the First World War. It was decided that all new or substantially enlarged states at the Peace Conference, and also any state thereafter applying for membership in the League of Nations, should be required to undertake certain international obligations with regard to their minorities. These obligations were placed under League "guarantee"; any member of the League Council had the right to bring a complaint to the Council's attention, and the Council could take whatever action was deemed "proper and effective." Each of these treaties intended to safeguard minority rights guaranteed the fundamental rights of life, liberty, and freedom of religion to all inhabitants. All nationals were declared equal before the law and had the right to the equal protection of the law. Additionally, the minorities were guaranteed freedom from discrimination, freedom of language, the right of establishment of minority institutions, and the right of access to public monies for minority institutions. It was thought that states would petition the League Council in the event of the violation by a state of its minority guarantees. This in fact hardly ever happened. Well over 90 percent of the petitions were lodged by members of the minorities themselves. This comparative lack of State complaints is of interest because it reveals the real reluctance of states to complain about the human rights violations of other states, a reluctance which has been seen with even greater clarity in recent years.

II

The remarkable developments in human rights law after the Second World War began with the inclusion of certain human rights provisions in the United Nations Charter. Article 1, which sets out the fundamental purposes of the United Nations, provides that one of the purposes is to "achieve international cooperation in promoting and encouraging respect for human rights and for fundamental freedoms for all without distinction as to race, sex, language or religion." In Article 55, it is provided that the United Nations shall promote ". . . universal respect for, and observance of, human rights and fundamental freedoms . . ." In Article 56, member states undertake "to take joint and separate action in cooperation with the Organization for the achievement of the Purposes set forth in Article 55."[9]

The precise legal significance of the pledge by member states to take joint and separate action to promote human rights has been a point of contention. It has been argued by many international lawyers that the cumulative legal effect of the human rights provisions of the Charter cannot be ignored and that the principle of good faith in treaty interpretation necessitates the conclusion that member states are under a duty to observe fundamental human rights. From this point of view, U.N. member states have undertaken definite, albeit not clearly delineated, legal obligations toward the inhabitants of their territories by the mere act of ratification of the United Nations Charter.[10] It has also been argued, on the other hand, that the language with regard to human rights used in the Charter does not admit of the interpretation that true legal obligations are imposed. The words of the Charter refer to "promoting," "encouraging," and "assisting in the realization of" human rights, and not to "guaranteeing" or "protecting" them.[11] It is emphasized, in addition, that the human rights provisions of the Charter do not identify those rights which are to be promoted and that it is impossible to speak of a "right" unless its precise legal content is known.[12] This issue was settled, finally, by the International Court of Justice in 1971 when the Court held, in the *Namibia Case*, that the Charter does indeed impose upon member states legal obligations with regard to human rights.[13]

No commentary on the human rights provisions of the Charter is complete without a reference to the Charter's "domestic jurisdiction" clause, though it in fact contains no explicit mention of human rights at all. Article 2 (7) of the Charter provides that "nothing contained in the present Charter shall authorize the United Nations to intervene in matters which are essentially within the domestic jurisdiction of any State. . . ." A state endeavoring to prevent U.N. discussion of a particular human rights situation, whether in its own country or in any other, has invariably invoked this provision as the legal basis for preventing discussion.[14] The invocation of Article 2 (7) in this manner is not without legal plausibility because, as has already been seen, hitherto a state's treatment of its nationals was a principal example of a matter of domestic jurisdiction. However, as the Permanent Court of International Justice emphasized over fifty years ago, "the question whether a certain matter is or is not solely within the domestic jurisdiction of a State is an essentially relative question; it depends upon the development of international relations."[15] The cumulative effect of the legal provisions of the Charter, of the Universal Declaration of Human Rights and other instruments, and of subsequent state practice, is that human rights are no longer matters of domestic jurisdiction alone. They have become internationalized both politically and in law. As a consequence, "whenever there has been a complaint on the grounds of violation of human rights, the near-uniform practice of the United Nations has been to ignore the claim of domestic jurisdiction when raised as an objection, to assume jurisdiction and to discuss the matter and adopt resolutions relatively freely, thus giving a restrictive interpretation to the domestic jurisdiction provision and making it practically ineffective with regard to the questions relating to human rights."[16]

The next achievement of the U.N. Charter, aside from the prominence given to human rights in the articles already mentioned, was to provide for the establishment of a commission "for the promotion of human rights."[17] This commission, the Commission on Human Rights,[18] was set up as a subsidiary organ of the Economic and Social Council in 1946. The Commission is presently composed of thirty-two members who act as representatives of their respective governments and who meet annually for a period of approximately six weeks. The Commission's principal activities have been the preparation of studies, recommendations, and instruments of a general character that serve to promote the observance of human rights. Undoubtedly the most important tasks of the Commission have been the drafting of the Universal Declaration of Human Rights and of the 1966 International Covenants on Political and Civil and on Economic, Social, and Cultural Rights, all of which will be discussed below. The Commission is assisted by a Subcommission on the Prevention of Discrimination and the Protection of Minorities,[19] which, unlike the Commission, is composed of eighteen individuals who are not, at least formally, representatives of governments. Rather, in theory, they act in their personal capacity, and for this reason the Subcommission is often seen as a far more vigorous and commendable body than the Commission itself.

The first task of the Commission on Human Rights was the preparation of an international bill of rights. It was decided in 1947 that the term "International bill of rights" should apply to the entirety of documents contemplated and in preparation: a declaration, a convention or covenant, and measures of implementation. The first of the documents prepared, the Universal Declaration of Human Rights, was passed unanimously by the General Assembly on December 10, 1948.[20] Many of the rights proclaimed in the Declaration are basic ones: the right to life, liberty, and security of person (Article 3); freedom from slavery (Article 4); freedom from torture (Article 5); the right to freedom from discrimination and to the equal protection of the law (Article 7); the presumption of innocence until proved guilty (Article 11); the right to freedom of thought, conscience, and religion (Article 18); and the right to freedom of opinion and expression (Article 19). But the Universal Declaration differs from classical catalogues of human rights because it deals not only with the traditional civil and political rights but also with economic, social, and cultural rights. The Declaration goes on to provide for the right to social security (Article 22), the right to work (Article 23), the right to equal pay for equal work (Article 23), the right to an adequate standard of living (Article 25), and the right to education (Article 26).

All the rights articulated in the Universal Declaration were not seen as rights in the technical sense of legally enforceable rights. The Universal Declaration, like most General Assembly resolutions, was not regarded as legally binding. This point was emphasized time and again by states when discussing the Declaration prior to its adoption. It is appropriate to ask, "What, then, is the significance of the Universal Declaration? How can we estimate its value to us?" Estimating its value is a difficult exercise. For one thing, we would have to know the effect in social psychology of exhortatory statements on states and on people. And we do not know that. But nevertheless, there are a number of categorical statements that can be made about the Universal Declaration because there are at least three areas in which the effect of the Declaration has been felt and can be measured: (1) *decisions made by the United Nations*—ever since the promulgation of the Declaration, it has been used as a standard of conduct and as a basis for appeals in urging governments to take measures to observe human rights;[21] (2) *treaties*—a number of global and regional treaties have been prepared that transform the Universal Declaration into international conventional law;[22] (3) *national constitutions, legislation, and court decisions*—the domestic law of many states has shown the marked influence of the Universal Declaration.[23] As a consequence, it can justifiably be said that influence of the Universal Declaration has been profound. Many scholars claim that the principles contained in the Declaration are now part of customary international law.

The undertaking by the United Nations to enact an international bill of human rights was completed in December 1966 with the adoption by the General Assembly of the International Covenant on Civil and Political Rights and of the International Covenant on Economic, Social and Cultural Rights. The covenants contain more detailed versions of the rights articulated in the Universal Declaration. Since the Universal Declaration may now be part of customary international law, and therefore binding upon all states in the international system, the chief interest in the covenants is that they contain enforcement procedures to ensure that states ratifying them fulfill their obligations in good faith. Each covenant provides for a reporting procedure under which states ratifying the covenant report periodically on the measures they have adopted which give effect to the rights contained therein and on the progress made in the enjoyment of those rights.[24] The reporting procedure is a technique adopted from the International Labor Organization, which has used the technique, or at least so it is traditionally argued, with real success with regard to the implementation of international labor conventions.[25]

In addition to the reporting procedure, the Civil and Political Covenant provides for an interstate complaints procedure. A state ratifying the Covenant may complain to the human rights committee established under the Covenant that another state party is not fulfilling its obligations under the Covenant. However, this procedure is optional. Only a state that has made a declaration recognizing the competence of the human rights committee to consider the complaints in regard to itself is authorized to set in motion the procedure with regard to another state party (which must also have recognized the committee's competence to hear complaints). Further, an interstate complaints procedure is an extremely weak technique for enforcing human rights obligations. The experience of both the Council of Europe, under the European Convention for the Protection of Human Rights, and of the International Labor Organization is that states rarely complain about rights violations in other states.[26] States are loathe to upset normal diplomatic relations by raising issues that bring them no substantial benefits.[27]

Mention must also be made of the Optional Protocol to the Civil and Political Covenant. Article 1 of the optional protocol provides that an individual may complain to the human rights committee that a state party to the optional protocol has violated the rights guaranteed to him under the Covenant.[28] This is an important development because, as has just been seen, states rarely use formal human rights complaints procedures against other states. It is highly desirable, therefore, to grant the allegedly wronged individual access to an international tribunal so that his grievance may both be considered and dealt with in at least a quasi-judicial fashion.

As both the Covenant and the optional protocol have only recently entered into force, it is still rather early to predict with total confidence how successful their complaints procedures will be in promoting the observance of human rights. But, given the rarity of state complaints under other international instruments, it seems possible to say that the Covenant's interstate complaints procedure is unlikely to be used with any real frequency or impact. As for the optional protocol, which opens up the possibility of individual complaints, it is likely to be ratified only by states with a relatively proud record of respect for civil and political liberties.[29]

The complaints procedures under the International Covenant and optional protocol are available only against certain states parties to the Covenant, as has been seen. However, another complaints procedure exists that is available against all member states of the United Nations, and it deserves at least a brief mention here. The procedure is available when a complaint reveals, or a number of complaints when read together reveal, a consistent pattern[30] of gross violations of human rights. The United Nations will consider the complaint or complaints in accordance with a confidential procedure established in outline by ECOSOC Resolution 1503.[31] The situation is, in the first instance, considered by a working group of the Subcommission on the Prevention of Discrimination and Protection of Minorities, with a view to bringing to the attention of the Subcommission those communications "which appear to reveal a consistent pattern of gross and reliably attested violations of human rights and fundamental freedoms." The Subcommission, in turn, considers the communications brought before it by the working group, together with any replies of governments, in order to decide whether to refer to the Commission on Human Rights "particular situations which appear to reveal a consistent pattern of gross and reliably attested violations of human rights requiring consideration by the Commission." Having examined any situation referred to it, the Commission may decide either to make a "thorough study" of it and report its recommendations to ECOSOC, or to appoint an *ad hoc* committee, if the state concerned consents, to conduct an investigation "in constant cooperation with that State and under conditions determined by agreement with it." The entire procedure remains confidential until such time as the Commission decides to make recommendations to ECOSOC.

The procedure under Resolution 1503 has so far proved something of a disappointment. Although it is understood that the Subcommission has referred a number of situations to the Commission on Human Rights as revealing, *prima facie*, consistent patterns of gross and reliably attested violations of human rights, the Commission has yet either to make a thorough study of any such situation or to appoint an *ad hoc* committee. This lack of political resolve has been the subject of considerable criticism,[32] and the meaningfulness of the procedure established under Resolution 1503 has been seriously questioned. Under Resolution 1503 the Commission has had referred to it substantial allegations of widespread political imprisonment, murder, torture, and even genocide; yet it has not seen fit to refer any of these situations to ECOSOC. Perhaps no feature of U.N. activity reveals so poignantly, and so desperately, the abyss between the U.N.'s attempt to promote human rights in theory and its efforts to protect them in fact.

In addition to the preparation of studies, recommendations, and treaties, the United Nations has also conducted a program of advisory services in the field of human rights. Under the U.N. advisory services program, the Secretary-General is authorized to make provision, at the request of governments, for advisory services of experts, seminars, and fellowships and scholarships. The program of advisory services of experts has never assumed great importance. Governments are reluctant to acknowledge that they are so weak, incompetent, or unenlightened as to require that kind of assistance. There are, however, some alternative methods. As one observer has commented, "The Secretariat was able to put some life into it by subverting its original purpose. One of the methods for extending assistance to countries asking for it was to be the organization of seminars in such countries. When it became apparent that Governments would not ask for seminars to be organized as part of a technical assistance program, the Secretariat adopted the line that to sponsor human rights seminars would be a sign of strength rather than of weakness and began to suggest to certain Governments that they sponsor seminars where their records were good."[33]

This strategy of the Secretariat succeeded, and seminars have become an important U.N. technique in promoting human rights. Regional seminars have been held on a great variety of human rights problems in every continent. For example, regional seminars have been held in Thailand, on the civic responsibilities and increased participation of Asian women in public life; in Argentina, on judicial and other remedies against the illegal exercise or abuse of administrative authority; in India, on freedom of information; and in Poland, on the realization of economic and social rights. In addition to the regional seminars, twelve worldwide seminars had been held by the end of 1972.

The program of fellowships and scholarships has also had modest success. Approximately fifty fellowships have been awarded each year since the mid-1960s. The candidates are generally selected from persons in developing countries having direct responsibilities in the implementation of human rights in their own countries, and successful candidates study in detail rights with which they are administratively concerned in their respective countries.

No account of the human rights techniques employed by the United Nations would be complete without a brief mention of one of its specialized agencies, the International Labor Organization, whose techniques of human rights promotion have been developed over the course of six decades.[34] By 1976, the International Labor Organization had adopted approximately 150 conventions and as many recommendations. Some of the conventions seek to guarantee basic human rights, such as freedom of association, freedom of labor, and freedom from discrimination. Others are concerned with narrower aspects of industrial relations, such as social security, the employment of women and children, migrant workers, and industrial safety.

The principal technique used by the ILO in the promotion of labor rights has been the ratification by states of international conventions. This technique can be said to be *the* fundamental human rights technique, because it is assumed that when a state ratifies a treaty, it does so in good faith. This assumption of "good faith" is fundamental to international law and to all international relations. It is assumed both politically and as a matter of law that a state will fulfill in good faith the international obligations it has voluntarily undertaken. But this assumption, however fundamental to the international system, may prove unfounded. As an assurance that states are in fact fulfilling their international obligations, Article 22 of the ILO Constitution provides that states shall make periodic reports on the labor conventions to which they are parties. These reports[35] are scrutinized by a committee of experts, who serve in their personal capacities and whose authority and objectivity has been seen over the years to be beyond doubt. The committee of experts makes a report concerning the extent to which governments are fulfilling their obligations under ratified conventions, and this report is submitted each year to the International Labor Conference that meets in June, where it is examined by the Committee on the Application of Conventions and Recommendations. States found to be in dereliction of fundamental obligations are put on a "black list" and hence subjected to that "mobilization of shame" that Sir Alfred Zimmern so many years ago called an effective restraint on state conduct. States rarely appear on the "black list" two years in a row, and human rights scholars have traditionally regarded the ILO system of supervision as an effective and successful strategy in promoting the observance of human rights. As a consequence, the ILO reporting procedure has been emulated in the UNESCO Convention against Discrimination in Education (1960), the European Social Charter (1961), the International Convention on the Elimination of All Forms of Racial Discrimination (1966), the International Covenants on Human Rights (1966), and the Arab Labor Standards Convention, (1967). The reporting procedure developed by the ILO has become a classic strategy in the promotion of human rights.[36]

III

Post-Second-World-War developments in human rights have also had an important regional aspect. The Council of Europe, the Organization of American States, the League of Arab States, and the Organization of African Unity have all been influenced by the human rights revolution established by the United Nations Charter and the Universal Declaration of Human Rights.

It is not surprising that the most significant developments have occurred in Western Europe. In 1950, the Council of Europe drafted the European Convention for the Protection of Human Rights and Fundamental Freedoms,[37] and in 1953, the Convention entered into force. The preamble to the Convention expressly recognizes its indebtedness to the Universal Declaration: The Preamble recites that the signatory governments are "resolved . . . to take the first steps for the collective enforcement of certain of the rights stated in the Universal Declaration."

European states ratifying the Convention solemnly promise in Article 1 to "secure to everyone within their jurisdiction the rights and freedoms" set forth therein. The Convention's principal interest to us is that it introduced, shortly after the promulgation of the Universal Declaration, the use of complaints procedures to ensure that the rights guaranteed by international treaty were not to be mere pieties. Under Article 24, a state party has the right to bring a complaint against another state party. Under Article 25 "any person, non-governmental organization or group of individuals claiming to be the victim of a violation by one of the High Contracting Parties of the rights set forth in this Convention" may lodge a petition, provided that the high contracting party concerned has accepted the right of individual petition.

The procedure under the Convention can be briefly summarized. Complaints are received by the European Commission of Human Rights, the members of which sit in their personal capacity. After having determined the admissibility of a complaint,[38] and after having established the facts, the Commission places itself at the disposal of the parties for a friendly settlement. If no friendly settlement is reached, the Commission draws up a report stating its opinion as to whether the facts as found disclose a breach of the Convention. The case may then be referred to the European Court of Human Rights by the Commission or by a state party concerned, so long as the defendant state has accepted the jurisdiction of the Court, which it may do either *ad hoc* or by making a general declaration under Article 46. If the case is not referred to the Court, the Commission's report goes to the Committee of Ministers of the Council of Europe, which decides whether there has been a violation of the Convention and prescribes measures to be taken by the defaulting state. Decisions of the European Court and of the Committee of Ministers are binding.

It is beyond the scope of this article to discuss the jurisprudence established under the Convention, but it can be said that the Convention's influence has been widespread and its effect profound. By December 31, 1974, the right of individual petition had been accepted by thirteen states, and this remedy was available to approximately 200 million persons within their jurisdiction.[39] It could be argued that this right of procedural access was the very *raison d'être* of the Convention itself, and the use made of the right of individual petition[40] since the Convention's entry into force has assured the Convention a place in international legal history. In addition to the individual complainants who have benefited from the terms of the Convention, there are numerous examples of states changing their legislation in order to bring certain legislative provisions into line with the terms of the Convention.[41] The European Convention is undoubtedly one of the greatest achievements of the Council of Europe.

The only regional organization that rivals the Council of Europe in the generality of its human rights program is the Organization of American States.[42] An American Declaration on the Rights and Duties of Man was passed unanimously in 1948, an Inter-American Commission on Human Rights was established in 1959, and in 1969, an American Convention on Human Rights was drafted.

The Inter-American Commission on Human Rights was created "to promote respect for human rights."[43] By a liberal construction of its statute, the Commission early asserted its power to study human rights situations in the member states of the OAS. And in 1965, a special Inter-American conference enlarged the powers of the Commission to enable it to consider individual complaints with regard to certain articles of the American Declaration of the Rights and Duties of Man.[44] Under this enlarged authority, the Commission has since 1966 considered complaints alleging violations of human rights directed against almost every member state of the OAS.

The American Convention on Human Rights, which was drafted in 1969, has not yet entered into force. The most striking difference between it and the European Convention is that, whereas under the European Convention the right of individual petition is an optional procedure, under the American Convention the right of individual petition is automatic, i.e., states ratifying the Convention automatically confer upon individuals the right of petition. It is precisely because this right of procedural access is thought to constitute a real safeguard of rights that the American Convention has been taking some time to enter into effect.

Developments in the Middle East and in Africa can be stated more briefly. In 1968, the League of Arab States established a Permanent Arab Commission on Human Rights.[45] The Commission is a promotional body, its chief task being to draft agreements to be submitted for approval to the Council of the League. It has not yet been given the power to receive complaints from either states or individuals, although it is contemplated that the Commission will eventually receive reports from member states on which it will make recommendations.[46] An African Commission on Human Rights has been proposed, but it has not yet been established.[47]

IV

The human rights developments over the last three decades have assumed a revolutionary character in international law. The individual is now a subject of the law, and the traditional theory of international law, according to which only states were the subjects of the law, has had to undergo a fundamental change. Not only is the individual now a subject of the law, but under certain treaties he has even been granted procedural access to international tribunals in order to seek his own remedies. It is difficult to exaggerate the profundity of these changes in legal terms.

This is not to say that broad and systematic violations of human rights do not occur. Even with regard to a right as basic as freedom from torture, the system-wide violation of the right is shattering.[48] The persistence of such gross violations in the face of the developing international law of human rights constitutes a challenge to legal scholars to develop strategies of protection more sensitive to the structural features of the international system and to the acknowledged behavior of states. Much, indeed almost all, international legal scholarship has been concerned with the textual exegesis of rights, obligations, and procedures. While this is not without value, there has been a failure to question the sanguine assumptions that underlie the basic techniques, such as reporting procedures, so far employed. Yet these assumptions must be tested, and their effectiveness established beyond doubt, if the human rights "rules" of the international system are not to be reduced to mere rhetorical legal flourishes.

NOTES

1. See, especially, Robert O. Keohane and Joseph S. Nye, *Power and Interdependence,* 1977.

2. The best general introductory work on the international protection of human rights is still Evan Luard, ed., *The International Protection of Human Rights,* 1967. For an extensive treatment of the legal issues, see Louis B. Sohn and Thomas Buergenthal, *International Protection of Human Rights,* 1973; and A. H. Robertson, *Human Rights in the World,* 1972. See also Hersch Lauterpacht, *International Law and Human Rights,* 1950; Manoucher Ganji, *The International Protection of Human Rights,* 1950; Manoucher Ganji, *The International Protection of Human Rights,* 1962; Moses Moscowitz, *International Concern with Human Rights;* Moscowitz, *The Politics and Dynamics of Human Rights,* 1968; Francis Vallat, *An Introduction to the Study of Human Rights,* 1972.

3. See Evan Luard, "The Origins of International Concern over Human Rights," in Luard, supra n.2, 7–21; Robertson, supra n.2, 15–22; Lauterpacht, supra n.2.

4. For the classical position, see E. M. Borchard, *The Diplomatic Protection of Citizens Abroad,* 1927.

5. A study of the right of freedom from slavery puts into relief some of the most fundamental problems to be faced in securing a right internationally: the value of bare treaty obligations (between 1829 and 1890 approximately 300 bilateral treaties on slavery were entered into, almost none of which was effective); the practical problems of international supervision (such as, in the case of slavery, patrolling the high seas for slave traders); the role of international organizational machinery; and the role of international nongovernmental organizations (NGOs). See, especially, C. W. W. Greenidge, *Slavery,* 1958.

6. Greenidge, supra n.5; Ganji, supra n.2, 88–112; Ved Nanda and Cherif Bassiouni, "Slavery and the Slave Trade: Steps Toward Eradication," 12 *Santa Clara Lawyer* (1972), 424–442.

7. See, generally, Jean Pictet, *Commentary on the Geneva Convention,* I–IV.

8. For a brief discussion, see C. A. Macartney, "The League of Nations' Protection of Human Rights," in Luard, supra n.2, 22–38. For more detailed discussion, see C. A. Macartney, *National States and National Minorities,* 1934; Julius Stone, *International Guarantee of Minority Rights,* 1932; Stone, *Regional Guarantee of Minority Rights: A Study of Minority Procedure in Upper Silesia,* 1933.

9. For the other human rights provisions of the Charter, see Articles 13, 62, 68, and 76.

10. No one has put this view more forcefully or persuasively than the late Sir Hersch Lauterpacht:

> Any construction of the Charter according to which Members of the UN are, in law, entitled to disregard—and to violate—human rights and fundamental freedoms runs counter to the cardinal principle of interpretation according to which treaties must be interpreted in good faith. It would be contrary both to these requirements and to the principle of effectiveness if the repeated and solemn provisions of the Charter in the matter of human rights and fundamental freedoms, coupled with the clear legal obligation to promote respect for them by joint and separate action, were interpreted as devoid of the obligation to respect them. *International Law and Human Rights,* supra n.2.

11. Contrast, for example, the language of Article 1 of the European Convention on Human Rights: "The High Contracting Parties *shall secure* to everyone within their jurisdiction the rights and freedoms defined in Section 1 of this Convention." (Italics added.)

12. Hans Kelsen, *The Law of the United Nations,* 1st ed. 1950, 29.

13. *International Court of Justice Reports 1971,* 16.

14. The discussion is usefully summarized in Moustafa El-Kayal, *The Role of the United Nations in the Protection of Human Rights* (J.S.D. thesis, University of Illinois at Champaign-Urbana, 1975), 127–148. See also Rosalyn Higgins, *The Development of International Law by the Political Organs of the United Nations,* 1963, 118–130; J. E. S. Fawcett, "Human Rights and Domestic Jurisdiction," in Luard, supra n.2, 286–303; Hersch Lauterpacht, supra n.2, 166–220.

15. Pub. Permanent Court of International Justice (1923), Series B, No. 4, 24.

16. El-Kayal, supra n.14, at 137.

17. Article 68.

18. See Sir Samuel Hoare, "The UN Commission on Human Rights," in Luard, supra n.2, 59–98. A nuclear Subcommission on the Status of Women was established by ECOSOC as a subcommission of the nuclear Commission on Human Rights. Shortly afterward ECOSOC decided to

constitute the subcommission a full commission, to be known as the Commission on the Status of Women. For the work of the Commission on the Status of Women, see Margaret Bruce, "The Work of the UN Relating to the Status of Women," 4 *Human Rights Journal* (1971), 365 et seq. See also Howard Taubenfeld and Rita Taubenfeld, "Achieving the Human Rights of Women; the Base Line, the Challenge, the Search for a Strategy," 4 *Human Rights* (1975), 125–169; Myres McDougal and others, "Human Rights for Women and World Public Order: the Outlawing of Sex-based Discrimination," 69 *American Journal of International Law* (1975), 497–533.

19. See, especially, John Paul Salzberg, *The United Nations Sub-Commission on Prevention of Discrimination and Protection of Minorities* (Ph.D. thesis, New York University, 1973). See also John P. Humphrey, "The Sub-Commission on the Prevention of Discrimination and the Protection of Minorities," 62 *American Journal of International Law* (1968), 869–888.

20. The vote was 48–0–8. The eight states abstaining were: Byelorussian S.S.R., Czechoslovakia, Poland, Saudi Arabia, Ukrainian S.S.R., Union of South Africa, U.S.S.R., and Yugoslavia.

21. For example, in Resolution 2144A of October 26, 1966 the General Assembly, convinced that "gross violations of the rights and fundamental freedoms set forth in the Universal Declaration of Human Rights continue to occur in certain countries," called upon states "to strengthen their efforts to promote the full observance of human rights and the right to self-determination in accordance with the Charter of the United Nations, and to attain the standards established by the Universal Declaration of Human Rights."

22. Chief among these treaties are the 1966 International Covenant on Civil and Political Rights and the 1966 International Covenant on Economic, Social and Cultural Rights, both of which entered into force in 1976. See also the following global or regional conventions: The European Convention for the Protection of Human Rights and Fundamental Freedoms (1950); the Convention relating to the Status of Refugees (1951), with a Protocol approved in 1966; the Equal Remuneration Convention (1951); the Convention on the Political Rights of Women (1952); the Convention on the Status of Stateless Persons (1954); the Supplementary Convention on the Abolition of Slavery, the Slave Trade, and Institutions and Practices Similar to Slavery (1956); the Convention on the Nationality of Married Women (1957); the Convention on the Abolition of Forced Labor (1957); the Discrimination (Employment and Occupation) Convention (1958); the Convention against Discrimination in Education (1960), with the Protocol of 1962; the Convention on the Reduction of Statelessness (1961); the Convention on Consent to Marriage, Minimum Age for Marriage, and Registration of Marriages (1962); the Employment Policy Convention (1964); the International Convention on the Elimination of All Forms of Racial Discrimination (1965); the American Convention on Human Rights (1969); and the International Convention on the Suppression and Punishment of the Crime of Apartheid (1973).

23. For example, by the mid-1960s the constitutions of eighteen new states had expressly referred to the Universal Declaration as a source of inspiration and guidance. Additionally, twenty-three other new constitutions had adopted in great part the phraseology of the Universal Declaration.

24. Under the Civil and Political Covenant, the reports are considered by a human rights committee composed of eighteen members elected by the states parties and serving in their personal capacity. Under the Economic, Social, and Cultural Covenant, the reports are considered by the Economic and Social Council of the United Nations.

25. See, especially, E. A. Landy, *The Effectiveness of International Supervision: Thirty Years of I.L.O. Experience*, 1966.

26. Only eight interstate complaints have been received under the European Convention in twenty-five years. In all of these cases the complainant state had a political ax to grind (the sole exception was the complaint lodged by the Scandinavian governments against Greece). Under Article 26 of the ILO Constitution, any member state may lodge a complaint if it is not satisfied that another member state is fulfilling its obligations under a convention which both states have ratified. There have been only six such complaints in six decades. Lastly, under the ILO's special machinery for examining allegations of violations of the right of freedom of association, both states and trade unions may lodge complaints. By mid-December 1975, 808 complaints had been lodged since 1951. All 808 cases had been lodged by trade unions. No state had ever lodged a complaint. These figures are remarkable. They suggest, beyond any shadow of a doubt, that states are unlikely to use available complaints procedures in the context of human rights (unless the complaint is politically motivated, as were almost all the state complaints under the European Convention). Yet one of the principal strategies developed in human rights law for protecting human rights has been the elaboration of interstate complaints procedures.

27. President Jimmy Carter's policy of upgrading human rights issues in assessing appropriate United States relations with other states is an unusual development. Its success as a strategy in promoting human rights has yet to be determined.

28. The procedural access granted to the individual in the optional protocol was not gained without a struggle. The inclusion of the right of individual petition in a separate protocol—and not in the body of the Covenant—was due to the fact that Communist states are opposed to the very idea of the individual's *locus standi* in international proceedings on the traditional theoretical ground that only states are the subjects of international law. The Communist states found support among a number of developing countries for the exclusion of the right of individual petition from the covenant, and hence the drafting of an optional protocol granting the right of individual petition became a compromise solution. For an account of the traditional view of the subjects of international law, see L. Oppenheim, *International Law*, 1st ed. 1905, I, 256. See also *Soviet Textbook of International Law* 1961, 89.

29. It is interesting to note which of the states parties to the Civil and Political Covenant (which includes the Soviet Union, Byelorussian S.S.R., Ukrainian S.S.R., Czechoslovakia, German Democratic Republic, Hungary, Romania, and Yugoslavia) have also accepted the right of individual petition under the optional protocol. None of the Communist states have. Two-thirds of the states which had, by December 1976, ratified the optional protocol were either Western European or liberal Latin American democracies. At the end of 1976, the states parties to the optional protocol were: Barbados, Colombia, Costa Rica, Denmark, Ecuador, Finland, Jamaica, Madagascar, Mauritius, Norway, Panama, Surinam, Sweden, Uruguay, Venezuela, and Zaire.

30. Hence, an isolated violation will not suffice. The complaint must reveal a consistent *pattern* of gross violations. Individual instances of violation are dealt with under ECOSOC Resolution 728F, according to which the United Nations asks the state concerned to comment on the alleged violation. If a comment is received, it is communicated to the complainant; but nothing further is done. Approximately 30,000 such complaints are received each year by the United Nations and are dealt with in this fashion.

31. For a good account of the historical development of Resolution 1503, see John P. Humphrey, "The Right of Petition in the UN," 4 *Human Rights Journal* (1971), 463–475. See also Malvina Guggenheim, "Key Provisions of the New United Nations Rules Dealing with Human Rights Petitions," 6 *New York University Journal of International Law and Politics* (1973), 427–454; Frank C. Newman, "The New United Nations Procedures for Human Rights Complaints: Reform, Status Quo, or Chambers of Horror?" 34 *Annales de Droit* (1974), 129–46.

32. See, for example, the article in *The London Sunday Times Weekly Review*, "Human Rights: A Conspiracy to Oppress," March 14, 1976.

33. John P. Humphrey, "The International Law of Human Rights in the Middle Twentieth Century," in Maarten Bos, ed., *The Present State of International Law*, 1973, 75–105, at 97.

34. For the best account of ILO techniques, see International Labour Organization, *The Impact of International Labour Conventions and Recommendations*, 1976. See also Wilfred Jenks, "The International Protection of Trade Union Rights," in Luard, supra n.2, 210–247; N. Valticos, "Fifty Years of Standard-Setting Activities by the International Labour Organization," *International Labour Review* (September 1969), 201–237.

35. For a detailed account of the reporting procedure, see Landy, supra n.25.

36. Also of interest, but beyond the scope of this essay, is the procedure developed by the ILO to protect the most basic of all trade union rights, the right of freedom of association. See, especially, Ernst Haas, *Human Rights and International Action: the Case of Freedom of Association*, 1970. See also G. von Potobsky, "Protection of Trade Union Rights: 20 Years' Work by the Committee on Freedom of Association," 105 *International Labour Review* (1972), 69–83; and K. Yokota, "International Standards of Freedom of Association for Trade Union Purposes," 144 *Hague Recueil* (1975), 317–379.

37. For a brief account of the operation of the Convention, see Ralph Beddard, *Human Rights and Europe*, 1973. For more detailed accounts, see, for a good legal and political assessment of the Convention, A. H. Robertson, *Human Rights in Europe*, 2nd ed. 1977. For detailed accounts of the jurisprudence under the Convention, see Francis G. Jacobs, *The European Convention on Human Rights*, 1975; and J. E. S. Fawcett, *The Application of the European Convention on Human Rights*, 1969.

38. The Commission may not deal with any complaint that is anonymous, repetitive, incompatible with the provisions of the Convention, manifestly ill-founded, abusive, or inadmissible for failure to exhaust local remedies. This stage is more important than it at first appears because the vast majority of complaints are declared inadmissible.

39. Robertson, supra n.37, at 151.

40. For which, see ibid., 149–153.

41. For example, Belgium changed its legislation with regard to vagrancy proceedings. Ibid., 58–59. Austria changed its criminal appeals procedure. Ibid., 67. And the United Kingdom changed its immigration appeals procedure. Ibid., 89.

42. For the most comprehensive account of the human rights activities of the OAS, see L. J.

LeBlanc, *The OAS and the Promotion and Protection of Human Rights* (Ph.D. thesis, University of Iowa, 1973).

43. On the work of the Commission, see A. P. Schreiber, *The Inter-American Commission on Human Rights*, 1970; Sohn and Buergenthal, supra n.2, 1284–1356.

44. These are: Article 1 (the right to life, liberty, and personal security); Article 2 (equality before the law); Article 3 (freedom of religion); Article 4 (freedom of expression); Article 18 (the right to a fair trial); Article 25 (freedom from arbitrary arrest); and Article 26 (due process of law).

45. See Robertson, supra n.2, 140–147.

46. Humphrey, supra n.33, at 100.

47. Robertson, supra n.2, 148–158.

48. Amnesty International, *Report on Torture*, 2nd ed., 1975.

DOCUMENTS
ON
HUMAN RIGHTS

PART I

The Philosophical Background

Introductory Note

The theoretical basis of human rights is the predominantly Western concept that individuals have a claim to autonomy and freedom in the face of governmental authority. Whether the justification for this lay in "natural rights," "the social contract," or the calculation of the "greatest good for the greatest number" as the *raison d'être* of political society, the purpose of government was to serve and protect citizens. This stood in sharp contrast to arguments that a regime need answer only to God or that the maintenance of order was an end in itself.

The idea of human rights was closely related to theories of democracy and liberalism. Further, the institutionalization of human rights, as expressed most clearly in the selection from John Stuart Mill, was seen as a guarantee of rapid social and economic progress and cultural creativity. During the eighteenth and nineteenth centuries, to foreign observers like Montesquieu and Voltaire, these virtues were best developed in Great Britain.

Naturally, the growing belief in human rights went hand in hand with the development of representative government and the overthrow of the old feudal order. The writings of John Locke and of the Baron de Montesquieu were influential in the formation of British law, while Jean-Jacques Rousseau and Voltaire provided an intellectual basis for the French Revolution.

All of these writings were, in turn, fundamental in shaping the minds of Thomas Jefferson and other leaders in the struggle for American independence. The Italian Enlightenment thinker Cesare Beccaria was widely translated and discussed in many countries. German writers of the period, including Immanuel Kant, were generally more interested in the prerogatives of the state, but Kant, albeit in a formalistic manner, expresses a German interpretation of contemporary thinking on the rights of the individual.

During the early and middle nineteenth century, utilitarian thinkers tried to develop a scientific approach to the duties of the state in allowing freedom for the individual. British philosophers such as Jeremy Bentham and John Stuart Mill extolled the empirical value of human rights to society and warned of the danger posed by the growing power of government.

Democratic intellectuals in the twentieth century, such as the American John Dewey, were often put on the defensive against new, totalitarian faiths. Mill's 1859 statement, "The time, it is to be hoped, is gone by, when any defence would be necessary of the 'liberty of the press' as one of the securities against corrupt or tyrannical government," seems ironic in a world where few countries can boast of a free press. In the midst of wartime hysteria, Dewey reminded Americans of the ever-present danger of accepting human rights only in theory. He rejected the urge to find some reason why the immediate situation —because of war, social unrest, economic difficulties, or the "obvious" righteousness of an ideology—would make it imperative or tempting to suspend these principles.

John Locke

Second Treatise of Government (1690)

Of Political or Civil Society

Man being born, as has been proved, with a title to perfect freedom and uncontrolled enjoyment of all the rights and privileges of the law of nature equally with any other man or number of men in the world, has by nature a power not only to preserve his property—that is, his life, liberty, and estate—against the injuries and attempts of other men, but to judge of and punish the breaches of that law in others as he is persuaded the offense deserves, even with death itself in crimes where the heinousness of the fact in his opinion requires it. But because no political society can be, nor subsist, without having in itself the power to preserve the property and, in order thereunto, punish the offenses of all those of that society, there and there only is political society where every one of the members has quitted his natural power, resigned it up into the hands of the community in all cases that exclude him not from appealing for protection to the law established by it. And thus all private judgment of every particular member being excluded, the community comes to be umpire by settled standing rules, indifferent and the same to all parties; and by men having authority from the community for the execution of those rules decides all the differences that may happen between any members of that society concerning any matter of right; and punishes those offenses which any member has committed against the society, with such penalties as the law has established; whereby it is easy to discern who are, and who are not, in political society together. Those who are united into one body, and have a common established law and judicature to appeal to, with authority to decide controversies between them, and punish offenders, are in civil society one with another; but those who have no such common appeal, I mean on earth, are still in the state of nature, each being, where there is no other, judge for himself, and executioner, which is, as I have before shown it, the perfect state of nature.

And thus the commonwealth comes by a power to set down what punishment shall belong to the several transgressions which they think worthy of it, committed among the members of that society (which is the power of making laws) as well as it has the power to punish any injury done unto any of its members, by anyone that is not of it (which is the power of war and peace): and all this for the preservation of the property of all the members of that society as far as is possible. But though every man who has entered into civil society, and is become a member of any commonwealth, has thereby quitted his power to punish offenses against the law of nature, in prosecution of his own private judgment; yet, with the judgment of offenses, which he has given up to the legislative in all cases, where he can appeal to the magistrate, he has given a right to the commonwealth to employ his force for the execution of the judgments of the commonwealth, whenever he shall be called to it; which, indeed, are his own judgments, they being made by himself or his representative. And herein we have the original of the legislative and executive power of civil society, which is to judge by standing laws how far offenses are to be punished when committed within the commonwealth, and also to determine, by occasional judgments founded on the present circumstances of the fact, how far injuries from without are to be vindicated; and in both these to employ all the force of all the members, when there shall be need.

Whenever, therefore, any number of men are so united into one society, as to quit every one his executive power of the law of nature, and to resign it to the public, there and there only is a political or civil society. And this is done wherever any number of men, in the state of nature, enter into society to make one people, one body politic, under one supreme government; or else when any one joins himself to, and incorporates with, any government already made; for hereby he authorizes the society or, which is all one, the legislative thereof, to make laws for him, as the public good of the society shall require, to the execution whereof his own assistance (as to his own decrees) is due. And this puts men out of a state of nature into that of a commonwealth by setting up a judge on earth, with authority to determine all the controversies, and redress the injuries that may happen to any member of the commonwealth; which judge is the legislative, or magistrate appointed by it. And wherever there are any number of men, however associated, that have no such decisive power to appeal to, there they are still in the state of nature.

Hence it is evident that absolute monarchy, which by some men is counted the only government in the world, is indeed inconsistent with civil society, and so can be no form of civil government at all; for the end of civil society being to avoid and remedy those inconveniences of the state of nature which necessarily follow from every man being judge in his own case, by setting up a known authority, to which everyone of that society may appeal upon any injury received or controversy that may arise, and which everyone of the society ought to obey. Wherever any persons are who have not such an authority to appeal to for the decision of any difference between them, there those persons are still in the state of nature; and so is every absolute prince, in respect of those who are under his dominion.

For he being supposed to have all, both legislative and executive power in himself alone, there is no judge to be found, no appeal lies open to anyone who may fairly and indifferently and with authority decide, and from whose decision relief and redress may be expected of any injury or inconvenience that may be suffered from the prince, or by his order; so that such a man, however entitled, "czar," or "grand seignior," or how you please, is as much in the state of nature with all under his dominion, as he is with the rest of mankind; for wherever any two men are who have no standing rule, and common judge to appeal to on earth, for the determination of controversies of right betwixt them, there they are still in the state of nature, and under all the inconveniences of it, with only this woeful difference to the subject, or rather slave, of an absolute prince: that whereas in the ordinary state of nature he has a liberty to judge of his right and, according to the best of his power, to maintain it; now, whenever his property is invaded by the will and order of his monarch, he has not only no appeal as those in society ought to have but, as if he were degraded from the common state of rational creatures, is denied a liberty to judge of, or to defend his right; and so is exposed to all the misery and inconveniences that a man can fear from one who, being in the unrestrained state of nature, is yet corrupted with flattery and armed with power. . . .

Of the Beginning of Political Societies

Men, being, as has been said, by nature all free, equal, and independent, no one can be put out of this estate and subjected to the political power of another without his own consent. The only way whereby anyone divests himself of his natural liberty and puts on the bonds of civil society is by agreeing with other men to join and unite into a community for their comfortable, safe, and peaceable living one among another, in a secure enjoyment of their properties and a greater security against any that are not of it. This any number of men may do, because it injures not the freedom of the rest; they are left as they were in the liberty of the state of nature. When any number of men have so consented to make one community or government, they are thereby presently incorporated and make one body politic wherein the majority have a right to act and conclude the rest. . . .

Though the legislative, whether placed in one or more, whether it be always in being, or only by intervals, though it be the supreme power in every commonwealth; yet:

First, it is not, nor can possibly be absolutely arbitrary over the lives and fortunes of the people; for it being but the joint power of every member of the society given up to that person or assembly which is legislator, it can be no more than those persons had in a state of nature before they entered into society and gave up to the community; for nobody can transfer to another more power than he has in himself, and nobody has an absolute arbitrary power over himself, or over any other, to destroy his own life, or take away the life or property of another. A man, as has been proved, cannot subject himself to the arbitrary power of another; and having in the state of nature no arbitrary power over the life, liberty, or possession of another, but only so much as the law of nature gave him for the preservation of himself and the rest of mankind, this is all he does or can give up to the commonwealth, and by it to the legislative power, so that the legislative can have no more than this. Their power, in the utmost bounds of it, is limited to the public good of the society. It is a power that has no other end but preservation, and therefore can never have a right to destroy, enslave, or designedly to impoverish the subjects. The obligations of the law of nature cease not in society but only in many cases are drawn closer and have by human laws known penalties annexed to them to enforce their observation. Thus the law of nature stands as an eternal rule to all men, legislators as well as others. The rules that they make for other men's actions must, as well as their own and other men's actions be comformable to the law of nature, i.e., to the will of God, of which that is a declaration, and the fundamental law of nature being the preservation of mankind, no human sanction can be good or valid against it.

Secondly, the legislative or supreme authority cannot assume to itself a power to rule by extemporary, arbitrary decrees, but is bound to dispense justice, and to decide the rights of the subject by promulgated, standing laws, and known authorized judges. For the law of nature being unwritten, and so nowhere to be found but in the minds of men, they who through passion or interest shall miscite or misapply it, cannot so easily be convinced of their mistake where there is no established judge; and so it serves not, as it ought, to determine the rights and fence the properties of those that live under it, especially where everyone is judge, interpreter, and executioner of it too, and that in his own case; and he that has right on his side, having ordinarily but his own single strength, has not force enough to defend himself from injuries or to punish delinquents. To avoid these inconveniences which disorder men's properties in the state of nature, men unite into societies that they may have the united strength of the whole society to secure and defend their properties, and may have standing rules to bound it by which everyone may know what is his. To this end it is that men give up all their natural power to the society which they enter into, and the community put the legislative power into such hands as they think fit with this trust, that they shall be governed by declared laws, or else their peace, quiet, and property will still be at the same uncertainty as it was in the state of nature.

Absolute arbitrary power or governing without settled standing laws can neither of them consist with the ends of society and government which men would not quit the freedom of the state of nature for, and tie themselves up under, were it not to preserve their lives, liberties, and fortunes, and by stated rules of right and property to secure their peace and quiet. It cannot be supposed that they should intend, had they a power so to do, to give to any one, or more, an absolute arbitrary power over their persons and estates, and put a force into the magistrate's hand to execute his unlimited will arbitrarily upon them. This were to put themselves into a worse condition than the state of nature, wherein they had a liberty to defend their right against the injuries of others, and were upon equal terms of force to maintain it, whether invaded by a single man or many in combination. Whereas, by supposing they have given up themselves to the absolute arbitrary power and will of a legislator, they have disarmed themselves, and armed him, to make a prey of them when he pleases; he being in a much worse condition who is exposed to the arbitrary power of one man, who has the command of 100,000, than he that is exposed to the arbitrary power of 100,000 single men, nobody being secure that his will, who has such a command, is better than that of other men, though his force be 100,000 times stronger. And therefore, whatever form the commonwealth is under, the ruling power ought to govern by declared and received laws and not by extemporary dictates and undetermined resolutions; for then mankind will be in a far worse condition than in the state of nature if they shall have armed one or a few men with the joint power of a multitude, to force them to obey at pleasure the exorbitant and unlimited decrees of their sudden thoughts, or unrestrained, and till that moment unknown wills, without having any measures set down which may guide and justify their actions. For all the power the government has being only for the good of the society, as it ought not to be arbitrary and at pleasure, so it ought to be exercised by established and promulgated laws; that both the people may know their duty and be safe and secure within the limits of the law; and the rulers, too, kept within their bounds, and not be tempted by the power they have in their hands to employ it to such purposes and by such measures as they would not have known, and own not willingly.

Thirdly, the supreme power cannot take from any man part of his property without his own consent; for the preservation of property being the end of government, and that for which men enter into society, it necessarily supposes and requires, that the people should have property; without which they must be supposed to lose that, by entering into society, which was the end for which they entered into it —too gross an absurdity for any man to own. . . .

But if they who say "it lays a foundation for rebellion" mean that it may occasion civil wars or intestine broils, to tell the people they are absolved from obedience when illegal attempts are made upon their liberties or properties, and may oppose the unlawful violence of those who were their magistrates when they invade their properties contrary to the trust put in them, and that therefore this doctrone is not to be allowed, being so destructive to the peace of the world; they may as well say, upon the same ground, that honest men may not oppose robbers or pirates because this may occasion disorder or bloodshed. If any mischief come in such cases, it is not to be charged upon him who defends his own right, but on him that invades his neighbor's. If the innocent honest man must quietly quit all he has, for peace's sake, to him who will lay violent hands upon it, I desire it may be considered, what a kind of peace there will be in the world, which consists only in violence and rapine, and which is to be maintained only for the benefit of robbers and oppressors. Who would not think it an admirable peace betwixt the mighty and the mean when the lamb without resistance yielded his throat to be torn by the imperious wolf? Polyphemus' den gives us a perfect pattern of such a peace and such a government, wherein Ulysses and his companions had nothing to do but quietly to suffer themselves to be devoured. And no doubt Ulysses, who was a prudent man, preached up passive obedience, and exhorted them to a quiet submission by representing to them of what concernment peace was to mankind, and by showing the inconveniences which might happen if they should offer to resist Polyphemus, who had now the power over them.

The end of government is the good of mankind. And which is best for mankind: that the people should be always exposed to the boundless will of tyranny, or that the rulers should be sometimes liable to be opposed when they grow exorbitant in the use of their power and employ it for the destruction and not the preservation of the properties of their people?

Baron de Montesquieu

The Spirit of Laws (1748)

Law in general is human reason, inasmuch as it governs all the inhabitants of the earth; the political and civil laws of each nation ought to be only the particular cases in which human reason is applied.

They should be adapted in such a manner to the people for whom they are framed, that it is a great chance if those of one nation suit another.

They should be relative to the nature and principle of each government; whether they form it, as may be said of political laws; or whether they support it, as in the case of civil institutions.

They should be relative to the climate of each country, to the quality of its soil, to its situation and extent, to the principal occupation of the natives, whether husbandmen, huntsmen, or shepherds: they should have a relation to the degree of liberty which the constitution will bear, to the religion of the inhabitants, to their inclinations, riches, numbers, commerce, manners, and customs. In fine, they have relations to each other, as also to their origin, to the intent of the legislator, and to the order of things on which they are established; in all which different lights they ought to be considered.

This is what I have undertaken to perform in the following work. These relations I shall examine, since all these together constitute what I call *The Spirit of Laws*.

Of Political Liberty and the Constitution of England

Democratic and aristocratic states are not in their own nature free. Political liberty is to be found only in moderate governments; and even in these it is not always found. It is there only when there is no abuse of power: but constant experience shews us that every man invested with power is apt to abuse it, and to carry his authority as far as it will go. Is it not strange, though true, to say, that virtue itself has need of limits?

To prevent this abuse, it is necessary, from the very nature of things, power should be a check to power. A government may be so constituted as no man shall be compelled to do things to which the law does not oblige him, nor forced to abstain from things which the law permits. . . .

The political liberty of the subject is a tranquility of mind arising from the opinion each person has of his safety. In order to have this liberty, it is requisite the government be so constituted as one man need not be afraid of another.

When the legislative and executive powers are united in the same person, or in the same body of magistrates, there can be no liberty; because apprehensions may arise, lest the same monarch or senate should enact tyrannical laws, to execute them in a tyrannical manner.

Again, there is no liberty if the judiciary power be not separated from the legislative and executive. Were it joined with the legislative, the life and liberty of the subject would be exposed to arbitrary control; for the judge would be then the legislator. Were it joined to the executive power, the judge might behave with violence and oppression.

There would be an end of every thing, were the same man, or the same body, whether of the nobles or of the people, to exercise those three powers, that of enacting laws, that of executing the public resolutions, and of trying the causes of individuals. . . .

The judiciary power ought not to be given to a standing senate; it should be exercised by persons taken from the body of the people, at certain times of the year, and consistently with a form and manner prescribed by law, in order to erect a tribunal that should last only so long as necessity requires.

By this method, the judicial power, so terrible to mankind, not being annexed to any particular state or profession, becomes, as it were, invisible. People have not then the judges continually present to their view; they fear the office, but not the magistrate. . . .

But, though the tribunals ought not to be fixed, the judgments ought; and to such a degree, as to be ever conformable to the letter of the law. Were they to be the private opinion of the judge, people would then live in society without exactly knowing the nature of their obligations.

Jean-Jacques Rousseau

The Social Contract (1762)

Slavery

Since no man has any natural authority over his fellow-men, and since force is not the source of right, conventions remain as the basis of all lawful authority among men.

If an individual, says Grotius, can alienate his liberty and become the slave of a master, why should not a whole people be able to alienate theirs, and become subject to a king? In this there are many equivocal terms requiring explanation; but let us confine ourselves to the word alienate. To alienate is to give or sell. Now, a man who becomes another's slave does not give himself; he sells himself at the very least for his subsistence. But why does a nation sell itself? So far from a king supplying his subjects with their subsistence, he draws his from them; and, according to Rabelais, a king goes not live on a little. Do subjects, then, give up their persons on condition that their property also shall be taken? I do not see what is left for them to keep.

It will be said that the despot secures to his subjects civil peace. Be it so; but what do they gain by that, if the wars which his ambition brings upon them, together with his insatiable greed and the vexations of his administration, harass them more than their own dissensions would? What do they gain by it if this tranquility is itself one of their miseries? Men live tranquilly also in dungeons; is that enough to make them contented there? The Greeks confined in the cave of Cyclops lived peacefully until their turn came to be devoured.

To say that a man gives himself for nothing is to say what is absurd and inconceivable; such an act is illegitimate and invalid, for the simple reason that he who performs it is not in his right mind. To say the same thing of a whole nation is to suppose a nation of fools, and madness does not confer rights.

Even if each person could alienate himself, he could not alienate his children; they are born free men; their liberty belongs to them, and no one has a right to dispose of it except themselves. Before they have come to years of discretion, the father can, in their name, stipulate conditions for their preservation and welfare, but not surrender them irrevocably and unconditionally; for such a gift is contrary to the ends of nature, and exceeds the rights of paternity. In order, then, that an arbitrary government might be legitimate, it would be necessary that the people in each generation should have the option of accepting or rejecting it; but in that case such a government would no longer be arbitrary.

To renounce one's liberty is to renounce one's quality as a man, the rights and also the duties of humanity. For him who renounces everything there is no possible compensation. Such a renunciation is incompatible with man's nature, for to take away all freedom from his will is to take away all morality from his actions. In short, a convention which stipulates absolute authority on the one side and unlimited obedience on the other is vain and contradictory. Is it not clear that we are under no obligations whatsoever towards a man from whom we have a right to demand everything? And does not this single condition, without equivalent, without exchange, involve the nullity of the act? For what right would my slave have against me, since all that he has belongs to me? His rights being mine, this right of me against myself is a meaningless phrase.

Grotius and others derive from war another origin for the pretended right of slavery. The victor having, according to them, the right of slaying the vanquished, the latter may purchase his life at the cost of his freedom; an agreement so much the more legitimate that it turns to the advantage of both.

But it is manifest that this pretended right of slaying the vanquished in no way results from the state of war. Men are not naturally enemies, if only for the reason that, living in their primitive independence, they have no mutual relations sufficiently durable to constitute a state of peace or a state of war. It is the relations of things and not of men which constitutes war; and since the state of war cannot arise from simple personal relations, but only from real relations, private war— war between man and man—cannot exist either in the state of nature, where there is no settled ownership, or in the social state, where everything is under the authority of the laws.

Private combats, duels, and encounters are acts which do not constitute a state of war; and with regard to the private wars authorised by the Establishments of Louis IX, king of France, and suspended by the Peace of God, they were abuses of the feudal government, an absurd system if ever there was one, contrary both to the principles of natural right and to all sound government.

War, then, is not a relations between man and man, but a relations between State and State, in which individuals are enemies only by accident, not as men, nor even as citizens, but as soldiers; not as members of the fatherland, but as its defenders. In short, each State can have as enemies only other States and not individual men, inasmuch as it is impossible to fix any true relations between things of different kinds.

This principle is also conformable to the established maxims of all ages and to the invariable practice of all civilized nations. Declarations of war are not so much warnings to the powers as to their subjects. The foreigner, whether king, or nation, or private person, that robs, slays, or detains subjects without declaring war against the government, is not an enemy, but a brigand. Even in open war, a just prince, while he rightly takes possession of all that belongs to the State in an enemy's country, respects the person and property of individuals; he respects the rights on which his own are based. The aim of war being the destruction of the hostile State, we have a right to slay its defenders so long as they have arms in their hands; but as soon as they lay them down and surrender, ceasing to be enemies or instruments of the enemy, they become again simply men, and no one has any further right over their lives. Sometimes it is possible to destroy the State without killing a single one of its members; but war confers no right except what is necessary to its end. These are not the principles of Grotius; they are not based on the authority of poets, but are derived from the nature of things, and are founded on reason.

With regard to the right of conquest, it has no other foundation than the law of the strongest. If war does not confer on the victor the right of slaying the vanquished, this right, which he does not possess, cannot be the foundation of a right to enslave them. If we have a right to slay an enemy only when it is impossible to enslave him, the right to enslave him is not derived from the right to kill him; it is, therefore, an iniquitous bargain to make him purchase his life, over which the victor has no right, at the cost of his liberty. In establishing the right of life and death upon the right of slavery, and the right of slavery upon the right of life and death, is it not manifest that one falls into a vicious circle?

Even if we grant this terrible right of killing everybody, I say that a slave made in war, or a conquered nation, is under no obligation at all to a master, except to obey him so far as compelled. In taking an equivalent for his life the victor has conferred no favour on the slave; instead of killing him unprofitably, he has destroyed him for his own advantage. Far, then, from having acquired over him any authority in addition to that of force, the state of war subsists between them as before, their relation even is the effect of it; and the exercise of the rights of war supposes that there is no treaty of peace. They have made a convention. Be it so; but this convention, far from terminating the state of war, supposes its continuance.

Thus, in whatever way we regard things, the right of slavery is invalid, not only because it is illegitimate, but because it is absurd and meaningless. These terms, slavery and right, are contradictory and mutually exclusive. Whether addressed by a man to a man, or by a man to a nation, such a speech as this will always be equally foolish: "I make an agreement with you wholly at your expense and wholly for my benefit, and I shall observe it as long as I please, while you also shall observe it as long as I please."

The passage from the state of nature to the civil state produces in man a very remarkable change, by substituting in his conduct justice for instinct, and by giving his actions the moral quality that they previously lacked. It is only when the voice of duty succeeds physical impulse, and law succeeds appetite, that man, who till then had regarded only himself, sees that he is obliged to act on other principles, and to consult his reason before listening to his inclinations. Although, in this state, he is deprived of many advantages that he derives from nature, he acquires equally great ones in return; his faculties are exercised and developed; his ideas are expanded; his feelings are ennobled; his whole soul is exalted to such a degree that, if the abuses of this new condition did not often degrade him below that from which he has emerged, he ought to bless without ceasing the happy moment that released him from it for ever, and transformed him from a stupid and ignorant animal into an intelligent being and a man.

Let us reduce this whole balance to terms easy to compare. What man loses by the social contract is his natural liberty and an unlimited right to anything which tempts him and which he is able to attain; what he gains is civil liberty and property in all that he possesses. In order that we may not be mistaken about these compensations, we must clearly distinguish natural liberty, which is limited by the general will; and possession, which is nothing but the result of force or the right of first occupancy, from property, which can be based only on a positive title.

Besides the preceding, we might add to the acquisitions of the civil state moral freedom, which alone renders man truly master of himself; for the impulse of mere appetite is slavery, while obedience to a self-prescribed law is liberty. But I have already said too much on this head, and the philosophical meaning of the term liberty does not belong to my present subject. . . .

If the State or city is nothing but a moral person, the life of which consists in the union of its members, and if the most important of its cares is that of self-preservation, it needs a universal and compulsive force to move and dispose every part in the manner most expedient for the whole. As nature gives every man an absolute power over all its members; and it is this same power which, when directed by the general will, bears, as I said, the name of sovereignty.

But besides the public person, we have to consider the private persons who compose it, and whose life and liberty are naturally independent of it. The question, then, is to distinguish clearly between the respective right of the citizens and of the sovereign, as well as between the duties which the former have to fulfil in their capacity as subjects and the natural rights which they ought to enjoy in their character as men.

It is admitted that whatever part of his power, property, and liberty each one alienates by the social compact is only the part of the whole of which the use is important to the community; but we must also admit that the sovereign alone is judge of what is important.

All the services that a citizen can render to the State he owes to it as soon as the sovereign demands them; but the sovereign, on its part, cannot impose on its subjects any burden which is useless to the community; it cannot even wish to do so, for, by the law of reason, just as by the law of nature, nothing is done without a cause.

The engagements which bind us to the social body are obligatory only because they are mutual; and their nature is such that in fulfilling them we cannot work for others without also working for ourselves. Why is the general will always right, and why do all invariably desire the prosperity of each, unless it is because there is no one but appropriates to himself this word each and thinks of himself in voting on behalf of all? This proves that equality of rights and the notion of justice that it produces are derived from the preference which each gives to himself, and consequently from man's nature; that the general will, to be truly such, should be so in its object as well as in its essence; that it ought to proceed from all in order to be applicable to all; and that it loses its natural rectitude when it tends to some individual and determinate object, because in that case, judging of what is unknown to us, we have no true principle of equity to guide us.

Indeed, so soon as a particular fact or right is in question with regard to a point which has not been regulated by an anterior general convention, the matter becomes contentious; it is a process in which the private persons interested are one of the parties and the public the other, but in which I perceive neither the law which must be followed, nor the judge who should decide. It would be ridiculous in such a case to wish to refer the matter for an express decision of the general will, which can be nothing but the decision of one of the parties, and which, consequently is for the other party only a will that is foreign, partial, and inclined on such an occasion to injustice as well as liable to error. Therefore, just as a particular will cannot represent the general will, the general will in turn changes its nature when it has a particular end, and cannot, as general, decide about either a person or a fact. When the people of Athens, for instance, elected or deposed their chiefs, decreed honours to one, imposed penalties on another, and by multitudes of particular decrees exercised indiscriminately all the functions of government, the people no longer had any general will properly so called; they no longer acted as a sovereign power, but as magistrates. This will appear contrary to common ideas, but I must be allowed time to expound my own.

From this we must understand that what generalizes the will is not so much the number of voices as the common interest which unites them; for, under this system, each necessarily submits to the conditions which he imposes on others—an admirable union of interest and justice, which gives to the deliberations of the community a spirit of equity that seems to disappear in the discussion of any private affair, for want of a common interest to unite and identify the ruling principle of the judge with that of the party.

By whatever path we return to our principle we always arrive at the same conclusion, viz. that the social compact establishes among the citizens such an equality that they all pledge themselves under the same conditions and ought all to enjoy the same rights. Thus, by the nature of the compact, every act of sovereignty, that is, every authentic act of the general will, binds of favours equally all the citizens so that the sovereign knows only the body of the nation, and distinguishes none of those that compose it.

What, then, is an act of sovereignty properly so called? It is not an agreement between a superior and an inferior, but an agreement of the body with each of its members; a lawful agreement because it has the social contract as its foundation; equitable because it is common to all; useful, because it can have no other object than the general welfare; and stable, because it has the public force and the supreme power as a guarantee. So long as the subjects submit only to such conventions, they obey no one, but simply their own will; and to ask how far the respective rights of the sovereign and citizens extend is to ask up to what point the latter can make engagements among themselves, each with all and all with each.

Thus we see that the sovereign power, wholly absolute, wholly sacred, and wholly inviolable as it is, does not, and cannot, pass the limits of general conventions, and that every man can fully dispose of what is left to him of his property and liberty by these conventions; so that the sovereign never has a right to burden one subject more than another, because then the matter becomes particular and his power is no longer competent.

Cesare Beccaria

Essay on Crimes and Punishments (1764)

The true relations between sovereigns and their subjects, and between nations, have been discovered. Commerce has been reanimated by the common knowledge of philosophical truths diffused by the art of printing, and there has sprung up among nations a tacit rivalry of industriousness that is most humane and truly worthy of rational beings. Such good things we owe to the productive enlightenment of this age. But very few persons have studied and fought against the cruelty of punishments and the irregularities of criminal procedures, a part of legislation that is as fundamental as it is widely neglected in almost all of Europe. Very few persons have undertaken to demolish the accumulated errors of centuries by rising to general principles, curbing, at least, with the sole force that acknowledged truths possess, the unbounded course of ill-directed power which has continually produced a long and authorized example of the most cold-blooded barbarity. And yet the groans of the weak, sacrificed to cruel ignorance and to opulent indolence; the barbarous torments, multiplied with lavish and useless severity, for crimes either not proved or wholly imaginary; the filth and horrors of a prison, intensified by that cruelest tormentor of the miserable, uncertainty—all these ought to have roused that breed of magistrates who direct the opinions of men. . . .

Adherence to a strictly logical sequence would now lead us to examine and distinguish the various kinds of crimes and modes of punishment; but these are by their nature so variable, because of the diverse circumstances of time and place, that the result would be a catalogue of enormous and boring detail. By indicating only the most general principles and the most dangerous and commonest errors, I will have done enough to disabuse both those who, from a mistaken love of liberty, would be ready to introduce anarchy, and those who would like to see all men subjected to a monastic discipline.

But what are to be the proper punishments for such crimes?

Is the death penalty really *useful* and *necessary* for the security and good order of society? Are torture and torments *just*, and do they attain the *end* for which laws are instituted? What is the best way to prevent crimes? Are the same punishments equally effective for all times? What influence have they on customary behavior? These problems deserve to be analyzed with that geometric precision which the mist of sophisms, seductive eloquence, and timorous doubt cannot withstand. If I could boast only of having been the first to present to Italy, with a little more clarity, what other nations have boldly written and are beginning to practice, I would account myself fortunate. But if, by defending the rights of man and of unconquerable truth, I should help to save from the spasm and agonies of death some wretched victim of tyranny or of no less fatal ignorance, the thanks and tears of one innocent mortal in his transports of joy would console me for the contempt of all mankind.

The Origin of Punishments, and the Right to Punish

No lasting advantage is to be hoped for from political morality if it is not founded upon the ineradicable feelings of mankind. Any law that deviates from these will inevitably encounter a resistance that is certain to prevail over it in the end—in the same way that any force, however small, if continuously applied, is bound to overcome the most violent motion that can be imparted to a body.

Let us consult the human heart, and we shall find there the basic principles of the true right of the sovereign to punish crimes.

No man ever freely sacrificed a portion of his personal liberty merely in behalf of the common good. That chimera exists only in romances. If it were possible, every one of us would prefer that the compacts binding others did not bind us; every man tends to make himself the center of his whole world.

The continuous multiplication of mankind, inconsiderable in itself yet exceeding by far the means that a sterile and uncultivated nature could offer for the satisfaction of increasingly complex needs, united the earliest savages. These first communities of necessity caused the formation of others to resist the first, and the primitive state of warfare thus passed from individuals to nations.

Laws are the conditions under which independent and isolated men united to form a society. Weary of living in a continual state of war, and of enjoying a liberty rendered useless by the uncertainty of preserving it, they sacrificed a part so that they might enjoy the rest of it in peace and safety. The sum of all these portions of liberty sacrificed by each for his own good constitutes the sovereignty of a nation, and their legitimate depositary and administrator is the sovereign. But merely to have established this deposit was not enough; it had to be defended against private usurpations by individuals each of whom always tries not only to withdraw his own share but also to usurp for himself that of others. Some tangible motives had to be introduced, therefore, to prevent the despotic spirit, which is in every man, from plunging the laws of society into its original chaos. These tangible motives are the punishments established against infractors of the laws. I say "tangible motives" because experience has shown that the multitude adopt no fixed principles of conduct and will not be released from the sway of that universal principle of dissolution which is seen to operate in both the physical and the moral universe, except for motives that directly strike the senses. These motives, by dint of repeated representation to the mind, counterbalance the powerful impressions of the private passions that oppose the common good. Not eloquence, not declamations, not even the most sublime truths have sufficed, for any considerable length of time, to curb passions excited by vivid impressions of present objects.

It was, thus, necessity that forced men to give up part of their personal liberty, and it is certain, therefore, that each is willing to place in the public fund only the least possible portion, no more than suffices to induce others to defend it. The aggregate of these least possible portions constitutes the right to punish; all that exceeds this is abuse and not justice; it is fact but by no means right.

Punishments that exceed what is necessary for protection of the deposit of public security are by their very nature unjust, and punishments are increasingly more just as the safety which the sovereign secures for his subjects is the more sacred and inviolable, and the liberty greater. . . .

Torture

A cruelty consecrated by the practice of most nations is torture of the accused during his trial, either to make him confess the crime or to clear up contradictory statements, or to discover accomplices, or to purge him of infamy in some metaphysical and incomprehensible way, or, finally, to discover other crimes of which he might be guilty but of which he is not accused.

No man can be called *guilty* before a judge has sentenced him, nor can society deprive him of public protection before it has been decided that he has in fact violated the conditions under which such protection was accorded him. What right is it, then, if not simply that of might, which empowers a judge to inflict punishment on a citizen while doubt still remains as to his guilt or innocence? Here is the dilemma, which is nothing new: the fact of the crime is either certain or uncertain; if certain, all that is due is the punishment established by the laws, and tortures are useless because the criminal's confession is useless; if uncertain, then one must not torture the innocent, for such, according to the laws, is a man whose crimes are not yet proved.

What is the political intent of punishments? To instill fear in other men. But what justification can we find, then, for the secret and private tortures which the tyranny of custom practices on the guilty and the innocent? It is important, indeed, to let no known crime pass unpunished, but it is useless to reveal the author of a crime that lies deeply buried in darkness. A wrong already committed, and for which there is no remedy, ought to be punished by political society only because it might otherwise excite false hopes of impunity in others. If it be true that a greater number of men, whether because of fear or virtue, respect the laws than break them, then the risk of torturing an innocent person should be considered greater when, other things being equal, the probability is greater that a man has rather respected the laws than despised them.

But I say more: it tends to confound all relations to require that a man be at the same time accuser and accused, that pain be made the crucible of truth, as if its criterion lay in the muscles and sinews of a miserable wretch.

Voltaire

Philosophical Dictionary (1764)

Government

In the time of William the Third it [the English constitution] was rebuilt of stone. Philosophy destroyed fanaticism, which convulses to their centres states even the most firm and powerful. We cannot easily help believing that a constitution which has regulated the rights of king, lords, and people, and in which every individual finds security, will endure as long as human institutions and concerns shall have a being.

We cannot but believe, also, that all states not established upon similar principles, will experience revolutions.

The English constitution has in fact arrived at that point of excellence, in consequence of which every man is restored to those natural rights, which, in nearly all monarchies, they are deprived of. These rights are, entire liberty of person and property; freedom of the press; the right of being tried in all criminal cases by a jury of independent men; the right of being tried only according to the strict letter of the law; and the right of every man to profess, unmolested, what religion he chooses, while he renounces offices, which the members of the Anglican or established church alone can hold. These are denominated privileges. And, in truth, invaluable privileges they are in comparison with the usages of most other nations of the world! To be secure on lying down that you shall rise in possession of the same property with which you retired to rest; that you shall not be torn from the arms of your wife, and from your children, in the dead of night, to be thrown into a dungeon or buried in exile in a desert; that, when rising from the bed of sleep, you will have the power of publishing all your thoughts; and that, if you are accused of having either acted, spoken, or written wrongly, you can be tried only according to law. These privileges attach to every one who sets his foot on English ground. A foreigner enjoys perfect liberty to dispose of his property and person; and, if accused of any offence, he can demand that half the jury shall be composed of foreigners.

I will venture to assert that, were the human race solemnly assembled for the purpose of making laws, such are the laws they would make for their security.

Intolerance

Read the article on "Intolerance" in the great Encyclopedia. Read the treatise on toleration composed on occasion of the dreadful assassination of John Calas, a citizen of Toulouse; and if, after that, you allow of persecution in matters of religion, compare yourself at once to Ravaillac. Ravaillac, you know, was highly intolerant.

The following is the substance of all the discourses ever delivered by the intolerant.

You monster! who will be burnt to all eternity in the other world, and whom I will myself burn as soon as ever I can in this; you really have the insolence to read De Thou and Bayle, who have been put into the index of prohibited authors at Rome! When I was preaching to you in the name of God, how Samson had killed a thousand men with the jawbone of an ass, your head, still harder than the arsenal from which Samson obtained his arms, showed me by a slight movement from left to right that you believed nothing of what I said. And when I stated, that the devil Asmodeus, who out of jealousy twisted the necks of the seven husbands of Sarah among the Medes, was put in chains in Upper Egypt, I saw a small contraction of your lips, in Latin called cachinnus (a grin) which plainly indicated to me, that in the bottom of your soul you held the history of Asmodeus in derision.

And as for you, Isaac Newton; Frederick the great, king of Prussia and elector of Brandenburgh; John Locke; Catherine, empress of Russia, victorious over the Ottomans; John Milton; the beneficent sovereign of Denmark; Shakespeare; the wise king of Sweden; Leibnitz; the august house of Brunswick; Tillotson; the emperor of China; the parliament of England; the Council of the great Mogul; in short, all you who do not believe one word which I have taught in my courses on divinity, I declare to you, that I regard you all as pagans and publicans, as, in order to engrave it on your unimpressible brains, I have often told you before. You are a set of callous miscreants; you will all go to the gehenna where the worm dies not and the fire is not quenched; for I am right, and you are all wrong; and I have grace, and you have none. I confess three devotees in my neighbourhood, while you do not confess a single one; I have executed the mandates of bishops, which has never been the case with you; I have abused philosophers in the language of the fish-market, while you have protected, imitated, or equalled them; I have composed pious defamatory libels, stuffed with infamous calumnies, and you have never so much as read them. I say mass every day in Latin for fourteen sous, and you are never even so much as present at it, any more than Cicero, Cato, Pompey, Caesar,

Horace, or Virgil, were ever present at it;—consequently you deserve each of you to have your right hand cut off, your tongue cut out, to be put to the torture, and at last burnt at a slow fire; for God is merciful.

Such, without the slightest abatement, are the maxims of the intolerant, and the sum and substance of all their books. How delightful to live with such amiable people!

Liberty of the Press

In general, we have as natural a right to make use of our pen as our language, at our peril, risk, and fortune. I know many books which fatigue, but I know of none which have done real evil. Theologians, or pretended politicians, cry—"Religion is destroyed, the government is lost, if you print certain truths or certain paradoxes. Never attempt to think, till you have demanded permission from a monk or an officer. It is against good order for a man to think for himself. Homer, Plato, Cicero, Virgil, Pliny, Horace, never published anything but with the approbation of the doctors of the Sorbonne and of the holy Inquisition.

"See into what horrible decay the liberty of the press brought England and Holland. It is true that they possess the commerce of the whole world, and that England is victorious on sea and land; but it is merely a false greatness, a false opulence; they hasten with long strides to their ruin. An enlightened people cannot subsist."

Toleration

What is toleration? It is the appurtenance of humanity. We are all full of weakness and errors; let us mutually pardon each other our follies,—it is the first law of nature.

When, on the exchange of Amsterdam, of London, of Surat, or of Bassora, the Guebre, the Banian, the Jew, the Mahometan, the Chinese Deist, the Brahmin, the Christian of the Greek Church, the Roman Catholic Christian, the Protestant Christian, and the Quaker Christian, traffic together, they do not lift the poniard against each other, in order to gain souls for their religion. Why then have we been cutting one another's throats almost without interruption since the first council of Nice? . . .

It is clear that every private individual who persecutes a man, his brother, because he is not of the same opinion, is a monster. This admits of no difficulty. But the government, the magistrates, the princes!—how do they conduct themselves towards those who have a faith different from their own? If they are powerful foreigners, it is certain that a prince will form an alliance with them. The Most Christian Francis I. will league himself with the Moslems against the Most Catholic Charles V. Francis I. will give money to the Lutherans in Germany, to support them in their rebellion against their emperor; but he will commence, as usual, by having the Lutherans in his own country burnt. He pays them in Saxony from policy; he burns them at Paris from policy. But what follows? Persecutions make proselytes. France will soon be filled with new Protestants. At first they will submit to be hanged, afterwards they will hang in their turn.

Immanuel Kant

On the Relationship of Theory to Practice in Political Right (1792)

Among all the contracts by which a large group of men unites to form a society, the contract establishing a *civil constitution* is of an exceptional nature. For while, so far as its execution is concerned, it has much in common with all others that are likewise directed towards a chosen end to be pursued by joint effort, it is essentially different from all others in the principle of its constitution. In all social contracts, we find a union of many individuals for some common end which they all *share*. But a union as an end in itself which they all *ought to share* and which is thus an absolute and primary duty in all external relationships whatsoever among human beings (who cannot avoid mutually influencing one another), is only found in a society in so far as it constitutes a civil state, i.e. a commonwealth. And the end which is a duty in itself in such external relationships, and which is indeed the highest formal condition of all other external duties, is the *right* of men *under coercive public laws* by which each can be given what is due to him and secured against attack from any others. But the whole concept of an external right is derived entirely from the concept of *freedom* in the mutual external relationships of human beings, and has nothing to do with the end which all men have by nature (i.e. the aim of achieving happiness) or with the recognised means of attaining this end. And thus the latter end must on no account interfere as a determinant with the laws governing external right. *Right* is the restriction of each individual's freedom so that it harmonises with the freedom of everyone else (in so far

From *Kant's Political Writings*, ed. Hans Reiss, trans. H. B. Nisbet (New York: Cambridge Univ. Press, 1970).

as this is possible within the terms of a general law). And *public right* is the distinctive quality of the *external laws* which make this constant harmony possible. Since every restriction of freedom through the arbitrary will of another party is termed *coercion*, it follows that a civil constitution is a relationship among *free* men who are subject to coercive laws, while they retain their freedom within the general union with their fellows. Such is the requirement of pure reason, which legislates *a priori*, regardless of all empirical ends (which can all be summed up under the general heading of happiness). Men have different views on the empirical end of happiness and what it consists of, so that as far as happiness is concerned, their will cannot be brought under any common principle nor thus under any external law harmonising with the freedom of everyone.

The civil state, regarded purely as a lawful state, is based on the following *a priori* principles:

1. The *freedom* of every member of society as a *human being*.
2. The *equality* of each with all the others as a *subject*.
3. The *independence* of each member of a commonwealth as a *citizen*.

These principles are not so much laws given by an already established state, as laws by which a state can alone be established in accordance with pure rational principles of external human right. Thus:

1. Man's *freedom* as a human being, as a principle for the constitution of a commonwealth, can be expressed in the following formula. No-one can compel me to be happy in accordance with his conception of the welfare of others, for each may seek his happiness in whatever way he sees fit, so long as he does not infringe upon the freedom of others to pursue a similar end which can be reconciled with the freedom of everyone else within a workable general law—i.e. he must accord to others the same right as he enjoys himself. A government might be established on the principle of benevolence towards the people, like that of a father towards his children. Under such a *paternal government*, the subjects, as immature children who cannot distinguish what is truly useful or harmful to themselves, would be obliged to behave purely passively and to rely upon the judgement of the head of state as to how they *ought* to be happy, and upon his kindness in willing their happiness at all. Such a government is the greatest conceivable *despotism*, i.e. a constitution which suspends the entire freedom of its subjects, who thenceforth have no rights whatsoever. The only conceivable government for men who are capable of possessing rights, even if the ruler is benevolent, is not a *paternal* but a *patriotic* government. A *patriotic* attitude is one where everyone in the state, not excepting its head, regards the commonwealth as a maternal womb, or the land as the

paternal ground from which he himself sprang and which he must leave to his descendants as a treasured pledge. Each regards himself as authorised to protect the rights of the commonwealth by laws of the general will, but not to submit it to his personal use at his own absolute pleasure. This right of freedom belongs to each member of the commonwealth as a human being, in so far as each is a being capable of possessing rights.

2. Man's *equality* as a subject might be formulated as follows. Each member of the commonwealth has rights of coercion in relation to all the others, except in relation to the head of state. For he alone is not a member of the commonwealth, but its creator or preserver, and he alone is authorised to coerce others without being subject to any coercive law himself. But all who are subject to laws are the subjects of a state, and are thus subject to the right of coercion along with all other members of the commonwealth; the only exception is a single person (in either the physical or the moral sense of the word), the head of state, through whom alone the rightful coercion of all others can be exercised. For if he too could be coerced, he would not be the head of state, and the hierarchy of subordination would ascend infinitely. But if there were two persons exempt from coercion, neither would be subject to coercive laws, and neither could do to the other anything contrary to right, which is impossible.

This uniform equality of human beings as subjects of a state is, however, perfectly consistent with the utmost inequality of the mass in the degree of its possessions, whether these take the form of physical or mental superiority over others, or of fortuitous external property and of particular rights (of which there may be many) with respect to others. Thus the welfare of the one depends very much on the will of the other (the poor depending on the rich), the one must obey the other (as the child its parents or the wife her husband), the one serves (the labourer) while the other pays, etc. Nevertheless, they are all equal as subjects *before the law*, which, as the pronouncement of the general will, can only be single in form, and which concerns the form of right and not the material or object in relation to which I possess rights. For no-one can coerce anyone else other than through the public law and its executor, the head of state, while everyone else can resist the others in the same way and to the same degree. No-one, however, can lose this authority to coerce others and to have rights towards them except through committing a crime. And no-one can voluntarily renounce his rights by a contract or legal transaction to the effect that he has no rights but only duties, for such a contract would deprive him of the right to make a contract, and would thus invalidate the one he had already made.

From this idea of the equality of men as subjects in a commonwealth, there emerges this further formula: every member of the common-wealth must be entitled to reach any degree of rank which a subject can earn through his talent, his industry and his good fortune. And his fellow-subjects may not stand in his way by *hereditary* prerogatives or privileges of rank and thereby hold him and his descendants back indefinitely.

Jeremy Bentham

Principles of Legislation (1802)

Of Political Good and Evil

It is with government, as with medicine. They have both but a choice of evils. Every law is an evil, for every law is an infraction of liberty: And I repeat that government has but a choice of evils: In making this choice, what ought to be the object of the legislator? He ought to assure himself of two things; 1st, that in every case, the incidents which he tries to prevent are really evils; and 2ndly, that if evils, they are greater than those which he employs to prevent them.

There are then two things to be regarded; the evil of the offense and the evil of the law; the evil of the malady and the evil of the remedy.

An evil comes rarely alone. A lot of evil cannot well fall upon an individual without spreading itself about him, as about a common center. In the course of its progress we see it take different shapes: we see evil of one kind issue from evil of another kind; evil proceed from good and good from evil. All these changes, it is important to know and to distinguish; in this, in fact, consists the essence of legislation. . . .

Of the Limits Which Separate Morals from Legislation

Morality in general is the act of directing the actions of men, so as to produce the greatest possible amount of happiness.

Legislation ought to have precisely the same object in view.

But although these two arts, or these two sciences have the same end in view, they differ much in their extent. All actions, whether public or private, are the springs of morals. It is a guide which may conduct an individual, as it were by the hand, through all the details of life, through all the relationships of society. Legislation cannot do this, and if it could, it ought not to exercise a continual and direct interference with the conduct of men. Morality prescribes to each individual to do whatever is advantageous to himself and to the community. But as there are many acts useful to the community which the legislator ought never to command: So are there many hurtful acts, which he ought not to forbid, although morality may. Legislation in a word has much the same center as morality, though not the same circumference.

There are two reasons for the difference: 1. Legislation cannot secretly influence the conduct of men but by punishment: these punishments are so many evils, which are no further justifiable, than as they produce a greater sum of good. But in many cases where we might wish to strengthen a moral precept by a penalty, the evil of the fault would be less than the evil of the penalty; the means necessary for securing the execution of the law would be of a nature to spread a degree of alarm more hurtful than the evil that we might wish to prevent.

2. Legislation is often stopped by the fear of including the innocent while striving to reach the guilty. Whence comes the danger? From the difficulty of defining the offense, of giving a clear and precise idea of it. For example, severity, ingratitude, perfidy, and other vices which the popular sanction punishes, cannot come within the supervision of the law, for we cannot give an exact definition of them, as of robbery, homicide, perjury, etc. . . .

General Rule. Leave to individuals the greatest possible latitude in every case where they can only injure themselves, for they are the best judges of their own interests. If they deceive themselves, the moment they perceive their error, it is to be presumed they will not persist. Do not suffer the power of the law to interfere, unless to prevent their injuring each other. It is there that law is necessary; it is there that the application of punishment is truly useful, since the rigor shown toward one may ensure the safety of all. . . .

Conclusion

I shall finish with a general observation. The language of error is always obscure, feeble, and changeable. A great abundance of words only serves to hide the poverty and falsity of ideas. The more the terms are varied, the more easy it is to lead people astray. The language of truth is uniform and simple: the same ideas, the same terms. All these refer to pleasures and to pains. We avoid all that may hide or intercept that familiar notion.—*From such or such an act, results such or such an impression of pain or pleasure.* Do not trust to me, trust to experience; and above all, to your own. *Between two opposite modes of action, would you know to which the preference is due? Calculate the effects, in good and ill, and decide for that which promises the greatest amount of happiness.*

John Stuart Mill

Essay on Liberty (1859)

But there is a sphere of action in which society, as distinguished from the individual, has, if any, only an indirect interest; comprehending all that portion of a person's life and conduct which affects only himself, or if it also affects others, only with their free, voluntary, and undeceived consent and participation. When I say only himself, I mean directly, and in the first instance: for whatever affects himself, may affect others *through* himself; and the objection which may be grounded on this contingency, will receive consideration in the sequel. This, then, is the appropriate region of human liberty. It comprises, first, the inward domain of consciousness; demanding liberty of conscience, in the most comprehensive sense; liberty of thought and feeling; absolute freedom of opinion and sentiment on all subjects, practical or speculative, scientific, moral, or theological. The liberty of expressing and publishing opinions may seem to fall under a different principle, since it belongs to that part of the conduct of an individual which concerns other people; but, being almost of as much importance as the liberty of thought itself, and resting in great part on the same reasons, is practically inseparable from it. Secondly, the principle requires liberty of tastes and pursuits; of framing the plan of our life to suit our own character; of doing as we like, subject to such consequences as may follow: without impediment from our fellow-creatures, so long as what we do does not harm them, even though they should think our conduct foolish, perverse, or wrong. Thirdly, from this liberty of each individual, follows the liberty, within the same limits, of combination among individuals; freedom to unite, for any purpose not involving harm to others: the persons combining being supposed to be of full age, and not forced or deceived.

No society in which these liberties are not, on the whole, respected, is free, whatever may be its form of government; and none is completely free in which they do not exist absolute and unqualified. The only freedom which deserves the name, is that of pursuing our own good in our own way, so long as we do not attempt to deprive others of theirs, or impede their efforts to obtain it. Each is the proper guardian of his own health, whether bodily, or mental and spiritual. Mankind are greater gainers by suffering each other to live as seems good to themselves, than by compelling each to live as seems good to the rest.

Though this doctrine is anything but new, and, to some persons, may have the air of a truism, there is no doctrine which stands more directly opposed to the general tendency of existing opinion and practice. Society has expended fully as much effort in the attempt (according to its lights) to compel people to conform to its notions of personal, as of social excellence. The ancient commonwealths thought themselves entitled to practise, and the ancient philosophers countenanced, the regulation of every part of private conduct by public authority, on the ground that the State had a deep interest in the whole bodily and mental discipline of every one of its citizens; a mode of thinking which may have been admissible in small republics surrounded by powerful enemies, in constant peril of being subverted by foreign attack or internal commotion, and to which even a short interval of relaxed energy and self-command might so easily be fatal, that they could not afford to wait for the salutary permanent effects of freedom. In the modern world, the greater size of political communities, and above all, the separation between spiritual and temporal authority (which placed the direction of men's consciences in other hands than those which controlled their worldly affairs), prevented so great an interference by law in the details of private life; but the engines of moral repression have been wielded more strenuously against divergence from the reigning opinion in self-regarding, than even in social matters; religion, the most powerful of the elements which have entered into the formation of moral feeling, having almost always been governed either by the ambition of a hierarchy, seeking control over every department of human conduct, or by the spirit of Puritanism. And some of those modern reformers who have placed themselves in strongest opposition to the religions of the past, have been no way behind either churches or sects in their assertion of the right of spiritual domination: M. Comte, in particular, whose social system, as unfolded in his *Traité de Politique Positive*, aims at establishing (though by moral more than by legal appliances) a despotism of society over the individual, surpassing anything contemplated in the political ideal of the most rigid disciplinarian among the ancient philosophers.

Apart from the peculiar tenets of individual thinkers, there is also in the world at large an increasing inclination to stretch unduly the powers of society over the individual, both by the force of opinion and even by that of legislation: and as the tendency of all the changes taking place in the world is to strengthen society, and diminish the power of the individual, this encroachment is not one of the evils which tend spontaneously to disappear, but, on the contrary, to grow more and more formidable. The disposition of mankind, whether as rulers or as fellow-citizens, to impose their own opinions and inclinations as a rule of conduct on others, is so energetically supported by some of the best and by some of the worst feelings incident to human nature, that it is hardly ever kept under restraint by anything but want of power; and as the power is not declining, but growing, unless a strong barrier of moral conviction can be raised against the mischief, we must expect, in the present circumstances of the world, to see it increase.

It will be convenient for the argument, if, instead of at once entering upon the general thesis, we confine ourselves in the first instance to a single branch of it, on which the principle here stated is, if not fully, yet to a certain point, recognised by the current opinions. This one branch is the Liberty of Thought: from which it is impossible to separate the cognate liberty of speaking and of writing. Although these liberties, to some considerable amount, form part of the political morality of all countries which profess religious toleration and free institutions, the grounds, both philosophical and practical, on which they rest, are perhaps not so familiar to the general mind, nor so thoroughly appreciated by many even of the leaders of opinion, as might have been expected. Those grounds, when rightly understood, are of much wider application than to only one division of the subject, and a thorough consideration of this part of the question will be found the best introduction to the remainder. Those to whom nothing which I am about to say will be new, may therefore, I hope, excuse me, if on a subject which for now three centuries has been so often discussed, I venture on one discussion more.

The time, it is to be hoped, is gone by, when any defence would be necessary of the 'liberty of the press' as one of the securities against corrupt or tyrannical government. No argument, we may suppose, can now be needed, against permitting a legislature or an executive, not identified in interest with the people, to prescribe opinions to them, and determine what doctrines or what arguments they shall be allowed to hear. This aspect of the question, besides, has been so often and so triumphantly enforced by preceding writers, that it needs not be specially insisted on in this place. Though the law of England, on the subject of the press, is as servile to this day as it was in the time of the Tudors, there is little danger of its being actually put in force against political discussion, except during some temporary panic, when fear of insurrection drives ministers and judges from their propriety;* and,

* These words has scarcely been written, when, as if to give them an emphatic contradiction, occurred the Government Press Prosecutions of 1858. That ill-judged interference with the liberty of public discussion has not, however, induced me to alter a single word in the text, nor has it at all weakened my conviction that, moments of panic excepted, the era of pains and penalties for political discussion has, in our own country, passed away. For, in the first place, the prosecutions were not persisted in; and, in the second, they were never, properly speaking, political prosecutions. The offence charged was not that of criticising institutions, or the acts or persons of rulers, but of circulating what was deemed an immoral doctrine, the lawfulness of Tyrannicide.

If the arguments of the present chapter are of any validity, there ought to exist the fullest liberty of professing and discussing, as a matter of ethical conviction, any doctrine, however immoral it may be

speaking generally, it is not, in constitutional countries, to be apprehended, that the government, whether completely responsible to the
people or not, will often attempt to control the expression of opinion,
except when in doing so it makes itself the organ of the general intolerance of the public. Let us suppose, therefore, that the government is
entirely at one with the people, and never thinks of exerting any power
of coercion unless in agreement with what it conceives to be their voice.
But I deny the right of the people to exercise such coercion, either by
themselves or by their government. The power itself is illegitimate.
The best government has no more title to it than the worst. It is as
noxious, or more noxious, when exerted in accordance with public
opinion, than when in opposition to it. If all mankind minus one, were
of one opinion, and only one person were of the contrary opinion,
mankind would be no more justified in silencing that one person, than
he, if he had the power, would be justified in silencing mankind. Were
an opinion a personal possession of no value except to the owner; if to
be obstructed in the enjoyment of it were simply a private injury, it
would make some difference whether the injury was inflicted only on
a few persons or on many. But the peculiar evil of silencing the expression of an opinion is, that it is robbing the human race; posterity as
well as the existing generation; those who dissent from the opinion,
still more than those who hold it. If the opinion is right, they are
deprived of the opportunity of exchanging error for truth: if wrong,
they lose, what is almost as great a benefit, the clearer perception and
livelier impression of truth, produced by its collision with error.

It is necessary to consider separately these two hypotheses, each of
which has a distinct branch of the argument corresponding to it. We
can never be sure that the opinion we are endeavouring to stifle is a
false opinion; and if we were sure, stifling it would be an evil still.

First: the opinion which it is attempted to suppress by authority may
possibly be true. Those who desire to suppress it, of course deny its
truth; but they are not infallible. They have no authority to decide the
question for all mankind, and exclude every other person from the
means of judging. To refuse a hearing to an opinion, because they are

---

considered. It would, therefore, be irrelevant and out of place to examine here, whether the doctrine
of Tyrannicide deserves that title. I shall content myself with saying, that the subject has been at all
times one of the open questions of morals; that the act of a private citizen in striking down a criminal,
who, by raising himself above the law, has placed himself beyond the reach of legal punishment or
control, has been accounted by whole nations, and by some of the best and wisest of men, not a
crime, but an act of exalted virtue; and that, right or wrong, it is not of the nature of assassination,
but of civil war. As such, I hold that the instigation to it, in a specific case, may be a proper subject
of punishment, but only if an overt act has followed, and at least a probable connexion can be
established between the act and the instigation. Even then, it is not a foreign government, but the
very government assailed, which alone, in the exercise of self-defence, can legitimately punish attacks
directed against its own existence.

sure that it is false, is to assume that *their* certainty is the same thing as *absolute* certainty. All silencing of discussion is an assumption of infallibility. Its condemnation may be allowed to rest on this common argument, not the worse for being common.

Unfortunately for the good sense of mankind, the fact of their fallibility is far from carrying the weight in their practical judgment, which is always allowed to it in theory; for while every one well knows himself to be fallible, few think it necessary to take any precautions against their own fallibility. . . .

The despotism of custom is everywhere the standing hindrance to human advancement, being in unceasing antagonism to that disposition to aim at something better than customary, which is called, according to circumstances, the spirit of liberty, or that of progress or improvement. The spirit of improvement is not always a spirit of liberty, for it may aim at forcing improvements on an unwilling people; and the spirit of liberty, in so far as it resists such attempts, may ally itself locally and temporarily with the opponents of improvement; but the only unfailing and permanent source of improvement is liberty, since by it there are as many possible independent centres of improvement as there are individuals. The progressive principle, however, in either shape, whether as the love of liberty or of improvement, is antagonistic to the sway of Custom, involving at least emancipation from that yoke; and the contest between the two constitutes the chief interest of the history of mankind. The greater part of the world has, properly speaking, no history, because the despotism of Custom is complete. This is the case over the whole East. Custom is there, in all things, the final appeal; justice and right mean conformity to custom; the argument of custom no one, unless some tyrant intoxicated with power, thinks of resisting. And we see the result. Those nations must once have had originality; they did not start out of the ground populous, lettered, and versed in many of the arts of life; they made themselves all this, and were then the greatest and most powerful nations in the world. What are they now? The subjects or dependents of tribes whose forefathers wandered in the forests when theirs had magnificent palaces and gorgeous temples, but over whom custom exercised only a divided rule with liberty and progress. A people, it appears, may be progressive for a certain length of time, and then stop: when does it stop? When it ceases to possess individuality. If a similar change should befall the nations of Europe, it will not be in exactly the same shape: the despotism of custom with which these nations are threatened is not precisely stationariness. It proscribes singularity, but it does not preclude change, provided all change together. We have discarded the fixed costumes of our forefathers; every one must still dress like other people, but the fashion may change once or twice a year. We thus take care that when there is change, it shall be for change's sake, and not from any idea of beauty or convenience; for the same idea of beauty or convenience would not strike all the world at the same moment, and be simultaneously thrown aside by all at another moment. But we are progressive as well as changeable: we continually make new inventions in mechanical things, and keep them until they are again superseded by better; we are eager for improvement in politics, in education, even in morals, though in this last our idea of improvement chiefly consists in persuading or forcing other people to be as good as ourselves. It is not progress that we object to; on the contrary, we flatter ourselves that we are the most progressive people who ever lived. It is individuality that we war against: we should think we had done wonders if we had made ourselves all alike; forgetting that the unlikeness of one person to another is generally the first thing which draws the attention of either to the imperfection of his own type, and the superiority of another, or the possibility, by combining the advantages of both, of producing something better than either. We have a warning example in China— a nation of much talent, and, in some respects, even wisdom, owing to the rare good fortune of having been provided at an early period with a particularly good set of customs, the work, in some measure, of men to whom even the most enlightened European must accord, under certain limitations, the title of sages and philosophers. They are remarkable, too, in the excellence of their apparatus for impressing, as far as possible, the best wisdom they possess upon every mind in the community, and securing that those who have appropriated most of it shall occupy the posts of honour and power. Surely the people who did this have discovered the secret of human progressiveness, and must have kept themselves steadily at the head of the movement of the world. On the contrary they have become stationary—have remained so for thousands of years; and if they are ever to be farther improved, it must be by foreigners. They have succeeded beyond all hope in what English philanthropists are so industriously working at—in making a people all alike, all governing their thoughts and conduct by the same maxims and rules; and these are the fruits. The modern *régime* of public opinion is, in an unorganized form, what the Chinese educational and political systems are in an organized; and unless individuality shall be able successfully to assert itself against this yoke, Europe, notwithstanding its noble antecedents and its professed Christianity, will tend to become another China.

What is it that has hitherto preserved Europe from this lot? What has made the European family of nations an improving, instead of a stationary portion of mankind? Not any superior excellence in them, which, when it exists, exists as the effect, not as the cause; but their remarkable diversity of character and culture. Individuals, classes, nations, have been extremely unlike one another: they have struck out a great variety of paths, each leading to something valuable; and although at every period those who travelled in different paths have been intolerant of one another, and each would have thought it an excellent thing if all the rest could have been compelled to travel his road, their attempts to thwart each other's development have rarely had any permanent success, and each has in time endured to receive the good which the others have offered. Europe is, in my judgment, wholly indebted to this plurality of paths for its progressive and many-sided development. But it already begins to possess this benefit in a considerably less degree. It is decidedly advancing towards the Chinese ideal of making all people alike. M. de Tocqueville, in his last important work, remarks how much more the Frenchmen of the present day resemble one another, than did those even of the last generation. The same remark might be made of Englishmen in a far greater degree. In a passage already quoted from Wilhelm von Humboldt, he points out two things as necessary conditions of human development, because necessary to render people unlike one another; namely, freedom, and variety of situations. The second of these two conditions is in this country every day diminishing. The circumstances which surround different classes and individuals, and shape their characters, are daily becoming more assimilated. Formerly, different ranks, different neighborhoods, different trades and professions lived in what might be called different worlds; at present, to a great degree in the same. Comparatively speaking, they now read the same things, listen to the same things, see the same things, go to the same places, have their hopes and fears directed to the same objects, have the same rights and liberties, and the same means of asserting them. Great as are the differences of position which remain, they are nothing to those which have ceased. And the assimilation is still proceeding. All the political changes of the age promote it, since they all tend to raise the low and to lower the high. Every extension of education promotes it, because education brings people under common influences, and gives them access to the general stock of facts and sentiments. Improvements in the means of communication promote it, by bringing the inhabitants of distant places into personal contact, and keeping up a rapid flow of changes of residence between one place and another. The increase of commerce and manufactures promotes it, by diffusing more widely the advantages of easy circumstances, and opening all objects of ambition, even the highest, to general competition, whereby the desire of rising becomes no longer the character of a particular class, but of all classes. A more powerful agency than even all these, in bringing about a general similarity among mankind, is the complete establishment, in this and other free countries, of the ascendancy of public opinion in the State.

As the various social eminences which enabled persons entrenched on them to disregard the opinion of the multitude, gradually become levelled; as the very idea of resisting the will of the public, when it is positively known that they have a will, disappears more and more from the minds of practical politicians; there ceases to be any social support for non-conformity—any substantive power in society, which, itself opposed to the ascendancy of numbers, is interested in taking under its protection opinions and tendencies at variance with those of the public.

The combination of all these causes forms so great a mass of influences hostile to Individuality, that it is not easy to see how it can stand its ground. It will do so with increasing difficulty, unless the intelligent part of the public can be made to feel its value—to see that it is good there should be differences, even though not for the better, even though, as it may appear to them, some should be for the worse. . . .

John Stuart Mill

Considerations on Representative Government (1862)

It is an inherent condition of human affairs that no intention, however sincere, of protecting the interests of others can make it safe or salutary to tie up their own hands. Still more obviously true is it that by their own hands only can any positive and durable improvement of their circumstances in life be worked out. Through the joint influence of these two principles, all free communities have both been more exempt from social injustice and crime, and have attained more brilliant prosperity than any others, or than they themselves after they lost their freedom. Contrast the free states of the world, while their freedom lasted, with the contemporary subjects of monarchical or oligarchical despotism: the Greek cities with the Persian satrapies, the Italian republics, and the free towns of Flanders and Germany, with the feudal monarchies of Europe; Switzerland, Holland, and England with Austria or ante-revolutionary France. Their superior prosperity was too obvious ever to have been gainsaid; while their superiority in good government and social relations is proved by the prosperity, and is manifest besides in every page of history. If we compare, not one age with another, but the different governments which coexisted in the same age, no amount of disorder which exaggeration itself can pretend to have existed amidst the publicity of the free states can be compared for a moment with the contemptuous trampling upon the mass of the people which pervaded the whole life of the monarchical countries, or the disgusting individual tyranny which was of more than daily occurrence under the systems of plunder which they called fiscal arrangements, and in the secrecy of their frightful courts of justice.

It must be acknowledged that the benefits of freedom, so far as they have hitherto been enjoyed, were obtained by the extension of its privileges to a part only of the community, and that a government in which they are extended impartially to all is a desideratum still unrealized. But, though every approach to this has an independent value, and in many cases more than an approach could not, in the existing state of general improvement, be made, the participation of all in these benefits is the ideally perfect conception of free government. In proportion as any, no matter who, are excluded from it, the interests of the excluded are left without the guaranty accorded to the rest, and they themselves have less scope and encouragement than they might otherwise have to that exertion of their energies for the good of themselves and of the community, to which the general prosperity is always proportioned.

Thus stands the case as regards present well-being—the good management of the affairs of the existing generation. If we now pass to the influence of the form of government upon character, we shall find the superiority of popular government over every other to be, if possible, still more decided and indisputable.

This question really depends upon a still more fundamental one, viz., which of two common types of character, for the general good of humanity, it is most desirable should predominate—the active or the passive type; that which struggles against evils or that which endures them; that which bends to circumstances, or that which endeavors to make circumstances bend to itself.

The commonplaces of moralists and the general sympathies of mankind, are in favor of the passive type. Energetic characters may be admired, but the acquiescent and submissive are those which most men personally prefer. The passiveness of our neighbors increases our own sense of security, and plays into the hands of our willfulness. Passive characters, if we do not happen to need their activity, seem an obstruction the less in our own path. A contented character is not a dangerous rival. Yet nothing is more certain than that improvement in human affairs is wholly the work of the uncontented characters; and, moreover, that it is much easier for an active mind to acquire the virtues of patience, than for a passive one to assume those of energy. . . .

The striving, go-ahead character of England and the United States is only a fit subject of disapproving criticism on account of the very secondary objects on which it commonly expends its strength. In itself it is the foundation of the best hopes for the general improvement of mankind. It has been acutely remarked, that whenever anything goes amiss, the habitual impulse of French people is to say, "Il faut de la patience"; and of English people, "What a shame." The people who think it a shame when anything goes wrong—who rush to the conclusion that the evil could and ought to have been prevented, are those who, in the long run, do most to make the world better. If the desires are low placed, if they extend to little beyond physical comfort, and the show of riches, the immediate results of the energy will not be much more than the continual extension of man's power over material objects; but even this makes room, and prepares the mechanical appliances for the greatest intellectual and social achievements; and while the energy is there, some persons will apply it, and it will be applied more and more, to the perfecting not of outward circumstances alone, but of man's inward nature. Inactivity, unaspiringness, absence of desire, is a more fatal hindrance to improvement than any misdirection of energy, and is that through which alone, when existing in the mass, any very formidable misdirection by an energetic few becomes possible. It is this, mainly, which retains in a savage or semi-savage state the great majority of the human race.

Now there can be no kind of doubt that the passive type of character is favored by the government of one or a few, and the active self-helping type by that of the many. Irresponsible rulers need the quiescence of the ruled more than they need any activity but that which they can compel. . . .

John Dewey

Conscription of Thought (1917)

I am not questioning the importance of social solidarity, of union of action, in war times. As with the soldier, so with the civil populations there is demand for closed ranks, for mass formations, for lining up with eyes right, and forward by platoons. Some surrenders and abandonments of the liberties of peace time are inevitable. Men pay more for flour and beefsteak whether they like it or not; and at countless social points they have to ask themselves whether they will make a sacrifice willingly from sense of union with their fellows, or sourly, peevishly, disgruntedly, in a sense of superior isolation. Moreover, the needed cohesion in action is best attained along with intellectual and emotional unity. Without a certain sweep of undivided beliefs and sentiments unity of outer action is likely to be mechanical and simulated. But what is denied is the efficacy of force to remove disunion of thought and feeling.

There is something strange in the history of toleration. Almost all men have learned the lesson of toleration with respect to past heresies and divisions. We wonder how men ever grew so hard and cruel about differences of opinion and faith. We are perplexed when we read how the heretic was regarded as a man with a plague which would surely spread unless he, the heretic, was extirpated. We reason with philosophic wisdom about the impossibility of conquering mind by brute force, of changing ideas by means of the truncheon or the nightstick. We recall that such attempts at direct suppression of thought have usually ended by increasing the vitality of obnoxious beliefs; we quote the saying that the blood of the martyrs is the seed of the church. We are surprised that leaders had not enough common sense to allow unpopular ideas to burn themselves out or die of inanition. But when some affair of our own day demands cohesive action and stirs deep feeling, we at once dignify the unpopular cause with persecution; we feed its flame with our excited suspicions; we make it the center of a factitious attention, and lend it importance by the conspicuousness of our efforts at suppression.

PART II

The Age of Democratic Revolution

Introductory Note

The definition and implementation of human rights took place in the drive toward democratic forms of government, most visible and dramatic in Great Britain, France, and the United States.

The Magna Charta, forced from King John in 1215 by the English barons, marked the beginning of this evolution. It embodied such principles as trial by a jury of peers, an end to feudal forced labor, no confiscation of property without compensation, equality of all before the law, and the right of free migration.

After the Glorious Revolution of 1688, a special session of Parliament presented a Declaration of Rights to William and Mary of Orange, introducing limited monarchy.

A century later, in the American colonies, a movement arose protesting that the rights of Englishmen had not been extended to them. The Declaration of Independence is a legal brief against King George III for violating the rights of his American subjects. The original U.S. Constitution, however, contained relatively few explicit guarantees of individual rights.

The Federalist Papers were written to defend the new Constitution before the New York electorate; in Number 84 Alexander Hamilton and John Jay answered objections about the lack of such provisions. The first ten amendments to the Constitution, generally called the Bill of Rights, remedied this shortcoming. At that time, full participation in political life was limited to white males. Additional amendments, adopted in succeeding years, guaranteed equal rights for racial minorities and for women.

After the French Revolution, the National Assembly adopted the Declaration of the Rights of Man and Citizen, analogous to the British and American statements. Alexis de Tocqueville, in *The Old Regime and the Revolution* provided an insightful analysis of the origins and course of belief in human rights in his country. The pattern of repression and degeneration which led to the French Revolution would become familiar in many countries in the following decades.

The European democratic revolutions in 1848, the reconstruction of political structures after World War I, and the formation of dozens of Third World governments after 1945, produced constitutions and legal systems based on these principles and expressing them in the clearest language. Yet enforcement of such provisions was extremely rare. One important exception was in India, where Mahatma Gandhi inculcated a deep commitment to democracy into the nationalist leadership of that nation, as can be seen by the statement by the great Indian poet Rabindranath Tagore, which was cited with approval by Gandhi.

The Magna Charta (1215)

1. We have in the first place granted to God and by this our present charter have confirmed, for us and our heirs forever, that the English Church shall be free and shall have her rights entire and her liberties inviolate. . . . We have also granted to all freemen of our kingdom, for us and our heirs forever, all the liberties hereinunder written, to be had and held by them and their heirs of us and our heirs. . . .

17. Common pleas shall not follow our Court, but shall be held in some fixed place.

20. A freeman shall be amerced for a small offence only according to the degree of the offence; and for a grave offence he shall be amerced according to the gravity of the offence, saving his contenement. And a merchant shall be amerced in the same way, saving his merchandise; and a villein in the same way, saving his wainage—should they fall into our mercy. And none of the aforesaid amercements shall be imposed except by the oaths of good men from the neighbourhood.

21. Earls and barons shall not be amerced except through their peers, and only in accordance with the degree of the offence.

22. No clergyman shall be amerced with respect to his lay holding, except in the manner of the other foregoing persons, and not according to the value of his church benefice.

23. No community or individual shall be compelled to make bridges at river banks, except those who from of old were legally bound to do so. . . .

28. No constable or other bailiff of ours shall take grain or other chattels of any one without immediately paying therefor in money (denarios), unless by the will of the seller he may secure postponement of that payment.

30. No sheriff or bailiff of ours, or any other person, shall take the horses or carts of any freeman for carrying service, *except by the will of that freeman.*

31. Neither we nor our bailiffs will take some one else's wood for [repairing] castles or for doing any other work of ours, except by the will of him to whom the wood belongs.

32. We will hold the lands of those convicted of felony only for a year and a day, and the lands shall then be given to the lords of the fiefs concerned. . . .

38. No bailiff for the future shall put any man to his "law" upon his own mere words of mouth, without credible witnesses brought for this purpose.

No freeman shall be arrested, or detained in prison, or deprived of his freehold, or outlawed, or banished, or in any way molested; and we will not set forth against him nor send against him, unless by the lawful judgment of his peers and by the law of the land. . . .

40. To no one will we sell, to no one will we deny or delay right or justice.

41. All merchants may safely and securely go away from England, come to England, stay in and go through England, by land or by water, for buying and selling under right and ancient customs and without any evil exactions, except in time of war if they are from the land at war with us. And if such persons are found in our land at the beginning of a war, they shall be arrested without injury to their bodies or goods until we or our chief justice can ascertain how the merchants of our land who may then be found in the land at war with us are to be treated. And if our men are to be safe, the others shall be safe in our land.

42. It shall be lawful in future for any one (excepting always those imprisoned or outlawed in accordance with the law of the kingdom, and natives of any country at war with us, and merchants, who shall be treated as is above provided) to leave our kingdom and to return, safe and secure by land and water, except for a short period in time of war, on grounds of pulic policy—reserving always the allegiance due to us. . . .

44. Men dwelling outside the forest shall no longer, in consequence of a general summons, come before our justices of the forest, unless they are [involved] in a plea [of the forest] or are sureties of some person or persons who have been arrested for offences against the forest.

45. We will appoint as justiciars, constables, sheriffs, or bailiffs only such men as know the law of the kingdom and well desire to observe it. . . .

54. No one shall be arrested or imprisoned upon the appeal of a woman, for the death of any other than her husband. . . .

60. Moreover, all the aforesaid customs and liberties, the observance of which we have granted in our kingdom as far as pertains to us towards our men, shall be observed by all of our kingdom, as well clergy as laymen, as far as pertains to them towards their men. . . .

63. Wherefore it is our will, and we firmly enjoin, that the English Church be free, and that the men in our kingdom have and hold all the

aforesaid liberties, rights, and concessions, well and peaceably, freely and quietly, fully and wholly, for themselves and their heirs, of us and our heirs, in all respects and in all places for ever, as is aforesaid. An oath, moreover, has been taken, as well on our part as on the part of the barons, that all these conditions aforesaid shall be kept in good faith and without evil intent. . . .

The English Bill of Rights (1689)

Whereas the late King James the Second, by the assistance of divers evil counsellors, judges, and ministers employed by him, did endeavour to subvert and extirpate the protestant religion, and the laws and liberties of this kingdom.

1. By assuming and exercising a power of dispensing with and suspending of laws, and the execution of laws, without consent of parliament.

2. By committing and prosecuting divers worthy prelates, for humbly petitioning to be excused from concurring to the said assumed power.

3. By issuing and causing to be executed a commission under the great seal for erecting a court called, The court of commissioners for ecclesiastical causes.

4. By levying money for and to the use of the crown, by pretence of prerogative, for another time, and in other manner, than the same was granted by parliament.

5. By raising and keeping a standing army within this kingdom in time of peace, without consent of parliament, and quartering soldiers contrary to law.

6. By causing several good subjects, being protestants, to be disarmed, at the same time when papists were both armed and employed, contrary to law.

7. By violating the freedom of election of members to serve in parliament.

8. By prosecutions in the court of King's bench, for matters and causes cognizable only in parliament; and by divers other arbitrary and illegal courses.

9. And whereas of late years, partial, corrupt, and unqualified persons have been returned and served on juries in trials, and particularly divers jurors in trials for high treason, which were not freeholders.

10. And excessive bail hath been required of persons committed in

criminal cases, to elude the benefit of the laws made for the liberty of the subjects.

11. And excessive fines have been imposed; and illegal and cruel punishments inflicted.

12. And several grants and promises made of fines and forfeitures, before any conviction or judgment against the persons, upon whom the same were to be levied.

All which are utterly and directly contrary to the known laws and statutes, and freedom of this realm.

And whereas the said late King James the Second having abdicated the government, and the throne being thereby vacant, his highness the prince of Orange (whom it hath pleased Almighty God to make the glorious instrument of delivering this kingdom from popery and arbitrary power) did (by the advice of the lords spiritual and temporal, and divers principal persons of the commons) cause letters to be written to the lords spiritual and temporal, being protestants; and other letters to the several counties, cities, universities, boroughs, and cinque-ports, for the choosing of such persons to represent them, as were of right to be sent to parliament, to meet and sit at Westminster upon the two and twentieth day of January, in this year one thousand six hundred eighty and eight, in order to such an establishment, as that their religion, laws, and liberties might not again be in danger of being subverted: upon which letters, elections have been accordingly made.

And thereupon the said lords spiritual and temporal, and commons, pursuant to their respective letters and elections, being now assembled in a full and free representative of this nation, taking into their most serious consideration the best means for attaining the ends aforesaid; do in the first place (as their ancestors in like case have usually done) for the vindicating and asserting their ancient rights and liberties, declare:

1. That the pretended power of suspending of laws, or the execution of laws, by regal authority, without consent of parliament, is illegal.

2. That the pretended power of dispensing with laws, or the execution of laws, by regal authority, as it hath been assumed and exercised of late, is illegal.

3. That the commission for erecting the late court of commissioners for ecclesiastical causes, and all other commissions and courts of like nature are illegal and pernicious.

4. That levying money for or to the use of the crown, by pretence of prerogative, without grant of parliament, for longer time, or in other manner than the same is or shall be granted, is illegal.

5. That it is the right of the subjects to petition the King, and all committments and prosecutions for such petitioning are illegal.

6. That the raising or keeping a standing army within the kingdom in time of peace, unless it be with consent of parliament, is against law.

7. That the subjects which are protestants, may have arms for their defence suitable to their conditions, and as allowed by law.

8. That election of members of parliament ought to be free.

9. That the freedom of speech, and debates or proceedings in parliament, ought not to be impeached or questioned in any court or place out of parliament.

10. That excessive bail ought not to be required, nor excessive fines imposed; nor cruel and unusual punishments inflicted.

11. That jurors ought to be duly impanelled and returned, and jurors which pass upon men in trials for high treason ought to be freeholders.

12. That all grants and promises of fines and forfeitures of particular persons before conviction, are illegal and void.

13. And that for redress of all grievances, and for the amending, strengthening, and preserving of the laws, parliaments ought to be held frequently.

And they do claim, demand, and insist upon all and singular the premisses, as their undoubted rights and liberties; and that no declarations, judgments, doings or proceedings, to the prejudice of the people in any of the said premisses, ought in any wise to be drawn hereafter into consequence or example.

To which demand of their rights they are particularly encouraged by the declaration of his highness the prince of Orange, as being the only means for obtaining a full redress and remedy therein.

Having therefore an entire confidence, that his said highness the prince of Orange will perfect the deliverance so far advanced by him, and will still preserve them from the violation of their rights, which they have here asserted, and from all other attempts upon their religion, rights, and liberties. . . .

The United States Declaration of Independence (1776)

When in the course of human events it becomes necessary for one people to dissolve the political bands which have connected them with another and to assume, among the powers of the earth, the separate and equal station to which the laws of nature and of nature's God entitle them, a decent respect to the opinions of mankind requires that they should declare the causes which impel them to the separation.

We hold these truths to be self-evident, that all men are created equal; that they are endowed by their Creator with certain unalienable rights; that among these are life, liberty, and the pursuit of happiness. That, to secure these rights, governments are instituted among men, deriving their just powers from the consent of the governed; that, whenever any form of government becomes destructive of these ends, it is the right of the people to alter or to abolish it, and to institute a new government, laying its foundation on such principles, and organizing its powers in such form, as to them shall seem most likely to effect their safety and happiness. Prudence, indeed, will dictate that governments long established should not be changed for light and transient causes; and, accordingly, all experience hath shown that mankind are more disposed to suffer, while evils are sufferable, than to right themselves by abolishing the forms to which they are accustomed. But when a long train of abuses and usurpations, pursuing invariably the same object, evinces a design to reduce them under absolute despotism, it is their right, it is their duty, to throw off such government and to provide new guards for their future security. Such has been the patient sufferance of these colonies, and such is now the necessity which constrains them to alter their former systems of government. The history of the present King of Great Britain is a history of repeated injuries and usurpations, all having, in direct object, the establishment of an absolute tyranny over these States. To prove this, let facts be submitted to a candid world:

He has refused his assent to laws the most wholesome and necessary for the public good.

He has forbidden his governors to pass laws of immediate and pressing importance, unless suspended in their operation till his assent should be obtained; and, when so suspended, he has utterly neglected to attend to them.

He has refused to pass other laws for the accommodation of large districts of people, unless those people would relinquish the right of representation in the legislature; a right inestimable to them and formidable to tyrants only.

He has called together legislative bodies at places unusual, uncomfortable, and distant from the depository of their public records, for the sole purpose of fatiguing them into compliance with his measures.

He has dissolved representative houses, repeatedly for opposing, with manly firmness, his invasions on the rights of the people.

He has refused, for a long time after such dissolutions, to cause others to be elected; whereby the legislative powers, incapable of annihilation, have returned to the people at large for their exercise; the state remaining, in the meantime, exposed to all the danger of invasion from without and convulsions within.

He has endeavored to prevent the population of these States; for that purpose, obstructing the laws for naturalization of foreigners, refusing to pass others to encourage their migration hither, and raising the conditions of new appropriations of lands.

He has obstructed the administration of justice by refusing his assent to laws for establishing judiciary powers.

He has made judges dependent on his will alone for the tenure of their offices and the amount and payment of their salaries.

He has erected a multitude of new offices and sent hither swarms of officers to harass our people and eat out their substance.

He has kept among us, in time of peace, standing armies, without the consent of our legislatures.

He has affected to render the military independent of, and superior to, the civil power.

He has combined with others to subject us to a jurisdiction foreign to our Constitution and unacknowledged by our laws, giving his assent to their acts of pretended legislation—

For quartering large bodies of armed troops among us;

For protecting them by a mock trial from punishment for any murders which they should commit on the inhabitants of these States;

For cutting off our trade with all parts of the world;

For imposing taxes on us without our consent;

For depriving us, in many cases, of the benefit of trial by jury;

For transporting us beyond seas to be tried for pretended offences;

For abolishing the free system of English laws in a neighboring province, establishing therein an arbitrary government, and enlarging its boundaries, so as to render it at once an example and fit instrument for introducing the same absolute rule into these colonies;

For taking away our charters, abolishing our most valuable laws and altering, fundamentally, the powers of our governments;

For suspending our own legislatures and declaring themselves invested with power to legislate for us in all cases whatsoever.

He has abdicated government here by declaring us out of his protection and waging war against us.

He has plundered our seas, ravaged our coasts, burnt our towns, and destroyed the lives of our people.

He is, at this time, transporting large armies of foreign mercenaries to complete the works of death, desolation, and tyranny already begun with circumstances of cruelty and perfidy scarcely paralleled in the most barbarous ages, and totally unworthy the head of a civilized nation.

He has constrained our fellow citizens, taken captive on the high seas, to bear arms against their country, to become the executioners of their friends and brethren, or to fall themselves by their hands.

He has excited domestic insurrections amongst us and has endeavored to bring on the inhabitants of our frontiers, the merciless Indian savages, whose known rule of warfare is an undistinguished destruction of all ages, sexes, and conditions.

In every stage of these oppressions, we have petitioned for redress in the most humble terms; our repeated petitions have been answered only by repeated injury. A prince whose character is thus marked by every act which may define a tyrant is unfit to be the ruler of a free people.

Nor have we been wanting in attention to our British brethren. We have warned them, from time to time, of attempts made by their legislature to extend an unwarrantable jurisdiction over us. We have reminded them of the circumstances of our emigration and settlement here. We have appealed to their native justice and magnanimity, and we have conjured them, by the ties of our common kindred, to disavow these usurpations, which would inevitably interrupt our connections and correspondence. They, too, have been deaf to the voice of justice and consanguinity. We must, therefore, acquiesce in the necessity which denounces our separation, and hold them, as we hold the rest of mankind, enemies in war, in peace, friends.

We, therefore, the representatives of the United States of America, in general Congress assembled, appealing to the Supreme Judge of the world for the rectitude of our intentions, do, in the name and by the authority of the good people of these colonies, solemnly publish and declare, that these united colonies are, and of right ought to be, free and independent states: that they are absolved from all allegiance to the British Crown, and that all political connection between them and the state of Great Britain is, and ought to be, totally dissolved; and that, as free and independent states, they have full power to levy war, conclude peace, contract alliances, establish commerce, and to do all other acts and things which independent states may of right do. And, for the support of this declaration, with a firm reliance on the protection of Divine Providence, we mutually pledge to each other our lives, our fortunes, and our sacred honor.

The United States Constitution (1789)

ARTICLE I, SECTION 9

2. The privilege of the writ of *habeas corpus* shall not be suspended, unless when in cases of rebellion or invasion the public safety may require it.

3. No bill of attainder or *ex-post-facto* law shall be passed.

ARTICLE III, SECTION 2

3. The trial of all crimes, except in cases of impeachment, shall be by jury; and such trial shall be held in the State where the said crimes shall have been committed; but when not committed within any State, the trial shall be at such place or places as the Congress may by law have directed.

ARTICLE III, SECTION 3

1. Treason against the United States shall consist only in levying war against them, or in adhering to their enemies, giving them aid and comfort. No person shall be convicted of treason unless on the testimony of two witnesses to the same overt act, or on confession in open court.

2. The Congress shall have power to declare the punishment of treason, but no attainder of treason shall work corruption of blood, or forfeiture, except during the life of the person attainted.

ARTICLE IV, SECTION 2

1. The citizens of each State shall be entitled to all privileges and immunities of citizens in the several States.

ARTICLE VI

3. The senators and representatives before mentioned, and the members of the several State legislatures, and all executive and judicial officers, both of the United States and of the several States, shall be bound by oath or affirmation to support this Constitution; but no religious test shall ever be required as a qualification to any office or public trust under the United States.

Alexander Hamilton and John Jay

The Federalist Number 84 (1788)

The most considerable of the remaining objections [to the proposed Constitution] is that the plan of the convention contains no bill of rights. Among other answers given to this, it has been upon different occasions remarked that the constitutions of several of the States are in a similar predicament. I add that New York is of the number. And yet the opposers of the new system, in this State, who profess an unlimited admiration for its constitution, are among the most intemperate partisans of a bill of rights. To justify their zeal in this matter, they allege two things: one is that, though the constitution of New York has no bill of rights prefixed to it, yet it contains, in the body of it, various provisions in favor of particular privileges and rights, which, in substance, amount to the same thing; the other is, that the Constitution adopts, in their full extent, the common and statute law of Great Britain, by which many other rights, not expressed in it, are equally secured.

To the first I answer, that the Constitution proposed by the convention contains, as well as the constitution of this State, a number of such provisions.

Independent of those which relate to the structure of the government, we find the following: Article 1, section 3, clause 7—"Judgment in cases of impeachment shall not extend further than to removal from office, and disqualification to hold and enjoy any office of honor, trust, or profit under the United States; but the party convicted shall, nevertheless, be liable and subject to indictment, trial, judgment, and punishment according to law." Section 9, of the same article, clause 2 —"The privilege of the writ of *habeas corpus* shall not be suspended, unless when in cases of rebellion or invasion the public safety may require it." Clause 3—"No bill of attainder or *ex-post-facto* law shall be passed." Clause 7—"No title of nobility shall be granted by the United States; and no person holding any office of profit or trust under them, shall, without the consent of the Congress, accept of any present, emolument, office, or title of any kind whatever, from any king, prince, or foreign state." Article 3, section 2, clause 3—"The trial of all crimes, except in cases of impeachment, shall be by jury; and such trial shall be held in the State where the said crimes shall have been committed; but when not committed within any State, the trial shall be at such place or places as the Congress may by law have directed." Section 3, of the same article—"Treason against the United States shall consist only in levying war against them, or in adhering to their enemies, giving them aid and comfort. No person shall be convicted of treason, unless on the testimony of two witnesses to the same overt act, or on confession in open court." And clause 3, of the same section—"The Congress shall have power to declare the punishment of treason; but no attainder of treason shall work corruption of blood, or forfeiture, except during the life of the person attainted."

It may well be a question, whether these are not, upon the whole, of equal importance with any which are to be found in the constitution of this State. The establishment of the writ of *habeas corpus*, the prohibition of *ex-post-facto* laws, and of titles of nobility, *to which we have no corresponding provision in our Constitution*, are perhaps greater securities to liberty and republicanism than any it contains. The creation of crimes after the commission of the fact, or, in other words, the subjecting of men to punishment for things which, when they were done, were breaches of no law, and the practice of arbitrary imprisonments, have been, in all ages, the favorite and most formidable instruments of tyranny. The observations of the judicious Blackstone, in reference to the latter, are well worthy of recital: "To bereave a man of life, [says he,] or by violence to confiscate his estate, without accusation or trial, would be so gross and notorious an act of despotism, as must at once convey the alarm of tyranny throughout the whole nation; but confinement of the person, by secretly hurrying him to jail, where his sufferings are unknown or forgotten, is a less public, a less striking, and therefore *a more dangerous engine* of arbitrary government." And as a remedy for this fatal evil he is everywhere peculiarly emphatical in his encomiums on the *habeas-corpus* act, which in one place he calls "the BULWARK of the British Constitution."

Nothing need be said to illustrate the importance of the prohibition of titles of nobility. This may truly be denominated the corner-stone of republican government; for so long as they are excluded, there can never be serious danger that the government will be any other than that of the people.

To the second—that is, to the pretended establishment of the common and statute law by the Constitution, I answer, that they are expressly made subject "to such alterations and provisions as the legislature shall from time to time make concerning the same." They are therefore at any moment liable to repeal by the ordinary legislative power, and of course have no constitutional sanction. The only use of the declaration was to recognize the ancient law, and to remove doubts which might have been occasioned by the Revolution. This consequently can be considered as no part of a declaration of rights, which under our constitutions must be intended as limitations of the power of the government itself.

It has been several times truly remarked that bills of rights are, in their origin, stipulations between kings and their subjects, abridgments of prerogative in favor of privilege, reservations of rights not surrendered to the prince. Such was Magna Charta, obtained by the barons, sword in hand, from King John. Such were the subsequent confirmations of that charter by succeeding princes. Such was the Petition of Right assented to by Charles I., in the beginning of his reign. Such, also, was the Declaration of Right presented by the Lords and Commons to the Prince of Orange in 1688, and afterwards thrown into the form of an act of parliament called the Bill of Rights. It is evident, therefore, that, according to their primitive signification, they have no application to constitutions, professedly founded upon the power of the people, and executed by their immediate representatives and servants. Here, in strictness, the people surrender nothing; and as they retain every thing they have no need of particular reservations. "We, the people of the United States, to secure the blessings of liberty to ourselves and our posterity, do *ordain* and *establish* this Constitution for the United States of America." Here is a better recognition of popular rights, than volumes of those aphorisms which make the principal figure in several of our State bills of rights, and which would sound much better in a treatise of ethics than in a constitution of government.

But a minute detail of particular rights is certainly far less applicable to a Constitution like that under consideration, which is merely intended to regulate the general political interests of the nation, than to a constitution which has the regulation of every species of personal and private concerns. If, therefore, the loud clamors against the plan of the convention, on this score, are well founded, no epithets of reprobation will be too strong for the constitution of this State. But the truth is, that both of them contain all which, in relation to their objects, is reasonably to be desired.

I go further, and affirm that bills of rights, in the sense and to the extent in which they are contended for, are not only unnecessary in the proposed Constitution, but would even be dangerous. They would contain various exceptions to powers not granted; and, on this very account, would afford a colorable pretext to claim more than were granted. For why declare that things shall not be done which there is no power to do? Why, for instance, should it be said that the liberty of the press shall not be restrained, when no power is given by which restrictions may be imposed? I will not contend that such a provision would confer a regulating power; but it is evident that it would furnish, to men disposed to usurp, a plausible pretence for claiming that power. They might urge with a semblance of reason, that the Constitution ought not to be charged with the absurdity of providing against the abuse of an authority which was not given, and that the provision against restraining the liberty of the press afforded a clear implication, that a power to prescribe proper regulations concerning it was intended to be vested in the national government. This may serve as a specimen of the numerous handles which would be given to the doctrine of constructive powers, by the indulgence of an injudicious zeal for bills of rights.

On the subject of the liberty of the press, as much as has been said, I cannot forbear adding a remark or two: in the first place, I observe, that there is not a syllable concerning it in the constitution of this State; in the next, I contend, that whatever has been said about it in that of any other State, amounts to nothing. What signifies a declaration, that "the liberty of the press shall be inviolably preserved"? What is the liberty of the press? Who can give it any definition which would not leave the utmost latitude for evasion? I hold it to be impracticable; and from this I infer, that its security, whatever fine declarations may be inserted in any constitution respecting it, must altogether depend on public opinion, and on the general spirit of the people and of the government.* And here, after all, as is intimated upon another occasion, must we seek for the only solid basis of all our rights.

There remains but one other view of this matter to conclude the point. The truth is, after all the declamations we have heard, that the Constitution is itself, in every rational sense, and to every useful purpose, a Bill of Rights. The several bills of rights in Great Britain form its Constitution, and conversely the constitution of each State is its bill of rights. And the proposed Constitution, if adopted, will be the bill of rights of the Union. Is it one object of a bill of rights to declare and specify the political privileges of the citizens in the structure and administration of the government? This is done in the most ample and precise manner in the plan of the convention; comprehending various precautions for the public security, which are not to be found in any of

* To show that there is a power in the Constitution by which the liberty of the press may be affected, recourse has been had to the power of taxation. It is said that duties may be laid upon the publications so high as to amount to a prohibition. I know not by what logic it could be maintained, that the declarations in the State constitutions, in favor of the freedom of the press, would be a constitutional impediment to the imposition of duties upon publications by the State legislatures. It cannot certainly be pretended that any degree of duties, however low, would be an abridgment of the liberty of the press. We know that newspapers are taxed in Great Britain, and yet it is notorious that the press nowhere enjoys greater liberty than in that country. And if duties of any kind may be laid without a violation of that liberty, it is evident that the extent must depend on legislative discretion, regulated by public opinion; so that, after all, general declarations respecting the liberty of the press, will give it no greater security than it will have without them. The same invasions of it may be effected under the State constitutions which contain those declarations through the means of taxation, as under the proposed Constitution, which has nothing of the kind. It would be quite as significant to declare that government ought to be free, that taxes ought not to be excessive, etc., as that the liberty of the press ought not to be restrained.

the State constitutions. Is another object of a bill of rights to define certain immunities and modes of proceeding, which are relative to personal and private concerns? This we have seen has also been attended to, in a variety of cases, in the same plan. Adverting therefore to the substantial meaning of a bill of rights, it is absurd to allege that it is not to be found in the work of the convention. It may be said that it does not go far enough, though it will not be easy to make this appear; but it can with no propriety be contended that there is no such thing. It certainly must be immaterial what mode is observed as to the order of declaring the rights of the citizens, if they are to be found in any part of the instrument which establishes the government. And hence it must be apparent, that much of what has been said on this subject rests merely on verbal and nominal distinctions, entirely foreign from the substance of the thing.

Amendments to the United States Constitution: The Bill of Rights and Other Amendments

AMENDMENT 1 [FIRST TEN AMENDMENTS RATIFIED DECEMBER 15, 1791]

Congress shall make no law respecting an establishment of religion, or prohibiting the free exercise thereof; or abridging the freedom of speech, or of the press; or the right of the people peaceably to assemble, and to petition the government for a redress of grievances.

AMENDMENT II

A well regulated militia, being necessary to the security of a free State, the right of the people to keep and bear arms, shall not be infringed.

AMENDMENT III

No soldier shall, in time of peace be quartered in any house, without the consent of the owner, nor in time of war, but in a manner to be prescribed by law.

AMENDMENT IV

The right of the people to secure in their persons, houses, papers, and effects, against unreasonable searches and seizures, shall not be violated, and no warrants shall issue, but upon probable cause, supported by oath or affirmation, and particularly describing the place to be searched, and the persons or things to be seized.

AMENDMENT V

No person shall be held to answer for a capital, or otherwise infamous crime, unless on a presentment or indictment of a grand jury, except in cases arising in the land or naval forces, or in the militia, when in actual service in time of war or public danger; nor shall any person be subject for the same offense to be twice put in jeopardy of life or limb; nor shall be compelled in any criminal case to be a witness against himself, nor be deprived of life, liberty, or property, without due process of law; nor shall private property be taken for public use, without just compensation.

AMENDMENT VI

In all criminal prosecutions, the accused shall enjoy the right to a speedy and public trial, by an impartial jury of the State and district wherein the crime shall have been committed, which district shall have been previously ascertained by law, and to be informed of the nature and cause of the accusation; to be confronted with the witnesses against him; to have compulsory process for obtaining witnesses in his favor, and to have the assistance of counsel for his defense.

AMENDMENT VII

In suits at common law, where the value in controversy shall exceed twenty dollars, the right of trial by jury shall be preserved, and no fact tried by a jury shall be otherwise reexamined in any court of the United States, than according to the rules of the common law.

AMENDMENT VIII

Excessive bail shall not be required, nor excessive fines imposed, nor cruel and unusual punishments inflicted.

AMENDMENT IX

The enumeration in the Constitution of certain rights shall not be construed to deny or disparage others retained by the people.

AMENDMENT X

The powers not delegated to the United States by the Constitution, nor prohibited by it to the States, are reserved to the States respectively, or to the people.

AMENDMENT XI [JANUARY 8, 1798]

The judicial power of the United States shall not be construed to extend to any suit in law or equity, commenced or prosecuted against one of the United States by citizens of another State, or by citizens or subjects of any foreign State.

AMENDMENT XIII [DECEMBER 18, 1865]

Section 1. Neither slavery nor involuntary servitude, except as a punishment for crime whereof the party shall have been duly convicted, shall exist within the United States, or any place subject to their jurisdiction.

Section 2. Congress shall have power to enforce this article by appropriate legislation.

AMENDMENT XIV [JULY 28, 1868]

Section 1. All persons born or naturalized in the United States, and subject to the jurisdiction thereof, are citizens of the United States and of the State wherein they reside. No State shall make or enforce any law which shall abridge the privileges or immunities of citizens of the United States; nor shall any State deprive any person of life, liberty, or property, without due process of law; nor deny to any person within its jurisdiction the equal protection of the laws.

Section 2. Representatives shall be apportioned among the several States according to their respective numbers, counting the whole number of persons in each State, excluding Indians not taxed. But when the right to vote at any election for the choice of electors for President and Vice President of the United States, representatives in Congress, the executive and judicial officers of a State, or the members of the legislature thereof, is denied to any of the male inhabitants of such State, being twenty-one years of age, and citizens of the United States, or in any way abridged, except for participating in rebellion, or other crime, the basis of representation therein shall be reduced in the proportion which the number of such male citizens shall bear to the whole number of male citizens twenty-one years of age in such State. . . .

Section 5. The Congress shall have power to enforce, by appropriate legislation, the provisions of this article.

AMENDMENT XV [MARCH 30, 1870]

Section 1. The right of citizens of the United States to vote shall not be denied or abridged by the United States or by any State on account of race, color, or previous condition of servitude.

Section 2. The Congress shall have power to enforce this article by appropriate legislation.

AMENDMENT XIX [AUGUST 26, 1920]

The right of citizens of the United States to vote shall not be denied or abridged by the United States or by any State on account of sex.

Congress shall have the power to enforce this article by appropriate legislation.

AMENDMENT XXIV [JANUARY 23, 1964]

Section 1. The right of citizens of the United States to vote in any primary or other election for President or Vice President, for electors for President or Vice President, or for Senator or Representative in Congress, shall not be denied or abridged by the United States or any State by reason of failure to pay any poll tax or other tax.

Section 2. The Congress shall have power to enforce this article by appropriate legislation.

The French Declaration of the Rights of Man and Citizen (1789)

The representatives of the French people, organized in National Assembly, considering that ignorance, forgetfulness, or contempt of the rights of man are the sole causes of public misfortunes and of the corruption of governments, have resolved to set forth in a solemn declaration the natural, inalienable, and sacred rights of man, in order that such declaration, continually before all members of the social body, may be a perpetual reminder of their rights and duties; in order that the acts of the legislative power and those of the executive power may constantly be compared with the aim of every political institution and may accordingly be more respected; in order that the demands of the citizens, founded henceforth upon simple and incontestable principles, may always be directed towards the maintenance of the Constitution and the welfare of all.

Accordingly, the National Assembly recognizes and proclaims, in the presence and under the auspices of the Supreme Being, the following rights of man and citizen.

1. Men are born and remain free and equal in rights; social distinctions may be based only upon general usefulness.

2. The aim of every political association is the preservation of the natural and inalienable rights of man; these rights are liberty, property, security, and resistance to oppression.

3. The source of all sovereignty resides essentially in the nation; no group, no individual may exercise authority not emanating expressly therefrom.

4. Liberty consists of the power to do whatever is not injurious to others; thus the enjoyment of the natural rights of every man has for its limits only those that assure other members of society the enjoyment of those same rights; such limits may be determined only by law.

5. The law has the right to forbid only actions which are injurious to society. Whatever is not forbidden by law may not be prevented, and no one may be constrained to do what it does not prescribe.

6. Law is the expression of the general will; all citizens have the right to concur personally, or through their representatives, in its formation; it must be the same for all, whether it protects or punishes. All citizens, being equal before it, are equally admissible to all public offices, positions, and employments, according to their capacity, and without other distinction than that of virtues and talents.

7. No man may be accused, arrested, or detained except in the cases determined by law, and according to the forms prescribed thereby. Whoever solicit, expedite, or execute arbitrary orders, or have them executed, must be punished; but every citizen summoned or apprehended in pursuance of the law must obey immediately; he renders himself culpable by resistance.

8. The law is to establish only penalties that are absolutely and obviously necessary; and no one may be punished except by virtue of a law established and promulgated prior to the offence and legally applied.

9. Since every man is presumed innocent until declared guilty, if arrest be deemed indispensable, all unnecessary severity for securing the person of the accused must be severely repressed by law.

10. No one is to be disquieted because of his opinions, even religious, provided their manifestation does not disturb the public order established by law.

11. Free communication of ideas and opinions is one of the most precious of the rights of man. Consequently, every citizen may speak, write, and print freely, subject to responsibility for the abuse of such liberty in the cases determined by law.

12. The guarantee of the rights of man and citizen necessitates a public force; such a force, therefore, is instituted for the advantage of all and not for the particular benefit of those to whom it is entrusted.

13. For the maintenance of the public force and for the expenses of administration a common tax is indispensable; it must be assessed equally on all citizens in proportion to their means.

14. Citizens have the right to ascertain, by themselves or through their representatives, the necessity of the public tax, to consent to it

freely, to supervise its use, and to determine its quota, assessment, payment, and duration.

15. Society has the right to require of every public agent an accounting of his administration.

16. Every society in which the guarantee of rights is not assured or the separation of powers not determined has no constitution at all.

17. Since property is a sacred and inviolable right, no one may be deprived thereof unless a legally established public necessity obviously requires it, and upon condition of a just and previous indemnity.

Alexis de Tocqueville

The Old Regime and the Revolution (1856)

It is impossible to form an accurate conception of the government of the old regime, and of the society which produced the Revolution, without pursuing somewhat farther the perusal of this book.

The spectacle of a people so divided and narrowed into cliques, with a royal authority so extensive and powerful, might lead to the impression that the spirit of independence had disappeared with public liberty, and that all Frenchmen were equally bowed in subjection. Nothing of the kind was the case. The government was sole and absolute manager of the public business, but it was not master of individual citizens.

Liberty survived in the midst of institutions already prepared for despotism; but it was a curious kind of liberty, not easily understood to-day. A very close inspection can alone discern the precise proportions of good and evil which it contained.

While the central government was displacing all the local authorities, and absorbing the whole power of the kingdom, its action was often impeded by institutions which it had either created or refrained from destroying, by old usages and customs, by rooted abuses. These nurtured a spirit of resistance in the minds of individuals, and preserved the characters of a good many from losing all their temper and outline. . . .

The art of stifling the sound of resistance was not brought to such perfection as it has been since. France was not so well deafened as it is in our day. It was, on the contrary, well adapted for the transmission of sound, and, though no political liberty could be seen, one had only to speak loud to be heard at a great distance.

The oppressed were secured a hearing in the courts of justice. The political and administrative institutions of the country were those of a despotism, but we were still a free people in our courts of law. The administration of justice under the old regime was cumbrous, complicated, slow, and costly—grave faults, no doubt; but it was never servile to the supreme power; and this is the very worst form of venality. That capital vice, which not only corrupts the judge, but soon infects the whole body of the people, was unknown in the old courts. Judges were not only irremovable, but looked for no promotion; both conditions are essential to independence, for the power of punishing may be dispensed with if that of rewarding be retained.

True, the royal authority had stripped the common courts of their jurisdiction over cases in which the government was interested, but it had not stripped them of their terrors. They might be prevented from judging cases, but they could not be hindered from receiving complaints and expressing their opinions. And as the judicial idiom had preserved the plain simplicity of the old French tongue, which called things by their right names, it was not uncommon for judges to qualify the measures of the government with such epithets as arbitrary and despotic. The irregular interference of the courts in the administration of government, which often proved a hindrance to the transaction of business, occasionally served as a safeguard of liberty; the greater evil was limited by the lesser.

In the heart of the magistracy and around it, the new ideas of the day had not wholly crushed out the vigorous habits of thought of olden time. No doubt the Parliaments thought more of themselves than of the public good; but still, when it was necessary to defend their independence and their honor, they were always intrepid, and gave heart to all who surrounded them.

When the Parliament of Paris was dissolved in 1770, every one of the magistrates who composed it submitted to the loss of rank and power rather than yield to the king. More than this: courts of another kind, such as the Court of Aids (*cour des aides*), which were neither assailed nor menaced, voluntarily exposed themselves to the same fate when that fate had become a matter of certainty. Nor was even this all. The leading advocates who had practiced before the Parliament spontaneously shared its fate. They resigned glory and profit, and preferred silence to pleading before a dishonored magistracy. I know of nothing grander than this in the history of any free people; and yet this took place in the eighteenth century, close to Louis the Fifteenth's court.

The nation had borrowed many habits from the courts. It was from the courts that we learned the only portion of the education of a free people which we owe to the old regime, that is to say, the principle that all decisions should be preceded by discussion, and subject to appeal; the use of publicity, and the love of forms. The government itself had borrowed largely from the language and usages of the courts. The king felt bound to assign reasons for his edicts; the Council's Orders were preceded by long preambles, intendants notified the public of their ordinances by the ministry of bailiffs. All the old administrative bodies, such as the Treasury Board, and the select-men, transacted business publicly, and heard rival petitioners or applicants by counsel. All their habits and forms were so many barriers against the arbitrary power of the sovereign. But the people proper, especially in the rural districts, had no means of resisting oppression except by violence. . . .

. . . Crushed for centuries under the weight of abuses which no one shared with them, living alone, and brooding silently over their prejudices, their jealousies, and their hatreds, they were hardened by their hard experience, and were as ready to inflict as to bear suffering.

Such was the French people when it laid hands on the government, and undertook to complete the work of the Revolution. It found in books a theory which it assumed to put in practice, shaping the ideas of the writers to suit its passions.

The careful student of France during the eighteenth century must have noticed in the preceding pages the birth and development of two leading passions, which were not coeval, and not always similar in their tendencies.

One—the deepest and most solidly rooted—was a violent, unquenchable hatred of inequality. It took its rise and grew in the face of marked inequalities; drove the French with steady, irresistible force to seek to destroy utterly all the remains of the medieval institutions; and prompted the erection on their ruins of a society in which all men should be alike, and as equal in rank as humanity dictates.

The other—of more recent date, and less solidly rooted—prompted men to seek to be free as well as equal.

Toward the close of the old regime these two passions were equally sincere, and apparently equally active; they met at the opening of the Revolution, and, blending together into one, they took fire from contact, and inflamed the whole heart of France. No doubt 1789 was a period of inexperience, but it was also a period of generosity, of enthusiasm, of manliness, of greatness—a period of immortal memory, upon which men will look back with admiration and respect when all who witnessed it, and we who follow them, shall have long since passed away. The French were then proud enough of their cause and of themselves to believe that they could enjoy freedom and equality together. They planted, therefore, free institutions in the midst of democratic institutions. Not content with pulverizing the superannuated laws which divided men into classes, castes, corporations, and endowed them with rights more unequal even than their ranks, they likewise annulled at a blow those other laws which were a later creation of the royal power, and which had stripped the nation of all control over itself, and set over every Frenchman a government to be his preceptor, his tutor, and, in case of need, his oppressor. Centralization fell with absolute monarchy.

But when the vigorous generation which began the Revolution perished or became enervated, as all generations must which undertake such enterprises; when, in the natural course of events of this character, the love of liberty had been discouraged and grown languid in the midst of anarchy and popular despotism, and the bewildered nation began to grope around for a master, immense facilities were offered for the restoration of absolute government; and it was easy for the genius of him who was destined both to continue and to destroy the Revolution to discover them.

The old regime contained, in fact, a large body of institutions of modern type which, not being hostile to equality, were susceptible of being used in the new order of things, and yet offered remarkable facilities for the establishment of despotism. They were sought for and found in the midst of the ruins. They had formerly given birth to habits, passions, and ideas which tended to keep men divided and obedient; they were restored and turned to account. Centralization was raised from its tomb and restored to its place; whence it happened that, all the checks which had formerly served to limit its power being destroyed, and not revived, there sprang out of the bosom of a nation which had just overthrown royalty a power more extensive, more detailed, more absolute than any of our monarchs had ever wielded. The enterprise seemed incredibly bold and unprecedentedly successful, because people only thought of what they saw before them, and forgot the past. The despot fell; but the most substantial portion of his work remained: his administrative system survived his government. And ever since, whenever an attempt has been made to overthrow an absolute government, the head of Liberty has been simply planted on the shoulders of a servile body.

During the period that has elapsed since the Revolution, the passion for liberty has frequently been extinguished again, and again revived. This will long be the case, for it is still inexperienced, ill regulated, easily discouraged, easily frightened away, easily overcome, superficial, and evanescent. Meanwhile, the passion for equality has retained its place at the bottom of the hearts it originally penetrated, and linked with their dearest sentiments. While the one is incessantly changing, now increasing, now diminishing, now gaining strength, now losing it, according to events, the other has remained uniformly the same, striving for its object with obstinate and often blind ardor, willing to sacrifice every thing to gain it, and ready to repay its grant from government by cultivating such habits, ideas, and laws as a despotism may require.

Rabindranath Tagore

The Poet on Civil Liberty (1937)

(The following is the text of the message which was sent by Dr. Tagore to the London Conference on Civil Liberty in India held on October 17th, and which was referred to approvingly by Mahatma Gandhi.)

Liberty is a privilege which the individual has to defend daily for himself; for even the most democratic government tends to be oppressive if its tyranny is tempted by the indifference or cowardice of its subjects. Hence the need for a Civil Liberties Union in any system of government, and hence the need for such unions to realize that they cannot safeguard liberty for the individual if they do not teach him to defend it for himself by his continual readiness to pay for it by sacrifice. The problem is one not of external organization so much as of inducing the appropriate moral qualities in the individual, of creating in him an awareness of his innate worth as an individual. Otherwise, if the individual is made to care for liberty as a means of attaining mere material satisfaction, then the State will easily tempt him to part with it by holding out to him the bait of better satisfactions; which is what is actually happening in party dictatorships—Red, Black or Brown.

The English people too, though they are traditionally supposed to cherish liberty for its own sake, have allowed other peoples to be robbed of it without any scruple whatsoever, simply because their greed for material satisfactions has been effectively appeased thereby. Perhaps my English friends will not agree with me there, but when the rivalry for colonial exploitation would become still more acute, the British citizens will find it necessary to arm their government at home with extraordinary powers to defend their possessions abroad. Then they will suddenly wake up to find that, without meaning it, they have forfeited their own liberty and drifted into a Fascist grip, and maybe, then they will realize that liberty has a true foundation only in the moral worth of the individuals who compose the State.

PART III

Diplomatic Intervention and the Protection of Minorities

Introductory Note

As human rights became accepted domestically by several countries, their governments attempted—or were pressured by public opinion to attempt—to apply them internationally. This was particularly true in the case of the protection of persecuted minorities, especially those with ethnic or religious compatriots at home. These concerns could become part of a power's attempt to increase its overseas influence, yet ambition often coincided with real humanitarian aims.

Two examples are traced here: Western attempts to aid non-Moslem minorities in the Ottoman Empire and the attempt of the United States to promote and protect democracy in Latin America.

By 1649, France was recognized as the protector of Catholics in the European provinces of the Ottoman Empire and attempts were made to extend this role to the Asian areas as well. The greatest pressure came, however, in the nineteenth century. European nations expressed their interests in the non-Moslem minorities in the Treaties of Paris and of Berlin. A significant reform lobby within the Ottoman bureaucracy utilized European pressure and military conflicts with Egypt and Russia, respectively, to promote two decrees—in 1839 and 1859— that promised minority protection and greater rights for all citizens. After a constitution had been achieved in 1876, these reforms were destroyed by a reactionary sultan. All of these measures had little lasting impact.

In fact, conditions became worse. Direct European intervention took place after a bloody intercommunal war in Lebanon in 1860. In 1904, President Theodore Roosevelt protested repression of the Armenians, which developed into wholesale genocide during World War I. Turkey's German allies attempted to dissociate themselves verbally from this behavior in 1915.

Although Thomas Jefferson, in an 1813 letter to the German scientist-explorer Alexander von Humboldt, expressed pessimism over the prospects of democracy in the new Latin American republics, the nurturing of such institutions became a major goal of U.S. policy. President James Monroe, in his Monroe Doctrine message to Congress, declared that America's well-being was connected to the existence of fellow democracies and the rejection of European autocracy in the Western Hemisphere.

Hatred of despotism was a major cause of U.S. intervention in Cuba in 1898, as seen in the speech of Senator Redfield Proctor, whose eloquence added momentum to the Congressional drive for a declaration of war on Spain, and in Senator Henry Teller's amendment to that resolution disclaiming territorial ambitions and supporting Cuban sovereignty. President Woodrow Wilson, who made the extension of democracy a high foreign-policy priority, outlined his thinking in two 1913 speeches. As time went on, however, such U.S. interventions created much resentment among South and Central Americans.

Wilson continued his liberal internationalism in the Fourteen Points speech, suggesting a settlement to World War I. The peace agreements involved a number of treaties, including the 1919 Polish accord, safeguarding minority rights in central and eastern Europe. These agreements were largely ignored.

World War II highlighted the need to reaffirm safeguards for minority and human rights, as seen in the 1941 Atlantic Charter, which sets out Anglo-American war aims. The 1947 Italian Peace Treaty offers an example of new attempts to protect minorities. Finally, a 1967 U.N. report summarizes some of the post-1945 minority treaties.

Proclamation of French Protection of the Maronite Community in Lebanon by Louis XIV (1649)

Louis, by the grace of God King of France and Navarre, to all whom these presents come, greeting: Let it be known: that we, by the advice of the Queen Regent, our very honored Lady and Mother, having taken and placed, as by these signs of our hand we do take and place in our protection and special safeguard the Most Reverend Patriarch and all the prelates, ecclesiastics, and Maronite Christian laics, who dwell particularly in Mount Lebanon: we desire that they should be aware of this at all times and, to this end, we command our beloved and trusty Sieur la Haye de Pentetet, Councilor in our Councils and our Ambassador in the Levant, and all those who succeed him in this post, to show favor to these former, together or separately, by their care, good offices, entreaty and protection, either before the Porte of our very dear and perfect friend the Grand Seigneur, or elsewhere as needs be, so that there will not be accorded to them any ill treatment, but, on the contrary, that they may continue freely their spiritual exercise and functions. We enjoin the Consuls and Vice-Consuls of the French Nation in the seaports of the Levant, or other flying the flag of France, now and in the future, to show all favor in their power to the said Lord Patriarch and to the said Maronite Christians of the said Mount Lebanon and to assist to embark on French or other vessels the young men and all other Christian Maronites who might wish to go over into Christian lands, either to study or for any other business, without taking or requiring of them any fee other than that which they may be able to give, treating them with all possible gentleness and charity.

We request and require the illustrious and magnificent Lords the Pashas and officers of His Highness to show favor to and assist the Lord Archbishop of Tripoli and all prelates and Maronite Christians offering on our part to do likewise for all those recommended by them.

Sultan Abdul-Mejid

Ottoman Imperial Rescript, "The Hatt-i Sherif of Gulhane" (1839)

All the world knows that in the first days of the Ottoman monarchy, the glorious precepts of the Koran and the laws of the empire were always honored.

The empire in consequence increased in strength and greatness, and all its subjects, without exception, had risen in the highest degree to ease and prosperity. In the last one hundred and fifty years a succession of accidents and divers causes have arisen which have brought about a disregard for the sacred code of laws and the regulations flowing therefrom, and the former strength and prosperity have changed into weakness and poverty; an empire in fact loses all its stability so soon as it ceases to observe its laws.

These considerations are ever present to our mind, and ever since the day of our advent to the throne the thought of the public weal, of the improvement of the state of the provinces, and of relief to the [subject] peoples, has not ceased to engage it. If, therefore, the geographical position of the Ottoman provinces, the fertility of the soil, the aptitude and intelligence of the inhabitants, are considered, the conviction will remain that by striving to find efficacious means, the result, which by the help of God we hope to attain, can be obtained within a few years. Full of confidence, therefore, in the help of the

Most High, and certain of the support of our Prophet, we deem it right to seek by new institutions to give to the provinces composing the Ottoman Empire the benefit of a good administration.

These institutions must be principally carried out under three heads, which are:

1. The guarantees insuring to our subjects perfect security for life, honor, and fortune.
2. A regular system of assessing and levying taxes.
3. An equally regular system for the levying of troops and the duration of their service.

And, in fact, are not life and honor the most precious gifts to mankind? What man, however much his character may be against violence, can prevent himself from having recourse to it, and thereby injure the government and country, if his life and honor are endangered? If, on the contrary, he enjoys in that respect perfect security, he will not depart from the ways of loyalty, and all his actions will contribute to the good of the government and of his brothers.

If there is an absence of security as to one's fortune, everyone remains insensible to the voice of the Prince and the country; no one interests himself in the progress of public good, absorbed as he is in his own troubles. If, on the contrary, the citizen keeps possession in all confidence of all his goods, then, full of ardor in his affairs, which he seeks to enlarge in order to increase his comforts, he feels daily growing and doubling in his heart not only his love for the Prince and country, but also his devotion to his native land.

These feelings become in him the source of the most praiseworthy actions.

As to the regular and fixed assessment of the taxes, it is very important that it be regulated; for the state which is forced to incur many expenses for the defense of its territory cannot obtain the money necessary for its armies and other services except by means of contributions levied on its subjects. Although, thanks be to God, our empire has for some time past been delivered from the scourge of monopolies, falsely considered in times of war as a source of revenue, a fatal custom still exists, although it can only have disastrous consequences; it is that of venal concessions, known under the name of "Iltizam."

Under that name the civil and financial administration of a locality is delivered over to the passions of a single man; that is to say, sometimes to the iron grasp of the most violent and avaricious passions, for if that contractor is not a good man, he will only look to his own advantage.

It is therefore necessary that henceforth each member of Ottoman society should be taxed for a quota of a fixed tax according to his fortune and means, and that it should be impossible that anything more could be exacted from him. It is also necessary that special laws should fix and limit the expenses of our land and sea forces.

Although, as we have said, the defense of the country is an important matter, and that it is the duty of all the inhabitants to furnish soldiers for that object, it has become necessary to establish laws to regulate the contingent to be furnished by each locality according to the necessity of the time, and to reduce the term of military service to four or five years. For it is at the same time doing an injustice and giving a mortal blow to agriculture and to industry to take, without consideration to the respective population of the localities, in the one more, in the other less, men than they can furnish; it is also reducing the soldiers to despair and contributing to the depopulation of the country by keeping them all their lives in the service.

In short, without the several laws, the necessity for which has just been described, there can be neither strength, nor riches, nor happiness, nor tranquility for the empire; it must, on the contrary, look for them in the existence of these new laws.

From henceforth, therefore, the cause of every accused person shall be publicly judged, as the divine law requires, after inquiry and examination, and so long as a regular judgment shall not have been pronounced, no one can secretly or publicly put another to death by poison or in any other manner.

No one shall be allowed to attack the honor of any other person whatever.

Each one shall possess his property of every kind, and shall dispose of it in all freedom, without let or hinderance from any person whatever; thus, for example, the innocent heirs of a criminal shall not be deprived of their legal rights, and the property of the criminal shall not be confiscated. These imperial concessions shall extend to all our subjects, of whatever religion or sect they may be; they shall enjoy them without exception. We therefore grant perfect security to the inhabitants of our empire in their lives, their honor, and their fortunes, as they are secured to them by the sacred text of the law.

As for the other points, as they must be settled with the assistance of enlightened opinions, our council of justice (increased by new members as shall be found necessary), to whom shall be joined, on certain days which we shall determine, our ministers and the notabilities of the empire, shall assemble in order to frame laws regulating the security of life and fortune and the assessment of the taxes. Each one in those assemblies shall freely express his ideas and give his advice.

Sultan Abdul-Mejid

Imperial Rescripts "Islahat Fermani" (1856)

I have therefore resolved upon, and I order the execution of the following measures:

The guarantees promised on our part by the Hatt-i Hamayoun of Gulhane, and in conformity with the Tanzimat, to all the subjects of my empire, without distinction of classes or of religion, for the security of their persons and property, and the preservation of their honor, are to-day confirmed and consolidated, and efficacious measures shall be taken in order that they may have their full entire effect.

All the privileges and spiritual immunities granted by my ancestors *ab antiquo*, and at subsequent dates, to all Christian communities or other non-Moslem persuasions established in my empire, under my protection, shall be confirmed and maintained.

Every Christian or other non-Moslem community shall be bound within a fixed period, and with the concurrence of a commission composed *ad hoc* of members of its own body, to proceed, with my high approbation and under the inspection of my Sublime Porte, to examine into its actual immunities and privileges, and to discuss and submit to my Sublime Porte the reforms required by the progress of civilization and of the age. The powers conceded to the Christian patriarchs and bishops by the Sultan Mahomet II and to his successors shall be made to harmonize with the new position which my generous and beneficient intentions insure to these communities.

The principle of nominating the patriarchs for life, after the revision of the rule of election now in force, shall be exactly carried out, conformably to the tenor of their firmans of investiture.

The patriarchs, metropolitans, archbishops, bishops, and rabbins shall take an oath, on their entrance into office, according to a form agreed upon in common by my Sublime Porte and the spiritual heads of the different religious communities. The ecclesiastical dues, of whatever sort or nature they be, shall be abolished and replaced by fixed revenues of the patriarchs and heads of communities, and by the allocations of allowances and salaries equitably proportioned to the importance, the rank, and the dignity of the different members of the clergy.

The property, real or personal, of the different Christian ecclesiastics shall remain intact; the temporal administration of the Christian or other non-Moslem communities shall, however, be placed under the safeguard of an assembly to be chosen from among the members, both ecclesiastics and laymen, of the said communities.

In the towns, small boroughs, and villages where the whole population is of the same religion, no obstacle shall be offered to the repair, according to their original plan, of buildings set apart for religious worship, for schools, for hospitals, and for cemeteries.

The plans of these different buildings, in case of their new erection, must, after having been approved by the patriarchs or heads of communities, be submitted to my Sublime Porte, which will approve of them by my imperial order, or make known its observations upon them within a certain time. Each sect, in localities where there are no other religious denominations, shall be free from every species of restraint as regards the public exercise of its religion.

In the towns, small boroughs, and villages where different sects are mingled together, each community inhabiting a distinct quarter shall, by conforming to the above-mentioned ordinances, have equal power to repair and improve its churches, its hospitals, its schools, and its cemeteries. When there is question of their erection of new buildings, the necessary authority must be asked for, through the medium of the patriarchs and heads of communities, from my Sublime Porte, which will pronounce a sovereign decision according that authority, except in the case of administrative obstacles.

The intervention of the administrative authority in all measures of this nature will be entirely gratuitous. My Sublime Porte will take energetic measures to insure to each sect, whatever be the number of its adherents, entire freedom in the exercise of its religion. Every distinction or designation pending to make any class whatever of the subjects of my empire inferior to another class, on account of their religion, language, or race, shall be forever effaced from administrative protocol. The laws shall be put in force against the use of any injurious or offensive term, either among private individuals or on the part of the authorities.

As all forms of religion are and shall be freely professed in my dominions, no subject of my empire shall be hindered in the exercise of the religion that he professes, nor shall he be in any way annoyed on this account. No one shall be compelled to change their religion.

The nomination and choice of all functionaries and other employés of my empire being wholly dependent upon my sovereign will, all the subjects of my empire, without distinction of nationality, shall be admissible to public employments, and qualified to fill them according to their capacity and merit, and conformably with rules to be generally applied.

All the subjects of my empire, without distinction, shall be received into the civil and military schools of the government, if they otherwise satisfy the conditions as to age and examination which are specified in the organic regulations of the said schools. Moreover, every community is authorized to establish public schools of science, art, and industry. Only the method of instructions and the choice of professors in schools of this class shall be under the control of a mixed council of public instruction, the members of which shall be named by my sovereign command.

All commercial, correctional, and criminal suits between Moslems and Christians, or other non-Moslem subjects, or between Christians or other non-Moslems of different sects, shall be referred to mixed tribunals.

The proceedings of these tribunals shall be public; the parties shall be confronted and shall produce their witnesses, whose testimony shall be received without distinction, upon an oath taken according to the religious law of each sect.

Suits relating to civil affairs shall continue to be publicly tried, according to the laws and regulations, before the mixed provincial councils, in the presence of the governor and judge of the place.

Special civil proceedings, such as those relating to successions or others of that kind, between subjects of the same Christian or other non-Moslem faith, may at the request of the parties, be sent before the councils of the patriarchs or of the communities.

Penal, correctional, and commercial laws, and rules of procedure for the mixed tribunals, shall be drawn up as soon as possible and formed into a code. Translations of them shall be published in all the languages current in the empire.

Proceedings shall be taken, with as little delay as possible, for the reform of the penitentiary system as applied to houses of detention, punishment, or correction, and other establishments of like nature, so as to reconcile the rights of humanity with those of justice. Corporal punishment shall not be administered, even in the prisons, except in conformity with the disciplinary regulations established by my Sublime Porte; and everything that resembles torture shall be entirely abolished.

Infractions of the law in this particular shall be severely repressed, and shall besides entail, as of right, the punishment, in conformity with the civil code, of the authorities who may order and of the agents who may commit them.

The organization of the police in the capital, in the provincial towns and in the rural districts, shall be revised in such a manner as to give to all the peaceable subjects of my empire the strongest guarantees for the safety both of their persons and property.

The equality of taxes entailing equality of burdens, as equality of duties entails that of rights, Christian subjects, and those of other non-Moslem sects, as it has been already decided, shall, as well as Moslems, be subject to the obligations of the law of recruitment.

The principle of obtaining substitutes, or of purchasing exemption, shall be admitted. A complete law shall be published, with as little delay as possible, respecting the admission into and service in the army of Christian and other non-Moslem subjects.

Proceedings shall be taken for a reform in the constitution of the provincial and communal councils in order to insure fairness in the choice of the deputies of the Moslem, Christian, and other communities and freedom of voting in the councils. My Sublime Porte will take into consideration the adoption of the most effectual means for ascertaining exactly and for controlling the result of the deliberations and of the decisions arrived at.

As the laws regulating the purchase, sale, and disposal of real property are common to all the subjects of my empire, it shall be lawful for foreigners to possess landed property in my dominions, conforming themselves to the laws and police regulations, and bearing the same charges as the native inhabitants, and after arrangements have been come to with foreign powers.

The taxes are to be levied under the same denomination from all the subjects of my empire, without distinction of class or of religion. The most prompt and energetic means for remedying the abuses in collecting the taxes, and especially the tithes, shall be considered.

The system of direct collections shall gradually, and as soon as possible, be substituted for the plan of farming, in all the branches of the revenues of the state. As long as the present system remains in force all agents of the government and all members of the medjlis shall be forbidden under the severest penalties, to become lessees of any farming contracts which are announced for public competition, or to have any beneficial interest in carrying them out. The local taxes shall, as far as possible, be so imposed as not to affect the sources of production or to hinder the progress of internal commerce.

Works of public utility shall receive a suitable endowment, part of which shall be raised from private and special taxes levied in the provinces, which shall have the benefit of the advantages arising from the establishment of ways of communication by land and sea.

A special law having been already passed, which declares that the budget of the revenue and the expenditure of the state shall be drawn up and made known every year, the said law shall be most scrupulously observed. Proceedings shall be taken for revising the emoluments attached to each office.

The heads of each community and a delegate, designated by my Sublime Porte, shall be summoned to take part in the deliberations of the supreme council of justice on all occasions which might interest the generality of the subjects of my empire. They shall be summoned specially for this purpose by my grand vizier. The delegates shall hold office for one year; they shall be sworn on entering upon their duties. All the members of the council, at the ordinary and extraordinary meetings, shall freely give their opinions and their votes, and no one shall ever annoy them on this account.

The laws against corruption, extortion, or malversation shall apply, according to the legal forms, to all the subjects of my empire, whatever may be their class and the nature of their duties.

Steps shall be taken for the formation of banks and other similar institutions, so as to effect a reform in the monetary and financial system, as well as to create funds to be employed in augmenting the sources of the material wealth of my empire. Steps shall also be taken for the formation of roads and canals to increase the facilities of communication and increase the sources of the wealth of the country.

Everything that can impede commerce or agriculture shall be abolished. To accomplish these objects means shall be sought to profit by the science, the art, and the funds of Europe, and thus gradually to execute them.

Such being my wishes and my commands, you, who are my grand vizier, will, according to custom, cause this imperial firman to be published in my capital and in all parts of my empire; and you will watch attentively and take all the necessary measures that all the orders which it contains be henceforth carried out with the most rigorous punctuality.

Treaty of Paris (1856)

Article IX. His Imperial Majesty the Sultan [Abdul-Aziz] having, in his constant solicitude for the welfare of his subjects, issued a Firman which, while ameliorating their condition without distinction of Religion or of Race, records his generous intentions towards the Christian population of his Empire, and wishing to give a further proof of his sentiments in that respect, has resolved to communicate to the Contracting Parties the said Firman, emanating spontaneously from his Sovereign will.

The Contracting Powers recognize the high value of this communication. It is clearly understood that it cannot, in any case, give to the said Powers the right to interfere, either collectively or separately, in the relations of His Majesty the Sultan with his subjects, nor in the internal Administration of his Empire.

Memorandums on European Intervention in Lebanon (1860)

Earl Cowley to Lord J. Russell, British Secretary of State for External Affairs, 5 July 1860

M. Thouvenel [French Minister of Foreign Affairs] . . . read me various reports which had reached him from Damascus and Beyrout . . . giving accounts of the massacres and horrors which the Christian population of the Lebanon, and more particularly the inhabitants of Hasbeya and Zahlé, had undergone at the hands of the Druses and Bedouin Arabs, under the eyes of the Turkish Authorities, without any protection from, if not with the connivance of, the latter.

As the Consuls of the Five Powers at Beyrout seem to have acted in complete accord, your Lordship will no doubt have received information direct from thence. The reports which have reached the French Government appear to be founded on information given by fugitive Christians alone. It is to be hoped, therefore, that there may be some exaggeration in them. Still, if but a tenth part be true, enough has occurred to excite universal reprobation, while the inability of the Turkish Authorities to maintain order and tranquility is clearly shown in the Minutes of the proceedings of the Consular Body at Beyrout.

M. Thouvenel was much moved while reading these reports to me. He said that it would be impossible to leave matters in this state in Syria; that when the horrible treatment to which the Christian populations had been exposed came to be known, there would be but one cry of indignation in France. Neither sex nor age had been spared; priests, women, and children, had been indiscriminately slain; the convents had been plundered, and the Sovereign Authority being impotent, or unwilling to act, there was no saying what the next intelligence might bring. The arrangement of 1845 ought not to be considered a dead-letter, and authorized the interference of Europe. It might be impossible for either France or England to send troops to restore order; but no doubt their ships-of-war would be able to protect their Consular

Great Britain, Command Papers No. 2800 (1861).

Officers, and such of their subjects as resided on the coast; but this would not be sufficient. Might not a Commission from the Five Powers be sent into the disturbed districts; and if it was found that the Porte was unable to furnish the force necessary to restore order, might not the Sultan be invited to ask for troops from the Viceroy of Egypt.

Lord J. Russell to Earl Cowley, Foreign Office, 6 July 1860

I have to inform your Excellency that Her Majesty's Government will press on the Porte the necessity of using the utmost efforts to repress the disturbances in Syria.

A British squadron will be sent to the coast of Syria, and, if necessary, Marines will be landed.

Earl Cowley to Lord J. Russell, Paris, 9 July 1860

With reference to your Lordship's despatch of the 6th instant, stating that Her Majesty's Government would direct a squadron to be sent to the coast of Syria, and Marines to be landed, if necessary, I have the honour to state that M. Thouvenel seems satisfied at the decision taken by the Porte to send Fuad Pasha, with extraordinary powers, to that country.

The French Government have also directed two men-of-war to proceed to the coast of Syria.

The instructions to the Officers commanding enjoin them to endeavour to act in concert with the men-of-war of any other nation with which they may meet.

M. Thouvenel to Count de Persigny, Paris, 16 July 1860

The events which have lately taken place in the Lebanon have, as might be expected, caused a profound emotion, and all the Cabinets have recognized that they have created duties for them. All have hastened to furnish to their Agents on the spot the means in their power for the protection of the Christian populations, and it is to be hoped that these measures, combined with the despatch of the Ottoman troops placed at the disposal of Fuad Pasha, will suffice at least to stop the effusion of blood. But after such scenes and such a complete derangement of affairs, it is not sufficient, in order to satisfy the principles of justice, and order, and to establish a durable state of things, to suppress the insurrection, and to oblige the Druses to lay down their arms. The situation requires measures calculated, at the same time, to repair frightful calamities and to prevent their recurrence. . . .

Lord J. Russell to Earl Cowley, Foreign Office, 28 July 1860

I am now enabled to give you the opinion of Her Majesty's Government respecting the Convention relating to the expedition to Syria.

The main points appear to be the necessity of obtaining the assent of the Porte explicitly given to the intervention of foreign troops in one of the provinces of the Sultan, and the equal necessity of fixing a term at the end of which such foreign intervention is to cease. . . .

The Protocol renouncing all views of separate advantage, territorial or commercial, and all exclusive influence, should be signed on the same day as the Treaty. . . .

It is to be hoped that the measures now taken may vindicate the rights of humanity, so cruelly outraged in Syria, and at the same time tend to maintain order and obedience in the dominions of the Sultan.

Lord J. Russell to Earl Cowley, Foreign Office, 28 July 1860

With respect to the proposal of Russia . . . to insert a declaration in favour of Christians generally in the Convention relating to the expedition to Syria, I have to instruct your Excellency to object to it, as altogether going beyond the present occasion; and if the Russian Ambassador presses it, you will refuse to sign a Convention or Protocol in which any Article to that effect is contained.

C. Musurus to Lord J. Russell, London, 30 July 1860

The Ambassador of the Sublime Porte at London has received from his Government a telegraphic despatch [according to which] His Imperial Majesty the Sultan, at the request of England and France, has authorized his Ambassador at Paris to negotiate and sign a Convention with the Powers, relative to sending a body of troops to Syria, if they should all agree to it.

Accordingly the Sublime Porte declares that her adoption of this decision is in order to give her Allies a proof of her confidence, and of her sincere desire to repress disorders which she regrets more than any one.

At the same time she has not failed to inform the Representatives of France and England at Constantinople of all the inconveniences and dangers which an intervention of this kind might produce. She has represented to them that the arrival of foreign troops at any point of the Ottoman Empire might awaken, from one end of the Empire to another, different sentiments amongst the different populations, the results of which might become most disastrous. In fact, the disaffected portion of the Christian population, considering the resolution of the Powers as a point in their favour against the Moslems, might deliver themselves over to excesses. On the other hand, such of the Moslems as are unable to appreciate the true intentions of Europe, in desperation, and annoyed at seeing themselves treated with so much mistrust, simply because the Druses and a few bad characters, who are only Moslems by name, have committed acts which they themselves deprecate, might respond to these excesses by committing excesses themselves. It is plain that the evils which might cause such a state of things would arouse those animosities which the Government is doing its utmost to extinguish.

Treaty of Berlin (1878)

Article XLIV. In Romania the difference of religious creeds and confessions shall not be alleged against any person as a ground for exclusion or incapacity in matters relating to the enjoyment of civil and political rights, admission to public employments, functions, and honours, or the exercise of the various professions and industries in any locality whatsoever.

The freedom and outward exercise of all forms of worship shall be assured to all persons belonging to the Romanian State, as well as to foreigners, and no hindrance shall be offered either to the hierarchical organization of the different communions, or to their relations with their spiritual chiefs.

The subjects and citizens of all the Powers, traders or others, shall be treated in Romania, without distinction of creed, on a footing of perfect equality.

Thomas Jefferson

On Latin America. Letter to Alexander von Humboldt (1813)

I think it most fortunate that your travels in those countries were so timed as to make them known to the world in the moment they were about to become actors on its stage. That they will throw off their European dependence I have no doubt; but in what kind of government their revolution will end I am not so certain. History, I believe, furnishes no example of a priest-ridden people maintaining a free civil government. This marks the lowest grade of ignorance, of which their civil as well as religious leaders will always avail themselves for their own purposes. The vicinity of New Spain to the United States, and their consequent intercourse, may furnish schools for the higher, and example for the lower classes of their citizens. And Mexico, where we learn from you that men of science are not wanting, may revolutionize itself under better auspices than the Southern provinces. These last, I fear, must end in military despotism. The different castes of their inhabitants, their mutual hatreds and jealousies, their profound ignorance and bigotry, will be played off by cunning leaders, and each be made the instrument of enslaving the others. But of all this you can best judge, for in truth we have little knowledge of them to be depended on, but through you. But in whatever governments they end they will be *American* governments, no longer to be involved in the never-ceasing broils of Europe. The European nations constitute a separate division of the globe; their localities make them part of a distinct system; they have a set of interests of their own in which it is our business never to engage ourselves. America has a hemisphere to itself. It must have its separate system of interests, which must not be subordinated to those of Europe. The insulated state in which nature has placed the American continent, should so far avail it that no spark of war kindled in the other quarters of the globe should be wafted across the wide oceans which separate us from them. And it will be so. In fifty years more the United States alone will contain fifty millions of inhabitants, and fifty years are soon gone over. The peace of 1763 is within that peroid. I was then twenty years old, and of course remember well all the transactions of the war preceding it. And you will live to see the epoch now equally ahead of us; and the numbers which will

The Writings of Thomas Jefferson, eds. Andrew A. Lipscomb and Albert E. Bergh (14:20–25).

then be spread over the other parts of the American hemisphere, catching long before that the principles of our portion of it, and concurring with us in the maintenance of the same system.

James Monroe

The Monroe Doctrine (1823)

At the proposal of the Russian Imperial Government, made through the minister of the Emperor residing here, a full power and instructions have been transmitted to the minister of the United States at St. Petersburg to arrange by amicable negotiation the respective rights and interests of the two nations on the northwest coast of this continent. A similar proposal had been made by His Imperial Majesty to the Government of Great Britain, which has likewise been acceded to. The Government of the United States has been desirous by this friendly proceeding of manifesting the great value which they have invariably attached to the friendship of the Emperor and their solicitude to cultivate the best understanding with his Government. In the discussions to which this interest has given rise and in the arrangements by which they may terminate the occasion has been judged proper for asserting, as a principle in which the rights and interests of the United States are involved, that the American continents, by the free and independent condition which they have assumed and maintain, are henceforth not to be considered as subjects for future colonization by any European powers. . . .

. . . It was stated at the commencement of the last session that a great effort was then making in Spain and Portugal to improve the condition of the people of those countries, and that it appeared to be conducted with extraordinary moderation. It need scarcely be remarked that the result has been so far very different from what was then anticipated. Of events in that quarter of the globe, with which we have so much intercourse and from which we derive our origin, we have always been anxious and interested spectators. The citizens of the United States cherish sentiments the most friendly in favor of the liberty and happiness of their fellow-men on that side of the Atlantic. In the wars of the European powers in matters relating to themselves we have never taken any part, nor does it comport with our policy so to do. It is only when our rights are invaded or seriously menaced that we resent injuries or make preparation for our defense. With the movements in this hemisphere we are of necessity more immediately connected, and by causes which must be obvious to all enlightened and impartial observers. The political system of the allied powers is essentially different in this respect from that of America. This difference proceeds from that which exists in their respective Governments; and to the defense of our own, which has been achieved by the loss of so much blood and treasure, and matured by the wisdom of their most enlightened citizens, and under which we have enjoyed unexampled felicity, this whole nation is devoted. We owe it, therefore, to candor and to the amicable relations existing between the United States and those powers to declare that we should consider any attempt on their part to extend their system to any portion of this hemisphere as dangerous to our peace and safety. With the existing colonies or dependencies of any European power we have not interfered and shall not interfere. But with the Governments who have declared their independence and maintained it, and whose independence we have, on great consideration and on just principles, acknowledged, we could not view any interposition for the purpose of oppressing them, or controlling in any other manner their destiny, by any European power in any other light than as the manifestation of an unfriendly disposition toward the United States. In the war between those new Governments and Spain we declared our neutrality at the time of their recognition, and to this we have adhered, and shall continue to adhere, provided no change shall occur which, in the judgment of the competent authorities of this Government, shall make a corresponding change on the part of the United States indispensable to their security.

The late events in Spain and Portugal shew that Europe is still unsettled. Of this important fact no stronger proof can be added than that the allied powers should have thought it proper, on any principle satisfactory to themselves, to have interposed by force in the internal concerns of Spain. To what extent such interposition may be carried, on the same principle, is a question in which all independent powers whose governments differ from theirs are interested, even those most remote, and surely none more so than the United States. Our policy in regard to Europe, which was adopted at an early stage of the wars which have so long agitated that quarter of the globe, nevertheless remains the same, which is, not to interfere in the internal concerns of any of its powers; to consider the government de facto as the legitimate government for us; to cultivate friendly relations with it, and to preserve those relations by a frank, firm, and manly policy, meeting in all instances the just claims of every power, submitting to injuries from none. But in regard to those continents circumstances are eminently and conspicuously different. It is impossible that the allied powers should extend their political system to any portion of either continent without endangering our peace and happiness; nor can anyone believe that our southern brethren, if left to themselves, would adopt it of their own accord.

Senator Redfield Proctor

Speech on Cuba (1898)

My trip was entirely unofficial and of my own motion, not suggested by anyone. The only mention I made of it to the President was to say to him that I contemplated such a trip and to ask him if there was any objection to it; to which he replied that he could see none. No one but myself, therefore, is responsible for anything in this statement.

Outside Habana all is changed. It is not peace nor is it war. It is desolation and distress, misery and starvation. Every town and village is surrounded by a "trocha" (trench), a sort of rifle pit, but constructed on a plan new to me, the dirt being thrown up on the inside and a barbed-wire fence on the outer side of the trench. These trochas have at every corner and at frequent intervals along the sides what are there called forts, but which are really small block houses, many of them more like large sentry boxes, loopholed for musketry, and with a guard of from two to ten soldiers in each.

The purpose of these trochas is to keep the reconcentrados in as well as to keep the insurgents out. From all the surrounding country the people have been driven in to these fortified towns and held there to subsist as they can. They are virtually prison yards and not unlike one in general appearance, except that the walls are not so high and strong; but they suffice, where every point is in range of a soldier's rifle, to keep in the poor reconcentrado women and children.

There are no domestic animals or crops on the rich fields and pastures except such as are under guard in the immediate vicinity of the towns. In other words, the Spaniards hold in these four western provinces just what their army sits on. Every man, woman, and child, and every domestic animal, wherever their columns have reached, is under guard and within their so-called fortifications. To describe one place is to describe all. To repeat, it is neither peace nor war. It is concentration and desolation. This is the "pacified" condition of the four western provinces.

All the country people in the four western provinces, about 400,000 in number, remaining outside the fortified towns when Weyler's* order

---

*The Spanish commander in Cuba responsible for putting civilians in concentration camps, to deprive nationalist guerrillas of support.

was made were driven into these towns, and these are the reconcentrados. They were the peasantry, many of them farmers, some landowners, others renting lands and owning more or less stock, others working on estates and cultivating small patches, and even a small patch in that fruitful clime will support a family. . . .

. . . Their huts are about 10 by 15 feet in size, and for want of space are usually crowded together very closely. They have no floor but the ground, no furniture, and, after a year's wear, but little clothing except such stray substitutes as they can extemporize; and with large families, or more than one, in this little space, the commonest sanitary provisions are impossible. Conditions are unmentionable in this respect. Torn from their homes, with foul earth, foul air, foul water, and foul food or none, what wonder that one-half have died and that one-quarter of the living are so diseased that they can not be saved? . . .

. . . Before Weyler's order, these people were independent and self-supporting. They are not beggars even now. There are plenty of professional beggars in every town among the regular residents, but these country people, the reconcentrados, have not learned the art. Rarely is a hand held out to you for alms when going among their huts, but the sight of them makes an appeal stronger than words. . . .

. . . I went to Cuba with a strong conviction that the picture had been overdrawn; that a few cases of starvation and suffering had inspired and stimulated the press correspondents, and that they had given free play to a strong, natural, and highly cultivated imagination. . . . I could not believe that out of a population of 1,600,000, two hundred thousand had died within these Spanish forts, practically prison walls, within a few months past from actual starvation and diseases caused by insufficient and improper food. My inquiries were entirely outside of sensational sources. They were made of our medical officers, of our consuls, of city alcades (mayors), of relief committees, of leading merchants and bankers, physicians, and lawyers. Several of my informants were Spanish born, but every time the answer was that the case had not been overstated. What I saw I can not tell so that others can see it. It must be seen with one's own eyes to be realized. . . .

. . . General Blanco's order of November 13 last somewhat modifies the Weyler order, but is of little or no practical benefit. Its application is limited to farms "properly defended," and the owners are obliged to build "centers of defense." Its execution is completely in the discretion of the local military authorities, and they know the terrible military efficiency of Weyler's order in stripping the country of all possible shelter, food, or source of information for an insurgent, and will be slow to surrender this advantage. In fact, though the order was issued four months ago, I saw no beneficent results from it worth mentioning.

United States Declaration of War on Spain (1898)

Whereas the abhorrent conditions which have existed for more than three years in the island of Cuba, so near our own borders, have shocked the moral sense of the people of the United States, have been a disgrace to Christian civilization, culminating, as they have, in the destruction of a United States battle ship, with 266 of its officers and crew, while on a friendly visit in the harbor of Havana, and can not longer be endured, as has been set forth by the President of the United States in his message to Congress of April 11, 1898, upon which the action of Congress was invited: Therefore,

Resolved by the Senate and House of Representatives of the United States of America in Congress assembled, First. That the people of the island of Cuba are and of right ought to be free and independent.

Second. That it is the duty of the United States to demand, and the Government of the United States does hereby demand, that the Government of Spain at once relinquish its authority and government in the island of Cuba and withdraws its land and naval forces from Cuba and Cuban waters.

Third. That the President of the United States be, and he hereby is, directed and empowered to use the entire land and naval forces of the United States and to call into the actual service of the United States the militia of the several States to such extent as may be necessary to carry these resolutions into effect.

Fourth.* That the United States hereby disclaims any disposition or intention to exercise sovereignty, jurisdiction, or control over said island except for the pacification thereof, and asserts its determination, when that is accomplished, to leave the government and control of the island to its people.

*Amendment proposed by Senator Henry Teller.

Theodore Roosevelt

On Human Rights in Foreign Policy (1904)

In asserting the Monroe Doctrine, in taking such steps as we have taken in regard to Cuba, Venezuela, and Panama, and in endeavoring to circumscribe the theater of war in the Far East, and to secure the open door in China, we have acted in our own interest as well as in the interest of humanity at large. There are, however, cases in which, while our own interests are not greatly involved, strong appeal is made to our sympathies. Ordinarily it is very much wiser and more useful for us to concern ourselves with striving for our own moral and material betterment here at home than to concern ourselves with trying to better the condition of things in other nations. We have plenty of sins of our own to war against, and under ordinary circumstances we can do more for the general uplifting of humanity by striving with heart and soul to put a stop to civic corruption, to brutal lawlessness and violent race prejudices here at home than by passing resolutions about wrongdoing elsewhere. Nevertheless there are occasional crimes committed on so vast a scale and of such peculiar horror as to make us doubt whether it is not our manifest duty to endeavor at least to show our disapproval of the deed and our sympathy with those who have suffered by it. The cases must be extreme in which such a course is justifiable. There must be no effort made to remove the mote from our brother's eye if we refuse to remove the beam from our own. But in extreme cases action may be justifiable and proper. What form the action shall take must depend upon the circumstances of the case; that is, upon the degree of the atrocity and upon our power to remedy it. The cases in which we could interfere by force of arms as we interfered to put a stop to intolerable conditions in Cuba are necessarily very few. Yet it is not to be expected that a people like ours, which in spite of certain very obvious shortcomings, nevertheless as a whole shows by its consistent practice its belief in the principles of civil and religious liberty and of orderly freedom, a people among whom even the worst crime, like the crime of lynching, is never more than sporadic, so that individuals and not classes are molested in their fundamental rights—it is inevitable that such a nation should desire eagerly to give expression to its horror on an occasion like that of the massacre of the Jews in Kishenef, or

From his State of the Union Message.

when it witnesses such systematic and long-extended cruelty and
oppression as the cruelty and oppression of which the Armenians have
been the victims, and which have won for them the indignant pity of
the civilized world. . . .

Woodrow Wilson

Speech on Latin America (1913)

One of the chief objects of my administration will be to cultivate the
friendship and deserve the confidence of our sister republics of Central
and South America, and to promote in every proper and honorable
way the interests which are common to the peoples of the two continents. . . .
. . . Cooperation is possible only when supported at every turn by
the orderly processes of just government based upon law, not upon
arbitrary or irregular force. We hold . . . that just government rests
always upon the consent of the governed, and that there can be no
freedom without order based upon law and upon the public conscience
and approval. . . . We shall lend our influence of every kind to the
realization of these principles in fact and practice, knowing that disorder, personal intrigues, and defiance of constitutional rights weaken
and discredit government and injure none so much as the people who
are unfortunate enough to have their common life and their common
affairs so tainted and disturbed. We can have no sympathy with those
who seek to seize the power of government to advance their own personal interests or ambition. We are the friends of peace, but we know
that there can be no lasting or stable peace in such circumstances. As
friends, therefore, we shall prefer those who act in the interest of peace
and honor, who protect private rights and respect the restraints of
constitutional provision. Mutual respect seems to us the indispensable
foundation of friendship between states as between individuals.
The United States has nothing to seek in Central and South America
except the lasting interests of the peoples of the two continents, the
security of governments intended for the people and for no special
group or interest, and the development of personal and trade relationships between the two continents which shall redound to the profit and
advantage of both and interfere with the rights and liberties of neither.

Woodrow Wilson

On Mexico (1913)

. . . There is but one cloud upon our horizon. That has shown itself to the south of us, and hangs over Mexico. There can be no certain prospect of peace in America until Gen. Huerta has surrendered his usurped authority in Mexico; until it is understood on all hands, indeed, that such pretended governments will not be countenanced or dealt with by the Government of the United States. We are the friends of constitutional government in America; we are more than its friends, we are its champions; because in no other way can our neighbors, to whom we would wish in every way to make proof of our friendship, work out their own development in peace and liberty. Mexico has no Government. The attempt to maintain one at the City of Mexico has broken down, and a mere military despotism has been set up which has hardly more than the semblance of national authority. It originated in the usurpation of Victoriano Huerta, who, after a brief attempt to play the part of constitutional President, has at last cast aside even the pretense of legal right and declared himself dictator. As a consequence, a condition of affairs now exists in Mexico which has made it doubtful whether even the most elementary and fundamental rights either of her own people or of the citizens of other countries resident within her territory can long be successfully safeguarded, and which threatens, if long continued, to imperil the interests of peace, order, and tolerable life in the lands immediately to the south of us. . . . But he has not succeeded. He has forfeited the respect and the moral support even of those who were at one time willing to see him succeed. Little by little he has been completely isolated. By a little every day his power and prestige are crumbling and the collapse is not far away. We shall not, I believe, be obliged to alter our policy of watchful waiting. And then, when the end comes, we shall hope to see constitutional order restored in distressed Mexico by the concert and energy of such of her leaders as prefer the liberty of their people to their own ambitions. . . .

From his State of the Union Message.

German Government Memorandum on the Armenians (1915)

The German Embassy in Turkey to the Turkish Ministry of Foreign Affairs

By its memorandum of July 4, the German Embassy had the honor to acquaint the Sublime Porte with the views of the Imperial German Government concerning the banishment of the Armenian inhabitants of the Anatolian provinces and to draw its attention to the fact that the measures had been attended in several places by acts of violence such as massacres and plundering which the end sought by the Ottoman Imperial Government could not justify.

The German Embassy regrets to state that it appears from information received subsequently from impartial and trustworthy sources that incidents of that character, instead of being prevented by the local authorities, have regularly occurred upon the expulsion of Armenians, so that most of them perished even before reaching their destination. These are reported mainly from the provinces of Trebizond, Diarbekr and Erzerum. In some places, at Mardin for instance, all the Christians without distinction of race or faith have had the same fate.

At the same time the Ottoman Imperial Government saw fit to extend the banishment order to the other provinces of Asia Minor, and quite recently the Armenian villages of the Izmid district were emptied of their inhabitants under like conditions.

In the presence of those events the German Embassy, by order of its Government, is constrained to remonstrate once more upon those horrible deeds and to decline any responsibility for the consequences they may involve. It finds itself under the necessity of drawing the attention of the Ottoman Government to that point all the more as public opinion is already inclined to believe that Germany as a friendly power allied to Turkey may have approved or even instigated those acts of violence.

Woodrow Wilson

On Self-Determination (1918)

. . . Free, open-minded, and absolutely impartial adjustment of all colonial claims, based upon a strict observance of the principle that in determining all such questions of sovereignty the interests of the population concerned must have equal weight with the equitable claims of the Government whose title is to be determined.

Point V of his Fourteen Points speech.

The League of Nations Covenant (1919)

Article 23. Subject to and in accordance with the provisions of international conventions existing or hereafter to be agreed upon, the Members of the League:

(a) will endeavor to secure and maintain fair and humane conditions of labor for men, women, and children, both in their own countries and in all countries to which their commercial and industrial relations extend, and for that purpose will establish and maintain the necessary international organizations;

(b) undertake to secure just treatment of the native inhabitants of territories under their control. . . .

Polish Minority Treaty (1919)

Whereas, The Allied and Associated Powers have by the success of their arms restored to the Polish nation the independence of which it had been unjustly deprived; and

Treaty Between the Allied and Associated Powers and Poland Concerning Protection of Minorities.

Whereas, By the proclamation of March 30, 1917, the Government of Russia assented to the re-establishment of an independent Polish State; and

Whereas, The Polish State, which now, in fact, exercises sovereignty over those portions of the former Russian Empire which are inhabited by a majority of Poles, has already been recognized as a sovereign and independent State by the Principal Allied and Associated Powers; and

Whereas, Under the Treaty of Peace concluded with Germany by the Allied and Associated Powers, a Treaty of which Poland is a signatory, certain portions of the former German Empire will be incorporated in the territory of Poland; and

Whereas, Under the terms of the said Treaty of Peace, the boundaries of Poland not already laid down are to be subsequently determined by the Principal Allied and Associated Powers;

The United States of America, the British Empire, France, Italy and Japan, on the one hand, confirming their recognition of the Polish State, constituted within the said limits as a sovereign and independent member of the Family of Nations, and being anxious to ensure the execution of the provisions of Article 93 of the said Treaty of Peace with Germany;

Poland, on the other hand, desiring to conform her institutions to the principles of liberty and justice, and to give a sure guarantee to the inhabitants of the territory over which she has assumed sovereignty;

For this purpose the High Contracting Parties . . . have agreed as follows:

Chapter I

ARTICLE 1

Poland undertakes that the stipulations contained in Articles 2 to 8 of this Chapter shall be recognized as fundamental laws, and that no law, regulation or official action shall conflict or interfere with these stipulations, nor shall any law, regulation or official action prevail over them.

ARTICLE 2

Poland undertakes to assure full and complete protection of life and liberty to all inhabitants of Poland without distinction of birth, nationality, language, race or religion.

All inhabitants of Poland shall be entitled to the free exercise, whether public or private, of any creed, religion or belief, whose practices are not inconsistent with public order or public morals.

ARTICLE 3

Poland admits and declares to be Polish nationals *ipso facto* and without the requirement of any formality, German, Austrian, Hungarian or Russian nationals habitually resident at the date of the coming into force of the present Treaty in territory which is or may be recognized as forming part of Poland, but subject to any provisions in the Treaties of Peace with Germany or Austria respectively relating to persons who became resident in such territory after a specified date.

Nevertheless, the persons referred to above who are over eighteen years of age will be entitled under the conditions contained in the said Treaties to opt for any other nationality which may be open to them. Option by a husband will cover his wife and option by parents will cover their children under eighteen years of age.

Persons who have exercised the above right to opt must, except where it is otherwise provided in the Treaty of Peace with Germany, transfer within the succeeding twelve months their place of residence to the State for which they have opted. They will be entitled to retain their immovable property in Polish territory. They may carry with them their movable property of every description. No export duties may be imposed upon them in connexion with the removal of such property.

ARTICLE 4

Poland admits and declares to be Polish nationals *ipso facto* and without the requirement of any formality, persons of German, Austrian, Hungarian or Russian nationality who were born in the said territory of parents habitually resident there, even if at the date of the coming into force of the present Treaty they are not themselves habitually resident there.

Nevertheless, within two years after the coming into force of the present Treaty, these persons may make a declaration before the competent Polish authorities in the country in which they are resident, stating that they abandon Polish nationality, and they will then cease to be considered as Polish nationals. In this connexion a declaration by a husband will cover his wife, and a declaration by parents will cover their children under eighteen years of age.

ARTICLE 5

Poland undertakes to put no hindrance in the way of the exercise of the right which the persons concerned have, under the Treaties concluded or to be concluded by the Allied and Associated Powers with Germany, Austria, Hungary or Russia, to choose whether or not they will acquire Polish nationality.

ARTICLE 6

All persons born in Polish territory who are not born nationals of another State shall *ipso facto* become Polish nationals.

ARTICLE 7

All Polish nationals shall be equal before the law and shall enjoy the same civil and political rights without distinction as to race, language or religion.

Differences of religion, creed or confession shall not prejudice any Polish national in matters relating to the enjoyment of civil or political rights, as for instance admission to public employments, functions and honours, or the exercise of professions and industries.

No restriction shall be imposed on the free use by any Polish national of any language in private intercourse, in commerce, in religion, in the press or in publications of any kind, or at public meetings.

Notwithstanding any establishment by the Polish Government of an official language, adequate facilities shall be given to Polish nationals of non-Polish speech for the use of their language, either orally or in writing, before the courts.

ARTICLE 8

Polish nationals who belong to racial, religious or linguistic minorities shall enjoy the same treatment and security in law and in fact as the other Polish nationals. In particular they shall have an equal right to establish, manage and control at their own expense charitable, religious and social institutions, schools and other educational establishments, with the right to use their own language and to exercise their religion freely therein.

ARTICLE 9

Poland will provide in the public educational system in towns and districts in which a considerable proportion of Polish nationals of other than Polish speech are resident adequate facilities for ensuring that in the primary schools the instruction shall be given to the children of such Polish nationals through the medium of their own language. This provision shall not prevent the Polish Government from making the teaching of the Polish language obligatory in the said schools.

In towns and districts where there is a considerable proportion of Polish nationals belonging to racial, religious or linguistic minorities, these minorities shall be assured an equitable share in the enjoyment and application of the sums which may be provided out of public funds under the State, municipal or other budget, for educational, religious or charitable purposes.

The provisions of this Article shall apply to Polish citizens of German speech only in that part of Poland which was German territory on August 1st, 1914.

ARTICLE 10

Educational Committees appointed locally by the Jewish communities of Poland will, subject to the general control of the State, provide for the distribution of the proportional share of public funds allocated to Jewish schools in accordance with Article 9, and for the organization and management of these schools.

The provisions of Article 9 concerning the use of languages in schools shall apply to these schools.

ARTICLE 11

Jews shall not be compelled to perform any act which constitutes a violation of their Sabbath, nor shall they be placed under any disability by reason of their refusal to attend courts of law or to perform any legal business on their Sabbath. This provision however shall not exempt Jews from such obligations as shall be imposed upon all other Polish citizens for the necessary purpose of military service, national defence, or the preservation of public order.

Poland declares her intention to refrain from ordering or permitting elections, whether general or local, to be held on a Saturday, nor will registration for electoral or other purposes be compelled to be performed on a Saturday.

ARTICLE 12

Poland agrees that the stipulations in the foregoing Articles, so far as they affect persons belonging to racial, religious or linguistic minorities, constitute obligations of international concern and shall be placed under the guarantee of the League of Nations. They shall not be modified without the assent of a majority of the Council of the League of Nations. The United States, the British Empire, France, Italy and Japan hereby agree not to withhold their assent from any modification in these Articles which is in due form assented to by a majority of the Council of the League of Nations.

Poland agrees that any Member of the Council of the League of Nations shall have the right to bring to the attention of the Council any infraction, or any danger of infraction, or any of these obligations, and that the Council may thereupon take such action and give such direction as it may deem proper and effective in the circumstances.

Poland further agrees that any difference of opinion as to questions of law or fact arising out of these Articles between the Polish Government and any one of the Principal Allied and Associated Powers or any other Power, a Member of the Council of the League of Nations, shall be held to be a dispute of an international character under Article 14 of the Covenant of the League of Nations. The Polish Government hereby consents that any such dispute shall, if the other party thereto demands, be referred to the Permanent Court of International Justice. The decision of the Permanent Court shall be final and shall have the same force and effect as an award under Article 13 of the Covenant.

The Atlantic Charter (1941)

. . . The President of the United States of America and the Prime Minister, Mr. Churchill . . . deem it right to make known certain common principles in the national policies of their respective countries on which they based their hopes for a better future for the world.

. . . they respect the right of all peoples to choose the form of government under which they will live; and they wish to see sovereign rights and self-government restored to those who have been forcibly deprived of them.

. . . they desire to bring about the fullest collaboration between all nations in the economic field with the object of securing, for all, improved labor standards, economic advancement, and social security.

. . . after the final destruction of the Nazi tyranny, they hope to see established a peace which will afford to all nations the means of dwelling in safety within their own boundaries, and which will afford assurance that all the men in all the lands may live out their lives in freedom from fear and want. . . .

Italian Peace Treaty (1947)

PART II,
SECTION 1,
ARTICLE 15

Italy shall take all measures necessary to secure to all persons under Italian jurisdiction, without distinction as to race, sex, language or religion, the enjoyment of human rights and of the fundamental freedoms, including freedom of expression, of press and publication, of religious worship, of political opinion and of public meeting.

United Nations Report on the Protection of Minorities (1967)

Special Protection Measures of an International Character for Ethnic, Religious or Linguistic Groups

General International Conventions. Three general international conventions adopted within the framework of the United Nations provide special protective measures for ethnic, religious or linguistic groups. In the Convention on the Prevention and Punishment of the Crime of Genocide, 1948, genocide is defined as any of a number of acts "committed with intent to destroy, in whole or in part, a national, ethnical, racial or religious group, as such," and the Contracting Parties "confirm that genocide, whether committed in time of peace or in time of war, is a crime under international law which they undertake to prevent and to punish." The Indigenous and Tribal Populations Convention, 1947, adopted by the General Conference of the International Labour Organisation, places upon Governments (Article 2) "the primary responsibility for developing co-ordinated and systematic action for the protection of the populations concerned and their progressive integration into the life of their respective countries," and provides, in particular (Article 3), that "so long as the social, economic and cultural conditions of the populations concerned prevent them from enjoying the benefits of the general laws of the country to which they belong, special measures shall be adopted for the protection of the institutions, persons, property and labour of these populations." In the Convention Against Discrimination in Education, 1960, adopted by the General Conference of the United Nations Educational, Scientific and Cultural Organization (UNESCO), the States Parties agree (Article 5c) that "it is essential to recognize the right of members of national minorities to carry on their own educational activities, including the maintenance of schools and, depending on their own language," and set out the circumstances in which this right may be exercised.

Regional Convention. The European Convention for the Protection of Human Rights and Fundamental Freedoms, signed in Rome on 4 November 1950, contains a provision (Article 14) in which "association with a national minority" is listed among a series of grounds upon which discrimination is prohibited.

Multilateral and Bilateral Instruments and Similar Measures. The peace settlements after the Second World War led to the conclusion of several multilateral and bilateral instruments and similar measures forbidding discrimination or providing special protective measures for ethnic, religious or linguistic groups. The Treaties of Peace with Bulgaria, Finland, Hungary, Italy and Romania of 10 February 1947, and the Austrian State Treaty of 15 May 1955, contain general provisions relating to the protection of human rights in those countries. The Peace Treaties with Hungary and Romania, and the Austrian State Treaty, contain in addition general provisions prohibiting discrimination. The preamble to the Peace Treaty with Japan of 8 September 1951 contains a general provision relating to the realization of the objectives of the Universal Declaration of Human Rights in Japan. The Austrian State Treaty also contains specific provisions (Article 7) relating to the rights of the Slovene and Croat minorities in three Austrian provinces, and the Agreement between the Austrian and Italian Governments of 5 September 1956, annexed to the Peace Treaty with Italy, contains provisions relating to the German-speaking inhabitants of the Bolzano Province and of the neighbouring bilingual townships of the Trento Province. The Special Statute annexed to the Memorandum of Understanding between Italy, the United Kingdom, the United States and Yugoslavia, regarding the Free Territory of Trieste, of 5 October 1954, contains provisions for the protection of the Yugoslav minority in that part of what was meant to become the Free Territory of Trieste which is now under Italian administration, and for the protection of the Italian minority in that part of the territory which is now under Yugoslav administration.

An Agreement between the Government of India and the Government of Pakistan, dated 8 April 1950, deals with the fundamental rights of the minorities in India and Pakistan and with the special situation created in West Bengal, Assam and Tripura, in India, and in East Pakistan, aiming particularly at the suppression of disorders wherever they may occur, ending the exodus of minorities by creating conditions necessary for the restoration of confidence, and the establishment of machinery for implementation of these purposes.

The Agreement reached between the United Kingdom Government and a Delegation from Singapore, at the Singapore Constitutional Conference, London, in 1957, provides special protective measures for certain ethnic, religious or linguistic groups.

Agreed statements made by the Governments of Denmark and the Federal Republic of Germany in 1955 include special measures to protect the German minority in Denmark and the Danish minority in the Federal Republic of Germany, respectively.

The Memorandum setting out the agreed foundation for the final settlement of the problem of Cyprus, 1959, contains detailed provisions concerning the rights of the Greek and Turkish minorities in that Republic.

The Agreement between France and Madagascar on the Status of the Population of the Island of Sainte-Marie, of 27 June 1960, contains special protective measures for that population. . . .

Decisions and Resolutions of Principal Organs of the United Nations. The General Assembly and the Economic and Social Council have on several occasions expressed an interest in a positive solution of the minorities problem. In resolution 217C (III) of 10 December 1948, on the "Fate of Minorities," the General Assembly stated "that the United Nations cannot remain indifferent to the fate of minorities," and added that "it is difficult to adopt a uniform solution of this complex and delicate question, which has special aspects in each State in which it arises." Later the General Assembly, in resolution 532B (VI), of 4 February 1952, expressed the view "that the prevention of discrimination and the protection of minorities are two of the most important branches of the positive work undertaken by the United Nations." The Economic and Social Council, in resolution 502F (XVI) of 3 August 1953, recommended that "in the preparation of any international treaties, decisions of international organs, or other acts which establish new States, or new boundary lines between States, special attention should be paid to the protection of any minority which may be created thereby."

Among the decisions of principal organs of the United Nations which have dealt with special protective measures for ethnic, religious or linguistic groups are three resolutions of the General Assembly; resolution 181 (II), on the future Government of Palestine; resolution 289 (IV), on the question of the disposal of the former Italian colonies; and resolution 390 (V), on the question of Eritrea. In addition, the Statute of the City of Jerusalem, approved by the Trusteeship Council on 4 April 1950, provides special protective measures for ethnic, religious or linguistic groups in articles dealing with human rights and fundamental freedoms (Article 9), the legislative council (Article 21), the judicial system (Article 28), official and working languages (Article 31), the educational system and cultural and benevolent institutions (Article 32), and broadcasting and television (Article 33).

PART IV

The Standpoint
of
International Law

Introductory Note

The views on various aspects of human rights taken by legal scholars have sharply changed over the last century. This transition can be seen clearly by comparing the attitudes of leading lawyers of their day on two main questions: First, do individuals and protection of their rights have any standing under international law? Second, can intervention be justified on humanitarian grounds against dictatorships oppressing their own people or mistreating racial, ethnic, or religious groups?

On the first issue, L. Oppenheim, a leading authority on international law, wrote in his classic book on the subject in 1912, "The Law of Nations is a law between States only and exclusively." In 1955, however, H. Lauterpacht, a British law professor, in updating Oppenheim's book, saw the situation quite differently. His changes and additions are italicized in the selection that follows.

As for the issue of intervention, British legal expert E. C. Hall, although sympathetic to the idea, saw little ground for such action in international law. "States so intervening," he wrote in 1895, "are going beyond their legal powers. Their excuse or their justification can only be a moral one." Yet by 1921, E. C. Stowell, a prestigious specialist in international law, found real legal justifications for states to seek to protect human rights abroad.

L. Oppenheim

International Law: A Treatise (1912)

Section 288. The importance of individuals to the Law of Nations is just as great as that of territory, for individuals are the personal basis of every State. Just as a State cannot exist without a territory, so it cannot exist without a multitude of individuals who are its subjects and who, as a body, form the people or the nation. The individuals belonging to a State can and do come in various ways in contact with foreign States in time of peace as well as of war. The Law of Nations is therefore compelled to provide certain rules regarding individuals.

Section 289. Now, what is the position of individuals in International Law according to these rules? Since the Law of Nations is a law between States only and exclusively, States only and exclusively are subjects of the Law of Nations. How is it, then, that, although individuals are not subjects of the Law of Nations, they have certain rights and duties in conformity with or according to International Law? Have not monarchs and other heads of States, diplomatic envoys, and even simple citizens certain rights according to the Law of Nations whilst on foreign territory? If we look more closely into these rights, it becomes quite obvious that they are not given to the favoured individual by the Law of Nations directly. For how could International Law, which is a law between States, give rights to individuals concerning their relations to a State? What the Law of Nations really does concerning individuals, is to impose the duty upon all the members of the Family of Nations to grant certain privileges to such foreign heads of States and diplomatic envoys, and certain rights to such foreign citizens as are on their territory. And, corresponding to this duty, every State has by the Law of Nations a right to demand that its head, its diplomatic envoys, and its simple citizens be granted certain rights by foreign States when on their territory. Foreign States granting these rights to foreign individuals do this by their Municipal Laws, and these rights are, therefore, not international rights, but rights derived from Municipal Laws. International Law is indeed the background of these rights in so far as the duty to grant them is imposed upon the single States by International Law. It is therefore quite correct to say that the individuals have these rights in conformity with or according to International Law, if it is only remembered that these rights would not exist had the single States not created them by their Municipal Law.

And the same is valid as regards special rights of individuals in foreign countries according to special international treaties between two or more Powers. Although such treaties mostly speak of rights which individuals shall have as derived from the treaties themselves, this is nothing more than an inaccuracy of language. In fact, such treaties do not create these rights, but they impose the duty upon the contracting States of calling these rights into existence by their Municipal Laws.

Again, in those rare cases in which States stipulate by international treaties certain favours for individuals other than their own subjects, these individuals do not acquire any international rights under these treaties. The latter impose the duty only upon the State whose subjects these individuals are of calling those favours into existence by its Municipal Law. Thus, for example, when articles 5, 25, 35, and 44 of the Treaty of Berlin, 1878, made it a condition of the recognition of

Bulgaria, Montenegro, Servia, and Roumania, that these States should not impose any religious disability upon their subjects, the latter did not thereby acquire any international rights. . . .

Now it is maintained that, although individuals cannot be subjects of International Law, they can nevertheless acquire rights and duties from International Law. But it is impossible to find a basis for the existence of such rights and duties. International rights and duties they cannot be, for international rights and duties can only exist between States. Likewise they cannot be municipal rights, for municipal rights and duties can only be created by Municipal Law. The opponents answer that such rights and duties nevertheless exist, and quote for example articles 4 and 5 of Convention XII (concerning the establishment of an International Prize Court) of the second Hague Peace Conference, according to which individuals have a right to bring an appeal before the International Prize Court. But is this a real right? Is it not more correct to say that the home States of the individuals concerned have a right to demand that these individuals can bring the appeal before the Court? Wherever International Law creates an independent organisation, such as the International Prize Court at the Hague or the European Danube Commission and the like, certain powers and claims must be given to the Courts and Commissions and the individuals concerned, but these powers and claims, and the obligations deriving therefrom, are neither international nor municipal rights and duties: they are powers, claims, and obligations existing only within the organisations concerned. To call them rights and duties —as indeed the respective treaties frequently do—is a laxity of language which is quite tolerable as long as one remembers that they neither comprise any relations between States nor any claims and obligations within the province of Municipal Law.

Section 290. But what is the real position of individuals in International Law, if they are not subjects thereof? The answer can only be that they are *objects* of the Law of Nations. They appear as such from many different points of view. When, for instance, the Law of Nations recognises the personal supremacy of every State over its subjects at home and abroad, these individuals appear just as much objects of the Law of Nations as the territory of the States does in consequence of the recognised territorial supremacy of the States. When, secondly, the recognised territorial supremacy of every State comprises certain powers over foreign subjects within its boundaries without their home State's having a right to interfere, these individuals appear again as objects of the Law of Nations. And, thirdly, when according to the Law of Nations any State may seize and punish foreign pirates on the Open Sea, or when belligerents may seize and punish neutral blockade-runners and carriers of contraband on the Open Sea without their home State's having a right to interfere, individuals appear here too as objects of the Law of Nations.

Section 291. If, as stated, individuals are never subjects but always objects of the Law of Nations, then nationality is the link between this law and individuals. It is through the medium of their nationality only that individuals can enjoy benefits from the existence of the Law of Nations. This is a fact which has its consequences over the whole area of International Law. Such individuals as do not possess any nationality enjoy no protection whatever, and if they are aggrieved by a State they have no way of redress, there being no State which would be competent to take their case in hand. As far as the Law of Nations is concerned, apart from morality, there is no restriction whatever to cause a State to abstain from maltreating to any extent such stateless individuals. On the other hand, if individuals who possess nationality are wronged abroad, it is their home State only and exclusively which has a right to ask for redress, and these individuals themselves have no such right. It is for this reason that the question of nationality is a very important one for the Law of Nations, and that individuals enjoy benefits from this law not as human beings but as subjects of such States as are members of the Family of Nations. . . .

Section 292. Several writers maintain that the Law of Nations guarantees to every individual at home and abroad the so-called rights of mankind, without regarding whether an individual be stateless or not, or whether he be a subject of a member-State of the Family of Nations or not. Such rights are said to comprise the right of existence, the right to protection of honour, life, health, liberty, and property, the right of practising any religion one likes, the right of emigration, and the like. But such rights do not in fact enjoy any guarantee whatever from the Law of Nations, and they cannot enjoy such guarantee, since the Law of Nations is a law between States, and since individuals cannot be subjects of this law. But there are certain facts which cannot be denied at the background of this erroneous opinion. The Law of Nations is a product of Christian civilisation and represents a legal order which binds States, chiefly Christian, into a community. It is therefore no wonder that ethical ideas which are some of them the basis of, others a development from, Christian morals, have a tendency to require the help of International Law for their realisation. When the Powers stipulated at the Berlin Congress of 1878 that the Balkan States should be recognised only under the condition that they did not impose any religious disabilities on their subjects, they lent their arm to the realisation of such an idea. Again, when the Powers after the beginning of the nineteenth century agreed to several international arrangements in the interest of the abolition of the slave trade, they fostered the realisation of another of these ideas. And the innumerable treaties between the different States as regards extradition of criminals, commerce, navigation, copyright, and the like, are inspired by the idea of affording ample protection to life, health, and property of individuals. Lastly, there is no doubt that, should a State venture to treat its own subjects or a part thereof with such cruelty as would stagger humanity, public opinion of the rest of the world would call upon the Powers to exercise intervention for the purpose of compelling such State to establish a legal order of things within its boundaries sufficient to guarantee to its citizens an existence more adequate to the ideas of modern civilisation. However, a guarantee of the so-called rights of mankind cannot be found in all these and other facts. Nor do the actual conditions of life to which certain classes of subjects are forcibly submitted within certain States show that the Law of Nations really comprises such guarantee.

H. Lauterpacht

Revision of Oppenheim (1955)

Section 288. The individuals belonging to a State can, and do, come in various ways in contact with foreign States in time of peace as well as war. *Moreover, apart from being nationals of their States, individuals are the ultimate objects of International Law—as they are, indeed, of all law. These are the reasons why the individual is often the object of international regulation and protection.*

Section 289. Since the Law of Nations is *primarily* a law between States, States are, to *that* extent, the only subjects of the Law of Nations. How is it, then, that, although individuals are not *normally* subjects of the Law of Nations, they have certain rights and duties in conformity with, or according to, International Law? Have not monarchs and other Heads of States, diplomatic envoys, and even private citizens, certain rights according to the Law of Nations whilst on foreign territory? The answer to these questions is that, *as a rule,* what the Law of Nations really does concerning individuals is to impose upon all States the duty to grant certain privileges to such foreign Heads of States and diplomatic envoys, and certain rights to such foreign citizens, as are on their territory. And, as corresponding to this duty, every State has by the Law of Nations a right to demand that its Head, its diplomatic envoys, and its citizens be granted certain rights by

Lauterpacht's changes and additions are italicized.

foreign States when on their territory. Foreign States granting these rights to foreign individuals do this by their Municipal Laws, and these rights are, *to that extent*, not international rights but rights derived from Municipal Laws. International Law is indeed the background of these rights, in so far as the duty to grant them is imposed upon the several States by International Law. It is therefore quite correct to say that individuals have these rights in conformity with, or according to, International Law, provided it is remembered that, *as a rule, these rights would not be enforceable before national courts* had the several States not created them by their Municipal Law.

The same applies as regards special rights of individuals in foreign countries according to treaties between two or more States. Although such treaties generally speak of rights which individuals shall have as derived from the treaties themselves, this is, *as a rule, not the normal position under the municipal law of States*. In fact, such treaties do not *normally* create these rights, but they impose the duty upon the contracting States of calling these rights into existence by their Municipal Laws. Again, where States stipulate by international treaties certain *benefits* for individuals other than their own subjects, these individuals do not, *as a rule*, acquire any international rights under these treaties, but the State whose subjects they are has an obligation towards the other States of granting such favours by its Municipal Law. *But although this is the normal and most convenient procedure, States may, and occasionally do, confer upon individuals, whether their own subjects or aliens, international rights stricto sensu, i.e. rights which they acquire without the intervention of municipal legislation and which they can enforce in their own name before international tribunals. Moreover, the quality of individuals as subjects of International Law is apparent from the fact that, in various spheres, they are, as such, bound by duties which International Law imposes directly upon them. The various developments since the two World Wars no longer countenance the view that, as a matter of positive law, States are the only subjects of International Law. In proportion as the realisation of that fact gains ground, there must be an increasing disposition to treat individuals, within a limited sphere, as subjects of International Law.*

Section 290. But what is the *normal* position of individuals in International Law, if they are not regularly subjects thereof? The answer can only be that, generally speaking, they are *objects* of the Law of Nations. They appear as such from many different points of view. When, for instance, the recognised territorial supremacy of every State is seen to comprise certain powers over foreign subjects within its boundaries with the exercise of which their home State has no right to interfere, these individuals appear again as objects of the Law of Nations. *The same applies to those rights of aliens which the territorial State is bound to respect and which the home State is entitled to protect. However, the fact that individuals are normally the object of International Law does not mean that they are not, in certain cases, the direct subjects thereof.*

Section 291. To the extent to which individuals are not subjects but objects of the Law of Nations, nationality is the link between them and International Law. It is through the medium of their nationality that individuals can normally enjoy benefits from the existence of the Law of Nations. This is a fact which has consequences over the whole area of International Law. Such individuals as do not possess any nationality enjoy, *in general*, no protection whatever, and if they are aggrieved by a State they have no means of redress, since there is no State which is competent to take up their case. As far as the Law of Nations is concerned, there is, apart from restraints of morality *or obligations expressly laid down by treaty—and in particular the general obligation, enshrined in the Charter of the United Nations, to respect human rights and fundamental freedoms*—no restriction whatever to cause a State to abstain from maltreating to any extent such stateless individuals. On the other hand, if individuals who possess nationality are wronged abroad, it is, *as a rule*, their home State only and exclusively which has a right to ask for redress, and these individuals themselves have no such right. It is for this reason that the question of nationality is very important for the Law of Nations.

Section 292. Writers have occasionally expressed the view that International Law guarantees to individuals, both at home and abroad and whether nationals of a State or stateless, certain fundamental rights usually referred to as rights of mankind. Such rights have been said to comprise the right of life, liberty, freedom of religion and conscience, and the like. *It is doubtful whether that view is expressive of the actual practice of States. For it is generally recognised that, apart from obligations undertaken by treaty, a State is entitled to treat both its own nationals and stateless persons at discretion and that the manner in which it treats them is not a matter with which International Law, as a rule, concerns itself.*

At the same time it cannot be said that the doctrine of the "rights of mankind" is altogether divorced from practice. In the first instance, it is clear that the State is bound to respect certain fundamental rights of aliens resident within its territory—although it is often said that the rights in question are not international rights of the aliens, but of their home State. Secondly, the principle and the practice of humanitarian intervention in defence of human rights ruthlessly trampled upon by the State have been frequently asserted and occasionally acted upon. Thirdly, the various treaties—such as those concluded at the Berlin Conference in 1878 or on the termination of the First World War—for the protection of religious and linguistic minorities signified the tendency to extend recognition, by means of international supervision and enforcement, to the elementary rights of at least some sections of the population of the State. Finally, an imposing array of treaties of a humanitarian character, such as those for the abolition of slavery, of slave trade, and of forced labour, for the protection of stateless persons and refugees, for safeguarding health and preventing abuses injurious to it, for securing humane conditions of work, and the like, have testified to the intimate connection between the interests of the individual and International Law. And although none of these developments have had the legal effect of incorporating the fundamental rights of man as part of the positive law of nations, they are not without significance for this aspect of International Law. It is probable that the Charter of the United Nations, with its repeated recognition of "human rights and fundamental freedoms," has inaugurated a new and decisive departure with regard to this abiding problem of law and government. In some instances—as, for example, in the European Convention on Human Rights—that development has assumed the complexion of explicit rules legally binding upon States.

W. E. Hall

A Treatise on International Law (1895)

International law professes to be concerned only with the relations of states to each other. Tyrannical conduct of a government towards its subjects, massacres and brutality in a civil war, or religious persecution, are acts which have nothing to do directly or indirectly with such relations. On what ground then can international law take cognizance of them? Apparently on one only, if indeed it be competent to take cognizance of them at all. It may be supposed to declare that acts of the kind mentioned are so inconsistent with the character of a moral being as to constitute a public scandal, which the body of states, or one or more states as representative of it, are competent to suppress. The supposition strains the fiction that states which are under international law form a kind of society to an extreme point, and some of the special grounds, upon which intervention effected under its sanction is based, are not easily distinguishable in principle from others which modern opinion has branded as unwarrantable. To some minds the excesses of a revolution would seem more scandalous than the tyranny of a sovereign. In strictness they ought, degree for degree, to be precisely equivalent in the eye of the law. While however it is settled that as a general rule a state must be allowed to work out its internal changes in its own fashion, so long as its struggles do not actually degenerate into internecine war, and intervention to put down a popular movement or the uprising of a subject race is wholly forbidden, intervention for the purpose of checking gross tyranny or of helping the efforts of a people to free itself is very commonly regarded without disfavour. Again, religious oppression, short of a cruelty which would rank as tyranny, has ceased to be recognised as an independent ground of intervention, but it is still used as between Europe and the East as an accessory motive, which seems to be thought by many persons sufficiently praiseworthy to excuse the commission of acts in other respects grossly immoral. Not only in fact is the propriety or impropriety of an intervention directed against an alleged scandal judged by the popular mind upon considerations of sentiment to the exclusion of law, but sentiment has been allowed to influence the more deliberately formed opinions of jurists. That the latter should have taken place cannot be too much regretted. In giving their sanction to interventions of the kind in question jurists have imparted an aspect of legality to a species of intervention, which makes a deep inroad into one of the cardinal doctrines of international law; of which the principle is not even intended to be equally applied to the cases covered by it; and which by the readiness with which it lends itself to the uses of selfish ambition becomes as dangerous in practice as it is plausible in appearance.

It is unfortunate that publicists have not laid down broadly and unanimously that no intervention is legal, except for the purpose of self-preservation, unless a breach of the law as between states has taken place, or unless the whole body of civilised states have concurred in authorising it. Interventions, whether armed or diplomatic, undertaken either for the reason or upon the pretexts of cruelty, or oppression, or the horrors of a civil war, or whatever the reason put forward, supported in reality by the justification which such facts offer to the popular mind, would have had to justify themselves, when not authorised by the whole body of civilised states accustomed to act together for common purposes, as measures which, being confessedly illegal in themselves, could only be excused in rare and extreme cases in consideration of the unquestionably extraordinary character of the facts causing them, and of the evident purity of the motives and conduct of the intervening state. The record of the last hundred years might not have been much cleaner than it is; but evil-doing would have been at least sometimes compelled to show itself in its true colours; it would have found more difficulty in clothing itself in a generous disguise; and international law would in any case have been saved from complicity with it. . . .

A somewhat wider range of intervention than that which is possessed by individual states may perhaps be conceded to the body of states, or to some of them acting for the whole in good faith with sufficient warrant. In the general interests of Europe, for example, an end might be put to a civil war by the compulsory separation of the parties to it, or a particular family or a particular form of government might be established and maintained in a country, if the interests to be guarded were strictly international, and if the maintenance of the state of things set up were a reasonable way of attaining the required object.

If a practice of this kind be permissible, its justification must rest solely upon the benefits which it secures. The body of states cannot be held to have a right of control, outside law, in virtue of the rudimentary social bond which connects them. More perfectly organised societies are contented with enforcing the laws that they have made; in doing this they consider themselves to have exhausted the powers which it is wise to assume; they do not go on to impose special arrangements or modes of life upon particular individuals; beyond the limits of law, direct compulsion does not take place; and evidently the community of states cannot in this respect have larger rights than a fully organised political society.

Is then such intervention justified by its probable or actual results? Certainly there must always be a likelihood that powers with divergent individual interests, acting in common, will prefer the general good to the selfish objects of a particular state. It is not improbable that this good may be better secured by their action than by free scope being given to natural forces. In one or two instances, as, for example, in that of the formation of Belgium, and in the recent one of the arrangements made by the Congress of Berlin, and of the minor interventions springing out of it, settlements have been arrived at, or collisions have been postponed, when without common action an era of disturbance might have been indefinitely prolonged, and its effects indefinitely extended. There is fair reason consequently for hoping that intervention by, or under the sanction of, the body of states on grounds forbidden to single states, may be useful and even beneficent. Still, from the point of view of law, it is always to be remembered that states so intervening are going beyond their legal powers. Their excuse or their justification can only be a moral one.

E. C. Stowell

Intervention in International Law (1921)

Humanitarian intervention may be defined as the reliance upon force for the justifiable purpose of protecting the inhabitants of another state from treatment which is so arbitrary and persistently abusive as to exceed the limits of that authority within which the soveriegn is presumed to act with reason and justice.

Westlake states the basic idea of humanitarian intervention and at the same time refutes the sterile doctrine of absolute non-intervention: "In considering anarchy and misrule as a ground for intervention the view must not be confined to the physical consequences which they may have beyond the limits of the territory in which they rage. Those are often serious enough, such as the frontier raids in which anarchy often boils over, or the piracy that may arise in seas in which an enfeebled government can no longer maintain the rule of law. The moral effect on the neighboring populations is to be taken into the account. Where these include considerable numbers allied by religion, language or race to the populations suffering from misrule, to restrain the former from giving support to the latter in violation of the legal rights of the misruled state may be a task beyond the power of their government, or requiring it to resort to modes of constraint irksome to its subjects, and not necessary for their good order if they were not excited by the spectacle of miseries which they must feel acutely. It is idle to argue in such a case that the duty of the neighboring peoples is to look on quietly. Laws are made for men and not creatures of the imagination, and they must not create or tolerate for them situations which are beyond the endurance, we will not say of average human nature, since laws may fairly expect to raise the standard by their operation, but of the best human nature that at the time and place they can hope to meet with." . . .

The legality of humanitarian intervention has the support of many authorities. The author of the *Vindicae Contra Tyrannos*, published in 1579 at the time of the religious wars in France, justifies interference "in behalf of neighboring peoples who are oppressed on account of adherence to the true religion or by any obvious tyranny." Since that time, a host of authorities have incidentally touched upon humanitarian intervention and recorded their approval of it. Only one of these [Antoine Rougier], as far as I am aware, has made a thorough study of this important institution. The list of the authorities who recognize the legality of humanitarian intervention includes: Grotius, Wheaton, Heiberg, Woolsey, Bluntschli, Westlake, and many others.

In 1625 Hugo Grotius wrote: "There is also another question, whether a war for the subjects of another be just, for the purpose of defending them from injuries inflicted by their ruler. Certainly it is undoubted that ever since civil societies were formed, the rulers of each claimed some especial right over his own subjects. Euripides makes his characters say that they are sufficient to right wrongs in their own city. And Thucydides puts among the marks of empire, the supreme authority in judicial proceedings. And so Virgil, Ovid, and Euripides in the *Hippolytus*. This is, as Ambrose says, that *peoples may not run into wars by usurping the care for those who do not belong to them.* The Corinthians in Thucydides say that it is right that each state should punish its own subjects. And Perseus says that he will not plead in defense of what he did against the Dolopians, since they were under his authority and he had acted upon his right. But all this applies when the subjects have really violated their duty; and we may add, when the case is doubtful. For that distribution of power was introduced for that case.

"But the case is different if the wrong be manifest. If a tyrant like Busiris, Phalaris, Diomede of Thrace, practises atrocities towards his subjects, which no just man can approve, the right of human social connection is not cut off in such a case. So Constantine took arms against Maxentius and Licinius; and several of the Roman emperors took or threatened to take arms against the Persians, except they prevented the Christians being persecuted on account of their religion."

In a recent work by Professor Edwin M. Borchard, we find a clear and emphatic statement. Referring to the minimum of rights which individuals enjoy under international law, this author remarks: "This view, it would seem, is confirmed by the fact that where a state under exceptional circumstances disregards certain rights of its own citizens, over whom presumably it has absolute sovereignty, the other states of the family of nations are authorized by international law to intervene on the grounds of humanity. When these 'human' rights are habitually violated, one or more states may intervene in the name of the society of nations and may take such measures as to substitute at least temporarily, if not permanently, its own sovereignty for that of the state thus controlled." . . .

Certain other publicists have, it is true, looked askance at humanitarian intervention, and even gone so far as to deny its legality. Starting from the premise of the independence of states, they fear to recognize the right of another state to step in as a policeman, even though a neighbor state should treat its nationals in a barbarous manner. Instead, they would proclaim as sacred and inviolable the right of every state to regulate its internal affairs and then condone as excusable violations of the law such corrective intervention as another state, urged on by public opinion, might undertake.

But why, we may ask, should the independence of a state be more sacred than the law which gives it that independence? Why adopt a system which makes it necessary to gloss over constant violations of the very principles which are declared to be most worthy of respect from all? If, where such intolerable abuses do occur, it be excusable to violate at one and the same time the independence of a neighbor and the law of nations, can such a precedent of disrespect for law prove less dangerous to international security than the recognition of the right, when circumstances justify, to ignore that independence which is the ordinary rule of state life? In any event, we find support for the view we hold from the weighty authorities to whom we have referred, and we may feel still more certain of our ground after we have examined the various instances in which the powers have intervened to prevent a neighbor from continuing to commit such abuses as constituted a violation of the universally recognized and generally respected rules of decent state conduct. And when so acting, the intervening states have proclaimed the legality of their course.

PART V

The Marxist Critique

Introductory Note

There are profound contradictions in Marxist thinking on human rights. In theory, communism's aim is to improve the lot of the vast majority. Its analysis, however, claims that the human rights most commonly enumerated are only "bourgeois" rights, benefiting one class exclusively. A "proletarian dictatorship" would spread fundamental rights, foremost among them being economic rights.

In rhetoric, Marxist states spend much time proclaiming their adherence to free speech, freedom of religion, and so forth. In practice, they restrict individual rights to a minimum with an efficiency hitherto little seen. While "class" ideology, on the one hand, is used to justify this behavior, on the other hand, there is an explicit legal acceptance of the basic human rights so important in the West. The conflict between theory and practice and the contradiction between state law and actual procedures are very sharp.

Whether or not they systematically adhere to Marxism, most Third World states have, in recent years, adopted this view and its political structure in dealing with human rights. Such a stance provides convenient explanations for the defense of authoritarian regimes.

Lenin, in selections from *The State and Revolution* and from his report to the First Congress of the Third International, provides the traditional Marxist view of human rights. The Soviet Communist Party, in its post-Stalin program, claims superiority over the West in its provision of such rights. The Yugoslav dissident and philosopher, Milovan Djilas, discusses the reasons behind the destruction of rights by Communist governments.

V. I. Lenin

The State and Revolution (1917)

In capitalist society, under the conditions most favorable to its development, we have more or less complete democracy in the democratic republic. But this democracy is always bound by the narrow framework of capitalist exploitation and consequently always remains, in reality, a democracy for the minority, only for the possessing classes, only for the rich. Freedom in capitalist society always remains just about the same as it was in the ancient Greek republics: freedom for the slave-owners. The modern wage slaves, owing to the conditions of capitalist exploitation, are so much crushed by want and poverty that "democracy is nothing to them," "politics is nothing to them"; that, in the ordinary peaceful course of events, the majority of the population is debarred from participating in social and political life.

The correctness of this statement is perhaps most clearly proved by Germany, just because in this state constitutional legality lasted and remained stable for a remarkably long time—for nearly half a century (1871–1914)—and because Social-Democracy in Germany during that time was able to achieve far more than in other countries in "utilizing legality" and was able to organize into a political party a larger proportion of the working class than anywhere else in the world.

What, then, is this largest proportion of politically conscious and active wage slaves that has so far been observed in capitalist society? One million members of the Social-Democratic Party—out of fifteen million wage workers! Three million organized in trade unions—out of fifteen million!

Democracy for an insignificant minority, democracy for the rich— that is the democracy of capitalist society. If we look more closely into the mechanism of capitalist democracy, everywhere, both in the "petty"—so-called petty—details of the suffrage (residential qualification, exclusion of women, etc.) and in the technique of the representative institutions, in the actual obstacles to the right of assembly (public buildings are not for "beggars"!), in the purely capitalist organization of the daily press, etc., etc.—on all sides we see restriction after restriction upon democracy. These restrictions, exceptions, exclusions, obstacles for the poor, seem slight, especially in the eyes of one who has himself never known want and has never been in close contact with the oppressed classes in their mass life (and nine-tenths, if not ninety-nine-hundredths, of the bourgeois publicists and politicians are of this class), but in their sum total these restrictions exclude and squeeze out the poor from politics and from an active share in democracy.

Marx splendidly grasped this *essence* of capitalist democracy when, in analyzing the experience of the Commune, he said that the oppressed were allowed, once every few years, to decide which particular representatives of the oppressing class should be in parliament to represent and repress them!

But from this capitalist democracy—inevitably narrow, subtly rejecting the poor, and therefore hypocritical and false to the core— progress does not march onward, simply, smoothly, and directly, to "greater and greater democracy," as the liberal professors and petty-bourgeois opportunists would have us believe. No, progress marches onward, *i.e.*, toward Communism, through the dictatorship of the proletariat; it cannot do otherwise, for there is no one else and no other way to *break the resistance* of the capitalist exploiters.

But the dictatorship of the proletariat—*i.e.*, the organization of the vanguard of the oppressed as the ruling class for the purpose of crushing the oppressors—cannot produce merely an expansion of democracy. *Together* with an immense expansion of democracy which *for the first time* becomes democracy for the poor, democracy for the people, and not democracy for the rich folk, the dictatorship of the proletariat produces a series of restrictions of liberty in the case of the oppressors, the exploiters, the capitalists. We must crush them in order to free humanity from wage slavery; their resistance must be broken by force; it is clear that where there is suppression there is also violence, there is no liberty, no democracy.

Engels expressed this splendidly in his letter to Bebel when he said, as the reader will remember, that "as long as the proletariat still *needs* the state, it needs it, not in the interests of freedom, but for the purpose of crushing its antagonists; and as soon as it becomes possible to speak of freedom, then the state, as such, ceases to exist."

Democracy for the vast majority of the people, and suppression by force, *i.e.*, exclusion from democracy, of the exploiters and oppressors of the people—this is the modification of democracy during the *transition* from capitalism to Communism.

Only in Communist society, when the resistance of the capitalists has been completely broken, when the capitalists have disappeared, when there are no classes (*i.e.*, there is no difference between the members of society in their relation to the social means of production), *only then* "the state ceases to exist," and "*it becomes possible to speak of freedom.*" Only then a really full democracy, a democracy without any exceptions, will be possible and will be realized. And only then will democracy itself begin to *wither away* due to the simple fact that, freed from capitalist slavery, from the untold horrors, savagery, absurdities, and infamies of capitalist exploitation, people will gradually *become accustomed* to the observance of the elementary rules of social life that have been known for centuries and repeated for thousands of years in all school books; they will become accustomed to observing them without force, without compulsion, without subordination, without the *special apparatus* for compulsion which is called the state.

The expression "the state *withers away*" is very well chosen, for it indicates both the gradual and the elemental nature of the process. Only habit can, and undoubtedly will, have such an effect; for we see around us millions of times how readily people get accustomed to observe the necessary rules of life in common, if there is no exploitation, if there is nothing that causes indignation, that calls forth protest and revolt and has to be *suppressed*.

Thus, in capitalist society, we have a democracy that is curtailed, poor, false; a democracy only for the rich, for the minority. The dictatorship of the proletariat, the period of transition to Communism, will, for the first time, produce democracy for the people, for the majority, side by side with the necessary suppression of the minority —the exploiters. Communism alone is capable of giving a really complete democracy, and the more complete it is, the more quickly will it become unnecessary and wither away of itself.

In other words: under capitalism we have a state in the proper sense of the word, that is, special machinery for the suppression of one class by another, and of the majority by the minority at that. Naturally, for the successful discharge of such a task as the systematic suppression by the exploiting minority of the exploited majority, the greatest ferocity and savagery of suppression are required, seas of blood are required, through which mankind is marching in slavery, serfdom, and wage labor.

Again, during the *transition* from capitalism to Communism, suppression is *still* necessary; but it is the suppression of the minority of exploiters by the majority of exploited. A special apparatus, special machinery for suppression, the "state," is *still* necessary, but this is now a transitional state, no longer a state in the usual sense, for the suppression of the minority of exploiters, by the majority of the wage slaves *of yesterday*, is a matter comparatively so easy, simple, and natural that it will cost far less bloodshed than the suppression of the risings of slaves, serfs, or wage laborers and will cost mankind far less. This is compatible with the diffusion of democracy among such an overwhelming majority of the population that the need for *special machinery* of suppression will begin to disappear. The exploiters are, naturally, unable to suppress the people without a most complex machinery for performing this task; but *the people* can suppress the exploiters even with very simple "machinery," almost without any "machinery," without any special apparatus, by the simple *organization of the armed masses* (such as the Soviets of Workers' and Soldiers' Deputies, we may remark, anticipating a little).

Finally, only Communism renders the state absolutely unnecessary, for there is *no one* to be suppressed—"no one" in the sense of a *class*, in the sense of a systematic struggle with a definite section of the population. We are not Utopians, and we do not in the least deny the possibility and inevitability of excesses on the part of *individual persons*, nor the need to suppress *such* excesses. But, in the first place, no special machinery, no special apparatus of repression is needed for this; this will be done by the armed people itself, as simply and as readily as any crowd of civilized people, even in modern society, parts a pair of combatants or does not allow a woman to be outraged. And, secondly, we know that the fundamental social cause of excesses which consist in violating the rules of social life is the exploitation of the masses, their want, and their poverty. With the removal of this chief cause, excesses will inevitably begin to *"wither away."* We do not know how quickly and in what succession, but we know that they will wither away. With their withering away, the state will also *wither away*.

Without going into Utopias, Marx defined more fully what can *now* be defined regarding this future, namely, the difference between the lower and higher phases (degrees, stages) of Communist society.

V. I. Lenin

Report to the First Congress of the Third International (1919)

7. "Freedom of assembly" can be taken as a sample of the requisites of "pure democracy". Every class-conscious worker who has not broken with his class will readily appreciate the absurdity of promising freedom of assembly to the exploiters at a time and in a situation when the exploiters are resisting the overthrow of their rule and are fighting to retain their privileges. When the bourgeoisie were revolutionary, they did not, either in England in 1649 or in France in 1793, grant "freedom of assembly" to the monarchists and nobles, who summoned foreign troops and "assembled" to organise attempts at restoration. If the present-day bourgeoisie, who have long since become reactionary, demand from the proletariat advance guarantees of "freedom of assembly" for the exploiters, whatever the resistance offered by the capitalists to being expropriated, the workers will only laugh at their hypocrisy.

The workers know perfectly well, too, that even in the most democratic bourgeois republic "freedom of assembly" is a hollow phrase, for the rich have the best public and private buildings at their disposal, and enough leisure to assemble at meetings, which are protected by the bourgeois machine of power. The rural and urban workers and the small peasants—the overwhelming majority of the population—are denied all these things. As long as that state of affairs prevails, "equality," i.e., "pure democracy" is a fraud. The first thing to do to win genuine equality and enable the working people to enjoy democracy in practice is to deprive the exploiters of all the public and sumptuous private buildings, to give the working people leisure and to see to it that their freedom of assembly is protected by armed workers, not by scions of the nobility or capitalist officers in command of downtrodden soldiers.

Only when that change is effected can we speak of freedom of assembly and of equality without mocking at the workers, at working people in general, at the poor. And this change can be effected only by the vanguard of the working people, the proletariat, which overthrows the exploiters, the bourgeoisie.

8. "Freedom of the press" is another of the principal slogans of "pure democracy." And here, too, the workers know—and socialists everywhere have admitted it millions of times—that this freedom is a deception while the best printing-presses and the biggest stocks of paper are appropriated by the capitalists, and while capitalist rule over the press remains, a rule that is manifested throughout the world all the more strikingly, sharply and cynically the more democracy and the republican system are developed, as in America for example. The first thing to do to win real equality and genuine democracy for the working people, for the workers and peasants, is to deprive capital of the possibility of hiring writers, buying up publishing houses and bribing newspapers. And to do that the capitalists and exploiters have to be overthrown and their resistance suppressed. The capitalists have always used the term "freedom" to mean freedom for the rich to get richer and for the workers to starve to death. In capitalist usage, freedom of the press means freedom of the rich to bribe the press, freedom to use their wealth to shape and fabricate so-called public opinion. In this respect, too, the defenders of "pure democracy" prove to be defenders of an utterly foul and venal system that gives the rich control over the mass media. They prove to be deceivers of the people, who, with the aid of plausible, fine-sounding, but thoroughly false phrases, divert them from the concrete historical task of liberating the press from capitalist enslavement. Genuine freedom and equality will be embodied in the system which the Communists are building, and in which there will be no opportunity for amassing wealth at the expense of others, no objective opportunities for putting the press under the direct or indirect power of money, and no impediments in the way of any workingman (or groups of workingmen, in any numbers) for enjoying and practising equal rights in the use of public printing-presses and public stocks of paper.

9. The history of the nineteenth and twentieth centuries demonstrated, even before the war, what this celebrated "pure democracy" really is under capitalism. Marxists have always maintained that the more developed, the "purer" democracy is, the more naked, acute and

merciless the class struggle becomes, and the "purer" the capitalist oppression and bourgeois dictatorship. The Dreyfus case in republican France, the massacre of strikers by hired bands armed by the capitalists in the free and democratic American republic—these and thousands of similar facts illustrate the truth which the bourgeoisie are vainly seeking to conceal, namely, that actually terror and bourgeois dictatorship prevail in the most democratic of republics and are openly displayed every time the exploiters think the power of capital is being shaken.

10. The imperialist war of 1914-18 conclusively revealed even to backward workers the true nature of bourgeois democracy, even in the freest republics, as being a dictatorship of the bourgeoisie. Tens of millions were killed for the sake of enriching the German or the British group of millionaires and multimillionaires, and bourgeois military dictatorships were established in the freest republics. This military dictatorship continues to exist in the Allied countries even after Germany's defeat. It was mostly the war that opened the eyes of the working people, that stripped bourgeois democracy of its camouflage and showed the people the abyss of speculation and profiteering that existed during and because of the war. It was in the name of "freedom and equality" that the bourgeoisie waged the war, and in the name of "freedom and equality" that the munition manufacturers piled up fabulous fortunes. Nothing that the yellow Berne International does can conceal from the people the now thoroughly exposed exploiting character of bourgeois freedom, bourgeois equality and bourgeois democracy.

11. In Germany, the most developed capitalist country of continental Europe, the very first months of full republican freedom, established as a result of imperialist Germany's defeat, have shown the German workers and the whole world the true class substance of the bourgeois-democratic republic. The murder of Karl Liebknecht and Rosa Luxemburg is an event of epoch-making significance not only because of the tragic death of these finest people and leaders of the truly proletarian, Communist International, but also because the class nature of an advanced European state—it can be said without exaggeration, of an advanced state on a world-wide scale—has been conclusively exposed. If those arrested, i.e., those placed under state protection, could be assassinated by officers and capitalists with impunity, and this under a government headed by social-patriots, then the democratic republic where such a thing was possible is a bourgeois dictatorship. Those who voice their indignation at the murder of Karl Liebknecht and Rosa Luxemburg but fail to understand this fact are only demonstrating their stupidity, or hypocrisy. "Freedom" in the German republic, one of the freest and advanced republics of the world, is freedom to murder arrested leaders of the proletariat with impunity.

Nor can it be otherwise as long as capitalism remains, for the development of democracy sharpens rather than dampens the class struggle which, by virtue of all the results and influences of the war and of its consequences, has been brought to boiling point.

Throughout the civilised world we see Bolsheviks being exiled, persecuted and thrown into prison. This is the case, for example, in Switzerland, one of the freest bourgeois republics, and in America, where there have been anti-Bolshevik pogroms, etc. From the standpoint of "democracy in general," or "pure democracy," it is really ridiculous that advanced, civilised, and democratic countries, which are armed to the teeth, should fear the presence of a few score men from backward, famine-stricken and ruined Russia, which the bourgeois papers, in tens of millions of copies, describe as savage, criminal, etc. Clearly, the social situation that could produce this crying contradiction is in fact a dictatorship of the bourgeoisie.

12. In these circumstances, proletarian dictatorship is not only an absolutely legitimate means of overthrowing the exploiters and suppressing their resistance, but also absolutely necessary to the entire mass of working people, being their only defence against the bourgeois dictatorship which led to the war and is preparing new wars.

The main thing that socialists fail to understand and that constitutes their short-sightedness in matters of theory, their subservience to bourgeois prejudices and their political betrayal of the proletariat is that in capitalist society, whenever there is any serious aggravation of the class struggle intrinsic to that society, there can be no alternative but the dictatorship of the bourgeoisie or the dictatorship of the proletariat. Dreams of some third way are reactionary, petty-bourgeois lamentations. That is borne out by more than a century of development of bourgeois democracy and the working-class movement in all the advanced countries, and notably by the experience of the past five years. This is also borne out by the whole science of political economy, by the entire content of Marxism, which reveals the economic inevitability wherever commodity economy prevails, of the dictatorship of the bourgeoisie that can only be replaced by the class which the very growth of capitalism develops, multiplies, welds together and strengthens, that is, the proletarian class.

13. Another theoretical and political error of the socialists is their failure to understand that ever since the rudiments of democracy first appeared in antiquity, its forms inevitably changed over the centuries as one ruling class replaced another. Democracy assumed different forms and was applied in different degrees in the ancient republics of Greece, the medieval cities and the advanced capitalist countries. It would be sheer nonsense to think that the most profound revolution in human history, the first case in the world of power being transferred

from the exploiting minority to the exploited majority, could take place within the timeworn framework of the old, bourgeois, parliamentary democracy, without drastic changes, without the creation of new forms of democracy, new institutions that embody the new conditions for applying democracy, etc.

14. Proletarian dictatorship is similar to the dictatorship of other classes in that it arises out of the need, as every other dictatorship does, to forcibly suppress the resistance of the class that is losing its political sway. The fundamental distinction between the dictatorship of the proletariat and the dictatorship of other classes—landlord dictatorship in the Middle Ages and bourgeois dictatorship in all the civilised capitalist countries—consists in the fact that the dictatorship of the landowners and bourgeoisie was the forcible suppression of the resistance offered by the vast majority of the population, namely, the working people. In contrast, proletarian dictatorship is the forcible suppression of the resistance of the exploiters, i. e., an insignificant minority of the population, the landowners and capitalists.

It follows that proletarian dictatorship must inevitably entail not only a change in democratic forms and institutions, generally speaking, but precisely such a change as provides an unparalleled extension of the actual enjoyment of democracy by those oppressed by capitalism —the toiling classes.

And indeed, the form of proletarian dictatorship that has already taken shape, i. e., Soviet power in Russia, the Räte-System in Germany, the Shop Stewards Committees in Britain and similar Soviet institutions in other countries, all this implies and presents to the toiling classes, i. e., the vast majority of the population, greater practical opportunities for enjoying democratic rights and liberties than ever existed before, even approximately, in the best and the most democratic bourgeois republics.

The substance of Soviet government is that the permanent and only foundation of state power, the entire machinery of state, is the massscale organisation of the classes oppressed by capitalism, i. e., the workers and the semi-proletarians (peasants who do not exploit the labour of others and regularly resort to the sale of at least a part of their own labour-power). It is the people, who even in the most democratic bourgeois republics, while possessing equal rights by law, have in fact been debarred by thousands of devices and subterfuges from participation in political life and enjoyment of democratic rights and liberties, that are now drawn into constant and unfailing, moreover, decisive, participation in the democratic administration of the state.

15. The equality of citizens, irrespective of sex, religion, race, or nationality, which bourgeois democracy everywhere has always promised but never effected, and never could effect because of the domina-

tion of capital, is given immediate and full effect by the Soviet system, or dictatorship of the proletariat. The fact is that this can only be done by a government of the workers, who are not interested in the means of production being privately owned and in the fight for their division and redivision.

16. The old, i. e., bourgeois, democracy and the parliamentary system were so organised that it was the mass of working people who were kept farthest away from the machinery of government. Soviet power, i. e., the dictatorship of the proletariat, on the other hand, is so organised as to bring the working people close to the machinery of government. That, too, is the purpose of combining the legislative and executive authority under the Soviet organisation of the state and of replacing territorial constituencies by production units—the factory.

17. The army was a machine of oppression not only under the monarchy. It remains as such in all bourgeois republics, even the most democratic ones. Only the Soviets, the permanent organisations of government authority of the classes that were oppressed by capitalism, are in a position to destroy the army's subordination to bourgeois commanders and really merge the proletariat with the army; only the Soviets can effectively arm the proletariat and disarm the bourgeoisie. Unless this is done, the victory of socialism is impossible.

The New Program of the Communist Party of the Soviet Union (1962)

The entire life of Socialist society is based on the principle of broad democracy. Working people take an active part, through the Soviets, trade unions and other mass organizations, in managing the affairs of the state and in solving problems of economic and cultural advancement. Socialist democracy includes both political freedoms—freedom of speech, of the press and of assembly, the right to elect and to be elected, and also social rights—the right to work, to rest and leisure, to education, to material security in old age and in case of illness or disability; equality of citizens of all races and nationalities; equal rights for women and men in all spheres of political, economic and cultural activity. Socialist democracy, unlike bourgeois democracy, does not merely proclaim the rights of the people, but makes it really possible for the people to exercise them. Soviet society insures the real liberty of the individual. The highest manifestation of this liberty is man's emancipation from exploitation, which is what primarily constitutes genuine social justice. . . .

Milovan Djilas

The New Class (1957)

Centralization of all forces and means as well as some kind of political unity of the revolutionary parties are essential conditions for every successful revolution. For the Communist revolution these conditions are even more important, since from the very beginning the Communists exclude every other independent political group or party from being an ally of their party. At the same time they demand uniformity of all viewpoints, including practical political views as well as theoretical, philosophical, and even moral views. The fact that the left-of-center SR's (Socialist-Revolutionaries) participated in the October Revolution, and that individuals and groups from other parties participated in the revolutions in China and Yugoslavia, does not disprove but rather confirms this proposition: these groups were only collaborators of the Communist Party, and only to a fixed degree in the struggle. After the revolution these collaborating parties were dispersed, or they dissolved of their own accord and merged with the Communist Party. The Bolsheviks routed the left-of-center SR's as soon as the latter wished to become independent, while the non-Communist groups in Yugoslavia and China that had supported the revolution had, in the meantime, renounced every one of their political activities.

The earlier revolutions were not carried out by a single political group. To be sure, in the course of a revolution individual groups pressured and destroyed one another; but, taken as a whole, the revolution was not the work of only one group. In the French revolution the Jacobins succeeded in maintaining their dictatorship for a brief period only. Napoleon's dictatorship, which emerged from the revolution, signified both the end of the Jacobin revolution and the beginning of the rule of the bourgeoisie. In every case, although one party played a decisive role in the earlier revolutions, the other parties did not surrender their independence. Although suppression and dispersion existed, they could be enforced only for a brief time. The parties could not be destroyed and would always emerge anew. Even the Paris Commune, which the Communists take as the forerunner of their revolution and their state, was a multi-party revolution.

A party may have played the chief, and even an exclusive, role in a particular phase of a revolution. But no previous party was ideologically, or as an organization, centralized to the degree that the Communist Party was. Neither the Puritans in the English revolution nor the Jacobins in the French revolution were bound by the same philosophical and ideological views, although the first belonged to a religious sect. From the organizational point of view the Jacobins were a federation of clubs; the Puritans were not even that. Only contemporary Communist revolutions pushed compulsory parties to the forefront, which were ideologically and organizationally monolithic.

In every case one thing is certain: in all earlier revolutions the necessity for revolutionary methods and parties disappeared with the end of civil war and of foreign intervention, and these methods and parties had to be done away with. After Communist revolutions, the Communists continue with both the methods and the forms of the revolution, and their party soon attains the fullest degree of centralism and ideological exclusiveness.

Lenin expressly emphasized this during the revolution itself in enumerating his conditions for acceptance in the Comintern:

> In the present epoch of acute civil war, a Communist Party will be able to perform its duty only if it is organized in the most centralized manner, only if iron discipline bordering on military discipline prevails in it, and if its party center is a powerful and authoritative organ, wielding wide powers and enjoying the universal confidence of the members of the party.

And to this, Stalin appended, in *Foundations of Leninism:*

> This is the position in regard to discipline in the party in the period of struggle preceding the achievement of the dictatorship.
> The same, but to an even greater degree, must be said about discipline in the party after the dictatorship has been achieved.

The revolutionary atmosphere and vigilance, insistence on ideological unity, political and ideological exclusiveness, political and other centralism do not cease after assuming control. On the contrary, they become even more intensified.

Ruthlessness in methods, exclusiveness in ideas, and monopoly in authority in the earlier revolutions lasted more or less as long as the revolutions themselves. Since revolution in the Communist revolution was only the first act of the despotic and totalitarian authority of a group, it is difficult to forecast the duration of that authority.

In earlier revolutions, including the Reign of Terror in France, superficial attention was paid to the elimination of real oppositionists. No attention was paid to the elimination of those who might become oppositionists. The eradication and persecution of some social or ideological groups in the religious wars of the Middle Ages was the only exception to this. From theory and practice, Communists know that they are in conflict with all other classes and ideologies, and behave accordingly. They are fighting against not only actual but also potential opposition. In the Baltic countries, thousands of people were liquidated overnight on the basis of documents indicating previously held ideological and political views. The massacre of several thousand Polish officers in the Katyń Forest was of similar character. In the case of Communism, long after the revolution is over, terrorist and oppressive methods continue to be used. Sometimes these are perfected and become more extensive than in the revolution, as in the case of the liquidation of the Kulaks. Ideological exclusiveness and intolerance are intensified after the revolution. Even when it is able to reduce physical oppression, the tendency of the ruling party is to strengthen the prescribed ideology—Marxism-Leninism.

Earlier revolutions, particularly the so-called bourgeois ones, attached considerable significance to the establishment of individual freedoms immediately following cessation of the revolutionary terror. Even the revolutionaries considered it important to assure the legal status of the citizenry. Independent administration of justice was an inevitable final result of all these revolutions. The Communist regime in the U.S.S.R. is still remote from independent administration of justice after forty years of tenure. The final results of earlier revolutions were often greater legal security and greater civil rights. This cannot be said of the Communist revolution.

There is another vast difference between the earlier revolutions and contemporary Communist ones. Earlier revolutions, especially the greater ones, were a product of the struggles of the working classes, but their ultimate results fell to another class under whose intellectual and often organizational leadership the revolutions were accomplished. The bourgeoisie, in whose name the revolution was carried out, to a considerable extent harvested the fruits of the struggles of the peasants and *sans-culottes*. The masses of a nation also participated in a Communist revolution; however, the fruits of revolution do not fall to them, but to the bureaucracy. For the bureaucracy is nothing else but the party which carried out the revolution. In Communist revolutions, the revolutionary movements which carried out the revolutions are not liquidated. Communist revolutions may "eat their own children," but not all of them.

In fact, on completion of a Communist revolution, ruthless and underhanded deals inevitably are made between various groups and factions which disagree about the path of the future.

Mutual accusations always revolve around dogmatic proof as to who is "objectively" or "subjectively" a greater counterrevolutionary or agent of internal and foreign "capitalism." Regardless of the manner in which these disagreements are resolved, the group that emerges victorious is the one that is the most consistent and determined supporter of industrialization along Communist principles, i.e., on the basis of total party monopoly, particularly of state organs in control of production. The Communist revolution does not devour those of its children who are needed for its future course—for industrialization. Revolutionaries who accepted the ideas and slogans of the revolution literally, naïvely believing in their materialization, are usually liquidated. The group which understood that revolution would secure authority, on a social-political-Communist basis, as an instrument of future industrial transformation, emerges victorious.

The Communist revolution is the first in which the revolutionaries and their allies, particularly the authority-wielding group, survived the revolution. Similar groups inevitably failed in earlier ones. The Communist revolution is the first to be carried out to the advantage of the revolutionaries. They, and the bureaucracy which forms around them, harvest its fruits. This creates in them, and in the broader echelons of the party, the illusion that theirs is the first revolution that remained true to the slogans on its banners.

PART VI

International Agreements

Introductory Note

A wide variety of international agreements have been formulated since 1945 to institutionalize and guarantee human rights. Many of these have come from the United Nations and its constituent bodies. Some have resulted from the actions of regional groups.

Unfortunately, these accords, while ratified by the requisite number of countries and sometimes provided with detailed machinery for implementation, have remained dead letters. The development of a new majority of nondemocratic states, the desire of governments to protect themselves from accusations of repression, the cynical employment of such issues for political advantage, and selectivity to the point of absurdity in application, have all vitiated these accords.

At the same time, the treaties *have* set forth detailed definitions of political and economic rights. Along with the Universal Declaration of Human Rights, there have been special statements on genocide, the rights of women, and racial discrimination. A European convention on human rights and two Western Hemisphere agreements have endorsed these principles. In practice, it is difficult to detect many material improvements resulting from all this diplomatic activity. Yet these agreements provided a basis for the renewed concern in the 1970s over the promotion of human rights, both by some governments (most notably that of the United States) and by a multitude of private organizations.

During the 1980s, there were efforts to expand the definition of human rights to cover additional groups and areas of life. These included rights to peace and economic development, a codification of rights for women, children, and handicapped people, as well as additional conventions against torture and religious discrimination. The reevaluation of Soviet policy under the rule of Mikhail Gorbachev and the spread of democracy in Latin America were encouraging, if perhaps temporary, signs of a human rights' resurgence. A symbol of the hope and problems involved in this process was in Nicaragua. The Sandinista government, brought to power there partly by an unprecedented Organization of American States' resolution condemning the Somoza dictatorship for human rights' violations then, itself, curtailed citizens' freedoms. The continuing prevalence of dictatorship in many parts of the world, the militant intolerance of Iran's Islamic regime, the use of chemical weapons by Iraq, and other events showed the continued hollowness of international agreements to defend human rights.

The United Nations Charter (1945)

Chapter I. Purposes and Principles

ARTICLE 1

The Purposes of the United Nations are:

3. To achieve international cooperation in solving international problems of an economic, social, cultural, or humanitarian character, and in promoting and encouraging respect for human rights and for fundamental freedoms for all without distinction as to race, sex, language, or religion. . . .

ARTICLE 2

7. Nothing contained in the present Chapter shall authorize the United Nations to intervene in matters which are essentially within the domestic jurisdiction of any state or shall require the Members to submit such matters to settlement under the present Charter. . . .

ARTICLE 13

1. The General Assembly shall initiate studies and make recommendations for the purpose of . . .

b. promoting international cooperation in the economic, social, cultural, educational, and health fields, and assisting in the realization of human rights and fundamental freedoms for all without distinction as to race, sex, language, or religion.

ARTICLE 55

. . . the United Nations shall promote:

c. universal respect for, and observance of, human rights and fundamental freedoms for all without distinction as to race, sex, language, or religion.

ARTICLE 56

All members pledge themselves to take joint and separate action in cooperation with the Organization for the achievement of the purposes set forth in Article 55.

ARTICLE 62

The Economic and Social Council . . . may make recommendations for the purpose of promoting respect for, and observance of, human rights and fundamental freedoms for all.

ARTICLE 68

The Economic and Social Council shall set up commissions in economic and social fields and for the promotion of human rights. . . .

ARTICLE 105

The Organization shall enjoy in the territory of each of its members such privileges and immunities as are necessary for the fulfillment of its purposes.

United Nations Universal Declaration of Human Rights (1948)

Whereas recognition of the inherent dignity and of the equal and inalienable rights of all members of the human family is the foundation of freedom, justice and peace in the world,

Whereas disregard and contempt for human rights have resulted in barbarous acts which have outraged the conscience of mankind, and the advent of a world in which human beings shall enjoy freedom of speech and belief and freedom from fear and want has been proclaimed as the highest aspiration of the common people,

Whereas it is essential, if man is not to be compelled to have recourse, as a last resort, to rebellion against tyranny and oppression, that human rights should be protected by the rule of law,

Whereas it is essential to promote the development of friendly relations between nations,

Whereas the peoples of the United Nations have in the Charter reaffirmed their faith in fundamental human rights, in the dignity and worth of the human person and in the equal rights of men and women and have determined to promote social progress and better standards of life in larger freedom,

Wheras Member States have pledged themselves to achieve, in cooperation with the United Nations, the promotion of universal respect for and observance of human rights and fundamental freedoms,

Whereas a common understanding of these rights and freedoms is of the greatest importance for the full realization of this pledge,

Now, therefore,

The General Assembly

Proclaims this Universal Declaration of Human Rights as a common standard of achievement for all peoples and all nations, to the end that every individual and every organ of society, keeping this Declaration constantly in mind, shall strive by teaching and education to promote respect for these rights and freedoms and by progressive measures, national and international, to secure their universal and effective recognition and observance, both among the peoples of Member States themselves and among the peoples of territories under their jurisdiction.

ARTICLE 1

All human beings are born free and equal in dignity and rights. They are endowed with reason and conscience and should act toward one another in a spirit of brotherhood.

ARTICLE 2

Everyone is entitled to all the rights and freedoms set forth in this Declaration, without distinction of any kind, such as race, color, sex, language, religion, political or other opinion, national or social origin, property, birth or other status.

Furthermore, no distinction shall be made on the basis of the political, jurisdictional or international status of the country or territory to which a person belongs, whether it be independent, trust, non-self-governing or under any other limitation of sovereignty.

ARTICLE 3

Everyone has the right to life, liberty and the security of person.

ARTICLE 4

No one shall be held in slavery or servitude; slavery and the slave trade shall be prohibited in all their forms.

ARTICLE 5

No one shall be subjected to torture or to cruel, inhuman or degrading treatment or punishment.

ARTICLE 6

Everyone has the right to recognition everywhere as a person before the law.

ARTICLE 7

All are equal before the law and are entitled without any discrimination to equal protection of the law. All are entitled to equal protection against any discrimination in violation of this Declaration and against any incitement to such discrimination.

ARTICLE 8

Everyone has the right to an effective remedy by the competent national tribunals for acts violating the fundamental rights granted him by the constitution or by law.

ARTICLE 9

No one shall be subjected to arbitrary arrest, detention or exile.

ARTICLE 10

Everyone is entitled to full equality to a fair and public hearing by an independent and impartial tribunal, in the determination of his rights and obligations and of any criminal charge against him.

ARTICLE 11

1. Everyone charged with a penal offense has the right to be presumed innocent until proved guilty according to law in a public trial at which he has had all the guarantees necessary for his defense.

2. No one shall be held guilty of any penal offense on account of any act or omission which did not constitute a penal offense, under national or international law, at the time when it was committed. Nor shall a heavier penalty be imposed than the one that was applicable at the time the penal offense was committed.

ARTICLE 12

No one shall be subjected to arbitrary interference with his privacy, family, home or correspondence, nor to attacks upon his honor and reputation. Everyone has the right to the protection of the law against such interference or attacks.

ARTICLE 13

1. Everyone has the right to freedom of movement and residence within the borders of each state.

2. Everyone has the right to leave any country, including his own, and to return to his country.

ARTICLE 14

1. Everyone has the right to seek and to enjoy in other countries asylum from persecution.

2. This right may not be invoked in the case of prosecutions genuinely arising from non-political crimes or from acts contrary to the purposes and principles of the United Nations.

ARTICLE 15

1. Everyone has the right to a nationality.

2. No one shall be arbitrarily deprived of his nationality nor denied the right to change his nationality.

ARTICLE 16

1. Men and women of full age, without any limitation due to race, nationality, or religion, have the right to marry and to found a family. They are entitled to equal rights as to marriage, during marriage and at its dissolution.

2. Marriage shall be entered into only with the free and full consent of the intending spouses.

3. The family is the natural and fundamental group unit of society and is entitled to protection by society and the State.

ARTICLE 17

1. Everyone has the right to own property alone as well as in association with others.

2. No one shall be arbitrarily deprived of his property.

ARTICLE 18

Everyone has the right to freedom of thought, conscience and religion; this right includes freedom to change his religion or belief, and freedom, either alone or in community with others and in public or private, to manifest his religion or belief in teaching, practice, worship and observance.

ARTICLE 19

Everyone has the right to freedom of opinion and expression; this right includes freedom to hold opinions without interference and to seek, receive and impart information and ideas through any media and regardless of frontiers.

ARTICLE 20

1. Everyone has the right to freedom of peaceful assembly and association.

2. No one may be compelled to belong to an association.

ARTICLE 21

1. Everyone has the right to take part in the Government of his country, directly or through freely chosen representatives.

2. Everyone has the right of equal access to public service in his country.

3. The will of the people shall be the basis of the authority of government; this will shall be expressed in periodic and genuine elections which shall be by universal and equal suffrage and shall be held by secret vote or by equivalent free voting procedures.

ARTICLE 22

Everyone, as a member of society, has the right to social security and is entitled to realization, through national effort and international cooperation and in accordance with the organization and resources of each State, of the economic, social and cultural rights indispensable for his dignity and the free development of his personality.

ARTICLE 23

1. Everyone has the right to work, to free choice of employment, to just and favorable conditions of work and to protection against unemployment.

2 Everyone, without any discrimination, has the right to equal pay for equal work.

3. Everyone who works has the right to just and favorable remuneration insuring for himself and his family an existence worthy of human dignity, and supplemented, if necessary, by other means of social protection.

4. Everyone has the right to form and to join trade unions for the protection of his interests.

ARTICLE 24

Everyone has the right to rest and leisure, including reasonable limitation of working hours and periodic holidays with pay.

ARTICLE 25

1. Everyone has the right to a standard of living adequate for the health and well-being of himself and of his family, including food, clothing, housing and medical care and necessary social services, and the right to security in the event of unemployment, sickness, disability, widowhood, old age or other lack of livelihood in circumstances beyond his control.

2. Motherhood and childhood are entitled to special care and assistance. All children, whether born in or out of wedlock shall enjoy the same social protection.

ARTICLE 26

1. Everyone has the right to education. Education shall be free, at least in the elementary and fundamental stages. Elementary education shall be compulsory. Technical and professional education shall be

made generally available and higher education shall be equally accessible to all on the basis of merit.

2. Education shall be directed to the full development of the human personality and to the strengthening of respect for human rights and fundamental freedoms. It shall promote understanding, tolerance and friendship among all nations, racial or religious groups, and shall further the activities of the United Nations for the maintenance of peace.

3. Parents have a prior right to choose the kind of education that shall be given to their children.

ARTICLE 27

1. Everyone has the right freely to participate in the cultural life of the community, to enjoy the arts and to share in scientific advancement and its benefits.

2. Everyone has the right to the protection of the moral and material interests resulting from any scientific, literary or artistic production of which he is the author.

ARTICLE 28

Everyone is entitled to a social and international order in which the rights and freedoms set forth in this Declaration can be fully realized.

ARTICLE 29

1. Everyone has duties to the community in which alone the free and full development of his personality is possible.

2. In the exercise of his rights and freedoms, everyone shall be subject only to such limitations as are determined by law solely for the purpose of securing due recognition and respect for the rights and freedoms of others and of meeting the just requirements of morality, public order and the general welfare in a democratic society.

3. These rights and freedoms may in no case be exercised contrary to the purposes and principles of the United Nations.

ARTICLE 30

Nothing in this Declaration may be interpreted as implying for any State, group or person any right to engage in any activity or to perform any act aimed at the destruction of any of the rights and freedoms set forth herein.

United Nations Convention on the Prevention and Punishment of the Crime of Genocide (1951)

The Contracting Parties,

Having considered the declaration made by the General Assembly of the United Nations in its resolution 96 (I) dated 11 December 1946 that genocide is a crime under international law, contrary to the spirit and aims of the United Nations and condemned by the civilized world;

Recognizing that at all periods of history genocide has inflicted great losses on humanity; and

Being convinced that, in order to liberate mankind from such an odious scourge, international cooperation is required:

Hereby agree as hereinafter provided.

ARTICLE I

The Contracting Parties confirm that genocide, whether committed in time of peace or in time of war, is a crime under international law which they undertake to prevent and to punish.

ARTICLE II

In the present Convention, genocide means any of the following acts committed with intent to destroy, in whole or in part, a national, ethnical, racial or religious group as such:

a. Killing members of the group;

b. Causing serious bodily or mental harm to members of the group;

c. Deliberately inflicting on the group conditions of life calculated to bring about its physical destruction in whole or in part;

d. Imposing measures intended to prevent births within the group;

e. Forcibly transferring children of the group to another group.

ARTICLE III

The following acts shall be punishable:

a. Genocide;

b. Conspiring to commit genocide;

c. Direct and public incitement to commit genocide;

d. Attempt to commit genocide;

e. Complicity in genocide.

ARTICLE IV
Persons committing genocide or any of the other acts enumerated in article III shall be punished, whether they are constitutionally responsible rulers, public officials or private individuals.

ARTICLE V
The Contracting Parties undertake to enact, in accordance with their respective Constitutions, the necessary legislation to give effect to the provisions of the present Convention and, in particular, to provide effective penalties for persons guilty of genocide or any of the other acts enumerated in article III.

ARTICLE VI
Persons charged with genocide or any of the other acts enumerated in article III shall be tried by a competent tribunal of the State in the territory of which the act was committed, or by such international penal tribunal as may have jurisidiction with respect to those Contracting Parties which shall have accepted its jurisdiction.

ARTICLE VII
Genocide and the other acts enumerated in article III shall not be considered as political crimes for the purpose of extradition.

The Contracting Parties pledge themselves in such cases to grant extradition in accordance with their laws and treaties in force.

ARTICLE VIII
Any Contracting Party may call upon the competent organs of the United Nations to take such actions under the Charter of the United Nations as they consider appropriate for the prevention and suppression of acts of genocide or any of the other acts enumerated in article III.

ARTICLE IX
Disputes between the Contracting Parties relating to the interpretation, application or fulfillment of the present Convention, including those relating to the responsibility of a State for genocide or any of the other acts enumerated in article III, shall be submitted to the International Court of Justice at the request of any of the parties to the dispute.

ARTICLE X
The present Convention of which the Chinese, English, French, Russian and Spanish texts are equally authentic, shall bear the date of 9 December 1948.

European Convention for the Protection of Human Rights and Fundamental Freedoms (1953)

The Governments signatory hereto, being Members of the Council of Europe,

Considering the Universal Declaration of Human Rights proclaimed by the General Assembly of the United Nations on 10th December 1948;

Considering that this Declaration aims at securing the universal and effective recognition and observance of the Rights therein declared;

Considering that the aim of the Council of Europe is achievement of greater unity between its Members and that one of the methods by which that aim is to be pursued is the maintenance and further realization of Human Rights and Fundamental Freedoms;

Reaffirming their profound belief in those Fundamental Freedoms which are the foundation of justice and peace in the world and are best maintained on the one hand by an effective political democracy and on the other by a common understanding and observance of the Human Rights upon which they depend;

Being resolved, as the Governments of European countries which are like-minded and have a common heritage of political traditions, ideals, freedom and the rule of law, to take the first steps for the collective enforcement of certain of the Rights stated in the Universal Declaration;

Have agreed as follows:

ARTICLE 1

The High Contracting parties shall secure to everyone within their jurisdiction the rights and freedoms defined in Section I of this Convention.

Section I

ARTICLE 2

1. Everyone's right to life shall be protected by law. No one shall be deprived of his life intentionally save in the execution of a sentence of a court following his conviction of a crime for which this penalty is provided by law.

2. Deprivation of life shall not be regarded as inflicted in contravention of this Article when it results from the use of force which is no more than absolutely necessary:

a. in defense of any person from unlawful violence;

b. in order to effect a lawful arrest or to prevent the escape of a person lawfully detained;

c. in action lawfully taken for the purpose of quelling a riot or insurrection.

ARTICLE 3

No one shall be subjected to torture or to inhuman or degrading treatment or punishment.

ARTICLE 4

1. No one shall be held in slavery or servitude.

2. No one shall be required to perform forced or compulsory labor.

3. For the purpose of this Article the term "forced or compulsory labor" shall not include:

a. any work required to be done in the ordinary course of detention imposed according to the provisions of Article 5 of this Convention or during conditional release from such detention;

b. any service of a military character or, in case of conscientious objectors in countries where they are recognized, service exacted instead of compulsory military service;

c. any service exacted in case of an emergency or calamity threatening the life or well-being of the community;

d. any work or service which forms part of normal civic obligations.

ARTICLE 5

1. Everyone has the right to liberty and security of person.

No one shall be deprived of his liberty save in the following cases and in accordance with a procedure prescribed by law:

a. the lawful detention of a person after conviction by a competent court;

b. the lawful arrest or detention of a person for noncompliance with the lawful order of a court or in order to secure the fulfilment of any obligation prescribed by law;

c. the lawful arrest or detention of a person effected for the purpose of bringing him before the competent legal authority on reasonable suspicion of having committed an offence or when it is reasonably considered necessary to prevent his committing an offence or fleeing after having done so;

d. the detention of a minor by lawful order for the purpose of educational supervision or his lawful detention for the purpose of bringing him before the competent legal authority;

e. the lawful detention of persons for the prevention of the spreading of infectious diseases, of persons of unsound mind, alcoholic or drug addicts or vagrants;

f. the lawful arrest or detention of a person to prevent his effecting an unauthorized entry into the country or of a person against whom action is being taken with a view to deportation or extradition.

2. Everyone who is arrested shall be informed promptly, in a language which he understands, of the reasons for his arrest and of any charge against him.

3. Everyone arrested or detained in accordance with the provisions of paragraph I (c) of this Article shall be brought promptly before a judge or other officer authorized by law to exercise judicial power and shall be entitled to trial within a reasonable time or to release pending trial. Release may be conditioned by guarantees to appear for trial.

4. Everyone who is deprived of his liberty by arrest or detention shall be entitled to take proceedings by which the lawfulness of his detention shall be decided speedily by a court and his release ordered if the detention is not lawful.

5. Everyone who has been the victim of arrest or detention in contravention of the provisions of this Article shall have an enforceable right to compensation.

ARTICLE 6

1. In the determination of his civil rights and obligations or of any criminal charge against him, everyone is entitled to a fair and public hearing within a reasonable time by an independent and impartial tribunal established by law. Judgment shall be pronounced publicly, but the press and public may be excluded from all or part of the trial in the interests of morals, public order or national security in a democratic society, where the interests of juveniles or the protection of the private life of the parties so require, or to the extent strictly necessary in the opinion of the court in special circumstances where publicity would prejudice the interests of justice.

2. Everyone charged with a criminal offence shall be presumed innocent until proved guilty according to law.

3. Everyone charged with a criminal offense has the following minimum rights:

a. to be informed promptly, in a language which he understands and in detail, of the nature and cause of the accusation against him;

b. to have adequate time and facilities for the preparation of his defense;

c. to defend himself in person or through legal assistance of his own choosing or, if he has not sufficient means to pay for legal assistance, to be given it free when the interests of justice so require;

d. to examine or have examined witnesses against him and to obtain the attendance and examination of witnesses on his behalf under the same conditions as witnesses against him;

e. to have the free assistance of an interpreter if he cannot understand or speak the language used in court.

ARTICLE 7

1. No one shall be held guilty of any criminal offence on account of any act or omission which did not constitute a criminal offense under national or international law at the time when it was committed. Nor shall a heavier penalty be imposed than the one that was applicable at the time the criminal offence was committed.

2. This Article shall not prejudice the trial and punishment of any person for any act or omission which, at the time when it was committed, was criminal according to the general principles of law recognized by civilized nations.

ARTICLE 8

1. Everyone has the right to respect for his private and family life, his home and his correspondence.

2. There shall be no interference by a public authority with the exercise of this right except such as in accordance with the law and is necessary in a democratic society in the interests of national security, public safety or the economic well-being of the country, for the prevention of disorder or crime, for the protection of health or morals, or for the protection of the rights and freedoms of others.

ARTICLE 9

1. Everyone has the right to freedom of thought, conscience and religion; this right includes freedom to change his religion or belief and freedom, either alone or in community with others and in public or private, to manifest his religion or belief, in worship, teaching, practice and observance.

2. Freedom to manifest one's religion or beliefs shall be subject only to such limitations as are prescribed by law and are necessary in a democratic society in the interests of public safety, for the protection of public order, health or morals, or for the protection of the rights and freedoms of others.

ARTICLE 10

1. Everyone has the right to freedom of expression. This right shall include freedom to hold opinions and to receive and impart information and ideas without interference by public authority and regardless of frontiers. This Article shall not prevent States from requiring the licensing of broadcasting, television or cinema enterprises.

2. The exercise of these freedoms, since it carries with it duties and responsibilities, may be subject to such formalities, conditions, restrictions or penalties as are prescribed by law and are necessary in a democratic society, in the interests of national security, territorial integrity or public safety, for the prevention of disorder or crime, for the protection of health or morals, for the protection of the reputation or rights of others, for preventing the disclosure of information received in confidence, or for maintaining the authority and impartiality of the judiciary.

ARTICLE 11

1. Everyone has the right to freedom of peaceful assembly and to freedom of association with others, including the right to form and to join trade unions for the protection of his interests.

2. No restrictions shall be placed on the exercise of these rights other than such as are prescribed by law and are necessary in a democratic society in the interests of national security or public safety, for the prevention of disorder or crime, for the protection of health or morals or for the protection of the rights and freedoms of others. This Article shall not prevent the imposition of lawful restrictions on the exercise of these rights by members of the armed forces, of the police or of the administration of the State.

ARTICLE 12

Men and women of marriageable age have the right to marry and to found a family, according to the national laws governing the exercise of this right.

ARTICLE 13

Everyone whose rights and freedoms as set forth in this Convention are violated shall have an effective remedy before a national authority notwithstanding that the violation has been committed by persons acting in an official capacity.

ARTICLE 14

The enjoyment of the rights and freedoms set forth in this Convention shall be secured without discrimination on any ground such as sex, race, color, language, religion, political or other opinion, national or social origin, association with a national minority, property, birth or other status.

ARTICLE 15

1. In time of war or other public emergency threatening the life of the nation any High Contracting Party may take measures derogating from its obligations under this Convention to the extent strictly required by the exigencies of the situation, provided that such measures are not inconsistent with its other obligations under international law.

2. No derogation from Article 2, except in the respect of deaths resulting from lawful acts of war, or from Articles 3, 4 (paragraph I) and 7 shall be made under this provision.

3. Any High Contracting Party availing itself of this right of derogation shall keep the Secretary-General of the Council of Europe fully informed of the measures which it has taken and the reasons therefor. It shall also inform the Secretary-General of the Council of Europe when such measures have ceased to operate and the provisions of the Convention are again being fully executed.

ARTICLE 16

Nothing in Articles 10, 11 and 14 shall be regarded as preventing the High Contracting Parties from imposing restriction on the political activity of aliens.

ARTICLE 17

Nothing in this Convention may be interpreted as implying for any State, group or person any right to engage in any activity or perform any act aimed at the destruction of any of the rights and freedoms set forth herein or at their limitation to a greater extent than is provided for in the Convention.

ARTICLE 18

The restrictions permitted under this Convention to the said rights and freedoms shall not be applied for any purpose other than those for which they have been prescribed.

Section II

ARTICLE 19

To ensure the observance of the engagements undertaken by the High Contracting Parties in the present Convention, there shall be set up:

1. A European Commission of Human Rights hereinafter referred to as "the Commission";

2. A European Court of Human Rights, hereinafter referred to as "the Court."

Section III

ARTICLE 20
The Commission shall consist of a number of members equal to that of the High Contracting Parties. No two members of the Commission may be nationals of the same State.

ARTICLE 21
1. The members of the Commission shall be elected by the Committee of Ministers by an absolute majority of votes, from a list of names drawn up by the Bureau of the Consultative Assembly; each group of the Representatives of the High Contracting Parties in the Consultative Assembly shall put forward three candidates, of whom two at least shall be its nationals.

2. As far as applicable, the same procedure shall be followed to complete the Commission in the event of other States subsequently becoming Parties to this Convention, and in filling casual vacancies. . . .

ARTICLE 25
1. The Commission may receive petitions addressed to the Secretary-General of the Council of Europe from any person, non-governmental organization or group of individuals claiming to be the victim of a violation by one of the High Contracting Parties of the rights set forth in this Convention, provided that the High Contracting Party against which the complaint has been lodged has declared that it recognizes the competence of the Commission to receive such petitions. Those of the High Contracting Parties who have made such a declaration undertake not to hinder in any way the effective exercise of this right.

2. Such declarations may be made for a specific period.

3. The declarations shall be deposited with the Secretary-General of the Council of Europe who shall transmit copies thereof to the High Contracting Parties and publish them.

4. The Commission shall only exercise the powers provided for in this Article when at least six High Contracting Parties are bound by declarations made in accordance with the preceding paragraphs.

Protocol No. 1 to the [European] Convention for the Protection of Human Rights and Fundamental Freedoms (1954)

The Governments signatory hereto, being Members of the Council of Europe,

Being resolved to take steps to ensure the collective enforcement of certain rights and freedoms other than those already included in Section I of the Convention for the Protection of Human Rights and Fundamental Freedoms signed at Rome on 4th November 1950 (hereinafter referred to as "the Convention"),

Have agreed as follows:

ARTICLE 1

Every natural or legal person is entitled to the peaceful enjoyment of his possessions. No one shall be deprived of his possessions except in the public interest and subject to the conditions provided for by law and by the general principles of international law.

The preceding provisions shall not, however, in any way impair the right of a State to enforce such laws as it deems necessary to control the use of property in accordance with the general interest or to secure the payment of taxes or other contributions or penalties.

ARTICLE 2

No person shall be denied the right to education. In the exercise of any functions which it assumes in relation to education and to teaching, the State shall respect the right of parents to ensure such education and teaching in conformity with their own religious and philosophical convictions.

ARTICLE 3

The High Contracting Parties undertake to hold free elections at reasonable intervals by secret ballot, under conditions which will ensure the free expression of the opinion of the people in the choice of the legislature.

ARTICLE 4

Any High Contracting Party may at the time of signature or ratification or at any time thereafter communicate to the Secretary-General of the Council of Europe a declaration stating the extent to which it undertakes that the provisions of the present Protocol shall apply to such of the territories for the international relations of which it is responsible as are named therein.

Any High Contracting Party which has communicated a declaration in virtue of the preceding paragraph may from time to time communicate a further declaration modifying the terms of any former declaration or terminating the application of the provisions of this Protocol in respect of any territory.

A declaration made in accordance with this Article shall be deemed to have been made in accordance with paragraph (1) of Article 63 of the Convention.

ARTICLE 5

As between the High Contracting Parties the provisions of Articles 1, 2, 3 and 4 of this Protocol shall be regarded as additional Articles to the Convention and all the provisions of the Convention shall apply accordingly.

ARTICLE 6

This Protocol shall be open for signature by the Members of the Council of Europe, who are the signatories of the Convention; it shall be ratified at the same time as or after the ratification of the Convention. It shall enter into force after the deposit of ten instruments of ratification. As regards any signatory ratifying subsequently, the Protocol shall enter into force at the date of the deposit of its instrument of ratification.

The instruments of ratification shall be deposited with the Secretary-General of the Council of Europe, who will notify all Members of the names of those who have ratified.

Protocol No. 4 to the [European] Convention for the Protection of Human Rights and Fundamental Freedoms (1963)

The Governments signatory hereto, being Members of the Council of Europe,

Being resolved to take steps to ensure the collective enforcement of certain rights and freedoms other than those already included in Section I of the Convention for the Protection of Human Rights and Fundamental Freedoms signed at Rome on 4th November 1950 (hereinafter referred to as "the Convention") and in Articles 1 to 3 of the First Protocol to the Convention, signed at Paris on 20th March 1952,

Have agreed as follows:

ARTICLE 1

No one shall be deprived of his liberty merely on the ground of inability to fulfill a contractual obligation.

ARTICLE 2

1. Everyone lawfully within the territory of a State shall, within that territory, have the right to liberty of movement and freedom to choose his residence.

2. Everyone shall be free to leave any country, including his own.

3. No restrictions shall be placed on the exercise of these rights other than such as are in accordance with law and are necessary in a democratic society in the interests of national security or public safety, for the maintenance of *ordre public*, for the prevention of crime, for the protection of health or morals, or for the protection of the rights and freedoms of others.

4. The rights set forth in paragraph 1 may also be subject, in particular areas, to restrictions imposed in accordance with law and justified by the public interest in a democratic society.

ARTICLE 3

1. No one shall be expelled, by means either of an individual or of a collective measure, from the territory of the State of which he is a national.

2. No one shall be deprived of the right to enter the territory of the State of which he is a national.

ARTICLE 4

Collective expulsion of aliens is prohibited.

ARTICLE 5

1. Any High Contracting Party may, at the time of signature or ratification of this Protocol, or at any time thereafter, communicate to the Secretary-General of the Council of Europe a declaration stating the extent to which it undertakes that the provisions of this Protocol shall apply to such of the territories for the international relations of which it is responsible as are named therein.

2. Any High Contracting Party which has communicated a declaration in virtue of the preceding paragraph may, from time to time, communicate a further declaration modifying the terms of any former declaration or terminating the application of the provisions of this Protocol in respect of any territory.

3. A declaration made in accordance with this Article shall be deemed to have been made in accordance with paragraph 1 of Article 63 of the Convention.

4. The territory of any State to which this Protocol applies by virtue of ratification or acceptance by that State, and each territory to which this Protocol is applied by virtue of a declaration by that State under this Article, shall be treated as separate territories for the purpose of the references in Articles 2 and 3 to the territory of a State.

ARTICLE 6

1. As between the High Contracting Parties the provisions of Articles 1 to 5 of this Protocol shall be regarded as additional Articles to the Convention, and all the provisions of the Convention shall apply accordingly.

2. Nevertheless, the right of individual recourse recognized by a declaration made under Article 25 of the Convention, or the acceptance of the compulsory jurisdiction of the Court by a declaration made under Article 46 of the Convention, shall not be effective in relation to this Protocol unless the High Contracting Party concerned has made a statement recognizing such right, or accepting such jurisdiction, in respect of all or any of Articles 1 to 4 of the Protocol. . . .

United Nations International Covenant on Civil and Political Rights (1966)

Preamble

The States Parties to the present Covenant,

Considering that, in accordance with the principles proclaimed in the Charter of the United Nations, recognition of the inherent dignity and of the equal and unalienable rights of all members of the human family is the foundation of freedom, justice and peace in the world,

Recognizing that these rights derive from the inherent dignity of the human person,

Recognizing that, in accordance with the Universal Declaration of Human Rights, the ideal of free human beings enjoying civil and political freedom and freedom from fear and want can only be achieved if conditions are created whereby everyone may enjoy his civil and political rights, as well as his economic, social and cultural rights,

Considering the obligation of States under the Charter of the United Nations to promote universal respect for, and observance of, human rights and freedoms,

Realizing that the individual, having duties to other individuals and to the community to which he belongs, is under a responsibility to strive for the promotion and observance of the rights recognized in the present Covenant,

Agree upon the following articles:

Part I

ARTICLE 1

1. All peoples have the right of self-determination. By virtue of the right they freely determine their political status and freely pursue their economic, social and cultural development.

2. All peoples may, for their own ends, freely dispose of their natural wealth and resources without prejudice to any obligations arising out of international economic cooperation, based upon the principle of mutual benefit, and international law. In no case may a people be deprived of its own means of subsistence.

3. The States Parties to the present Covenant, including those having responsibility for the administration of Non-Self-Governing and Trust Territories, shall promote the realization of the right of self-determination, and shall respect that right, in conformity with the provisions of the United Nations Charter.

Part II

ARTICLE 2

1. Each State Party to the present Covenant undertakes to respect and to ensure to all individuals within its territory and subject to its jurisdiction the rights recognized in the present Covenant, without distinction of any kind, such as race, color, sex, language, religion, political or other opinion, national or social origin, property, birth or other status.

2. Where not already provided for by existing legislative or other measures, each State Party to the present Covenant undertakes to take the necessary steps, in accordance with its constitutional processes and with the provisions of the present Covenant, to adopt such legislative or other measures as may be necessary to give effect to the rights recognized in the present Covenant.

3. Each State Party to the present Covenant undertakes:

a. To ensure that any person whose rights or freedoms as herein recognized are violated shall have an effective remedy notwithstanding that the violation has been committed by persons acting in an official capacity;

b. To ensure that any person claiming such a remedy shall have his right thereto determined by competent judicial, administrative or legislative authorities, or by any other competent authority provided for by the legal system of the State, and to develop the possibilities of judicial remedy;

c. To ensure that the competent authorities shall enforce such remedies when granted.

ARTICLE 3

The States Parties to the present Covenant undertake to ensure the equal right of men and women to the enjoyment of all civil and political rights set forth in the present Covenant.

ARTICLE 4

1. In time of public emergency which threatens the life of the nation and the existence of which is officially proclaimed, the States Parties to the present Covenant may take measures derogating from their obligations under the present Covenant to the extent strictly required by the exigencies of the situation, provided that such measures are not inconsistent with their other obligations under international law and do not involve discrimination solely on the ground of race, color, sex, language, religion or social origin.

2. No derogation from articles 6, 7, 8 (paragraphs 1 and 2), 11, 15, 16 and 18 may be made under this provision.

3. Any State Party to the present Covenant availing itself of the right of derogation shall inform immediately the other States Parties to the present Covenant, through the intermediary of the Secretary-General of the United Nations of the provisions from which it has derogated and of the reasons by which it was actuated. A further communication shall be made, through the same intermediary, on the date on which it terminates such derogation.

ARTICLE 5

1. Nothing in the present Covenant may be interpreted as implying for any State, group or person any right to engage in any activity or perform any act aimed at the destruction of any of the rights and freedoms recognized herein or at their limitation to a greater extent than is provided for in the present Covenant.

2. There shall be no restriction upon or derogation from any of the fundamental human rights recognized or existing in any State Party to the present Covenant pursuant to law, conventions, regulations or custom on the pretext that the present Covenant does not recognize such rights or that it recognizes them to a lesser extent.

Part III

ARTICLE 6

1. Every human being has the inherent right to life. This right shall be protected by law. No one shall be arbitrarily deprived of his life.

2. In countries which have not abolished the death penalty, sentence of death may be imposed only for the most serious crimes in accordance with law in force at the time of the commission of the crime and not contrary to the provisions of the present Covenant and to the Convention on the Prevention and Punishment of the Crime of Genocide. This penalty can only be carried out pursuant to a final judgment rendered by a competent court.

3. When deprivation of life constitutes the crime of genocide, it is understood that nothing in this article shall authorize any State Party to the present Covenant to derogate in any way from any obligation assumed under the provisions of the Convention on the Prevention and Punishment of the Crime of Genocide.

4. Anyone sentenced to death shall have the right to seek pardon or commutation of the sentence. Amnesty, pardon or commutation of the sentence of death may be granted in all cases.

5. Sentence of death shall not be imposed for crimes committed by persons below eighteen years of age and shall not be carried out on pregnant women.

6. Nothing in this article shall be invoked to delay or to prevent the abolition of capital punishment by any State Party to the present Covenant.

ARTICLE 7

No one shall be subjected to torture or to cruel, inhuman or degrading treatment or punishment. In particular, no one shall be subjected without his free consent to medical or scientific experimentation.

ARTICLE 8

1. No one shall be held in slavery; slavery and the slave trade in all their forms shall be prohibited.

2. No one shall be held in servitude.

3. (a) No one shall be required to perform forced or compulsory labor;

   (b) The preceding subparagraph shall not be held to preclude in countries where imprisonment with hard labor may be imposed as a punishment for a crime, the performance of hard labor in pursuance of a sentence to such punishment by a competent court;

(c) For the purpose of this paragraph the term "forced or compulsory labor" shall not include:

i. Any work or service, not referred to in subparagraph (b), normally required of a person who is under detention in consequence of a lawful order of a court, or of a person during conditional release from such detention;

ii. Any service of a military character and, in countries where conscientious objection is recognized, any national service required by law of conscientious objectors;

iii. Any service exacted in cases of emergency or calamity threatening the life or well-being of the community;

iv. Any work or service which forms part of normal civil obligations.

ARTICLE 9

1. Everyone has the right to liberty and security of person. No one shall be subjected to arbitrary arrest or detention. No one shall be deprived of his liberty except on such grounds and in accordance with such procedures as are established by law.

2. Anyone who is arrested shall be informed, at the time of arrest, of the reasons for his arrest and shall be promptly informed of any charges against him.

3. Anyone arrested or detained on a criminal charge shall be brought promptly before a judge or other officer authorized by law to exercise judicial power and shall be entitled to trial within a reasonable time or to release. It shall not be the general rule that persons awaiting trial shall be detained in custody, but release may be subject to guarantees to appear for trial, at any other stage of the judicial proceedings, and, should occasion arise, for execution of the judgement.

4. Anyone who is deprived of his liberty by arrest or detention shall be entitled to take proceedings before a court, in order that such court may decide without delay on the lawfulness of his detention and order his release if the detention is not lawful.

5. Anyone who has been the victim of unlawful arrest or detention shall have an enforceable right to compensation.

ARTICLE 10

1. All persons deprived of their liberty shall be treated with humanity and with respect for the inherent dignity of the human person.

2. (a) Accused persons shall, save in exceptional circumstances, be segregated from convicted persons, and shall be subject to separate treatment appropriate to their status as unconvicted persons;

(b) Accused juvenile persons shall be separated from adults and brought as speedily as possible for adjudication.

3. The penitentiary system shall comprise treatment of prisoners the essential aim of which shall be their reformation and social rehabilitation. Juvenile offenders shall be segregated from adults and be accorded treatment appropriate to their age and legal status.

ARTICLE 11

No one shall be imprisoned merely on the ground of inability to fulfill a contractual obligation.

ARTICLE 12

1. Everyone lawfully within the territory of a State shall, within that territory, have the right to liberty of movement and freedom to choose his residence.

2. Everyone shall be free to leave any country, including his own.

3. The above-mentioned rights shall not be subject to any restrictions except those which are provided by law, are necessary to protect national security, public order ("*ordre public*"), public health or morals or the rights and freedoms of others, and are consistent with the other rights recognized in the present Covenant.

4. No one shall be arbitrarily deprived of the right to enter his own country.

ARTICLE 13

An alien lawfully in the territory of a State Party to the present Covenant may be expelled therefrom only in pursuance of a decision reached in accordance with law and shall, except where compelling reasons of national security otherwise require, be allowed to submit the reasons against his expulsion and to have his case reviewed by, and be represented for the purpose before, the competent authority or a person or persons especially designated by the competent authority.

ARTICLE 14

1. All persons shall be equal before the courts and tribunals. In the determination of any criminal charge against him, or of his rights and obligations in a suit at law, everyone shall be entitled to a fair and public hearing by a competent, independent and impartial tribunal established by law. The Press and the public may be excluded from all or part of a trial for reasons of morals, public order ("*ordre public*") or national security in a democratic society, or when the interest of the private lives of the parties so requires, or to the extent strictly necessary in the opinion of the court in special circumstances where publicity would prejudice the interests of justice; but any judgment rendered in a criminal case or in a suit at law shall be made public except where the interest of juveniles otherwise requires

or the proceedings concern matrimonial disputes or the guardianship of children.

2. Everyone charged with a criminal offense shall have the right to be presumed innocent until proved guilty according to law.

3. In the determination of any criminal charge against him, everyone shall be entitled to the following minimum guarantees, in full equality:

a. To be informed promptly and in detail in a language which he understands of the nature and cause of the charge against him;

b. To have adequate time and facilities for the preparation of his defense and to communicate with counsel of his own choosing;

c. To be tried without undue delay.

d. To be tried in his presence, and to defend himself in person or through legal assistance of his own choosing; to be informed, if he does not have legal assistance, of this right; and to have legal assistance assigned to him, in any case where the interests of justice so require, and without payment by him in any such case if he does not have sufficient means to pay for it;

e. To examine, or have examined, the witnesses against him and to obtain the attendance and examination of witnesses on his behalf under the same conditions as witnesses against him;

f. To have the free assistance of an interpreter if he cannot understand or speak the language used in court;

g. Not to be compelled to testify against himself, or to confess guilt.

4. In the case of juveniles, the procedure shall be such as will take account of their age and the desirability of promoting their rehabilitation.

5. Everyone convicted of a crime shall have the right to his conviction and sentence being reviewed by a higher tribunal according to law.

6. When a person has by a final decision been convicted of a criminal offense and when subsequently his conviction has been reversed or he has been pardoned on the ground that a new or newly discovered fact shows conclusively that there has been a miscarriage of justice, the person who has suffered punishment as a result of such conviction shall be compensated according to law, unless it is proved that the nondisclosure of the unknown fact in time is wholly or partly attributable to him.

7. No one shall be liable to be tried or punished again for an offense for which he has already been finally convicted or acquitted in accordance with the law and penal procedure of each country.

ARTICLE 15

1. No one shall be held guilty of any criminal offense on account of any act or omission which did not constitute a criminal offense, under

national or international law, at the time when it was committed. Nor shall a heavier penalty be imposed than the one that was applicable at the time when the criminal offense was committed. If, subsequently to the commission of the offense, provision is made by law for the imposition of a lighter penalty, the offender shall benefit thereby.

2. Nothing in this article shall prejudice the trial and punishment of any person for any act or omission which, at the time when it was committed, was criminal according to the general principles of law recognized by the community of nations.

ARTICLE 16

Everyone shall have the right to recognition everywhere as a person before the law.

ARTICLE 17

1. No one shall be subjected to arbitrary or unlawful interference with his privacy, family, home or correspondence, nor to unlawful attacks on his honor and reputation.

2. Everyone has the right to the protection of the law against such interference or attacks.

ARTICLE 18

1. Everyone shall have the right to freedom of thought, conscience and religion. This right shall include freedom to have or to adopt a religion or belief of his choice, and freedom either individually or in community with others and in public or private, to manifest his religion or belief in worship, observance, practice and teaching.

2. No one shall be subject to coercion which would impair his freedom to have or to adopt a religion or belief of his choice.

3. Freedom to manifest one's religion or beliefs may be subject only to such limitations as are prescribed by law and are necessary to protect public safety, order, health, or morals or the fundamental rights and freedoms of others.

4. The States Parties to the present Covenant undertake to have respect for the liberty of parents and, when applicable, legal guardians, to ensure the religious and moral education of their children in conformity with their own convictions.

ARTICLE 19

1 Everyone shall have the right to hold opinions without interference.

2. Everyone shall have the right to freedom of expression; this right shall include freedom to seek, receive and impart information and ideas of all kinds, regardless of frontiers, either orally, in writing or in print, in the form of art, or through any other media of his choice.

3. The exercise of the rights provided for in the foregoing paragraph carries with it special duties and responsibilities. It may therefore be subject to certain restrictions, but these shall be such only as are provided by law and are necessary, (1) for respect of the rights or reputations of others, (2) for the protection of national security or of public order ("*ordre public*"), or of public health or morals.

ARTICLE 20

1. Any propaganda for war shall be prohibited by law.
2. Any advocacy of national, racial, or religious hatred that constitutes incitement to discrimination, hostility or violence shall be prohibited by law.

ARTICLE 21

The right of peaceful assembly shall be recognized. No restrictions may be placed on the exercise of this right other than those imposed in conformity with the law and which are necessary in a democratic society in the interests of national security or public safety, public order ("*ordre public*"), the protection of public health or morals or the protection of the rights and freedoms of others.

ARTICLE 22

1. Everyone shall have the right to freedom of association with others, including the right to form and join trade unions for the protection of his interests.
2. No restrictions may be placed on the exercise of this right other than those prescribed by law and which are necessary in a democratic society in the interests of national security or public safety, public order ("*ordre public*"), the protection of public health or morals or the protection of the rights and freedoms of others. This article shall not prevent the imposition of lawful restrictions on members of the armed forces and of the police in their exercise of this right.
3. Nothing in this article shall authorize States Parties to the International Labor Convention of 1948 on Freedom of Association and Protection of the Right to Organize to take legislative measures which would prejudice, or to apply the law in such a manner as to prejudice, the guarantees provided for in the Convention.

ARTICLE 23

1. The family is the natural and fundamental group unit of society and is entitled to protection by society and the State.
2. The right of men and women of marriageable age to marry and to found a family shall be recognized.

3. No marriage shall be entered into without the free and full consent of the intending spouses.

4. States Parties to the present Covenant shall take appropriate steps to ensure equality of rights and responsibilities of spouses as to marriage, during marriage and at its dissolution. In the case of a dissolution, provision shall be made for the necessary protection of any children.

ARTICLE 24

1. Every child shall have, without any discrimination as to race, color, sex, language, religion, national or social origin, property or birth, the right to such measures of protection as required by his status as a minor, on the part of his family, the society and the State.

2. Every child shall be registered immediately after birth and shall have a name.

3. Every child has the right to acquire a nationality.

ARTICLE 25

Every citizen shall have the right and the opportunity, without any of the distinctions mentioned in article 2 and without unreasonable restrictions:

a. To take part in the conduct of public affairs, directly or through freely chosen representatives;

b. To vote and to be elected at genuine periodic elections which shall be by universal and equal suffrage and shall be held by secret ballot, guaranteeing the free expression of the will of the electors;

c. To have access, on general terms of equality, to public service in his country.

ARTICLE 26

All persions are equal before the law and are entitled without any discrimination to equal protection of the law. In this respect the law shall prohibit any discrimination and guarantee to all persons equal and effective protection against discrimination on any ground such as race, color, sex, language, religion, political or other opinion, national or social origin, property, birth or other status.

ARTICLE 27

In those States in which ethnic, religious or linguistic minorities exist, persons belonging to such minorities shall not be denied the right, in community with the other members of their group, to enjoy their own culture, to profess and practice their own religion, or to use their own language.

United Nations International Covenant on Economic, Social and Cultural Rights (1966)

Preamble

The States Parties to the present Covenant,

Considering that, in accordance with the principles proclaimed in the Charter of the United Nations, recognition of the inherent dignity and of the equal and inalienable rights of all members of the human family is the foundation of freedom, justice and peace in the world,

Recognizing that these rights derive from the inherent dignity of the human person,

Recognizing that, in accordance with the Universal Declaration of Human Rights, the ideal of free human beings enjoying freedom from fear and want can only be achieved if conditions are created whereby everyone may enjoy his economic, social and cultural rights, as well as his civil and political rights,

Considering the obligation of States under the Charter of the United Nations to promote universal respect for, and observance of, human rights and freedoms,

Realizing that the individual, having duties to other individuals and to the community to which he belongs, is under a responsibility to strive for the promotion and observance of the rights recognized in the present Covenant,

Agree upon the following articles:

Part I

ARTICLE 1

1. All peoples have the right of self-determination. By virtue of the right they freely determine their political status and freely pursue their economic, social and cultural development.

2. All peoples may, for their own ends, freely dispose of their natural wealth and resources without prejudice to any obligations arising out of international economic cooperation, based upon the principle of mutual benefit, and international law. In no case may a people be deprived of its own means of subsistence.

3. The States Parties to the present Covenant, including those having responsibility for the administration of Non-Self-Governing

and Trust Territories, shall promote the realization of the right of self-determination, and shall respect that right, in conformity with the provisions of the United Nations Charter.

Part II

ARTICLE 2

1. Each State Party to the present Covenant undertakes to take steps, individually and through international assistance and cooperation especially economic and technical, to the maximum of its available resources, with a view to achieving progressively the full realization of the rights recognized in the present Covenant by all appropriate means, including particularly the adoption of legislative measures.

2. The States Parties to the present Covenant undertake to guarantee that the rights enunciated in the present Covenant will be exercised without discrimination of any kind as to race, color, sex, religion, political or other opinion, national or social origin, property, birth or other status.

3. Developing countries, with due regard to human rights and their national economy, may determine to what extent they would guarantee the economic rights recognized in the present Covenant to non-nationals.

ARTICLE 3

The States Parties to the present Covenant undertake to ensure the equal right of men and women to the enjoyment of all economic, social and cultural rights set forth in this Covenant.

ARTICLE 4

The States Parties to the present Covenant recognize that in the enjoyment of those rights provided by the State in conformity with the present Covenant, the State may subject such rights only to such limitations as are determined by law only in so far as this may be compatible with the nature of these rights and solely for the purpose of promoting the general welfare in a democratic society.

ARTICLE 5

1. Nothing in the present Covenant may be interpreted as implying for any State, group or person, any right to engage in any activity or to perform any act aimed at the destruction of any of the rights or freedoms recognized herein, or at their limitation to a greater extent than is provided for in the present Covenant.

2. No restriction upon or derogation from any of the fundamental

human rights recognized or existing in any country in virtue of law, conventions, regulations or custom shall be admitted on the pretext that the present Covenant does not recognize such rights or that it recognizes them to a lesser extent.

Part III

ARTICLE 6

1. The States Parties to the present Covenant recognize the right to work, which includes the right of everyone to the opportunity to gain his living by work which he freely chooses or accepts, and will take appropriate steps to safeguard this right.

2. The steps to be taken by a State Party to the present Covenant to achieve the full realization of this right shall include technical and vocational guidance and training programs, policies and techniques to achieve steady economic, social and cultural development and full and productive employment under conditions safeguarding fundamental political and economic freedoms to the individual.

ARTICLE 7

The States Parties to the present Covenant recognize the right of everyone to the enjoyment of just and favorable conditions of work, which ensure, in particular:

a. Remuneration which provides all workers as a minimum with:

i. Fair wages and equal remuneration for work of equal value without distinction of any kind, in particular women being guaranteed conditions of work not inferior to those enjoyed by men, with equal pay for equal work; and

ii. A decent living for themselves and their families in accordance with the provisions of the present Covenant;

b. Safe and healthy working conditions;

c. Equal opportunity for everyone to be promoted in his employment to an appropriate higher level, subject to no considerations other than those of seniority and competence;

d. Rest, leisure and reasonable limitation of working hours and periodic holidays with pay, as well as remuneration for public holidays.

ARTICLE 8

1. The States Parties to the present Covenant undertake to ensure:

a. The right to everyone to form trade unions and join the trade union of his choice subject only to the rules of the organization concerned, for the promotion and protection of his economic and social interests. No restrictions may be placed on the exercise of this right other than those prescribed by law and which are necessary in a democratic society in the interests of national security or public order or for the protection of the rights and freedoms of others;

b. The right of trade unions to establish national federations or confederations and the right of the latter to form or join international trade-union organizations;

c. The right of trade unions to function freely subject to no limitations other than those prescribed by law and which are necessary in a democratic society in the interests of national security or public order or for the protection of the rights and freedoms of others;

d. The right to strike, provided that it is exercised in conformity with the laws of the particular country.

2. This article shall not prevent the imposition of lawful restrictions on the exercise of these rights by members of the armed forces, or of the police, or of the administration of the State.

3. Nothing in this article shall authorize State Parties to the International Labor Convention of 1948 on Freedom of Association and Protection of the Right to Organize to take legislative measures which would prejudice, or apply the law in such a manner as would prejudice, the guarantees provided for in that Convention.

ARTICLE 9

The States Parties to the present Covenant recognize the right of everyone to social security including social insurance.

ARTICLE 10

The States Parties to the present Covenant recognize that:

1. The widest possible protection and assistance should be accorded to the family, which is the natural and fundamental group unit of society, particularly for its establishment and while it is responsible for the care and education of dependent children. Marriage must be entered into with the free consent of the intending spouses;

2. Special protection should be accorded to mothers during a reasonable period before and after childbirth. During such periods working mothers should be accorded paid leave or leave with adequate social security benefits;

3. Special measures of protection and assistance should be taken on behalf of all children and young persons without any discrimination for reasons of parentage or other conditions. Children and younger persons should be protected from economic and social exploitation. Their employment in work harmful to their morals or health or

dangerous to life or likely to hamper their normal development should be punishable by law. States should also set several age limits below which the paid employment of child labor should be prohibited and punishable by law.

Article 11

1. The States Parties to the present Covenant recognize the right of everyone to an adequate standard of living for himself and his family, including adequate food, clothing and housing, and to the continuous improvement of living conditions. The States Parties will take appropriate steps to ensure the realization of this right, recognizing to this effect the essential importance of international cooperation based on free consent.

2. The States Parties to the present Covenant, recognizing the fundamental right of everyone to be free from hunger, shall take, individually and through international cooperation, the measures, including specific programs, which are needed:

    a. To improve methods of production, conservation and distribution of food by making full use of technical and scientific knowledge, by disseminating knowledge of the principles of nutrition and by developing or reforming agrarian systems in such a way as to achieve the most efficient development and utilization of natural resources; and

    b. Take into account the problems of both food-importing and food-exporting countries, to ensure an equitable distribution of world food supplies in relation to need.

Article 12

1. The States Parties to the present Covenant recognize the right of everyone to the enjoyment of the highest attainable standard of physical and mental health.

2. The steps to be taken by the States Parties to the present Covenant to achieve the full realization of this right shall include those necessary for:

    a. The provision for the reduction of the still-birth-rate and of infant mortality and for the healthy development of the child;

    b. The improvement of all aspects of environmental and industrial hygiene;

    c. The prevention, treatment and control of epidemic, endemic, occupational and other diseases;

    d. The creation of conditions which would assure to all medical service and medical attention in the event of sickness.

ARTICLE 13

1. The States Parties to the present Covenant recognize the right of everyone to education. They agree that education shall be directed to the full development of the human personality and the sense of its dignity, and shall strengthen the respect for human rights and fundamental freedoms. They further agree that education shall enable all persons to participate effectively in a free society, promote understanding, tolerance and friendship among all nations and all racial ethnic or religious groups, and further the activities of the United Nations for the maintenance of peace.

2. The States Parties to the present Covenant recognize that, with a view to achieving the full realization of this right:

a. Primary education shall be compulsory and available free to all;

b. Secondary education in its different forms, including technical and vocational secondary education, shall be made generally available and accessible to all by every appropriate means, and in particular by the progressive introduction of free education;

c. Higher education shall be made equally accessible to all, on the basis of capacity, by every appropriate means, and in particular by the progressive introduction of free education;

d. Fundamental education shall be encouraged or intensified as far as possible for those persons who have not received or completed the whole period of their primary education;

e. The development of a system of schools at all levels shall be actively pursued, an adequate fellowship system shall be established, and the material conditions of teaching staff shall be continuously improved.

3. The States Parties to the present Covenant undertake to have respect for the liberty of parents and, when applicable, legal guardians, to choose for their children schools other than those established by the public authorities which conform to such minimum education standards as may be laid down or approved by the State and to ensure the religious and moral education of their children in conformity with their own convictions.

4. No part of this article shall be construed so as to interfere with the liberty of individuals and bodies to establish and direct educational institutions, subject always to the observance of the principles set forth in paragraph 1 and to the requirement that the education given in such institutions shall conform to such minimum standards as may be laid down by the State.

ARTICLE 14

Each State Party to the present Covenant which, at the time of becoming a Party, has not been able to secure in its metropolitan territory or other territories under its jurisdiction compulsory primary education, free of charge, undertakes, within two years, to work out and adopt a detailed plan of action for the progressive implementation, within a reasonable number of years, to be fixed in the plan, of the principle of compulsory education free of charge for all.

ARTICLE 15

1. The States Parties to the present Covenant recognize the right of everyone:
    a. To take part in cultural life;
    b. To enjoy the benefits of scientific progress and its applications;
    c. To benefit from the protection of the moral and material interests resulting from any scientific, literary or artistic production of which he is the author.
2. The steps to be taken by the States Parties to the present Covenant to achieve the full realization of this right shall include those necessary for the conservation, the development and the diffusion of science and culture.
3. The States Parties to the present Covenant undertake to respect the freedom indispensable for scientific research and creative activity.
4. The States Parties to the present Covenant recognize the benefits to be derived from the encouragement and development of international contracts and cooperation in the scientific and cultural fields.

Part IV

ARTICLE 16

1. The States Parties to the present Covenant undertake to submit in conformity with this part of the Covenant reports on the measures which they have adopted and the progress made in achieving the observance of the rights recognized herein.
2. (a) All reports shall be submitted to the Secretary-General of the United Nations who shall transmit copies to the Economic and Social Council for consideration in accordance with the provisions of the present Covenant.
    (b) The Secretary-General of the United Nations shall also transmit to the specialized agencies copies of the reports, or any relevant parts therefrom, from States Parties to the present Covenant which are also members of these specialized agencies in so far as these

reports, or parts therefrom, relate to any matters which fall within the responsibilities of the said agencies in accordance with their constitutional instruments.

ARTICLE 17

1. The States Parties to the present Covenant shall furnish their reports in stages, in accordance with a program to be established by the Economic and Social Council within one year of the entry into force of the present Covenant after consultation with the States Parties and the specialized agencies concerned.

2. Reports may indicate factors and difficulties affecting the degree of fulfillment of obligations under the present Covenant.

3. Where relevant information has previously been furnished to the United Nations or to any specialized agency by any State Party to the present Covenant it will not be necessary to reproduce that information but a precise reference to the information so furnished will suffice.

ARTICLE 18

Pursuant to its responsibilities under the Charter in the field of human rights and fundamental freedoms, the Economic and Social Council may make arrangements with the specialized agencies in respect of their reporting to it on the progress made in achieving the observance of the provisions of the present Covenant falling within the scope of their activities. These reports may include particulars of decisions and recommendations on such implementation adopted by their competent organs.

ARTICLE 19

The Economic and Social Council may transmit to the Commission on Human Rights for study and general recommendation or as appropriate for information the reports concerning human rights submitted by States in accordance with articles 16 and 17, and those concerning human rights submitted by the specialized agencies in accordance with article 18.

ARTICLE 20

The States Parties to the present Covenant and the specialized agencies concerned may submit comments to the Economic and Social Council on any general recommendation under article 19 or reference to such general recommendation in any report of the Commission or any documentation referred to therein.

ARTICLE 21

The Economic and Social Council may submit from time to time to the General Assembly reports with recommendations of a general nature and a summary of the information received from the States Parties to the present Covenant and the specialized agencies on the measures taken and the progress made in achieving general observance of the rights recognized in the present Covenant.

ARTICLE 22

The Economic and Social Council may bring to the attention of other organs of the United Nations, their subsidiary organs and specialized agencies concerned with furnishing technical assistance, any matters arising out of the reports referred to in this part of the present Covenant which may assist such bodies in deciding each within its field of competence, on the advisability of international measures likely to contribute to the effective progressive implementation of the present Covenant.

ARTICLE 23

The States Parties to the present Covenant agree that international action for the achievement of the rights recognized in the present Covenant includes such methods as the conclusion of conventions, the adoption of recommendations, the furnishing of technical assistance and the holding of regional meetings and technical meetings for the purpose of consultation and study organized in conjunction with the Governments concerned.

ARTICLE 24

Nothing in the present Covenant shall be interpreted as impairing the provisions of the Charter of the United Nations and of the constitutions of the specialized agencies which define the respective responsibilities of the various organs of the United Nations and of the specialized agencies in regard to the matters dealt with in the present Covenant.

ARTICLE 25

Nothing in the present Covenant shall be interpreted as impairing the inherent right of all peoples to enjoy and utilize fully and freely their natural wealth and resources.

United Nations International Convention on the Elimination of All Forms of Racial Discrimination (1969)

The States Parties to This Convention,

Considering that the Charter of the United Nations is based on the principles of the dignity and equality inherent in all human beings, and that all Member States have pledged themselves to take joint and separate action in cooperation with the Organization for the achievement of one of the purposes of the United Nations which is to promote and encourage universal respect for and observance of human rights and fundamental freedoms for all without distinction as to race, sex, language or religion,

Considering that the Universal Declaration of Human Rights proclaims that all human beings are born free and equal in dignity and rights and that everyone is entitled to all the rights and freedoms set out therein, without distinctions of any kind, in particular as to race, color or national origin,

Considering that all human beings are equal before the law and are entitled to equal protection of the law against any discrimination and against any incitement to discrimination,

Considering that the United Nations has condemned colonialism and all practices of segregation and discrimination associated therewith, in whatever form and wherever they exist, and that the Declaration on the Granting of Independence to Colonial Countries and Peoples of 14 December 1960 (General Assembly resolution 1514 (XV)) has affirmed and solemnly proclaimed the necessity of bringing them to a speedy and unconditional end,

Considering that the United Nations Declaration on the Elimination of All Forms of Racial Discrimination of 20 November 1963 (General Assembly resolution 1904 (XVIII)) solemnly affirms the necessity of speedily eliminating racial discrimination throughout the world in all its forms and manifestations and of securing understanding of and respect for the dignity of the human person,

Convinced that any doctrine of superiority based on racial differentiation is scientifically false, morally condemnable, socially unjust and dangerous, and that there is no justification for racial discrimination, in theory or in practice, anywhere,

Reaffirming that discrimination between human beings on the grounds of race, color, or ethnic origin is an obstacle to friendly and peaceful relations among nations and is capable of disturbing peace and security among peoples and the harmony of persons living side by side even within one and the same State,

Convinced that the existence of racial barriers is repugnant to the ideals of any human society,

Alarmed by manifestations of racial discrimination still in evidence in some areas of the world and by governmental policies based on racial superiority or hatred, such as policies of *apartheid*, segregation or separation,

Resolved to adopt all necessary measures for speedily eliminating racial discrimination in all its forms and manifestations and to prevent and combat racist doctrines and practices in order to promote understanding between races and to build an international community free from all forms of racial segregation and racial discrimination,

Bearing in mind the Convention on Discrimination in Respect of Employment and Occupation adopted by the International Labor Organization in 1958, and the Convention Against Discrimination in Education adopted by the United Nations Educational, Scientific and Cultural Organization in 1960,

Desiring to implement the principles embodied in the United Nations Declaration on the Elimination of All Forms of Racial Discrimination and to secure the earliest adoption of practical measures to that end,

Have agreed as follows:

Part I

ARTICLE 1

1. In this Convention the term "racial discrimination" shall mean any distinction, exclusion, restriction or preference based on race, color, descent, or national or ethnic origin which has the purpose or effect of nullifying or impairing the recognition, enjoyment or exercise, on an equal footing, of human rights and fundamental freedoms in the political, economic, social, cultural or any other field of public life.

2. This Convention shall not apply to distinctions, exclusions, restrictions or preferences made by a State Party to this Convention between citizens and non-citizens.

3. Nothing in this Convention may be interpreted as affecting in any way the legal provisions of States Parties concerning nationality, citizenship or naturalization, provided that such provisions do not discriminate against any particular nationality.

4. Special measures taken for the sole purpose of securing adequate

advancement of certain racial or ethnic groups or individuals requiring such protection as may be necessary in order to ensure to such groups or individuals equal enjoyment or exercise of human rights and fundamental freedoms shall not be deemed racial discrimination, provided, however, that such measures do not, as a consequence, lead to the maintenance of separate rights for different racial groups and that they shall not be continued after the objectives for which they were taken have been achieved.

ARTICLE 2

1. States Parties condemn racial discrimination and undertake to pursue by all appropriate means and without delay a policy of eliminating racial discrimination in all its forms, and promoting understanding among all races, and to this end:

a. Each State Party undertakes to engage in no act or practice of racial discrimination against persons, groups of persons or institutions and to ensure that all public authorities and public institutions, national and local, shall act in conformity with this obligation;

b. Each State Party undertakes not to sponsor, defend or support racial discrimination by any persons or organizations;

c. Each State Party shall take effective measures to review governmental, national and local policies, and to amend, rescind or nullify any laws and regulations which have the effect of creating or perpetuating racial discrimination wherever it exists;

d. Each State Party shall prohibit and bring to an end, by all appropriate means, including legislation as required by circumstances, racial discrimination by any persons, group or organization;

e. Each State Party undertakes to encourage, where appropriate, integrationist multi-racial organizations and movements and other means of eliminating barriers between races, and to discourage anything which tends to strengthen racial division.

2. States Parties shall, when the circumstances so warrant, take, in the social, economic, cultural and other fields, special and concrete measures to ensure the adequate development and protection of certain racial groups or individuals belonging to them for the purpose of guaranteeing them the full and equal enjoyment of human rights and fundamental freedoms. These measures shall in no case entail as a consequence the maintenance of unequal or separate rights for different racial groups after the objectives for which they were taken have been achieved.

ARTICLE 3

States Parties particularly condemn racial segregation and *apartheid* and undertake to prevent, prohibit and eradicate, in territories under their jurisdiction, all practices of this nature.

ARTICLE 4

States Parties condemn all propaganda and all organizations which are based on ideas or theories of superiority of one race or group of persons of one color or ethnic origin, or which attempt to justify or promote racial hatred and discrimination in any form, and undertake to adopt immediate and positive measures designed to eradicate all incitement to, or acts of, such discrimination, and to this end, with due regard to the principles embodied in the Universal Declaration of Human Rights and the rights expressly set forth in article 5 of this Convention, *inter alia:*

a. Shall declare an offense punishable by law all dissemination of ideas based on racial superiority or hatred, incitement to racial discrimination, as well as all acts of violence or incitement to such acts against any race or group of persons of another color or ethnic origin, and also the provision of any assistance to racist activities, including the financing thereof;

b. Shall declare illegal and prohibit organizations, and also organized and all other propaganda activities, which promote and incite racial discrimination, and shall recognize participation in such organizations or activities as an offense punishable by law;

c. Shall not permit public authorities or public institutions, national or local, to promote or incite racial discrimination.

ARTICLE 5

In compliance with the fundamental obligations laid down in article 2, States Parties undertake to prohibit and to eliminate racial discrimination in all its forms and to guarantee the right of everyone, without distinction as to race, color, or national or ethnic origin, to equality before the law, notably in the enjoyment of the following rights:

a. The right to equal treatment before the tribunals and all other organs administering justice;

b. The right to security of person and protection by the State against violence or bodily harm, whether inflicted by Government officials or by any individual, group or institution;

c. Political rights, in particular the rights to participate in elections, to vote and to stand for election—on the basis of universal and equal suffrage, to take part in the Government as well as in the conduct of public affairs at any level and to have equal access to public service;

d. Other civil rights, in particular:

i. the right to freedom of movement and residence within the border of the State;

ii. the right to leave any country, including his own, and to return to his country;

iii. the right to nationality;

iv. the right to marriage and choice of spouse;

v. the right to own property alone as well as in association with others;

vi the right to inherit;

vii. the right to freedom of thought, conscience and religion;

viii. the right to freedom of opinion and expression;

ix. the right to freedom of peaceful assembly and association;

e. Economic, social and cultural rights, in particular:

i. the rights to work, free choice of employment, just and favorable conditions of work, protection against unemployment, equal pay for equal work, just and favorable remuneration;

ii. the right to form and join trade unions;

iii. the right to housing;

iv. the right to public health, medical care and social security and social services;

v. the right to education and training;

vi. the right to equal participation in cultural activities;

f. The right of access to any place or service intended for use by the general public such as transport, hotels, restaurants, cafés, theatres, parks.

ARTICLE 6

States Parties shall assure to everyone within their jurisdiction effective protection and remedies through the competent national tribunals and other State institutions against any acts of racial discrimination which violate his human rights and fundamental freedoms contrary to this Convention, as well as the right to seek from such tribunals just and adequate reparation or satisfaction for any damage suffered as a result of such discrimination.

American Convention on Human Rights (1969)

Preamble

The American states signatory to the present Convention,

Reaffirming their intention to consolidate in this hemisphere, within the framework of democratic institutions, a system of personal liberty and social justice based on respect for the essential rights of man;

Recognizing that the essential rights of man are not derived from one's being a national of a certain state, but are based upon attributes of the human personality, and that they therefore justify international protection in the form of a convention reinforcing or complementing the protection provided by the domestic law of the American states;

Considering that these principles have been set forth in the Charter of the Organization of American States, in the American Declaration of the Rights and Duties of Man, and in the Universal Declaration of Human Rights, and that they have been reaffirmed and refined in other international instruments, worldwide as well as regional in scope;

Reiterating that, in accordance with the Universal Declaration of Human Rights, the ideal of free men enjoying freedom from fear and want can be achieved only if conditions are created whereby everyone may enjoy his economic, social, and cultural rights, as well as his civil and political rights; and

Considering that the Third Special Inter-American Conference (Buenos Aires, 1967) approved the incorporation into the Charter of the Organization itself of broader standards with respect to economic, social, and educational rights and resolved that an inter-American convention on human rights should determine the structure, competence, and procedure of the organs responsible for these matters,

Have agreed upon the following:

Signed at Inter-American Specialized Conference on Human Rights, San José, Costa Rica.

Part I. State Obligations and Rights Protected

CHAPTER I. GENERAL OBLIGATIONS

ARTICLE 1. OBLIGATION TO RESPECT RIGHTS

1. The States Parties to this Convention undertake to respect the rights and freedoms recognized herein and to ensure to all persons subject to their jurisdiction the free and full exercise of those rights and freedoms, without any discrimination for reasons of race, color, sex, language, religion, political or other opinion, national or social origin, economic status, birth, or any other social condition.

2. For the purposes of this Convention, "person" means every human being.

ARTICLE 2. DOMESTIC LEGAL EFFECTS

Where the exercise of any of the rights or freedoms referred to in Article 1 is not already ensured by legislative or other provisions, the States Parties undertake to adopt, in accordance with their constitutional processes and the provisions of this Convention, such legislative or other measures as may be necessary to give effect to those rights or freedoms.

CHAPTER II. CIVIL AND POLITICAL RIGHTS

ARTICLE 3. RIGHT TO JURIDICAL PERSONALITY

Every person has the right to recognition as a person before the law.

ARTICLE 4. RIGHT TO LIFE

1. Every person has the right to have his life respected. This right shall be protected by law and, in general, from the moment of conception. No one shall be arbitrarily deprived of his life.

2. In countries that have not abolished the death penalty, it may be imposed only for the most serious crimes and pursuant to a final judgment rendered by a competent court and in accordance with a law establishing such punishment, enacted prior to the commission of the crime. The application of such punishment shall not be extended to crimes to which it does not presently apply.

3. The death penalty shall not be reestablished in states that have abolished it.

4. In no case shall capital punishment be inflicted for political offenses or related common crimes.

5. Capital punishment shall not be imposed upon persons who, at the time the crime was committed, were under 18 years of age or over 70 years of age; nor shall it be applied to pregnant women.

6. Every person condemned to death shall have the right to apply for amnesty, pardon, or commutation of sentence, which may be granted in all cases. Capital punishment shall not be imposed while such a petition is pending decision by the competent authority.

ARTICLE 5. RIGHT TO HUMANE TREATMENT

1. Every person has the right to have his physical, mental, and moral integrity respected.

2. No one shall be subjected to torture or to cruel, inhuman, or degrading punishment or treatment. All persons deprived of their liberty shall be treated with respect for the inherent dignity of the human person.

3. Punishment shall not be extended to any person other than the criminal.

4. Accused persons shall, save in exceptional circumstances, be segregated from convicted persons, and shall be subject to separate treatment appropriate to their status as unconvicted persons.

5. Minors while subject to criminal proceedings shall be separated from adults and brought before specialized tribunals, as speedily as possible, so that they may be treated in accordance with their status as minors.

6. Punishment consisting of deprivation of liberty shall have as an essential aim the reform and social readaptation of the prisoners.

ARTICLE 6. FREEDOM FROM SLAVERY

1. No one shall be subject to slavery or to involuntary servitude, which are prohibited in all their forms, as are the slave trade and traffic in women.

2. No one shall be required to perform forced or compulsory labor. This provision shall not be interpreted to mean that, in those countries in which the penalty established for certain crimes is deprivation of liberty at forced labor, the carrying out of such a sentence imposed by a competent court is prohibited. Forced labor shall not adversely affect the dignity or the physical or intellectual capacity of the prisoner.

3. For the purposes of this article, the following do not constitute forced or compulsory labor:

   a. work or service normally required of a person imprisoned in execution of a sentence or formal decision passed by the competent judicial authority. Such work or service shall be carried out under the supervision and control of public authorities, and any persons performing such work or service shall not be placed at the disposal of any private party, company, or juridical person;

   b. military service and, in countries in which conscientious objectors are recognized, national service that the law may provide for in lieu of military service;

   c. service exacted in time of danger or calamity that threatens the existence or the well-being of the community; or

   d. work or service that forms part of normal civic obligations.

ARTICLE 7. RIGHT TO PERSONAL LIBERTY

1. Every person has the right to personal liberty and security.

2. No one shall be deprived of his physical liberty except for the reasons and under the conditions established beforehand by the constitution of the State Party concerned or by a law established pursuant thereto.

3. No one shall be subject to arbitrary arrest or imprisonment.

4. Anyone who is detained shall be informed of the reasons for his detention and shall be promptly notified of the charge or charges against him.

5. Any person detained shall be brought promptly before a judge or other officer authorized by law to exercise judicial power and shall be entitled to trial within a reasonable time or to be released without prejudice to the continuation of the proceedings. His release may be subject to guarantees to assure his appearance for trial.

6. Anyone who is deprived of his liberty shall be entitled to recourse to a competent court, in order that the court may decide without delay on the lawfulness of his arrest or detention and order his release if the arrest or detention is unlawful. In States Parties whose laws provide that anyone who believes himself to be threatened with deprivation of his liberty is entitled to recourse to a competent court in order that it may decide on the lawfulness of such threat, this remedy may not be restricted or abolished. The interested party or another person in his behalf is entitled to seek these remedies.

7. No one shall be detained for debt. This principle shall not limit the orders of a competent judicial authority issued for non-fulfillment of duties of support.

ARTICLE 8. RIGHT TO A FAIR TRIAL

1. Every person has the right to a hearing, with due guarantees and within a reasonable time, by a competent, independent, and impartial tribunal, previously established by law, in the substantiation of any accusation of a criminal nature made against him or for the determination of his rights and obligations of a civil, labor, fiscal, or any other nature.

2. Every person accused of a criminal offense has the right to be presumed innocent so long as his guilt has not been proven according to law. During the proceedings, every person is entitled, with full equality, to the following minimum guarantees:

a. the right of the accused to be assisted without charge by a translator or interpreter, if he does not understand or does not speak the language of the tribunal or court;

b. prior notification in detail to the accused of the charges against him;

c. adequate time and means for the preparation of his defense;

d. the right of the accused to defend himself personally or to be assisted by legal counsel of his own choosing, and to communicate freely and privately with his counsel;

e. the inalienable right to be assisted by counsel provided by the state, paid or not as the domestic law provides, if the accused does not defend himself personally or engage his own counsel within the time period established by law;

f. the right of the defense to examine witnesses present in the court and to obtain the appearance, as witnesses, of experts or other persons who may throw light on the facts;

g. the right not to be compelled to be a witness against himself or to plead guilty; and

h. the right to appeal the judgment to a higher court.

3. A confession of guilt by the accused shall be valid only if it is made without coercion of any kind.

4. An accused person acquitted by a non-appealable judgment shall not be subjected to a new trial for the same cause.

5. Criminal proceedings shall be public, except insofar as may be necessary to protect the interests of justice.

ARTICLE 9. FREEDOM FROM EX POST FACTO LAWS

No one shall be convicted of any act or omission that did not constitute a criminal offense, under the applicable law, at the time it was committed. A heavier penalty shall not be imposed than the one that was applicable at the time the criminal offense was committed. If subsequent to the commission of the offense the law provides for the imposition of a lighter punishment, the guilty person shall benefit therefrom.

ARTICLE 10. RIGHT TO COMPENSATION

Every person has the right to be compensated in accordance with the law in the event that he has been sentenced by a final judgment through a miscarriage of justice.

ARTICLE 11. RIGHT TO PRIVACY

1. Everyone has the right to have his honor respected and his dignity recognized.

2. No one may be the object of arbitrary or abusive interference with his private life, his family, his home, or his correspondence, or of unlawful attacks on his honor or reputation.

3. Everyone has the right to the protection of the law against such interference or attacks.

ARTICLE 12. FREEDOM OF CONSCIENCE AND RELIGION

1. Everyone has the right to freedom of conscience and of religion. This right includes freedom to maintain or to change one's religion or beliefs and freedom to profess or disseminate one's religion or beliefs, either individually or together with others, in public or in private.

2. No one shall be subject to restrictions that might impair his freedom to maintain or to change his religion or beliefs.

3. Freedom to manifest one's religion and beliefs may be subject

only to the limitations prescribed by law that are necessary to protect public safety, order, health, or morals, or the rights or freedoms of others.

4. Parents or guardians, as the case may be, have the right to provide for the religious and moral education of their children or wards that is in accord with their own convictions.

ARTICLE 13. FREEDOM OF THOUGHT AND EXPRESSION

1. Everyone has the right to freedom of thought and expression. This right includes freedom to seek, receive, and impart information and ideas of all kinds, regardless of frontiers, either orally, in writing, in print, in the form of art, or through any other medium of one's choice.

2. The exercise of the right provided for in the foregoing paragraph shall not be subject to prior censorship but shall be subject to subsequent imposition of liability, which shall be expressly established by law to the extent necessary to ensure:

    a. respect for the rights or reputations of others; or

    b. the protection of national security, public order, or public health or morals.

3. The right of expression may not be restricted by indirect methods or means, such as the abuse of government or private controls over newsprint, radio broadcasting frequencies, or equipment used in the dissemination of information, or by any other means tending to impede the communication and circulation of ideas and opinions.

4. Notwithstanding the provisions of paragraph 2 above, public entertainments may be subject by law to prior censorship for the sole purpose of regulating access to them for the moral protection of childhood and adolescence.

5. Any propaganda for war and any advocacy of national, racial, or religious hatred that constitute incitements to lawless violence or to any other similar illegal action against any person or group of persons on any grounds including those of race, color, religion, language, or national origin shall be considered as offenses punishable by law.

ARTICLE 14. RIGHT OF REPLY

1. Anyone injured by inaccurate or offensive statements or ideas disseminated to the public in general by a legally regulated medium of communication has the right to reply or to make a correction using the same communications outlet, under such conditions as the law may establish.

2. The correction or reply shall not in any case remit other legal liabilities that may have been incurred.

3. For the effective protection of honor and reputation, every pub-

lisher, and every newspaper, motion picture, radio, and television company, shall have a person responsible who is not protected by immunities or special privileges.

ARTICLE 15. RIGHT OF ASSEMBLY

The right of peaceful assembly, without arms, is recognized. No restrictions may be placed on the exercise of this right other than those imposed in conformity with the law and necessary in a democratic society in the interest of national security, public safety or public order, or to protect public health or morals or the rights or freedoms of others.

ARTICLE 16. FREEDOM OF ASSOCIATION

1. Everyone has the right to associate freely for ideological, religious, political, economic, labor, social, cultural, sports, or other purposes.

2. The exercise of this right shall be subject only to such restrictions established by law as may be necessary in a democratic society, in the interest of national security, public safety or public order, or to protect public health or morals or the rights and freedoms of others.

3. The provisions of this article do not bar the imposition of legal restrictions, including even deprivation of the exercise of the right of association, on members of the armed forces and the police.

ARTICLE 17. RIGHTS OF THE FAMILY

1. The family is the natural and fundamental group unit of society and is entitled to protection by society and the state.

2. The right of men and women of marriageable age to marry and to raise a family shall be recognized, if they meet the conditions required by domestic laws, insofar as such conditions do not affect the principle of nondiscrimination established in this Convention.

3. No marriage shall be entered into without the free and full consent of the intending spouses.

4. The States Parties shall take appropriate steps to ensure the equality of rights and the adequate balancing of responsibilities of the spouses as to marriage, during marriage, and in the event of its dissolution. In case of dissolution, provision shall be made for the necessary protection of any children solely on the basis of their own best interests.

5. The law shall recognize equal rights for children born out of wedlock and those born in wedlock.

ARTICLE 18. RIGHT TO A NAME

Every person has the right to a given name and to the surnames of his parents or that of one of them. The law shall regulate the manner in which this right shall be ensured for all, by the use of assumed names if necessary.

ARTICLE 19. RIGHTS OF THE CHILD

Every minor child has the right to the measures of protection required by his condition as a minor on the part of his family, society, and the state.

ARTICLE 20. RIGHT TO NATIONALITY

1. Every person has the right to a nationality.
2. Every person has the right to the nationality of the state in whose territory he was born if he does not have the right to any other nationality.
3. No one shall be arbitrarily deprived of his nationality or of the right to change it.

ARTICLE 21. RIGHT TO PROPERTY

1. Everyone has the right to the use and enjoyment of his property. The law may subordinate such use and enjoyment to the interest of society.
2. No one shall be deprived of his property except upon payment of just compensation, for reasons of public utility or social interest, and in the cases and according to the forms established by law.
3. Usury and any other form of exploitation of man by man shall be prohibited by law.

ARTICLE 22. FREEDOM OF MOVEMENT AND RESIDENCE

1. Every person lawfully in the territory of a State Party has the right to move about in it, and to reside in it subject to the provisions of the law.
2. Every person has the right to leave any country freely, including his own.
3. The exercise of the foregoing rights may be restricted only pursuant to a law to the extent necessary in a democratic society to prevent crime or to protect national security, public safety, public order, public morals, public health, or the rights or freedoms of others.
4. The exercise of the rights recognized in paragraph 1 may also be restricted by law in designated zones for reasons of public interest.
5. No one can be expelled from the territory of the state of which he is a national or be deprived of the right to enter it.
6. An alien lawfully in the territory of a State Party to this Convention may be expelled from it only pursuant to a decision reached in accordance with law.

7. Every person has the right to seek and be granted asylum in a foreign territory, in accordance with the legislation of the state and international conventions, in the event he is being pursued for political offenses or related common crimes.

8. In no case may an alien be deported or returned to a country, regardless of whether or not it is his country of origin, if in that country his right to life or personal freedom is in danger of being violated because of his race, nationality, religion, social status, or political opinions.

9. The collective expulsion of aliens is prohibited.

ARTICLE 23. RIGHT TO PARTICIPATE IN GOVERNMENT

1. Every citizen shall enjoy the following rights and opportunities:

a. to take part in the conduct of public affairs, directly or through freely chosen representatives;

b. to vote and to be elected in genuine periodic elections, which shall be by universal and equal suffrage and by secret ballot that guarantees the free expression of the will of the voters; and

c. to have access, under general conditions of equality, to the public service of his country.

2. The law may regulate the exercise of the rights and opportunities referred to in the preceding paragraph only on the basis of age, nationality, residence, language, education, civil and mental capacity, or sentencing by a competent court in criminal proceedings.

ARTICLE 24. RIGHT TO EQUAL PROTECTION

All persons are equal before the law. Consequently, they are entitled, without discrimination, to equal protection of the law.

ARTICLE 25. RIGHT TO JUDICIAL PROTECTION

1. Everyone has the right to simple and prompt recourse, or any other effective recourse, to a competent court or tribunal for protection against acts that violate his fundamental rights recognized by the constitution or laws of the state concerned or by this Convention, even though such violation may have been committed by persons acting in the course of their official duties.

2. The States Parties undertake:

a. to ensure that any person claiming such remedy shall have his rights determined by the competent authority provided for by the legal system of the state;

b. to develop the possibilities of judicial remedy; and

c. to ensure that the competent authorities shall enforce such remedies when granted.

CHAPTER III. ECONOMIC, SOCIAL, AND CULTURAL RIGHTS

ARTICLE 26. PROGRESSIVE DEVELOPMENT

The States Parties undertake to adopt measures, both internally and through international cooperation, especially those of an economic and technical nature, with a view to achieving progressively, by legislation or other appropriate means, the full realization of the rights implicit in the economic, social, educational, scientific, and cultural standards set forth in the Charter of the Organization of American States as amended by the Protocol of Buenos Aires.

CHAPTER IV. SUSPENSION OF GUARANTEES, INTERPRETATION, AND APPLICATION

ARTICLE 27. SUSPENSION OF GUARANTEES

1. In time of war, public danger, or other emergency that threatens the independence or security of a State Party, it may take measures derogating from its obligations under the present Convention to the extent and for the period of time strictly required by the exigencies of the situation, provided that such measures are not inconsistent with its other obligations under international law and do not involve discrimination on the ground of race, color, sex, language, religion, or social origin.

2. The foregoing provision does not authorize any suspension of the following articles: Article 3 (Right to Juridical Personality), Article 4 (Right to Life), Article 5 (Right to Humane Treatment), Article 6 (Freedom from Slavery), Article 9 (Freedom from *Ex Post Facto* Laws), Article 12 (Freedom of Conscience and Religion), Article 17 (Rights of the Family), Article 18 (Right to a Name), Article 19 (Rights of the Child), Article 20 (Right to Nationality), and Article 23 (Right to Participate in Government), or of the judicial guarantees essential for the protection of such rights.

3. Any State Party availing itself of the right of suspension shall immediately inform the other States Parties, through the Secretary General of the Organization of American States, of the provisions the application of which it has suspended, the reasons that gave rise to the suspension, and the date set for the termination of such suspension.

ARTICLE 28. FEDERAL CLAUSE

1. Where a State Party is constituted as a federal state, the national government of such State Party shall implement all the provisions of the Convention over whose subject matter it exercises legislative and judicial jurisdiction.

2. With respect to the provisions over whose subject matter the constituent units of the federal state have jurisdiction, the national government shall immediately take suitable measures, in accordance with its constitution and its laws, to the end that the competent authorities of the constituent units may adopt appropriate provisions for the fulfillment of this Convention.

3. Whenever two or more States Parties agree to form a federation or other type of association, they shall take care that the resulting federal or other compact contains the provisions necessary for continuing and rendering effective the standards of this Convention in the new state that is organized.

ARTICLE 29. RESTRICTIONS REGARDING INTERPRETATION
No provision of this Convention shall be interpreted as:

a. permitting any State Party, group, or person to suppress the enjoyment or exercise of the rights and freedoms recognized in this Convention or to restrict them to a greater extent than is provided for herein;

b. restricting the enjoyment or exercise of any right or freedom recognized by virtue of the laws of any State Party or by virtue of another convention to which one of the said states is a party;

c. precluding other rights or guarantees that are inherent in the human personality or derived from representative democracy as a form of government; or

d. excluding or limiting the effect that the American Declaration of the Rights and Duties of Man and other international acts of the same nature may have.

ARTICLE 30. SCOPE OF RESTRICTIONS
The restrictions that, pursuant to this Convention, may be placed on the enjoyment or exercise of the rights or freedoms recognized herein may not be applied except in accordance with laws enacted for reasons of general interest and in accordance with the purpose for which such restrictions have been established.

ARTICLE 31. RECOGNITION OF OTHER RIGHTS
Other rights and freedoms recognized in accordance with the procedures established in Articles 76 and 77 may be included in the system of protection of this Convention.

Chapter V. Personal Responsibilities

Article 32. Relationship Between Duties and Rights

1. Every person has responsibilities to his family, his community, and mankind.

2. The rights of each person are limited by the rights of others, by the security of all, and by the just demands of the general welfare, in a democratic society.

Part II. Means of Protection

Chapter VI. Competent Organs

Article 33

The following organs shall have competence with respect to matters relating to the fulfillment of the commitments made by the States Parties to this Convention:

a. the Inter-American Commission on Human Rights, referred to as "The Commission"; and

b. the Inter-American Court of Human Rights, referred to as "The Court."

Chapter VII. Inter-American Commission on Human Rights

Section 1. Organization

Article 34

The Inter-American Commission on Human Rights shall be composed of seven members, who shall be persons of high moral character and recognized competence in the field of human rights.

Article 35

The Commission shall represent all the member countries of the Organization of American States.

Article 36

1. The members of the Commission shall be elected in a personal capacity by the General Assembly of the Organization from a list of candidates proposed by the governments of the member states.

2. Each of those governments may propose up to three candidates,

who may be nationals of the states proposing them or of any other member state of the Organization of American States. When a slate of three is proposed, at least one of the candidates shall be a national of a state other than the one proposing the slate.

International Convention on the Suppression and Punishment of the Crime of Apartheid (1973)

The States Parties to the present Convention,

Recalling the provisions of the Charter of the United Nations, in which all Members pledged themselves to take joint and separate action in cooperation with the Organization for the achievement of universal respect for, and observance of, human rights and fundamental freedoms for all without distinction as to race, sex, language or religion,

Considering the Universal Declaration of Human Rights, which states that all human beings are born free and equal in dignity and rights and that everyone is entitled to all the rights and freedoms set forth in the Declaration, without distinction of any kind, such as race, color or national origin.

Considering the Declaration on the Granting of Independence to Colonial Countries and Peoples, in which the General Assembly stated that the process of liberation is irresistible and irreversible and that, in the interests of human dignity, progress and justice, an end must be put to colonialism and all practices of segregation and discrimination associated therewith,

Observing that, in accordance with the International Convention on the Elimination of all Forms of Racial Discrimination, States particularly condemn racial segregation and *apartheid* and undertake to prevent, prohibit and eradicate all practices of this nature in territories under their jurisdiction,

Observing that, in the Convention on the Prevention and Punishment of the Crime of Genocide, certain acts which may also be qualified as acts of *apartheid* constitute a crime under international law,

Observing that, in the Convention on the Non-Applicability of Statutory Limitations to War Crimes and Crimes Against Humanity, "inhuman acts resulting from the policy of *apartheid*" are qualified as crimes against humanity,

Observing that the General Assembly of the United Nations has adopted a number of resolutions in which the policies and practices of *apartheid* are condemned as a crime against humanity,

Observing that the Security Council has emphasized that *apartheid* and its continued intensification and expansion seriously disturb and threaten international peace and security,

Convinced that an International Convention on the Suppression and Punishment of the Crime of *Apartheid* would make it possible to take more effective measures at the international and national levels with a view to the suppression and punishment of the crime of *apartheid*.

Have agreed as follows:

ARTICLE I

1. The States Parties to the present Convention declare that *apartheid* is a crime against humanity and that inhuman acts resulting from the policies and practices of *apartheid* and similar policies and practices of racial segregation and discrimination, as defined in article II of the Convention, are crimes violating the principles of international law, in particular the purposes and principles of the Charter of the United Nations, and constituting a serious threat to international peace and security.

2. The States Parties to the present Convention declare criminal those organizations, institutions and individuals committing the crime of *apartheid*.

ARTICLE II

For the purpose of the present Convention, the term "the crime of *apartheid*," which shall include similar policies and practices of racial segregation and discrimination as practiced in southern Africa, shall apply to the following inhuman acts committed for the purpose of establishing and maintaining domination by one racial group of persons over any other racial group of persons and systematically oppressing them:

(a) Denial to a member or members of a racial group or groups of the right to life and liberty of person:

(i) By murder of members of a racial group or groups;

(ii) By the infliction upon the members of a racial group or groups of serious bodily or mental harm by the infringement of their freedom or dignity, or by subjecting them to torture or to cruel, inhuman or degrading treatment or punishment;

(iii) By arbitrary arrest and illegal imprisonment of the members of a racial group or groups;

(b) Deliberate imposition on a racial group or groups of living conditions calculated to cause its or their physical destruction in whole or in part;

(c) Any legislative measures and other measures calculated to prevent a racial group or groups from participation in the political, social, economic and cultural life of the country and the deliberate creation of conditions preventing the full development of such a group or groups, in particular by denying to members of a racial group or groups basic human rights and freedoms, including the right to work, the right to form recognized trade unions, the right to education, the right to leave and to return to their country, the right to a nationality, the right to freedom of movement and residence, the right to freedom of opinion and expression, and the right to freedom of peaceful assembly and association;

(d) Any measures, including legislative measures, designed to divide the population along racial lines by the creation of separate reserves and ghettos for the members of a racial group or groups, the prohibition of mixed marriages among members of various racial groups, the expropriation of landed property belonging to a racial group or groups or to members thereof;

(e) Exploitation of the labor of the members of a racial group or groups, in particular by submitting them to forced labor;

(f) Persecution of organizations and persons, by depriving them of fundamental rights and freedoms, because they oppose *apartheid*.

The Helsinki Agreement (1975)

VI. NON-INTERVENTION IN INTERNAL AFFAIRS

The participating States will refrain from any intervention, direct or indirect, individual or collective, in the internal or external affairs falling within the domestic jurisdiction of another participating State, regardless of their mutual relations.

They will accordingly refrain from any form of armed intervention or threat of such intervention against another participating State.

They will likewise in all circumstances refrain from any other act of military, or of political, economic or other coercion designed to subordinate to their own interest the exercise by another participating State of the rights inherent in its sovereignty and thus to secure advantages of any kind.

Accordingly, they will, inter alia, refrain from direct or indirect assistance to terrorist activities, or to subversive or other activities directed towards the violent overthrow of the regime of another participating State.

VII. RESPECT FOR HUMAN RIGHTS AND FUNDAMENTAL FREEDOMS, INCLUDING THE FREEDOM OF THOUGHT, CONSCIENCE, RELIGION OR BELIEF

The participating States will respect human rights and fundamental freedoms, including the freedom of thought, conscience, religion or belief, for all without distinction as to race, sex, language or religion.

They will promote and encourage the effective exercise of civil, political, economic, social, cultural and other rights and freedoms all of which derive from the inherent dignity of the human person and are essential for his free and full development.

Within this framework the participating States will recognize and respect the freedom of the individual to profess and practice, alone or in community with others, religion or belief acting in accordance with the dictates of his own conscience.

The participating States on whose territory national minorities exist will respect the right of persons belonging to such minorities to equality before the law, will afford them the full opportunity for the actual enjoyment of human rights and fundamental freedoms and will, in this manner, protect their legitimate interests in this sphere.

The participating States recognize the universal significance of human rights and fundamental freedoms, respect for which is an essential factor for the peace, justice and well-being necessary to ensure the development of friendly relations and cooperation among themselves as among all States.

They will constantly respect these rights and freedoms in their mutual relations and will endeavor jointly and separately, including in cooperation with the United Nations, to promote universal and effective respect for them.

They confirm the right of the individual to know and act upon his rights and duties in this field.

In the field of human rights and fundamental freedoms, the participating States will act in conformity with the purposes and principles of the Charter of the United Nations and with the Universal Declaration of Human Rights. They will also fulfill their obligations as set forth in the international declarations and agreements in this field, including inter alia the International Covenants on Human Rights, by which they may be bound.

VIII. EQUAL RIGHTS AND SELF-DETERMINATION OF PEOPLES

The participating States will respect the equal rights of peoples and their right to self-determination, acting at all times in conformity with the purposes and principles of the Charter of the United Nations and with the relevant norms of international law, including those relating to territorial integrity of States.

By virtue of the principle of equal rights and self-determination of peoples, all peoples always have the right, in full freedom, to determine, when and as they wish, their internal and external political status, without external interference, and to pursue as they wish their political, economic, social and cultural development.

The participating States reaffirm the universal significance of respect for and effective exercise of equal rights and self-determination of peoples for the development of friendly relations among themselves as among all States; they also recall the importance of the elimination of any form of violation of this principle. . . .

Cooperation in Humanitarian and Other Fields

The participating States,
Desiring to contribute to the strengthening of peace and understanding among peoples and to the spiritual enrichment of the human personality without distinction as to race, sex, language or religion,
Conscious that increased cultural and educational exchanges, broader dissemination of information, contacts between people, and the solution of humanitarian problems will contribute to the attainment of these aims,
Determined therefore to cooperate among themselves, irrespective of their political, economic and social systems, in order to create better conditions in the above fields, to develop and strengthen existing forms of cooperation and to work out new ways and means appropriate to these aims,
Convinced that this cooperation should take place in full respect for the principles guiding relations among participating States as set forth in the relevant document,
Have adopted the following:

1. HUMAN CONTACTS

The participating States,
Considering the development of contacts to be an important element in the strengthening of friendly relations and trust among peoples,
Affirming, in relation to their present effort to improve conditions in this area, the importance they attach to humanitarian considerations,
Desiring in this spirit to develop, with the continuance of détente, further efforts to achieve continuing progress in this field
And conscious that the questions relevant hereto must be settled by the States concerned under mutually acceptable conditions,
Make it their aim to facilitate freer movement and contacts, individually and collectively, whether privately or officially, among persons,

institutions and organizations of the participating States, and to contribute to the solution of the humanitarian problems that arise in that connection,

Declare their readiness to these ends to take measures which they consider appropriate and to conclude agreements or arrangements among themselves, as may be needed, and

Express their intention now to proceed to the implementation of the following:

(A) CONTACTS AND REGULAR MEETINGS ON THE BASIS OF FAMILY TIES

In order to promote further development of contacts on the basis of family ties the participating States will favorably consider applications for travel with the purpose of allowing persons to enter or leave their territory temporarily, and on a regular basis if desired, in order to visit members of their families.

Applications for temporary visits to meet members of their families will be dealt with without distinction as to the country of origin or destination: existing requirements for travel documents and visas will be applied in this spirit. The preparation and issue of such documents and visas will be effected within reasonable time limits; cases of urgent necessity—such as serious illness or death—will be given priority treatment. They will take such steps as may be necessary to ensure that the fees for official travel documents and visas are acceptable.

They confirm that the presentation of an application concerning contacts on the basis of family ties will not modify the rights and obligations of the applicant or of members of his family.

(B) REUNIFICATION OF FAMILIES

The participating States will deal in a positive and humanitarian spirit with the applications of persons who wish to be reunited with members of their family, with special attention being given to requests of an urgent character—such as requests submitted by persons who are ill or old.

They will deal with applications in this field as expeditiously as possible.

They will lower where necessary the fees charged in connection with these applications to ensure that they are at a moderate level.

Applications for the purpose of family reunification which are not granted may be renewed at the appropriate level and will be reconsidered at reasonably short intervals by the authorities of the country of residence or destination, whichever is concerned; under such circumstances fees will be charged only when applications are granted.

Persons whose applications for family reunification are granted may bring with them or ship their household and personal effects; to this end the participating States will use all possibilities provided by existing regulations.

Until members of the same family are reunited, meetings and contacts between them may take place in accordance with the modalities for contacts on the basis of family ties.

The participating States will support the efforts of Red Cross and Red Crescent Societies concerned with the problems of family reunification.

They confirm that the presentation of an application concerning family reunification will not modify the rights and obligations of the applicant or of members of his family.

The receiving participating State will take appropriate care with regard to employment for persons from other participating States who take up permanent residence in that State in connection with family reunification with its citizens and see that they are afforded opportunities equal to those enjoyed by its own citizens for education, medical assistance and social security.

(c) Marriage between Citizens of Different States

The participating States will examine favorably and on the basis of humanitarian considerations requests for exit or entry permits from persons who have decided to marry a citizen from another participating State.

The processing and issuing of the documents required for the above purposes and for the marriage will be in accordance with the provisions accepted for family reunification.

In dealing with requests from couples from different participating States, once married, to enable them and the minor children of their marriage to transfer their permanent residence to a State in which either one is normally a resident, the participating States will also apply the provisions accepted for family reunification.

(d) Travel for Personal or Professional Reasons

The participating States intend to facilitate wider travel by their citizens for personal or professional reasons and to this end they intend in particular:

- gradually to simplify and to administer flexibly the procedures for exit and entry;
- to ease regulations concerning movement of citizens from the other participating States in their territory, with due regard to security requirements.

They will endeavor gradually to lower, where necessary, the fees for visas and official travel documents.

They intend to consider, as necessary, means—including, in so far as appropriate, the conclusion of multilateral or bilateral consular conventions or other relevant agreements or understandings—for the improvement of arrangements to provide consular assistance.

They confirm that religious faiths, institutions and organizations, practicing within the constitutional framework of the participating States, and their representatives can, in the field of their activities, have contacts and meetings among themselves and exchange information.

(E) Improvement of Conditions for Tourism on an Individual or Collective Basis

The participating States consider that tourism contributes to a fuller knowledge of the life, culture and history of other countries, to the growth of understanding among peoples, to the improvement of contacts and to the broader use of leisure. They intend to promote the development of tourism, on an individual or collective basis, and, in particular, they intend:

- to promote visits to their respective countries by encouraging the provision of appropriate facilities and the simplification and expediting of necessary formalities relating to such visits;
- to increase, on the basis of appropriate agreements or arrangements where necessary, cooperation in the development of tourism, in particular by considering bilaterally possible ways to increase information relating to travel to other countries and to the reception and service of tourists, and other related questions of mutual interest.

(F) Meetings Among Young People

The participating States intend to further the development of contacts and exchanges among young people by encouraging:

- increased exchanges and contacts on a short or long term basis among young people working, training or undergoing education through bilateral or multilateral agreements or regular programs in all cases where it is possible;
- study by their youth organizations of the question of possible agreements relating to frameworks of multilateral youth cooperation;
- agreements or regular programs relating to the organization of exchanges of students, of international youth seminars, of courses of professional training and foreign language study;
- the further development of youth tourism and the provision to this end of appropriate facilities;
- the development, where possible, of exchanges, contacts and cooperation on a bilateral or multilateral basis between their organi-

zations which represent wide circles of young people working, training or undergoing education;

- awareness among youth of the importance of developing mutual understanding and of strengthening friendly relations and confidence among peoples.

(G) SPORT

In order to expand existing links and cooperation in the field of sport that participating States will encourage contacts and exchanges of this kind, including sports meetings and competitions of all sorts, on the basis of the established international rules, regulations and practice.

(H) EXPANSION OF CONTACTS

By way of further developing contacts among governmental institutions and non-governmental organizations and associations, including women's organizations, the participating States will facilitate the convening of meetings as well as travel by delegations, groups and individuals.

2. INFORMATION

The participating States,

Conscious of the need for an ever wider knowledge and understanding of the various aspects of life in other participating States,

Acknowledging the contribution of this process to the growth of confidence between peoples,

Desiring, with the development of mutual understanding between the participating States and with the further improvement of their relations, to continue further efforts toward progress in this field,

Recognizing the importance of the dissemination of information from the other participating States and of a better acquaintance with such information,

Emphasizing therefore the essential and influential role of the press, radio, television, cinema and news agencies and of the journalists working in these fields,

Make it their aim to facilitate the freer and wider dissemination of information of all kinds, to encourage cooperation in the field of information and the exchange of information with other countries, and to improve the conditions under which journalists from one participating State exercise their profession in another participating State, and

Express their intention in particular:

(A) IMPROVEMENT OF THE CIRCULATION OF, ACCESS TO, AND EXCHANGE OF INFORMATION

(i) Oral Information

- To facilitate the dissemination of oral information through the encouragement of lectures and lecture tours by personalities and specialists from the other participating States, as well as exchanges of opinions at round table meetings, seminars, symposia, summer schools, congresses and other bilateral and multilaterial meetings.

(ii) Printed Information

- To facilitate the improvement of the dissemination, on their territory, of newspapers and printed publications, periodical and nonperiodical, from the other participating States. For this purpose:

they will encourage their competent firms and organizations to conclude agreements and contracts designed gradually to increase the quantities and the number of titles of newspapers and publications imported from the other participating States. These agreements and contracts should in particular mention the speediest conditions of delivery and the use of the normal channels existing in each country for the distribution of its own publications and newspapers, as well as forms and means of payment agreed between the parties making it possible to achieve the objectives aimed at by these agreements and contracts;

where necessary, they will take appropriate measures to achieve the above objectives and to implement the provisions contained in the agreements and contracts.

- To contribute to the improvement of access by the public to periodical and non-periodical printed publications imported on the bases indicated above. In particular:

they will encourage an increase in the number of places where these publications are on sale;

they will facilitate the availability of these periodical publications during congresses, conferences, official visits and other international events and to tourists during the season;

they will develop the possibilities for taking out subscriptions according to the modalities particular to each country;

they will improve the opportunities for reading and borrowing these publications in large public libraries and their reading rooms as well as in university libraries.

They intend to improve the possibilities for acquaintance with bulletins of official information issued by diplomatic missions and distributed by those missions on the basis of arrangements acceptable to the interested parties.

(iii) Filmed and Broadcast Information

- To promote the improvement of the dissemination of filmed and broadcast information. To this end:

they will encourage the wider showing and broadcasting of a greater variety of recorded and filmed information from the other participating States, illustrating the various aspects of life in their countries and received on the basis of such agreements or arrangements as may be necessary between the organizations and firms directly concerned;

they will facilitate the import by competent organizations and firms of recorded audio-visual material from the other participating States.

The participating States note the expansion in the dissemination of information broadcast by radio, and express the hope for the continuation of this process, so as to meet the interest of mutual understanding among peoples and the aims set forth by this Conference.

(B) COOPERATION IN THE FIELD OF INFORMATION

- To encourage cooperation in the field of information on the basis of short or long term agreements or arrangements. In particular:

they will favor increased cooperation among mass media organizations, including press agencies, as well as among publishing houses and organizations;

they will favor cooperation among public or private, national or international radio and television organizations, in particular through the exchange of both live and recorded radio and television programs, and through the joint production and the broadcasting and distribution of such programs;

they will encourage meetings and contacts both between journalists' organizations and between journalists from the participating States;

they will view favorably the possibilities of arrangements between periodical publications as well as between newspapers from the participating States, for the purpose of exchanging and publishing articles;

they will encourage the exchange of technical information as well as the organization of joint research and meetings devoted to the exchange of experience and views between experts in the field of the press, radio and television.

(C) IMPROVEMENT OF WORKING CONDITIONS FOR JOURNALISTS

The participating States, desiring to improve the conditions under which journalists from one participating State exercise their profession in another participating State, intend in particular to:

- examine in a favorable spirit and within a suitable and reasonable time scale requests from journalists for visas;
- grant to permanently accredited journalists of the participating States, on the basis of arrangements, multiple entry and exit visas for specified periods;
- facilitate the issue to accredited journalists of the participating States of permits for stay in their country of temporary residence and, if and when these are necessary, of other official papers which it is appropriate for them to have;
- ease, on a basis of reciprocity, procedures for arranging travel by journalists of the participating States in the country where they are exercising their profession, and to provide progressively greater opportunities for such travel, subject to the observance of regulations relating to the existence of areas closed for security reasons;
- ensure that requests by such journalists for such travel receive, in so far as possible, an expeditious response, taking into account the time scale of the request;
- increase the opportunities for journalists of the participating States to communicate personally with their sources, including organizations and official institutions;
- grant to journalists of the participating States the right to import, subject only to its being taken out again, the technical equipment (photographic, cinematographic, tape recorder, radio and television) necessary for the exercise of their profession,*
- enable journalists of the other participating States, whether permanently or temporarily accredited, to transmit completely, normally and rapidly by means recognized by the participating States to the information organs which they represent, the results of

---

* While recognizing appropriate local personnel are employed by foreign journalists in many instances, the participating States note that the above provisions would be applied, subject to the observance of the appropriate rules, to persons from the other participating States, who are regularly and professionally engaged as technicians, photographers or cameramen of the press, radio, television or cinema. [Footnote in original.]

their professional activity, including tape recordings and undeveloped film, for the purpose of publication or of broadcasting on the radio or television.

Convention on the Elimination of All Forms of Discrimination Against Women (1979)

The States Parties to the present Convention,

Noting that the Charter of the United Nations reaffirms faith in fundamental human rights, in the dignity and worth of the human person and in the equal rights of men and women,

Noting that the Universal Declaration of Human Rights affirms the principle of the inadmissibility of discrimination and proclaims that all human beings are born free and equal in dignity and rights and that everyone is entitled to all the rights and freedoms set forth therein, without distinction of any kind including distinction based on sex,

Noting that States Parties to the International Covenant on Human Rights have the obligation to secure the equal rights of men and women to enjoy all economic, social, cultural, civil and political rights,

Considering the international conventions concluded under the auspices of the United Nations and the specialized agencies promoting equality of rights of men and women,

Noting also the resolutions, declarations and recommendations adopted by the United Nations and the specialized agencies promoting equality of rights of men and women,

Concerned, however, that despite these various instruments extensive discrimination against women continues to exist,

Recalling that discrimination against women violates the principles of equality of rights and respect for human dignity, is an obstacle to the participation of women, on equal terms with men, in the political, social, economic and cultural life of their countries, hampers the growth of the prosperity of society and the family, and makes more difficult the full development of the potentialities of women in the service of their countries and of humanity,

Concerned that in situations of poverty women have the least access to food, health, education, training and opportunities for employment and other needs,

Convinced that the establishment of the new international economic order based on equity and justice will contribute significantly towards the promotion of equality between men and women,

Emphasizing that the eradication of *apartheid*, of all forms of racism, racial discrimination, colonialism, neocolonialism, aggression, foreign occupation and domination and interference in the internal affairs of States is essential to the full enjoyment of the rights of men and women,

Affirming that the strengthening of international peace and security, relaxation of international tension, mutual cooperation among all States irrespective of their social and economic systems, general and complete disarmament and in particular nuclear disarmament under strict and effective international control, the affirmation of the principles of justice, equality and mutual benefit in relations among countries, and the realization of the right of peoples under alien and colonial domination and foreign occupation to self-determination and independence as well as respect for national sovereignty and territorial integrity will promote social progress and development and as a consequence will contribute to the attainment of full equality between men and women,

Convinced that the full and complete development of a country, the welfare of the world and the cause of peace require the maximum participation of women on equal terms with men in all fields,

Bearing in mind the great contribution of women to the welfare of the family and to the development of society, so far not fully recognized, the social significance of maternity and the role of both parents in the family and in the upbringing of children, and aware that the role of women in procreation should not be a basis for discrimination but that the upbringing of children requires a sharing of responsibility between men and women and society as a whole,

Aware that a change in the traditional role of men as well as the role of women in society and in the family is needed to achieve full equality between men and women,

Determined to implement the principles set forth in the Declaration on the Elimination of Discrimination against Women and, for that purpose, to adopt the measures required for the elimination of such discrimination in all its forms and manifestations,

Have agreed on the following:

Part I

ARTICLE 1

For the purposes of the present Convention, the term "'discrimination against women" shall mean any distinction, exclusion or restriction made on the basis of sex which has the effect or purpose of impairing or nullifying the recognition, enjoyment or exercise by women, irrespective of their marital status, on a basis of equality of men and women, of human rights and fundamental freedoms in the political, economic, social, cultural, civil or any other field.

ARTICLE 2

States parties condemn discrimination against women in all its forms, agree to pursue, by all appropriate means and without delay, a policy of eliminating discrimination against women and, to this end, undertake:

a. To embody the principle of the equality of men and women in their national Constitutions or other appropriate legislation if not yet incorporated therein, and to ensure, through law and other appropriate means, the practical realization of this principle;

b. To adopt appropriate legislative and other measures, including sanctions where appropriate, prohibiting all discrimination against women;

c. To establish legal protection of the rights of women on an equal basis with men and to ensure through competent national tribunals and other public institutions the effective protection of women against any act of discrimination;

d. To refrain from engaging in any act or practice of discrimination against women and to ensure that public authorities and institutions shall act in conformity with this obligation;

e. To take all appropriate measures to eliminate discrimination against women by any person, organization or enterprise;

f. To take all appropriate measures, including legislation, to modify or abolish existing laws, regulations, customs and practices which constitute discrimination against women;

g. To repeal all national penal provisions which constitute discrimination against women.

ARTICLE 3

States Parties shall take in all fields, in particular in the political, social, economic and cultural fields, all appropriate measures, including legislation, to ensure the full development and advancement of women, for the purpose of guaranteeing them the exercise and enjoyment of human rights and fundamental freedoms on a basis of equality with men.

ARTICLE 4

1. Adoption by States Parties of temporary special measures aimed at accelerating *de facto* equality between men and women shall not be considered discrimination as defined in this Convention, but shall in no way entail, as a consequence, the maintenance of unequal or separate standards; these measures shall be discontinued when

the objectives of equality of opportunity and treatment have been achieved.

2. Adoption by States Parties of special measures, including those measures contained in the present Convention, aimed at protecting maternity, shall not be considered discriminatory.

ARTICLE 5

States Parties shall take all appropriate measures:

a. To modify the social and cultural patterns of conduct of men and women, with a view to achieving the elimination of prejudices and customary and all other practices which are based on the idea of the inferiority or the superiority of either of the sexes or on stereotyped roles for men and women;

b. To ensure that family education includes a proper understanding of maternity as a social function and the recognition of the common responsibility of men and women in the upbringing and development of their children, it being understood that the interest of the children is the primordial consideration in all cases.

ARTICLE 6

States Parties shall take all appropriate measures, including legislation, to suppress all forms of traffic in women and exploitation of prostitution of women.

Part II

ARTICLE 7

States Parties shall take all appropriate measures to eliminate discrimination against women in the political and public life of the country and, in particular, shall ensure, on equal terms with men, the right:

a. To vote in all elections and public referenda and to be eligible for election to all publicly elected bodies;

b. To participate in the formulation of government policy and the implementation thereof and to hold public office and perform all public functions at all levels of government;

c. To participate in non-governmental organizations and associations concerned with the public and political life of the country.

ARTICLE 8

States Parties shall take all appropriate measures to ensure to women on equal terms with men, and without any discrimination, the opportunity to represent their Governments at the international level and to participate in the work of international organizations.

ARTICLE 9

1. States Parties shall grant women equal rights with men to acquire, change or retain their nationality. They shall ensure in particular that neither marriage to an alien nor change of nationality by the husband during marriage shall automatically change the nationality of the wife, render her stateless or force upon her the nationality of the husband.

2. States Parties shall grant women equal rights with men with respect to the nationality of their children.

Part III

ARTICLE 10

States Parties shall take all appropriate measures to eliminate discrimination against women in order to ensure to them equal rights with men in the field of education and in particular to ensure, on a basis of equality of men and women:

a. The same conditions for career and vocational guidance, for access to studies and for the achievement of diplomas in educational establishments of all categories in rural as well as in urban areas; this equality shall be ensured in pre-school, general, technical, professional and higher technical education, as well as in all types of vocational training;

b. Access to the same curricula, the same examinations, teaching staff with qualifications of the same standard and school premises and equipment of the same quality;

c. The elimination of any stereotyped concept of the roles of men and women at all levels and in all forms of education by encouraging coeducation and other types of education which will help to achieve this aim and, in particular, by the revision of textbooks and school programs and the adaptation of teaching methods;

d. The same opportunities to benefit from scholarships and other study grants;

e. The same opportunities for access to programs of continuing education, including adult and functional literacy programs, particularly those aimed at reducing, at the earliest possible time, any gap in education existing between men and women;

f. The reduction of female student drop-out rates and the organization of programs for girls and women who have left school prematurely;

g. The same opportunities to participate actively in sports and physical education;

h. Access to specific educational information to help to ensure the health and well-being of families, including information and advice on family planning.

ARTICLE 11

1. States Parties shall take all appropriate measures to eliminate discrimination against women in the field of employment in order to ensure, on a basis of equality of men and women, the same rights, in particular:

a. The right to work as an inalienable right of all human beings;

b. The right to the same employment opportunities, including the application of the same criteria for selection in matters of employment;

c. The right to free choice of profession and employment, the right to promotion, job security and all benefits and conditions of service and the right to receive vocational training and retraining, including apprenticeships, advanced vocational training and recurrent training;

d. The right to equal remuneration, including benefits, and to equal treatment in respect of work of equal value, as well as equality of treatment in the evaluation of the quality of work;

e. The right to social security, particularly in cases of retirement, unemployment, sickness, invalidity and old age and other incapacity to work, as well as the right to paid leave;

f. The right to protection of health and to safety in working conditions, including the safeguarding of the function of reproduction.

2. In order to prevent discrimination against women on the grounds of marriage or maternity and to ensure their effective right to work, States Parties shall take appropriate measures:

a. To prohibit, subject to the imposition of sanctions, dismissal on the grounds of pregnancy or of maternity leave and discrimination in dismissals on the basis of marital status;

b. To introduce maternity leave with pay or with comparable social benefits without loss of former employment, seniority or social allowances;

c. To encourage the provision of the necessary supporting social services to enable parents to combine family obligations with work responsibilities and participation in public life, in particular through promoting the establishment and development of a network of child-care facilities;

d. To provide special protection to women during pregnancy in types of work proved to be harmful to them.

3. Protective legislation relating to matters covered in this article

shall be reviewed periodically in the light of scientific and technological knowledge and shall be revised, repealed or extended as necessary.

ARTICLE 12

1. States Parties shall take all appropriate measures to eliminate discrimination against women in the field of health care in order to ensure, on a basis of equality of men and women, access to health care services, including those related to family planning.

2. Notwithstanding the provisions of paragraph 1 above, States Parties shall ensure to women appropriate services in connection with pregnancy, confinement and the post-natal period, granting free services where necessary, as well as adequate nutrition during pregnancy and lactation.

ARTICLE 13

States Parties shall take all appropriate measures to eliminate discrimination against women in other areas of economic and social life in order to ensure, on a basis of equality of men and women, the same rights, in particular:

a. The right to family benefits;

b. The right to bank loans, mortgages and other forms of financial credit;

c. The right to participate in recreational activities, sports and in all aspects of cultural life.

ARTICLE 14

1. States Parties shall take into account the particular problems faced by rural women and the significant roles which they play in the economic survival of their families, including their work in the non-monetized sectors of the economy, and shall take all appropriate measures to ensure the application of the provisions of this Convention to women in rural areas.

2. States Parties shall take all appropriate measures to eliminate discrimination against women in rural areas in order to ensure, on a basis of equality of men and women, that they participate in and benefit from rural development and, in particular, shall ensure to such women the right:

a. To participate in the elaboration and implementation of development planning at all levels;

b. To have access to adequate health care facilities, including information, counseling and services in family planning;

c. To benefit directly from social security programs;

d. To obtain all types of training and education, formal and non-formal, including that relating to functional literacy, as well as the benefit of all community and extension services, *inter alia*, in order to increase their technical proficiency;

e. To organize self-help groups and cooperatives in order to obtain equal access to economic opportunities through employment or self-employment;

f. To participate in all community activities;

g. To have access to agricultural credit and loans, marketing facilities, appropriate technology and equal treatment in land and agrarian reform as well as in land resettlement schemes;

h. To enjoy adequate living conditions, particularly in relation to housing, sanitation, electricity and water supply, transport and communications.

Part IV

ARTICLE 15

1. States Parties shall accord to women equality with men before the law.

2. States Parties shall accord to women, in civil matters, a legal capacity identical to that of men and the same opportunities to exercise that capacity. They shall in particular give women equal rights to conclude contracts and to administer property and treat them equally in all stages of procedure in courts and tribunals.

3. States Parties agree that all contracts and all other private instruments of any kind with a legal effect which is directed at restricting the legal capacity of women shall be deemed null and void.

4. States Parties shall accord to men and women the same rights with regard to the law relating to the movement of persons and the freedom to choose their residence and domicile.

ARTICLE 16

1. States Parties shall take all appropriate measures to eliminate discrimination against women in all matters relating to marriage and family relations and in particular shall ensure, on a basis of equality of men and women:

a. The same right to enter into marriage;

b. The same right freely to choose a spouse and to enter into marriage only with their free and full consent;

c. The same rights and responsibilities during marriage and at its dissolution;

d. The same rights and responsibilities as parents, irrespective of their marital status, in matters relating to their children. In all cases the interests of the children shall be paramount;

 e. The same rights to decide freely and responsibly on the number and spacing of their children and to have access to the information, education and means to enable them to exercise these rights;

 f. The same rights and responsibilities with regard to guardianship, wardship, trusteeship and adoption of children, or similar institutions where these concepts exist in national legislation. In all cases the interest of the children shall be paramount;

 g. The same personal rights as husband and wife, including the right to choose a family name, a profession and an occupation;

 h. The same rights for both spouses in respect of the ownership, acquisition, management, administration, enjoyment and disposition of property, whether free of charge or for a valuable consideration.

 2. The betrothal and the marriage of a child shall have no legal effect and all necessary action, including legislation, shall be taken to specify a minimum age for marriage and to make the registration of marriages in an official registry compulsory. . . .

Organization of American States

Report on Human Rights in Nicaragua (1979)

On June 23, 1979, the XVII *Meeting of Consultation* approved *a resolution* which, for the first time in the history of the OAS and perhaps for the first time in the history of any international organization, deprived an incumbent government of a member state of the *Organization of Legitimacy*, based on the human rights violations committed by that government against its own population. The text of the resolution reads as follows:

Whereas:

 The people of Nicaragua are suffering the horrors of a fierce armed conflict that is causing grave hardships and loss of life, and has thrown the country into a serious political, social, and economic upheaval;

 The inhumane conduct of the dictatorial regime governing the country, as evidenced by the report of the Inter-American Commission on Human Rights, is the fundamental cause of the dramatic situation faced by the Nicaraguan people and;

The spirit of solidarity that guides Hemisphere relations places an unavoidable obligation on the American countries to exert every effort within their power, to put an end to the bloodshed and to avoid the prolongation of this conflict which is disrupting the peace of the Hemisphere;

The Seventh Meeting of Consultation of Ministers of Foreign Affairs declares:

That the solution of the serious problem is exclusively within the jurisdiction of the people of Nicaragua.

That in the view of the Seventh Meeting of Consultation of Ministers of Foreign Affairs this solution should be arrived at on the basis of the following:

1. Immediate and definitive *replacement of the Somoza regime*.
2. Installation in *Nicaraguan territory of a democratic government*, the composition of which should include the principal representative groups which oppose the Somoza regime and which reflects the free will of the people of Nicaragua.
3. Guarantee of the respect for human rights of all Nicaraguans without exception.
4. The holding of free elections as soon as possible, that will lead to the establishment of a truly democratic government that guarantees peace, freedom, and justice. . . .

C. The Establishment of the Government of National Reconstruction

1. On June 17, 1979, from San José, Costa Rica, the Sandinista National Liberation Front (FSLN) announced the formation of a five person Junta, or governing council, of the Provisional Government of National Reconstruction. Less than one month later, the FSLN appeared assured of a military victory; it controlled the cities of León, Chinandega, Estelí, Matagalpa and Masaya.

2. On July 13, 1979, at a press conference held in Costa Rica, the Junta announced that it was convinced that the "people's armed forces could take Managua and annihilate the National Guard." However, at the same time, the Junta put forward a "Plan to Achieve Peace." One day earlier, on July 12, 1979, the Junta, seeking OAS support, sent a copy of the Plan to the Secretary General of the Organization, Alejandro

Orfila, to be transmitted to the member states. The text of this document is as follows:

Mr. Secretary General:

As we are doing with the Foreign Ministers of the member countries of that Organization, it is our pleasure to place in your hands the document that contains our "Plan to Achieve Peace" in our heroic and long-suffering homeland, now that the people of Nicaragua have established their political and military victory over the dictatorship.

We have developed that plan on the basis of the resolution adopted by the Seventeenth Meeting of Consultation on June 23, 1979, a Resolution that is historic in every respect, as it demands the immediate replacement of the genocidal Somoza dictatorship, which has now met its end, and backs the installation in our country of a broad-based, democratic government of the kind we ourselves are establishing.

Further, in stating that the solution to the serious problem is exclusively within the jurisdiction of the people of Nicaragua, that Resolution calls for hemispheric solidarity in preserving our people's right to self-determination.

In our "Plan to Achieve Peace," we are presenting to the community of nations in this hemisphere the purposes that have inspired our Government since its establishment and as set forth in our documents and policy statements, some of which we would like to ratify here:

I. Our firm intention to establish full respect for human rights in our country, in accordance with the United Nations Universal Declaration of the Rights and Duties of Man and the Charter on Human Rights of the OAS. . . .

Stages of the Plan

I. Somoza submits his resignation to his Congress, which in turn accepts it and turns over the reins of power to the Government of National Reconstruction in recognition of the backing it has received from all sectors of Nicaraguan society.

II. Installation of the Government of National Reconstruction. This Government is made up of representatives of all sectors of Nicaraguan politics and has received the official support of all.

III. Immediately after the Government of National Reconstruction has installed itself in Nicaragua, the member countries of the OAS, especially those that sponsored or voted in favor of the Resolution, will then recognize it officially as the legitimate Government of Nicaragua.

IV. The Government of National Reconstruction will immediately do the following:

1. Repeal the Somoza Constitution.
2. Decree the Fundamental Statute which shall provisionally govern the Government of National Reconstruction.
3. Dissolve the National Congress.
4. Order the National Guard to cease hostilities and immediately confine them to barracks with the guarantees that their lives and other rights will be respected. The officials, noncommissioned officers and soldiers of the National Guard that so desire may join the new national army or civilian life.

   The Sandinista Army will enforce the cease-fire to facilitate fulfillment of these agreements by maintaining the positions won as of the time of the Decree.
5. Maintain order by means of those sectors of the National Guard which have honored the cease-fire and were appointed to these functions by the Government of National Reconstruction, a task which they will carry out in coordination with the combatants of the Sandinista Army.
6. Decree the organic law that will govern the institutions of the State.
7. Implement the program of the Government of National Reconstruction.
8. Guarantee the departure from the country of all those military personnel, Somoza's functionaries who wish to leave and who are found not to have been involved in serious crimes against the people. . . .

V. Those who have collaborated with the regime and who wish to leave the country, and who are not responsible for the genocide that we have suffered or for other serious crimes that demand trial by the civil courts, may do so with all necessary guarantees, guarantees which the Government of National Reconstruction will demonstrate now and henceforth. The departure of these individuals may be supervised by the Inter-American Commission on Human Rights and by the International Red Cross.

VI. The plan to call Nicaraguans to the first free elections that our country will have in this century, so that they may elect their representatives to the city councils and to a constitutional assembly, and the country's highest-ranking authorities.

Now, Mr. Secretary General, the governments of this hemisphere have their opportunity to publicly declare their solidarity with the fight that our people have waged to bring democracy and justice to Nicaragua.

With the request that you convey the text of this letter to the foreign ministers of the OAS, we present our compliments.

JUNTA OF THE GOVERNMENT OF NATIONAL RECONSTRUCTION
VIOLETA DE CHAMORRO, SERGIO RAMIREZ MERCADO, ALFONSO ROBELO
CALLEJAS, DANIEL ORTEGA SAAVEDRA, MOISES HASSAN MORALES.

Plan of the Government of National Reconstruction to Achieve Peace

Our premise is that while it is true that the solution to Nicaragua's serious problem is the exclusive competence of the Nicaraguan people, hemispheric solidarity, essential for this plan to take hold, will be accorded in fulfillment of the Resolution of the Seventeenth Meeting of Consultation of Ministers of Foreign Affairs of the OAS, approved on June 23, 1979.

The following steps will ensure the immediate and definitive replacement of the Somoza regime, already destroyed by the heroic and combative people of Nicaragua and their vanguard, the Sandinista National Liberation Front. Rejection of this plan in favor of a political solution would leave military destruction of Somocismo as the only recourse; this could go on for weeks and would lead, unnecessarily, to many more deaths and destruction. . . .

On July 16, 1979, General Anastasio Somoza tendered his letter of resignation to the Nicaraguan Congress, the text of which reads as follows:

Honorable National Congress
People of Nicaragua
Having consulted the governments that truly have an interest in bringing peace to the country, I have decided to respect the decision of the Organization of American States and do hereby resign the Office of the Presidency to which I was elected by popular vote. My resignation is irrevocable.

I have fought against communism and believe that when the truth emerges history will vindicate me.

A. Somoza
President of the Republic

As a constitutional formality, in the early morning hours of July 18, the Nicaraguan Congress unanimously elected Francisco Urcuyo Maliaños, the President of the Chamber of Deputies, to replace Somoza and to facilitate the transfer of power to the Junta once it reached Managua from Costa Rica.

However, the newly elected President refused to relinquish the Office of the Presidency and announced that he intended to complete

General Somoza's term, in other words, to serve until May 1981. Instead of arranging a speedy transfer of power, Urcuyo delivered an address in which he praised the National Guard and demanded that "all irregular forces lay down their arms." Next, he proceeded to fill all the key posts in the National Guard with young colonels and lieutenant colonels, following the departure, with General Somoza, of almost all the senior military officers. The new Director of the National Guard, Lt. Col. Federico Mejía González, called on the National Guard "to redouble . . . their efforts in the current fight."

5. Wednesday morning, July 18, three members of the Junta, Sergio Ramírez, Alfonso Robelo, and Violeta Chamorro, left San José, Costa Rica, for León, Nicaragua, where they joined fourth Junta member, Daniel Ortega, and declared León to be the new provisional capital. Interim President Urcuyo fled to Guatemala, leaving the new National Guard Director in charge. According to information received, Mejía, now promoted to General, began negotiations with a Sandinista representative and with Archbishop Obando y Bravo in the "bunker" of General Somoza, regarding the terms of National Guard surrender. In view of the posture that Urcuyo had assumed, the negotiations were no longer possible on the original cease-fire terms; as a consequence, the FSLN now demanded the unconditional surrender of the National Guard. After the meeting, one of the participants stated that the talks had reached an impasse because the Sandinistas insisted on a surrender rather than a cease-fire in place. At approximately 2:00 A.M., General Mejía presented a list of the National Guard's demands, which included retention of all property belonging to individual officers in exchange for a surrender. The Sandinistas refused to accept these conditions and all communications broke off. Shortly before dawn on July 19, General Mejía, the General Staff of the National Guard, as well as most of the high-ranking officers, left Nicaragua by plane.

After a night of chaos, which some observers called "the worst night in the seven weeks of battle," the Nicaraguan civil war ended early on the morning of July 19, as Sandinista guerrillas took control of Managua and called for a cease-fire. At approximately noon that same day, the last of the commanders of the National Guard, Lt. Col. Fulgencio Largaespada Baez, ordered his soldiers to surrender. The text of his communiqué is as follows:

> Attention, Nicaraguans, attention: To the Commands and headquarters, officers, noncommissioned officers and enlisted personnel of the Nicaraguan National Guard:
> In the name of the General Staff of the Nicaraguan National Guard and with the approval of the Sandinista National Liberation Front

(FSLN) and of the Junta of the Government of National Reconstruction, I, Lt. Col. Fulgencio Largaespada Baez, do hereby inform you of the following:

1. The withdrawal of the General Staff of the National Guard, under the command of General Federico Mejía has led to the disintegration of our armed corps.
2. The victorious position that the Sandinista Front has held and continues to hold throughout the entire national territory has brought an end to the war waged against the Sandinista Front and the defeat of the National Guard.
3. To prevent further bloodshed and useless loss of innocent lives, National Guard noncommissioned officers and enlisted personnel are to obey the following orders:
   a. Immediate cease-fire at all command posts and on all war fronts.
   b. Deposition of weapons in your respective headquarters or posts at the following shelters: Red Cross stations, churches and embassies. All these places will be respected by the victorious forces of the Sandinista National Liberation Front.
   c. White flags are to be displayed wherever armed soldiers are to be found; this will be regarded as a sign of unconditional surrender.
   d. Once the orders issued by the joint National Directorate of the Sandinista National Liberation Front and the Junta of the Government of National Reconstruction have been carried out, the life and physical safety of every soldier who surrenders will be guaranteed.

This call does not constitute a betrayal of anyone or of anything. To the contrary, it represents the dignity invested in the National Guard, on behalf of the well-being of our long-suffering people. This I swear before the altar of country and of God, our Lord.

The present communiqué has been drafted jointly and with the authorization of Commander Humberto Ortega Saavedra, on behalf of the joint National Directorate of the FSLN and of the Junta of the Government of National Reconstruction.

Effective immediately.

(signed) Fulgencio Largaespada Baez, Chief of the General Staff of the Nicaraguan National Guard.

On July 20, the Junta of the Government of National Reconstruction was installed in Managua.

United Nations Declaration on the Elimination of All Forms of Intolerance and of Discrimination Based on Religion or Belief (1981)

ARTICLE 1

1. Everyone shall have the right to freedom of thought, conscience and religion. This right shall include freedom to have a religion or whatever belief of his choice, and freedom, either individually or in community with others and in public or private, to manifest his religion or belief in worship, observance, practice and teaching.

2. No one shall be subject to coercion which would impair his freedom to have a religion or belief of his choice.

3. Freedom to manifest one's religion or belief may be subject only to such limitations as are prescribed by law and are necessary to protect public safety, order, health or morals or the fundamental rights and freedoms of others.

ARTICLE 2

1. No one shall be subject to discrimination by any State, institution, group of persons, or person on the grounds of religion or other belief.

2. For the purposes of the present Declaration, the expression "intolerance and discrimination based on religion or belief" means any distinction, exclusion, restriction or preference based on religion or belief and having as its purpose or as its effect nullification or impairment of the recognition, enjoyment or exercise of human rights and fundamental freedoms on an equal basis.

ARTICLE 3

Discrimination between human beings on the grounds of religion or belief constitutes an affront to human dignity and a disavowal of the principles of the Charter of the United Nations, and shall be condemned as a violation of the human rights and fundamental freedoms proclaimed in the Universal Declaration of Human Rights and enunciated in detail in the International Covenants on Human Rights, and as an obstacle to friendly and peaceful relations between nations.

ARTICLE 4

1. All States shall take effective measures to prevent and eliminate discrimination on the grounds of religion or belief in the recognition, exercise and enjoyment of human rights and fundamental freedoms in all fields of civil, economic, political, social and cultural life.

2. All States shall make all efforts to enact or rescind legislation where necessary to prohibit any such discrimination, and to take all appropriate measures to combat intolerance on the grounds of religion or other beliefs in this matter.

ARTICLE 5

1. The parents or, as the case may be, the legal guardians of the child have the right to organize the life within the family in accordance with their religion or belief and bearing in mind the moral education in which they believe the child should be brought up.

2. Every child shall enjoy the right to have access to education in the matter of religion or belief in accordance with the wishes of his parents or, as the case may be, legal guardians, and shall not be compelled to receive teaching on religion or belief against the wishes of his parents or legal guardians, the best interests of the child being the guiding principle.

3. The child shall be protected from any form of discrimination on the grounds of religion or belief. He shall be brought up in a spirit of understanding, tolerance, friendship among peoples, peace and universal brotherhood, respect for freedom of religion or belief of others, and in full consciousness that his energy and talents should be devoted to the service of his fellow men.

4. In the case of a child who is not under the care either of his parents or of legal guardians, due account shall be taken of their expressed wishes or of any other proof of their wishes in the matter of religion or belief, the best interests of the child being the guiding principle.

5. Practices of a religion or belief in which a child is brought up must not be injurious to his physical or mental health or to his full development, taking into account article 1, paragraph 3, of the present Declaration.

ARTICLE 6

In accordance with article 1 of the present Declaration, and subject to the provisions of article 1, paragraph 3, the right to freedom of thought, conscience, religion or belief shall include, *inter alia*, the following freedoms:

a. To worship or assemble in connection with a religion or belief, and to establish and maintain places for these purposes;

b. To establish and maintain appropriate charitable or humanitarian institutions;

c. To make, acquire and use to an adequate extent the necessary articles and materials related to the rites or customs of a religion or belief;

d. To write, issue and disseminate relevant publications in these areas;

e. To teach a religion or belief in places suitable for these purposes;

f. To solicit and receive voluntary financial and other contributions from individuals and institutions;

g. To train, appoint, elect or designate by succession appropriate leaders called for by the requirements and standards of any religion or belief;

h. To observe days of rest and to celebrate holidays and ceremonies in accordance with the precepts of one's religion or belief;

i. To establish and maintain communications with individuals and communities in matters of religion and belief at the national and international levels. . . .

United Nations Declaration on the Right of Peoples to Peace (1984)

The General Assembly,

Reaffirming that the principal aim of the United Nations is the maintenance of international peace and security.

Bearing in mind the fundamental principles of international law set forth in the Charter of the United Nations,

Expressing the will and the aspirations of all peoples to eradicate war from the life of mankind and, above all, to avert a world-wide nuclear catastrophe,

Convinced that life without war serves as the primary international prerequisite for the material well-being, development and progress of countries, and for the full implementation of the rights and fundamental human freedoms proclaimed by the United Nations,

Aware that in the nuclear age the establishment of a lasting peace on Earth represents the primary condition for the preservation of human civilization and the survival of mankind,

Recognizing that the maintenance of a peaceful life for people is the sacred duty of each State,

1. *Solemnly proclaims* that the peoples of our planet have a sacred right to peace;

2. *Solemnly declares* that the preservation of the right of peoples to peace and the promotion of its implementation constitute a fundamental obligation of each State;

3. *Emphasizes* that ensuring the exercise of the right of peoples to peace demands that the policies of States be directed toward the elimination of the threat of war, particularly nuclear war, the renunciation of the use of force in international relations and the settlement of international disputes by peaceful means on the basis of the Charter of the United Nations;

4. *Appeals* to all States and international organizations to do their utmost to assist in implementing the right of peoples to peace through the adoption of appropriate measures at both the national and the international level.

Convention Against Torture and Other Cruel, Inhuman or Degrading Treatment or Punishment (1984)

The States Parties to this Convention,

Considering that, in accordance with the principles proclaimed in the Charter of the United Nations, recognition of the equal and inalienable rights of all members of the human family is the foundation of freedom, justice and peace in the world,

Recognizing that those rights derive from the inherent dignity of the human person,

Considering the obligation of States under the Charter, in particular Article 55, to promote universal respect for, and observance of, human rights and fundamental freedoms,

Having regard to article 5 of the Universal Declaration of Human Rights and article 7 of the International Covenant on Civil and Political Rights, both of which provide that no one shall be subjected to torture or to cruel, inhuman or degrading treatment or punishment,

Having regard also to the Declaration on the Protection of All Persons from Being Subjected to Torture and Other Cruel, Inhuman or Degrading Treatment or Punishment, adopted by the General Assembly on 9 December 1975,

Desiring to make more effective the struggle against torture and other cruel, inhuman or degrading treatment or punishment throughout the world,

Have agreed as follows:

Part I

ARTICLE 1

1. For the purposes of this Convention, the term "torture" means any act by which severe pain or suffering, whether physical or mental, is intentionally inflicted on a person for such purposes as obtaining from him or a third person information or a confession, punishing him for an act he or a third person has committed or is suspected of having committed, or intimidating or coercing him or a third person, or for any reason based on discrimination of any kind, when such pain or suffering is inflicted by or at the instigation of or with the consent or acquiescence of a public official or other person acting in an official capacity. It does not include pain or suffering arising only from, inherent in or incidental to lawful sanctions.

2. This article is without prejudice to any international instrument or national legislation which does or may contain provisions of wider application.

ARTICLE 2

1. Each State Party shall take effective legislative, administrative, judicial or other measures to prevent acts of torture in any territory under its jurisdiction.

2. No exceptional circumstances whatsoever, whether a state of war or a threat of war, internal political instability or any other public emergency, may be invoked as a justification of torture.

3. An order from a superior officer or a public authority may not be invoked as a justification of torture.

ARTICLE 3

1. No State Party shall expel, return ("refouler") or extradite a person to another State where there are substantial grounds for believing that he would be in danger of being subjected to torture.

2. For the purpose of determining whether there are such grounds, the competent authorities shall take into account all relevant considerations including, where applicable, the existence in the State concerned of a consistent pattern of gross, flagrant or mass violations of human rights.

ARTICLE 4

1. Each State Party shall ensure that all acts of torture are offenses under its criminal law. The same shall apply to an attempt to commit torture and to an act by any person which constitutes complicity or participation in torture.

2. Each State Party shall make these offenses punishable by appropriate penalties which take into account their grave nature.

ARTICLE 5

1. Each State Party shall take such measures as may be necessary to establish its jurisdiction over the offenses referred to in article 4 in the following cases:

a. When the offenses are committed in any territory under its jurisdiction or on board a ship or aircraft registered in that State;

b. When the alleged offender is a national of that State;

c. When the victim is a national of that State if that State considers it appropriate.

2. Each State Party shall likewise take such measures as may be necessary to establish its jurisdiction over such offenses in cases where the alleged offender is present in any territory under its jurisdiction and it does not extradite him pursuant to article 8 to any of the States mentioned in paragraph 1 of this article.

3. This Convention does not exclude any criminal jurisdiction exercised in accordance with internal law.

ARTICLE 6

1. Upon being satisfied, after an examination of information available to it, that the circumstances so warrant, any State Party in whose territory a person alleged to have committed any offenses referred to in article 4 is present shall take him into custody or take other legal measures to ensure his presence. The custody and other legal measures shall be as provided in the law of that State but may be continued only for such time as is necessary to enable any criminal or extradition proceedings to be instituted.

2. Such State shall immediately make a preliminary inquiry into the facts.

3. Any person in custody pursuant to paragraph 1 of this article shall be assisted in communicating immediately with the nearest appropriate representative of the State of which he is a national, or, if he is a stateless person, with the representative of the State where he usually resides.

4. When a State, pursuant to this article, has taken a person into custody, it shall immediately notify the States referred to in article 5, paragraph 1, of the fact that such person is in custody and of the circumstances which warrant his detention. The State which makes the preliminary inquiry contemplated in paragraph 2 of this article shall promptly report its findings to the said States and shall indicate whether it intends to exercise jurisdiction.

ARTICLE 7

1. The State Party in the territory under whose jurisdiction a person alleged to have committed any offense referred to in article 4 is found shall in the cases contemplated in article 5, if it does not extradite him, submit the case to its competent authorities for the purpose of prosecution.

2. These authorities shall take their decision in the same manner as in the case of any ordinary offense of a serious nature under the law of that State. In the cases referred to in article 5, paragraph 2, the standards of evidence required for prosecution and conviction shall in no way be less stringent than those which apply in the cases referred to in article 5, paragraph 1.

3. Any person regarding whom proceedings are brought in connection with any of the offenses referred to in article 4 shall be guaranteed fair treatment at all stages in the proceedings.

ARTICLE 8

1. The offenses referred to in article 4 shall be deemed to be included as extraditable offenses in any extradition treaty existing between States Parties. States Parties undertake to include such offenses as extraditable offenses in every extradition treaty to be concluded between them.

2. If a State Party which makes extradition conditional on the existence of a treaty receives a request for extradition from another State Party with which it has no extradition treaty, it may consider this Convention as the legal basis for extradition in respect of such offenses. Extradition shall be subject to the other conditions provided by the law of the requested State.

3. States Parties which do not make extradition conditional on the existence of a treaty shall recognize such offenses as extraditable offenses between themselves subject to the conditions provided by the law of the requested State.

4. Such offenses shall be treated, for the purpose of extradition between States Parties, as if they had been committed not only in the place in which they occurred but also in the territories of the States required to establish their jurisdiction in accordance with article 5, paragraph 1.

ARTICLE 9

1. States Parties shall afford one another the greatest measure of assistance in connection with criminal proceedings brought in respect of any of the offenses referred to in article 4, including the supply of all evidence at their disposal necessary for the proceedings.

2. States Parties shall carry out their obligations under paragraph 1 of this article in conformity with any treaties on mutual judicial assistance that may exist between them.

ARTICLE 10

1. Each State Party shall ensure that education and information regarding the prohibition against torture are fully included in the training of law enforcement personnel, civil or military, medical personnel, public officials and other persons who may be involved in the custody, interrogation or treatment of any individual subjected to any form of arrest, detention or imprisonment.

2. Each State Party shall include this prohibition in the rules or instructions issued in regard to the duties and functions of any such persons.

ARTICLE 11

Each State Party shall keep under systematic review interrogation rules, instructions, methods and practices as well as arrangements for the custody and treatment of persons subjected to any form of arrest, detention or imprisonment in any territory under its jurisdiction, with a view to preventing any cases of torture.

ARTICLE 12

Each State Party shall ensure that its competent authorities proceed to a prompt and impartial investigation, wherever there is reasonable ground to believe that an act of torture has been committed in any territory under its jurisdiction.

ARTICLE 13

Each State Party shall ensure that any individual who alleges he has been subjected to torture in any territory under its jurisdiction has the right to complain to, and to have his case promptly and impartially examined by, its competent authorities. Steps shall be taken to ensure that the complainant and witnesses are protected against all ill-treatment or intimidation as a consequence of his complaint or any evidence given.

ARTICLE 14

1. Each State Party shall ensure in its legal system that the victim of an act of torture obtains redress and has an enforceable right to fair and adequate compensation, including the means for as full rehabilitation as possible. In the event of the death of the victim as a result of an act of torture, his dependents shall be entitled to compensation.

2. Nothing in this article shall affect any right of the victim or other persons to compensation which may exist under national law.

ARTICLE 15

Each State Party shall ensure that any statement which is established to have been made as a result of torture shall not be invoked as evidence in any proceedings, except against a person accused of torture as evidence that the statement was made.

ARTICLE 16

1. Each State Party shall undertake to prevent in any territory under its jurisdiction other acts of cruel, inhuman or degrading treatment or punishment which do not amount to torture as defined in article 1, when such acts are committed by or at the instigation of or with the consent or acquiescence of a public official or other person acting in an official capacity. In particular, the obligations contained in articles 10, 11, 12 and 13 shall apply with the substitution for references to torture of references to other forms of cruel, inhuman or degrading treatment or punishment.

2. The provisions of this Convention are without prejudice to the provisions of any other international instrument or national law which prohibits cruel, inhuman or degrading treatment or punishment or which relates to extradition or expulsion. . . .

Inter-American Convention to Prevent and Punish Torture (1985)

The American States signatory to the present Convention,

Aware of the provision of the American Convention on Human Rights that no one shall be subjected to torture or to cruel, inhuman, or degrading punishment or treatment;

Reaffirming that all acts of torture or any other cruel, inhuman, or degrading treatment or punishment constitute an offense against human dignity and a denial of the principles set forth in the Charter of the Organization of American States and in the Charter of the United Nations and are violations of the fundamental human rights and freedoms proclaimed in the American Declaration of the Rights and Duties of Man and the Universal Declaration of Human Rights;

Noting that, in order for the pertinent rules contained in the aforementioned global and regional instruments to take effect, it is necessary to draft an Inter-American Convention that prevents and punishes torture;

Reaffirming their purpose of consolidating in this hemisphere the conditions that make for recognition of and respect for the inherent dignity of man, and ensure the full exercise of his fundamental rights and freedoms,

Have agreed upon the following:

ARTICLE 1

The States Parties undertake to prevent and punish torture in accordance with the terms of this Convention.

ARTICLE 2

For the purposes of this Convention, torture shall be understood to be any act intentionally performed whereby physical or mental pain or suffering is inflicted on a person for purposes of criminal investigation, as a means of intimidation, as personal punishment, as a preventive measure, as a penalty, or for any other purpose. Torture shall also be understood to be the use of methods upon a person intended to obliterate the personality of the victim or to diminish his physical or mental capacities, even if they do not cause physical pain or mental anguish.

The concept of torture shall not include physical or mental pain or suffering that is inherent in or solely the consequence of lawful measures, provided that they do not include the performance of the acts or use of the methods referred to in this article.

ARTICLE 3

The following shall be held guilty of the crime of torture:

a. A public servant or employee who acting in that capacity orders, instigates, or induces the use of torture, or who directly commits it or who, being able to prevent it, fails to do so.

b. A person who at the instigation of a public servant or employee mentioned in subparagraph (a) orders, instigates or induces the use of torture, directly commits it, or is an accomplice thereto.

ARTICLE 4

The fact of having acted under orders of a superior shall not provide exemption from the corresponding criminal liability.

ARTICLE 5

The existence of circumstances such as a state of war, threat of war, state of siege or of emergency, domestic disturbance or strife, suspension of constitutional guarantees, domestic political instability, or other public emergencies or disasters shall not be invoked or admitted as justification for the crime of torture.

Neither the dangerous character of the detainee or prisoner, nor the

lack of security of the prison establishment or penitentiary shall
justify torture.

ARTICLE 6

In accordance with the terms of Article 1, the States Parties shall
take effective measures to prevent and punish torture within their
jurisdiction.

The States Parties shall ensure that all acts of torture and attempts
to commit torture are offenses under their criminal law and shall make
such acts punishable by severe penalties that take into account their
serious nature.

The States Parties likewise shall take effective measures to prevent
and punish other cruel, inhuman, or degrading treatment or punishment within their jurisdiction.

ARTICLE 7

The States Parties shall take measures so that, in the training of
police officers and other public officials responsible for the custody of
persons temporarily or definitively deprived of their freedom, special
emphasis shall be put on the prohibition of the use of torture in
interrogation, detention, or arrest.

The States Parties likewise shall take similar measures to prevent
other cruel, inhuman, or degrading treatment or punishment.

ARTICLE 8

The States Parties shall guarantee that any person making an accusation of having been subjected to torture within their jurisdiction
shall have the right to an impartial examination of his case.

Likewise, if there is an accusation or well-grounded reason to
believe that an act of torture has been committed within their jurisdiction, the States Parties shall guarantee that their respective authorities
will proceed properly and immediately to conduct an investigation
into the case and to initiate, whenever appropriate, the corresponding
criminal process.

After all the domestic legal procedures of the respective State and
the corresponding appeals have been exhausted, the case may be
submitted to the international fora whose competence has been
recognized by that State.

ARTICLE 9

The States Parties undertake to incorporate into their national
laws regulations guaranteeing suitable compensation for victims of
torture.

None of the provisions of this article shall affect the right to receive compensation that the victim or other persons may have by virtue of existing national legislation.

ARTICLE 10

No statement that is verified as having been obtained through torture shall be admissible as evidence in a legal proceeding, except in a legal action taken against a person or persons accused of having elicited it through acts of torture, and only as evidence that the accused obtained such statement by such means.

ARTICLE 11

The States Parties shall take the necessary steps to extradite anyone accused of having committed the crime of torture or sentenced for commission of that crime, in accordance with their respective national laws on extradition and their international commitments on this matter.

ARTICLE 12

Every State Party shall take the necessary measures to establish its jurisdiction over the crime described in this Convention in the following cases:

a. When torture has been committed within its jurisdiction;

b. When the alleged criminal is a national of that State; or

c. When the victim is a national of that State and it so deems appropriate.

Every State Party shall also take the necessary measures to establish its jurisdiction over the crime described in this Convention when the alleged criminal is within the area under its jurisdiction and it is not appropriate to extradite him in accordance with Article 11.

This Convention does not exclude criminal jurisdiction exercised in accordance with domestic law.

ARTICLE 13

The crime referred to in Article 2 shall be deemed to be included among the extraditable crimes in every extradition treaty entered into between States Parties. The States Parties undertake to include the crime of torture as an extraditable offense in every extradition treaty to be concluded between them.

Every State Party that makes extradition conditional on the existence of a treaty may, if it receives a request for extradition from another State Party with which it has no extradition treaty, consider this Convention as the legal basis for extradition in respect of the crime of torture. Extradition shall be subject to the other conditions that may be required by the law of the requested State.

States Parties which do not make extradition conditional on the existence of a treaty shall recognize such crimes as extraditable offenses between themselves, subject to the conditions required by the law of the requested State.

Extradition shall not be granted nor shall the person sought be returned when there are grounds to believe that his life is in danger, that he will be subjected to torture or to cruel, inhuman or degrading treatment, or that he will be tried by special or ad hoc courts in the requesting State.

ARTICLE 14

When a State Party does not grant the extradition, the case shall be submitted to its competent authorities as if the crime had been committed within its jurisdiction, for the purposes of investigation, and when appropriate, for criminal action, in accordance with its national law. Any decision adopted by these authorities shall be communicated to the State that has requested the extradition.

ARTICLE 15

No provision of this Convention may be interpreted as limiting the right to asylum, when appropriate, nor as altering the obligations of the States Parties in the matter of extradition. . . .

United Nations Declaration on the Right to Development (1986)

The General Assembly,

Bearing in mind the purposes and principles of the Charter of the United Nations relating to the achievement of international cooperation in solving international problems of an economic, social, cultural, or humanitarian nature, and in promoting and encouraging respect for human rights and fundamental freedoms for all without distinction as to race, sex, language or religion,

Recognizing that development is a comprehensive economic, social, cultural and political process, which aims at the constant improvement of the well-being of the entire population and of all individuals on the basis of their active, free and meaningful participation in development and in the fair distribution of benefits resulting therefrom,

Considering that under the provisions of the Universal Declaration of Human Rights everyone is entitled to a social and international order in which the rights and freedoms set forth in that Declaration can be fully realized,

Recalling the provisions of the International Covenant on Economic, Social and Cultural Rights and of the International Covenant on Civil and Political Rights,

Recalling further the relevant agreements, conventions, resolutions, recommendations and other instruments of the United Nations and its specialized agencies concerning the integral development of the human being, economic and social progress and development of all peoples, including those instruments concerning decolonization, the prevention of discrimination, respect for and observance of human rights and fundamental freedoms, the maintenance of international peace and security and the further promotion of friendly relations and cooperation among States in accordance with the Charter,

Recalling the right of peoples to self-determination, by virtue of which they have the right freely to determine their political status and to pursue their economic, social and cultural development,

Recalling also the right of peoples to exercise, subject to the relevant provisions of both International Covenants on Human Rights, full and complete sovereignty over all their natural wealth and resources,

Mindful of the obligation of States under the Charter to promote universal respect for and observance of human rights and fundamental freedoms for all without distinction of any kind such as race, colour, sex, language, religion, political or other opinion, national or social origin, property, birth or other status,

Considering that the elimination of the massive and flagrant violations of the human rights of the peoples and individuals affected by situations such as those resulting from colonialism, neo-colonialism, *apartheid*, all forms of racism and racial discrimination, foreign domination and occupation, aggression and threats against national sovereignty, national unity and territorial integrity and threats of war would contribute to the establishment of circumstances propitious to the development of a great part of mankind,

Concerned at the existence of serious obstacles to development, as well as to the complete fulfilment of human beings and of peoples, constituted, *inter alia*, by the denial of civil, political, economic, social and cultural rights, and considering that all human rights and fundamental freedoms are indivisible and interdependent and that, in order to promote development, equal attention and urgent consideration should be given to the implementation, promotion and protection of civil, political, economic, social and cultural rights and that, accordingly, the promotion of, respect for and enjoyment of certain human rights and fundamental freedoms cannot justify the denial of other human rights and fundamental freedoms,

Considering that international peace and security are essential elements for the realization of the right to development,

Reaffirming that there is a close relationship between disarmament and development and that progress in the field of disarmament would considerably promote progress in the field of development and that resources released through disarmament measures should be devoted to the economic and social development and well-being of all peoples and, in particular, those of the developing countries,

Recognizing that the human person is the central subject of the development process and that development policy should therefore make the human being the main participant and beneficiary of development,

Recognizing that the creation of conditions favorable to the development of peoples and individuals is the primary responsibility of their States,

Aware that efforts at the international level to promote and protect human rights should be accompanied by efforts to establish a new international economic order,

Confirming that the right to development is an inalienable human right and that equality of opportunity for development is a prerogative both of nations and of individuals who make up nations,

Proclaims the following Declaration on the Right to Development:

ARTICLE 1

1. The right to development is an inalienable human right by virtue of which every human person and all peoples are entitled to participate in, contribute to and enjoy economic, social, cultural and political development, in which all human rights and fundamental freedoms can be fully realized.

2. The human right to development also implies the full realization of the right of peoples to self-determination, which includes, subject to the relevant provisions of both International Covenants on Human Rights, the exercise of their inalienable right to full sovereignty over all their natural wealth and resources.

ARTICLE 2

1. The human person is the central subject of development and should be the active participant and beneficiary of the right to development.

2. All human beings have a responsibility for development, individually and collectively, taking into account the need for full respect to their human rights and fundamental freedoms as well as their duties to the community, which alone can ensure the free and complete fulfillment of the human being, and they should therefore promote and protect an appropriate political, social and economic order for development.

3. States have the right and the duty to formulate appropriate national development policies that aim at the constant improvement of the well-being of the entire population and of all individuals, on the basis of their active, free and meaningful participation in development and in the fair distribution of the benefits resulting therefrom.

ARTICLE 3

1. States have the primary responsibility for the creation of national and international conditions favorable to the realization of the right to development.

2. The realization of the right to development requires full respect for the principles of international law concerning friendly relations and cooperation among States in accordance with the Charter of the United Nations.

3. States have the duty to cooperate with each other in ensuring development and eliminating obstacles to development. States should realize their rights and fulfill their duties in such a manner as to promote a new international economic order based on sovereign equality, interdependence, mutual interest and cooperation among all States, as well as to encourage the observance and realization of human rights.

ARTICLE 4

1. States have the duty to take steps, individually and collectively, to formulate international development policies with a view to facilitating the full realization of the right to development.

2. Sustained action is required to promote more rapid development of developing countries. As a complement to the efforts of developing countries, effective international cooperation is essential in providing these countries with appropriate means and facilities to foster their comprehensive development.

ARTICLE 5

States shall take resolute steps to eliminate the massive and flagrant violations of the human rights of peoples and human beings affected by situations such as those resulting from apartheid, all forms of racism and racial discrimination, colonialism, foreign domination and occupation, aggression, foreign interference and threats against national sovereignty, national unity and territorial integrity, threats of war and refusal to recognize the fundamental right of peoples of self-determination.

ARTICLE 6

1. All States should cooperate with a view to promoting, encouraging and strengthening universal respect for and observance of all

human rights and fundamental freedoms for all without any distinction as to race, sex, language or religion.

2. All human rights and fundamental freedoms are indivisible and interdependent; equal attention and urgent consideration should be given to the implementation, promotion and protection of civil, political, economic, social and cultural rights.

3. States should take steps to eliminate obstacles to development resulting from failure to observe civil and political rights, as well as economic, social and cultural rights.

ARTICLE 7

All States should promote the establishment, maintenance and strengthening of international peace and security and, to that end, should do their utmost to achieve general and complete disarmament under effective international control, as well as to ensure that the resources released by effective disarmament measures are used for comprehensive development, in particular that of the developing countries.

ARTICLE 8

1. States should undertake, at the national level, all necessary measures for the realization of the right to development and shall ensure, inter alia, equality of opportunity for all in their access to basic resources, education, health services, food, housing, employment and the fair distribution of income. Effective measures should be undertaken to ensure that women have an active role in the development process. Appropriate economic and social reforms should be carried out with a view to eradicating all social injustices.

2. States should encourage popular participation in all spheres as an important factor in development and in the full realization of all human rights.

ARTICLE 9

1. All the aspects of the right to development set forth in the present Declaration are indivisible and interdependent and each of them should be considered in the context of the whole.

2. Nothing in the present Declaration shall be construed as being contrary to the purposes and principles of the United Nations, or as implying that any State, group or person has a right to engage in any activity or to perform any act aimed at the violation of the rights set forth in the Universal Declaration of Human Rights and in the International Covenants on Human Rights.

ARTICLE 10

Steps should be taken to ensure the full exercise and progressive enhancement of the right to development, including the formulation, adoption and implementation of policy, legislative and other measures at the national and international levels.

Conference on Security and Cooperation in Europe (1989)
Cooperation in Humanitarian and Other Fields

The participating States,

Considering that cooperation in humanitarian and other fields is an essential factor for the development of their relations,

Agreeing that their cooperation in these fields should take place in full respect for the principles guiding relations between participating States as set forth in the Final Act as well as for the provisions in the Madrid Concluding Document and in the present Document pertaining to those principles,

Confirming that, in implementing the provisions concerning cooperation in humanitarian and other fields in the framework of their laws and regulations, they will ensure that THOSE laws and regulations conform with their obligations under international law and are brought into harmony with their CSCE commitments,

Recognizing that the implementation of the relevant provisions of the Final Act and of the Madrid Concluding Document requires continuous and intensified efforts,

Have adopted and will implement the following:

Human Contacts

1. In implementing the human contacts provisions of the Final Act, the Madrid Concluding Document and the present Document, they will fully respect their obligations under international law as referred to in the subchapter of the present Document devoted to principles, in particular that everyone shall be free to leave any country, including

From "A Framework for Europe's Future," concluding document of the Vienna meeting.

his own, and to return to his country, as well as their international commitments in this field.

2. They will ensure that their policies concerning entry into their territories are fully consistent with the aims set out in the relevant provisions of the Final Act, the Madrid Concluding Document and the present Document.

3. They will take the necessary steps to find solutions as expeditiously as possible, but in any case within six months, to all applications based on the human contacts provisions of the Final Act and the Madrid Concluding Document, outstanding at the conclusion of the Vienna Follow-up Meeting.

4. Thereafter they will conduct regular reviews in order to ensure that all applications based on the human contacts provisions of the Final Act and of the other aforementioned CSCE documents are being dealt with in a manner consistent with those provisions.

5. They will decide upon applications relating to family meetings in accordance with the Final Act and the other aforementioned CSCE documents in as short a time as possible and in normal practice within one month.

6. In the same manner they will decide upon applications relating to family reunification or marriage between citizens of different States, in normal practice within three months.

7. In dealing favorably with applications relating to family meetings, they will take due account of the wishes of the applicant, in particular on the timing and sufficiently long duration of such meetings, and on traveling together with other members of his family for joint family meetings.

8. In dealing favorably with applications relating to family meetings, they will also allow visits to and from more distant relatives.

9. In dealing favorably with applications relating to family reunification or marriage between citizens of different States, they will respect the wishes of the applicants on the country of destination ready to accept them.

10 They will pay particular attention to the solution of problems involving the reunification of minor children with their parents. In this context and on the basis of the relevant provisions of the Final Act and of the other aforementioned CSCE documents, they will ensure

- that an application in this regard submitted while the child is a minor will be dealt with favorably and expeditiously in order to effect the reunification without delay; and
- that adequate arrangements are made to protect the interests and welfare of the children concerned.

11. They will consider the scope for gradually reducing and eventually eliminating any requirements which might exist for travelers to obtain local currency in excess of actual expenditure, giving priority to persons traveling for the purpose of family meetings. They will accord such persons the opportunity in practice to bring in or to take out with them personal possessions or gifts.

12. They will pay immediate attention to applications for travel of an urgent humanitarian nature and deal with them favorably as follows:

- They will decide within three working days upon applications relating to visits to a seriously ill or dying family member, travel to attend the funeral of a family member or travel by those who have a proven need of urgent medical treatment or who can be shown to be critically or terminally ill.
- They will decide as expeditiously as possible upon applications relating to travel by those who are seriously ill or by the elderly, and other travel of an urgent humanitarian nature.

They will intensify efforts by their local, regional and central authorities concerned with the implementation of the above, and ensure that charges for giving priority treatment to such applications do not exceed costs actually incurred.

13. In dealing with applications for travel for family meetings, family reunification or marriage between citizens of different States, they will ensure that acts or omissions by members of the applicant's family do not adversely affect the rights of the applicant as set forth in the relevant international instruments.

14. They will ensure that all documents necessary for applications based on the human contacts provisions of the Final Act and of the other aforementioned CSCE documents are easily accessible to the applicant. The documents will remain valid throughout the application procedure. In the event of a renewed application the documents already submitted by the applicant in connection with previous applications will be taken into consideration.

15. They will simplify practices and gradually reduce administrative requirements for applications based on the human contacts provisions of the Final Act and of the other aforementioned CSCE documents.

16. They will ensure that, when applications based on the human contacts provisions of the Final Act and of the other aforementioned CSCE documents are refused for reasons specified in the relevant international instruments, the applicant is promptly provided in writing with an official notification of the grounds on which the decision was based. As a rule and in all cases where the applicant so requests,

he will be given the necessary information about the procedure for making use of any effective administrative or judicial remedies against the decision available to him as envisaged in the above-mentioned international instruments. In cases where exit for permanent settlement abroad is involved, this information will be provided as part of the official notification foreseen above.

17. If in this context an individual's application for travel abroad has been refused for reasons of national security, they will ensure that, within strictly warranted time limits, any restriction on that individual's travel is as short as possible and is not applied in an arbitrary manner. They will also ensure that the applicant can have the refusal reviewed within six months and, should the need arise, at regular intervals thereafter so that any changes in the circumstances surrounding the refusal, such as the time elapsed since the applicant was last engaged in work or duties involving national security, are taken into account. Before individuals take up work or duties involving national security, they will be formally notified if and how this could affect applications they might submit for such travel.

18. Within one year of the conclusion of the Vienna Follow-up Meeting they will publish and make easily accessible, where this has not already been done, all their laws and statutory regulations concerning movement by individuals within their territory and travel between States.

19. In dealing favorably with applications based on the human contacts provisions of the Final Act and of the other aforementioned CSCE documents, they will ensure that these are dealt with in good time in order, *inter alia*, to take due account of important family, personal or professional considerations significant for the applicant.

20. They will deal favorably with applications for travel abroad without distinction of any kind, such as race, color, sex, language, religion, political or other opinion, national or social origin, property, birth, age or other status. They will ensure that any refusal does not affect applications submitted by other persons.

21. They will further facilitate travel on an individual or collective basis for personal or professional reasons and for tourism, such as travel by delegations, groups and individuals. To this end they will reduce the time for the consideration of applications for such travel to a minimum.

22. They will give serious consideration to proposals for concluding agreements on the issuing of multiple entry visas and the reciprocal easing of visa processing formalities, and consider possibilities for the reciprocal abolition of entry visas on the basis of agreements between them.

23. They will consider adhering to the relevant multilateral instru-

ments as well as concluding complementary or other bilateral agreements, if necessary, in order to improve arrangements for ensuring effective consular, legal and medical assistance for citizens of other participating States temporarily on their territory.

24. They will take any necessary measures to ensure that citizens of other participating States temporarily on their territory for personal or professional reasons, *inter alia* for the purpose of participating in cultural, scientific and educational activities, are afforded appropriate personal safety, where this is not already the case.

25. They will facilitate and encourage the establishment and maintenance of direct personal contacts between their citizens as well as between representatives of their institutions and organizations through travel between States and other means of communication.

26. They will facilitate such contacts and cooperation among their peoples through such measures as direct sports exchanges on a local and regional level, the unimpeded establishment and implementation of town-twinning arrangements, as well as student and teacher exchanges.

27. They will encourage the further development of direct contacts between young people, as well as between governmental and non-governmental youth and student organizations and institutions; the conclusion between such organizations and institutions of bilateral and multilateral arrangements and programs; and the holding on a bilateral and multilateral basis of educational, cultural and other events and activities by and for young people.

28. They will make further efforts to facilitate travel and tourism by young people, *inter alia*, by recommending to those of their railway authorities which are members of the International Union of Railways (UIC) that they expand the Inter-Rail system to cover all their European networks and by recommending to those of their railway authorities which are not members of the UIC that they consider establishing similar facilities.

29. In accordance with the Universal Postal Convention and the International Telecommunication Convention, they will

- guarantee the freedom of transit of postal communication;
- ensure the rapid and unhindered delivery of correspondence, including personal mail and parcels;
- respect the privacy and integrity of postal and telephone communications; and
- ensure the conditions necessary for rapid and uninterrupted telephone calls, including the use of international direct dialing systems, where they exist, and their development.

30. They will encourage direct personal contacts between the citizens of their States, *inter alia* by facilitating individual travel within their countries and by allowing foreigners to meet their citizens as well as, when invited to do so, to stay in private homes.

31. They will ensure that the status of persons belonging to national minorities or regional cultures on their territories is equal to that of other citizens with regard to human contacts under the Final Act and the other aforementioned CSCE documents and that these persons can establish and maintain such contacts through travel and other means of communication, including contacts with citizens of other States with whom they share a common national origin or cultural heritage.

32. They will allow believers, religious faiths and their representatives, in groups or on an individual basis, to establish and maintain direct personal contacts and communication with each other, in their own and other countries, *inter alia* through travel, pilgrimages and participation in assemblies and other religious events. In this context and commensurate with such contacts and events, those concerned will be allowed to acquire, receive and carry with them religious publications and objects related to the practice of their religion or belief.

33. They heard accounts of the Meeting of Experts on Human Contacts held in Bern from 15 April to 26 May 1986. Noting that no conclusions had been agreed upon at the Meeting, they regarded both the frankness of the discussion and the greater degree of openness in the exchanges as welcome developments. In this respect they noted the particular importance of the fact that proposals made at the Meeting had received further consideration at the Vienna Follow-up Meeting.

Information

34. They will continue efforts to contribute to an ever wider knowledge and understanding of life in their States, thus promoting confidence between peoples.

They will make further efforts to facilitate the freer and wider dissemination of information of all kinds, to encourage cooperation in the field of information and to improve the working conditions for journalists.

In this connection and in accordance with the International Covenant on Civil and Political Rights, the Universal Declaration of Human Rights and their relevant international commitments concerning seeking, receiving and imparting information of all kinds, they will ensure that individuals can freely choose their sources of information. In this context they will

- ensure that radio services operating in accordance with the ITU Radio Regulations can be directly and normally received in their states; and
- allow individuals, institutions and organizations, while respecting intellectual property rights, including copyright, to obtain, possess, reproduce and distribute information material of all kinds.

To these ends they will remove any restrictions inconsistent with the above-mentioned obligations and commitments.

35. They will take every opportunity offered by modern means of communication, including cable and satellites, to increase the freer and wider dissemination of information of all kinds. They will also encourage cooperation and exchanges between their relevant institutions, organizations and technical experts, and work toward the harmonization of technical standards and norms. They will bear in mind the effects of these modern means of communication on their mass media.

36. They will ensure in practice that official information bulletins can be freely distributed on their territory by the diplomatic and other official missions and consular posts of the other participating States.

37. They will encourage radio and television organizations, on the basis of arrangements between them, to broadcast live, especially in the organizing countries, programs and discussions with participants from different States and to broadcast statements of and interviews with political and other personalities from the participating States.

38. They will encourage radio and television organizations to report on different aspects of life in other participating States and to increase the number of telebridges between their countries.

39. Recalling that the legitimate pursuit of journalists' professional activity will neither render them liable to expulsion nor otherwise penalize them, they will refrain from taking restrictive measures such as withdrawing a journalist's accreditation or expelling him because of the content of the reporting of the journalists or of his information media.

40. They will ensure that, in pursuing this activity, journalists, including those representing media from other participating States, are free to seek access to and maintain contacts with public and private sources of information and that their need for professional confidentiality is respected.

41. They will respect the copyright of journalists.

42. On the basis of arrangements between them, where necessary, and for the purpose of regular reporting, they will grant accreditation, where it is required, and multiple entry visas to journalists from other participating States, regardless of their domicile. On this basis they will reduce to a maximum of two months the period for issuing both accreditation and multiple entry visas to journalists.

43. They will facilitate the work of foreign journalists by providing relevant information, on request, on matters of practical concern, such as import regulations, taxation and accommodation.

44. They will ensure that official press conferences and, as appropriate, other similar official press events are also open to foreign journalists, upon accreditation, where this is required.

45. They will ensure in practice that persons belonging to national minorities or regional cultures on their territories can disseminate, have access to, and exchange information in their mother tongue.

46. They agree to convene an Information Forum to discuss improvement of the circulation of, access to and exchange of information; cooperation in the field of information; and the improvement of working conditions for journalists. The Forum will be held in London from 18 April to 12 May 1989. It will be attended by personalities from the participating States in the field of information. The agenda, time-table and other organizational modalities are set out in Annex VIII.

Cooperation and Exchanges in the Field of Culture

47. They will promote and give full effect to their cultural cooperation, *inter alia* through the implementation of any relevant bilateral and multilateral agreements concluded among them in the various fields of culture.

48. They will encourage non-governmental organizations interested in the field of culture, to participate, together with state institutions, in the elaboration and implementation of these agreements and specific projects, as well as in the elaboration of practical measures concerning cultural exchange and cooperation.

49. They will favor the establishment, by mutual agreement, of cultural institutes or centers of other participating States on their territory. Unhindered access by the public to such institutes or centers as well as their normal functioning will be assured.

50. They will assure unhindered access by the public to cultural events organized on their territory by persons or institutions from

other participating States and ensure that the organizers can use all means available in the host country to publicize such events.

51. They will facilitate and encourage direct personal contacts in the field of culture, on both an individual and a collective basis, as well as contacts between cultural institutions, associations of creative and performing artists and other organizations in order to increase the opportunities for their citizens to acquaint themselves directly with the creative work in and from other participating States.

52. They will ensure the unimpeded circulation of works of art and other cultural objects, subject only to those restrictions aimed at preserving their cultural heritage which are based on respect for intellectual and artistic property rights or derive from their international commitments on the circulation of cultural property.

53. They will encourage cooperation between and joint artistic endeavors of persons from different participating states who are engaged in cultural activities; as appropriate, facilitate specific initiatives to this end by such persons, institutions and organizations and encourage the participation of young people in such initiatives. In this context they will encourage meetings and symposia, exhibitions, festivals and tours by ensembles or companies, and research and training programs in which persons from the other participating States may also freely take part and make their contribution.

54. The replacement of persons or groups invited to participate in a cultural activity will be exceptional and subject to prior agreement by the inviting party.

55. They will encourage the holding of film weeks including, as appropriate, meetings of artists and experts as well as lectures on cinematographic art; facilitate and encourage direct contacts between film directors and producers with a view to coproducing films; and encourage cooperation in the protection of film material and the exchange of technical information and publications about the cinema.

56. They will explore the scope for computerizing bibliographies and catalogues of cultural works and productions in a standard form and disseminating them.

57. They will encourage museums and art galleries to develop direct contacts, *inter alia* with a view to organizing exhibitions, including loans of works of art, and exchanging catalogs.

58. They will renew their efforts to give effect to the provisions of the Final Act and the Madrid Concluding Document relating to less widely spoken languages. They will also encourage initiatives aimed at increasing the number of translations of literature from and into these languages and improving their quality, in particular by the

holding of workshops involving translators, authors and publishers, by the publication of dictionaries and, where appropriate, by the exchange of translators through scholarships.

59. They will ensure that persons belonging to national minorities or regional cultures on their territories can maintain and develop their own culture in all its aspects, including language, literature and religion; and that they can preserve their cultural and historical monuments and objects. . . .

Cooperation and Exchanges in the Field of Education

63. They will ensure access by all to the various types and levels of education without discrimination as to race, color, sex, language, religion, political or other opinion, national or social origin, property, birth or other status.

64. In order to encourage wider cooperation in science and education, they will facilitate unimpeded communication between universities and other institutions of higher education and research. They will also facilitate direct personal contacts, including contacts through travel, between scholars, scientists and other persons active in these fields.

65. In this context they will also ensure unimpeded access by scholars, teachers and students from the other participating States to open information material available in public archives, libraries, research institutes and similar bodies.

66. They will facilitate exchanges of schooolchildren between their countries on the basis of bilateral arrangements, where necessary, including meeting and staying with families of the host country in their homes, with the aim of acquainting schoolchildren with life, traditions and education in other participating States.

67. They will encourage their relevant government agencies or educational institutions to include, as appropriate, the Final Act as a whole in the curricula of schools and universities.

68. They will ensure that persons belonging to national minorities or regional cultures on their territories can give and receive instruction on their own culture, including instruction through parental transmission of language, religion and cultural identity to their children.

69. They will encourage their radio and television organizations to inform each other of the educational programs they produce and to consider exchanging such programs.

70. They will encourage direct contacts and cooperation between

relevant governmental institutions or organizations in the field of education and science.

71. They will encourage further cooperation and contacts between specialized institutions and experts in the field of education and rehabilitation of handicapped children. . . .

PART VII

Speeches, Policy Statements and Other Documents

Introductory Note

The issue of human rights has gained a continuing, if not consistent, place on the agenda of international issues. Yet the gap between theory and practice is still a wide one. A growing number of speeches, constitutions, U.N. resolutions, and international treaties defined the principles of human rights and promised to observe them. Virtually every regime and opposition group—sometimes the more repressive most of all—talked of its allegiance to these ideas. Yet the vast quantity of rhetoric went hand-in-hand with the worst violations of human rights in dozens of countries.

At least, however, the modern world had defined human rights as a proper way of behavior. This was a view quite different from previous decades when such principles were unknown and unacknowledged in much of the world. The practices of a government within its own territory was maintained to be no one else's business. There was even some recognition that human rights had a functional value in producing a successful, modern industrial society. In the U.S.S.R., the People's Republic of China, Poland, and elsewhere, popular support for the government and their ability to exchange ideas more freely, for example, began to be related to the society's ability to produce technical innovation, respond flexibly to citizens' needs, reduce waste, and motivate its people to work more effectively.

One important development in the post-1945 period was the extention of human rights to economic issues. This was by no means the exclusive innovation of Marxist and Third World thought, as indicated by President Franklin Roosevelt's 1944 call for an "Economic Bill of Rights." A 1968 report by José Figueres, as economist and former President of Costa Rica, evaluates these concepts within the context of Third World demands.

Human rights also became a central question in East-West relations. The Jackson Amendment to the Trade Reform Act, which tied U.S.-U.S.S.R. economic relations to Russian emigration policy, was introduced in 1972 and signed into law three years later. Soviet dissidents publicized the denial of rights in their country and pleaded for Western assistance, as in Andrei Sakharov's 1973 open letter.

The Helsinki Agreement incorporated a number of clauses supporting fundamental freedoms. Dissident groups attempted to utilize the accord, most dramatically in the Czechoslovakian Charter 77. As demonstrated in the report of the Russian Group for Implementation of the Helsinki Agreement, however, Communist governments ignored their pledges.

Within the U.S. Congress, there was strong support for using American power in support of human rights overseas. In addition to the Jackson Amendment, the Inter-American Development Bank Act and the International Security Assistance and Arms Export Control Act, both passed in 1976, sought to deny military aid and oppose loans to countries violating human rights.

President Jimmy Carter's administration launched a public campaign to support human rights, defining and explaining its scope in speeches by the President and by Secretary of State Cyrus Vance.

A number of responses were made to this program. Soviet President Leonid Brezhnev rejected Western pressure, and the new Constitution of the U.S.S.R. promised extensive human rights, many of them previously pledged—and unenforced—in the preceding 1936 Constitution. Dr. Luis Reque, former executive secretary of the Inter-American Commission on Human Rights, sought to use the Carter campaign against rights violations by many Western Hemisphere regimes. While several United States allies were unenthusiastic about Carter's initiatives, British Foreign Minister David Owen pledged his government to strongly back human rights efforts.

Other countries besides the U.S.S.R. that became particular targets in the human rights campaign include South Africa, Chili, where Catholic bishops called for more democracy under the military dictatorship, and Uganda, where the British Commonwealth passed an unprecedented resolution against President Idi Amin's reign of terror.

Many new issues appeared in the 1970s which claimed or invoked the slogan of human rights. These include the struggles for racial and sexual equality, national self-determination, equal justice under the law, environmental protection, and freedom of information, among others. Much interesting debate has taken place over the right of individuals to privacy in an increasingly intrusive society.

But the Carter Administration's human rights policy was less popular in 1981, when he left office, than it had been four years earlier. The Iranian and Nicaraguan revolutions and the Soviet invasion of Afghanistan were perceived by many Americans as indicating U.S. weakness. Human rights as interpreted by Carter, conservatives charged, had been used to undermine U.S. allies with devastating results. Perhaps the most important of these critics was Jeane Kirkpatrick, who became the Reagan Administration's ambassador to the United Nations.

In the 1980s, then, the debate became more complex. President

José Napoleón Duarte led a reformist government in El Salvador trying to maintain human rights against the challenge of Marxist guerrillas as well as rightist soldiers and death squads. A new kind of regime, the Islamic Republic of Iran, promulgated its interpretation of Islamic fundamentalist law at home, ruthlessly crushing opponents. A number of countries, including Iran, Libya, and Syria, became increasingly brazen in their assistance to international terrorism.

The neoconservative intellectual Irving Kristol charged that the concept of human rights was being manipulated for political purposes. Assistant Secretary of State Richard Schifter defended that approach in terms of American tradition. President Ronald Reagan argued that human rights criticism should focus on the U.S.S.R. and leftist dictatorships in the Third World.

Yet the new thinking about human rights that had marked the 1970s was also embodied in a set of U.S. laws, including the International Workers Rights, the Torture Victim Protection Act, and legislation opposing apartheid in South Africa. There were, however, debates on how these and other laws should be interpreted and enforced.

By the eve of the 1990s there were both positive and worrisome developments. The most inspiring developments was a mass antidictatorship, pro-democratic upsurge in the Philippines which swept Corazon Aquino, widow of a murdered opposition leader, into the presidency. There were also strong popular movements for democracy and human rights in South Korea, Argentina, and a number of other countries. Most of Latin America came under the rule of elected civilian governments though economic and other problems threatened to make this a relatively temporary situation.

Particularly startling was the new era in the Soviet Union under the leadership of Mikhail Gorbachev. His call for *glasnost* and *perestroika* was motivated by the necessity of coping with the U.S.S.R.'s severe economic problems. There was much opposition in the Communist Party and government hierarchy. The regime persisted in its efforts, both supported and criticized by dissidents like Andre Sakharov. Gorbachev had no intention of yielding political power, but Soviet society became more open than perhaps at any time since the revolution.

On the more pessimistic side, the spread of chemical and biological weapons and missiles and the reinforcement of an unapologetic doctrine of Third World dictatorship created some terrible situations. The mass murders in Cambodia during the 1970s were possibly the greatest atrocity since the Holocaust.

The eight-year-long Iran-Iraq war, for example, was marked by numerous human rights' violations. Children were pressed into frontline fighting, missiles were fired at civilian targets, prisoners of war were put under tremendous pressure to change sides, and terrorism was employed as a tool against third parties. Iraq's use of chemical weapons against its own citizens was an innovation in repression, while Iran's death threat against Salman Rushdie—whose book was deemed insulting to Islam and part of an international imperialist conspiracy—became the first global civil liberties case.

The future outlook for human rights depends on how they are defined and dealt with by individual countries and on the international political atmosphere. The seven centuries following the Magna Charta witnessed steady growth in the breadth of recognized political, social, and economic rights. The efficiency and ruthlessness of totalitarian regimes in this century have thrown into question the continuation of this progress and the optimism that has accompanied it. Powerful doctrines have arisen that seek to justify the virtue of submerging individual rights under the requirements of nation-states or of ideological goals. Technology too has sometimes been put at the service of such systems.

Despite myriad conferences and treaties, there is still little practical agreement on the boundaries of human rights. Although the trend toward broadening them in North America and in Western Europe has continued, those hoping for some mellowing of Communist regimes have often been disappointed. Many of the new Afro-Asian polities have been captured by military regimes whose treatment of their own citizens has varied from the genially arbitrary to the aggressively brutal.

Contemporary debate over human rights generally resolves itself into two categories. First, is democracy a necessary concomitant of development? Those who answer "yes" believe that the Western experience will repeat itself in this area and that individualization and human rights are embedded in the industrialization process. Others believe that such a process is blocked both by elites who wish to remain in power and by cultures whose values often conflict with the value changes that are implied by Western concepts of human rights. Some would go so far as to argue that the strains and pressures required in the mobilization of resources for modernization are antithetical to increases in human rights and representative government.

In addition to the longer-range questions, there are immediate issues for Western policymakers. Does the whole concept of a human rights policy interfere with the pursuit of national interests and of national survival? Or can the West only prosper by struggling to maintain strong and representative allied regimes with an authentic commitment to human rights? Do not democratic and popular governments make for more stable and reliable friends than dictatorships? Does not a human rights policy supply both a weapon against foes and a way of winning popular support among those still undecided? How can influence be brought to bear on allies and enemies? When does intervention, even one directed by humanitarian motivations, become overbearing or counterproductive?

Beyond and behind all of these considerations it should be reaffirmed that human rights are—in the most profound sense—a just cause. Whether the tremendous interest in human rights in the 1970s will continue is not clear; there can be no doubt that it *should* continue.

Franklin Roosevelt

Economic Bill of Rights (1944)

. . . an equally basic essential to peace is a decent standard of living for all individual men and women and children in all nations. Freedom from fear is eternally linked with freedom from want. . . .

We have come to a clear realization of the fact that true individual freedom cannot exist without economic security and independence. "Necessitous men are not freemen." People who are hungry and out of a job are the stuff of which dictatorships are made.

In our day these economic truths have become accepted as self-evident. We have accepted, so to speak, a second Bill of Rights under which a new basis of security and prosperity can be established for all—regardless of station, race, or creed.

Among these are:

The right to a useful and remunerative job in the industries, or shops or farms or mines of the Nation;

The right to earn enough to provide adequate food and clothing and recreation;

The right of every farmer to raise and sell his products at a return which will give him and his family a decent living;

The right of every businessman, large and small, to trade in an atmosphere of freedom from unfair competition and domination by monopolies at home or abroad;

The right of every family to a decent home;

The right to adequate medical care and the opportunity to achieve and enjoy good health;

The right to adequate protection from the economic fears of old age, sickness, accident, and unemployment;

The right to a good education.

All of these rights spell security. And after this war is won, we must be prepared to move forward, in the implementation of these rights, to new goals of human happiness and well-being.

America's own rightful place in the world depends in large part upon how fully these and similar rights have been carried into practice for our citizens. For unless there is security here at home, there cannot be lasting peace in the world.

One of the great American industrialists of our day—a man who has rendered yeoman service to his country in this crisis—recently emphasized the grave dangers of rightist reaction in this Nation. All clear-thinking businessmen share his concern. Indeed, if such reaction should develop—if history were to repeat itself and we were to return to the so-called normalcy of the 1920's—then it is certain that, even though we shall have conquered our enemies on the battlefields abroad, we shall have yielded to the spirit of fascism here at home.

I ask the Congress to explore the means for implementing this economic bill of rights—for it is definitely the responsibility of the Congress to do so. . . .

Nelson R. Mandela

"No Easy Walk to Freedom," Presidential Address (1953)

Since 1912 and year after year thereafter, in their homes and local areas, in provincial and national gatherings, on trains and buses, in the factories and on the farms, in cities, villages, shanty towns, schools and prisons, the African people have discussed the shameful misdeeds of those who rule the country. Year after year, they have raised their voices in condemnation of the grinding poverty of the people, the low wages, the acute shortage of land, the inhuman exploitation and the whole policy of white domination. But instead of more freedom, repression began to grow in volume and intensity and it seemed that all their sacrifices would end up in smoke and dust. Today the entire country knows that their labours were not in vain, for a new spirit and new ideas have gripped our people. Today the people speak the language of action: there is a mighty awakening among the men and women of our country and the year 1952 stands out as the year of this upsurge of national consciousness.

In June, 1952, the *African National Congress* and the *South African*

Indian Congress, bearing in mind their responsibility as the representatives of the downtrodden and oppressed people of South Africa, took the plunge and launched the Campaign for the Defiance of the Unjust Laws. Starting off in Port Elizabeth in the early hours of June 26 and with only thirty-three defiers in action and then in Johannesburg in the afternoon of the same day with one hundred and six defiers, it spread throughout the country like wild fire. Factory and office workers, doctors, lawyers, teachers, students and the clergy; Africans, Coloureds, Indians and Europeans, old and young, all rallied to the national call and defied the pass laws and the curfew and the railway apartheid regulations. At the end of the year, more than 8,000 people of all races had defied. The Campaign called for immediate and heavy sacrifices. Workers lost their jobs, chiefs and teachers were expelled from the service, doctors, lawyers and businessmen gave up their practices and businesses and elected to go to jail. Defiance was a step of great political significance. It released strong social forces which affected thousands of our countrymen. It was an effective way of getting the masses to function politically; a powerful method of voicing our indignation against the reactionary policies of the Government. It was one of the best ways of exerting pressure on the Government and extremely dangerous to the stability and security of the State. It inspired and aroused our people from a conquered and servile community of yes-men to a militant and uncompromising band of comrades-in-arms. The entire country was transformed into battle zones where the forces of liberation were locked up in immortal conflict against those of reaction and evil. Our flag flew in every battlefield and thousands of our countrymen rallied around it. We held the initiative and the forces of freedom were advancing on all fronts. It was against this background and at the height of this Campaign that we held our last annual provincial Conference in Pretoria from the 10th to the 12th of October last year. In a way, that Conference was a welcome reception of those who had returned from the battlefields and a farewell to those who were still going to action. The spirit of defiance and action dominated the entire conference.

Today we meet under totally different conditions. By the end of July last year, the Campaign had reached a stage where it had to be suppressed by the Government or it would impose its own policies on the country.

The Government launched its reactionary offensive and struck at us. Between July last year and August this year forty-seven leading members from both Congresses in Johannesburg, Port Elizabeth and Kimberley were arrested, tried and convicted for launching the Defiance Campaign and given suspended sentences ranging from three months to two years on condition that they did not again participate in the defiance of the unjust laws. In November last year, a proclamation was passed which prohibited meetings of more than ten Africans and made it an offence for any person to call upon an African to defy. Contravention of this proclamation carried a penalty of three years or a fine of three hundred pounds. In March this year the Government passed the so-called Public Safety Act which empowered it to declare a state of emergency and to create conditions which would permit the most ruthless and pitiless methods of suppressing our movement. Almost simultaneously, the Criminal Laws Amendment Act was passed which provided heavy penalties for those convicted of Defiance offences. This Act also made provision for the whipping of defiers including women. . . .

The Congresses realized that these measures created a new situation which did not prevail when the Campaign was launched in June 1952. The tide of defiance was bound to recede and we were forced to pause and to take stock of the new situation. We had to analyse the dangers that faced us, formulate plans to overcome them and evolve new plans of political struggle. A political movement must keep in touch with reality and the prevailing conditions. Long speeches, the shaking of fists, the banging of tables and strongly worded resolutions out of touch with the objective conditions do not bring about mass action and can do a great deal of harm to the organization and the struggle we serve. The masses had to be prepared and made ready for new forms of political struggle. We had to recuperate our strength and muster our forces for another and more powerful offensive against the enemy. To have gone ahead blindly as if nothing had happened would have been suicidal and stupid. The conditions under which we meet today are, therefore, vastly different. The Defiance Campaign together with its thrills and adventures has receded. The old methods of bringing about mass action through public mass meetings, press statements and leaflets calling upon the people to go to action have become extremely dangerous and difficult to use effectively. The authorities will not easily permit a meeting called under the auspices of the A.N.C., few newspapers will publish statements openly criticizing the policies of the Government and there is hardly a single printing press which will agree to print leaflets calling upon workers to embark on industrial action for fear of prosecution under the Suppression of Communism Act and similar measures. These developments require the evolution of new forms of political struggle which will make it reasonable for us to strive for action on a higher level than the Defiance Campaign. The Government, alarmed at the indomitable upsurge of national consciousness, is doing everything in its power to crush our movement by removing the genuine representatives of the people from the organizations. . . .

Meanwhile the living conditions of the people, already extremely difficult, are steadily worsening and becoming unbearable. The purchasing power of the masses is progressively declining and the cost of living is rocketing. Bread is now dearer than it was two months ago. The cost of milk, meat and vegetables is beyond the pockets of the average family and many of our people cannot afford them. The people are too poor to have enough food to feed their families and children. They cannot afford sufficient clothing, housing and medical care. They are denied the right to security in the event of unemployment, sickness, disability, old age and where these exist, they are of an extremely inferior and useless nature. Because of lack of proper medical amenities, our people are ravaged by such dreaded diseases as tuberculosis, venereal disease, leprosy, pellagra, and infantile mortality is very high. The recent state budget made provision for the increase of the cost-of-living allowances for Europeans and not a word was said about the poorest and most hard-hit section of the population—the African people. The insane policies of the Government which have brought about an explosive situation in the country have definitely scared away foreign capital from South Africa and the financial crisis through which the country is now passing is forcing many industrial and business concerns to close down, to retrench their staffs and unemployment is growing every day. The farm laborers are in a particularly dire plight. You will perhaps recall the investigations and exposures of the semi-slave conditions on the Bethal farms made in 1948 by the Reverend Michael Scott and a *Guardian* Correspondent; by the *Drum* last year and the *Advance* in April this year. You will recall how human beings, wearing only sacks with holes for their heads and arms, never given enough food to eat, slept on cement floors on cold nights with only their sacks to cover their shivering bodies. You will remember how they are woken up as early as 4 A.M. and taken to work on the fields with the *indunas sjamboking*, those who tried to straighten their backs, who felt weak and dropped down because of hunger and sheer exhaustion. You will also recall the story of human beings toiling pathetically from the early hours of the morning till sunset, fed only on mealie meal served on filthy sacks spread on the ground and eating with their dirty hands. People falling ill and never once being given medical attention. You will also recall the revolting story of a farmer who was convicted for tying a labourer by his feet from a tree and had him flogged to death, pouring boiling water into his mouth whenever he cried for water. These things which have long vanished from many parts of the world still flourish in S. A. today. None will deny that they constitute a serious challenge to Congress and we are in duty bound to find an effective remedy for these obnoxious practices.

The Government has introduced in Parliament the Native Labour (Settlement of Disputes) Bill and the Bantu Education Bill. Speaking on the Labour Bill, the Minister of Labour, Ben Schoeman, openly stated that the aim of this wicked measure is to bleed African trade unions to death. By forbidding strikes and lockouts, it deprives Africans of the one weapon the workers have to improve their position. The aim of the measure is to destroy the present African trade unions which are controlled by the workers themselves and which fight for the improvement of their working conditions in return for a Central Native Labor Board controlled by the Government and which will be used to frustrate the legitimate aspirations of the African worker. The Minister of Native Affairs, Verwoerd, has also been brutally clear in explaining the objects of the Bantu Education Bill. According to him, the aim of this law is to teach our children that Africans are inferior to Europeans. African education would be taken out of the hands of people who taught equality between black and white. When this Bill becomes law, it will not be the parents but the Department of Native Affairs which will decide whether an African child should receive higher or other education. It might well be that the children of those who criticise the Government and who fight its policies will almost certainly be taught how to drill rocks in the mines and how to plough potatoes on the farms of Bethal. High education might well be the privilege of those children whose families have a tradition of collaboration with the ruling circles.

The attitude of the Congress on these bills is very clear and unequivocal. Congress totally rejects both bills without reservation. The last provincial Conference strongly condemned the then proposed Labour Bill as a measure designed to rob the African workers of the universal right of free trade unionism and to undermine and destroy the existing African trade unions. Conference further called upon the African workers to boycott and defy the application of this sinister scheme which was calculated to further the exploitation of the African worker. To accept a measure of this nature even in a qualified manner would be a betrayal of the toiling masses. At a time when every genuine Congressite should fight unreservedly for the recognition of African trade unions and the realisation of the principle that everyone has the right to form and to join trade unions for the protection of his interests, we declare our firm belief in the principles enunciated in the Universal Declaration of Human Rights that everyone has the right to education; that education shall be directed to the full development of human personality and to the strengthening of respect for human rights and fundamental freedoms. It shall promote understanding, tolerance and friendship among the nations, racial or religious groups and shall further the activities of the United Nations for the maintenance of peace. That parents have the right to choose the kind of education that shall be given to their children.

The cumulative effect of all these measures is to prop up and perpetuate the artificial and decaying policy of the supremacy of the white men. The attitude of the government to us is that: "Let's beat them down with guns and batons and trample them under our feet. We must be ready to drown the whole country in blood if only there is the slightest chance of preserving white supremacy."

But there is nothing inherently superior about the *herrenvolk* idea of the supremacy of the whites. In China, India, Indonesia and Korea, American, British, Dutch and French Imperialism, based on the concept of the supremacy of Europeans over Asians, has been completely and perfectly exploded. In Malaya and Indo-China, British and French imperialisms are being shaken to their foundations by powerful and revolutionary national liberation movements. In Africa, there are approximately 190,000,000 Africans as against 4,000,000 Europeans. The entire continent is seething with discontent and already there are powerful revolutionary eruptions in the Gold Coast, Nigeria, Tunisia, Kenya, the Rhodesias and South Africa. The oppressed people and the oppressors are at loggerheads. *The day of reckoning* between the forces of freedom and those of reaction is not very far off. I have not the slightest doubt that when that day comes, truth and justice will prevail.

The intensification of repressions and the extensive use of the bans is designed to immobilise every active worker and to check the national liberation movement. But gone forever are the days when harsh and wicked laws provided the oppressors with years of peace and quiet. The racial policies of the Government have pricked the conscience of all men of good will and have aroused their deepest indignation. The feelings of the oppressed people have never been more bitter. If the ruling circles seek to maintain their position by such inhuman methods, then a clash between the forces of freedom and those of reaction is certain. The grave plight of the people compels them to resist to the death the stinking policies of the gangsters that rule our country. . . .

Nelson R. Mandela

Statement During the Rivonia Trial (1964)

Our fight is against real, and not imaginary, hardships, or to use the language of the State Prosecutor, "so-called hardships." Basically, we fight against two features which are the hallmarks of African life in South Africa and which are entrenched by legislation which we seek to have repealed. These features are poverty and lack of human dignity, and we do not need Communists or so-called "agitators" to teach us about these things.

South Africa is the richest country in Africa, and could be one of the richest countries in the world. But it is a land of extremes and remarkable contrasts. The Whites enjoy what may well be the highest standard of living in the world, whilst Africans live in poverty and misery. Forty percent of the Africans live in hopelessly overcrowded and, in some cases, drought-stricken reserves, where soil erosion and the overworking of the soil, make it impossible for them to live properly off the land. Thirty percent are labourers, labour tenants and squatters on White farms and work and live under conditions similar to those of the serfs of the Middle Ages. The other thirty percent live in towns where they have developed economic and social habits which bring them closer in many respects to White standards. Yet most Africans, even in this group, are impoverished by low incomes and high cost of living.

The highest paid and the most prosperous section of urban African life is in Johannesburg. Yet their actual position is desperate. The latest figures were given on the 25th March, 1964, by Mr. Carr, Manager of the Johannesburg Non-European Affairs Department. The poverty datum line for the average African family in Johannesburg (according to Mr. Carr's department) is R42.84 per month. He showed that the average monthly wage if R32.24 and that 46% of all African families in Johannesburg do not earn enough to keep them going.

Poverty goes hand in hand with malnutrition and disease. The incidence of malnutrition and deficiency diseases is very high amongst Africans. Tuberculosis, pellagra, kwashiorkor, gastroenteritis and scurvy

Source: Nelson R. Mandela, "Statement during the Rivonia Trial" (April 20, 1964).

bring death and destruction of health. The incidence of infant mortality is one of the highest in the world. According to the Medical Officer of Health for Pretoria, tuberculosis kills forty people a day (almost all Africans), and in 1961 there were 58,491 new cases reported. These diseases not only destroy the vital organs of the body, but they result in retarded mental conditions and lack of initiative, and reduce powers of concentration. The secondary results of such conditions affect the whole community and the standard of work performed by African labourers.

The complaint of Africans, however, is not only that they are poor and the Whites are rich, but that the laws which are made by the Whites are designed to preserve this situation. There are two ways to break out of poverty. The first is by formal education, and the second is by the worker acquiring a greater skill at his work and thus higher wages. As far as Africans are concerned, both these avenues of advancement are deliberately curtailed by legislation.

The present Government has always sought to hamper Africans in their search for education. One of their early acts, after coming into power, was to stop subsidies for African school feeding. Many African children, who attended schools, depended on this supplement to their diet. This was a cruel act.

There is compulsory education for all White children at virtually no cost to their parents, be they rich or poor. Similar facilities are not provided for the African children, though there are some who receive such assistance. African children, however, generally have to pay more for their schooling than Whites. According to figures quoted by the South African Institute of Race Relations in its 1963 journal, approximately 40% of African children in the age group between 7 to 14 do not attend school. For those who do attend school, the standards are vastly different from those afforded to White children. In 1960/61 the per capita Government spending on African students at State-aided schools was estimated at R12.46. In the same years, the per capita spending on White children in the Cape Province (which are the only figures available to me) was R144.57. Although there are no figures available to me, it can be stated, without doubt, that the White children on whom R144.57 per head was being spent all came from wealthier homes than African children on whom R12.46 per head was being spent.

The quality of education is also different. According to the Bantu Education Journal, only 5,660 African children in the whole of South Africa passed their J.C. in 1962, and in that year only 362 passed matric. This is presumably consistent with the policy of Bantu education about which the present Prime Minister said, during the debate on the Bantu Education Bill in 1953:—

"When I have control of Native education, I will reform it so that Natives will be taught from childhood to realise that equality with Europeans is not for them ... People who believe in equality are not desirable teachers for Natives. When my Department controls Native education it will know for what class of higher education a Native is fitted, and whether he will have a chance in life to use his knowledge."

The other main obstacle to the economic advancement of the African is the industrial colour bar under which all the better jobs of industry are reserved for Whites only. Moreover, Africans who do obtain employment in the unskilled and semi-skilled occupations which are open to them, are not allowed to form Trade Unions which have recognition under the Industrial Conciliation Act. This means that strikes of African workers are illegal, and that they are denied the right of collective bargaining which is permitted to the better-paid White workers. The discrimination in the policy of successive South African Governments towards African workers is demonstrated by the so-called "civilised labour policy" under which sheltered unskilled Government jobs are found for those White workers who cannot make the grade in industry, at wages which far exceeded the earnings of the average African employee in industry.

The Government often answers its critics by saying that Africans in South Africa are economically better off than the inhabitants of the other countries in Africa. I do not know whether this statement is true and doubt whether any comparison can be made without having regard to the cost of living index in such countries. But even if it is true, as far as the African people are concerned it is irrelevant. Our complaint is not that we are poor by comparison with people in other countries, but that we are poor by comparison with the White people in our own country, and that we are prevented by legislation from altering this imbalance.

The lack of human dignity experienced by Africans is the direct result of the policy of White supremacy. White supremacy implies Black inferiority. Legislation designed to preserve White supremacy entrenches this notion. Menial tasks in South Africa are invariably performed by Africans. When anything has to be carried or cleaned, the White man will look around for an African to do it for him, whether the African is employed by him or not. Because of this sort of attitude, Whites tend to regard Africans as a separate breed. They do not look upon them as people with families of their own; they do not realise that they have emotions—that they fall in love like White people do; that they want to be with their wives and children like White people want to be with theirs; that they want to earn enough money to support their families properly, to feed and clothe them and send them to school. And what "house-boy" or "garden-boy" or labourer can ever hope to do this?

Pass Laws, which to the Africans are among the most hated bits of legislation in South Africa, render any African liable to police surveillance at any time. I doubt whether there is a single African male in South Africa who has not at some stage had a brush with the police over his pass. Hundreds and thousands of Africans are thrown into gaol each year under pass laws. Even worse than this is the fact that pass laws keep husband and wife apart and lead to the breakdown of family life.

Poverty and the breakdown of family life have secondary effects. Children wander about the streets of the Townships because they have no schools to go to, or no money to enable them to go to school, or no parents at home to see that they go to school, because both parents (if there be two) have to work to keep the family alive. This leads to a breakdown in moral standards, to an alarming rise in illegitimacy and to growing violence which erupts, not only politically, but everywhere. Life in the townships is dangerous. There is not a day that goes by without somebody being stabbed or assaulted. And violence is carried out of the townships in the White living areas. People are afraid to walk alone in the streets after dark. Housebreakings and robberies are increasing, despite the fact that the death sentence can now be imposed for such offences. Death sentences cannot cure the festering sore.

Africans want to be paid a living wage. Africans want to perform work which they are capable of doing, and not work which the Government declares them to be capable of. Africans want to be allowed to live where they obtain work, and not be endorsed out of an area because they were not born there. Africans want to be allowed to own land in places where they work, and not to be obliged to live in rented houses which they can never call their own. Africans want to be part of the general population, and not confined to living in their own ghettos. African men want to have their wives and children to live with them where they work, and not be forced into an unnatural existence in men's hostels. African women want to be with their menfolk and not be left permanently widowed in the reserves. Africans want to be allowed out after 11 o'clock at night and not to be confined to their rooms like little children. Africans want to be allowed to travel in their own country and to seek work where they want to and not where the Labour Bureau tells them to. Africans want a just share in the whole of South Africa; they want security and a stake in society.

Above all, we want equal political rights, because without them our disabilities will be permanent. I know this sounds revolutionary to the Whites in this country, because the majority of voters will be Africans. This makes the White man fear democracy.

But this fear cannot be allowed to stand in the way of the only solution which will guarantee racial harmony and freedom for all. It is not true that the enfranchisement of all will result in racial domination. Political division, based on colour, is entirely artificial and, when it disappears, so will the domination of one colour group by another. The A.N.C. has spent half a century fighting against racialism. When it triumphs it will not change that policy. . . .

José Figueres

Some Economic Foundations of Human Rights (1968)

INTRODUCTION

1. The Secretary-General of the United Nations, in his statement to the Economic and Social Council at its forty-third session in 1967, declared that *faith in the dignity of man*, and in the equal rights of men and women, is the basic reason for the Organization to promote social progress and better standards of living for all (A/6703, introduction).

2. His statement affirms that *economic and social development* is an indispensable means to the full realization of human rights in the modern world.

3. This theme has been steadily and progressively elaborated by the United Nations and its organs during the twenty-two years of the Organization's growth.

4. There have been numerous pronouncements. The Universal Declaration of Human Rights, article 22, states that everyone is entitled to the realization of the economic, social and cultural rights indispensable for the full development of his personality. This requires national and international efforts in accordance with the resources of each State.

5. Article 23 of the Declaration recognizes the right of everyone to work, to free choice of employment, to just and favorable conditions

Official U.N. document from the International Conference on Human Rights, held at Teheran. The author is former President of Costa Rica.

of work, to protection against unemployment and to equal pay for equal work.

6. Also affirmed is the right of everyone who works to a remuneration ensuring for his family an existence consistent with human dignity. His income being supplemented, if necessary, by other means of social protection.

7. Another right proclaimed by the Declaration, article 25, is that of everyone to an adequate standard of health and well-being for himself and his family.

8. Of particular interest for the purposes of this study is article 28 of the Declaration, which states that everyone is entitled to a *social and international order* in which the rights and freedoms of the Declaration can be fully realized.

9. The Declaration on Permanent Sovereignty over Natural Resources contained in General Assembly resolution 1803 (XVII) of 14 December 1962 (article 1), provides that the rights of peoples and nations to permanent sovereignty over their natural resources must be exercised in their own interest.

10. It further states (article 2) that the exploration, development and disposition of such resources, as well as the foreign capital required for these purposes, should conform to the rules that the nations consider to be necessary for the authorization, restriction or prohibition of such activities.

11. It stipulates (article 6) that international cooperation for development, whether public or private investments, exchange of goods or services, technical assistance or exchange of scientific information shall be so conducted as to further the independent national life and the sovereignty of the developing nations.

12 The International Covenant on Economic, Social and Cultural Rights (a binding legal instrument adopted in 1966 by the General Assembly) not only contains the basic economic and social rights first enunciated in the Universal Declaration, but also in some cases strengthens and supplements them.

13. One right, however, which was omitted in the Declaration but is now included in the Covenant (article 1) states that all peoples are entitled to self-determination and may therefore freely determine their political status and the pursuit of their economic, social and cultural development. In no case may a people be deprived of its means of subsistence.

14. Article 2 (i) imposes another important obligation. Each State Party shall take steps, individually and internationally, to the maximum of its available resources, to achieve progressively the full realization of the rights recognized in the Covenant. This shall be done by

all appropriate means, including particularly the adoption of legislative measures.

15. Article 11 (1) of the International Covenant on Economic, Social and Cultural Rights, after recognizing the right of everyone to an adequate standard of living for himself and his family, goes beyond the Universal Declaration and adds that everyone has the right to the continuous improvement of living conditions.

16. Of interest to the present study is also article 11 (2) of the Covenant. It provides that the States Parties, recognizing the fundamental right of everyone to be free from hunger, commit themselves to undertake the measures and programs that may be needed to improve methods of production, conservation and distribution of *food*.

17. Among other things, agrarian systems shall be developed or reformed so as to achieve the highest utilization of natural and human resources.

18. Also, an efficient distribution of the world food supplies should be ensured, taking into account the problems of both food importing and food exporting nations.

19. Worth noting for this study is also article 23, which stipulates that international action for the purposes of the Covenant includes such methods as conventions, agreements, recommendations, international assistance, regional meetings and technical consultations organized in conjunction with the Governments concerned.

20. The preceding paragraphs illustrate the unceasing efforts of the United Nations to ensure for everyone the fullest measure of human dignity. These efforts include setting goals and standards in the economic and social spheres, and prescribing means and methods for their attainment.

21. This paper is written by one who fully shares the objectives of the United Nations, and is guided by them in his study. It is intended to serve a dual purpose, broadly speaking: (*a*) it seeks to identify the obstacles to the full enjoyment of human rights encountered in the economic and social struggles by the peoples of the less developed world; (*b*) it attempts to suggest some measures that should be taken if economic and social factors are to stop denying to those peoples their full range of human rights.

22. The nature of the subject may help explain why the body of this study contains some of the features of an essay in economics. Indeed, it may be described as a study in "The Economic Foundations of Human Rights."

I. ENUNCIATIONS

23. We live at a time when human rights have been beautifully enunciated in numerous documents, subscribed to by many nations. These enunciations, in themselves, are no small accomplishment.

24. Ethical codes have always preceded ethical conduct. A certain time is needed for education and adaptation. Even afterward, perfection is never attained.

25. The Universal Declaration of Human Rights and the Covenants are now in the period of education and adaptation. Actual life in many nations is still far behind the principles. Men tend to be impatient about the apparent slow progress, because they forget that the lives of nations, of institutions, of mankind, are longer than the lives of individuals.

26. The Latin American Republics organized themselves under democratic principles when they won their independence during the first quarter of the nineteenth century.

27. For a hundred and fifty years these societies have been in the process of education and adaptation.

28. Later the principles were vigorously reiterated in the Charter of the Organization of American States, and in the documents of several subsequent conferences. Whatever the remaining shortcomings, these countries are now relatively advanced toward democratic life. It would be inconceivable to adopt today a non-democratic credo, except by force.

29. If it had not been for the enunciation of principles that were difficult to fulfill, the progress that has been made by these nations would not exist, and probably the vices of dictatorship would be officially sanctioned today.

30. I do not mean that it will take a hundred and fifty years for the Declaration of Human Rights to be implemented throughout the world. All processes move faster in our time. I do mean, however, that we would not be discouraged by differences between principle and fact.

II. SOVEREIGNTY

31. The new nations that have emerged since the Second World War, are still in a state of mind inclined to eradicate the remnants of colonialism and to consolidate political independence or sovereignty. There is a tendency to believe that national sovereignty automatically brings personal liberties. This is not so, as Latin America has well learned through its history.

32. It takes some time to understand that independence, however

costly, should really be a means to an end. The end should be the full comprehension and enjoyment of human rights by all the people.

33. Another temporary disillusion that the emerging countries find is that independence, by itself, does not bring about economic development and social well-being.

34. Some socialists of the nineteenth century thought that general welfare was only a matter of equitable distribution of existing wealth and income, not realizing how small wealth and income were. Some of the revolutionary heroes of independence in our time, and their followers, seem to have underestimated the difficulties of development. Abundance for all the people does not come automatically with sovereignty.

35. Human rights, in their economic and social aspects, can only be achieved by a combination of high production and fair distribution. In theory at least, you could even have a society juridically so constituted that everybody enjoys civil rights and everybody is poor.

36. In actual practice, however, aspirations are so high in all modern countries that you cannot maintain political stability in the unrest provoked by the lack of fulfillment of human wants.

III. ECONOMIC RIGHTS

37. The two Covenants of the United Nations correctly equate economic and social rights with civil and political rights.

38. The dignity of man is not respected, by himself or by others, when he is not allowed to earn a decent living. By the same token, in the international field a nation is not sufficiently respected, whatever her political independence, while her work and her trade with other nations do not allow her fully to support all her citizens.

39. The provision of an adequate standard of living for all members of society requires a high degree of economic development.

40. Before the Industrial Revolution such abundance of goods and services would have been unthinkable. It was tacitly agreed, except by some reformers, that the work of the community could only produce the welfare of a privileged minority. Today, for the first time in human history, some countries are producing enough for practically all their citizens.

41. The poorer nations, which still constitute the majority of mankind, want to do likewise. They want to develop.

42. It is of common interest to all peoples, and to the harmony of the human family, that these retarded nations should develop. The economic and social rights cannot be universally fulfilled until the necessary amount of goods and services are produced by all nations.

IV. INTERNAL OBSTACLES

43. In their development efforts, poor countries encounter two sets of difficulties: internal and international. The internal obstacles to development are, among others, the following:

44. Lack of capital, which is a consequence of insufficient savings, and in turn, of low income; deficient technology; improper land tenure and tax systems; rapid population growth; poor general education; bad health, largely caused by malnutrition.

45. It would be hard to tell which of these internal deficiencies is more serious. They all cause one another in a series of vicious circles. Some people mention political instability first. I wonder if political instability is not also the effect of the other deficiencies.

V. INTERNATIONAL OBSTACLES

46. The international causes of underdevelopment are less generally recognized. Small nations cannot develop without an intense trade with the advanced countries, (*a*) because their people want to consume the products of foreign industry or agriculture; (*b*) because industrialization requires capital goods produced in the developed countries; and (*c*) because indispensable services such as communications and transportation are largely the property of the rich countries.

47. The poor countries have to pay for all three—consumer goods, capital goods, services—with their natural resources, such as minerals, and with their agricultural labor turned into a few commodities like coffee, tea, cocoa, bananas and sugar.

48. There is a close association between human rights and the objectives of the United Nations Conference on Trade and Development, established in New York and Geneva in 1964. The Conference was convened for the purpose of studying trade between the rich and poor countries, and to try to find means of correcting the trends that are widening the gap between the two groups.

49. Trade between rich and poor nations *could* be an instrument of uniform world development. If economic and social rights were universally effective, one hour of human work spent in one country would be traded for one hour spent in another. This rule, still a distant goal, would give most retarded countries sufficient foreign income for their development.

VI. PRODUCTIVITY

50. There are activities in which the product of one hour of work depends largely on the amount of capital investment behind the worker. Also, on the amount of applied technology. A trained driver

with a power shovel moves a hundred times more earth than a laborer with a hand shovel.

51. When a poor nation can export products in which investment and technology increase production per man-hour of work, it should be the common interest of both traders, the buying and the selling countries, to make such capital and such knowledge available.

52. The field for improvement of productivity through larger investment is more restricted in agriculture than in industry. Little more could be done to improve the advanced methods already applied in some areas to the production of coffee, tea, cocoa, bananas. Yet, when the coffee farmer buys a truck from an industrial country, he exchanges hours of work at the rate of ten or twenty to one.

53. Internally, in an advanced society, there are activities where productivity per man-hour has increased greatly, like the steel industry. There are other activities where there has been no increased productivity, like the work of the barber, or, for that matter, the teacher or the musician. Logically, the compensation has increased more or less uniformly for the steelworker and for the barber, thus relating wages to the productivity of the whole economy, and not of a particular activity. The barber who serves the steelworker, indirectly produces steel also. This is in accord with the aspirations of the economic and social rights.

54. In an integrated mankind, the same principles should apply internationally. Fantastic as it may sound in our time, there is no moral reason why the Colombian laborer who supplies the Detroit worker who makes his truck, with his morning cup of coffee, should earn less (sometimes twenty times less) than his northern colleague. The fair rule should be 'equal pay for equal effort'.

VII. SLAVE LABOR

55. The advanced societies of today abhor even the remnants of slave labor. Minimum wage legislation prevents the economically strong employer from hiring cheap labor, when labor is weak. No low wages for foreign workers are allowed. The United States, with a legal minimum wage of $1.50 an hour, could import millions and millions of laborers for one third that legal wage. Such bargain is prevented not only by the power of the trade unions, but also by the moral sense of the nation, expressed in its legislation. It would be contrary to the economic and social rights of man.

56. Yet, the toil of countless workers at cheap wages is imported to the rich countries in the form of raw materials or primary products, particularly agricultural products. "Free trade" is allowed between private importers who bargain from the strength of a rich economy, and private exporters who are part of the weakness of a poor economy.

57. Private exporters in poor countries are not responsible for the well-being of their people. Their interest is to have a margin between what they pay to local producers and workers, and the price they get from foreign importers. They continue to do a good business, at any level of prices and wages, unintentionally retarding economic development and social improvement.

58. This shows the need of more study for reasonable regulations of international trade, at least in the relation between rich and poor nations.

59. Such trade might to some extent be entrusted to public institutions with a social responsibility. Or it could be regulated by such means as the International Wheat Agreement which, in times of surplus, has protected the farming communities against undeliberate exploitation in international trade.

60. The goal might be: when two or more countries trade intensely, supplying each other with needed goods and services, their joint economies should provide uniformly adequate standards of living for all their people.

VIII. Surpluses

61. Surpluses of certain commodities are one of the paradoxes of our time, when two thirds of mankind suffer from scarcities of nearly everything.

62. In the rich countries, agricultural surpluses are the result of market stabilization programs, without which the development of the rural areas would have been impossible. Large though this problem is sometimes thought to be, it is really small by comparison to the problem of export surpluses in poor countries.

63. For the less developed nations, the prices of a few exports, easily depressed by overproduction, are a question of development or stagnation. And stagnation produces social and political unrest, with all the chain reaction of ill effects.

64. The anomaly is that even at the present (1967) depressed prices, the tendency continues to overproduction in coffee and other tropical products. As the economic situation in the producing countries deteriorates, the prices of other crops diminish and the temptation increases to produce more coffee.

65. Furthermore, the tendency to consume imported articles is growing constantly, spurred by the variety of desirable gadgets from the industrial countries, by advertising and by installment payment sales. All this has negative effects on developing societies.

66. Neither the balance of payments nor the economy as a whole can afford to have too many people rapidly improving their standard of living at the same time. Color television in one family deprives

several families of the bare essentials of life. This is one of the effects of trade between rich and poor nations.

IX. DIVERSIFICATION

67. The other effect of overstimulated consumption for commercial aims in the poor countries is a tendency to further overproduce coffee, cocoa, tea, as the only possible means of payment for increasing imports. This depresses prices even more, and the vicious circle goes on.

68. It is easy to recommend crop diversification and industrialization. Yet substitute crops for coffee, for example, are extremely difficult to find. Latitude, altitude, the rain system, soil, the local culture of whole societies that have grown together with coffee culture, all these factors present great obstacles to change. There are some flat areas of Brazil where coffee can be changed for something else at a bearable cost. Over one billion trees have been uprooted there. But on the hills of Columbia, the five Central American countries and others, nobody has found even a half-economical way of substituting crops.

69. Industrialization is going on everywhere at the slow pace permitted by the low prices of exports. It will be a long uphill effort. . . .

XXI. CONCLUSION

141. I have read the documents that tell the story of the accomplishments of the United Nations in the field of human rights.

142. While a long road lies ahead in this field of man's progress, those achievements, that some persons might be tempted to regard as modest, plus the undoubtable greatness and permanency of the Declaration and the Covenants, make the last two decades of initiation in human rights the best spent period in the history of mankind.

143. Much that I have said in this paper belongs to the realm of enunciations. More ideas, more time, more education, more adaptation will be needed. Yet, the rate of progress is an accelerating movement.

144. According to these views, the fulfillment of human rights *requires* economic and social development.

145. Development requires not only corrections to the internal causes of poverty in the retarded nations, but also a full revision of all economic relations with the advanced countries.

146. Since several of these relations are difficult to change, an overall compensation may have to be given for a time, in the form of increased foreign aid.

147. The increase in foreign aid may be dependent on the reduction of war expenses. This is no surprise. Human rights and world peace

dwell side by side in the hearts of men. The United Nations is endeavoring to achieve both.

148. Peace will help development. Development will engender peace. They are both causes and effects. They strengthen each other. Their common goal is the reign of human rights.

The Jackson Amendment to the Trade Reform Act (1972)

EAST-WEST TRADE AND FREEDOM OF EMIGRATION

Sec. 507. (a) To assure the continued dedication of the United States to fundamental human rights, and notwithstanding any other provision of this Act or any other law, after October 25, 1972, no nonmarket economy country shall be eligible to receive most-favored-nation treatment or to participate in any program of the Government of the United States which extends credits or credit guarantees or investment guarantees, directly or indirectly, during the period beginning with the date on which the President of the United States determines that such country—

1. denies its citizens the right or opportunity to emigrate; or

2. imposes more than a nominal tax on emigration or on the visas or other documents required for emigration, for any purpose or cause whatsoever; or

3. imposes more than a nominal tax, levy, fine, or other charge on any citizen as a consequence of the desire of such citizen to emigrate to the country of his choice and ending on the date on which the President determines that such country is no longer in violation of paragraph (1), (2), or (3).

(b) After October 15, 1972, a nonmarket economy country may participate in a program of the Government of the United States which extends credits or credit guarantees or investment guarantees, and shall be eligible to receive most-favored-nation treatment, only after the President of the United States has submitted to the Congress a report indicating that such country is not in violation of paragraph (1), (2), or (3) of subsection (a). Such report with respect to such country, shall include information as to the nature and implementation of emigration laws and policies and restrictions or discrimination applied to or against persons wishing to emigrate. The report required by this subsection shall be submitted initially as provided herein and semiannually thereafter so long as any agreement entered into pursuant to the exercise of such authority is in effect.

Andrei Sakharov

Open Letter to the United States Congress (1973)

Moscow. At a time when the Congress is debating fundamental issues of foreign policy, I consider it my duty to express my view on one such issue—protection of the right to freedom of residence within the country of one's choice. That right was proclaimed by the United Nations in 1948 in the Universal Declaration of Human Rights.

If every nation is entitled to choose the political system under which it wishes to live, this is true all the more of every individual person. A country whose citizens are deprived of this minimal right is not free even if there were not a single citizen who would want to exercise that right.

But, as you know, there are tens of thousands of citizens in the Soviet Union—Jews, Germans, Russians, Ukrainians, Lithuanians, Armenians, Estonians, Latvians, Turks and members of other ethnic groups—who want to leave the country and who have been seeking to exercise that right for years and for decades at the cost of endless difficulty and humiliation.

You know that prisons, labor camps and mental hospitals are full of people who have sought to exercise this legitimate right.

You surely know the name of the Lithuanian, Simas A. Kudirka, who was handed over to the Soviet authorities by an American vessel, as well as the names of the defendants in the tragic 1970 hijacking trial in Leningrad. You know about the victims of the Berlin Wall.

There are many more lesser known victims. Remember them, too!

For decades the Soviet Union has been developing under conditions of an intolerable isolation, bringing with it the ugliest consequences. Even a partial preservation of those conditions would be highly perilous for all mankind, for international confidence and detente.

In view of the foregoing, I am appealing to the Congress of the United States to give its support to the Jackson Amendment, which represents in my view and in the view of its sponsors an attempt to protect the right of emigration of citizens in countries that are entering into new and friendlier relations with the United States.

The Jackson Amendment is made even more significant by the fact that the world is only just entering on a new course of detente and it is therefore essential that the proper direction be followed at the outset. This is a fundamental issue, extending far beyond the question of emigration.

Those who believed that the Jackson Amendment is likely to undermine anyone's personal or governmental prestige are wrong. Its provisions are minimal and not demeaning.

It should be no surprise that the democratic process can add its corrective to the actions of public figures who negotiate without admitting the possibility of such an amendment. The amendment does not represent interference in the internal affairs of socialist countries, but simply a defense of international law, without which there can be no mutual trust.

Adoption of the amendment therefore cannot be a threat to Soviet-American relations. All the more, it would not imperil international detente.

There is a particular silliness in objections to the amendment that are founded on the alleged fear that its adoption would lead to outbursts of anti-Semitism in the U.S.S.R. and hinder the emigration of Jews.

Here you have total confusion, either deliberate or based on ignorance about the U.S.S.R. It is as if the emigration issue affected only Jews. As if the situation of those Jews who have vainly sought to emigrate to Israel was not already tragic enough and would become even more hopeless if it were to depend on the democratic attitudes and on the humanity of OVIR [the Soviet visa agency]. As if the techniques of "quiet diplomacy" could help anyone, beyond a few individuals in Moscow and some other cities.

The abandonment of a policy of principle would be a betrayal of the thousands of Jews and non-Jews who want to emigrate, of the hundreds in camps and mental hospitals, of the victims of the Berlin Wall.

Such a denial would lead to stronger repressions on ideological grounds. It would be tantamount to total capitulation of democratic principles in face of blackmail, deceit and violence. The consequences of such a capitulation for international confidence, detente and the entire future of mankind are difficult to predict.

I express the hope that the Congress of the United States, reflecting the will and the traditional love of freedom of the American people, will realize its historical responsibility before mankind and will find the strength to rise above temporary partisan considerations of commercialism and prestige.

I hope that the Congress will support the Jackson Amendment.

(signed) A. SAKHAROV.

Czechoslovakian Charter 77 Declaration (1976)

On 13 October 1976 the Collection of Laws of the C.S.S.R. (no. 120) published the "International Pact on Civil and Political Rights" and the "International Pact on Economic, Social and Cultural Rights" which had been signed in the name of our Republic in 1968, confirmed in Helsinki in 1975, and which acquired validity here on 23 March 1976. From that day our citizens have the right and our State the duty to be guided by them.

The freedoms and rights of people which are guaranteed by these pacts are important values of civilisation for which the efforts of many progressive forces have been directed in history and their statement in law can significantly assist human development in our society.

We therefore welcome the fact that the Czechoslovak Socialist Republic has entered into these pacts.

Their publication, however, reminds us with new urgency how many fundamental civil rights remain, unfortunately, only on paper in our country.

Quite illusory, for instance, is the right to freedom of expression, guaranteed by Article 19 of the first pact: tens of thousands of citizens are prevented from working in their occupations merely because they hold views differing from the official views. At the same time they are often subjected to all kinds of discrimination and harassment by the authorities and public organisations; deprived of all means to defend themselves, they are, in effect, the victims of a type of apartheid.

Hundreds of thousands of further citizens are denied "freedom from fear" (preamble to the first pact) because they are obliged to live in permanent danger of losing the opportunity to work, and other opportunities, if they voice their views.

In conflict with Article 13 of the second pact, ensuring the right to education for all, numerous young people are prevented from studying purely on account of their views, or even the views of their parents. Countless citizens have to live in fear that if they were to express themselves in accordance with their convictions, they or their children could be denied the right to education.

Exercising the right "to seek, receive and spread information and ideas of all kinds, regardless of frontiers, orally, in writing or in print" or "through art" (point 2, Article 19 of the first pact) is attacked not only extrajudicially, but also judicially, often in the guise of criminal prosecution (witness to this are, for instance, the trials of young musicians now proceeding).

Freedom of public expression is suppressed by the central control over all communications media and publishing and cultural facilities. No political, philosophical, scientific or artistic expression which however slightly deviates from the official ideological or aesthetic bounds can be published; public criticism of crisis symptoms in society is barred; there is no opportunity for public defence against false and offensive accusations by official propaganda (the legal protection against "attacks on honour and reputation," explicitly guaranteed by Article 17 of the first pact, does not exist in practice); false accusations cannot be refuted and every attempt to get restitution through the courts is in vain; open debate in the area of intellectual and cultural work is excluded. Many scholars and cultural workers and other citizens are discriminated against merely because in earlier years they legally or openly voiced opinions which are condemned by the present political power.

The freedom of religious confession, emphatically guaranteed by Article 18 of the first pact, is systematically restricted by arbitrary authority: by curtailing the activities of priests, who are permanently threatened by the possibility that state consent to the performance of their office may be refused or withdrawn; by job or other sanctions against those who express their religious beliefs in word or deed; by suppressing religious teaching etc.

As an instrument for restricting, and often completely suppressing, many civil rights we have the system whereby, in effect, all institutions and organisations of state are subordinated to the political directives from the apparatus of the ruling party and to the decisions of individuals influential in the power structure. The Constitution of the C.S.S.R. and the other laws and legal norms give no authority either for the content and form, nor for the making and application of such decisions; they are often purely verbal, entirely unknown to citizens, and uncontrollable by them; their originators are responsible to none but themselves and their hierarchy, yet they exert a decisive influence on the legislative and executive organs of state administration, the judiciary, the trade unions, organisations around special interest and other public organisations, other political parties, enterprises, factories, institutes, offices, and other establishments, and their orders take precedence over the law. When an organisation or individual comes into conflict with such an order in their interpretation of their rights and duties, they cannot turn to an impartial institution, because none exists. All this gravely limits the rights deriving from Articles 21 and 22 of the first pact (the right of association and the prohibition of any restriction on implementing it) and Article 25 (the equal right to share in managing public affairs), Article 26 (excluding all discrimination before the law). The present situation also prevents workers and other employees from establishing, without restriction trade union and other organisations to protect their economic and social interests and freely to exercise the right to strike (point 1, Article 8 of the second pact).

Other civil rights, including the explicit prohibition of "arbitrary interference in private life, in the family, home or correspondence" (Article 17 of the first pact), are also gravely infringed by the many ways in which the Ministry of the Interior controls citizens' lives, for instance by tapping telephones, listening devices in homes, checking on mail, personal surveillance, house searches, forming a network of informers from among the public (often won over by impermissable threats, or promises) etc. The Ministry also frequently intervenes in employers' decisions, inspires discriminatory actions by official bodies and organisations, campaigns in the media. This activity is not regulated by law, it is secret and the citizen has no defence against it.

In cases of politically motivated prosecution, the examining and judicial organs infringe the rights of the accused and of their defence, although these are guaranteed by Article 14 of the first pact and Czechoslovak law. People convicted in this manner are treated in prison in a way which denies their human dignity, endangers their health and attempts to break them morally.

There is also a general infringement of point 2 of Article 12 of the first pact, which guarantees the right of the citizen to leave his country; under the pretext of "protecting national security" (point 3), this right is tied to various impermissible conditions. Arbitrary procedure is also employed in issuing entry visas to foreign nationals, many of whom are unable to visit Czechoslovakia merely because they have had working or friendly contacts with people who are discriminated against here.

Some citizens call attention to the constant infringement of human rights and democratic freedoms—either privately at their places of work, or publicly, which is possible in practice only through the foreign media—and demand remedy in concrete cases; but their voices usually get no response, or they become the subjects of investigation.

The responsibility for maintaining civil rights in the land belongs, of course, to the political and state power. But not to it alone. Everyone bears their share of responsibility for public matters, and hence also for the observance of pacts valid in law, which are, in any case, binding not only on governments but on all citizens.

The sense of this co-responsibility, the belief in the meaning of the citizens' commitment, the will for it, and the common need to seek a new and more effective expression of it, has led us to think of drawing up CHARTER 77, the origin of which we are publicly announcing today.

CHARTER 77 is a free, informal and open association of people of varied opinions, varied beliefs and professions, who are united by the will individually and jointly to work for the respecting of civil and human rights in our country and in the world—the rights which both the international pacts recognise for man, the final act of the Helsinki conference, various other international documents against war, force and social and spiritual oppression, and which are stated in sum in the United Nations General Declaration on Human Rights.

CHARTER 77 is rooted in the solidarity and friendship of people who share a concern for the ideals which they have seen, and still see, as part of their lives and work.

CHARTER 77 is not an organisation, it has no statues, no permanent bodies or formally organised membership. Anyone who agrees with its ideas, takes part in its work and supports it belongs to it.

CHARTER 77 is not a basis for activity as a political opposition. It aims to serve the general interest as do many similar initiatives by citizens in various countries in the West and the East. Thus it is not intended to put forward its own programmes of political or social reform or changes, but to conduct in its sphere a constructive dialogue with the political and state power, especially by calling attention to various cases where human and civil rights are infringed, to propose solutions, submit more general proposals aimed at strengthening these rights and their guarantees, to act as an intermediary in possible conflict situations which may be caused by the lack of political rights, etc.

By its symbolical name CHARTER 77 stresses its origin on the threshold of a year declared as the year of political prisoners and in which the Belgrade conference is to examine how the Helsinki undertakings have been implemented.

As signatories to his declaration, we empower Prof. Dr. Jan Patocka, Dr. h.c. Vaclav Havel and Prof. Jiri Hajek DrSc to be spokesmen for CHARTER 77. These spokesmen are authorised to represent the Charter both in relation to state and other organisations, and to the public here and abroad, and they guarantee by their signatures the authenticity of the documents. In us, and in other citizens who join in, they will have their associates who will take part with them in any necessary negotiations, will undertake specific tasks and will share all responsibility with them.

We believe that CHARTER 77 will contribute to enabling all Czechoslovak citizens to live and work as free people.

One Year After Helsinki: A Group of Soviet Citizens' Reports (1976)

During the first months following the Conference in Helsinki, official offices concerned with questions of emigration from the U.S.S.R. simply ignored the humanitarian articles of the Final Act. Those who referred to this Declaration were told that it had nothing to do with emigration to Israel inasmuch as Israel did not sign it, or that since their name was not mentioned in the Declaration there was no use in referring to the document. Subsequently, however, as the attention of the West to the problem of human rights in the U.S.S.R. grew, this approach was changed. On February 16, 1976, the deputy head of the Department of Administrative Organs of the CPSU Central Committee, at a meeting with Jews seeking to emigrate to Israel, stated that Soviet authorities intended to fulfill and were fulfilling their international obligations without, however, harming the state. He emphasized that with regard to settling the issue of reunification of families, just as with other issues connected with human rights, Soviet organs operate on the principle that "the interests of the state are higher than human rights."

Finally, in June, Vladimir Obidin, the head of the All-Union OVIR, explained that the competent Soviet organs, in granting permission to emigrate from the U.S.S.R, would be strictly guided by the Final Act of the Helsinki Conference and would give visas only for the reunification of families and that, in accordance with the Code on Marriage and the Family, only spouses and their unmarried children would be considered as a family. Refusals because of "an insufficient degree of kinship" are now becoming as common a phenomenon as those "for reasons of secrecy." In this way the Final Act of the Helsinki Conference has become a fulcrum for . . . the restriction of emigration.

There is no need to expound on the hypocrisy of such an interpretation of the Helsinki Declaration, the humanitarian articles of which are aimed at the liberalization of emigration policy. This is corroborated as well by the obligation of the participants of the Helsinki Conference to act in accordance with the aims and principles of the Declaration of Human Rights and the Covenant on Civil and Political Rights, which directly affirm the right of every individual to leave any country, including his own. Furthermore, the actions of the Soviet authorities are inconsistent even given their unique interpretation of the question of the reunification of families, since there are cases of refusals of emigration to family members recognized as such by the Soviet Code on Marriage and the Family (see Document No. 5 of the Group).

It is necessary to emphasize that the intolerable interpretation of the Final Act that the authorities now embrace makes leaving the country impossible for Soviet citizens who wish to emigrate not for reasons of family reunification, but for religious, political, national, professional, and other reasons.

The Inter-American Development Bank Act (1976)

SECTION 28

a. The United States Executive Director of the Bank is authorized and directed to vote against any loan, any extension of financial assistance, or any technical assistance to any country which engages in a consistent pattern of gross violations of internationally recognized human rights, including torture or cruel, inhumane, or degrading treatment or punishment, prolonged detention without charges, or other flagrant denial of the right of life, liberty, and the security of person, unless such assistance will directly benefit the needy people in such country.

The International Security Assistance and Arms Export Control Act (1976)

SECTION 502B. HUMAN RIGHTS.

(a)(1) It is the policy of the United States, in accordance with its international obligations as set forth in the Charter of the United Nations and in keeping with the constitutional heritage and traditions of the United States, to promote and encourage increased respect for human rights and fundamental freedoms for all without distinction as to race, sex, language, or religion. To this end, a principal goal of the foreign policy of the United States is to promote the increased observance of internationally recognized human rights by all countries.

(2) It is further the policy of the United States that, except under

circumstances specified in this section, no security assistance may be provided to any country the government of which engages in a consistent pattern of gross violations of internationally recognized human rights.

(3) In furtherance of the foregoing policy the President is directed to formulate and conduct international security assistance programs of the United States in a manner which will promote and advance human rights and avoid identification of the United States, through such programs, with governments which deny to their people internationally recognized human rights and fundamental freedoms, in violation of international law or in contravention of the policy of the United States as expressed in this section or otherwise.

(b) The Secretary of State shall transmit to the Congress, as part of the presentation materials for security assistance programs proposed for each fiscal year, a full and complete report, prepared with the assistance of the Coordinator for Human Rights and Humanitarian Affairs, with respect to practices regarding the observance of and respect for internationally recognized human rights in each country proposed as a recipient of security assistance. In determining whether a government falls within the provisions of subsection (a) (3) and in the preparation of any report or statement required under this section, consideration shall be given to—

(1) the relevant findings of appropriate international organizations, including nongovernmental organizations, such as the International Committee of the Red Cross; and

(2) the extent of cooperation by such government in permitting an unimpeded investigation by any such organization of alleged violations of internationally recognized human rights.

(c)(1) Upon the request of the Senate or the House of Representatives by resolution of either such House, or upon the request of the Committee on Foreign Relations of the Senate or the Committee on International Relations of the House of Representatives, the Secretary of State shall, within thirty days after receipt of such request, transmit to both such committees a statement, prepared with the assistance of the Coordinator for Human Rights and Humanitarian Affairs, with respect to the country designated in such request, setting forth—

(A) all the available information about observance of and respect for human rights and fundamental freedom in that country, and a detailed description of practices by the recipient government with respect thereto;

(B) the steps the United States has taken to—

(i) promote respect for and observance of human rights in that country and discourage any practices which are inimical to internationally recognized human rights, and

(ii) publicly or privately call attention to, and disassociate the United States and any security assistance provided for such country from, such practices;

(C) whether, in the opinion of the Secretary of State, notwithstanding any such practices—

(i) extraordinary circumstances exist which necessitate a continuation of security assistance for such country, and, if so, a description of such circumstances and the extent to which such assistance should be continued (subject to such conditions as Congress may impose under this section), and

(ii) on all the facts it is in the national interest of the United States to provide such assistance; and

(D) such other information as such committee or such House may request.

Cyrus Vance

Law Day Speech on Human Rights and Foreign Policy (1977)

. . . I speak today about the resolve of this Administration to make the advancement of human rights a central part of our foreign policy.

Many here today have long been advocates of human rights within our own society. And throughout our Nation that struggle for civil rights continues.

In the early years of our civil rights movement, many Americans treated the issue as a "Southern" problem. They were wrong. It was and is a problem for all of us. Now, as a Nation, we must not make a comparable mistake. Protection of human rights is a challenge for all countries, not just for a few.

Our human rights policy must be understood in order to be effective. So today I want to set forth the substance of that policy and the results we hope to achieve.

Our concern for human rights is built upon ancient values. It looks with hope to a world in which liberty is not just a great cause but the common condition. In the past it may have seemed sufficient to put our name to international documents that spoke loftily of human rights. That is not enough. We will go to work, alongside other people and governments, to protect and enhance the dignity of the individual.

Let me define what we mean by "human rights."

First, there is the right to be free from governmental violation of the integrity of the person. Such violations include torture; cruel, inhuman, or degrading treatment or punishment; and arbitrary arrest or imprisonment. And they include denial of fair public trial, and invasion of the home.

Second, there is the right to the fulfillment of such vital needs as food, shelter, health care, and education. We recognize that the fulfillment of this right will depend, in part, upon the stage of a nation's economic development. But we also know that this right can be violated by a Government's action or inaction—for example, through corrupt official processes which divert resources to an elite at the expense of the needy, or through indifference to the plight of the poor.

Third, there is the right to enjoy civil and political liberties—freedom of thought, of religion, of assembly; freedom of speech; freedom of the press; freedom of movement both within and outside one's own country; freedom to take part in government.

Our policy is to promote all these rights. They are all recognized in the Universal Declaration of Human Rights, a basic document which the United States helped fashion and which the United Nations approved in 1948. There may be disagreement on the priorities these rights deserve, but I believe that, with work, all of these rights can become complementary and mutually reinforcing.

The philosophy of our human rights policy is revolutionary in the intellectual sense, reflecting our Nation's origin and progressive values. As Archibald MacLeish wrote during our Bicentennial a year ago, "The cause of human liberty is now the one great revolutionary cause. . . ."

President Carter put it this way in his speech before the United Nations:

> . . . All the signatories of the United Nations Charter have pledged themselves to observe and respect basic human rights. Thus, no member of the United Nations can claim that mistreatment of its citizens is solely its own business. Equally, no member can avoid its responsibilities to review and to speak when torture or unwarranted deprivation occurs in any part of the world. . . .

Since 1945 international practice has confirmed that a nation's obligations to respect human rights is a matter of concern in international law.

Our obligations under the U.N. Charter is written into our own legislation. For example, our Foreign Assistance Act now reads: "A principal goal of the foreign policy of the United States is to promote the increased observance of internationally recognized human rights by all countries." In these ways our policy is in keeping with our tradition, our international obligations, and our laws.

In pursuing a human rights policy, we must always keep in mind the limits of our power and of our wisdom. A sure formula for defeat of our goals would be a rigid, hubristic attempt to impose our values on others. A doctrinaire plan of action would be as damaging as indifference.

We must be realistic. Our country can only achieve our objectives if we shape what we do to the case at hand. In each instance we will consider these questions as we determine whether and how to act:

First, we will ask ourselves, what is the nature of the case that confronts us? For example, what kind of violations or deprivations are there? What is their extent? Is there a pattern to the violations? If so, is the trend toward concern for human rights or away from it? What is the degree of control and responsibility of the Government involved? And, finally, is the Government willing to permit independent, outside investigation?

A second set of questions concerns the prospects for effective action. Will our action be useful in promoting the overall cause of human rights? Will it actually improve the specific conditions at hand? Or will it be likely to make things worse instead? Is the country involved receptive to our interest and efforts? Will others work with us, including official and private international organizations dedicated to furthering human rights? Finally, does our sense of values and decency demand that we speak out or take action anyway, even though there is only a remote chance of making our influence felt?

We will ask a third set of questions in order to maintain a sense of perspective. Have we steered away from the self-righteous and strident, remembering that our own record is not unblemished? Have we been sensitive to genuine security interests, realizing that outbreak of armed conflict or terrorism could in itself pose a serious threat to human rights? Have we considered all the rights at stake? If, for instance, we reduce aid to a Government which violates the political rights of its citizens, do we not risk penalizing the hungry and poor who bear no responsibility for the abuses of their Government?

If we are determined to act, the means available range from quiet diplomacy in its many forms through public pronouncements to withholding of assistance. Whenever possible, we will use positive steps of encouragement and inducement. Our strong support will go to countries that are working to improve the human condition. We will always try to act in concert with other countries through international bodies.

In the end, a decision whether and how to act in the cause of human rights is a matter for informed and careful judgment. No mechanistic formula produces an automatic answer.

It is not our purpose to intervene in the internal affairs of other countries, but as the President has emphasized, no member of the United Nations can claim that violation of internationally protected human rights is solely its own affair. It is our purpose to shape our policies in accord with our beliefs and to state them without stridency or apology when we think it is desirable to do so.

Our policy is to be applied within our society as well as abroad. We welcome constructive criticism at the same time as we offer it.

No one should suppose that we are working in a vacuum. We place great weight on joining with others in the cause of human rights. The U.N. system is central to this cooperative endeavor. That is why the President stressed the pursuit of human rights in his speech before the General Assembly last month. That is why he is calling for U.S. ratification of four important human rights covenants and conventions, and why we are trying to strengthen the human rights machinery within the United Nations.

And that is an important reason why we have moved to comply with U.N. sanctions against Rhodesia. In one of our first acts, this Administration sought and achieved repeal of the Byrd amendment, which had placed us in violation of these sanctions and thus in violation of international law. We are supporting other diplomatic efforts within the United Nations to promote basic civil and political rights in Namibia and throughout southern Africa.

Regional organizations also play a central role in promoting human rights. The President has announced that the United States will sign and seek Senate approval of the American Convention on Human Rights. We will continue to work to strengthen the machinery of the Inter-American Commission on Human Rights. This will include efforts to schedule regular visits to all members of the Organization of American States, annual debates on human rights conditions, and the expansion of the inter-American educational program on human rights.

The United States is seeking increased consultation with other nations for joint programs on economic assistance and more general efforts to promote human rights. We are working to assure that our efforts reach out to all, with particular sensitivity to the problems of women.

We will meet in Belgrade later this year to review implementation of the Final Act of the Conference on Security and Cooperation in Europe—the so-called Helsinki conference. We will take this occasion to work for progress there on important human issues: family reunification, binational marriages, travel for personal and professional reasons, and freer access to information.

The United States looks to use of economic assistance—whether bilateral or through international financial institutions—as a means to foster basic human rights.

- We have proposed a 20 percent increase in U.S. foreign economic assistance for Fiscal Year 1978.
- We are expanding the program of the Agency of International Development for "new initiatives in human rights" as a complement to present efforts to get the benefits of our aid to those most in need abroad.
- The programs of the U.S. Information Agency and the State Department's Bureau of Educational and Cultural Affairs stress support for law in society, a free press, freedom of communication, an open educational system, and respect for ethnic diversity.

This Administration's human rights policy has been framed in collaboration and consultation with Congress and private organizations. We have taken steps to assure firsthand contact, consultation, and observation when members of Congress travel abroad to review human rights conditions.

We are implementing current laws that bring human rights considerations directly into our decisions in several international financial institutions. At the same time, we are working with the Congress to find the most effective way to fulfill our parallel commitment to international cooperation in economic development.

In accordance with human rights provisions of legislation governing our security assistance programs, we recently announced cuts in military aid to several countries.

Outside the Government, there is much that can be done. We welcome the efforts of individual American citizens and private organizations—such as religious, humanitarian, and professional groups—to work for human rights with commitments of time, money, and compassion.

All these initiatives to further human rights abroad would have a hollow ring if we were not prepared to improve our own performance at home. So we have removed all restrictions on our citizens' travel abroad and are proceeding with plans to liberalize our visa policies.

We support legislation and administrative action to expand our refugee and asylum policies and to permit more victims of repressive regimes to enter the United States. During this last year, the United States spent some $475 million on assistance to refugees around the world, and we accepted 31,000 refugees for permanent resettlement in this country.

What results can we expect from all these efforts?

We may justifiably seek a rapid end to such gross violations as those cited in our law: ". . . torture, or cruel, inhuman or degrading treatment or punishment, or prolonged detention without charges. . . ." Just last week our Ambassador at the United Nations, Andrew Young, suggested a series of new ways to confront the practice of torture around the world.

The promotion of other human rights is a broader challenge. The results may be slower in coming but are no less worth pursuing, and we intend to let other countries know where we stand.

We recognize that many nations of the world are organized on authoritarian rather than democratic principles—some larger and powerful, others struggling to raise the lives of their people above bare subsistence levels. We can nourish no illusions that a call to the banner of human rights will bring sudden transformation in authoritarian societies.

We are embarked on a long journey. But our faith in the dignity of the individual encourages us to believe that people in every society, according to their own traditions, will in time give their own expression to this fundamental aspiration.

Our belief is strengthened by the way the Helsinki principles and the U.N. Declaration of Human Rights have found resonance in the hearts of people of many countries. Our task is to sustain this faith by our example and our encouragement.

In his inaugural address, three months ago, President Carter said: "Because we are free, we can never be indifferent to the fate of freedom elsewhere." Again, at a meeting of the Organization of American States two weeks ago, he said: "You will find this country . . . eager to stand beside those nations which respect human rights and which promote democratic ideals."

We seek these goals because they are right, and because we too will benefit. Our own well-being, and even our security, are enhanced in a world that shares common freedoms and in which prosperity and economic justice create the conditions for peace. And let us remember that we always risk paying a serious price when we become identified with repression.

Nations, like individuals, limit their potential when they limit their goals. The American people understand this. I am confident they will support foreign policies that reflect our traditional values. To offer less is to define America in ways we should not accept.

America fought for freedom in 1776 and in two World Wars. We have offered haven to the oppressed. Millions have come to our shores in times of trouble. In time of devastation abroad, we have shared our resources.

Our encouragement and inspiration to other nations and other peoples have never been limited to the power of our military or the bounty of our economy. They have been lifted up by the message of our Revolution, the message of individual human freedom. That message has been our great national asset in times past. So it should be again.

Jimmy Carter

Speech on Humane Purposes in Foreign Policy (1977)

In his twenty-five years as president of Notre Dame, Father Hesburgh has spoken more consistently and more effectively in the support of the rights of human beings than any other person I know. His interest in the Notre Dame Center for Civil Rights has never wavered, and he played an important role in broadening the scope of the Center's work—and I have visited there last fall to see this work—to include now all people in the world, as shown by last month's conference here on human rights and American foreign policy.

And that concern has been demonstrated again today in a vivid fashion by the selection of Bishop Donal Lamont, Paul Cardinal Arns, and Stephen Cardinal Kim, to receive honorary degrees. In their fight for human freedoms in Rhodesia, Brazil, and South Korea, these three religious leaders typify all that is best in their countries and in their church. I am honored to join you in recognizing their dedication and their personal sacrifice and their supreme courage.

Quite often, brave men like these are castigated and sometimes punished, sometimes even put to death, because they enter the realm where human rights is a struggle, and sometimes they are blamed for the very circumstance which they helped to dramatize. But it has been there for a long time, and the flames which they seek to extinguish concern us all and are increasingly visible around the world.

Last week, I spoke in California about the domestic agenda for our Nation to provide more efficiently for the needs of our people, to demonstrate—against the dark faith of our times—that our government can be both competent and more humane.

But I want to speak to you today about the strands that connect our actions overseas with our essential character as a Nation. I believe we can have a foreign policy that is democratic, that is based on funda-

Delivered at the Commencement Exercises of the University of Notre Dame.

mental values, and that uses power and influence which we have for humane purposes. We can also have a foreign policy that the American people both support and, for a change, know about and understand.

I have a quiet confidence in our own political system. Because we know that democracy works, we can reject the arguments of those rulers who deny human rights to their people. We are confident that democracy's example will be compelling, and so we seek to bring that example closer to those from whom in the past few years we have been separated and who are not yet convinced about the advantages of our kind of life.

We are confident that democratic methods are the most effective, and we are not tempted to employ improper tactics here at home or abroad.

We are confident of our own strength, so we can seek substantial mutual reductions in the nuclear arms race.

And we are confident of the good sense of the American people, and so we let them share in the process of making foreign policy decisions. We can thus speak with the voices of 215 million, and not just of an isolated handful.

Democracy's great recent successes—in India, Portugal, Spain, Greece—show that our confidence in this system is not misplaced. Being confident of our own future, we are now free of that inordinate fear of communism which once led us to embrace any dictator who joined us in that fear. I am glad that that is being changed.

For too many years, we have been willing to adopt the flawed and erroneous principles and tactics of our adversaries, sometimes abandoning our own values for theirs. We have fought fire with fire, never thinking that fire is better quenched with water. This approach failed, with Vietnam the best example of its intellectual and moral poverty. But through failure, we have now found our way back to our own principles and values, and we have regained our lost confidence.

By the measure of history, our Nation's 200 years are very brief and our rise to world eminence is briefer still. It dates from 1945 when Europe and the old international order lay in ruins. Before then America was largely on the periphery of world affairs, but since then we have inescapably been at the center of world affairs.

Our policy during this period was guided by two principles; a belief that Soviet expansion was almost inevitable, but it must be contained, and the corresponding belief in the importance of an almost exclusive alliance among non-Communist nations on both sides of the Atlantic. That system could not last forever unchanged. Historical trends have weakened its foundation. The unifying threat of conflict with the Soviet Union has become less intensive, even though the competition has become more expensive.

The Vietnamese war produced a profound moral crisis, sapping worldwide faith in our own policy and our system of life, a crisis of confidence made even more grave by the covert pessimism of some of our own leaders.

In less than a generation we have seen the world change dramatically. The daily lives and aspirations of most human beings have been transformed. Colonialism is nearly gone. A new sense of national identity now exists in almost 100 new countries that have been formed in the last generation. Knowledge has become more widespread; aspirations are higher.

As more people have been freed from traditional constraints, more have been determined to achieve for the first time in their lives social justice.

The world is still divided by ideological disputes, dominated by regional conflicts, and threatened by the danger that we will not resolve the differences of race and wealth without violence or without drawing into combat the major military powers. We can no longer separate the traditional issues of war and peace from the new global questions of justice, equity, and human rights.

It is a new world—but America should not fear it. It is new world and we should help to shape it. It is a new world that calls for a new American foreign policy—a policy based on constant decency in its values and on optimism in our historical vision.

We can no longer have a policy solely for the industrial nations as the foundation of global stability, but we must respond to the new reality of a politically awakening world.

We can no longer have a policy solely for the industrial nations as the foundation of global stability, but we must respond to the new reality of a politically awakening world.

We can no longer expect that the other 150 nations will follow the dictates of the powerful, but we must continue—confidently—our efforts to inspire, to persuade, and to lead.

Our policy must reflect our belief that the world can hope for more than simple survival, and our belief that dignity and freedom are fundamental spiritual requirements. Our policy must shape an international system that will last longer than secret deals.

We cannot make this kind of policy by manipulation. Our policy must be open and it must be candid; it must be one of constructive global involvement, resting on five cardinal premises.

I have tried to make these premises clear to the American people since last January. Let me review what we have been doing and discuss what we intend to do.

Human Rights

First, we have reaffirmed America's commitment to human rights as a fundamental tenet of our foreign policy. In ancestry, religion, color, place of origin, and cultural background, we Americans are as diverse a nation as the world has ever seen. No common mystique of blood or soil unites us. What draws us together, perhaps more than anything else, is a belief in human freedom. We want the world to know that our Nation stands for more than financial prosperity.

This does not mean that we can conduct our foreign policy by rigid moral maxims. We live in a world that is imperfect and which will always be imperfect—a world that is complex and confused, and which will always be complex and confused.

I understand fully the limits of moral suasion. We have no illusion that changes will come easily or soon. But I also believe that it is a mistake to undervalue the power of words and of ideas that words embody. In our own history, that power has ranged from Thomas Paine's "Common Sense" to Martin Luther King, Jr.'s, "I Have a Dream."

In the life of the human spirit, words are action, much more so than many of us may realize who live in countries where freedom of expression is taken for granted. The leaders of totalitarian nations understand this very well. The proof is that words are precisely the action for which dissidents in those countries are being prosecuted.

Nonetheless, we can already see dramatic worldwide advances in the protection of the individual from the arbitrary power of the state. For us to ignore this trend would be to lose influence and moral authority in the world. To lead it will be to regain the moral stature that we once had.

The great democracies are not free because we are strong and prosperous. I believe we are strong and influential because we are free.

Throughout the world today, in free nations and in totalitarian countries as well, there is a preoccupation with the subject of human freedom, human rights, and I believe it is incumbent on us in this country to keep that discussion, that debate, that contention alive. No other country is as well qualified as we to set an example. We have our own shortcomings and faults, and we should strive constantly and with courage to make sure that we are legitimately proud of what we have. . . .

Archbishop Oscar Romero

The Last Sermon (1980)

Let no one be offended because we use the divine words read at our mass to shed light on the social, political and economic situation of our people. Not to do so would be unchristian. Christ desires to unite himself with humanity, so that the light he brings from God might become life for nations and individuals.

I know many are shocked by this preaching and want to accuse us of forsaking the gospel for politics. But I reject this accusation. I am trying to bring to life the message of the Second Vatican Council and the meetings at Medellin and Puebla. The documents from these meetings should not just be studied theoretically. They should be brought to life and translated into the real struggle to preach the gospel as it should be for our people. Each week I go about the country listening to the cries of the people, their pain from so much crime, and the ignominy of so much violence. Each week I ask the Lord to give me the right words to console, to denounce, to call for repentance. And even though I may be a voice crying in the desert, I know that the church is making the effort to fulfill its mission. . . .

Every country lives its own "exodus"; today El Salvador is living its own exodus. Today we are passing to our liberation through a desert strewn with bodies and where anguish and pain are devastating us. Many suffer the temptation of those who walked with Moses and wanted to turn back and did not work together. It is the same old story. God, however, wants to save the people by making a new history. . . .

History will not fail; God sustains it. That is why I say that insofar as historical projects attempt to reflect the eternal plan of God, to that extent they reflect the kingdom of God. This attempt is the work of the church. Because of this, the church, the people of God in history, is not attached to any one social system, to any political organization, to any party. The church does not identify herself with any of those forces because she is the eternal pilgrim of history and is indicating at every historical moment what reflects the kingdom of God and what does not reflect the kingdom of God. She is the servant of the kingdom of God.

The great task of Christians must be to absorb the spirit of God's kingdom and, with souls filled with the kingdom of God, to work on the projects of history. It's fine to be organized in popular groups; it's all right to form political parties; it's all right to take part in the government. It's fine as long as you are a christian who carries the reflection of the kingdom of God and tries to establish it where you are working, and as long as you are not being used to further worldly ambitions. This is the great duty of the people of today. My dear Christians, I have always told you, and I will repeat, that the true liberators of our people must come from us Christians, from the people of God. Any historical plan that's not based on what we spoke of in the first point—the dignity of the human being, the love of God, the kingdom of Christ among people—will be a fleeting project. Your project, however, will grow in stability the more it reflects the eternal design of God. It will be a solution of the common good of the people every time, if it meets the needs of the people. . . . Now I invite you to look at things through the eyes of the church, which is trying to be the kingdom of God on earth and so often must illuminate the realities of our national situation.

We have lived through a tremendously tragic week. I could not give you the facts before, but a week ago last Saturday, on 15 March, one of the largest and most distressing military operations was carried out in the countryside. The villages affected were La Laguna, Plan de Ocotes and El Rosario. The operation brought tragedy: a lot of ranches were burned, there was looting, and—inevitably—people were killed. In La Laguna, the attackers killed a married couple, Ernesto Navas and Audelia Mejía de Navas, their little children, Martin and Hilda, thirteen and seven years old, and eleven more peasants.

Other deaths have been reported, but we do not know the names of the dead. In Plan de Ocotes, two children and four peasants were killed, including two women. In El Rosario, three more peasants were killed. That was last Saturday.

Last Sunday, the following were assassinated in Arcatao by four members of ORDEN: peasants Marcelino Serrano, Vincente Ayala, twenty-four years old, and his son, Freddy. That same day, Fernando Hernández Navarro, a peasant, was assassinated in Galera de Jutiapa, when he fled from the military.

Last Monday, 17 March, was a tremendously violent day. Bombs exploded in the capital as well as in the interior of the country. The damage was very substantial at the headquarters of the Ministry of Agriculture. The campus of the national university was under armed siege from dawn until 7 P.M. Throughout the day, constant bursts of machine-gun fire were heard in the university area. The archbishop's

From *The Church and Human Liberation*, March 24, 1980.

office intervened to protect people who found themselves caught inside.

On the Hacienda Colima, eighteen persons died, at least fifteen of whom were peasants. The administrator and the grocer of the ranch also died. The armed forces confirmed that there was a confrontation. A film of the events appeared on TV, and many analyzed interesting aspects of the situation.

At least fifty people died in serious incidents that day: in the capital, seven persons died in events at the Colonia Santa Lucía; on the outskirts of Tecnillantas, five people died; and in the area of the rubbish dump, after the evacuation of the site by the military, were found the bodies of four workers who had been captured in that action.

Sixteen peasants died in the village of Montepeque, thirty-eight kilometers along the road to Suchitoto. That same day, two students at the University of Central America were captured in Tecnillantas: Mario Nelson and Miguel Alberto Rodríguez Velado, who were brothers. The first one, after four days of illegal detention, was handed over to the courts. Not so his brother, who was wounded and is still held in illegal detention. Legal Aid is intervening on his behalf.

Amnesty International issued a press release in which it described the repression of the peasants, especially in the area of Chalatenango. The week's events confirm this report in spite of the fact the government denies it. As I entered the church, I was given a cable that says, "Amnesty International confirmed today [that was yesterday] that in El Salvador human rights are violated to extremes that have not been seen in other countries." That is what Patricio Fuentes (spokesman for the urgent action section for Central America in Swedish Amnesty International) said at a press conference in Managua, Nicaragua.

Fuentes confirmed that, during two weeks of investigations he carried out in El Salvador, he was able to establish that there had been eighty-three political assassinations between 10 and 14 March. He pointed out that Amnesty International recently condemned the government of El Salvador, alleging that it was responsible for six hundred political assassinations. The Salvadorean government defended itself against the charges, arguing that Amnesty International based its condemnation on unproved assumptions.

Fuentes said that Amnesty had established that in El Salvador human rights are violated to a worse degree than the repression in Chile after the coupe d'état. The Salvadorean government also said that the six hundred dead were the result of armed confrontations between army troops and guerrillas. Fuentes said that during his stay in El Salvador, he could see that the victims had been tortured before their deaths and mutilated afterward.

The spokesman of Amnesty International said that the victims' bodies characteristically appeared with the thumbs tied behind their backs. Corrosive liquids had been applied to the corpses to prevent identification of the victims by their relatives and to prevent international condemnation, the spokesman added. Nevertheless, the bodies were exhumed and the dead have been identified. Fuentes said that the repression carried out by the Salvadorean army was aimed at breaking the popular organizations through the assassination of their leaders in both town and country.

According to the spokesman of Amnesty International, at least three thousand five hundred peasants have fled from their homes to the capital to escape persecution. "We have complete lists in London and Sweden of young children and women who have been assassinated for being organized," Fuentes stated. . . .

I would like to make a special appeal to the men of the army, and specifically to the ranks of the National Guard, the police and the military. Brothers, you come from our own people. You are killing your own brother peasants when any human order to kill must be subordinate to the law of God which says, "Thou shalt not kill." No soldier is obliged to obey an order contrary to the law of God. No one has to obey an immoral law. It is high time you recovered your consciences and obeyed your consciences rather than a sinful order. The church, the defender of the rights of God, of the law of God, of human dignity, of the person, cannot remain silent before such an abomination. We want the government to face the fact that reforms are valueless if they are to be carried out at the cost of so much blood. In the name of God, in the name of this suffering people whose cries rise to heaven more loudly each day, I implore you, I beg you, I order you in the name of God: stop the repression.

The church preaches your liberation just as we have studied it in the holy Bible today. It is a liberation that has, above all else, respect for the dignity of the person, hope for humanity's common good, and the transcendence that looks before all to God and only from God derives its hope and its strength.

Jeane Kirkpatrick

Establishing a Viable Human Rights Policy (1981)

In this paper I deal with three broad subjects:

- First, the content and consequences of the Carter administration's human rights policy;
- Second, the prerequisites ·of a more adequate theory of human rights;
- And third, some characteristics of a more successful human rights policy.

The Carter Human Rights Policy

How the Carter administration came to be outspokenly committed to the cause of human rights is far from clear. As Daniel Patrick Moynihan has observed, "Human rights as an issue in foreign policy was by no means central to Jimmy Carter's campaign for the presidency. It was raised in the Democratic platform drafting committee, and at the Democratic Convention, but in each instance the Carter representatives were at best neutral, giving the impression of not having heard very much of the matter before and not having any particular views." Indeed, some of candidate Carter's remarks suggested that he was far from wedded to an activist human rights policy. "Our people have now learned," he told the Foreign Policy Association in June 1976, "the folly of our trying to inject our power into the internal affairs of other nations."

Nevertheless, by the time of his inaugural address, Jimmy Carter had become adamant on the subject of human rights. "Our commitment to human rights," the new president informed the nation, "must be absolute." Within weeks of his inauguration, President Carter replied to a letter from Andrei Sakharov, and met with the noted

NOTE: This paper was prepared by Ambassador Jeane J. Kirkpatrick, United States permanent representative to the United Nations, for Kenyon College's Human Rights Conference, April 4, 1981.

Soviet dissident Vladimir Bukovsky in the White House. These symbolic acts generated a great deal of excitement, yet they hardly constituted a human rights policy. On April 30, 1977, however, Secretary of State Vance delivered a major policy address in which he set out to explain just what it was the Carter administration meant by "human rights" and how it intended to promote them. According to Vance, by "human rights" the administration meant three things:

1. The right to be free from governmental violation of the integrity of the person. Such violations include torture; cruel, inhuman, or degrading treatment or punishment; and arbitrary arrest or imprisonment. And they include denial of fair public trial and invasion of the home.

2. The right to the fulfillment of such vital needs as food, shelter, health care, and education. We recognize that the fulfillment of this right will depend, in part, upon the stage of a nation's economic development. But we also know that this right can be violated by a government's action or inaction—for example, through corrupt official processes which divert resources to an elite at the expense of the needy or through indifference to the plight of the poor.

3. The right to enjoy civil and political liberties: freedom of thought, of religion, of assembly; freedom of speech; freedom of the press; freedom of movement both within and outside one's own country; freedom to take part in government.

U.S. policy, Vance stated, "is to promote all these rights." "If we are determined to act," he continued, "the means available range from quiet diplomacy in its many forms, through public pronouncements, to withholding of assistance." Significantly, nowhere in his speech did Vance indicate that human rights rest on specific institutions and that, where these institutions do not exist, neither quiet diplomacy nor public pronouncements nor the withholding of assistance can conjure human rights into being.

In accepting the notion that economic and social "rights" are just as important as civil and political rights, Secretary Vance went well beyond any previous U.S. understanding of human rights. Another prominent administration spokesman on human rights, U.N. Ambassador Andrew Young, went further still. "For most of the world," Young declared, "civil and political rights . . . come as luxuries that are far away in the future." Young called on the U.S. to recognize that there are various equally valid concepts of human rights in the world. The Soviets, for example, "have . . . developed a completely different concept of human rights. For them, human rights are essentially not civil and political but economic. . . ."

President Carter, meanwhile, was busy trying to erase the impression, resulting from his letter to Sakharov and his meeting with

Bukovsky, that his advocacy of human rights implied an anti-Soviet bias. "I have never had an inclination to single out the Soviet Union as the only place where human rights are being abridged," he told a press conference on February 23, 1977. "I've tried to make sure that the world knows that we're not singling out the Soviet Union for criticism," he again told a press conference on March 24. "I've never made the first comment that personally criticized General Secretary Brezhnev," he told a press conference on June 13. In fact, so eager was the Carter administration not to single out the Soviet Union for criticism that, within a year of its coming into office, Secretary Vance privately instructed the U.S. ambassador to the U.N. Human Rights Commission that under no circumstances was he even to mention the name of the recently arrested Soviet dissident Yuri Orlov.

President Carter's disinclination to single out the Soviet Union for criticism extended to a number of other communist regimes, as well. On April 12, 1978, for example, President Carter informed President Ceausescu of Rumania that "our goals are also the same, to have a just system of economics and politics, to let the people of the world share in growth, in peace, in personal freedom." And on March 4, 1978, in greeting President Tito of Yugoslavia, Carter said, "Perhaps as much as any other person, he exemplifies in Yugoslavia the eagerness for freedom, independence, and liberty that exists throughout Eastern Europe and indeed throughout the world."

But while the Carter administration was notably unwilling to criticize communist states for their human rights violations—not until April 21, 1978, did the administration denounce Cambodia for its massive human rights violations, despite the fact that it had known of these violations for quite some time—it showed no similar reticence when it came to criticizing authoritarian recipients of U.S. aid. In 1976, before the Carter administration came into office, Congress had passed an amendment to the Foreign Assistance Act which, inter alia, required the State Department to submit annual reports to Congress describing the human rights performance of states receiving U.S. aid, and which prohibited the U.S. from assisting states which consistently violated the human rights of their citizens unless the president "certifies in writing that extraordinary circumstances exist." On the basis of the annual reports required by the 1976 law, the Carter administration withheld economic credits and military assistance to Chile, Argentina, Paraguay, Brazil, Nicaragua, and El Salvador. South Korea and the Philippines continued to receive U.S. aid, on the president's recommendation that such aid served the security interests of the U.S. Nonetheless, the public criticism of those governments helped delegitimize them, at the same time it rendered them *less* susceptible to our views.

These tendencies were exacerbated by the nearly exclusive focus of Carter doctrine and policymakers on violations of human rights by governments. By definition, activities of terrorists and guerrillas could not qualify as violations of human rights, whereas a government's efforts to repress terrorism would quickly run afoul of Carter human rights standards.

This focus not only permitted Carter policymakers to focus on government "repression" while ignoring guerrilla violence, it encouraged consideration of human rights violations independently of context.

Various major actions undertaken by the Carter administration appear to have been derived, either in whole or in part, from its "absolute" commitment to human rights: President Carter's decision, in 1977, to press for ratification of the U.N. Covenants on Economic, Social and Cultural Rights and on Civil and Political Rights; the 1977 decision to support the mandatory U.N. arms embargo against South Africa; the decision, during President Carter's official visit to South Korea in mid-1979, to present the South Korean foreign minister with a privately compiled list of the names of over 100 alleged South Korean political prisoners; Secretary Vance's call, before a meeting of the Organization of American States in June 1979, for the departure of Nicaragua's President Somoza; the decision, in 1979, to withhold U.S. support for the Shah of Iran; and President Carter's decision, in June 1979, not to lift economic sanctions against the Muzorewa government in Zimbabwe Rhodesia.

Viewing the Carter administration's human rights policy in retrospect, it seems fair to conclude that its principal aims were to infuse U.S. foreign policy with "moral content," to create a broad domestic consensus behind the administration's foreign policy goals, and, generally speaking, to make Americans feel good about themselves. Whether the policy succeeded in achieving any of these objectives is debatable. One thing, however, is clear: the thrust of U.S. human rights policy, as it evolved under the Carter administration, was directed against U.S. allies. Instead of using the human rights issue to place the totalitarian states on the defensive, the U.S. frequently joined the totalitarians in attacking pro-Western authoritarian states, and actually helped to destabilize pro-Western regimes in Nicaragua and Iran.

Toward a More Adequate Conception of Human Rights

It is always necessary to know what one is talking about. Although debate about the existential and cognitive status of human rights has occupied philosophical giants in past centuries, recent discussions

could profit from renewed and systematic attention to some fundamental distinctions. Four of these seem to me crucial. They are:

- first distinction: between ideas and institutions;
- second distinction: between rights and goals;
- third distinction: between intentions and consequences;
- fourth distinction: between morals and politics.

IDEAS AND INSTITUTIONS

There are several important reasons that, in thinking about "rights"
(as about all other plans for social systems), it is important to bear in
mind the differences between ideas and institutions. Ideas are the
product of the mind. They are abstractions which may have no
empirical referents. Anything is possible in the domain of abstract
reason that does not violate analytical canons which are themselves the
products of mind. Robert Owen, for example, proposed "a world
convention to emancipate the human race from ignorance, poverty,
division, sin, and misery." In our times we propose declarations and
laws to attempt to hold other nations responsible for the disappearance of some of these evils to which Owen referred.

Since the world has not arrived at Hegel's promised end where the
rational becomes the real and the real rational, there exists no experience with the realization of abstract ideas in society. Many ideas can
probably never be realized. Not everything that can be conceived can
be created. One can, for example, conceive a unicorn, describe it,
destroy whole forests in a determined effort to find one, and still fail.
Ideas are readily brought into being and are readily manipulable by
their creators. They are susceptible to being changed merely because
a decision is made to change them. Their relationship to context is
therefore also manipulable—subject to being held constant or altered
depending on the decision of their creators.

But institutions have very different characteristics. Institutions are
stabilized patterns of human behavior. They involve millions, they
rest on *expectations* shaped by experience—or they rest on habit and
internalized values and beliefs—or on coercion.

These internalized expectations become inextricably bound up with
identity. They are extremely resistant to change. Since institutions
exist not in the minds of philosophers but in the habits and beliefs of
actual people, they can be brought into existence only as people are
persuaded or coerced into conforming their thoughts, preferences, and
behavior to the necessary patterns. History and recent experience
indicate that some kinds of goals and plans cannot finally be implemented, no matter how much persuasion or coercion is employed.
Moreover, in the absence of experience there is no way to estimate

accurately the feasibility, the costs, even the concrete desirability of an idea or ideal.

Therefore, though rights are easy to claim, they are extremely difficult to translate into reality. In actual societies, unlike in definitions, political principles do not exist in isolation; they interact and the effort at maximization begins at some point to undermine some other value. Frequently the relations among values are themselves embedded in tradition and habit, and profoundly resistant to alteration.

Burke focused on the distinction between ideas and institutions. He said, therefore, of the French Revolution:

> I should therefore suspend my congratulations on the liberty of France until I was informed as to how it had been combined with government, with public force, with discipline, with obedience of armies, with the collection and effectiveness of a well-distributed revenue, with morality and religion, with solidity and property, with peace and order, with civil and social manners. All these are good things, too. Without them liberty is of no benefit whilst it lasts and is not likely long to continue.

The failure to distinguish between the domains of rhetoric and politics is the essence of *rationalism*—which encourages us to believe anything that can be conceived can be realized. Rationalism not only encourages utopianism, utopianism is a form of rationalism. It shares the characteristic features, including a disregard of the experience, the concrete probability, in favor of the affirmation of rationality, abstraction, and possibility.

Applied to human rights and foreign policy, disregard of the distinction between ideas and institutions leads to an expectation that declarations of rights have existential status—and constitute valid, practical programs of action.

RIGHTS AND GOALS

The second distinction I want to emphasize is that between rights and goals. In our times, "rights" proliferate at the rhetorical level, with extraordinary speed. To the rights to life, liberty, and security of person have been added the rights to nationality, to privacy, to equal rights in marriage, to education, to culture, to the full development of personality, to self-determination, to self-government, to adequate standards of living.

The United Nations Universal Declaration of Human Rights claims as a universal every political, economic, social right yet conceived.

The Declaration consists of a Preamble and thirty articles, setting forth the human rights and fundamental freedoms to which all men and women, everywhere in the world, are entitled, without any discrimination. Article 1, which lays down the philosophy upon which the Declaration is based, reads: "All human beings are born free and equal in dignity and rights. They are endowed with reason and conscience and should act toward one another in a spirit of brotherhood." Article 2, which sets out the basic principle of equality and nondiscrimination as regards the enjoyment of human rights and fundamental freedoms, forbids "distinction of any kind, such as race, color, sect, language, religion, political or other opinion, national or social origin, property, birth, or other status."

Article 3, a cornerstone of the Declaration, proclaims the right to life, liberty, and security of person: rights which are essential to the enjoyment of all other rights. It introduces the series of articles (4 to 21) in which the human rights of every individual are elaborated further.

The civil and political rights recognized in Articles 4 to 21 of the Declaration include: the right to life, liberty, and security of person; freedom from slavery and servitude; freedom from torture or cruel, inhuman, or degrading treatment or punishment; the right to recognition everywhere as a person before the law; the right to an effective judicial remedy; freedom from arbitrary arrest, detention, or exile; the right to a fair and public hearing by an independent and impartial tribunal; the right to be presumed innocent until proved guilty; freedom from arbitrary interference with privacy, family, home, or correspondence; freedom of movement and residence; the right of asylum; the right to a nationality; the right to marry and found a family; the right to own property; freedom of thought, conscience, and religion; freedom of opinion and expression; the right to peaceful assembly and association; the right of everyone to take part in the government of his country; and the right of everyone to equal access to public service in his country.

Article 22, the second cornerstone of the Declaration, introduces Articles 23 to 27, in which economic, social, and cultural rights—the rights to which everyone is entitled "as a member of society"—are set out. Article 22 reads: "Everyone, as a member of society, has the right to social security and is entitled to realization, through national effort and international cooperation and in accordance with the organization and resources of each state, of the economic, social, and cultural rights indispensable for his dignity and the full development of his personality."

The economic, social, and cultural rights recognized in Articles 23 to 27 include the right to social security, the right to work, the right to equal pay for equal work, the right to leisure, the right to a standard of living adequate for health and well-being, the right to education, and the right to participate in the cultural life of the community.

The concluding articles, Articles 28 to 30, stress that everyone "is entitled to a social and international order in which the rights and freedoms set forth in this Declaration can be fully realized" (Article 28); that "everyone has duties to the community in which alone the free and full development of his personality is possible" (Article 29.1); and that "nothing in this Declaration may be interpreted as implying for any State, group or person any right to engage in any activity aimed at the destruction of any of the rights and freedoms set forth herein."

Recently, in Geneva, the United Nations Commission on Human Rights affirmed a "right to development" which carries its own comitant list of "rights" including the right to a new economic order, peace, and an end to the arms race.

Such declarations of human "rights" take on the character of "a letter to Santa Claus"—as Orwin and Prangle noted. They can multiply indefinitely because "no clear standard informs them, and no great reflection produced them." For every goal toward which human beings have worked, there is in our time a "right." Neither nature, experience, nor probability informs these lists of "entitlements," which are subject to no constraints except those of the mind and appetite of their authors. The fact that such "entitlements" may be without possibility of realization does not mean they are without consequences.

The consequence of treating goals as rights is grossly misleading about how goals are achieved in real life. "Rights" are vested in persons; "goals" are achieved by the efforts of persons. The language of rights subtly vests the responsibility in some other. When the belief that one has a right to development coincides with facts of primitive technology, hierarchy, and dictatorship, the tendency to blame someone is almost overwhelming. If the people of the world do not fully enjoy their economic rights, it must be because some *one*—some monopoly capitalist, some Zionist, some man—is depriving them of their rightful due.

Utopian expectations concerning the human condition are compounded then by a vague sense that Utopia is one's due; that citizenship in a perfect society is a reasonable expectation for real persons in real societies.

INTENTIONS AND CONSEQUENCES

The third distinction with special relevance to human rights and foreign policy is the distinction between intentions and consequences.

In political philosophy as in ethics there are theories that emphasize motives and those that emphasize consequences.

Preoccupation with motives is a well-known characteristic of a breed of political purist that has multiplied in our times. The distinguishing characteristic of this breed is emphasis on internal criteria, on what one believes and feels is right. Doing what one "knows" is right then becomes more important than producing desired results.

In human rights and foreign policy this position leads to an overweening concern with purity of intentions. When the morality of the motive is more important than the consequences, we are less concerned about creating new traditionalist tyranny than by the morality of our own intentions, and the principal function of a purist policy of human rights is to make us feel good about ourselves.

PERSONAL AND POLITICAL MORALITY

The fourth distinction important to thinking about human rights and foreign policy is that between personal and political morality. Where personal morality derives from the characteristics of single individuals and depends on the cultivation of personal virtues such as faith, hope, charity, and discipline, political morality depends on the structured *interactions* of persons—depends, that is, on institutions.

Justice, democracy, liberty are all the products of arrangements of offices and distributions of power. These arrangements and distributions embodied in *constitutions* produce *political* goods by respecting and harmonizing the diverse parts of a political community. The political goods—democracy, due process, protection of "rights" to free speech, assembly—are, as Plato, Aristotle, and the American founding fathers understood, the consequences of wisely structured constitutions.

Rights, then, are embodied in institutions—not rhetoric. They are the consequences of prudential judgments, not good motives. They are always complex and rest on patterns of social life, not on individual virtues.

The consequences of trying to base a human rights policy on private virtue is failure. Where institutions are not constructed on the basis of human proclivities and habits, failure is the inevitable result. Human rights can be, should be, must be, will be, taken into account by U.S. foreign policy, but we have had enough of rationalism and purism, of private virtues and public vices.

Amnesty International

Twelve-Point Program for the Prevention of Torture (1983)

Torture is a fundamental violation of human rights, condemned by the General Assembly of the United Nations as an offense to human dignity and prohibited under national and international law.

Yet torture persists, daily and across the globe. In Amnesty International's experience, legislative prohibition is not enough. Immediate steps are needed to confront torture and other cruel, inhuman or degrading treatment or punishment wherever they occur and to eradicate them totally.

Amnesty International calls on all governments to implement the following 12-Point Program for the Prevention of Torture. It invites concerned individuals and organizations to join in promoting the program. Amnesty International believes that the implementation of these measures is a positive indication of a government's commitment to abolish torture and to work for its abolition worldwide.

1. OFFICIAL CONDEMNATION OF TORTURE

The highest authorities of every country should demonstrate their total opposition to torture. They should make clear to all law enforcement personnel that torture will not be tolerated under any circumstances.

2. LIMITS ON INCOMMUNICADO DETENTION

Torture often takes place while the victims are held incommunicado—unable to contact people outside who could help them or find out what is happening to them. Governments should adopt safeguards to ensure that incommunicado detention does not become an opportunity for torture. It is vital that all prisoners be brought before a judicial authority promptly after being taken into custody and that relatives, lawyers and doctors have prompt and regular access to them.

3. NO SECRET DETENTION

In some countries torture takes place in secret centers, often after the victims are made to "disappear." Governments should ensure that prisoners are held in publicly recognized places, and that accurate information about their whereabouts is made available to relatives and lawyers.

4. SAFEGUARDS DURING INTERROGATION AND CUSTODY
Governments should keep procedures for detention and interrogation under regular review. All prisoners should be promptly told of their rights, including the right to lodge complaints about their treatment. There should be regular independent visits of inspection to places of detention. An important safeguard against torture would be the separation of authorities responsible for detention from those in charge of interrogation.

5. INDEPENDENT INVESTIGATION OF REPORTS OF TORTURE
Governments should ensure that all complaints and reports of torture are impartially and effectively investigated. The methods and findings of such investigations should be made public. Complainants and witnesses should be protected from intimidation.

6. NO USE OF STATEMENTS EXTRACTED UNDER TORTURE
Governments should ensure that confessions or other evidence obtained through torture may never be invoked in legal proceedings.

7. PROHIBITION OF TORTURE IN LAW
Governments should ensure that acts of torture are punishable offenses under the criminal law. In accordance with international law, the prohibition of torture must not be suspended under any circumstances, including states of war or other public emergency.

8. PROSECUTION OF ALLEGED TORTURERS
Those responsible for torture should be brought to justice. This principle should apply wherever they happen to be, wherever the crime was committed and whatever the nationality of the perpetrators or victims. There should be no "safe haven" for torturers.

9. TRAINING PROCEDURES
It should be made clear during the training of all officials involved in the custody, interrogation or treatment of prisoners that torture is a criminal act. They should be instructed that they are obliged to refuse to obey any order to torture.

10. COMPENSATION AND REHABILITATION
Victims of torture and their dependents should be entitled to obtain financial compensation. Victims should be provided with appropriate medical care and rehabilitation.

11. INTERNATIONAL RESPONSE

Governments should use all available channels to intercede with governments accused of torture. Inter-governmental mechanisms should be established and used to investigate reports of torture urgently and to take effective action against it. Governments should ensure that military, security or police transfers or training do not facilitate the practice of torture.

12. RATIFICATION OF INTERNATIONAL INSTRUMENTS

All governments should ratify international instruments containing safeguards and remedies against torture, including the International Covenant on Civil and Political Rights and its Optional Protocol which provides for individual complaints.

Pablo Antonio Cuadra

Notes on Culture in the New Nicaragua (1984)

In Nicaragua today a dramatic struggle is going on between ideology and culture. The ideology of the Sandinista Front has lost its utopian aspect, and what remains in its place is somewhat elemental and gray: a Marxism-Leninism which crudely apes the wretched Soviet notions of man and society, retailed secondhand by Cuba, and which—retailed once more by our own social realities—amount to nothing more than a complete and total failure, sustainable only through the mechanisms of totalitarian propaganda. This sounds strong—I know it—but is true nonetheless. From the point of view of culture, at least, our situation could not be worse. The reigning ideology, for its very survival, *requires* the negation of freedom and of the right to critical thought, elements which are, after all, indispensable for cultural work.

The ideology of the Sandinista Front has been presented to us, somewhat presumptuously, as the expression of "modernity": its Marxism is an advance, so it is said, in all areas, while the Nicaraguan culture that preceded it is represented as a tradition of failure. The

From *Vuelta* (Mexico City), August 1984. Translated from the Spanish by Mark Falcoff.

"progressive" pyrotechnics of Sandinismo rather stupidly deny history: everything new is good, everything previous to it is bad. It is certainly true that the democratic tradition in Nicaragua, which is a substantial part of our culture, has nothing to point to but defeats. On the other hand, the germinal aspect of our history resides in the fact that the near totality of our civil wars and insurrections have represented frustrated efforts to achieve democracy.

All our dictators disguised themselves as paladins of democracy, and began their governments by raising high its banners against the previous frustrated attempt. What we derive from our history is a tradition of *democratic aspirations*. There is nothing particularly "modern" about the effort to frustrate once more this secular desire of the Nicaraguan people by establishing instead some sort of new dictatorship, which offers what culture has always rejected, and presents in the guise of the new and the modern, what is, in fact, the definitive defeat of these historic efforts. What is tragic is that this failure is essential to Marxism-Leninism: it is the failure of Marx who proposed a system intended to achieve the complete freedom of man, and only managed—thanks to the work of Lenin—to generate the most oppressive and totalitarian power in history. That failure is the result of a dialectic that, to our misfortune, functioned with the same brutal logic in Nicaragua, where the real movement of history was a heroic libertarian revolution against Somoza, a movement that was derailed by Marxist-Leninist interference, and brought us back to our point of departure—from dictatorship to dictatorship—which is to say, a reinforcement of the state machinery left behind by Somoza. A sad compensation for the rivers of blood shed by the thousands of Nicaraguans who fell in the struggle for liberty!

But the paradox is even deeper and more cruel than that: within that movement, the entire literary and philosophical production of our intellectuals expressed the same libertarian goal. We knew very well, from our own cultural tradition, what a highly admired novelist—Gabriel García Marquez—had said to us in a lapidary fashion: "When one reaches absolute power, one loses total contact with reality." Absolute power, the "progressive" ideal of Marxism-Leninism, means not only placing the state in opposition to culture, but sealing it off from the basic realities of our society. It is for this reason that the entire Nicaraguan literary movement, which played a vital role in the gestation of the revolution against Somoza, never contemplated the emergence of a totalitarian state, or even the enlargement of apparatus which was already too powerful, much less redeem the poor with the Communist formula "dictatorship of the proletariat."

For this reason "ideology" has had to impose itself slowly, operating, as it were, in various disguises, never calling things by their proper names, always denying and hiding behind false colors. Today the Sandinista leaders affirm and they do not affirm; another day they punish or insult those who call them Marxist-Leninists or Communists. For a long time the daily newspaper *La Prensa* was censured or operated under virtual siege conditions, because it persisted in documenting the totalitarian nature of certain acts or measures taken by the government. If we have learned anything in Nicaragua, it is that Communism advances to the degree to which it can do so unobserved or unmarked. From the point of view of culture, this is a terrible, profoundly sterilizing attitude. Hypocrisy, false labels, can create slogans but no poems; propaganda but not life: there are no roots, there are no realities to nurture creative work, and this accounts for the fact that in six years of the revolutionary regime the literature production of Nicaragua has been astonishingly poor. This is all the more dramatic when we recall that it was the earlier effervescence of creative literary energy which first brought the Nicaraguan revolution to the attention of the world. Not only was that revolution betrayed on the political plane, but also on that of literature and art. The triumph of Sandinismo represents a crime against the spirit.

In November, 1979, when it was still possible to imagine that the Nicaraguan people were or could be united behind a single revolutionary project, we organized a symposium on "The Writer and the Revolution." To preside over it we invited the Minister of Culture, Ernesto Cardenal, and the Argentine writer Ernesto Cortázar. Seven Nicaraguan writers, representing the entire range of living generations, assembled before a numerous public made up of the intellectual, political, and university communities. Both Cortázar and the Minister of Culture ended by declaring themselves in favor of the absolute freedom of poetic creation, without any demands on the part of the state for political compatibility.

Those ideas, which were unanimously accepted by all who participated in the symposium, were the prelude to something truly original (and of course heretical for totalitarian ideologues). We thought it might be the single most important contribution of the Nicaraguan revolution to the world. I remember two Cuban poets, who had just arrived, expressing to me something more than their pleasure, their enthusiasm for those resolutions pertaining to creative liberty and intellectual independence. Inevitably, they suggested, such things eventually would influence developments in Cuba. Nonetheless, precisely the opposite occurred: two years later, in October, 1982, this commitment to freedom had been so completely abandoned that *Ventans*, the cultural supplement to the official daily *Barricada*, published on its first page the antique discourse of Fidel Castro, so reminiscent of

Mussolini, entitled, "Everything Within the Revolution; Nothing Against the Revolution," the interpretations of which—made by political functionaries and police officials—have condemned a significant number of Cuban writers and artists to jail and exile.

Those empowered to outline the new official doctrine in cultural matters, or rather, to discard the first mask of freedom and to place over their faces another more severe (let us not forget that in Communist praxis all masks are ultimately designed to be discarded) were Commander Bayardo Arce, and novelist and Junta member Sergio Ramírez. The auditorium was packed by intellectuals from all corners of the country for the First Convention of Cultural Workers in February, 1980. In their speeches they began to reveal the Orwellian face of the supreme "commissary" whose job it is to define what revolutionary culture ought to be—what is permitted and what is not; which is to say, they proclaimed that by virtue of possessing power, they were converted into supermen, individuals of extraordinary talent, and therefore qualified to send all of the intellectuals and artists of the country to a ramshackle schoolhouse, where they would be taught how they ought to be and how they ought to work; and they believed themselves competent as well to outline the parameters of future Nicaraguan culture. These were the first orders given to militarize our culture.

Arce expounded thus? "The artist *ought* to try to encounter the means to represent the values we inherited from the heroic career of General Sandino. *We* [referring here to the nine commanders; power, the revolution] should not like to see culture ever again assume the *decadent* forms it has taken in the past." Hitler used the word decadent to exile an entire vanguard school of art. What would be decadent for the State-Become-Critic in Nicaragua?

Sergio Ramírez simply echoed the same ideas: "We never thought to admit the existence of a culture isolated from the revolutionary process"—words that reminded us of the words of Octavio Paz written in 1956, "There is no more pernicious, barbarous prejudice than to attribute powers to the state in the sphere of artistic creation. An artistic style is a living entity, a continuous process of invention. It can never be imposed from without; born of the profoundest tendencies within a society, its direction is to a certain extent unpredictable, in much the same way as the eventual configuration of a tree's branches. In contrast, official style is the very negation of creative spontaneity. Power immobilizes; it freezes with a single gesture—grandiose, terrible, theatrical, or finally, simply monotonous—the variety which is life."

The negation of spontaneity in Nicaragua continued to be defined by Arce: "*We want* to retain artistic quality, but remember, please, that art is of no value if it is not understood by workers and peasants. *We want* [a situation] where, every time someone paints a picture or writes a poem, publishes a book or arranges a song, that person asks himself, first, to what degree is it going to assist our people in the process of self-transformation. . . ." Wouldn't it be better, however, to educate people to understand art? What Arce asks for is precisely what Cortázar called "a hateful personalism." Moreover, his definitions completely ignore the astronomical difference between the voluntary voice of, say, a poet to write some verses, and the imposition of the state which is, finally, the very essence of tyranny.

Sergio Ramírez continued the process of demolition: "Nicaraguan culture prior to June 19, 1979, was a failure," he said. But Ramírez forgets that that very culture, with its edges badly charred by the drama of our struggle, was never an attempt to produce a full-dress result, but rather, the surviving fragments of a lengthy agony. Ramírez's fatuous remark consigns, as it were, to the dust-heap of history an entire epoch in Nicaraguan history, whose leading figures include Rubén Dario, Alfonso Cortés, Azarias Pallais, José Coronel, Joaquín Pasos, Carlos Martínez Rivas, even Ernesto Cardenal himself. It puts the stamp of failure—much as one might put an entire library to the revolutionary torch—upon a national tradition of painting, architecture, music, and other "bourgeois" artifices such as the novel. If our tradition were less valuable than in fact it is, there would be *even less reason* to discard the lot in the name of something which has yet to come into existence. Ramírez, like all Marxists who pretend to use a "scientific" method to analyze the past, falls into the realm of fantasy whenever the time comes to describe the future. "Revolutionary culture, just because it is revolutionary, *cannot fail to be* authentic, and cannot fail to be a culture of quality," Ramírez says in one speech, thus simply sweeping aside the entire history of a nation.

"Nicaraguan history begins with the Sandinista Front." Such is the slogan of the regime—an attitude that might be, in the context of political liberty, nothing more than a case of understandable exaggeration, the pretentious boasting of some inexperienced young people suddenly come upon political power for the first time. In this case, however, it represents a statist ideology that seeks to abolish every cultural manifestation which is not fully coherent with it. The most dramatic and painful example was—and still is—the treatment of the Miskito Indians, an event which in all probability will have catastrophic consequences for our nationality. In this case, we are dealing with a cultural and historic problem which has been rendered virtually insoluble, pushed to the point of civil war, largely because those who sought to resolve it began by purposely denying the past.

At the time that the relationship between the Miskitos and the Sandinista Front began to break down (1981), I invited to the offices of *La Prensa* the representatives of Misurasata, the leaders of all of the political parties, and representing the FSLN and the government, the local authorities on the Atlantic coast. My purpose was to provoke a serious and sincere dialogue. The Miskito leaders explained their grievances, and in the process I learned something I had not previously known, namely, that they were asking for nothing that had not already been granted them in 1895 by legislative degree, at the time that the Mosquito Reserve was formally incorporated into the Republic of Nicaragua. The conditions of that incorporation were: investment in the Atlantic Coast to encourage development; respect for local religion, language, and customs; the right of the Indian communities to elect their own authorities; respect for their communal forestlands; liberty for some of their political prisoners, etc. In spite of our efforts to persuade them to the contrary, the Sandinista *comandantes* insisted upon regarding these demands as "separatist"; in their view, the Miskitos were being manipulated by "imperialism," and the only response to their requests was a hard and unyielding refusal. To make things worse, instead of dispatching their own people to the Atlantic Coast, they sent Cubans. That produced a massive uprising on the part of the people of Bluefields, followed by a chain of misunderstandings, violence, massive migration (into exile), repression, and other incidents that have done so much to damage the revolution's image abroad.

But Sandinista ideology has failed not only because it begins by rejecting or ignoring our culture, but also because of its specific philosophic content. Marxist collectivism—in the same way, be it said, as capitalist individualism—is incompatible with self-governing, self-sufficient communities. Let us recall that in Nicaragua, it was the Liberal dictator José Santos Zelaya who decreed the dissolution of collective property in land and the Indian communities in 1906. Thus the "socialist man" turns out to be not so very different from his capitalist antecedent; the difference resides in the fact that Communist is statist, but not communitarian.

We have betrayed the two underlying currents of our long-suffering Nicaraguan and Hispanic-American culture: *calling ourselves enemies of imperialism, we mask from view a more fundamental loss of independence. Calling ourselves paladins of liberation, we have lost, in our conception of the state, the proper measure of man.* We insist upon this double paradox, for from its springs practically all of the danger which the Sandinista Front is likely to inflict upon us, and will in fact inflict upon us, if nothing is done to counteract it—and soon.

In the official version, Sandinismo is defending the independence of our culture. But under this rubric, to reject one model only to choose another—apart from being a contradiction in terms—is even more dangerous. At least in the prerevolutionary period we knew what it meant to surrender our sovereignty: now, however, we are not even permitted to call things by their proper names. In the days of Bolívar, after all, we often said that we did not fight for independence from Spain simply to fall under the tutelage of another colonial power. We said the same thing during the 1920s, when General Sandino was fighting the U.S. Marines. It seems to be the tragic destiny of tiny Nicaragua to represent the medular point of Spanish-America in its conflict with the United States. But, in that conflict, our strength (and in the final analysis, our victory) will consist in the reaffirmation of our Hispanic-American personality and the strengthening of an independent culture. Our anti-imperialism is meant to obligate the United States to act as a democracy in its relations with other American nations. We do not want war; we do not want to be allies in a war—nor satellites of the other superpower, so that it can win its victories with proxy forces; what we want is a Spanish-American alliance, the dream of Bolívar, and also, the dream of General Sandino. The purpose of that alliance would be to obligate the United States to behave toward our countries in a civilized manner, on a plane of equality and mutual respect. In this Fidel Castro has forfeited what might otherwise be his claim to continental leadership, since he legitimized the loss of his own country's (and ultimately our) independence to the Soviet Union. In 1979 the entire world believed that the new Nicaraguan revolution would rectify this Cuban error and that it would offer—in bringing about social change—the proper reponse of an independent nation. To date this has not been the case. The land of Dario is no more independent now than it has ever been.

In the same fashion, our sister republics of Latin America believed and hoped—wrongly, as it turned out—that our revolution would be not merely the autumn, but the definitive death of the Patriarch. The fall of Somoza was, symbolically, the end of an entire epoch in history of Spanish-American culture: the elimination of that aberrant, monstrous form of power, which appeared and reappeared throughout our collective history, thus frustrating what would have been our truer, more noble purpose as independent nations.

In Arce's speech cited above, he counseled thus: "The task of Nicaraguan intellectuals, whether they have or have not been committed thus far to the revolutionary process, to take their stand: those who are already with us, to reaffirm their commitment still further, and for those who were not involved, to do so now, so as to participate in this transition which is, of course, cultural, but at the same time and fundamentally political, economic, and social." In one fell swoop literature and art were converted into branches of the bureaucracy.

Slowly the pressures began to close in upon us. First came veiled threats. Then the purposeful exclusion of "uncooperative" writers and artists. Internal exile. A ban on the citation of books or articles by the nonaligned or the uncommitted. The Union of Cultural Workers began to threaten with sanctions those writers and artists who contributed to the literary supplement of *La Prensa*. It is painful to report that many young dissident poets have asked me, in my capacity as editor of that magazine, to publish their work under pen names—so as to avoid reprisals, and to be able to continue to work with some measure of tranquillity. This is how more than one writer or poet will eventually enter the anthologies of our national literature—under an assumed name!

In the much-discussed (and properly controversial) "workshops" sponsored by the Ministry of Culture, they teach one not merely how to sing, but what verses. Sergio Ramírez has said as much in one of his speeches: "The workshops on popular poetry which have been organized in Nicaragua since July 19 [1979], reflect the poetry of young combatants, a poetry often anonymous, spun of the experiences of daily life, of reality, which seems to me to be vastly more important than the poetry which is the product of elitist dilettantism, the poetry which, after all, is all we have produced thus far as a nation. This phenomenon—how to break with that tradition—is something to which we should focus all of our energies."

In truth, I wish that this enthusiastic critical judgment, made by Ramírez the politician, were the same as that made by Ramírez the writer. I shall only add that in a propaganda exercise for Sandinista Television, a young apprentice poet declared, "Before now I was in error: I went about writing love poems. In the workshop I have learned why my poetry was bad—it had no political message." Perhaps that poor lad was destined, nonetheless, to be the author of some very great love poems. We shall never know. What is certain is that from here on, he will be scratching out forced, pedestrian (or derivative) verses, unless his own genius comes to his rescue, if in fact he is so fortunate.

It is precisely because I believe our revolution possessed magnificent roots and our culture ample reserves to produce a really original, Nicaraguan response to the challenge of history, that I have remained at *La Prensa* to resist a dictatorial ideology which is increasingly totalitarian. After all, what is at issue is the destiny of an entire people. At times I close my eyes and contemplate the *via crucis* of that newspaper since the triumph of the very revolution to which it contributed with 45 years of struggle—not to mention the blood of its martyred publisher, Pedro Joaquín Chamorro, and the ashes of his enterprise, destroyed by the last dictator. What has been our fortune since then? Ceaseless pressures, threats to news agents and to reporters, death threats to some editors who have been forced into exile, mobs attacking our physical installations, jail sentences, violence, withdrawal of passports, tapped telephones, tampered correspondence, and—from official organs—insults and lies, employing a crude and obscene language never before heard in our country. Without any question, this kind of treatment does not announce the advent of a *new man;* instead, it repeats the barbarous practices which are, unfortunately, the warp and woof of Nicaraguan political history. Perhaps some sort of excuse could be made for it by calling it the characteristic conduct of a new militarism. What is intolerable, however, is the representation of censorship as some sort of culmination of a liberation movement; as the final "conquest" of that revolution which was, after all, ignited by the death of a newspaperman, of an intellectual whom even the hated regime felt obligated to officially proclaim "martyr to public liberties." To escape the clutches of three Somozas merely to fall into the pit of censorship—really, for this there is no excuse! It amounts to crowning with fear the libertarian struggle of those who were not afraid to die.

Let us be clear: censorship is cowardice. On the part of the authorities it institutionalizes the abuse of power. It masks corruption. It is a school of torture: it teaches, and accustoms one to the use of force against an idea, to submit thought to an alien "other." But worst still, censorship destroys criticism, which is the essential ingredient of culture. The human condition, after all, is defined by the aspiration to always supersede oneself, which in turn requires nonconformity. As the Spanish poet Antonio Machado has his character Juan de Mairena say, "Even if we could teach a chimpanzee everything we know, he still would be unable to replicate the human condition, since that requires an essential willingness to question one's own nature, to desire to be other than what one is." What makes it impossible for the chimpanzee to mount the final scale in the animal kingdom is a lack of criticism, the only recourse that makes possible human and cultural progress. As I have told my Sandinista friends and former friends until I am blue in the face: any revolution which denies the right to criticize is bound to wallow in stagnation and backwardness. But in Latin America, something even worse will happen—the chimpanzee will become a gorilla.

For a writer there is nothing more depressing than to receive an editorial or an article mutilated by censorship—I leave aside an act of intellectual thuggery far worse, which is tampering with a poem!

Nonetheless, a poet like the American Lawrence Ferlinghetti—I admit, a man of surpassing naïveté—was quite unmoved when I showed him mountains of censored manuscripts originally destined for *La Prensa*. They dealt with topics very far from the civil war or the particular themes proscribed by the Law of Emergency. Nonetheless, in due course his publishing house in San Francisco saw fit to bring out a piece of Sandinista propaganda entitled *Seven Days in Nicaragua Libre*, wherein Ferlinghetti, to counteract my complaints about censorship and also to wash his hands of the matter, asked Ernesto Cardenal, also a poet and Minister of Culture, for an official declaration on censorship. Among other lies, it affirms, "With respect to censorship, I don't believe there is a single important document by any of our leaders defending it. In fact, we don't like it, and we don't want it; we have imposed it only because we are at war. . . . The newspaper *La Prensa* openly defends the enemy, the actions of the CIA, and employs all of the arguments of the Reagan administration. . . . In any event, this censorship ended in May, 1984, when the electoral campaign began. Since then there has been no basis for attacking Nicaragua on this score, but of course they will find others."

With respect to this letter I should merely like to point out that (1) for Cardenal, whose status as a priest seems not to inhibit him from misrepresenting facts, to demand democracy and liberty is to somehow provide Reagan and the CIA with arguments to attack our country; (2) Cardenal lies when he says that censorships was imposed by wartime conditions. Censorship was established in Nicaragua—for the radio as well as for newspapers—long before. I refer Mr. Ferlinghetti to Decrees 511 and 512 of September, 1980; almost immediately thereafter, the Ministry of Defense began intermittently closing down my newspaper. In 1981 alone, between January and September, there were fourteen such incidents. (3) Censorship was not lifted in May. It was maintained before the electoral campaign, during it, and after it. It continues to this date. How it pains me to see an admired, even beloved poet—now drunk with power—repeating the same formulas and falsehoods as the Somoza dictatorship used to employ when it wanted to deceive *its* naive Yankee "friends" . . .

José Napoleón Duarte

Inaugural Address (1984)

The achievement of democracy has never been easy for any people throughout history. El Salvador, all of its people, have paid a high price for it. . . . I wish to address all who kept their faith in democracy in the most adverse conditions, and who went to vote in the three democratic elections that we have held in the 80's. . . .

The significance of this unique, unprecedented, and new historical moment in our fatherland is that it is the product of the unmistakable and iron will of all of the Salvadoran people, who on two consecutive occasions—26 March and 6 May 1984—went massively to the polls to freely elect their legitimate rulers. . . .

Why did we vote? When over eighty percent of the Salvadoran people turned out to vote, it was not only because of their profound faith in the democratic system and in freedom. At the bottom of their hearts, each Salvadoran has also expressed, in voting, his profound desire to achieve peace and to create the necessary conditions for all of us to have work, the means for a decent life, and access to products in accordance with the potentials of each of us.

Salvadorans, we must bravely, frankly, and realistically acknowledge the fact that our homeland is immersed in an armed conflict that affects each and every one of us; that this armed conflict has gone beyond our borders and has become a focal point in the struggle between the big world power blocs. With the aid of Marxist governments like Nicaragua, Cuba, and the Soviet Union, an army has been trained and armed and has invaded our homeland.

Its actions are directed from abroad. Armed with the most sophisticated weapons, the Marxist forces harass our Armed Forces and constantly carry out actions intended to destroy our economy, with the loss of countless human lives and the suffering of hundreds of thousands of Salvadorans. For its part, our Army has been considerably enlarged, it has received better training, and it is imbued with a profound patriotic commitment to defend the people and to keep us from falling into the hands of Marxist subversion, which seeks to establish a totalitarian dictatorship in our homeland.

From *FBIS: Latin America*, June 4, 1984.

In the face of these realities, many Salvadorans have wondered why our Armed Forces have not yet managed to defeat the guerrillas. Many foreigners ask themselves the same question. Others, overwhelmed by international Marxist propaganda, wonder why the guerrillas have not yet managed to seize the country. The response to this is very simple: It has been clearly seen that the immense majority of the people have chosen the democratic solution by means of the vote, and this obviously makes it impossible for the guerrillas to seize the country. Then there is another truth. This is that many of us Salvadorans view the conflict as spectators, concerned only about our own interests, without contributing to the economic recovery, our national defense, or the solution of our social conflicts. This is the gist of the matter. So far, the people have rejected the violence and the war, but have not taken dynamic action, alongside the Armed Forces, to defend democracy, even though the situation has changed drastically. This is why it is important to point out our position on dialogue and the negotiation.

I have often said that if dialogue and negotiation are taken to mean a discussion of power quotas with weapons on the table, this would be denying the very essence of democracy, distorting the very essence of civilian power, and making a mockery of the mandate that the people have bestowed upon us. It is tantamount to accepting and admitting that power on both sides is exclusively in the hands of those who wield weapons. I have often said that differences should not be settled through violence and death, but through reason. I wish to recall my own words when, speaking to the nation, I said: If they were capable of taking up weapons, they should now be audacious in laying them down.

I receive the presidency of the Republic directly from the people, because democracy has triumphed and the Constitution prevails. Therefore, the Armed Forces are fulfilling their specific mission with upright discipline, changing the course of history, leaving behind the sad past when the Armed Forces were used as a tool of repression by the political groups that controlled power while the opposition that struggled for justice and freedom was subjugated.

This achievement, which was well explained by President Magaña, contrasts with the subjugation that leftist political sectors find themselves in with regard to the military guerrilla sector. The truth is that they have fallen under the authority of the guerrilla commanders, whom they must obey, and have not demonstrated so far that they are the leaders of the subversive movement. For this reason, to achieve credibility, they must demonstrate their authority over the armed sector, because in this way, any decision like that made by the subversive groups in Colombia would be heeded by the entire subversive movement. This would be an important signal, and one which the entire nation and all of our people expect, so that dialogue is not held with weapons on the table, but serves instead to find the political paths necessary to bring all Salvadorans into the democratic process. Since this is of momentous importance, allow me to repeat this: This would be an important signal, and one which the entire nation expects, so that dialogue is not held with weapons on the table, but serves instead to find the political paths to bring all Salvadorans into the democratic process.

For its part, my government will make efforts to promote a climate of security and confidence that will permit us, as a prior step, to begin as soon as possible a national dialogue among all democratic forces and majority sectors so that together we can draw up a formula of peace that will be the faithful reflection of the real feelings of the Salvadoran people and that will be vigorously supported so that no one can doubt that such a formula is a genuine decision and an expression of the will of all of the people and that should be turned into a common, energetic, and supreme effort capable of overcoming all obstacles and of achieving the great objective of peace. For this purpose, we will appeal to the law, international solidarity, patriotic responsibility, and, when circumstances demand, to the legitimate right of defense.

The structural crisis: The crisis we currently face has its origins in the unequal structures that have characterized our political, economic, and social process. But we have also recognized our weakness and errors so as to implement adequate reforms and begin to build democracy, social justice, and respect for human rights, and to achieve the peace that we need and desire so much. In the face of this reality, El Salvador does not need foreign ideologies. It does not need to hear the deafening language of sophisticated weapons or the materialistic clamor of an alleged specific destiny. It does not need to be an area of international dispute.

However, we need to build a new fatherland, free of an unjust past and in whose foundations there will be a predominant place for human development and freedom within a context of participatory institutions that will guarantee respect for the rights of all individuals without regard to their political position, economic condition, or social situation. . . .

These in turn can offer us the common good and the participation of the majority, values for which these great Salvadoran people have always fought; values on which misguided, impatient, and frustrated sectors even claim to support themselves, and which they have used as the primary reason for their struggle to obtain by means of blind and irreconcilable violence that which we are achieving peacefully as a majority. Those sectors do not realize that they are being treacherously used to establish an all-embracing dictatorship at all levels of the social structure, a totalitarian and atheist dictatorship in which the human being is stripped of his most elemental rights. These minority sectors are joined by others which, also by means of terror, stubbornly seek to return to a system of privileges which no longer have either a place or a reason for being in this new and emerging society, which has been called upon to grow deep roots.

For this reason I urge both sectors to abandon their violent stands and adopt the social pact so that together we may create a suitable climate so the peasants, the workers, the artisans, the small business-men, in short, the sectors traditionally excluded from economic, so-cial, political, and cultural development in El Salvador, may find and enjoy the betterment they yearn for in their lives and their work and for their descendants. Only in this way can we overcome the crisis. Only in this way can we achieve peace, the peace for which the people voted bravely, the peace that the innermost recesses of our nationality claim, the peace that the people conceive of not as a mere absence of armed violence but as an environment resulting from a system where there is no room for structural violence based on anach-ronistic forms of participation in the economic, social, political, and cultural life of our country. . . .

José Napoleón Duarte

Terrorism and Democracy (1985)

Events of the past years have led to brutal actions of the past weeks, making it crystal clear that in El Salvador a battle is being fought between diametrically opposed principles: humanism and terrorism.

Terrorism has grown as a world wide cancer. With few exceptions democratic nations have been unable to eliminate or significantly reduce its criminal consequences and disastrous effects.

I must make clear here today something that no well-meaning individual can dare reject. There is a symbiotic relationship between totalitarianism and terrorism. This is possible thanks to those who promote, use, protect and guarantee its impunity. Moreover, totalitar-ianism feeds endlessly on terrorism.

As a counterpart to totalitarianism, there exist in open societies laws

From a speech at National Press Club, November 1, 1985.

and principles based in humanism: A frame of reference within which the human beings can develop as individuals and as members of society. Nonetheless, open societies are susceptible to threats, to danger and to the thirst for power of those who profess totalitarian doctrines. To attempt against these rights, is to attempt against humanity.

The language used by totalitarians and terrorists, who are one and the same, may at times sound suggestive, but I invite you to bear in mind at all times that those who preach and practice hatred and violence cannot or will not ever be champions of justice. . . .

To better understand the process that has brought my country to the present confrontation between humanism and terrorism, let me remind you that the extreme left in El Salvador has gone through three different easily identifiable stages.

In the first stage, it publicly declared war against what the subversives termed the "national oligarchy," and the extreme left expressed its intent to fight for a democratic and representative government. These positions won them the support of leaders of parties within the Socialist International and of some free-thinking intellectuals around the world. However, when the Salvadoran Government enacted the land reform which turned over large land holdings to campesino cooperatives and the rented land to the tenant farmers, when it nationalized the banks and foreign trade, the extreme left turned to assassinations of campesino leaders, to burning crops picked by the cooperatives. When the first free elections in national history were held, the guerrillas shot against civilians who were in line to cast their ballots, burned ballot boxes and put fire to city halls and schools where balloting was taking place.

The people of El Salvador confronted the threats of the Marxist guerrillas and in the midst of bullet fire turned out to cast their votes in larger numbers than ever.

In the second stage, faced with the will of the Salvadoran population, the extreme left changed its objectives and stated that its fight was against the armed forces and the Government, who it considered "puppets of Yankee imperialism." The guerrillas then, besides their military operation, committed themselves to the merciless destruction of our infrastructure—blowing up bridges, schools, health care centers, city halls, railroads, electric pylons, water reservoirs, roads and anything in their path—that, to a poor nation like mine, required the efforts of generations to build. In indiscriminately denying the population the basic services such as water, education, health, electricity and telephones, the Communists, saying that these were military objectives, were damaging the majority of the Salvadorans, who not only have turned their backs on subversion but have defied it openly in the elections. During that period, the violent actions of the extreme left, in their alliance against democracy, joined with the violence of the extreme rightist individuals who brutally and in the name of Nazi inspired anticommunism and fascism tortured and killed civilians through their infamous death squads.

Two facts altered the strategy of the extreme left and of their foreign allies. The people of El Salvador enacted a new Constitution, elected freely a President and a new Congress in an electoral contest that gave a resounding victory to the Christian Democratic Party, to which I am proud to belong. At the same time, the armed forces increased its capacity through unprecedented technical improvement and demonstrated its commitment to law and the Constitution.

As the air we breathe and the freedom we enjoy, peace can only be appreciated in its full context when it is missing, when it is lost. The fight for national peace was not only the result of my devotion for the human being but a mandate that the people had given me at my election. Because of that mandate, on October 15, 1984, as the world witnessed our fervent desire for peace, I called in the United Nations for a serious and honest dialogue with the subversives to serve as a vehicle for them to become part of the democratic process and to compete for power through elections.

I left our meeting at the church in La Palma feeling optimistic and satisfied that my idealism had been vindicated. Among other factors, had the dialogue continued only among Salvadorans, if the guerrillas had not had so many commitments to their patrons in Cuba, Nicaragua, Bulgaria, the Soviet Union, Libya, the PLO, and others, then, even in the midst of the storm, we would have found a rainbow of peace.

Criticized by national and international opinion, stunned by the improvement of our soldiers and weakened by the will of the people, the Salvadoran guerrillas accepted Yasir Arafat's thesis of terror as submitted to the Palestinian leadership. In this third stage they have joined the criminal fanatics who believed they could obtain their goals by murdering a handicapped old man aboard the *Achille Lauro*, those who kicked to death a young sailor on the TWA flight, and those who have placed bombs in airports.

This is not different from what is happening in El Salvador. The guerrillas have begun this third stage by spraying bullets on innocent people in a sidewalk café and by terrorizing families, including my own. They kidnapped many Salvadorans, among whom were 33 mayors and municipal employees of small villages, young Ana Cecilia Villeda Sosa and my daughter Inés Guadalupe, mother of three young children, arguing that they too were military objectives. I will not speak today about my suffering. I have vivid memories of the tears in my grandchildren's eyes when they asked about their mother. Obviously, these kidnappings were not only a declaration of war. They had a well-defined objective: to provoke repression, introduce disagreement within the armed forces and my government, and frighten the civilian population by showing that no one, not even the President, was safe from terrorism.

I rejected the idea to capture the families of the guerrilla commanders, because of my Christian and humanitarian convictions.

The spontaneous solidarity nationally and internationally in rejecting the condemnable act of kidnapping was so overpowering that the ex-guerrillas and now terrorists at first even denied the act, as PLO terrorists initially denied the murder of Mr. Leon Klinghoffer.

This crime against helpless individuals underscored the irrelevancy of the FMLN's political arm, the "Democratic Revolutionary Front" (FDR). The president of the FDR, when interviewed by reporters and members of the Socialist International, answered that he did not know anything about the kidnapping and later that he could not order or propose the release of the kidnapped. But a year ago, on October 15, 1984, in La Palma, the same president of the FDR maintained that the guerrillas and the FDR were the same thing, indivisible.

To prove that their crime was not an isolated case but a new stage of terrorism, the FMLN-FDR in El Salvador kidnapped last Saturday Colonel Napoleón Avalos, the Director of Civil Aviation, when he was with his children, and thus unable to defend himself without endangering their lives.

In Central America, in my own country, countless persons from all walks of life, and in the case of my family, my daughter Inés Guadalupe, would not have been victims of the merciless violence of the terrorists if terrorists did not have the support, direction, approval and timely protection of the terrorist dictatorship in Nicaragua. Nicaragua is the Central American source for totalitarianism and violence, and is the sanctuary for terrorists.

The Salvadoran guerrillas, whose headquarter is in Managua, have been trained, sheltered, armed, helped by the totalitarian governments of Nicaragua and Cuba with the support of the PLO and countries such as Libya.

I ask if terrorism could be possible without the assistance given by governments that, like Nicaragua, show total disregard to all the principles and rules of international law. . . .

Amnesty International

Human Rights in Nicaragua (1986)

3. Amnesty International's principal concerns today

3.1 PRISONERS OF CONSCIENCE

Leaders and members of political opposition parties and their affiliated trade unions have been subjected to arrest and short-term imprisonment in what Amnesty International believes to be a pattern of intimidation and harassment. These arrests were carried out under the state of emergency in force since March 1982. Most of these prisoners were released before their cases were brought to trial, however, and those prisoners of conscience believed to have been wrongfully convicted of crimes have, with few exceptions, been released under the law of pardon, not long after sentencing.

However, some trade union and political party leaders who Amnesty International believes to have been prisoners of conscience have been detained repeatedly, sometimes for a year or more. They have also been required to present themselves at the State Security Service's public relations office "Casa 50" for further interviews and questioning by officials. Many short-term detainees have reported that interrogators threatened them with further, prolonged imprisonment without trial in the custody of the State Security Service, or trial under the Public Order Law, as a consequence of further independent trade union or political party activism. . . .

3.4 CONSCRIPTION AND CONSCIENTIOUS OBJECTION TO MILITARY SERVICE

. . . After the revolution the provisions of the previous constitution for compulsory military service were reflected in the new government's Fundamental Statute (Article 24). Only in 1983, however, was legislation introduced by which obligatory military service was to be implemented. A law of compulsory military service, the *Ley del Servicio Militar Patriotico*, Law of Patriotic Military Service (Decree 1337), was enacted on 13 September 1983 under which all men aged 18 (subsequently modified to 17) to 40 were required to register for military service, and were subject to call up for active or reserve duty. Those

From Amnesty International, "Nicaragua: The Human Rights Record."

aged 18 to 25 were subject to immediate recruitment for two-year periods of active service. Women aged between 18 and 40 are eligible for voluntary registration for military service under the law.

Exemptions from military service are provided under the law for illness or disabilities, as well as for men with certain specified family responsibilities. The law makes no provision for conscientious objection to military service, or for service to be performed as an alternative to military duty.

A series of penalties are established in the law for people who fail to register for military service, who do not present themselves when called for interviews or examinations, or who provide false information on registration. Those who fail to register or to report when called for active service may be imprisoned for up to four years.

Opposition to the conscription law was voiced by some sectors of the Roman Catholic clergy and by political opposition groups, which claimed that the new army was in the hands of a political party (the FSLN) and so was not a legitimate national army. In 1984 some parents' groups protested against the implementation of the law after high casualty rates were reported from Honduran border areas. They claimed that young recruits were sent into combat inadequately trained and armed. Further protests related to the manner in which conscription was enforced during the law's first year of application. In late 1983 and the first months of 1984 young people in some areas were reportedly picked up by army recruiters virtually at random in press gang operations, including many who were under or over draft age, or who were otherwise exempt under the law. An inter-ministerial commission was reportedly set up in mid-1984 to supervise a review of conscription procedures, and to investigate and remedy reported abuses. . . .

3.6 DETENTION AND INTERROGATION PROCEDURES: THE STATE SECURITY SERVICE

Since the creation of a new government in 1979 the Ministry of Interior's State Security Service has taken primary responsibility for the detention and interrogation of most suspects in political cases. Incommunicado detention is the norm for prisoners in State Security Service custody, with prisoners frequently held incommunicado for from fifteen to thirty days and sometimes for several months. Although the State Security Service maintains offices and detention facilities in most major towns, the principal detention and interrogation facility is at its headquarters in Managua. Known as "El Chipote," it is located on the slope of the Loma de Tiscapa volcano behind Managua's Intercontinental Hotel. Most political detainees are reportedly brought for interrogation to "El Chipote" and held there pending indictment or release. . . .

* * *

In practice, the State Security Service's actions under the state of emergency and suspension of most civil rights appear to be largely unrestricted by the judiciary or any other civil authority. Optometrist Alejandro Pereira was detained on 6 June 1983 and taken to "El Chipote" on suspicion that on recent visits to Honduras he had contacted FDN and CIA officials, a charge he denied. Held totally incommunicado for seventy days, Alejandro Pereira was taken before a court only in January 1984. He was charged with violation of the Public Order Law Articles 1 b) and g), after he had signed a "confession" that he had provided political, military, and economic information to the FDN and CIA. During his seven months at "El Chipote," the State Security Service's Director refused to comply with a Supreme Court *habeas corpus* order to permit access to an examining magistrate to establish the condition of his health—he had previously had several operations for a duodenal ulcer and was hospitalized at the order of the court after his first court appearance in January.

While he was held incommunicado, an elaborate effort was made to convince Alejandro Pereira that his wife, too, had been detained, and that she would remain at "El Chipote" until he "confessed." Sra. Pereira had been taken to "El Chipote" on 9 June, dressed in a prison overall, and been walked past Alejandro Pereira as he stood in an open doorway; neither was permitted to speak. Sra. Pereira was then permitted to return to her home. For the next 70 days of incommunicado detention Alejandro Pereira was told his wife was also undergoing interrogation at "El Chipote."

After receiving a seven year sentence passed by the TPA court on 23 February 1984, based exclusively on his testimony while held incommunicado, Alejandro Pereira denied that his statement had been made freely, and claimed that he had been both psychologically and physically tortured. On appeal his sentence was raised to fifteen years' imprisonment, the court rejecting his allegations out of hand. Amnesty International was given access by the president of the TPA court to the trial record, including the original copy of the "confession." The organization expressed concern to the authorities that the statement had been produced while the prisoner was incommunicado in the State Security Service's custody, and that his allegations of coercion had not resulted in any investigation of the State Security Service's procedures in the case. Further concern was expressed at the general failure of the Ministry of Justice (the public prosecutor's office) or the courts to challenge the validity of such "confessions" recorded by the State Security Service while prisoners were held incommunicado. In October 1984 Alejandro Pereira was released on health grounds through a pardon by the Council of State.

Amnesty International was concerned that in other cases the State Security Service appeared to have fabricated evidence and to have manipulated the government news media in order to denigrate political opponents, and justify to the Nicaraguan public their detention and prosecution. One such case was the prosecution and house arrest of Father Amado Peña, a priest well known for his outspoken criticism of the government in sermons in his Managua church, who is considered close to Cardinal Monseñor Miguel Obando y Bravo, a critic of the current government. On 22 June 1984 the State Security Service broadcast a video film which showed Father Peña leaving a car holding a bag, which, when opened by police officers, revealed a "terrorist kit" implicating the church in armed violence: several hand grenades, dynamite, and a white and yellow Vatican flag on which the letters FDN had been sewn.

According to Father Peña, however, who was interviewed by Amnesty International delegates in July 1984 while under house arrest, after celebrating mass on 22 June he had accepted a lift from a man at the service and, when the driver pulled up behind a parked car, was asked to hand a bag to a man in the other car. A video was recorded by the State Security Service as he stepped from the car holding the bag and shows the appearance of police officers on the scene and the opening of the bag in their presence. The drivers of the two cars were apparently neither questioned, detained, nor publicly identified by the State Security Service and Father Peña was told he could go home when the filming was completed. However, four days later, after the government news media denounced him as a terrorist accomplice, he was placed under house arrest, and confined to a Church seminary outside Managua. Ten foreign priests who had been critical of government policies, some of whom had been residents in Nicaragua for over 30 years, were summarily expelled from Nicaragua after protesting against the government news media's attacks on Father Peña. Amnesty International considered Father Peña a prisoner of conscience, falsely implicated in criminal activity by the State Security Service because of his expression of his political views. Although charges were brought against Father Peña before the Popular Tribunal, the case never went to trial and the charges were dismissed by a legislative pardon in September 1984.

In a June 1985 letter to President Ortega, Amnesty International stressed its concern at the extraordinary *de facto* powers accorded the State Security Service under the state of emergency, and the consequent scope for abuse of these powers. The organization noted that the State Security Service routinely carried out detentions without apparent basis in law; that long periods of incommunicado detention subject to no known regulation were the norm for State Security

Service prisoners in pre-trial detention; that in some cases even members of the judiciary were denied access to prisoners by the state Security Service and that State Security Service prisoners were routinely denied consultation with defense lawyers, or contact with families or doctors. Concern was also expressed about the lack of accountability of the State Security Service to the judiciary. State Security Service officers carrying out arrests and interrogations, who are responsible for determining the conditions and duration of incommunicado, administrative detention, are apparently accountable in practice only to the Minister of the Interior, and not to any court of law or other supervisory authority. . . .

In a similar case, forestry technicians Fausto Cristy and Jorge Canales, both Nicaraguans, and Regine Schmemann, a citizen of the Federal Republic of Germany, were seized on 14 June 1985 by forces of the largely Miskito Indian group MISURA while working north of Puerto Cabezas in Zelaya Department. They were subsequently taken into Honduran territory to the MISURA camp at Srum Laya. Following international protests, Regine Schmemann was removed from Srum Laya on 2 July by a delegation of three men, one whom was identified as a Honduran army officer. According to Regine Schmemann's testimony, the army escort was made aware that her two companions remained in custody at Srum Laya, but made no effort to assist them. She was subsequently taken first to a Honduran army command post in Gracias a Dios province, and then to the capital, Tegucigalpa, where she was handed over to a representative from her country's embassy and members of the International Committee of the Red Cross.

According to the account given to Amnesty International by Regine Schmemann, each of the three captives was threatened with execution while in MISURA custody. It is believed that her presence, as a citizen of the Federal Republic of Germany, may have provided some protection for her companions, and that there is now considerable danger to the lives of these Nicaraguan civilians. On 12 August 1985 Amnesty International telexed the president of the Republic of Honduras to welcome the reported steps taken by the Honduran army to secure the release of Regine Schmemann, and urged that similar measures be taken to ensure the physical safety of Fausto Cristy and Jorge Canales and to secure their immediate release.

While some prisoners were reportedly taken to bases outside Nicaragua by opposition forces, the forces of the FDN were more frequently reported to retain no prisoners, killing captives on the spot or after brief field interrogations. In some areas they reportedly killed their captives before the assembled residents of target communities. Witnesses of such killings of relatives and neighbors, and FDN personnel who have deserted the force, have described in detailed testimonies made available to Amnesty International execution-style killings in which captives were bound, tortured, and their throats slit by FDN forces. In some cases captives were shot dead or beheaded. The number of captives tortured and put to death by FDN forces since 1981 is impossible to determine, but is believed to total several hundred.

3.8 ALLEGATIONS, INVESTIGATIONS AND PUNISHMENT OF OTHER ABUSE

Amnesty International has also received reports of other serious abuses of the rights of detainees. These have in past years included allegations of physical torture, "disappearance," and arbitrary killings. The organization has, however, welcomed a recent pattern whereby such allegations have been investigated and the police and military forces alleged to be responsible for such abuses have been brought to justice.

A number of cases of torture, "disappearance," and arbitrary killing were reported from the Pantasma area, in the Jinotega department, near the Honduran border, in late 1983 and the first days of 1984. The reports followed a series of major attacks there by Honduran based troops of the FDN in which some forty civilians were reported killed, some of them after capture. Nicaraguan army officers at Pantasma responded with a wave of human rights violations directed at individuals suspected to be supporters of the FDN. Abuses reported included the torture of detainees, at least six extrajudicial executions, and the apparent "disappearance" of four local people. In January 1984 a special prosecutor was appointed to investigate the Pantasma case and forty-one military personnel were detained. In March 1984 a court martial in open session sentenced the region's army commander to forty-four years' imprisonment (although a maximum of thirty years of the sentence can be served under Nicaraguan law), on two counts of murder, and for the torture of four captives; twelve subordinates received sentences of up to fourteen years. The trial and convictions were widely publicized by the government inside Nicaragua. . . .

4.1 ALLEGATIONS OF TORTURE AND SUMMARY EXECUTIONS OF DETAINEES BY OPPOSITION FORCES

Since 1981 reports have been regularly received of detentions, torture and summary execution by armed opposition forces, with most reports coming from the areas of Jinotega and Matagalpa bordering Honduras, and the Atlantic Coast region. Victims of reported summary execution by forces associated with the FDN included a Miskito, José Cornejo, who was released in the December 1983 amnesty, and his wife. José Cornejo was reportedly accused by opposition forces of collaborating with the Nicaraguan authorities and as a consequence he and his wife were reportedly captured and killed in late January 1984 near the hamlet Yulo.

Others captured were reportedly taken to bases in Honduras or Costa Rica. Amnesty International appealed to the Honduran authorities in December 1982 after lay church leaders María Eugenia de Barreda and her husband Felipe Barreda were seized by FDN forces while working as teachers near the Honduran border, taken across the border, and reportedly transported by Honduran army forces to the town of Danli where they and other Nicaraguan captives were reportedly held and interrogated. According to the detailed reports, from captives who escaped FDN/Honduran custody at Danli, the Barredas had been severely beaten. Other reports maintained that María Eugenia de Barreda had been repeatedly raped and was held bound and gagged. The bodies of the two were reportedly found near Danli several months later.

More recently, Amnesty International appealed to the Honduran authorities after the seizure by FDN forces in Nicaragua's Jinotega department of five student teachers on 28 September, 1984, and another on 5 October and their reported removal across the border to Honduras. In mid-November 1985 it was reported that one of them had escaped. She told a press conference in Managua that she had been held inside Honduras for part of her captivity, where she was raped and tortured. She believed that four of her colleagues may have been killed by the FDN. The detention of the fifth teacher remains unconfirmed and the Honduran authorities have made no response to inquiries about her fate and that of other captives reportedly taken to the FDN's Las Vegas camp.

Irving Kristol

"Human Rights": The Hidden Agenda (1986/87)

To the best of my knowledge, the first time the issue of "human rights" became a focus for a major foreign policy debate in a Western democracy occurred a little more than a century ago in Britain, when Gladstone divided the country because of the massacre of some 12,000 Bulgarians by their Turkish rulers.

From *The National Interest-Winter 1986/7*.

Gladstone was a believing Christian, with an intensity of religious commitment that, in the United States today, would surely be regarded as a disqualification for high office. He was appalled that the British government, under Disraeli, seemed unmoved by the massacre of Bulgarian Christians by Turkish Muslims. And Disraeli was indeed unmoved. Though nominally a Christian, he could hardly be called a believer, much less a true believer. What he did care very much about was preventing Russia, the self-appointed Slavic "protector" of Bulgarians and other Balkan peoples under Turkish rule, from liquidating the Turkish empire and acquiring Constantinople and the Dardanelles in the process. He saw this as a serious threat to the new British empire he was in the process of creating—an empire that would include India and Cyprus, with the area in between (Afghanistan, Egypt, etc.) a British sphere of influence. For Disraeli, Russia's imperial ambitions were the main enemy, and it was to frustrate these ambitions that he tried to preserve the integrity of the Turkish empire— even if it meant a war with Russia, which he was prepared to contemplate. In the event, the Turkish empire was beyond salvaging, but at the Congress of Berlin Disraeli was still able to come away with "peace and honor"—i.e., with Cyprus in hand and the Dardanelles out of Soviet reach. As a concession to the Tsar, the Bulgarians did get some dilution of Turkish sovereignty, but for Disraeli this was distinctly a minor matter.

In the brief period that intervened between the original Bulgarian massacre and the Congress of Berlin, Gladstone did more than denounce Disraeli for lack of Christian compassion. He elaborated an alternative view of Britain's role in the world and of an appropriate British foreign policy. It was, quite simply, an anti-imperialist view, a candidly "little England" view. He thought it ridiculous for Queen Victoria to become Empress of India, saw no point in having Cyprus as a colony or in establishing military outposts in Afghanistan. He believed in self-determination for the Christian peoples of the Balkans and did not give a damn for the Turkish empire, which he regarded as a barbaric relic—but he was not about to do anything to "liberate" those Christian peoples. And while he did not like the idea of Russia acquiring the Dardanelles, he did not think it was worth a war to prevent it. This was not just a point of view, it was a program.

When Gladstone returned to office in 1880, however, the "facts" that Disraeli had created, the public opinion that had been solidified behind them, as well as the coercive necessities of international power politics, prevented Gladstone from carrying out his program. He never left any doubt as to what he would have preferred to do, had he been free to do it. But he was not free, and the issue of "human rights" slid once again to the distant margins of British foreign policy.

When one looks back at this episode, one is struck by what one can only call the "innocence" with which the issue was raised and debated. Ever since the end of World War II, in contrast, when "human rights" again became of international concern, the entire discussion has been tainted with disingenuousness. For the past four decades, a concern for "human rights" has not simply and mainly been opposed to a hardheaded and hard-hearted realpolitik. On the contrary, despite the sea of sentimentality on which the issue of "human rights" has floated, that issue has, as often as not, been an accessory to a certain kind of ideological politics.

Today, most discussions of "human rights" are misleading because beneath the surface there is almost always a hidden agenda. An issue of "human rights" today is all too likely to be an issue exploited in bad faith.

Am I questioning the sincerity of the thousands of "human rights" activists in the United States and elsewhere? Well, sincerity in politics is a tricky affair. It is more common in politics than cynics think, but even political activists can have difficulty knowing what it is they are being sincere *about*. It is not always easy to distinguish between sincerity and a passionate self-righteousness that cares only for the purity of conscience which inhabits a posturing self. Many of the most ardent Northern abolitionists, prior to the Civil War, were so offended by slavery that they urged that the South be encouraged to secede. Were they being sincere about slavery, or about their own moral fastidiousness? God only knows.

There is no doubt that most Americans who exhibit a passionate interest in "human rights" are moved primarily by humanitarian motives—usually by an understandable, even commendable, outrage at one particular abuse directed against a particular person or group of persons. It is then very easy for them to slide into a feverish humanitarian*ism* which disorients their senses when they confront issues of foreign policy. In such a condition, they are easily manipulable by those who have a professional, as distinct from a simple, humanitarian interest in "human rights."

Yes, one must certainly respect the courage of those human rights activists who live and operate in countries and under circumstances where self-sacrifice is a possible consequence of their commitment. Yet it also has to be said that even some of those who make this exemplary commitment do not necessarily care about "human rights" in any general sense. Thus, I do not share the widespread admiration for Archbishop Tutu of South Africa, because I am reasonably certain that if and when the African National Congress comes to power, he will be a vocal apologist for its tyranny and brutality. My certainty on this score derives from his placid acquiescence in the brutality and tyranny of existing black African regimes.

On the whole, then, I think the question of "sincerity" is best left aside when discussing "human rights" agitation. Much human rights agitation today appears to exemplify what Hegel called "negative activity"—a fanaticism of the abstract that assaults the actual without having in mind any practical plans for improving the actual. In politics such "negative activity," whatever its motivation, always ends up serving a positive political purpose. It seems to me that the key question today is whether such activity is linked to a "hidden agenda." Much of the time, I would argue, this is the case. Moreover, it is this linkage that explains why the issue of "human rights" has achieved such extraordinary prominence in our time.

The era of bad faith in "human rights" began soon after the conclusion of World War II, with the United Nations' Universal Declaration of Human Rights in 1948. This document has been widely criticized for the bland way it equates "social and economic rights" (the right to a job, the right to medical care, vacations with pay) with the kinds of traditional political rights (government by consent of the governed, due process off law, etc.) that have prevailed in the liberal democracies. But there was more than intellectual error or enthusiastic idealism at work here. The document was an important first step in establishing something like a moral equivalence between liberal capitalist democracies and communist or self-styled socialist regimes. This was the hidden agenda that gave birth to this text.

It is probable that most of those in the West who endorsed the Declaration did not realize what was happening. They shortsightedly perceived only immediate advantages to their own political agendas. The trade unions were delighted to see their long-standing demands elevated to the level of "human rights." Liberals eager to construct a welfare state were pleased to think that they were now enlarging the sphere of "human rights." So, naturally, were social democrats, for whom the welfare state is a necessary transitional regime toward some kind of socialist society. To the degree that these groups shared a common ideological purpose it was the denigration of "old-fashioned" property rights in order to create a more egalitarian society—and to this same degree, they were complicitous with the "hidden agenda," even if they didn't fully realize its implications. On the other hand, some of those involved in the composition and promulgation of this text knew exactly what they were doing, and were fully aware of its implications.

Those implications, spelled out over the succeeding decades, have been momentous. To begin with, the Declaration legitimized the notion that totalitarian or authoritarian societies that emphasize "social and economic rights" as part of an official egalitarian ideology have their own distinctive virtues as well as their obvious vices, to be balanced against the virtues and vices of liberal-capitalist societies. While this did not usually result in a literal "moral equivalence," it did frustrate any effort at a strong comparative moral judgment. It is not too much to say that what was involved was nothing less than a firm step toward the *moral disarmament* of the West.

Perhaps an even more important intellectual consequence of this new conception of "human rights" was the near-magical transvaluation of a venerable political idea: the idea of tyranny. Clearly, any authoritarian or totalitarian regime officially dedicated to an egalitarian ideology and officially committed to the entire spectrum of "social and economic rights" could not simply be described as tyranny, even though the kinds of political rights distinctive of liberal societies were nonexistent. This helps to explain what to many thoughtful people is otherwise a mystery, or a sheer perversity: why the majority of liberals in the West extend such an extraordinary tolerance toward "left-wing" tyrants.

Traditional liberalism spoke not of "human rights" but of *individual rights*, these being almost exclusively rights vis-à-vis government. It explicitly recognized only one "social or economic right": the right to property, including the "property" of one's labor power. This right was thought to be the cornerstone of all those political rights that collectively defined a liberal order. In and of itself, of course, it was not a sufficient basis for those rights—but it was deemed a necessary basis for those rights. Nothing in the experience of the past three centuries has invalidated this thesis. Political liberties exist only in societies that respect individual rights, including property rights. True, the degree of respect (or non-respect) will vary from country to country, and from time to time. Moreover, in all liberal societies today, property rights have been limited by various entitlements that some would call "social and economic rights," although they are never constitutionally defined as such. But wherever these entitlements are given a massive priority as part of an egalitarian ethos, a liberal society either will not exist or will not endure for long.

To put it bluntly: the effect of the "hidden agenda" was to help delegitimate the market economy ("capitalism") that is an indispensable precondition of a traditional liberal ("bourgeois") society. It had the further implication of casting into doubt the moral status of American foreign policy, which has never thought it appropriate to concern itself with "social and economic rights" in other countries. The importance of this latter implication has been gradually revealed over the course of the past two decades. It is today the primary "hidden agenda" of most activist organizations concerned with "human rights."

I have to emphasize (lest I seem paranoid) that many of the people involved in these organizations are naive innocents. But among the organizers and leaders there are always some full-time professionals who are sophisticated enough to know exactly what they are doing. "Human rights" indeed is only one aspect of their endeavors. It has been documented—though little notice has been taken of this—that many of the same people who are among the leaders of "human rights" agitation are also active in antinuclear agitation, arms control agitation, extremist environmentalist agitation, unilaterial disarmament agitation, anti-aid-to-the-*contras* agitation, radical feminist agitation, as well as all sorts of organizations that sponsor "friendship" programs with left-wing regimes. Since these are not only energetic people, but very intelligent as well, they have been very successful in giving the issue of "human rights" a special "spin" in a certain direction.

Take, for instance, the question of "torture" which has become so prominent in "human rights" agitation. Note that I put the word in quotation marks, because one of the successes of the "human rights" movement has been to broaden the definition of "torture" to include what would otherwise be classified as "police brutality." Americans would be disapproving of but not outraged at police brutality or the use of third-degree methods against prisoners in distant lands; we are, after all, familiar enough with this phenomenon at home, and would not be surprised to learn that it is far more common in "less civilized" (i.e., most other) countries. But torture, real torture, is an abomination to the bourgeois-liberal sensibility, a violation of that sense of human dignity which is at the very root of our liberal individualism. So a focus on torture is a brilliant bit of public relations.

The question that should be asked, but isn't, is: Why is torture such an issue now, when in years past it never even entered any discussion of international relations? Is torture more common today than it was, say, thirty years ago? There is no reason to think so. In a country like Turkey there has always been a thin line between sheer brutality and outright torture in its prisons. But Turkey, a member of Nato, is an important military ally of the United States. Are we really willing to help destabilize its government in the interest of prison reform? And are those who are so willing really more interested in prison reform than in such destabilization?

In fact, torture (and police brutality, too) may well be less common in the world today because of the power of the media to expose such abuses. In general, actual torture is used today mainly in countries where it has been a traditional practice for centuries. It is also likely to be used in circumstances of a guerilla insurrection (urban or rural) where the police and military—themselves targets (and often victims) of assassination—are determined to acquire information that might help them suppress the rebellion. That there is provocation to torture is not, of course, a justification, since civilized opinion properly decided long ago that there is no justification, whatever the circumstances. But by focusing on instances of torture (or of police brutality now counted as torture) the "human rights" activists score an important point: They help legitimate the insurrection that today generally comes from the left, while doing their bit to discredit those governments that are trying to suppress the insurrection.

Critics of the "human rights" organizations assert that these organizations operate on a double standard—they seek out authoritarian governments that are on good terms with the United States and emphasize the violations (real or supposed) of "human rights" that occur there, but tend to be relatively unexcited, or at least much less excited, about violations of "human rights" by authoritarian or totalitarian anti-American governments. Indeed, the government that gains this privileged status need not even be left-wing, so long as it is clearly anti-American. Note the disproportionate lack of interest in the state of "human rights" in Syria or Iran, as contrasted with the intense interest in Israel.

To this the "human rights" activists reply, with plausibility, that it makes sense for them to direct their energies to situations where it is reasonable to assume that the United States government is capable of exercising some benign influence—and where, therefore, it bears a degree of moral responsibility for failing to exercise this influence. To which the critics retort that the "human rights" activists are themselves guilty of moral turpitude because of their failure to distinguish between what Joshua Muravchik calls "individual abuses" and "systemic deformities," the latter characterizing totalitarian communist regimes as distinct from merely authoritarian regimes. To which the "human rights" spokesmen then reply that this distinction between "totalitarian" and "authoritarian" regimes is a species of "cold war" sophistry, since the suffering of the victim of torture or police brutality under either regime is unvarnished, indistinguishable suffering.

I must confess that, though my sympathies are all with the critics of the "human rights" movement, I find this debate to be essentially sterile. To begin with, the perspective of the victim—whether in war or peace—is the stuff of which poetry (or perhaps theology) is made, not politics, and certainly not foreign policy. To invert Tolstoy's aphorism, all victims are alike in their suffering and humiliation. But not all political regimes in which suffering and humiliation exist are alike. The difference between totalitarian *societies* and authoritarian *governments* is obvious enough—though one of the purposes of focusing on the individual indignities suffered under both regimes is precisely to blur this obvious distinction. True, not all totalitarian societies are identical—there are important national differences that create shades and hues of totalitarianism—nor are they immune to change. But though there may arise an occasional instance where the distinction between an authoritarian and totalitarian policy is less easy to make, the distinction is of crucial significance for an understanding of twentieth-century history and politics.

Authoritarian governments have existed throughout history and may fairly be regarded as *pre*-liberal realities. Whether they are "destined" to become liberal or totalitarian societies, or to evolve into some social form still unimaginable, is an interesting question of political philosophy. But no one can seriously claim that the numerous authoritarian regimes now scattered all over the world constitute any kind of threat to liberal America or the liberal West. Totalitarian societies, on the other hand, are *post*-liberal realities—they emerge out of an explicit rejection of the Western liberal tradition, are the declared enemies of this tradition, and aim to supercede it. It is impossible to write a history of international relations in the twentieth century without making the rise of post-liberal totalitarianism (whether of the right or left) *the* central event of the era, or without making the "cold war" between the liberal democracies and the new totalitarian states the central focus around which everything else revolves. It is, in contrast, perfectly possible to write a history of international relations in the twentieth century without ever bothering to mention something called "authoritarianism." In fact, the histories that have been written all do exemplify both this impossibility and this possibility.

It is not an accident that most "human rights" activists, and all "human rights" publicists or theorists, insist on denying either the existence or the importance of the totalitarian-authoritarian distinction. In the abstract, there would seem to be no need for them to do so. There are actually some "human rights" activists who do ignore this whole issue—like the clergy of yesteryear, they are impelled by the simple desire to alleviate human suffering, without paying attention to politics. But these are a minority, even among the clergy of today. The "human rights" *movement* is decidedly political. Its need to obfuscate the totalitarian-authoritarian distinction flows from its political intentions, its desire to deny that the "cold war" is anything but a paranoid fantasy of a bourgeois-capitalist establishment, to minimize the totalitarian threat to liberal-democratic nations, to unnerve American foreign policy by constantly exposing the "immorality" of its relations with authoritarian allies, etc. In short, to repeat: Its purpose—

the hidden agenda of its "negative activity"—is the moral disarmament of the bourgeois-capitalist West.

It is interesting, by the way, to note that the "human rights" movement is far less influential in Western Europe, and is taken far less seriously by governments there, than is the case in the United States. No European foreign office has to engage in the idiotic political arithmetic which Congress has imposed on our State Department, whereby every year it solemnly tots up the "human rights" situation in dozens of countries. It is an inherently absurd enterprise. If women in Switzerland don't have the vote, while they do in Romania, does that make Romania in any way more respectful of "human rights" than Switzerland? And how does one even apply the concept of "human rights" to Saudi Arabia—a medieval nation rather than a modern state? Why are we so silly as to get involved in this sort of thing, while European governments do not? Are the peoples across the Atlantic less concerned with human rights than we are?

I don't think so. I believe, rather, than the difference is that Western Europe has real, live, important socialist parties, while the United States does not. The result is that those Americans who, in Europe, would belong to socialist or social-democratic parties are forced to channel their political energies into "causes" which, in sum, approximate as closely as possible to those parties' programs. The upshot is that the European left is far more candid than its American counterpart, and has less need for any hidden agendas. When one reads books by European socialists on foreign affairs—the recent writings of Regis Debray can serve as an example—"human rights" is, at most, a very subordinate theme and the theme is sometimes not struck at all. These writings suffer from all kinds of illusions, but they are illusions that flow from avowed ideological convictions. In the United States, where it is imprudent to avow a socialist ideology, those convictions go underground and then emerge in "causes" such as "human rights" or "arms control" or "unilateral nuclear disarmament," which present themselves as apolitical or transpolitical.

Precisely because they seem so nonpolitical or transpolitical, they can actually be more radical in substance. No European country has an Arms Control and Disarmament Agency, whose function is presumably to thwart the militarist proclivities of our Defense Department. Similarly, no European country has an Assistant Secretary of State for Human Rights, whose function is presumably to thwart the immoral proclivities of our State Department. True, the notion of negotiating an "arms control" agreement with the Soviet Union is at least as popular in Western Europe as in the United States. But in Western Europe this notion is often based on a real (or not-unrealistic) anxiety, that a conflict between the two superpowers would easily and quickly result in Western Europe becoming a devastated nuclear battlefield, even if the source of this conflict lies outside Western Europe itself or is marginal to Western Europe interests. It is this fear that motivates many of the more serious "antinuclear" activists over there. In the United States, however, "antinuclear" and "arms control" publicists are more akin to the anti-American, pro-Soviet left in Europe. They are persuaded that it is a "cold war" American foreign policy which threatens the world with nuclear devastation, and that a more "conciliatory" (i.e., appeasing) posture toward the Soviet Union and its allies will avert such a catastrophe. They display little fear of Soviet intentions, much fearful anxiety about our own White House, Pentagon, and State Department. It is this distrust of the United States and of its status as a world power—what in Europe would be called "anti-Americanism"—that motivates our more passionate "antinuclear" advocates and impels them to support *any* formula acceptable to the Soviets, and to adopt an appeasing mode in foreign policy. Such appeasement is their hidden—not deeply hidden, it must be said—agenda.

There is no other explanation, so far as I can see, for the pertinacity of various leading "arms control" advocates, when by now one would have expected them to be thoroughly disillusioned with the whole affair. This includes many who were involved in the negotiation of the SALT I agreement, an agreement that never would have been signed, never could have been signed, if it had been understood beforehand that the Soviets would promptly install over 500 intermediate-range warheads aimed at Western Europe—something that, it turned out, was permitted (though certainly never envisaged) under the SALT I agreement. The lack of subsequent disillusionment among such knowledgeable people, the fact that their passion for the "arms control process" remains undiminished, is something that requires interpretation.

What makes American foreign policy so vulnerable to "human rights" agitation? The explanation is not far to seek: This foreign policy has—must have—an ineradicable moral-ideological component. We are indeed engaged in a profound ideological conflict with the Soviet Union, a conflict that dominates world politics. But it is both a simplification and a distortion to describe it as a conflict about "human rights." It is, rather, a conflict over the very *definition* of "human rights," and the point of this conflict is to determine who will have the *power* to define "human rights" for future generations. In that sense, the United States cannot evade the urgencies and the ambiguities of "power politics."

The relation of such "power politics" to the American "public philosophy" makes for tension and complications in our foreign policy. Realpolitik à la Disraeli is unthinkable in America, since it runs against the very grain of our political ethos. Ours is a nation based on a universal creed, and there is an unquenchable missionary element in our foreign policy. We do aim to "make the world safe for democracy"—eventually, and in those places and at those times where conditions permit democracy to flourish. Every American administration in our history has felt compelled—though some have been more enthusiastic than others—to use our influence, wherever possible, to see that other governments respect our conception of individual rights as the foundation of a just regime and a good society.

On the other hand, only two presidents in our history have tried to emulate Gladstone in making the missionary element the very centerpiece of American foreign policy. The first was Woodrow Wilson, who believed that his enterprise would achieve its success by creating a world organization that in turn would form a "community of nations" pledged to respect the principles we hold dear—with disrespect being curbed by a broadened (Wilson would have said "heightened") definition of international law, to be enforced by this new "world community." It was a utopian vision to which many eminent Americans still pay lip service, but which no serious person can any longer take at face value. Today, all that is left of the Wilsonian dream is a host of international organizations that are at best debating societies, at worst sinks of corruption. There is also an array of treaty obligations that the United States thoughtlessly entered into and from which we are now gingerly trying to free ourselves.

The second president, of course, was Jimmy Carter, who fully accepted the expanded version of "human rights" (including social and economic rights) and who then tried to give the American missionary impulse a unilateralist thrust. But he soon was forced to recognize that the world is a complex and recalcitrant place, full of other peoples with other ideas, and that while proclaiming high-minded principles was one thing, unilateral American efforts to reshape world realities according to our national vision were an enterprise necessarily limited in scope—often very limited. The rights of individuals in other lands are a matter of concern for Americans. One may even say it is an integral part of our national interest. But it is usually a concern that claims no centrality in our foreign policy, since it has to be weighed against all those other interests which make up our national interest.

Secretary of State Cyrus Vance, one of the original "human rights" enthusiasts, was not in office more than a month before he felt constrained to issue the following statement:

We will speak frankly about injustice both at home and abroad. We do not intend, however, to be strident or polemical, but we do believe that an abiding respect for human rights is a human value of fundamental importance and that it must be nourished. We will not comment on each and every issue, but we will from time to time comment when we see a threat to human rights, when we believe it constructive to do so.

Well—yes. If one is willing to stipulate that by "human rights" one means pretty much what used to be called "individual rights," then any American president could have endorsed that statement. Ronald Reagan, I am certain, would be happy to endorse it. The United States (in this respect like the Soviet Union) does *stand* for something in the world and its foreign policy must, to the degree that the world permits, respect the principles of its establishment. But it is the nature of foreign policy to operate, most of the time, in the realm of necessity rather than the realm of freedom. So while it is fair to assert that the ideological basis of American foreign policy gives it a permanent moral dimension which itself delimits the scope of any purely "realistic" policy, these limits have to be broad enough to permit foreign policy to be effective.

Just how broad or narrow these limits are will depend on circumstances. Probably the "purest"—most moral, least self-interested— foreign policy action ever taken on behalf of "human rights" was the British navy's suppression of the slave trade in the nineteenth century. This action was made possible by many factors: Britain's massive superiority in sea power, the unimportance of the "Third World" countries involved, the nonexistence (as compared with today) of a complex structure of international law and international organizations. So while Britain's action was wholly admirable, one also has to point out that it was costless, or as close to costless as makes no matter.

It is conceivable that the United States might, one of these days, find itself in a more or less comparable situation, and it is certainly to be hoped that it would then take a comparable action. But such situations are likely to be rare. Like all great nations, the United States does conceive itself as having some kind of "civilizing mission." But, lacking an "imperialist" impulse, we are not usually inclined to accomplish this mission through forceful intervention. Presumably if a Pol Pot regime came to power in Central America and began a genocidal campaign against its own people, we might very well intervene. On the other hand, we did not intervene in Cambodia, nor have we even dreamed of intervening in Africa, where tribal genocide is not uncommon. Unilateral military intervention by the United States on behalf of "human rights" would have to overcome resistance from both our enemies and our allies. And steps short of military intervention will almost always be more symbolic than real. True, symbolic action may sometimes be better than no action at all. But over time the impact, both at home and aboard, of a series of mainly symbolic actions will be negligible. Worse, they will be interpreted as a sign of weakness, not strength, of moralistic importance rather than moral energy.

If this is our situation today—and the experience of the Carter administration had confirmed that it is—why has the message failed to get through to the "human rights" constituency? The reason, I suggest, is that this constituency has its own agenda, and that "human rights" is a useful rhetoric in which to promote it.

A final point: There are some conservative (or non-left) "human rights" activists who feel that this theme can be exploited for purposes of anticommunist and antitotalitarian propaganda. It is impossible not to admire the diligence with which they expose the sufferings of people under communism, and this kind of candid ideological warfare does serve to remind us of the nature of the enemy—a reminder that is always timely. But there is reason to wonder whether this strategy, on its own, can be effective over the longer term. There cannot be many people who do not already know about conditions in the Soviet Union. The question is: Why don't they care? Why are most of the major Christian churches in the United States so utterly indifferent to the persecution of Christianity in the Soviet Union and in Soviet-occupied Eastern Europe? If this be ignorance, it is a special kind of willful ignorance.

Such willful ignorance, I would suggest, has two sources. First, since the Soviet Union has its own (Marxist) conception of "human rights," about which it is brutally assertive and in no way apologetic, it does seem quixotically futile to criticize it for not sharing our traditional-liberal political philosophy. Second, and more important, there are many who believe the Soviet model is flawed but who nevertheless regard it as a respectable alternative to our own, which they perceive as at least equally flawed, or even flawed to a greater degree. The sad and simple truth is that, once one has lost faith in the traditional-liberal model, one feels deprived of the moral authority to challenge the Soviet model and one then loses all interest in doing so. It is this loss of faith that feeds the organized "human rights" movement, and gives it an "anti-American" bias. To this loss of faith, mere anticommunism is no answer.

There is also a significant cost involved in such an anticommunist "human rights" campaign. To avoid accusations of unprincipled conservative bias, it is inevitably pushed toward making "human rights" a central issue in determining American policy toward South Korea, Chile, Indonesia, the Philippines, etc.—which is, after all, exactly what our anti-American "human rights" activists wish. In effect, the conservative campaign has the unintended consequence of legitimating the "human rights" efforts of the left.

The so-called "human rights" activists inside the Soviet Union—or at least the more sophisticated among them—understand this problem well enough. They certainly do appreciate efforts in the West to alleviate the suffering of those who oppose particular policies of the Soviet system. This is justification enough for such efforts, whatever their limited success. But those activists inside the Soviet Union also have a hidden agenda, one of which I thoroughly approve. To the extent that the "human rights" issue offers them some protection as well as some leverage, they are morally entitled to use it. It is also politically prudent for them to emphasize it. Unfortunately, such hidden agendas are easily read by the Soviet authorities, who have had so much experience in writing them.

Richard Schifter

Human Rights in the Reagan Years: A Reply to Irving Kristol (1987)

I find myself in agreement with many of the observations and comments in Irving Kristol's article (Winter 19867). And yet I profoundly disagree with his principal thesis that for the United States to adopt a human rights policy is foolhardy. . . .

The principal targets of Kristol's article are the advocacy groups, the organizations which make up what has occasionally been called the "human rights movement." Kristol contends that these groups use the human rights cause to cloak a political agenda whose purposes are (a) to disrupt United States foreign policy by alienating authoritarian governments which are on good terms with us, and (b) to broaden the definition of human rights to add so-called "social and economic rights" to the traditional inherent rights of the individual against government oppression. While focusing his attention on the "movement," Kristol says little about how the United States government has in recent years sought to carry out a consistent human-rights policy. When he does so, he tends to denigrate it. Yet he does recognize that the American people expect their government "to use our influence

From *The National Interest, Fall 1987*.

wherever possible, to see that other governments respect our conception of individual rights as the foundation of a just regime and a good society. . . ."

Only slightly more than forty years have gone by, a relatively short period in the history of nation states, since "human rights," in earlier times referred to as the "rights of man," were recognized as an issue suitable for discussion in the field of diplomacy. Since that recognition occurred, we have witnessed a great deal of posturing on that subject, and a great deal of fruitless debate, and also some utterly dishonest use of the human rights cause by groups and states which have no commitment to it whatever. However, throughout this period there have also been those who have been honorable and sincere in devotion to that cause, whose outlook reflected what Kristol calls "an unquenchable missionary element in our foreign policy," and who have over time helped the United States government evolve a human rights policy which compacts with both that "missionary element" and our national interest. . . . An attempt will be made, within tight space limitations, to present an outline of the role played by governments, particularly the United States, in espousing human rights in international diplomacy. . . .

Though American Presidents have throughout this century spoken out to express their disapproval of human rights violations by foreign governments . . . human rights considerations have not until very recently been systematically infused into the practice of United States diplomacy. American diplomats, as did their colleagues in other countries, had always adhered to the tradition that what a sovereign government did to its own citizens within its own territory was the concern of that government only. In the wake of World War II, to be sure, the issue of human rights was permanently anchored in the Charter of the United Nations and had thereafter become the subject of discussion and debate in United Nations fora. But initially it was assumed that the Charter provision authorized the United Nations merely to discuss human rights in the abstract, to establish universally accepted standards of human rights, but not to engage in discussions of specific human rights cases or problems as they arose. To do so, it was assumed, would run afoul of Article II, Section 7 of the United Nations Charter, which provides that the United Nations must not "intervene in matters which are essentially within the domestic jurisdiction of any state. . . ."

But there were those who thought that more should be expected of the United Nations system than mere norm-setting. They insisted that the United Nations could not be said to live up to its commitment to the cause of human rights by merely adopting norm-setting documents, while turning a blind eye to consistent patterns of egregious violations of the most basic precepts of human rights. They argued further that mere discussion of specific human rights violations in United Nations fora would not constitute "intervention" as proscribed by Article II, Section 7 of the Charter. . . .

This was by no means quickly accepted. On the contrary, years went by as the United Nations slowly inched its way toward free discussion of specific situations violating human rights, progress in that direction being slowed down both by Western adherence to diplomatic custom and Soviet bloc concern that such discussion could set precedents which might ultimately haunt the practitioners of Leninism. . . .

Precisely because it foresaw that human rights debates in international fora could ultimately be turned against it, the Soviet Union was most hesitant about what in the United Nations is referred to as the "implementation" of human rights instruments. Only when they saw a political issue of overriding importance to their interests did the Soviets join in support of the discussion of specific human rights situations. . . .

In the 1970s, the composition of the United Nations underwent substantial change. The center of gravity shifted to the Third World. The concerns of Western diplomats over the principle of noninterference in the domestic affairs of sovereign states were cast aside. Yet human rights violations were taken up only if they took place in countries which were friendless. Any state that was closely associated with a regional bloc could effectively escape United Nations censure. This was particularly true of states over which the Soviet Union extended its protecting wings.

The onesidedness of the United Nations human rights agenda became increasingly a topic of concern to those whose commitment to human rights reflected a universal approach to the subject rather than a cloak for a particular political philosophy. They noted that the United States was prepared to go along with United Nations campaigns against South Africa, Chile, Somoza's Nicaragua, and other countries placed on the list of human rights violators, countries with powerful enemies and few friends, but did very little to try to take on the most serious human rights violators—the totalitarian states of the Soviet bloc.

There had been differences of opinion in the State Department as to the position of the United States. U.S. representatives to the United Nations Human Rights Commission were increasingly eager to speak out on the subject of Soviet human rights violations, but were held back by those who clung to the noninterference principle as well as those who were concerned that U.S.–U.S.S.R. relations not be disturbed.

A major breakthrough on the issue of U.S. discussion of consistent patterns of Soviet human rights violations occurred not in the setting of the United Nations, but at the 1977 Belgrade follow-up meeting of the Conference on Security and Cooperation in Europe, the conference which had produced the Helsinki Final Act. The head of the United States Delegation, Justice Arthur Goldberg, insisted on discussing the pattern of increased repression in the Soviet Union in 1977 and, after some bureaucratic in-fighting, succeeded in gaining approval for his approach, which was to recite the facts of Soviet human rights violations in detail, and to name names. After thirty-two years of discussing human rights at international conferences, during which time the Soviet Union was literally allowed to get away with murder, the United States had finally taken the initiative to call the Soviets to account.

The international human rights debate has not been the same since. At Belgrade our allies were appalled. Not one of them spoke up in support of the United States delegation. The meeting ultimately adjourned without having reached any substantive agreement. But the ice had been broken. When the next Helsinki meeting began in Madrid in 1980, the new head of the U.S. delegation, Max Kampelman, continued the approach and Soviet human rights abuse became the principal theme of the meeting. This time our allies were no longer silent, many joining the United States in speaking up for the rights of the individual as spelled out so clearly in the Helsinki Final Act.

The new United States policy on the Helsinki Final Act did not immediately spill over onto its approach at the United Nations. Circumspection was the order of the day in that forum for a while longer, even after Arthur Goldberg's *tour de force* at Belgrade. The restrictions on our U.N. delegations were, however, relaxed in 1980, following the invasion of Afghanistan and abandoned entirely in 1981, after the Reagan Administration took office. Soviet human rights violations were thenceforth discussed freely. Moreover, once the United States had decided to take the lead in the debate of Soviet human rights violations and to persist, some of the other Western democracies decided to follow suit.

Kristol's comment on efforts to expose Soviet human rights violations is that "[t]here cannot be many people who do not already know about conditions in the Soviet Union." This observation, I believe, overestimates the general public's knowledge and even the knowledge of some diplomats and other government officials as to the egregiousness of Soviet human rights abuse. . . . Only when cases are spelled out clearly, when the commitment of sane persons to institutions for the mentally ill is described, when the case of a poet is described who was sentenced to twelve years of deprivation of freedom for writing poetry, when the specifics are presented as to repression of national culture or freedom of religion do people fully comprehend that the Soviet Union violates human rights.

Even after the adoption of the United Nations Charter and its human rights provisions, Joseph Stalin knew that he could persecute, kill and torture people without fearing that his regime might be called to account for such actions in some international forum. Today, by contrast, Soviet leaders and the leaders of Warsaw Pact nations know that these repressive moves may have consequences in the international scene. There is good reason to believe that that fact helps modify their behavior.

I have so far discussed the evolution of United States human rights policy as it relates to what the State Department calls multilateral diplomacy. But there is another area in which such evolution has taken place: in bilateral diplomacy, direct dealings between the United States and foreign countries accused of human rights violations.

In the 1970s, unquestionably in response to appeals from advocacy groups, Congress had begun to write provisions into laws which compelled the Executive Branch to take human rights into account in making decisions which affect foreign policy. . . .

The Executive Branch was called upon to take human rights into account in granting foreign aid, in votes on loans from international development banks and in the export of equipment for potential police and military use. The State Department was also mandated to prepare an annual report, broken down country-by-country on human rights conditions throughout the world. That statute, which Kristol dismisses as requiring the State Department "to engage in . . . idiotic political arithmetic" turned out to be a law which had consequences far greater than those envisaged by its authors. The law's purpose was simply to enable the members of Congress to have information on human rights conditions readily available to them, initially only as to foreign countries that were the recipients of American assistance, later concerning others as well.

But the bureaucratic results of this law were great. Each of our embassies is now required to prepare an initial draft on the human rights situation in the country in which it was located. That, in turn, makes it necessary for an officer at each embassy to be assigned the task of observing human rights conditions in the country in question in order to collect the data needed for the preparation of the annual report. Foreign service officers are not in the habit of merely collecting information and filing it away for use once a year. The custom of the Service is to report on observations currently and send these reports to Washington. . . . Washington has received these reports in increasing numbers during the last ten years. They have created an awareness of human rights problems that simply did not exist before.

The reporting requirement has thus stimulated the State Department to confront human rights problems and seek to deal with them.

The statute requiring the preparation of the annual reports has also had one other important consequence. The more repressive the country, the less the information about human rights conditions is obtainable through its public media. This means that information can be obtained primarily through persons outside that government who are aware of human rights conditions. As a result, in a wide variety of repressive states throughout the world, United States Embassy personnel have routinely developed contacts with adherents of democracy living in these states.

Human rights concerns are understandably not the only factor on which our international relations are based. Security objectives and our national interest must always be the centerpiece of our diplomacy. But rarely is there direct conflict between our security interests and our interest in the support and scrutiny of international respect for human rights. In many instances they can be dealt with simultaneously. More often than not they are mutually reinforcing.

There are still a few American spokesmen for the notion that compelling our diplomats to concern themselves with matters other than our security and economic interests is inherently wrong, that we should return to the traditional precept that what a foreign government does to its own citizens is none of our business. George Kennan is today probably the most vigorous advocate of that position. A good many arguments can be advanced against Kennan, but the simplest and to me the most persuasive one is that there is an overwhelming domestic popular consensus in favor of our human rights policy. Americans want their government to protect the national interest but also to give moral content to our foreign policy. Congress has responded to this popular interest by enacting legislation which requires the Executive Branch to give weight to human rights concerns in the formulation of foreign policy. The State Department adheres both to the spirit and the letter of the law.

Irving Kristol is clearly in agreement with the proposition just set forth, namely that the American people want their government to factor human rights into its foreign policy. As he puts it, *"Realpolitik* à la Disaraeli is unthinkable in America, since it runs against the very grain of our political ethos. Ours is a nation based on a universal creed, and there is an unquenchable missionary element in our foreign policy. We do aim to make the world safe for democracy. . . ."

Irving Kristol has evidently missed the success of the United States government in recent years in infusing the ideals of that universal democratic creed into our day-by-day foreign policy operations, without endangering our national interest. The person who led the way, my predecessor Elliott Abrams, did not view his job, as Mr. Kristol thinks, as one "to thwart the immoral proclivities of our State Department," but as one of seeing to it that human rights concerns receive appropriate attention in foreign policy formulation. Nor are our annual Country Reports the "absurd enterprise" depicted by Mr. Kristol. They are thoughtful, balanced analyses of international human rights conditions, which leave the reader without any doubt that these conditions are far better in Switzerland than in Romania, to use Mr. Kristol's example. The Reports are now respected and valued reference works throughout the democratic world and sought after, not surprisingly, in many parts of the nondemocratic world.

As I have noted, the United States government uses its own resources to gather information on human rights conditions and builds its policy on the data base thus accumulated. Though we note what advocacy groups have to say, we check their reports against the information which reaches us through our own channels. This means that however valid Irving Kristol's criticism of human rights advocacy groups, it is not relevant to the human rights policy of the United States government. The United States government is aware of the fact that the organizations which identify themselves with the human rights cause run the spectrum from those sincerely and impartially concerned with human rights to organizations which are nothing other than transmission belts for Soviet propaganda. . . . In our assessments of human rights we rely in the first instance on the data which we, in the government, have collected. In the process we develop our own notions as to which outside reports are to be taken seriously and which are not.

Kristol argues that human rights advocacy groups are trying to broaden the definition of human rights to include "social and economic rights."

Though some human rights advocacy groups tend to express some interest in the so-called "social and economic rights," most of their material and argumentation focuses on violations of political and civil rights, occasionally on invented violations of such rights. The argument of "social and economic rights," which appears to preoccupy Irving Kristol, is an argument of yesteryear; . . . what the 1980s have brought is a full understanding worldwide that socialism and planned economies, though they may promise social and economic improvement, have failed to deliver on the promise, and that market economies and private initiative, which do not promise a higher standard of living, have succeeded in bringing that result about. Increasingly, therefore, in recent years the discussion of human rights has reverted to the assertion of the inherent rights of the individual against undue state interference with his life, liberty, freedom of expression and association, freedom of religion, etc. . . . .

Kristol is most assuredly off-the-mark in his critique of the Universal Declaration of Human Rights, approved by the United Nations General Assembly in December 1948. If, as he says, it was "an important first step in establishing something like a moral equivalence between liberal capitalist democracies and communist or self-styled socialist regimes," why did the Soviets refuse support?

The Soviets knew what they were doing. In its first twenty-one articles the Declaration raised to internationally-recognized human rights the basic principles of limited government inherent in liberal capitalist democracy, including, in Article 17, "the right to own property" and not to "be arbitrarily deprived of" it. To these 21 articles which constitute an elaboration of our own Bill of Rights, the Declaration's drafters added four articles raising key elements of the New Deal legislative program of the Thirties to a level equal to these traditional rights, doing so in a clearly democratic context. The right to work and to protection against unemployment is combined with the right to free choice of employment and the right of the individual to form and join trade unions.

Whatever the theoretical arguments of earlier decades on the subject of political civil rights *versus* social and economic rights may have been, the verdict of the 1980's is clear: the capitalist democracies respect the former and as "goals of government" rather than "rights" deliver on the latter. The Communist dictatorships, by contrast, fail across the board.

To sum up, the term "human rights" is indeed one which is now widely abused and trivialized but that should not lead us to the conclusion that one cannot be honestly and sincerely devoted to the cause of human rights and engage in serious efforts to see these rights respected worldwide. What individuals and nongovernmental groups can do to advance the cause can also be done and, as I have pointed out, is being done by the United States government. We do indeed, as Kristol phrases it, "use our influence, whenever possible, to see that other governments respect our conception of individual rights as the foundation of a just regime and a good society."

Rudy Oswald

AFL-CIO on International Workers' Rights (1987)

The inclusion by Congress of worker rights criteria in both the Generalized System of Preferences (GSP) and the Overseas Private Investment Corporation (OPIC) is an extremely significant step in the continuing development of the United States government's international economic policies. We are disappointed however with the Administration's recent determinations concerning the implementation of the worker rights criteria in GSP and OPIC. While those decisions are a beginning, we believe they fall far short of complying with the laws' intent.

The notion that international trade and investment should contribute positively to the economic and social development of both the home and host country is not new. The Preamble of the GATT states:

> ". . . relations in the field of trade and economic endeavor should be conducted with a view to raising standards of living, ensuring full employment and a large and steadily growing volume of real income and effective demand . . ."

This goal however, is undermined when workers overseas are unable to share equitably in the fruits of their labor. American workers are also harmed through unemployment and lost income as domestic production is displaced by products manufactured under repressive conditions.

Sad to say, many workers overseas do not earn enough to buy the products that they produce. Their standard of living should be raised so that they can purchase the goods produced by their labor.

The AFL-CIO has long believed that competitive advantage in trade must not be derived through the abuse of workers and the

Rudy Oswald, Director of Research, American Federation of Labor and Congress of Industrial Organizations, in "International Workers' Rights," hearing before the Subcommittee on Human Rights and International Organizations of the Committee on Foreign Affairs. House of Representatives, One Hundredth Congress, first session, June 30, 1987. U.S. Government Printing Office, Washington, 1987.

suppression of basic rights and freedoms. If trade and investment are in fact going to provide benefits to all parties involved, adherence to certain minimum standards of behavior regarding labor rights and conditions is essential.

Almost 100 years ago, Congress passed a trade law which linked workers rights to trade by forbidding imports of products made by convict labor. In 1930 products made by forced labor were added to the list of forbidden imports.

The Commission on Security and Cooperation in Europe

Reform and Human Rights: The Gorbachev Record (1988)
Liberties and the Law

No visitor to the Soviet capital who had known its atmosphere before 1985 can miss the freedom Gorbachev's rule has brought to civic discourse among the intelligentsia, the stratum of pre-Revolutionary and of Soviet society defined by its engagement in independent thought.[1] "Remarkably," reported a one-time spokesman for Jewish refuseniks, "most of the people I met in Moscow were not afraid to speak their minds in terms unthinkable twelve years ago."[2]

Especially after the arrests of Orlov, Shcharansky and others in early 1977 and the heavy sentences imposed on them for having tried to hold the Soviet Union publicly accountable for its human rights conduct, speaking one's mind in Moscow became a perilous activity. Ten years later, dissenters are still harassed. But in no reported instance from September 1986 until March 1988 have any been arrested, tried or convicted on charges of either disseminating "slander" against the Soviet Union or conducting "anti-Soviet agitation and propaganda."

The laws forbidding and severely punishing dissent are still on the books, articles 190-1 and 70 of the Criminal Code of the Russian Republic, for instance. In Gorbachev's third year, at least, the authorities were not only not enforcing those statutes; they were also releasing several hundred political prisoners who had been incarcerated for

From report submitted by the CSC to the U.S. Congress.

violating them. And, Gorbachev indicated in early 1987, the laws were soon to be dropped or notably softened.

POLITICAL PRISONERS—FREE AND NOT

Although some of the better-known prisoners of conscience—men like Shcharansky (traded for a Czech spy on the KGB payroll) and Orlov (part of the Daniloff-for-Zakharov swap)—were given their freedom and often their ticket to Western exile in 1985 and 1986, the gates of the Soviet gulag did not seem to open wide until after the December 1986 death of Anatoly Marchenko, one of the most revered and stubborn dissidents. Many observers believe that the shock and protest over his death in a prison hospital touched a high-level political nerve. In any event, less than two weeks later, Mikhail Gorbachev telephoned Andrei Sakharov to tell the famed dissenter that his Gorky exile had been lifted. And within a few months the process of amnestying large numbers of prisoners with permission to remain in the U.S.S.R. got underway.

When Sakharov returned to Moscow on December 23, 1986, his first public statement repeated one of his long-standing appeals: freedom for all political dissenters serving terms in Soviet labor camps, prisons, and exile.[3] Less than two months later, *Izvestiya* announced that the Supreme Soviet was pardoning 140 people convicted under articles 70 and 190-1 after they pledged "that in the future they would not be involved in illegal activities." A Soviet spokesperson said that another 140 cases were under review.[4]

By the end of March—in the largest Soviet mass release of political prisoners since the Khrushchev era—two hundred had been freed with pardons, though not formal rehabilitations, that left them exposed to reincarceration if and when the authorities decide they have violated their promises of obedient conduct. The actual oaths seemed to vary, depending on the camp or prison authorities and the negotiating skills of the inmates. As Sergei Grigoryants joked, "They asked me to write a statement that amounted to a promise that I would not take to the streets with a machine gun."[5]

Following the February decree, a June 1987 amnesty in honor of the seventieth anniversary of the Bolshevik Revolution, gave freedom to first-time offenders under article 190-1 and reduced sentences handed down under article 70. One result was to empty the camps of all the women "politicals" in detention.

For the 329 political prisoners released last year, however, freedom is still a relative matter. Many have experienced difficulty in finding employment or residence permission from local authorities. Paradoxically, a July 1987 letter received in the West from several former prisoners, complains that those who completed their sentences before the first pardon remain under "administrative surveillance" (an ill-defined practice whereby former prisoners are still accountable for their movements to the local police) and, hence, have more problems in resettling.

For them and for others, Andrei Sakharov's mixed verdict on the nature and pace of human rights progress under Gorbachev is a fitting one: "The times are changing slowly and in some ways, not at all. But the changes are real."[6]

In the Camps: For the approximately three hundred and fifty men and women—twelve of them, former Helsinki Accord monitors—still incarcerated or in exile by the count of the International Helsinki Federation and for the perhaps six hundred others whom some Soviet sources tally, "life in prison," said the U.S. State Department in 1987, "continues to be marked by isolation, poor diet, and malnutrition, compulsory hard labor, beatings, frequent illness and inadequate medical care."

Through 1986, in fact, reports received by the Commission indicated that labor camp conditions had worsened, even that guards and criminal inmates were intensifying the level of political violence and isolation used to demoralize political prisoners.[7] Writing his mother from Perm camp 36-1, former Estonian activist Mart Niklus, who is still in confinement, reported: "In Kuchino . . . everything is unchanged."[8]

By the end of December of last year, eight months after low-key criticism of the labor camps appeared briefly in the Soviet press, Niklus at least had more company. All political prisoners had by then been moved to Perm 36, from a camp in Mordovia and from Perm camps 35 and 37.[9] And, with no inmates left, the women's prison at Barashevo in Mordovia had been closed.

Sergei Grigoryants, who went from Chistopol Prison in February 1987 to found and edit the unofficial journal, *Glasnost*, has noted that the June 1987 amnesty did not include provisions to reduce the camps' production quotas. Failure to meet these heavy work norms, he added, can give wardens the pretext for cutting down on releases by trumping up insubordination charges. "The zone has proven immune to reform," he declared.[10] Despite official Soviet claims that fifty thousand prisoners—the vast majority of them ordinary criminals—have been freed, Grigoryants said that his diverse sources indicate that "no more than ten percent of the prison population has been released."[11]

PSYCHIATRIC ABUSE

Aside from the release of sixty-four Soviet citizens committed to psychiatric hospitals as punishment for political crimes,[12] candor has been the most notable 1987 change in Soviet practices in the field of mental health. Not only did the official press begin to reveal the sorry state of the discipline—although not the abuse of psychiatry as a weapon against dissent, but Soviet psychiatrists visiting the United States also agreed "in principle" to let American colleagues visit them, and, presumably, examine their patients.[13]

Along with a TASS announcement in January 1988, that the police would no longer run maximum security "special" clinics and that new regulations would give mental patients the right to contest their commitment in court, recent developments suggest a decided effort to correct one of the ugliest forms of Soviet repression.[14]

The new trend, however, makes few concessions to long-standing criticisms. Nor has it brought freedom to ninety-five political prisoners known to be still undergoing treatment or dismissal to doctors associated with past abuses. In fact, Dr. Marat Vartanyan, one of the best-known apologists for Soviet psychiatric practices, has been appointed to head the All-Union Center for Mental Health.

"Psychiatry as a weapon in the fight against dissidence still exists," said religion activist Alexander Ogorodnikov, a prisoner from 1978 to 1987, after the TASS announcement. "I think the changes are aimed at limiting the purely nonpolitical abuse of psychiatry" to regain respectability in the international psychiatric community.[15]

Inside Stories: Until last year the official press did not admit that the reputation of Soviet psychiatry was in any way stained. But beginning with a July 11 *Izvestiya* piece, "Without Defense," Soviet journalists have written several exposés of the improper commitment of sane men and women, even of corruption among their doctors. The most candid article appeared November 11, 1987 in *Komsomolskaya Pravda* with the direct attack on the diagnosis of "sluggish schizophrenia" that the late Dr. Andrei Snezhevsky had used to describe mental illness "with no obvious symptoms." Although the paper did not disclose that the diagnosis had been imposed extensively on dissenters, the report did say that it was "very broad and used very frequently" and "can be applied to practically anyone, even someone sane by conventional definition."

Moreover, the paper reported cases of doctors granting false certificates of insanity to common criminals evading prosecution and of orderlies raping women patients and forcibly removing the gold crowns from inmates' teeth. Some drug treatments, it added, "can even turn a sane person into an insane one," and some forms of "rehabilitation" amount to "an assault on human dignity."[16]

Dr. Georgy Morozov, head of the Serbsky Institute over which Snezhevsky once presided, has dismissed such reports as "incompetent" and "slanderous" journalism. He also claims that the new regulations, far from requiring significant changes, simply reflect instructions long in effect in Soviet psychiatry.[17] The Health Ministry's chief psychiatrist, however, announced that the new rules should mean dropping two million people from the Government's registry of mental patients, a stigmatic listing that limits civil rights, such as travel and employment and that raises risks of involuntary commitment.[18]

Prognosis: Seeking readmission to the World Psychiatric Association it left in 1983, on the verge of expulsion, the Soviet mental health profession still has a lot to explain and to correct. Few who have followed its history are likely to forget first-hand reports like the one of the brutal treatment administered to Serafim Yesyukov, incarcerated after he sought to emigrate:

> He refused (to take pills). They first tried jamming the pills into his mouth. Then the orderly strapped him to the bed and employed two mentally ill inmates to help hold him down while they closed his nostrils and tried to force him to open his mouth. His nose bled. Finally they gave up and injected instead—with a promise to repeat the process if he refused the pills the next time.[19]

CITIZEN ACTION, CIVIC DISCOURSE

In a handful of unofficial but increasingly widely circulated journals, in thousands of lively gatherings of private groups and clubs and in scores of public demonstrations, Mikhail Gorbachev's *glasnost* is bringing a semblance of civil society back to life in a country from which it had seemed, after 1917, to be all but erased. And unlike the brief emergence of such energies during Nikita Khrushchev's thaws, the discourse in the streets and meeting rooms is not in the elliptical form of daring poetry but in the direct language of social and political agitation.

Glasnost creates many dilemmas for party officials. None pose greater problems than the outpouring of such organized but independent citizen action. Launched by the party leadership but still unsanctioned by legal guarantees, this tide of self-expression is beginning to elude party control and to generate forceful but intermittent police reaction.

Not yet a movement—rather a spectrum of interests newly given their voice—the spread of civic action is as closely watched by outsiders as by the Kremlin. Given its head, it could eventually transform Soviet politics. Violently repressed, it will remind the West that the Soviet regime cannot tolerate change.

Independent Presses: Having failed in their campaign of arrests and intimidation to abolish the multiform *samizdat* publication of the 1960's and 1970's, Soviet authorities by 1985 had at least managed to silence the most respected human rights journals—the *Chronicle of Current*

Events, established in 1968, and the *Documents of the Moscow Helsinki Group*, begun in 1976. Once released from imprisonment, however, the editors of the earlier publications returned to their typewriters with restored zeal and extended contact networks.

The result has been the appearance of an array of *samizdat* bulletins in Moscow and Leningrad and, to a lesser extent, in other major cities. Earliest and best known is the journal *Glasnost*, edited by Sergei Grigoryants. His former collaborator Lev Timofeyev has also begun circulating *Referendum*, while a Leningrad group puts out *Mercury*. The first two concentrate on human rights issues: *Mercury* focuses on local and environmental affairs; other specialized journals report on the arts, economics and religion.[20]

Devoid of comment but packed with news, *Express-Khronika* first appeared on street corners in central Moscow in August 1987, the product of Aleksandr Podrabinek, whose compaign against the political abuse of psychiatry earned him two terms in the labor camps before his thirty-fifth birthday. A weekly, averaging about 20 pages and an initial press run of 150-170 copies, *Express-Khronika* feeds a hunger for human rights news that authorized reporting only teases. "We are starved for information, not points of view," Podrabinek says. "Facts—we need facts."

"In the past, of course," adds his colleague, Sergei Lyozov, "the official press would publish nothing at all. *Glasnost* means they are now publishing bits and scraps, always distorted and always weeks late."[21]

With its reports on demonstrations and nationalities, activities around the U.S.S.R., on treatment of political prisoners and demonstrations by Crimean Tatars in Central Asia, *Express-Khronika* amounts to a real-time news service from the Soviet underground. The challenge it presents to the authorities is being answered in two ways. *Sovetskaya Rossiya* on March 27, 1988, labeled Podrabinek a "dealer in slander," and KGB plainclothesmen attacked him with their fists the same day, as he hawked copies of the purple-covered journal in downtown Moscow.[22]

Indepent groups: According to the February 1, 1988 issue of *Pravda*, there are now over thirty thousand citizens groups in the Soviet Union, representing, as do the independent publications, a wide range of social interests and viewpoints. Some are openly political, such as the reestablished Ukrainian Helsinki Monitoring Group; others pursue such interests as preserving cultural monuments, protecting the environment, advancing music and the arts.

Groups with political agendas, such as the Pacifist Group for Trust Between the East and West, tend to be called "unofficial," while those considered to be apolitical are usually referred to as "informal." Both kinds are, in theory, legal instances of civic organizations. But according to a 1932 law, the groups must have as their goal "active participation in the building of socialism" in the U.S.S.R. or in the defense of the country.

They must also be controlled by the party. While visiting Moscow in November 1987, former Soviet citizen Vladimir Kozlovsky was told by Moscow acquaintances that the Russian Nationalist *Pamyat* Society, a linguistics society and a homosexuals' club had all applied for registration with the Moscow City Council. A member of the linguistic club reported that it had been refused on the grounds that "no one in the city council had enough knowledge of linguistics to exert control over it."[23]

Some independent citizens groups have been granted permission by local authorities to meet in public buildings. One group that was not was the Press Club *Glasnost*. When it organized the independent human rights seminar in Moscow in December 1987, authorities closed a building that had been rented for the group's opening plenary session, allegedly for reasons of public health. Nevertheless, the seminar was allowed to take place in separate apartments in the city, where working groups met to discuss various issues. Approximately four hundred persons, including Western observers, discussed such issues as "law and society," "human contacts," "nationality issues," "religious freedom" and "culture." Although some would-be participants from outside Moscow were prevented from attending, the meeting was a milestone in the Soviet human rights movement.

In the Streets: Article 190-3 of the RSFSR Criminal Code provides labor camp sentences up to three years long for "organization of, or active participation in group actions disrupting the peace." It is not being stringently enforced. As a *New York Times* correspondent wrote in mid-1987:

> A few months ago it would have been inconceivable for a human rights protest to occur in the heart of the capital without the participants being quickly whisked away by the police.[24]

By late 1987, in fact, public demonstrations in the city on a wide spectrum of issues had become almost commonplace by Soviet standards. Noting the rallies held in the Baltic States that year to commemorate significant dates in their history, Latvian dissident and protest organizer Roland Silaraups testified to the Commission in October:

> . . . in Latvia today, it is easier to express one's opinions—opinions which are independent of those held by the authorities—without fear of immediate arrest, than has been the case in the past.

Aside from the major and often sustained protest demonstrations by nationality activists described in the next section, a variety of other protesters have appeared in the Soviet streets. In Lvov, for example, twenty members of the Ukrainian branch of the Trust Group demonstrated against Soviet policy in Afghanistan. And environmentalists in Leningrad have protested destruction of cultural monuments and dangers to the ecology in the area.

Demonstrations were even held in support of deposed Moscow city party head, Boris Yeltsin, both in Moscow and Sverdlovsk, his former home. The February 9, 1988 issue of *Novoe Russkoe Slovo*, features a photo of animal rights activists picketing at Moscow's "Dynamo" Metro Station.

The response to demonstrations seems to vary with location, timing and circumstances. Following Crimean Tatar protests in the summer of 1987, a delegation was allowed to meet with Council of Ministers President Gromyko to discuss the Tatars' grievances. Some of the most active participants, however, were fined forty to fifty rubles, about a week's average wage, and forced to leave the capital.

Conflicting Signals: Shortly thereafter the Moscow City Council passed a measure barring demonstrations on or in the Red Square area or on the main streets of central Moscow. New laws have also been adopted by municipal authorities in areas with high concentrations of Crimean Tatars to crack down on their continuing demonstrations. Authorities in Sverdlovsk passed similar regulations in response to the pro-Yeltsin demonstrations, as did the city authorities of Ufa, after citizens took to the streets to protest urban air pollution. Ufa officials did, however, promise to consult with Moscow about ending construction of additional chemical plants. Demonstrations and public meetings in late winter of 1988 with city officials in Nizhny Tagil, produced a promise to cease operations at a local coke smelting plant that had, according to protesters, dangerously raised the level of pollution in the city, and had caused 54 children to be stillborn in 1987.[25]

In Estonia, city officials met ahead of time with organizers of the August 23, 1987 demonstration and worked out a tenuous framework for the rally. While the first Latvian demonstration in June 1987 went unmolested, violence broke out at its August successor when police attacked organizers in Riga. By November 14, the Latvian authorities had developed another technique: filling the city with their own "demonstrators," a method subsequently emulated in Moscow, keeping some organizers under house arrest and expelling others from the U.S.S.R.

In—and perhaps because of—the presence of observers from the International Helsinki Federation, one hundred Jewish refuseniks were allowed to demonstrate in central Moscow on January 28, 1988 without interference. On other occasions, demonstrators have been beaten by plainclothes police or kept under preemptive house arrest. Only a handful, however, have been jailed and these for two weeks or less under what is termed "administrative arrest."

So while demonstrators are not immediately whisked away by the police in every case, article 190-3 is still on the books. In his Commission testimony, Silaraups warned that, . . . the KGB continues to collect information about these people so, if there is a change in the political climate, they can be held accountable. And *Pravda* wrote on December 27, 1987:

> There are groups who, under the label of independent organizations, directly carry out provocatory work, press for the creation of opposition parties, "free" labor unions, push phony culture instead of genuine values. Their activities sometimes acquire a clearly illegal nature: without permission from the authorities, they organize demonstrations, and at times, disorders, illegally print and distribute documents inimicable to socialism.

On October 7, 1987, Soviet Constitution Day, police detained about fifteen citizens who publicly called for revision of the 10-year-old Constitution to reflect *glasnost* and *democratizatsia*. One of the KGB officers told the group: "*Perestroika* is already over."[26]

PROTECTION OF THE LAW

To gauge the progress Soviets have made in the field of human rights, it is necessary to look beyond activities they have tolerated under Gorbachev's rule to liberties they have guaranteed. It is a short search that turns up little.

Despite public promises in early 1987 of major reforms in the Criminal Code, either the complexity of the task or political resistance to it have left old laws in force and new ones largely in abeyance. Following a call by Gorbachev himself for review and reform of Soviet laws to bring them in line with his program of social change, the Party Central Committee formally ordered "the first systematic examination of criminal laws since the existing code was drawn up in 1961."[27] The order, in turn, formalized a campaign by Soviet spokesmen to herald sweeping liberalization—even, it was suggested, abolition of the statutes that made political actions into crimes.

Publicity outpaced performance. More recent Soviet statements promise only to drop article 190-1 punishing "dissemination of clearly false fabrications slandering the Soviet political and social system" and to abolish provisions for sentencing offenders to internal exile. Considering that the slander statute was added to the code in 1966 without previous public discussion, it is discouraging that it has not been erased with similar dispatch.

Article 190-3, giving the courts grounds to punish public demonstrations, was another Brezhnev era addition to the laws that could be—but have not been—summarily dropped. Even if they were removed, Soviet legal expert Vladimir Kudryatsev indicated in early 1988 that article 70 on "anti-Soviet agitation" will remain, albeit rewritten. "It is now important," he said, "for us to draw a clear line, through clear formulations, between the desired free statement of opinion, on the one hand, and the fanning of anti-State activities on the other."[28] Since article 70 carries stiffer penalties—up to seven years in labor camps—than article 190 (up to three years), its retention could leave dissenters exposed to harsher treatment than before.

Even the one legal liberalization that has taken effect turns out to have limited impact. A new law giving Soviet citizens the right to appeal acts by officials, came into force on New Year's Day, 1988, but a commentary on it published since, specifies that it does not apply to decisions by any but individual officials, presumably abusing their power, or by any officials in the Office of Visas and Registration (OVIR) that grants or denies permission to emigrate.

As exiled Soviet criminal defense lawyer Dina Kaminskaya has told Commission staff, earlier laws already provided legal recourse, in theory, against arbitrary acts of housing authorities and employers. In practice, such disputes were rarely pursued through the courts and rarely to the satisfaction of individual citizens.

One other small sign of progress is a Moscow City Council decree at the end of 1987 that will allow former prisoners with a single conviction for a "serious crime" to be registered with spouses or parents as legal residents of the capital. Those with more than one conviction—Aleksandr Podrabinek, for example—are still barred from residence in the city except in cases of medical necessity.

The greatest change for the better remains the nonenforcement of repressive laws. Until that practice is made permanent by real revisions of the Criminal Code and by a judiciary independent of official pressure, the rights of Soviet citizens to question the state openly are in the hands of the state itself, subject to whatever restrictions this regime or its successors decide to impose.

LOOKING FORWARD

Mikhail Gorbachev's calls for a more open Soviet society, for more initiative and involvement by Soviet citizens in shaping their lives and implementing his reforms, have already had remarkable effects on correcting past abuses of human rights. But he has not changed the system of political rule by a single, all-powerful party, and he has indicated that he does not seek more than a measure of political competition *within* the Communist Party—certainly not from forces outside or opposed to it.

Given that built-in limitation to his reform goals, civil liberty as the West conceives it, can never be the broad foundation of Soviet law and society. The latitude Gorbachev has granted for dissent—energetically exploited by many who have suffered before for having the courage of their convictions—is new in Soviet experience. But it is a freedom that can be curtailed as easily as it was granted.

Andrei Sakharov judges progress in these cautionary words sent to a June 14, 1987 graduation ceremony at the College of Staten Island:

> The changes in the internal life of the Soviet Union which have been proposed by Gorbachev are important and necessary. I want to believe that his intentions are serious.
>
> But what has been accomplished to date is merely a beginning. It has only scratched the surface of the monolith of Soviet society.

Beneath that surface, expectations are rising. A young Socialist, a veteran of 13 months in the KGB's Lefortovo Prison in Moscow in 1982–83, presses the case for parliamentary elections, opposition political parties, a free press and broad civil liberties. In meetings of groups like the Club for Social Initiatives or Democratic *Perestroika*, 29-year-old Boris Kagarlitsky argues for radical change:

> The young have not lived through the Stalin crimes or the thaw under Khrushchev. We have different experiences and a different psychology and cultural background . . . We've never really even had socialism here. It's time we tried.[29]

NOTES

1. See Tibor Szamuely, *The Russian Tradition*, New York: McGraw-Hill, 1974.

2. Alex Goldfarb, "Testing *Glastnost*, An Exile Visits His Homeland," *New York Times Magazine*, Dec. 6, 1987.

3. Gary Lee, "Sakharov Returns, Calls for Release of Prisoners," Dec. 24, 1986.

4. "Humane Act," *Izvestiya*, Feb. 14, 1987.

5. Bill Keller, "Soviet Releasing Some Prisoners Under New Law," *New York Times*, Feb. 7, 1987.

6. Bill Keller, "Sakharov Emerges, Freer But Still in Limbo," *New York Times*, Nov. 7, 1987.

7. "Memorandum on Recent Intensification of the Regime in Soviet Prisons and Concentration Camps," Research Center for Prisons, Psychoprisons, and Forced-Labor Camps in the Soviet Union, April 1986.

8. Mart Niklus, letter provided by Relief Committee for Estonian Prisoners of Conscience.

9. Kronid Lubarsky, *USSR News Brief*, Dec. 31, 1987.

10. Bill Keller, "Where Cold and Food Are the Tools of Torture," *New York Times*, Feb. 22, 1987.

11. Sergei Grigoryants, "The Pitiful Results of the Amnesty," *Russkaya Mysl'*, Feb. 5, 1988.

12. "Soviet Abuse of Psychiatry for Political Purposes," Helsinki Watch, New York, January 1988, p. 2.

13. Associated Press, "Soviets to Allow Visits to Mental Hospitals," *Washington Post*, March 27, 1988.

14. Paul Quinn-Judge, "Soviet Dissidents Give New Psychiatric Law Mixed Reviews," *Christian Science Monitor*, Jan. 7, 1988.

15. *Ibid.*

16. "Soviet Abuse of Psychiatry," *op. cit.*, p. 4.

17. "International Helsinki Federation Mission to Moscow," *News from the Helsinki Watch*, Feb. 22, 1988.

18. Associated Press, "Two Million to Quit Soviet Mental-Patient Rolls," *Washington Post*, Feb. 12, 1988.

19. Joyce Barnathan, "Inside a Mind Jail," *Newsweek*, Aug. 11, 1986.

20. David Remnick, "Dissident Paper Reports the News *Pravda* Won't Print," *Washington Post*, Mar. 28, 1988.

21. *Ibid.*

22. *Ibid.*

23. Vladimir Kozlovsky, "Return," *Novoe Russkoe Slovo*, Dec. 20, 1987.

24. Philip Taubman, "In Moscow, A New Era?" *New York Times*, July 29, 1987.

25. Associated Press, "Smog-Covered Soviet City Site of Mass Anti-Pollution Protest," Apr. 8, 1988.

26. Vladimir Kozlovsky, "Return to Moscow," *Novoe Russkoe Slovo*, Jan. 26, 1988.

27. Celestine Bohlen, "Soviets Would Drop Law Used to Jail Dissidents," *Washington Post*, Sept. 22, 1987.

28. Quoted in *Der Spiegel*, Jan. 25, 1988.

29. David Remnick, "New Soviet Dissidents Urge 'Genuine' Socialism," *Washington Post*, March 3, 1988.

President's Report to the Congress Pursuant to Section 501 of the Comprehensive Anti-Apartheid Act of 1986

Pursuant to Section 501 of the Comprehensive Anti-Apartheid Act of 1986, the President has transmitted to the Speaker of the House of Representatives and the Chairman of the Committee on Foreign Relations of the Senate a report on the extent to which significant progress has been made toward ending the system of apartheid. Included is the President's recommendation on which suggested additional measures, if any, should be imposed on South Africa.

The Administration has concluded that the additional U.S. economic sanctions mandated by the Act to date have not been successful in moving the South African Government toward the set of goals outlined in Title I of the Act, goals that are shared by the Administration and Congress. Moreover, the South African Government's response to the Act so far gives no grounds for hope that more sanctions will produce better results. The Act has, instead, reduced U.S. leverage, hardened the South African Government's determination to resist outside pressure, and increased the appeal to South African whites of isolationist, ultra-conservative, and white supremacist movements. Indeed, South Africa's response to sanctions has been to place our goals even further from achievement.

Because the economic sanctions embodied in the 1986 Act have not been effective in advancing the goals on which Congress and the Administration agree, and the conviction that additional measures would be counterproductive, the President recommends the imposition of no additional sanctions at this time.

We must build on those elements of current policy that are designed to use our influence with all segments of South African society on behalf of change, and to assist black South Africans to overcome the handicaps imposed by apartheid. U.S. willingness to stay involved in South Africa and to facilitate dialogue among South Africans is the correct approach to helping South Africans peacefully resolve their country's profound political problems.

The Act states that United States policy toward South Africa shall be designed to bring about reforms leading to the establishment of a nonracial democracy and that the United States will work toward this goal by encouraging the Government of South Africa to:

- "repeal the present state of emergency and respect the principle of equal justice under law for citizens of all races,"
- "release Nelson Mandela, Govan Mbeki, Walter Sisulu, black trade union leaders, and all political prisoners,"
- "permit the free exercise by South Africans of all races of the right to form political parties, express political opinions and otherwise participate in the political process,"
- "establish a timetable for the elimination of apartheid laws,"
- "negotiate with representatives of all racial groups in South Africa the future political system in South Africa,"
- "end military and paramilitary activities aimed at neighboring states." . . .

THE STATUS OF APARTHEID: OCTOBER 1987 TO OCTOBER 1988

I am again unable to report significant progress leading to the end of apartheid and the establishment of a nonracial democracy in South Africa. The sanctions enacted in 1986 have not had their intended effect of weakening the resolve of South Africa's white minority to retain its monopoly of political power; indeed, they appear in some respects to have had the opposite effect. There is no indication that the South African Government is preparing initiatives that would address adequately the aspirations of the country's black majority. The South African Government's determination to demonstrate that it will not be swayed by pressure from abroad has further decreased the capacity of the United States to influence positively the course of events in that country. Repression of government opponents has intensified in the past year.

INTERNAL POLITICAL SITUATION: STATUS OF RACE RELATIONS

Viewed against the objectives outlined in Section 101 of the Act, the following developments over the past year argue strongly in favor of a reevaluation of the effectiveness of punitive sanctions as a means of promoting positive change in South Africa.

- Freedom of expression, association, movement, and the press have been further restricted. The past year has seen a clampdown on campus activisim and the virtual banning of the panoply of antiapartheid organizations, including the United Democratic Front and the National Education Crisis Committee. The political activities of the Congress of South African Trade Unions have also been severely limited. In August, the End Conscription Campaign was effectively banned. Throughout the period under review, restrictions on the press have been rigidly enforced, and the flow of information both within and from South Africa has been further reduced.
- In June the State of Emergency was renewed for another year. Although Govan Mbeki was released from prison in November, 1987 restrictions were placed on his activity and movements shortly thereafter. Nelson Mandela, Walter Sisulu, and Zeph Mothopeng remain in government custody. Several thousand others remain in detention, including a majority of the leaders of the broadly based United Democratic Front. New detentions continue to occur weekly. Since the imposition of the 1986 sanctions, the South African Government has been far less responsive to U.S. and other foreign government representations on behalf of antiapartheid activists.

- Although there was steady progress in scrapping apartheid laws through mid-1986, this progress has since ground to a halt. In mid-1988 the South African Government proposed legislation which would strengthen provisions of the Group Areas Act, thereby entrenching residential apartheid and facilitating a resumption of forced removals. No timetable has been established for abolishing the Group Areas Act or eliminating other important apartheid laws, and the prospects for this happening in the near future seem, if anything, to have worsened.

- The South African Government has given no sign that it is ready to negotiate with credible black leaders except within narrowly defined contexts established by the government itself.

POLITICAL CLIMATE: A WHITE SHIFT TO THE RIGHT

Heightened repression and the continuing erosion of civil liberties have taken place in an atmosphere of growing white support for isolationist, ultraconservative, and white supremacist political groups. The Conservative Party (CP), which became the official opposition in Parliament through its success in the May 1987 general election, won resounding victories in three key by-elections in early 1988 and is poised to make significant inroads into the ruling National Party's (NP) hold on local governments in the election scheduled for October 26. The groundswell of white support for the CP caused the NP to postpone indefinitely even modest plans for the political accommodation of the black majority. In part, the CP's appeal derives from its strident rejection of international pressure to end apartheid and its ability to capitalize on the growing sense of international hostility and ostracism that sanctions have helped to foster among white voters.

SOUTH AFRICA IN A REGIONAL CONTEXT

Although the South African Government has failed to tackle severe domestic problems over the last year, it has—with U.S. encouragement—launched initiatives designed to ease tensions with neighboring states. Under U.S. mediation, South Africa currently is engaged in negotiations with Angola and Cuba which have already led to the withdrawal of South African troops from Angolan territory, a cessation of hostilities along th Angolan/Namibian border, and establishment of a joint military commission to monitor the ceasefire. All parties have agreed to the target date of November 1, 1988 for the beginning of implementation of U.N. Security Council Resolution 435, which will lead to independence for Namibia. A successful negotiation will also achieve the withdrawal of more than fifty thousand Cuban troops from Angola under a mutually agreed timetable. Vigorous efforts involving numerous African leaders are underway to promote an end to the civil war in Angola and national reconciliation. As this report is being submitted, U.S. mediation efforts have intensified. The negotiating parties have compromised sufficiently that a definitive settlement is in reach which would end more than seventy years of South African occupation of Namibia, allow more than one million citizens of that country to elect their own government, and establish peace where war has raged for the past thirteen years. . . .

UNITED STATES POLICY

Within South Africa, U.S. influence has continued to decline since the implementation of the Act in 1986. Our ability to counsel restraint, to promote human rights, and to provide incentives for constructive South African Government behavior has diminished. In view of this trend, it has been necessary to measure carefully the ways in which we use our remaining influence with Pretoria.

Of particular importance, the United States was able earlier this year to argue persuasively for a stay of execution for the Sharpeville Six. Similarly, quiet persuasion was a factor in Pretoria's decision to withdraw legislation that could have severely restricted the flow of foreign funds to internal grass roots groups—including recipients of U.S. aid. Although we have yet to achieve our goal, I have appealed directly to State President Botha to release Nelson Mandela. Such a humanitarian gesture would, I believe, help to create the conditions needed for a negotiated solution to South Africas political dilemma. Throughout the period under review, the United States has persisted in efforts to maintain and expand contacts with all parties having a stake in South Africa's future. We have impressed upon South Africans the need to abandon stereotypes and nonnegotiable demands. We have promoted dialogue and compromise and underlined the ultimate futility of violence. We remain prepared to facilitate negotiations, which represent South Africa's best hope for a peaceful transition to a nonracial democracy. At the same time, we have continued an innovative program of assistance to South Africa's disadvantaged majority.

U.S. aid is being used to promote educational opportunities, provide managerial and leadership skills, and bolster the position of trade unions and certain grass roots organizations working for peaceful change.

ECONOMIC EFFECTS OF SANCTIONS AGAINST SOUTH AFRICA

According to the most optimistic current projections, South Africa's real gross domestic product will grow at a rate of approximately 2.5

percent in 1988. This falls far short of the country's economic potential and needs.

International sanctions have resulted in an estimated two percent decrease in South Africa's total foreign trade over the past two years. Pretoria has reacted to sanctions, and the threat of future sanctions, by developing new domestic industries to provide key products, by locating new external suppliers, and by continuing to stockpile key imports and raw materials, such as petroleum. South Africa's capacity for circumventing sanctions is in large part explained by the character of its exports. Over sixty percent of the nation's export earnings come from low bulk, high value commodities, such as gold and other precious metals.

The one area in which sanctions may have had a more significant effect is in the ability of South Africa to attract sufficient foreign capital to meet its debt repayment obligations and to finance economic growth. Sanctions-related restrictions coupled with shaky business confidence have reduced foreign lending and investment, forcing South Africa to rely more heavily on trade surpluses. However, a deterioration in the balance of trade in the first half of 1988, combined with annual debt service obligations of over $300 million and other capital outflows, has led the South African Government to contain domestic economic growth and to impose new controls on imports. These steps are also meant to increase import substitution and raise the degree of South African economic self-sufficiency. Recently announced dramatic increases in the cost of consumer credit, as well as tariff increases of 110 percent on imported cars, 60 percent on luxury imported consumer goods, and 20 percent on capital goods reflect this trend.

Slow growth and a lack of new investment have a direct economic impact on black South Africans. The expected 2.5 percent rate of growth is far short of the 5 percent needed to create jobs for an estimated 350,000 new job seekers each year, most of whom are black. The shortage of new foreign capital and tax revenue from a slow growing economy has led the government to consider drastic cuts in the previously planned major increase in expenditures on black education and housing.

Holly Burkhalter, Human Rights Watch

The Reagan Administration's Human Rights Record (1988)

In some countries, such as Cuba and the U.S.S.R., the Reagan Administration vigorously promoted the cause of human rights and spoke out forthrightly when violations occurred. In other countries, such as El Salvador and Honduras, the Administration squandered its extensive opportunities to promote human rights by denying that violations occurred, and attacked human rights organizations that told a different story.

One theme which emerges from our analysis of human rights policies around the world is that the Reagan Administration has a too narrow view of democracy, and has missed opportunities to support and protect the rule of law and those civilian institutions which are required for real democracy to flourish: an independent judiciary, a free press, functioning trade unions, opposition political parties.

Haiti provides a striking illustration of this approach: since it took office in February 1986, the CNG (the interim military government) committed gross abuses of human rights, and failed to discipline the police or the armed forces. Even after June, when the military government attempted to take over the civilian-run electoral process in violation of the constitution, and in November, when the military passively tolerated machine-gun and firebomb attacks on the civilian electoral council, the Administration stuck faithfully by the military government in the stubborn belief that, despite its repeated actions to the contrary, it would somehow see elections through. The administration's failure to denounce the sham elections of January 17th, and its refusal to publicly call upon the Manigat Government to conduct proper elections in accordance with the Haitian constitution have been a great disservice to the future of democracy in that country.

Another regrettable feature of the Reagan Administration's policy has been its failure to denounce attacks on persons or institutions with which it disagrees, or with whom its allies disagree. For example, in

From a speech before the Subcommittee on Human Rights and International Organizations of the Committee on Foreign Affairs, House of Representatives, One Hundredth Congress, Second Session (February 1988)

January, 1988, two human rights advocates in Taiwan were sentenced to ten and eleven years imprisonment because the charter of their organization, the Formosan Political Prisoners Association, advocated the independence of Taiwan. The Draconian sentences for the peaceful expression of a political view—albeit one with which neither the U.S. nor the government on Taiwan agrees—is a tremendous setback for human rights in Taiwan, and deserved to be condemned. To our knowledge, the Administration has been silent. In the case of Tibet the executive branch played down the seriousness of the PRC's suppression of dissent in Lhasa and even voiced support for China's efforts to restore its authority in Tibet. For example, just a few days after the violent suppression of demonstrations in October, the Administration criticized the U.S. Senate for failing to acknowledge "significant changes" by China which had led to an improvement in human rights in Tibet. This was an inappropriate signal to send at a tense moment in Tibet. Not until Congress initiated several strong resolutions did the Administration modify its protective stance towards the PRC and speak more frankly about abuses in Tibet.

A particularly flagrant example of the Administration refusing to acknowledge abuses against those with whom it disagrees is the case of labor unionists in El Salvador. At last week's hearing before this Subcommittee, Secretary Schifter justified the Administration's failure to take up the Americas Watch petition on worker rights in El Salvador before the U.S. Trade Representative on the grounds that the victims were guerilla sympathizers. This stance invites attacks against activist labor unions and peasant associations, and is a disservice to the cause of human rights and the development of independent institutions in El Salvador. Moreover, the Administration's refusal to accept the Americas Watch's well-documented labor rights petition on El Salvador is a clear violation of Section 502(b) (c) of the Trade Act. In fact, the Salvadoran government has harshly suppressed labor and peasant organizing activities by pro-government, antigovernment, and nonaligned unions. . . .

The Administration's support for human rights monitors around the world has been similarly distorted by ideology. Human rights monitoring and reporting by local groups is essential to the cause of human rights and the development of civilian institutions. The protection of human rights monitors—whatever their political views—should be a high priority of our government, and should be the particular cause of the Human Rights Bureau. Yet the Administration has been quick to denounce certain human rights monitors who condemn abuses by governments allied to the U.S. One particularly vivid example of the Administration's selective support of human rights monitors is the case of Dr. Ramon Custodio, the president of the Committee for the

Defense of Human Rights in Honduras (CODEH). Dr. Custodio has responsibly documented abuses by the Honduran armed forces and by the Nicaraguan *contras* against Honduran civilians, at great personal risk. The U.S. Ambassador in Tegucigalpa and State Department officials in Washington have regularly denounced Dr. Custodio as a "communist" and brushed aside reports of threats against him and other CODEH members. Such an attitude deprives CODEH of the international protection it needs and deserves, and invites attacks upon the group. CODEH's vulnerability can be seen in the assassination of the its Vice President, Miguel Pavon, on January 14, 1988. Pavon was a leading witness before the Inter-American Court in a landmark case brought by the Inter-American Commission on Human Rights against the Government of Honduras for gross violations of human rights.

On the positive side, the Administration has strongly supported human rights monitors in some countries and spoken out about abuses of human rights forthrightly. The executive branch is to be particularly commended for the high profile afforded human rights issues during the U.S.-U.S.S.R. summit. By giving praise where it is due but condemning persistent shortcomings, the Administration maintained a forceful advocacy of human rights throughout the year, even as it pursued an improvement in Soviet-American relations. A particular priority of Helsinki Watch is monitoring the development of independent organizations in the U.S.S.R., Poland, East Germany, and Czechoslovakia. "Clubs" dealing with numerous issues such as peace, disarmament, the environment, religion, and human rights, are springing up in the U.S.S.R. and in several Eastern European countries. While some controls on such independent activity have been lifted, others have been imposed. The Reagan Administration supports the development of civil society in the East Bloc. We would urge the executive branch to adopt this posture with respect to another Helsinki signatory—Turkey—and speak out frankly about continued repression of the Kurdish minority, continued restrictions on the press and labor unions, and continued political imprisonment and torture.

Another welcome human rights development was the Reagan Administration's resumption of normal immigration policy with Cuba, which will allow released political prisoners to emigrate to the U.S. in addition to some twenty thousand other Cubans yearly. It is very important that in administering the return of certain of the Mariel "excludables" the rights of the detainees be observed, and that all Cuban detainees be given a hearing in accordance with due process. Another important human rights initiative last year was the Reagan Administration's use of the United Nations as a forum in which to raise the issue of human rights in Cuba. Although the Administration's initiative at the United Nations Commission on Human Rights in March 1987 was defeated, it succeeded in calling attention to the human rights situation in Cuba. We would welcome a similarly energetic effort at the United Nations on Chile: in March, the U.S. supported a resolution condemning General Pinochet's repressive practices, but in November and December at the U.N. General Assembly, the U.S. abstained on a similar resolution. Since the Administration has improved its human rights position on Chile in other respects, including the imposition of trade sanctions because of worker rights violations, this stance at the United Nations is an anomaly. . . .

I would be remiss if I did not comment on the role of the Congress in promoting human rights. While the Administration possesses many more opportunities and has more diplomatic tools at its disposal, the Congress can and does have an important role to play. The activities of this particular Subcommittee in monitoring and reporting on human rights abuses are an important contribution to the promotion of human rights around the world. On a more critical note, however, the Congress appears to be taking less and less seriously its responsibilities towards monitoring military and police aid to governments engaged in gross abuses of human rights. Generic human rights laws, such as Section 502(B) and 116 of the Foreign Assistance Act have become virtually irrelevant, since countries engaged in systematic violations of human rights regularly receive U.S. assistance without debate. The Administration has become particularly adept at defending its requests for military and police aid on human rights grounds, and the majority in Congress appear to accept such justifications.

In one particular case last year, that of Guatemala, the Congress itself took the lead in earmarking significant military and police assistance to a country with one of the worst human rights records in the hemisphere. The Guatemalan president himself lobbied influential senators and representatives for increased military aid, and the Guatemalan Foreign Minister even went so far as to ask for military aid "with human rights conditions." Clearly, the Foreign Minister did not mean to suggest that money should be withheld if the Army committed abuses; he knows full well that Army abuses against civilians continue. Rather, the request for military aid "with human rights conditions" was an explicit acknowledgment that human rights restrictions attached to foreign aid do not prevent aid from flowing, but do tend to diminish liberal opposition to military assistance to repressive military forces. Accordingly, the Congress earmarked $7 million in military aid (upping the Administration's $5 request by $2 million) and $2 million in police aid, which the Administration didn't request at all.

The Congress has played an important role in speaking out about human rights abuses around the world—in the past year, for example, Congressional activism on human rights in South Korea, South Africa, Tibet, Haiti, and Romania have been particularly helpful. Yet oversight of foreign aid appears to be less and less of a priority. Furthermore, labor rights conditions have been attached to certain U.S. trade benefits, but the Administration has resisted administering the statute evenhandedly. . . . I would urge this Subcommittee to maintain and expand your legislative oversight activities and insist that both the executive branch and your own colleagues apply human rights laws responsibly.

Amnesty International

Human Rights and U.S. Foreign Policy: A Mandate for Leadership (1988)
Introduction

Amnesty International USA urges U.S. Government officials to accept the challenge of leadership in the promotion and protection of human rights. Amnesty International USA's 200,000 members work with Amnesty International members in over 150 other countries. We encourage the U.S. Government and elected officials to contribute to safeguarding the fundamental rights of all people. U.S. political leaders who support the standards in international human rights agreements will find that their position resonates throughout the United States and the world.

Responding to the human rights abuses of World War II, the international community, with strong U.S. leadership, adopted in 1948 the Universal Declaration of Human Rights. Forty years later, one-third of the world's governments condone or permit torture. More than 100 governments jail real or perceived political opponents. Dozens of governments still punish offenders by killing them, all in contravention of international human rights norms. It is past time to end these abuses.

Amnesty International USA calls on U.S. Government officials to reaffirm U.S. leadership in protecting human rights, to stand firm in opposition to these abuses and to state clearly what actions they will take in this endeavor.

U.S. interests are best served when our domestic and foreign policies support the values embodied in the founding documents of our nation: the Declaration of Independence and the Constitution. These values of individual liberty, freedom of expression, freedom of association, and security of the person, rightfully stand enshrined in the heritage of this country. We identify ourselves and our government as instruments to protect these rights. U.S. policies, therefore, must clearly show our commitment to end political imprisonment, torture, and killing wherever they occur.

I. Human Rights Protection Supports National Interests

Human rights interests cannot be separated from national security interests. Respect for human rights guarantees every nation's security and a peaceful and stable world. The Universal Declaration of Human Rights states: "Recognition of the inherent dignity and of the equal and inalienable rights of all members of the human family is the foundation of freedom, justice, and peace in the world."

Amnesty International USA encourages all U.S. Government officials to state clearly their awareness of the fundamental relationship between national security and the protection of human rights.

In the short term, U.S. Government actions in pursuit of perceived national security interests often tend too override human rights concerns when applied to specific countries.

Amnesty International USA urges all U.S. Government officials to pledge to resolve any seeming conflict of interest in ways that protect human rights as well as national security interests.

II. The Human Rights Policy of the United States Must be Universal in its Conception, Effective in its Implementation, and Cooperative in its Method

1. HUMAN RIGHTS STANDARDS CROSS IDEOLOGICAL FRONTIERS
The fundamental human rights recognized by the Universal Declaration and other international instruments are, by definition, universal. Universal rights have no place in ideological arsenals, to be invoked or ignored according to the dictates of shifting partisan politics. Selective attention weakens human rights protection worldwide, thereby undermining a secure and just world order consonant with U.S. national interests.

Elected officials must develop a foreign policy that serves this country's national interests by giving priority to universal human rights concerns. U.S. support for the rights of citizens living under a repressive government, whatever that government's ideology, gains the friendship of that country's people. A people's perception that the U.S. Government supports their oppression engenders their long-term enmity.

Amnesty International USA calls upon U.S. Government officials to endorse the universal application of human rights standards.

2 EFFECTIVENESS IS KEY TO HUMAN RIGHTS POLICY

The basic criterion for choosing human rights strategies and programs must be effectiveness. Particular methods of protecting human rights may be successful in some circumstances and ineffective in others. The debate on quiet diplomacy versus public denunciation, like any argument which separates methodology from goals, is essentially sterile. Yet it is clear that a policy of private communication with friendly governments and open denunciation of hostile governments is counterproductive. When the U.S. Government publicly ignores violations committed by its friends, while condemning its adversaries for the same violations, it reduces human rights to a propaganda tool and generates cynicism rather than hope.

A government committed to human rights develops a corps of foreign service professionals trained and experienced in human rights work. A strong and active bureau of human rights is central to a strong and active human rights policy. Systematic briefings of all policymakers and clear instructions on human rights promotion are important aspects of an effective human rights program.

Successive Administrations and Congresses have enacted during recent years laws linking a country's human rights performance to U.S. policy and actions toward that country. The effective implementation of this legislation is critical to an effective human rights policy. The integrity of the information that is used in implementing the legislation is crucial. Attempts to circumvent the law by ignoring or distorting information on particular countries signal offending governments that the United states is not serious in its human rights advocacy.

Amnesty International USA calls upon U.S. Government officials to define an effective U.S. human rights policy and support implementation of existing human rights legislation.

3. INTERNATIONAL COOPERATION HELPS ENFORCE HUMAN RIGHTS NORMS

The United States must promote human rights in both the bilateral and multilateral foreign policy channels. Its efforts, however, are

Amnesty International USA. Human Rights Policy Paper (February, 1988)

undercut by the inexplicable failure to rafify basic human rights treaties, such as the International Human Rights Covenants. These covenants, as well as the Convention Against Torture and the American Convention on Human Rights, must be promptly ratified.

, *Amnesty International USA calls upon U.S. Government officials* to express clear support for ratification of international human rights instruments without crippling reservations.

Support for international human rights laws and conventions, as well as United Nations procedures and mechanisms for protecting human rights, moves that protection from philosophical discussion to positive action. That support is best expressed when the United States itself abides by international norms and uses its considerable influence to ensure that partisan ideological currents do not override the spirit of universal protection and promotion of human rights.

Amnesty International USA calls on U.S. Government officials to signal their commitment to establishing effective and impartial enforcement mechanisms for protecting human rights within the international system.

III. Selected Actions Suggested to Eradicate Specific Human Rights Violations

Amnesty International works globally and impartially on specific concerns: release of prisoners of conscience (men, women, and children imprisoned solely for their ethnic origins or beliefs, provided they have neither used nor advocated violence), fair and prompt trials for all political prisoners, and abolition of torture and executions. Amnesty International USA's 200,000 members, who work with Amnesty members in over 150 other countries, urge the U.S. Government to safeguard the human rights of all people by monitoring events abroad, raising human rights concerns in public and private forums, and taking other actions enumerated below to protect basic human rights.

Amnesty International USA urges U.S. Government officials to endorse a human rights policy for this country that incorporates efforts to eradicate specific categories of violations, namely, political imprisonment, torture, and executions.

1. TAKE ACTION TO FREE PRISONERS OF CONSCIENCE AND TO PROMOTE FAIR TRIALS IN POLITICAL CASES

Amnesty International has documented thousands of prisoner of conscience cases. Governments in every region of the world have arrested and detained their citizens, sometimes jailing them for years without charge or trial.

Amnesty International USA calls on U.S. Government officials to:
- Use their good offices to intervene for the release of individual prisoners of conscience.
- Promote attendance at political trials by U.S. embassy personnel.
- Gather information from human rights activists and others knowledgeable in human rights issues during official visits abroad to supplement that provided by government sources.

2. TAKE ACTION TO END TORTURE

President Reagan signed into law in September 1984 a Congressional Resolution Against Torture (P.L. 98-447). The resolution specifies measures to be taken by U.S. Government officials against torture practiced by foreign governments.

Amnesty International USA calls on U.S. Government officials to commit themselves to achieve the goals of the resolution by:

- Publicly condemning torture wherever it occurs.
- Pressuring governments to abolish practices which facilitate torture, including incommunicado or secret detention.
- Pressuring governments to investigate reports of torture, prosecute torturers, and compensate victims or their dependents.
- Prohibiting transfer of military, police, or security equipment or expertise when it can be reasonably assumed that these transfers play a direct role in torture or related human rights abuses.

3. TAKE ACTION TO ELIMINATE ARBITRARY AND DISCRIMINATORY CAPITAL SENTENCING

There is an adverse relationship between capital punishment and existing international human rights standards. The Universal Declaration of Human Rights states in Article 5: "No one shall be subjected to torture or to cruel, inhuman, or degrading treatment or punishment." In addition, imposition of the death penalty in the United States and other countries which still permit capital punishment results in arbitrary and discriminatory executions. The United States has a responsibility to review the existence of discrimination in the administration and application of capital sentencing. The United States can promote human rights abroad by demonstrating its commitment to protecting human rights at home.

The United States is one of the member states of the United Nations. It shows little sign, however, of joining the world trend toward abolishing state-sanctioned killing. Therefore, the United States contravenes the United Nations declaration that "in order to guarantee fully the right to life, provided for in Article 3 of the Universal Declaration of Human Rights," member states should progressively seek to restrict "the number of offenses for which capital punishment may be imposed with a view to the desirability of abolishing this punishment in all countries."

Amnesty International USA calls on U.S. Government officials to commit themselves to work toward abolition of the death penalty in the United States and specifically to:

• Prohibit the execution of juvenile offenders, a practice which contravenes the International Covenant on Civil and Political Rights and the American Convention on Human Rights.
• Prohibit execution of the mentally impaired, a practice which contravenes the guidelines of the United Nations Economic and Social Council.
• Eliminate discrimination in application of the death penalty.

4. TAKE ACTION TO ENSURE JUST TREATMENT OF REFUGEES

The United States has condemned torture and political killing. This government should not send asylum seekers back to countries where there are reasonable grounds to believe that they may become victims of unjust imprisonment, torture, or political killing. People subjected to or threatened with human rights abuses often have no choice but flight, and this country has a tradition of receiving refugees.

Amnesty International USA calls on U.S. Government officials to:

• Support continuation of the U.S. humanitarian custom of granting asylum, seeking evenhanded treatment of refugees from countries of differing ideologies.
• Support guarantees that all asylum seekers will receive legal assistance and due process in pursuing their cases with U.S. immigration officials.
• Support a policy of providing safe haven to refugees from our own region fleeing from civil strife in their own countries.

Conclusion

Disregard for human rights exacerbates conflicts both within and between nations. U.S. Government policies and actions that give priority to human rights concerns contribute to the resolution of these conflicts. When U.S. officials and legislators publicly promote human rights, they demonstrate the political will necessary to create a just and peaceful environment both at home and abroad.

Amnesty International USA urges U.S. Government officials to state publicly their determination to place human rights at the core of U.S. foreign policy and take specific actions in pursuit of that goal.

Richard Schifter

Human Rights: A Western Cultural Bias? (1988)

"That to secure these Rights, Governments are instituted among Men, deriving their just Powers from the Consent of the Governed," says the U.S. Declaration of Independence. The rights referred to are the rights to life, liberty, and the pursuit of happiness.

The Declaration thus rejected the fundamental notion, which had persisted for so long in human history, of the divine right of kings, which held that the ruler had an inherent right to exercise power and that the subjects had a responsibility to obey. It turned that relationship around by defining the right of the citizen as the principal reason for the existence of state authority.

The writers of the American Declaration of Independence were, in 1776, not the originators of this idea. The thoughts which were incorporated into the Declaration were those that had been discussed and written about for more than a century—the thoughts of the Enlightenment. Thirteen years later, in 1789, the same thoughts were reflected in France's Declaration of the Rights of Man and the Citizen. And, almost simultaneously, the United States followed up on its Declaration with the Bill of Rights.

Anyone who compares these documents of the late 18th century with the Universal Declaration of Human Rights will recognize the close similarity. What the Universal Declaration has clearly done has been to elevate to the international scene the principles of government enunciated by the writers and thinkers of the Enlightenment.

From an address by Richard Schifter, Assistant Secretary for Human Rights and Humanitarian Affairs, before the European Workshop on the Universal Declaration of Human Rights sponsored by the UN Center for Human Rights, Milan, Italy, September 7, 1988.

Cultural Experience and Attitudes Toward Human Rights

Do I, by making these observations, lend support to the criticism of the Universal Declaration that it is culture bound, that it narrowly reflects the attitude and thinking of what is generally known as Western civilization, and that it is really not applicable to societies which have different cultural roots? In other words, have I given support to the proposition that the Universal Declaration is not truly universal?

To focus on the issue thus posed, let me suggest that we think of how some British observers of political developments in France might have responded in the year 1789 to the news of the promulgation of the Declaration of the Rights of Man and the Citizen. It would have been slightly more than 100 years after the glorious revolution, many decades after the development of a constitutional monarchy in Britain had begun. Wouldn't it be likely that a good many observers in London would have exclaimed: "Rights of citizens in France? All these people have ever known is absolute monarchy. What does the average Frenchman understand about the rights of the citizen?"

Let us also consider the American experience. To be sure, the writers of the Declaration of Independence and of the Bill of Rights represented a burgeoning new country in which government with the consent of the governed and respect for individual rights were recognized concepts. But was it government by consent of *all* the governed? And were the rights of *all* individuals respected?

The answer to both of these questions was "no." The most egregious form of repression—chattel slavery—was practiced in many of the states that made up that new country, which had been brought into being by the Declaration of Independence of 1776. Slavery was an institution that lasted 87 years after the country's founders had proudly proclaimed that "all men are created equal." And it took a civil war—the most costly war in American history—to expunge slavery from American life.

The point I want to make is that the principles set forth in such documents as the American Declaration of Independence or the French Declaration of the Rights of Man and the Citizen were not deeply rooted in the practices of either of these countries.

Corazon C. Aquino

Speech on the Fortieth Anniversary of the Universal Declaration of Human Rights (1988)

This celebration of the fortieth Anniversary of the Universal Declaration of Human Rights pays tribute to the common bond of decency that proclaims all men as brothers. That bond is the Universal Declaration of Human Rights.

We call it universal because all men, by their humanity, declare an unwavering commitment to respect those rights. The preamble of the Declaration is clear on this:

"The General Assembly of the United Nations proclaims this Universal Declaration of Human Rights as a common standard of achievement for all peoples and nations,

- to the end that every individual and every organ of society shall strive
- by teaching and education
- to promote respect for these rights and freedoms
- and by progressive measures
- to secure their universal and effective recognition and observance."

I have quoted the preamble at length because we must return to the root for the true meaning and spirit of the commitment that the world made to itself after history's most terrible conflict.

Wars had never been like this. It was not a war for economic advantage and military glory only, but one aimed at the annihilation of whole peoples simply for being who they were.

The war was a crime against humanity, for the aggressors denied the humanity of all who did not belong to their race and follow their creed.

It was a war where single acts of human endurance were overwhelmed by shocking acts of inhuman cruelty. Acts committed by individuals against individuals—in military prisons, in concentration camps, in the charnel houses of the great dictatorships.

It is not surprising therefore that the Universal Declaration of Human Rights marks out the individual, and not just governments, as carrying a special obligation to promote, by teaching and education, respect for human rights; and, by progressive measures, secure their universal and effective recognition and observance. Thus:

By specific order of the Human Rights Commission, detainees are accorded liberal visitation rights and their persons are secured against mental or bodily abuse.

By executive order, an extensive education and information campaign has been conducted to spread awareness and respect for human rights.

And finally, by living example, we, the Filipino people, taught the world how to respect human rights.

Our people stood up unarmed for their human rights and for the human rights of the soldiers who opposed them.

[The] army responded with equal respect for human rights by not firing on the unarmed multitude. No army in the Western world would have shown such forbearance. What might have been the tragedy of Kent State became [a] miracle.

There are those who question the human rights commitment of this nation and this government. I want them to prove their accusations. I, and everyone concerned about the safety of democracy, have a stake in punishing the human rights violators in the military. The hand that can abuse a prisoner will have the mind to plot a coup d'etat. Such violations show an indiscipline and inclination to anarchy that a democracy cannot tolerate in its armed forces.

Until that time, I must say what the facts proclaim: That this new government has never adopted, by neglect or design, a policy or pattern of human rights violations for any purpose.

That there are sporadic violations of human rights in this country, I must acknowledge.

We are only in the third year of regained democracy. The inhumanity of people obsessed by power or possessed by dogma, whether in the uniform of the regular army or in the casual wear of the insurgency, will be with us for some time yet.

But for as long as Filipinos have a democracy, human rights violations will never become the pattern and policy of government in this country.

Sadly, I cannot speak for all Filipinos. I cannot speak for those who refuse to adopt peaceful means to express their rejection of democracy. If there is a pattern of human rights violations, if there is a conscious policy of terrorism in this country, you will find it among them.

The government does not shoot traffic policemen to secure the fearful respect and cooperation of the people.

The government does not demand ransom from individuals as the price of their lives.

And we do not execute our fellow workers for their mistakes.

As every individual must respect the human rights of everyone, so must his human rights be respected by all.

"Everyone has the right of life, liberty, and security of person. No one shall be subjected to torture or to cruel, inhuman, or degrading treatment or punishment."

"Everyone," says the Declaration, "is entitled to all the rights and freedoms" set forth therein.

That includes the policeman who falls to the pavement with a shattered head.

That includes the poor farmer whose children are killed or horribly disfigured because their homesteads have been chosen as the battleground of ideology.

That includes the insurgent who is executed because he gave a second thought to democracy.

That includes the leftists and labor leaders who were tortured and assassinated by the rightwing elements in the military.

Yet the same obligation to respect human rights that binds governments bind the killers of these people as well.

I cannot allow any accusation against the human rights commitment of this country and this government to go unchallenged—or univestigated and unpunished.

It is not a matter of pride, but of memory. It is a matter of self-preservation.

Those of us who lived in the shadow of violence under the dictatorship, will not allow it again to darken the door to human rights and freedom that we have opened for our people.

That there are violations, the Lupao massacre proves. That they will occur again is inevitable in any country riven by a rebellion led by fanatics.

I have made it clear that I intend to win the war against the insurgency. There will be no substitute for the permanent victory for democracy.

I have given the order for the vigorous prosecution of the war so that its early end will shorten the agony of this nation and hasten the recovery of its former strength and status in this region.

Yet, I will not accept the heat of battle as an excuse for brutality—towards the people we are pledged to protect, and even toward our enemies. Democracy needs force, but this government will not stoop to terrorism to survive.

I welcome the continuing concern of human rights groups, both here and from abroad, about the human rights situation in the Philippines. We need all the eyes that can be spared to uncover the abuses that still occur, even as we need every pair of hands to bind the wounds and bring the perpetrators to justice. I welcome most specially the recent vigilance of congress, particularly the Senate. . . .

Andrei Sakharov

Towards Democracy (1988)

In the context of perestroika, such questions as state structure, especially the Constitution and the electoral system, are of critical importance. Similarly significant are freedom of association and assembly, and such traditional issues as freedom of conviction and the free choice of country of residence.

On October 22-23, Soviet newspapers carried draft amendments to the U.S.S.R. Constitution and electoral law. It has been announced that, after a month-long discussion, they will be presented to the U.S.S.R. Supreme Soviet for endorsement. I must confess that I am worried by such haste in so serious a matter. The Constitution and electoral law define the country's political structure for years to come, and any mistake here is fraught with unpredictable consequences. We should therefore make quite sure that all factors have been taken into consideration so that there is no casting of votes for a list drawn up by officials in elections to the Supreme Soviet, as in that case the popularly elected deputies will not be able to discharge their functions.

There is likewise a need to make provision in the Supreme Soviet representation for new public organizations, including any that might appear in the foreseeable future. Why is there no place on the list of organizations empowered to nominate deputies to the Soviets for the popular fronts currently emerging in the different constituent republics? I think it would be beneficial to extend the period of discussion by, say, three months, as within this period independent teams of experts could clarify and complement the drafts. Why not call an all-union referendum as provided for in the Constitution? Another reason I suggest this is that, in the last few months the U.S.S.R. Supreme Soviet has, by a majority vote, endorsed edicts concerned with the procedure for holding meetings and demonstrations and with the powers enjoyed by the troops of the Ministry of the Interior.

From *New Times*, November 1988.

They have, however, been criticized in the news media, by legal experts and in the Supreme Soviet itself. . . .

The concept of a *law-governed state* implies, above all, the preeminence of the law. All instances, all state bodies, all persons, however high their office, are equal with all citizens in the eyes of the law. In turn, the laws fully conform to, and do not conflict with, the Constitution, and likewise fully accord with international norms and the country's international commitments. . . . Indeed, international commitments must necessarily come first and they may be directly invoked, even in the case of judicial rulings and decisions. There must also be due and appropriate constitutional control and supervision in the shape of a constitutional court or other analogous body that would ensure that legislation accords with the Constitution and international commitments. The Committee of Constitutional Supervision envisaged by the draft constitutional amendments could be such a body. The entire system for appealing against judicial decisions and rulings also stands in need of revision. Incidentally, it is important to enhance the standard of jurisprudence, as all transgressions and abuses of the law in the process of interrogation must necessarily be identified. All interrogation conducted by unlawful means must be declared illegal. It must be established that the defendant's confession has no legal force, as then the interrogating officer will not attempt to elicit a confession, which is often coerced by unlawful means.

In a law-governed state the rights of citizens must be protected unconditionally.

Freedom of Conviction

We had and indeed still have articles in our criminal code in conformity with which people have been sentenced for their conviction or for non-violent action associated therewith. Most of these people have been released, and it is now necessary to release and reinstate all such persons.

How the appropriate articles of the new criminal code are formulated is important. So far we only have sketchy information as to how this code is being drafted. Apparently Article 190, Section 1, of the Russian Federation Criminal Code is to be dropped, as has been noted in the Soviet media. I think it essential to state precisely that criminal prosecution for one's convictions and for non-violent action associated therewith is intolerable. I think this should be reflected in the Fundamentals of U.S.S.R. Criminal Legislation.

I also think the "religious" articles should be so worded as to prevent harassment for non-violent action relating to beliefs and religious convictions.

Free Choice of Country of Residence

Soviet law, at any rate Soviet practice, declares that with us emigration is admissible in the case of the reunion of families, for which purpose what are known as invitations are required.

The Universal Declaration of Human Rights and the human rights treaties that the Soviet Union has ratified imply the totally unrestricted right to choose one's country of residence. This right is unrestricted in the sense that no conditions are required other than the person's own wish. Naturally, in cases when exit is denied for reason of national security, the authorities are entitled to refuse permission. That is reasonable and provision should be made for it in Soviet legislation. This must all be strictly legalized and it must be possible to appeal to the law courts against such decisions, as each denial must be justified.

Freedom of Assembly and Demonstrations

The only constitutional solution to this problem in a given case would be one according to which citizens notify local government bodies of a forthcoming assembly or demonstration. Meanwhile, the authorities should take steps to ensure that such assemblies proceed with due observance of law and order, allowing nobody to obstruct them. However, if they believe that the said meeting should be forbidden, such a ban should be justified.

National Problems and Problems of the National-State Constitutional Structure of the U.S.S.R.

In its initial version, the U.S.S.R. Constitution was drafted in the 1920s, and subsequently in the 1930s in conditions when considerable aberrations already existed in state structure.

The state's national structure conforms to the hierarchical principle of the branching-tree type. The picture is one of the state, followed by the constituent republics and such autonomous formations as republics, regions and national areas administratively subordinated to it.

In itself this system gives rise to acute national contradictions and problems, insofar as minorities and ethnic groups have found themselves subordinated to larger ethnic groups.

As I see it, the new, modified Constitution should introduce not a hierarchical system of links, but what is known as a horizontal one, incorporating a central supranational government and equal formations based on national characteristics, though not necessarily equal in size and level of development.

The Right of Citizens to Control and Supervise State Decisions

Millions of destinies hinge on the implementation of this right. It relates to decisions taken on social and economic issues, as, for instance, price reform, and likewise on matters of foreign policy. I maintain, for instance, that such decisions as the sending of Soviet troops into Afghanistan should not have been taken without discussion, without popular involvement.

Dissidents and Society

Today the moral condition of our society is changing drastically. It is being shaken up. People are being deluged with information about what really happened in this country and what is happening now. I see this as a cleansing, purging factor, which must help us, or at least the young, to acquire a more democratic mentality. That, in turn, implies respect for people who think differently, as well as the desire to take stock of everything for oneself without blind faith in authority. Society needs its dissidents. Generally, I want to say that only ideas can conflict with ideas.

Mikhail Gorbachev

Interview by *The Washington Post* and *Newsweek(1988)*

About the similarities and dissimilarities of economic policy in this country and in the West. Of course, it is possible to find a likeness, formal at least, in anything and such a likeness does exist if you do not go into the essence of one reform or another. However, it is the difference of principle that matters. What is taking place in the U.S.S.R. is an all-embracing process of revolutionary renovation of socialist society on the basis of the historical choice which we do not doubt and which proved, in principle, the only correct one of our people seventy years ago. Otherwise the country with which you are discussing things that affect the future of the world as a whole would not exist. Of course, combating stagnation in the course of perestroika and dismantling the mechanism of retardation require that inflexibility and conservatism be overcome. Sometimes we are confronted with hectic impatience. There is also conscious resistance on the part of those whose narrow selfish interests are incompatible with perestroika, socially, economically or morally.

However, this is precisely what we mean by perestroika, in the course of which we want to renovate our society, upgrade it qualitywise. Perestroika is proceeding in width and depth, encompassing all public groups and all our territory. Perestroika is growing and gaining momentum.

As for glasnost, it and freedom of speech are, of course, interconnected. However, these are not identical things. I would put it this way: while freedom of speech is indispensable for glasnost, we see glasnost as a broader phenomenon. For us it is not just the right of every citizen to openly say what he or she thinks about all social and political questions, but also the duty of the ruling Party and all bodies of authority and administration to ensure openness in decision-making, be accountable for their actions, act on criticism, and consider advice and recommendations from the shop floor, public organizations and individuals.

Glasnost accentuates an environment allowing citizens to effectively participate in discussing all of the country's affairs, in elaborating and making decisions that affect the interests of all of us and in monitoring the implementation of these decisions.

Question: Could you discuss what ideas from abroad have had influence in the formation of your political and economic thinking and your mode of action? Conversely, what is the effect of glasnost and perestroika in other socialist countries?

Answer: In my book on perestroika published by Harper and Row, I wrote that our new political thinking is a result of our comprehension of the realities of the nuclear age, of deep and self-critical reflections on the past and present of our own country and of the surrounding world.

The new thinking took into account and absorbed the conclusions and demands of the Non-Aligned Movement, of the public and of the scientific community, of the movements of physicians, scientists and ecologists, and of various anti-war organizations. We also take into consideration the experience of other socialist countries just as they take ours into account. The process of mutual enrichment with experience, in which no one tries to impose any models on others, is under way.

Yes, all of us really do understand our dependence on one another better and feel that we live in an interrelated world and that all of us are inseparable parts of the single present-day civilization.

Question: Judging by the President's statements, you disagree with him on human rights. At the same time, your dramatic decision to free Andrei Sakharov and to ease the conditions of emigration for some Soviet Jews who desire to live abroad have attracted attention around the world. What further steps do you plan in this direction?

Answer: Our perestroika, the main factor of which is creative effort, also includes doing away with all deformations of the past years, with everything that hampers manifestation of the humanitarian essence of socialism.

We know our problems and speak honestly and openly about them. The process of democratization does not bypass the sphere of human rights and liberties. We are enhancing the political and public status of the personality. Many issues have already been resolved within the framework of the democratic process, while others will be resolved as Soviet society changes qualitatively in the course of perestroika. But that is our job. We are resolving these issues not because we want to play up to somebody or to please somebody, but because this meets the interests of our society, because perestroika cannot be carried out without it, and, last but not least, because it is wanted by the Soviet people who have long outgrown the restrictions which they put up with in the past and which were to a certain extent an inevitable part of the unusual revolutionary development which we have gone through.

Once I said, and it seems to me, to an American: please, show me a country that has no problems. Each country has problems of its own, human rights included. Of course, we are well informed about the situation with political, social, economic and other rights in the United States. We know well the achievements and problems, but also the flaws of American society. But we do not allow interference in your home affairs, though we deem it right to express our views on the processes taking place in American society, on your Administration's policy. But we do not want to make all this a reason for confrontation. We consider such an approach to be correct, fair; we see it as meeting the interests of Soviet-American relations and their future. I want to emphasize once again that we do not try to impose anything on the United States, but at the same time we rebuff attempts by any side to meddle in our affairs, no matter who tries to do so in your country.

Such is, in principle, our approach. At the same time, there are problems in the human rights sphere which require joint consideration. The mechanism of cooperation in that area has begun to take shape of late. Scientists, specialists and public representatives have been widely drawn into it. Specific issues are analyzed at their meetings in a calm atmosphere and businesslike manner.

We also welcome the accord on setting up a permanent body on human rights with the participation of Deputies to the U.S.S.R. Supreme Soviet and U.S. Congressmen. It is the duty of legislators in both countries to show concern for observance of the citizens' rights.

We are prepared to go on acting in this spirit.

Taking advantage of this opportunity, I would like to say the following. As it seems to me, pragmatism, preparedness to seek new decisions if what has been tested does not work is the Americans' forte. But they also have a trait—please, do not resent my frankness—which sometimes makes it difficult to deal with them. I mean their confidence that everything American is the best, while what others have is at least worse if not altogether bad and unfit for use. I am not talking about anti-communism, which has been implanted in the U.S.A. for decades, despite the fact that Albert Einstein called it the greatest lie of the 20th century many years ago.

For the sake of our mutual understanding, please, do not try to teach us to live according to American rules—it is altogether useless. And I repeat that, for our part, we do not intend to suggest our values to the Americans.

Let each side live in its own way, respecting each other's choice and voluntary exchanging the fruits of our labor in all the spheres of human activity.

I am sure that each nation, each people does not lose but, conversely, wins if it looks at itself critically and does not ignore others' experience, if it is open to understanding of and respect for a different culture, a different way of thinking, different customs, lastly, a different political system, of course, if it is not terrorist, fascist or dictatorial.

Question: Does your policy of perestroika require fundamental changes in the way relations among Soviet nationalities are structured? Does this policy offer new ways of promoting their cultural diversity and internationalism?

Answer: The question of changing the socialist principles of relations among the peoples, big and small, in our country is not on the agenda in the U.S.S.R. But we will set right the violations of these principles. It is such violations that caused the recent developments in some of our Republics. The West has displayed, I would say, a morbid interest in them, not infrequently with anti-Soviet innuendo and bad intentions. It made lavish use of speculations aimed at weakening our multinational Union.

Problems certainly do exist, and they are linked with the legacy we inherited from the time of the personality cult and the period of stagnation—in the economy, social policy, cultural life and human relations. Internationalism, which is deeply rooted in the hearts and minds of Soviet people of all nationalities will help us resolve the problems in this sphere, too. And we will resolve them in the spirit of perestroika and in close linkage with the accomplishment of all the main tasks it involves, in the process of radical renewal of society.

Mikhail Gorbachev

Speech to the United Nations General Assembly (1988)

I would like to join the voice of my country in the expressions of high appreciation of the significance of the Universal Declaration of Human Rights adopted 40 years ago on Dec. 10, 1948.

Today, this document retains its significance. It, too, reflects the universal nature of the goals and objectives of the United Nations.

The most fitting way for a state to observe this anniversary of the declaration is to improve its domestic conditions for respecting and protecting the rights of its own citizens. . . .

Our country is going through a period of truly revolutionary uplifting.

The process of perestroika is gaining momentum. We began with the formulation of the theoretical concept of perestroika. We had to evaluate the nature and the magnitude of problems, to understand the lessons of the past and express that in the form of political conclusions and programs. This was done.

Theoretical work, a reassessment of what is happening, the finalization, enrichment and readjustment of political positions have not been completed. They are continuing.

But it was essential to begin with an overall concept, which, as now confirmed by the experience of these past years, has generally proved to be correct and which has no alternative.

For our society to participate in efforts to implement the plans for

From *The Washington Post* December 8, 1988.

perestroika, it had to be democratized in practice. Under the sign of democratization, perestroika has now spread to politics, the economy, intellectual life and ideology.

We have initiated a radical economic reform. We have gained experience. At the start of next year the entire national economy will be redirected to new forms and methods of operation. This also means profoundly reorganizing relations of production and releasing the tremendous potential inherent in socialist property.

Undertaking such bold revolutionary transformations, we realized that there would be mistakes, and also opposition, that new approaches would generate new problems. We also foresaw the possibility of slowdowns in some areas.

But the guarantee that the overall process of perestroika will steadily move forward and gain strength lies in a profound democratic reform of the entire system of power and administration.

With the recent decisions by the U.S.S.R. Supreme Soviet on amendments to the Constitution and the adoption of the Law on Elections, we have completed the first stage of the process of political reform.

Without pausing, we have begun the second stage of this process with the main task of improving the relationship between the center and the republics, harmonizing interethnic relations on the principles of Leninist internationalism that we inherited from the Great Revolution, and at the same time reorganizing the local system of Soviet power.

A great deal of work lies ahead. Major tasks will have to be dealt with concurrently.

We are full of confidence. We have a theory and a policy, and also the vanguard force of perestroika—the party, which also is restructuring itself in accordance with new tasks and fundamental changes in society as a whole.

What is most important is that all our peoples and all generations of citizens of our great country support perestroika.

We have become deeply involved in building a socialist state based on the rule of law. Work on a series of new laws has been completed or is nearing completion.

Many of them will enter into force as early as in 1989, and we expect them to meet the highest standards from the standpoint of ensuring the rights of the individual.

Soviet democracy will be placed on a solid normative base. I am referring, in particular, to laws on the freedom of conscience, glasnost, public associations and organizations, and many others.

In places of confinement there are no persons convicted for their political or religious beliefs.

Additional guarantees are to be included in the new draft laws that rule out any form of persecution on those grounds.

Naturally this does not apply to those who committed actual criminal offenses or state crimes such as espionage, sabotage, terrorism, etc., whatever their political or ideological beliefs.

Draft amendments to the penal code have been prepared and are awaiting their turn. Among the articles being revised are those related to capital punishment.

The problem of exit from and entry to our country, including the question of leaving it for family reunification, is being dealt with in a humane spirit.

As you know, one of the reasons for refusal to leave is a person's knowledge of secrets. Strictly warranted time limitations on the secrecy rule will not be applied. Every person seeking employment at certain agencies or enterprises will be informed of this rule. In case of disputes, there is a right of appeal under the law.

This removes from the agenda the problem of the so-called "refusniks."

We intend to expand the Soviet Union's participation in the United Nations and CSCE [Conference of Security and Cooperation in Europe] human rights monitoring arrangements. We believe that the jurisdiction of the International Court of Justice at the Hague as regards the interpretation and implementation of agreements on human rights should be binding on all states.

We regard as part of the Helsinki process the cessation of jamming of all foreign radio broadcasts beamed at the Soviet Union.

Overall, this is our credo. Political problems must be solved only by political means, human problems, only in a humane way.

Amnesty International

Report on Iran (1988)

Thousands of political prisoners, including prisoners of conscience, were reported to be detained without trial and suspected government opponents who were brought to trial continued to be denied legal representation and the right to appeal to a higher court. Torture of political prisoners remained widespread and thousands of people were subjected to lashings and other judicial punishments which constitute torture or cruel, inhuman or degrading treatment. There were at least 158 executions, although the true number was probably higher as executions of political prisoners continued to occur in secret.

Ayatollah Montazeri, Ayatollah Khomeini's designated successor, and Hojatoleslam Hashemi Rafsanjani, the Speaker of the Iranian Parliament, made statements during 1987 recognizing the importance of human rights. In June Ayatollah Montazeri urged military court officers to "be satisfied with the minimum number of arrests possible" and called for offenders to be prosecuted and brought to trial promptly. Later the same month, while addressing the Supreme Judicial Council, the highest judicial authority in Iran, he said that the state judicial apparatus should safeguard people's rights, and criticized the continued detention of people after their sentences had expired. He added, "If we can make our country a judicial example to other nations, our revolution will be imitated." Hojatoleslam Hashemi Rafsanjani was reported in August to have acknowledged the excesses of the early years of the revolution and to have expressed support for international human rights standards.

Despite these positive developments, many alleged opponents of the government arrested in previous years continued to be detained without trial throughout 1987 or to serve sentences imposed after unfair trials. Some political prisoners were released under amnesties, reportedly on condition that they repented and undertook to take no further part in political activity. However, many other suspected government opponents were arrested. In March the Deputy Minister of Information announced the arrest of some 700 members and supporters of the People's Feda'i Organization. During 1987 many suspected supporters of the People's Mojahedine Organization and other opposition political organizations were also detained. Some had been involved in armed opposition to the government, but others were believed to be prisoners of conscience. Many were still held at the end of 1987. Some were not released despite having served their prison sentences.

Political prisoners were reported to have gone on hunger-strikes in Evin and Gohardasht prisons in protest against the continued detention of prisoners after the expiry of their sentences, the alleged increase in the number of secret executions, and the persistent torture and ill-treatment of detainees. Similar protest strikes are reported to have taken place in Qasr and Qezel Hesar prisons.

Torture of prisoners was reported to be widespread and many political prisoners held in Evin Prison were said to have been beaten. Many were reported to have been beaten on the soles of their feet. Former prisoners who left Iran in 1987 provided detailed testimonies of torture: some were subsequently examined by doctors who found injuries consistent with their allegations. In one such case, there was medical evidence corroborating a former prisoner's allegation that torturers using an electric drill had pierced her ankle and big toe.

Thousands of people were also subjected to judicial punishments which constituted torture or cruel, inhuman or degrading treatment for criminal offenses. In March an official stated that 4,467 corporal punishments were carried out in the Iranian calendar year 1365 (March 1986 to March 1987) in the Tehran district alone. Most of these punishments were lashings, but some victims had their fingers amputated as a punishment for theft. Similar punishments were carried out in all parts of the country.

At least 158 people were executed during 1987, but as some executions were carried out secretly the true number may have been considerably higher. Most executions reported in the official press were of people convicted of murder or drug offenses. In September Ayatollah Khomeini was reported to have instructed the Supreme Judicial Council to take action against drug traffickers: this may have contributed to an increase in reported executions in the following weeks. In at least eight cases, victims were flogged before they were hanged. One person was also reported to have been stoned to death and three to have jumped to their deaths from a cliff after having been made to choose one from among three methods of execution.

A number of people were executed on account of their political or religious views or activities. In October the Supreme Judicial Council was reported to have approved death sentences imposed on seven alleged members of "atheistic and hypocritical mini-groups" by Islamic Courts in west Azerbaijan, Isfahan and Ham. Another six alleged members of "counter-revolutionary mini-groups" had their death sentences approved in November. Four adherents of the Baha'i faith were reported to have been executed, two in September and two in March, apparently because of their religious beliefs. A further seventeen Baha'is were said to be at risk of execution in November. However, five of these were reportedly released on bail in December. The fate of the other twelve was unknown at the end of the year. Three alleged supporters of a Kurdish opposition organization were also said to have been executed at Orumieh, after they had been forcibly repatriated from Turkey in November 1986.

Scores of political detainees were alleged to have been executed in secret. Among them was a group of forty allegedly executed in Evin Prison for leading or taking part in prisoners' hunger strikes. There were also allegations that Iranian government personnel, or individuals acting on the instructions of the government, had been involved in attacks on Iranians abroad. Iranian exiles were killed during 1987 in Austria, the United Kingdom, Pakistan and elsewhere.

Prisoners sentenced to death by the courts had no right to appeal to a higher court as required by the International Covenant on Civil and Political Rights, to which Iran is a party. Instead, such death sentences are considered by the Supreme Judicial Council, a body composed of senior clerics with an expertise in Islamic jurisprudence. The Supreme Judicial Council may exercise the authority to confirm death sentences or to refer them back to the courts for review.

Peter Galbraith and Christopher Van Hollen, Jr.

Iraqi Chemical Weapons Use in Kurdistan (1988)

Overwhelming evidence exists that Iraq used chemical weapons on Kurdish civilians in a major offensive in northern Iraq that began August 25, 1988. The offensive is intended to break the Kurdish insurgency and appears to be accomplishing that objective. As reported by Kurdish refugees, cumulative civilian casualties from chemical weapons and other military operations are in the thousands. Information is available only on attacks taking place in a narrow band of territory along the Iraq-Turkey border. Virtually no refugees have been able to escape from deeper inside Iraqi Kurdistan. If the same kinds of military operations are taking place there as in the border regions, the Kurdish death toll could be in the hundreds of thousands.

Iraq is engaged in a military policy intended to depopulate Iraqi Kurdistan. Elements of the policy include: (1) the destruction of villages and towns throughout Kurdistan; (2) the relocation of the Kurdish population to concentrated new settlements where military control can be exercised; (3) the deportation of Kurds to areas outside Kurdistan; and (4) the use of terror tactics, including chemical weapons, to drive civilians out of the areas to be depopulated. The end result of this policy will be the destruction of the Kurdish identity, Kurdish culture, and a way of life that has endured for centuries.

The principle evidence for the Iraqi chemical weapons attacks are the eyewitness accounts of the Kurdish refugees in Turkey. The attacks were widely observed and reported in detail with regard to location, timing, and method of attack. The credibility of these extensive firsthand accounts is enhanced when viewed in the context of

Staff Report to the Senate Foreign Relations Committee.

Iraq's documented four-year record of chemical weapons use in the Iran-Iraq war and in the context of its brutal Kurdish policies.

There is physical evidence of chemical weapons attacks but the evidence available in Turkey is limited. Symptoms are hard to diagnose among the lightly injured survivors of the attacks, and only the lightly injured were able to make the rugged trek across the mountains to Turkey. However, the absence of certain physical evidence is more consistent with a chemical attack than with any other form of attack that might have driven the seasoned Pesh Merga fighters and more than 65,000 Iraqi Kurds into Turkey. Had the Iraqis launched a conventional weapons attack against the Kurds, one would expect to see bullet wounds and other evidence of such attack. Chemical weapons, by contrast, leave fewer detectable traces. . . .

Since 1984 Iraq has used chemical weapons on a large scale without paying any price in political or economic relations with other countries. Global acquiescence in previous Iraqi use of chemical weapons has undoubtedly been a factor in Iraq's belief it could use gas on the Kurds with no international consequences. The Reagan administration has been denouncing Iraqi use of chemical weapons since 1984. It has not followed up with action to deter such use.

We believe a compelling case exists that Iraq used chemical weapons on a broad scale against its Kurdish population beginning August 25, 1988. Almost all the Kurdish refugees in Turkey came from regions of Iraq adjacent to Turkey. Among those who lived in villages closest to the Turkish border, there existed a substantial opportunity for escape and we believe casualties for these villagers were limited to those who died in the initial attacks. For those who lived further inside Iraq, the Iraqi Army was able to cut most of the avenues of escape and in this region the casualties could be quite high. The survivors were generally the most fit; that is, the men associated with Pesh Merga or the Kurdish insurgents. Casualties among women and children appear to have been very high. We have no information on the substantial Kurdish population that lives along the Iran-Iraq border and those at a distance of more than fifty miles from Turkey. If Iraq's conduct in the Turkish border regions has been repeated in the interior, the death toll could be very high, with no witnesses to tell the tale.

The chemical weapons attacks on Kurdish villages appear to be part of a broader Iraqi policy of ending the Kurdish insurgency by depopulating Iraqi Kurdistan. Since 1986 Iraq has been systematically dynamiting and leveling all but the largest towns in Kurdistan. The local population has been transferred to lower altitudes, where they can more easily be controlled. At a minimum, this policy is destroying a centuries-old Kurdish way of life. It has also been accompanied by large loss of civilian life, as in the case of August's chemical attacks.

Whether Iraq's policy constitutes genocide, within the meaning of the Genocide Convention, may be debated if the standard used for genocide is that of the elimination of an entire race. However, Iraq's policy in Kurdistan does appear to have many of the characteristics of genocide, as defined by the Genocide Convention. Under Article II of the Convention, genocide is defined to mean, "any of the following acts committed with intent to destroy, in whole or in part, a national, ethnical, racial, or religious group, as such: (*a*) killing members of the group; (*b*) causing serious bodily or mental harm to members of the group; (*c*) deliberately inflicting on the group conditions of life calculated to bring about its physical destruction in whole or in part." . . .

With the August 20 ceasefire in the Iran-Iraq war, Iraq initiated what it termed the "final offensive" to end the Kurdish insurgency. The following is a narrative account constructed from eyewitness accounts of Kurdish refugees who fled from Iraq to Turkey.

On August 20, 1988, the day the Iran-Iraq ceasefire went into effect, Iraqi President Saddam Hussein turned his forces against the Kurdish population in northern Iraq. Some of Iraq's most battle-tested forces were dispatched to wrest control of the area from Kurdish fighters, drop poison gas on Kurdish villagers, and destroy Kurdish villages. On August 21, the Iraqi military began building up its forces along the major roads in Iraqi Kurdistan, and on August 25 launched chemical attacks against scores of Kurdish villages. On August 28, Iraqi forces began to destroy evacuated Kurdish villages.

During the early morning hours of August 25, 1988 Iraqi war planes and helicopters dropped chemical weapons on a series of villages in regions of Iraqi Kurdistan. In each of these regions, the Kurdish fighters, or Pesh Merga, had established camps outside of villages to protect them. For the most part, however, Iraqi bombs did not fall on these camps, as might have been expected, but on the villages themselves. In the Dihok region alone, more than 30 villages were exposed to various concentrations of poison gas. Among the villages in the Zakho, Dihok, and Amadiyah regions that suffered the most severe attacks were: Vermil, Bergini, Tika (Duka), Ekmala, Hese, Xirabe, Blecane, Siyare, Meze, Afuke, Belut, Sernae, Sivye, Zeweshkan, Mergeti, Zinawa, Dergel, Dubanche, Ermisht, Berkevre, Bergabore, Borghule, Bilejane, Warneze, Zavita, Nazdure, Berkule, Rudaniyo, Sarki, Berchi, and Ruyse.

As described by the villagers, the bombs that fell on the morning of August 25 did not produce a large explosion. Only a weak sound could be heard and then a yellowish cloud spread out from the center of the explosion and became a thin mist. The air became filled with a mixture of smells—"bad garlic," "rotten onions," and "bad apples."

Those who were very close to the bombs died almost instantly. Those who did not die instantly found it difficult to breathe and began to vomit. The gas stung the eyes, skin, and lungs of the villagers exposed to it. Many suffered temporary blindness.

After the bombs exploded, many villagers ran and submerged themselves in nearby streams to escape the spreading gas. They placed wet cloth over their noses, eyes, and mouths to block the gas. Many of those who made it to the streams survived. Those who could not run from the growing smell, mostly the very old and the very young died.

The survivors who saw the dead reported that blood could be seen trickling out of the mouths of some of the bodies. A yellowish fluid could also be seen oozing out the noses and mouths of some of the dead. Some said the bodies appeared frozen. Many of the dead bodies turned blackish blue. Most of the villagers quickly abandoned the contaminated areas, leaving the bodies unburied in the sun. In some cases, they later returned to the poisoned villages to bury the bodies. The few who ventured to look at the shattered pieces of the bomb casings said they were colored green.

In every village where chemical bombs were dropped the livestock— mostly donkeys and goats—died. Birds are also reported to have been killed by the gas.

The Iraquis continued to drop chemical weapons on Kurdish villages on August 26. Turkish villagers living less than a kilometer from the Turkey-Iraq border could see the Iraqi helicopters flying above a mountain ridge. Iraqi Kurds living close to the Turkish border left their contaminated villages to seek refuge in Turkey. Those from villages farther from the Turkish border did not immediately flee to Turkey. They first sought safety in nearby areas that had not been bombed. Many fled to the Pesh Merga camps outside the villages.

On August 27 the chemical bombs continued to fall on villages in the Zakho, Dihok, and Amadiyah regions. Villagers who had fled to nearby villages after their own had been gassed found themselves again under attack. No area in the northeastern reaches of Iraqi Kurdistan was safe from chemical attack. As a result, thousands of Iraqi Kurds from the Zakho, Dihok, and Amadiyah regions began to make their way on foot and animal back across the rough mountain terrain to Turkey.

On August 28 villagers fleeing from areas farther from the Turkish border found their escape routes almost fully impeded by deployments of Iraqi soldiers. The key east-west road from Amadiyah to Zakho was effectively blocked. Kurdish villagers south of the road suddenly found themselves trapped inside of Iraq. Those Kurds who attempted to cross the road were fired on by Iraqi soldiers. An Iraqi Kurd who managed to cross the road said, "Whatever they saw they shot—children, women, young, and old." Some still managed to make their way across the road. By September 5, however, the Iraqi troops had established camps all along the Turkey-Iraq border and the flow of refugees slowed to a trickle. More than 65,000 Kurdish refugees had arrived in Turkey. No one knows how many remain trapped on the other side. One Pesh Merga estimated that 70 percent of those who lived south of the Zakho-Amadiyah road found their way blocked by Iraqi soldiers. Information is available only on attacks that took place in a narrow band of territory along the Iraqi-Turkish border. The fate of those left behind is uncertain. If the same kind of military operations are taking place deeper inside of Iraqi Kurdistan as in the border regions, the Kurdish death toll could be in the hundreds of thousands.

In at least one village where Kurds remained—the village of Baze— survivors report that Iraqi forces opened fire with machine-guns on everyone in the village and then used bulldozers to push the bodies into mass graves.

On August 28, the day the Iraqi soldiers sealed off the Zakho-Amadiyah road, the chemical bombings stopped. Iraqi forces began to destroy the evacuated villages. Turkish truck drivers who regularly use the roads in Iraqi Kurdistan report that all the villages along the road have been destroyed and the trees have dried out. Kurdish fighters said the Iraqi soldiers entered the contaminated areas with gas masks. . . .

Standing alone, the eyewitness accounts provide compelling evidence of Iraqi use of chemical weapons. These accounts, however, do not stand alone. Rather, they occur in the context of a documented record of Iraqi use of chemical weapons and in the context of a recent history of a particularly brutal suppression of the Kurds. That the eyewitness accounts are consistent with a known Iraqi modus operandi in the Iran-Iraq war and with Iraqi policy objectives in Iraqi Kurdistan clearly enhances the credibility of these accounts.

Iran first complained about Iraqi use of chemical weapons in a letter to the Secretary-General dated November 3, 1983. Following a February 27, 1984, Iraqi chemical attack, Iran sent the soldier/victims to hospitals throughout Western Europe for treatment. Doctors in Belgium, Sweden, and West Germany confirmed that the soldiers were victims of mustard gas.

In the four years following, Iraq repeatedly and effectively used poison gas on Iran. U.N. missions were sent to the region in March 1984, April 1985, February–March 1986, April–May 1987, March–April 1988, twice in July 1988, and most recently in mid-August 1988. In each instance the United Nations found that poison gas had been used, and in circumstances that clearly indicated Iraqi use.

By February 1988, Iran's military had achieved its high watermark of wartime success. Its forces occupied Iraq's Fao Peninsula in the south and substantial territory in the vicinity of Basra. In the north, Iranian-supported Kurdish insurgents had effective control of much of that rugged region's countryside, including the important city of Halabja. Feeling pressed, Iraq stepped up its use of chemical weapons and extended their use to Kurdish and Iranian civilian targets.

In March, the Iraqi Air Force attacked Halabja, a city of 70,000, with chemical weapons. The results, documented by Western journalists and television cameras, were grisly. Over 4,000 were dead, almost all Iraqi Kurds and almost all civilians. Entire families were wiped out and the streets were littered with the corpses of men, women, and children. Other forms of life in and around the city—horses, housecats, cattle—perished as well.

The pictures of Halabja (and other chemical weapons victims) were shown on Iranian television. Intended to bolster the national will by showing the sins of the enemy, the pictures had an opposite effect. Recruitment into Iranian armed forces plummeted, Iranian military morale wavered, and in a few short months Iraq was able to retake its lost territory (making extensive use of chemical weapons). Iran was forced to accept an unwanted peace.

After Iran announced it would accept Resolution 598 providing for a ceasefire in the Iran-Iraq war, Iraq made one final chemical weapons attack on Iran. This time the target was an Iranian village near the two countries' border in the north. Many of the victims were Iranian civilians and the attack was seen both as a means to enhance Iraq's position at the negotiating table and as a warning to Iran against a resumption of the war.

While Iraq has hotly denounced United States allegations of chemical use on the Kurds, it has admitted using chemical weapons in the war. In a July 1, 1988, Bonn press conference, Iraq's Foreign Minister, Tariq Aziz, stated that both sides used chemical weapons and asserted a right to so do: "Every nation has the right to protect itself against invasion."

Iraq's use of chemical weapons on the Kurds in the August offensive is simply an extension of a military policy of indiscriminate use of chemical weapons against both military and civilian targets. Vehement denials of chemical weapon use in the latest offensive lose credibility in the face of this record.

The eyewitness accounts of chemical weapons use should also be viewed in the context of Iraqi policy toward its Kurdish population. Since 1985 this policy has been one of severe repression.

Iraq's Kurdish policy provides a second context for evaluating the chemical weapons charges. The stated aims of Iraq's Kurdish policy are: (1) to deprive the insurgents of a population base from which to operate; (2) to punish those areas which attacked the motherland at its hour of supreme national crisis; and (3) to provide the Kurds the benefits of modern life. In reality, the policy is to depopulate Iraqi Kurdistan, and poison gas is an instrument of the policy. After the 1975 Algiers Accord put an end to an earlier phase of the Kurdish insurrection, the Iraqi Government created a security zone along its Iranian border. Villages within a certain distance of the border were demolished and the inhabitants relocated.

Following the intensification of the Kurdish insurgency in 1985, the Iraqi Government vastly extended the village demolition program. During a September 1987 staff trip through Iraqi Kurdistan, some 20 demolished towns and villages were observed on the roads leading from Baghdad and Baquba to Sulamanyeh (the capital of the Kurdish autonomous region) and along the road from Sulamanyeh to Kirkuk.

The scope of the destruction was impressive. Villages were dynamited and leveled with a bulldozer to ensure the population did not return. Some of the villages were vast, with over a one-mile road frontage.

According to the refugees, Iraqi troops have entered the gassed villages (after an interval to allow for the dissipation of the poison gas) and dynamited the villages. The pattern seems widespread and insurgent leaders provided us a list of 245 villages that have been destroyed in this manner, a list which itself represents only a small part of the total destruction.

Those Kurds moved out of the destroyed villages have been relocated to areas more securely under central government control. There they are provided building materials and told to construct new housing along a designated grid pattern. Some of these new villages are located in the lower parts of Iraqi Kurdistan. In each there is a military presence which enables the Iraqi Government to exercise control over the population's movements and to ensure docility through coercion and intimidation.

Some of the Kurds have apparently relocated to areas outside Kurdistan, including areas in Iraq's hot, flat south. For a people with millennia-old tradition of independence in a rugged mountain environment, these relocations are difficult. Many are unable to make the adjustments.

The relocation policy has been accompanied by substantial violence. Poison gas is, of course, one tool for ending resistance to such moves. More conventional atrocities also occur.

Iraqi Kurdistan is fast becoming a mountainous wasteland. Outside of Sulaymaniyya, Halabja, and two or three other large towns, there will be no permanent inhabitants. A centuries-old way of life will disappear from a region that has been continuously inhabited from near the beginning of human civilization.

Legislation passed by the U.S. Senate (S. 2763, The Prevention of Genocide Act of 1988) describes Iraq's conduct in Kurdistan as genocide. Under the Genocide Convention, the crime is defined as the destruction of a distinct religious, ethnic, or racial group. Iraq's policy of killings, gassings, and relocations does seem designed to destroy Kurdish culture, the Kurdish identity, and the Kurdish way of life. If not genocide under the terms of the treaty, Iraq's conduct certainly has many characteristics of this crime.

The powerful eyewitness accounts, the threads of physical evidence, and the pattern of past Iraqi use of chemical weapons provide overwhelming evidence that Iraq dropped chemical weapons on its Kurdish population in the northeastern reaches of Iraq from August 25 through August 27. That conclusion is supported by a September 15 New York Times report that the United States intercepted Iraqi military communications indicating that Iraq used chemical weapons against the Kurds in late August. The eyewitness accounts of the Iraqi Kurds suggest that a variety of chemical agents were used against them. Nerve gasses and lewisite, which contains arsenic, act immediately. Other victims complained of the symptoms typically associated with other types of poison gas—severe nausea, vomiting, burnt and itchy skin, and blurry vision. This portrait is consistent with earlier findings made by U.N. expert teams that investigated use of chemical weapons in the Iran-Iraq war and concluded that a variety of chemical agents were probably used.

The Kurdish Pesh Merga have been battling the Iraqi Government intermittently for 30 years. During that period they have become seasoned fighters. Like the Mujahidin who know every peak and valley in Afghanistan, the Pesh Merga know every nook and cranny in the rough mountain terrain of Iraqi Kurdistan. In 30 years of fighting, the Iraqi Army has been unable to snuff out the insurgency using conventional military means. Poison gas has provided them with a weapon of terror that the Kurdish fighters cannot hide from or defend against. As one Pesh Merga told us, before the use of poison gas "we could go into the caves in our region and hide. But the chemical gas goes into the caves as well and that's why we left."

Having used gas with effect against the Iranian Army, the Iraqis decided it could also be used to put a final end to the Kurdish insurgency. The Iraqis have not only used gas to ferret out fighters hiding in caves, they have used it indiscriminately against Kurdish villagers. The chemical massacre of Kurdish villagers in Halabja last March demonstrated the Iraqi's willingness to use chemical weapons not just as instruments of war, but as tools for mass murder. Indeed, the late August attacks were directed primarily against Kurdish villages, not the Pesh Merga camps. The Iraqi Government has concluded that if it destroys the families of the insurgents, the fighters will give up. As one Pesh Merga told us, "our families refused to stay in Iraq after the Iraqi army started using poison gas. We could not allow them all to be destroyed and we could not let them flee alone." Thus, poison gas is Iraq's ultimate weapon against its Kurdish insurrection.

Hojjat ol-Eslam 'Ali Akbar Hashemi-Rafsanjani

Speech on the Salman Rushdie Affair (1989)

In the name of God, the merciful, the compassionate. Our esteemed deputies and people are aware of this act of sedition [fitneh] which global infidelity has planned for the world of Islam. They are following specific targets with specific motives in mind with regard to their insults to Islamic sanctities. It is possible that some rascals and satanic people in society may warp the minds of the people by making such insinuations as: What importance does a book, or a writer who has done something wrong, possess to merit such a sensation, or measures or a public holiday throughout society or to cause demonstrations in the Islamic world? Therefore, this point needs to be thrashed out. It is necessary to do so because if our nation is to be exposed to such temptations, it must know that this is not the problem. This is only as it appears.

What can be surmised from the summation of the events—events that prompted our great leader, the imam of the ummah, to embark on such spirited confrontation and also outraged the deputy leader, the grand ayatollahs, the clerics, and people throughout the world—is that such outrage and confrontation are caused by both what goes on behind the scenes and what one can see.

What one can perceive through current events is that planning and

From (Foreign Broadcast Information Series:) Near East and South Asia, February 16, 1989.

organizational work has been carried out that is aimed at bringing about a very dangerous move; one that is worse than an officially declared war.

Following the blows they received from Iran, which they saw in Lebanon and Afghanistan, as well as the dynamism and awareness they saw in Muslims all over the world, they arrived at the conclusion—in their analysis—that all this stems from the holiness that covers everything sacred in Islam. This keeps the minds of the Muslims clean. This gives dynamism and happiness to the world of Islam.

Materialism and all kinds of political forces failed to break this holiness, so they chose this method of action: choosing a person who seemingly comes from India and who apparently is separate from the Western world and has a misleading name. They begin their work in this fashion. Advance royalties were given to that person. One can see that they appoint guards for him in advance because they knew what they were doing. One can see that a Zionist publishing establishment is involved, and that translations already have been prepared in countries like the United States and Italy.

We see that the publicity encourages the people to buy the book. All this tells us of an organized and planned effort. It is not an ordinary work so that one might say that many books have been written so far, that insults to Islam have been frequent, that many others have said evil things against God and everything else, and that that is the way it has been throughout history. Yes, this true, but I believe there has not previously been such a well-planned act as the way this is being done. This is a confrontation to break the sanctity of Islam and all that is sacred in Islam.

Therefore, the importance of the issue merits that our great leader, who usually does not involve himself in personal issues, should involve himself forcefully in order to express his anger. It is always incumbent upon us to obey his orders. We know he always raises issues related to Islam in a timely manner and that he creates confrontation well in time.

It is incumbent upon the Islamic world to regard this issue seriously so that Islam's enemies may learn such methods will not lead them anywhere and so that those who allow themselves to be manipulated into such acts by Islam's enemies may learn that they are involved in dangerous issues.

Well, the logic of Islam is clear. The Koran, from the very early days, instructed Muslims: Revile not ye those whom they call upon besides God, lest they out of spite revile God in their ignorance. This is the logic of the Koran—not to use bad language, or insulting ways either in the sacred schools or in anything sacred to the nations. The

Koran does not indulge in bad language, nor does it accept it: nor does it shirk from opposing insults to the sacred things of other peoples. For us this applies to other religions. If today somebody insults His Holiness Moses, Abraham, or His Holiness Jesus, then we must stand up against such insults with the same intensity.

These are sanctities in which the majority of the people believe. You see how the Koran campaigns against accusations inflicted on Her Holiness Mary.

Such a method is an unreasonable one. We expect the world's Christians and Jews—those who do not espouse the Zionist spirit—to protest seriously to obstruct such a foul move. The issue is more serious than the mere publication of a book or a novel so that one may say that some book has been written and the matter is closed.

Leon Wieseltier

On Salman Rushdie and Civil Liberties (1989)

When the mob in Islamabad marched against Salman Rushdie and his book, it marched on the American cultural center. Many were baffled by the association. But in truth the association was beautifully appropriate. If you are for the banning and the burning of books, if you deny the right of a writer to write and the right of a publisher to publish and the right of a reader to read, if you believe that an opinion may be met by a bullet, then you are, supremely, anti-American.

The persecution of Rushdie and his book is precisely the sort of challenge for which the traditions of America have prepared us. Philosophically and politically, we have been bred to recoil from this sort of darkness, and to fight it. For that reason, the behavior of our government in this affair has been an extraordinary disappointment. It spoke late, it spoke listlessly, it spoke equivocally. It spoke at the prodding of reporters, or through institutional spokesmen at routine briefings. It spoke without enthusiasm for principle, without anger at the assault on principle.

We have been given two reasons for the grudging behavior of our government. The first is its respect for geo-politics. The second is its respect for religion. Both, of course, are worthy of respect. But

From testimony before the Senate Foreign Relations Committee, Subcommittee on Terrorism, Narcotics, and International Operations, March 8, 1989.

neither must be allowed to impede our will as a state, to interfere with our lucidity as a society.

The questions for which this subcommittee, and indeed the whole of the American government, must find answers, and the answers are not far to seek, are these: What has a novel to do with reasons of state? What has blasphemy to do with freedom?

The strategic significance of Iran is perfectly obvious. A look at the map suffices. . . . In this region the United States must expect opportunism from the Soviet Union and an utterly amoral agility, its reform notwithstanding. We may all agree, moreover, that there is a difference between a foreign policy and a crusade. In the articulation of foreign policy, there will often be a tension, even a contradiction, between American values and American interests.

But there are times when the distinction between American values and American interests must disappear, when our values are our interests, when the coincidence of our values and our interests is so complete that it would be a corruption not to see it. This is such a time. The inquisition against Salman Rushdie is an inquisition against the reason that this country was brought into being. If we do not represent ourselves with clarity, the world will not view us with clarity. If we do not powerfully denounce, and efficiently act against, the persecution of a writer and a book, then in the name of what, exactly, shall we praise the developments in Moscow, deplore the developments in Prague and Havana, worry about the developments in Managua and Santiago, detest the developments in Johannesburg and Tehran? For how long will the foreign policy of the United States be held hostage to hostages? I cannot believe that we are without instruments of policy. Must we wait for some poor soul to act on the Ayatollah's threat before we consider sanctions against Iran? Are those states which have banned or burned books to feel only the less than withering impact of comment on the Sunday talk shows?

Finally, there is the matter of blasphemy, of the wounded feelings of believers, about which we have been reading and hearing a lot lately, not least from the former president of the United States. The American writer Ambrose Bierce, in a book whose title brings to mind the title of the book whose fate we are here to discuss, in *The Devil's Dictionary*, proposed a definition of impiety. Impiety, said Bierce, is "your irreverence toward my deity." That is not cynicism. That is democracy.

I am a religous man, and I have devoted many years of my life to the study of religion. I know something about the sanctity of the Divine Name, about the sanctity of the revealed word, about the sanctity of the received tradition. I have read, and heard, my own faith insulted; and I have started in pain, and in rage, at the insults.

And yet, if the mockery of my faith is the price that I must pay for the freedom to study my faith, for the freedom of others to study my faith, for the freedom to study the faith of others, for the confidence that neither I nor others will suffer in any way for the study of any faith, then I will eagerly pay the price. I will gladly, in the same breath, cherishing the contradiction, serve my God and defend the blasphemer. For blasphemy is proof of liberty. Since I want liberty, I welcome blasphemy.

Selected Bibliography on Human Rights

This book has sought to provide a starting point for an understanding of the tradition of thought and debate over human rights. Up to now, further scholarship has been handicapped by lack of a comprehensive bibliography on the subject. Although partial collations exist, there was nothing which facilitated a comparative approach involving philosophical, political, and legal aspects of the human rights question.

The following bibliography is intended to help solve this difficulty. We have not listed here the original works by the thinkers cited (of which selections are included in the text) as those lists are readily available elsewhere. Rather, we have concentrated on works of commentary which might be of assistance to anyone interested in further reading on the development of the concept of human rights.

General

Abram, Morris B. The United Nations and human rights. 1969. 47 For. Aff. 3633-74.

Abranches, C. A. D. de. Proteção internacional dos direitos humanos. Rio de Janeiro, Freitas, 1964.

Bassiouni, M. C. The human rights program: the veneer of civilization thickens. 1971. 21 De Paul L. Rev. 271-85.

Becker, Carl L. The heavenly city of the eighteenth-century philosophers. New Haven, Yale Univ. Press, 1959.

Bilder, Richard B. Rethinking international human rights: some basic questions. (Summ. in French) 1969. 2 Rev. Droits de l'Homme 557-608.

Birnbaum, K. E. "Human rights and east-west relations." 1977. 55 For. Aff. 783-99.

Bissell, Thomas St. G. Negotiation by international bodies and the protection of human rights, 1968. 7 Colum. J. Transnat'l. L. 90-134.

Compiled by Anthony P. Grech, Librarian, The Association of the Bar of the City of New York, and Lenore F. Tarley, Assistant to the Librarian, The Association of the Bar of the City of New York.

Bite, Vita. Primer of human rights treaties. Washington, Library of Congress, Congressional Research Service, 1977.

Bossuyt, Marc. L'interdiction de la discrimination dans le droit international des droits de l'homme. Préf. de Georges Abi-Saab. Bruxelles, Bruylant, 1976. 1v.

Buergenthal, Thomas. International and regional human rights, law and institutions: some examples of their interaction. 1977. 12 Texas Int'l. L. J. 321-30.

Buergenthal, Thomas and Torney, Judith V. International human rights and international education. Washington, Dep't. of State, Nat'l Comm'n for UNESCO, 1976.

Brownlie, Ian, comp. Basic documents on human rights. Oxford, Clarendon Press, 1971.

Cassin, René.
   Comment protéger les droits de l'homme. 1970. 25 Comunità Internazionale. 455-68.
   Commission des droits de l'homme de l'ONU 1947-1971 (In Ganshof van der Meersch collection, I, 397-433, Bruxelles, Bruylant; Paris, Librairie Générale de Droit et de Jurisprudence, 1972).
   La Pensée et l'action. Boulogne-sur-Seine, F. Lalou. 1972.

Chafee, Zechariah, ed. Documents on fundamental human rights. Cambridge, Harvard Univ. Press, 1951-52. 3v.

Chappelle, P. de la. "Droits de l'homme," exigence d'universalism (In Cassin collection, 164, Paris, Pédone, 1969).

Clark, Roger Stenson. A United Nations high commissioner for human rights. The Hague, Nijhoff, 1972.

Claude, Richard P., ed. Comparative human rights. Baltimore, Johns Hopkins Univ. Press, 1976.

Cohn, Haim A. The right and duty of resistance (summ. in French) 1968. 1 Rev. Droits de l'Homme, 491-517.

Cranston, Maurice William. What are human rights? New York, Taplinger, 1973.

Daubie, Christian.
   Concilliation et protection européenne des droits de l'homme. 1973. 9 Rev. Belge Droit International 403-46.
   Cyrus le Grand: un précurseur dans la domaine des droits de l'homme. 1972. 5 Rev. Droits de l'Homme 293-304.

Derechos humanos. Numéro spécial consacré à un bilan de la théorie et de la pratique dans ce domaine. 1972. 2 Anales Cátedra Francisco Suarez 9-328.

Dinstein, Yoram. Collective human rights of peoples and minorities. 1976. 25 Int'l. & Comp. L. Q. 102-30.

Doimi di Delupis, Ingrid. Bibliography of international law. London and New York, Bowker, 1975. 207-49.

Duchacek, Ivo D. Rights and liberties in the world today; constitutional promise and reality. Santa Barbara, Calif. and Oxford, Eng., ABC-Clio Press, 1973.

The enlightenment; a comprehensive anthology. Ed. with introd. notes by Peter Gay. New York, Simon & Schuster, 1973.

Ermacora, Felix. Procedure to deal with human rights violations: a hopeful start in the United Nations? 1974. 7 Rev. Droits de l'Homme 670-89.

Fischer, Georges. Les états multiraciaux. 1972. 5 Rev. Droits de l'Homme 535-607.

Galey, M. E. Indigenous people, international consciousness raising and the development of international law on human rights. 1975. 8 Rev. Droits de l'Homme 21-39.

Ganshof van der Meersch collection. Bruxelles, Bruylant; Paris, Librairie Générale de Droit et de Jurisprudence. 1972. 3v.

Garibaldi, Oscar M. General limitations on human rights: the principle of legality. 1976. Harv. Int'l. L. J. 503-57.

Golsong, H. Implementation of international protection of human rights (In Hague, Academy of international law. Recueil des cours 1963, v.3, 1-151).

Green, James Frederick. Changing approaches to human rights: the United Nations, 1954 and 1974. 1977. 12 Texas Int'l. L. J. 223-38.

Green, L. C. Human rights and the general principles of law (In his Law and society. Leyden, Sijthoff; Dobbs Ferry, N.Y., Oceana, 1975, 283-320).

Hammarskjöld Forum, 12th, December 12, 1967, New York. International protection of human rights; background and proceedings. John Carey, author . . . working paper, editor . . . proceedings. Dobbs Ferry, N.Y., Pub. for The Association of the Bar of the City of New York by Oceana Pub. 1968. (bibliography, 71-90).

Human rights bibliography (In United Nations juridical yearbook 1975. New York, United Nations, 1977, 235-38).

Humphrey, John P.
The international law of human rights in the middle twentieth century (In Boss, M., ed. The present state of international law and other essays. Deventer, Kluwer, 1973, 75-105).

The revolution in the international law of human rights. 1975. 8 Rev. Droits de l'Homme 205-16.

International commission of jurists review 1954— (combines former bulletin and journal).

Ireland, Patricia. International protection of human rights. 1975. Law. of the Americas 318-36.

Israel, Fred L., comp. Major peace treaties of modern history, 1648-
1967. Commentaries by Emanuel Chill. Introd. essay by Arnold
J. Toynbee. New York, Chelsea House, 1967. 4v.

Konvitz, Milton R. and Rossiter, Clinton. Aspects of liberty. Ithaca,
Cornell Univ. Press, 1958.

Kutner, Luis, ed. The human right to individual freedom: a symposium on world habeas corpus. Coral Gables, Univ. of Miami
Press, 1970.

Lador-Lederer, Joseph J. International group protection. Leyden Sijthoff, 1968.

Lannung, Hermod. Human rights and the multiplicity of European
systems for international protection. 1972. 5 Rev. Droits de
l'Homme 651-72.

Lauterpacht, Hersch.
An international bill of rights for man. New York, Columbia Univ.
Press, 1946.
International law and human rights. Hamden, Conn., Archon
Books, 1968.
The international protection of human rights (In Hague. Academy
of international law. Recueil des cours 1947, I. v.70, 1-108).
The law of nations, the law of nature and the rights of man (In
Grotius society transactions, v.29, 1944, 1-33).

Liskofsky, Sidney. Coping with the "question of the violation of
human rights and fundamental freedoms." 1975. 8 Rev. Droits de
l'Homme 883-914.

Luard, David Evan Trant, ed. & trans. The international protection of
human rights. London, Thames & Hudson; New York, Praeger,
1967.

Mansuy, Gérard. Un médiateur des Nations unies pour les droits de
l'homme? 1973. 6 Rev. Droits de l'Homme 235-62.

Marie, Jean-Bernard. La commission des droits de l'homme de
l'O.N.U. Paris, Pédone, 1975.

M'Baye, Kéba. Le droit au développement comme un droit de
l'homme. 1972. 5 Rev. Droits de l'Homme 505-34.

McCarthy, Thomas E. The international protection of human rights:
ritual and reality. 1976. 25 Int'l. & Comp. L. Q. 261-91.

MacDonald, R. St. J. A United Nations high commissioner for human
rights: the decline and fall of an initiative. 1972. Can. Yb. Int'l. L.
40-64.

McDougal, Myres S. Human rights and world public order: principles
of content and procedure for clarifying general community policies. 1973/74. 14 Va. J. Int'l. L. 387-449.

McDougal, Myres S., Lasswell, Harold D., and Chen, Lung-chu.

Nationality and human rights: the protection of the individual in external areas. 1973/74. 83 Yale L. J. 900-98.

Non-conforming political opinion and human rights: trans-national protection against discrimination. 1975. 2 Yale Studies in World Public Order 1-31.

Meuwissen, D. H. M. The relationship between international and municipal law and fundamental rights. 1977. 24 (spec. iss. 1/2) Netherlands Int'l. L. Rev. 189-204.

Midgley, E. B. F. Natural law and fundamental rights. 1976. 21 Am. J. Juris. 144-55.

Modinos collection . . . problèmes des droits de l'homme et de l'unification européenne. Paris, Pédone, 1968.

Modinos, Polys.
Les droits de l'homme ou la recherche d'une éthique. 1975. 8 (no. spécial) Rev. Droits de l'Homme 637-47.

Introduction à l'étude des droits de l'homme. 1975. 8 (no. spécial) Rev. Droits de l'Homme 648-58.

Peidro Pastor, I. Aspectos filosófico-jurídicos de los pactos internacionales sobre derechos humanos. 1970/71. 9 Anuario de Derecho (Rev. Jurídica Panameña) 67—.

Pollack, Ervin H., ed. Human rights . . . "Amintaphil I." Buffalo, Jay Stewart Pub., 1971.

Przetacznik, Franciszek.
L'attitude des états socialistes à l'égard de la protection internationale des droits de l'homme. 1974. 7 Rev. Droits de l'Homme 175-206.

Les mésures de la mise en application des droits de l'homme selon les traités internationaux. 1974. Rev. Droit Int'l. Sciences Diplomatiques, Politiques et Sociales, 1-25.

René Cassin amicorum discipulorumque liber. Paris, Pédone. 1969-72. 4v. (V.1, Problèmes de protection internationale des droits de l'homme; v.2, Le difficile progrès du règne de la justice et de la paix internationales par le droit, des origines à la société des nations; v.3, Protection des droits de l'homme dans les rapports entre personnes privées; v. 4, Méthodologie de droits de l'homme).

Revue des droits de l'homme (Human rights journal). V. 1—1968—. Paris, Pédone.

Robertson, A. H. Human rights in Europe. 2d ed. Manchester, Eng., Manchester Univ. Press, 1977.

Robinson, Jacob. International protection of minorities; a global view. 1971. 1 Israel Yb. on Human Rights 61-91.

Rubin, Barry and Elizabeth Spiro. Human rights and U.S. foreign policy. Boulder, Westview, 1979.

Sandifer, Durward V. and Scheman, L. R. The foundations of freedom: the interrelationship between democracy and human rights. New York, Praeger, 1966.

Schreiber, Marc. La pratique récente des nations unies dans le domaine de la protection des droits de l'homme (In Hague. Academy of international law. Recueil des cours 1975, II, v.145, 299-398).

Schreuer, C. H. The impact of international institutions on the protection of human rights in domestic courts. 1974. 4 Israel Yb. on Human Rights 60-88.

Schwelb, Egon. The law of treaties and human rights. 1973. 16 Archiv des Völkerrechts 1-27.

Sélection bibliographiques des ouvrages concernant le droit international et le droit comparé des droits de l'homme. 1973. 6 Rev. Droits de l'Homme 208-16.

Sohn, Louis B. and Buergenthal, Thomas. International protection of human rights. With a companion volume: Basic documents on international protection of human rights. Indianapolis, Bobbs-Merrill, 1973.

Symposium on the international law of human rights. 1965. 11 Howard L. J. 257-623 (entire issue, no. 2).

Tardu, Maxime. Quelques questions relative à la coexistence des procédures universelles et régionales de plainte individuelle dans le domaine des droits de l'homme. 1971. 4 Rev. Droits de l'Homme 589-625.

Torelli, M. and Baudouin, R. Les droits de l'homme et les libertés publiques par les textes. Québec, Presses Univ. de Québec, 1973.

United Nations. Yearbook on human rights. New York, 1946—.

U.S. Congress. House Comm. on Foreign Affairs. Subcom. on Internal Organizations and Movements. (93.1) International protection of human rights; the work of international organizations and the role of U.S. foreign policy. Hearings . . . Washington, Gov't. Print. Off., 1974.

U.S. Congress. Senate. Comm. on Government Operations. Permanent Subcom. on Investigations. International human rights; selected declarations and agreements. Washington, Gov't. Print. Off., 1977.

Vallat, Francis. An introduction to the study of human rights. London, Europa Pub., 1972.

van Boven, Theo C. Partners in the promotion and protection of human rights. 1977. 24 (spec. iss. 1/2) Netherlands Int'l. L. Rev. 55-84.

van Niekerk, Barend V. D. The mirage of liberty. 1973. 3 Human Rights 283-99.

Vasak, Karel. Dimensions internationales des droits de l'homme: perspectives d'avenir. 1975. 8 Rev. Droits de l'Homme 605-22.

Vasak, Karel. Le droit international des droits de l'homme (In Hague. Academy of international law. Recueil des cours 1974, IV, v.140, 335-415).

Veenhoven, William A. and Ewing, Winifred C. Case studies on human rights and fundamental freedoms. A world survey. The Hague, Nijhoff. 1975. 2v.

Veinte años de evolución de los derechos humanos; [actas del] seminario internacional. Colaboradores: R. Cassin and others. México, Univ. Nacional, Instituto de Investigaciones Jurídicas, 1974.

Venturi, Franco. Utopia and reform in the enlightenment. Cambridge, Cambridge Univ. Press, 1971.

Vierdag, E. W. The concept of discrimination in international law. With special reference to human rights. The Hague, Nijhoff, 1973.

Vlachos, Georges. La structure des droits de l'homme et le problème de leur réglementation en régime pluraliste. 1972. 24 Rev. Int'l. Droit Comparé 279-355.

Walter, H. Die rechtsprechung des europäischen gerichtshofs für menschenrechte 1959-1974. 1975. 24 Jahrbuch Offentlichen Rechts Gegenwart 25-60.

Woetzel, Robert K. The philosophy of freedom. Dobbs Ferry, N.Y., Oceana Pub., 1966.

The Philosophers

JOHN LOCKE

Aaron, Richard Ithamar. John Locke. 2d ed. Oxford, Clarendon Press, 1965.

Arenilla, L. Propriété et liberté chez Locke. 1960. 99 (sér. M No. 7) Cahiers l'Institut de Science Economique Appliquée. 87-99.

Ashcraft, Richard.
  Locke's state of nature: historical fact or moral fiction? 1968. 62 Am. Pol. Sci. Rev. 898-915. [Reply with rejoinder R. A. Goldwin. 64:595-96 (1970).]
  Political theory and political reform: John Locke's essay on Virginia. 1969. 22 W. Polit. Q. 742-58.

Bennett, Jonathan Francis. Locke, Berkeley, Hume: central themes. Oxford, Clarendon Press, 1971.

Bianca, Giuseppe G. La credenza come fondamento dell'attività pratica in Locke e in Hume. Catania, Edizioni B., 1948.

Bobbio, Norberto. Studi lockiani (studies on Locke). 1965. 77 Riv. Storia Diritto Italiano 96-130.

Bourne, H. R. Fox. The life of John Locke. New York, Harper & Brothers, 1876. 2v. (V.2, pp. 169-80; Second treatise on government.)

Cox, Richard Howard. Locke on war and peace. Oxford, Clarendon Press, 1960.

Cranston, Maurice William. John Locke, a biography. London and New York, Longmans Green, 1957.

Dunn, J. M.
Justice and the interpretation of Locke's political theory. Feb. 1968. 16 Polit. Studies (Oxford) 68-87.
The political thought of John Locke: an historical account of the *Two treatises on government*. London, Cambridge Univ. Press, 1969.

Edwards, S. Political philosophy belimed: the case of Locke. 1969. 17 Polit. Studies (Oxford) 273-93.

Gale, George. John Locke on territoriality: an unnoticed aspect of the second treatise. 1973. 1 Polit. Theory 472-85.

Goldwin, Robert A. Locke's state of nature in political society. 1976. 29 W. Polit. Q. 126-45.

Gough, John W. John Locke's political philosophy: eight studies. 2d ed. Oxford, Clarendon Press, 1973.

Larkin, Paschal. Property in the eighteenth century, with special reference to England and Locke. With a pref. by J. L. Stocks. Port Washington, N.Y., Kennikat Press, 1968.

Laski, Harold J. Political thought in England from Locke to Bentham. New York, Holt & Co., 1920.

Laslett, Peter. The English revolution and Locke's *Two treatises of government*. 1956. 12 Cambridge Hist. J. 40—.

Leyden, W. von. La loi, la liberté et la prérogative dans la pensée de John Locke. 1973. 98 Rev. Philosophique France et l'Etranger 187-203.

Locke, John.
Essai sur le pouvoir civil. Trad. par J.-L. Fyot. Préf. de B. Mirkine-Guetzevitch et M. Prelot. Paris, Presses Univ. de France, 1953.
Two treatises of government: a critical edition with an introduction and apparatus criticus by Peter Laslett. 2d ed. London, Cambridge Univ. Press, 1967.

MacPherson, C. B. The social bearing of Locke's political theory. 1954. 7 W. Polit. Q. 1-22.

Marini, F. John Locke and the revision of classical democratic theory. 1969. 22 W. Polit. Q. 5-18.

Ogden, H. V. S. The state of nature and the decline of Lockian political theory in England, 1760-1800. 1941. 46 Am. Hist. Rev. 21-44.

Parsons, J. E., Jr. Locke's doctrine of property. 1969. 36 Social Research 389-411.

Rostock, Michael. Die lehre von der gewalteinteilung in der politischen theorie von John Locke. Meisenheim am Glan, A. Hain, 1974.

Sabetti, Alfredo. La filosofia politica di John Locke. Anno accademico 1970-71. Napoli, Liguori. 1971.

Sandler, S. G. Lockean ideas in Thomas Jefferson's bill for establishing religious freedom. 1960. J. Hist. of Ideas 110-16.

Sandoz, E. The civil theology of liberal democracy; Locke and his predecessors. 1972. 34 J. Polit. 2-36.

Schmidt, H. Seinserkenntnis und staatsdenken; der subjekts-und erkenntnisbegriff von Hobbes, Locke und Rousseau als grundlage des rechtes und der geschichte (Knowledge and state thought; Hobbes', Locke's and Rousseau's notions as a basis of law and history). Tübingen, M. Niemeyer, 1965.

Schochet, Gordon J., comp. Life, liberty and property; essays on Locke's political ideas. Belmont, Calif., Wadsworth Pub., 1971.

Singh, R. John Locke and the theory of natural law. 1961. 9 Polit. Studies (Oxford) 105-18.

Yolton, John W.

John Locke and the way of ideas. London, Oxford Univ. Press, 1956.

Ed. John Locke: problems and perspectives. A new collection of essays. New York, Cambridge Univ. Press, 1969.

CHARLES LOUIS DE (BARON DE) MONTESQUIEU

Cabeen, David Clark. The esprit of the *Esprit des lois*. 1939. 54 Pub. Mod. Language Ass'n. 439-53.

Cotta, S. Montesquieu e la scienza della società. Torino, Ramella, 1953.

Destutt de Tracy, Antoine Louis Claude. A commentary and review of Montesquieu's *Spirit of the laws*. Prepared . . . from the original manuscript in the hands of the publisher. Translated by Thomas Jefferson. To which are annexed: Observations on the thirty-first, i.e., twenty-ninth book by M. Condorcet, and two letters of Helvetius on the merits of the same work. New York, B. Franklin, 1969.

Faguet, Emile. La politique comparée de Montesquieu, Rousseau et Voltaire. New York, B. Franklin, 1971. (Reprint of 1902 ed.)

Foriers, P. L'égalité chez Montesquieu (In Bruxelles, Université libre, centre de philosophie du droit. L'égalité 1971, v.1, 247-57).

Hazard, Paul. La pensée européenne au XVIIIe siècle: de Montesquieu à Lessing. Paris, Boivin, 1946. 3v. (Pub. in Eng. trans. by J. Lewis May. London, Hollis & Ward; Yale Univ. Press; 1954).

Imbert, P.-H. Destutt de Tracy critique de Montesquieu, ou de la liberté en matière politique. Paris, A. G. Nizet, 1974.

Keller, H. G. Montesquieu's *Esprit des lois*. 1968. 17 Jahrbuch Offentlichen Rechts Gegenwart 33-63.

Keohane, N. O. Virtuous republics and glorious monarchies: two models in Montesquieu's political thought. 1972. 20 Polit. Studies (Oxford) 383-96.

Landucci, Sergio. Montesquieu e l'origine della scienzà sociale. Firenze, Sansoni, 1973.

Gentile, F. L'esprit classique nel pensiero di Montesquieu. Padova, Cedam, 1965.

Levin, Lawrence Meyer. The political doctrine of Montesquieu's *Esprit des lois;* its classical background. Westport, Conn., Greenwood Press, 1973. (Reprint of 1936 ed.)

Lowenthal, David. Book I of Montesquieu's *The spirit of the laws.* 1959. 53 Am. Pol. Sci. Rev. 485-98.

Mason, Sheila Mary. Montesquieu's idea of justice. The Hague, Nijhoff, 1975.

Masterson, M. P. Montesquieu's grand design: the political sociology of *Esprit des lois.* 1972. 2 Brit. J. Polit. Sci. 283-318.

Merry, H. J. Montesquieu's system of natural government. West Lafayette, Ind., Purdue Univ. Press, 1970.

Mirkine-Guetzevitch, B. De l'*Esprit des lois* au constitutionnalisme moderne. 1952. 4 Rev. Int'l. Droit Comparé 205-16.

Mirkine-Guetzevitch, B. and Puget, H. Montesquieu: sa pensée politique et constitutionnelle. Bicentaire de l'*Esprit des lois* (1748-1948). Paris, Librairie Sirey, 1952.

Morkel, A. Montesquieus begriff der despotie (his concept of despotism). 1966. 13 (1) Zeitschrift für Politik 14-32.

Oudin, Charles.
    De l'unité de l'*Esprit des lois* de Montesquieu. (Réimpr. de l'éd. de Paris, 1910) Genève, Slatkine Reprints, 1970.
    Le spinozisme de Montesquieu; étude critique. Genève, Slatkine Reprints, 1971.

Pangle, Thomas L. Montesquieu's philosophy of liberalism: a commentary on the *Spirit of the laws.* Chicago, Univ. of Chicago Press, 1973.

Richter, Melvin.
    Comparative political analysis in Montesquieu and Tocqueville. 1969. 1 Comp. Polit. 129-60.
    The political theory of Montesquieu. New York, Cambridge Univ. Press, 1977.

Ritter, R. *Esprit des lois* et l'esprit de 1789 (In Brethe de la Gressaye collection, 627, Bordeaux, Bière, 1967).

Shackleton, Robert.
"Essai touchant les lois naturelles" est-il de Montesquieu? (In Brethe de la Gressaye collection, 763, Bordeaux, Bière, 1967).
La genèse de l'*Esprit des lois*. 1952. 52 Rev. Histoire Littéraire France 425-38.
Montesquieu: a critical biography. London, Oxford Univ. Press, 1961.

Torrey, N. L., ed. Les philosophes (Montesquieu, Rousseau, La Mettrie). New York, G. P. Putnam's, 1961.

Vidal, Enrico. Saggio sul Montesquieu; con particolare riguardo alla sua concezione dell'uomo, del diritto e della politica. Milano, Giuffrè, 1950.

Vlachos, Georges. La politique de Montesquieu: notion et méthode. Paris, Ed. Montchrétien, 1974.

JEAN-JACQUES ROUSSEAU

Althusser, L. Sur le *Contrat social* (les décalages). May/June 1967. 8 Cahiers Analyse 5-42.

Brandt, Richard. Rousseaus philosophie der gesellschaft. Stuttgart-Bad Cannstatt, Frommann-Holzboog, 1973.

Bruno, A. Aspetti del problema politico moderno: Rousseau, Green, Dewey, Croce. Catania, Giannatta, 1968.

Cassirer, Ernst.
The question of Jean-Jacques Rousseau; trans. by Peter Gay. New York, Columbia Univ. Press, 1954.
Rousseau, Kant and Goethe. Hamden, Conn., Archon Books, 1961. (Reprint of 1945 ed.)

Charvet, J. The social problem in the philosophy of Rousseau. London, Cambridge Univ. Press, 1974.

Cobban, Alfred. Rousseau and the modern state. London, Allen & Unwin, 1934.

Crocker, Lester G. Rousseau's *Social contract*: an interpretative essay. Cleveland, Case-W. Reserve Univ. Press, 1968.

Dobinson, Charles Henry. Jean-Jacques Rousseau: his thought and its relevance today. London, Methuen, 1969.

Echeverria, D. The pre-revolutionary influence of Rousseau's *Contrat social*. 1972. 33 J. Hist. of Ideas 543-60.

Emery, Léon. De Montaigne à Teilhard de Chardin via Pascal et Rousseau. Lyon, Cahiers Libres, 1965.

Favre, P. Unanimité et majorité dans le *Contrat social* de Jean-Jacques Rousseau. 1976. Rev. Droit Public et Sci. Politique, France et Etranger 111-86.

Fay, Bernard. Jean-Jacques Rousseau: ou le rêve de la vie. Paris, Librairie Académique Perrin, 1974.

Fetscher, Irving.
Rousseau's concepts of freedom in the light of his philosophy of history (In Friedrich, C. J., ed., Liberty, Nomos IV, 1962, 29-56).
Rousseaus politische philosophie; zur geschichte des demokratischen freiheitsbegriffs. 2. erw. aufl. Neuweid am Rhein, Luchterhand, 1968.

Green, Frederick Charles. Jean-Jacques Rousseau: a study of his life and writings. Cambridge, Cambridge Univ. Press, 1955.

Griffin-Collart, E. L'égalité: condition de l'harmonie sociale pour J.-J. Rousseau (In Bruxelles, Université libre, centre de philosophie du droit. L'égalité 1971, v.1, 258-71.)

Grimsley, Ronald. The philosophy of Rousseau. London, Oxford Univ. Press, 1973.

Guéhenno, Jean. Jean-Jacques Rousseau. Trans. by John and Doreen Weightman. London, Routledge & Kegan Paul; New York, Columbia Univ. Press. 1966-67. 2v. (First pub. in French 1962.)

Haegi, Klaus Donat. Die politische freiheit im werk von Jean-Jacques Rousseau. Winterthur, P. G. Keller, 1963.

Höffding, Harald. Jean-Jacques Rousseau and his philosophy. Trans. from the 2d Danish ed. by William Richards and Leo E. Saidla . . . with a new pref. by the author. New Haven, Yale Univ. Press; London, H. Milford, Oxford Univ. Press. 1930.

Kelly, G. A. Rousseau, Kant and history. 1968. 29 J. Hist. of Ideas 347-64.

Lacharrière, R. de. Jean-Jacques Rousseau: interprétation et permanence. 1961. 77 Rev. Droit Public Sci. Polit. 469-531.

Launay, Michel. Jean-Jacques Rousseau, écrivain politique. Cannes, C. E. L., 1972.

Lemos, Ramon M. Rousseau's political philosophy: an exposition and interpretation. Athens, Univ. of Georgia Press, 1977.

Levin, M. Uses of the *social contract* method: Vaughan's interpretation of Rousseau. 1967. 28 J. Hist. of Ideas 521-36.

Lüthy, K. Diritti dell'uomo e diritti del cittadino in Rousseau, Hegel e Marx. 1965. 3 Cultura 113-28.

Machado, Lourival Gomes. A política de Jean-Jacques Rousseau. Homem e sociedade na teoria política de Jean-Jacques Rousseau (man and society in Rousseau's political theory). ed. by O. S. Ferreira. São Paulo, Liv. Martins, 1968.

Nisbet, Robert. Rousseau and equality. 1974. 43 (3) Encounter 40-51.

Noone, J. B., Jr.
Rousseau's theory of natural law as conditional. 1972. 33 J. Hist. of Ideas 23-42.

The *social contract* and the idea of sovereignty in Rousseau. 1970. 32 J. Polit. 696-708.

Rousseau, Jean-Jacques.

The social contract and the *discourses*. Trans. by G. D. H. Cole. London and Baltimore, Penguin, 1973.

The social contract and discourse on the origin and foundation of inequality among mankind. Ed. and with an introd. by Lester G. Crocker. New York, Washington Square Press, 1967.

Rouvier, J. Les grandes idées politiques, des origines à J.-J. Rousseau. Paris, Bordas, 1973.

Shklar, Judith N. Men and citizens: a study of Rousseau's social theory. London, Cambridge Univ. Press, 1969.

Sylwestrzak, A. Idea umowy spolecznej w doktrynie polityczene J.-J. Rousseau (the notion of social contract in the political doctrine of Rousseau). 1974. 21 Annales Univ. M. Curie-Sklodowska 163-83.

Williams, Alfred Tuttle. The concept of equality in the writings of Rousseau, Bentham and Kant. New York, AMS Press, 1972. (Reprint of 1907 ed., Teachers College, Columbia Univ.)

CESARE BECCARIA

Corpaci, Francesco.

Ideologia e politica in Cesare Beccaria. Milano, Giuffrè, 1965.

Utile, diritto e giustizia nel pensiero di Beccaria. 1961. 38 Riv. Internazionale Filosofia Diritto 668—.

Dalma, J. Actualidad de Césare Beccaria. Aug. 1970. 29 La Justicia (México) 37—.

Jacomella, Sergio. L'attualità del pensiero di Cesare Beccaria. (Per una giustizia penale più civile e più umana.) Lugano, Cenobio, 1964.

Maestro, Marcello T.

Cesare Beccaria and the origins of penal reform. Fwd. by Norval Morris. Philadelphia, Temple Univ. Press, 1973.

Pioneer for the abolition of capital punishment: Cesare Beccaria. 1973. 34 J. Hist. of Ideas 463-68.

Voltaire and Beccaria as reformers of criminal law. New York, Octagon Books. 1972. (Reprint of 1942 ed., Columbia Univ. Press.)

Marongiu, A. Muratori, Beccaria, Pietro Verri e la scienza del diritto. 1975. 18 Riv. Italiana Diritto e Procedura Penale 744-76.

Phillipson, Coleman. Three criminal law reformers (Beccaria, Romilly and Bentham). Montclair, N.J., Patterson Smith, 1970.

Sabino Júnior, Vicente. Cesare Beccaria e o seu livro *Dos delitos e das penas* (estudo biográfico e critico). São Paulo, Editora Juriscredi, 1972.

Spurlin, Paul M. Beccaria's essay on crimes and punishments in eighteenth-century America (In 17 Studies on Voltaire and the eighteenth century, 1963, 1489-1504).

VOLTAIRE

Aldridge, Alfred Owen. Voltaire and the century of light. Princeton, Princeton Univ. Press, 1975.

Barr, Mary Margaret Harrison. A century of Voltaire study; a bibliography of writings on Voltaire, 1825-1925. New York, B. Franklin, 1972. (Reprint of 1929 ed.)

Brandes, George. Voltaire. New York, A. & C. Boni, 1930. 2v.

Deneckere, M. La conscience européenne chez Voltaire. March 1952. 1 Cahiers Bourges 43-54.

Gay, Peter. The philosophe in his dictionary (In The party of humanity; essays in the French enlightenment, 1st ed. New York, Knopf, 1964).

Philosophical dictionary. Trans. with an introd. and glossary by Peter Gay. Pref. by André Maurois. New York, Basic Books, 1962. 2v.

Price, E. H. Voltaire and Montesquieu's three principles of government. 1942. 57 Pub. Mod. Language Ass'n. 1046-52.

Trapnell, William H. Voltaire and his portable dictionary. Frankfurt am Main, V. Klostermann, 1972.

Vial, Fernand. Voltaire: sa vie et son oeuvre. Paris, Didier, 1955.

Waldinger, R. Voltaire and reform in the light of the French revolution. Genève, E. Droz, 1959.

IMMANUEL KANT

Beck, Lewis White. Studies in the philosophy of Kant. 1st ed. Indianapolis, Bobbs-Merrill, 1965.

Bobbio, Norberto. Diritto e stato nel pensiero di Emanuele Kant. 2. ed. riveduta ed ampliata. Torino, G. Giappichelli, 1969.

Cassirer, Ernst. Kants leben und lehre. Darmstadt, Wissenschaftliche Buchgesellschaft, 1972. (reprint)

Delbos, Victor. La philosophie pratique de Kant. 3e éd. Paris, Presses Univ. de France, 1969.

Diemer, Alwin. Gesamtregister der Kantstudien. Meisenheim am Glan, A. Hain, 1969—. 1v.—.

Ebbinghaus, J. Das Kantische system der rechte des menschen und bürgers in seiner geschichtlichen und aktuellen bedeutung. 1964. Archiv Rechts-und Sozialphilosophie 23-56.

Jaspers, Karl. Kant: leben, werk, wirkung. München, R. Piper, 1975.

Kant as a political thinker. Ed. by Eduard Gerresheim; trans. by Patricia Crampton. Bonn, Inter Nationes, 1974.

Kant's political writings. Ed. with an introd. and notes by Hans Reiss. Trans. by H. B. Nisbet. Cambridge, Cambridge Univ. Press, 1970.

Kelly, G. A. The structure and spirit of legality in Kant. 1969. 31 J. Polit. 513-27.

Kojève, Alexander. Kant. Paris, Gallimard, 1973.

Lacroix, Jean. Kant et le kantisme. 4ᵉ éd. mise à jour. Paris, Presses Univ. de France, 1973.

Lasky, M. J. Sweet dream: Kant and the revolutionary hope for utopia. Oct. 1969. 33 Encounter 14-27.

Levine, Andrew. The politics of autonomy: a Kantian reading of Rousseau's *Social contract*. Amherst, Univ. of Massachusetts Press, 1976.

Lodigiani, G. Fondamento ed i caratteri dell'idèa internazionalistica e cosmopolitica di Kant. 1967. 20 Jus (Milano) 18—.

Lumia, G. La dottrina kantiana del diritto e dello stato. Milano, Giuffrè, 1960.

Lunati, Giancarlo. La libertà; saggi su Kant, Hegel e Croce. Napoli, Giannini, 1959.

Margiotta, Umberto. Kant e la formazione dell'uomo moderno. Roma, A. Signorelli, 1974?.

Pasini, Dino. Diritto, società e stato in Kant. Milano, Giuffrè, 1957.

Pasqualucci, Paolo.
    Rapporto Rousseau-Kant. 1973. 50 Riv. Internazionale Filosofia Diritto 450-97.
    Rousseau e Kant. Milano, Giuffrè, 1974—. V.1—.

Pecilli, D. Diritto e valore. Alcune considerazioni sulla filosofia giuridica de Emanuele Kant. 1963. 40 Riv. Internazionale Filosofia Diritto 378.

Saage, Richard. Besitzindividualistische perspektiven der politischen theorie Kants. 1972. 2 Neue Polit. Literatur 168-93.

Saner, Hans. Kant's political thought; its origins and development. Trans. by E. B. Ashton. Chicago, Univ. of Chicago Press, 1973–. V.1–.

Scalia, Archimede. Da Kant a Croce. Pensatori e correnti. S. Maria degli Angeli/Assisi, Tip. Porziuncola, 1968.

Sellars, W. Some remarks on Kant's theory of experience. 1967. 64 J. Philosophy 633-47.

Symposium: Kant on revolution. 1971. 32 J. Hist. of Ideas 411-40.

Toyama, Yoshitaka. Kants praktische philosophie mit rücksicht auf eine theorie des friedens. Hamburg, H. Buske, 1973.

Vancourt, Raymond. Kant, sa vie, son oeuvre, avec un exposé de sa philosophie et un choix de textes de Kant. Paris, Presses Univ. de France, 1967.

Vlachos, Georges. Fédération des peuples et coexistence pacifique chez Kant (In Mélanges Séferiadès, v.I, Athènes, Ecole des sciences politiques "Panteios," 1961, 367-86).

Volkmann-Schluck, Karl Heinz. Politische philosophie: Thukydides, Kant, Tocqueville. Frankfurt am Main, Klostermann, 1974.

Vorländer, Karl. Immanuel Kants leben. Neu. hrsg. von Rudolf Malter. 3., unverand. aufl. Hamburg, Meiner, 1974.

Wolff, Robert Paul, comp. Kant; a collection of critical essays. 1st ed. Garden City, N.Y., Anchor Books, 1967.

JEREMY BENTHAM

Atkinson, Charles Milner. Jeremy Bentham; his life and work. 1st AMS ed. London, Methuen; New York, AMS Press. 1971.

Dicey, A. V. The period of Benthamism or individualism (In Lectures on the relation between law and public opinion in England during the nineteenth century. London, Macmillan, 1914, 26-210).

Griffin-Collart, E.
Egalité et justice dans l'utilitarisme; Bentham, J. S. Mill, H. Sidgwick. Bruxelles, Bruylant, 1974.
Le principe d'utilité et l'égalité: Bentham et J. S. Mill. 1971. 1 L'Egalité 272-90.

Gunn, J. A. W. Jeremy Bentham and the public interest. 1968. 1 Can. J. Pol. Sci. 398-413.

Halévy, Elie. The growth of philosophical radicalism; trans. from the French by Mary Morris. New ed., with a new pref. by John Plamenatz. London, Faber, 1972.

Hart, H. L. A. Bentham and the demystification of the law. 1973. 36 (1) Modern L. Rev. 2-17.

Holdsworth, William. Bentham's place in English legal history. 1940. 28 Calif. L. Rev. 568-86.

Larrabee, H., ed. Bentham's handbook of political fallacies. Baltimore, Johns Hopkins Press, 1952.

The limits of jurisprudence defined, being part two of "An introduction to the principles of morals and legislation." Now first printed from the author's manuscript, with an introd. by Charles Warren Everett. New York, Columbia Univ. Press; London, H. Milford. 1945.

Long, Douglas G. Bentham on liberty: Jeremy Bentham's idea of liberty in relation to his utilitarianism. Toronto, Univ. of Toronto Press, 1977.

Lyons, David B. In the interest of the governed; a study in Bentham's philosophy of utility and law. Oxford, Clarendon Press, 1973.

Parekh, Bhikhu C. Bentham's theory of equality. 1970. 18 Polit. Studies (Oxford) 478-95.

Parekh, Bhikhu C., comp. Jeremy Bentham; ten critical essays. London, Cass., 1974.

Rockow, Lewis. Bentham on the theory of second chambers. 1928. 22 Am. Pol. Sci. Rev. 576-90.

Rodman, B. S. Bentham and the paradox of penal reform. 1968. 29 J. Hist. of Ideas 197-210.

Steele, Anita. An essay on *An introduction to the principles of morals and legislation* by Jeremy Bentham. 1972. 65 Law Lib. J. 50-57.

Steintrager, James. Bentham. Ithaca, Cornell Univ. Press, 1977.

Wilson, Roland Knyvet. Life and work of Bentham; the writings of Bentham (In History of modern English law. London, Rivingtons, 1875, 133-56).

ALEXIS DE TOCQUEVILLE

Barth, N. Die idee der freiheit und der demokratie bei Alexis de Tocqueville. Aaran, Keller, 1953.

Berlin, Isaiah. The thought of de Tocqueville. 1965. 50 History 199-206.

Cavallaro, R. Dall'individualismo al controllo democratico: aspetti del pensiero di Alexis de Tocqueville sull'associazionismo volontario. 1973/74. 28 Critica Sociologica 99-125.

Drescher, Seymour.
  Dilemmas of democracy; Tocqueville and modernization. Pittsburgh, Univ. of Pittsburgh Press, 1968.
  Tocqueville's two democracies. 1964. 25 J. Hist. of Ideas 201-16.

Freund, Dorrit. Alexis de Tocqueville und die politische kultur der demokratie. Bern; Stuttgart, Paul Haupt. 1974.

Geiss, Imanuel. Tocqueville und das zeitalter der revolution. München, Nymphenburger Verlagshandlung, 1972.

Herr, R. Tocqueville and the old regime. Princeton, Princeton Univ. Press, 1962.

Lively, J. The social and political thought of Alexis de Tocqueville. Oxford, Clarendon Press, 1962.

Negro Pavon, D. Individualismo y collectivismo en la ciencia social. Ensayo sobre Tocqueville y Stuart Mill. 1970. 28 Rev. Internacional Sociologia 5-32; 1971. 29:47-76.

Polin, Claude. De la *Démocratie en Amérique*, Tocqueville, analyse critique. Paris, Hatier, 1973.

Probst, G. E., ed. The happy republic: a reader in Tocqueville's America. New York, Harper & Row, 1962.

Resh, R. W. Alexis de Tocqueville and the negro: *Democracy in America* reconsidered. 1963. J. Negro Hist. 251-59.

Rosenberg, B. and Wrong, D. H. La *Démocratie en Amérique*. 1961. 33 Diogène 132-42. (Idées et méthodes de Tocqueville.)

Strout, C. Tocqueville's duality: describing America and thinking of Europe. Spring 1969. 21 Am. Q. 87-99.

Vossler, Otto. Alexis de Tocqueville; freiheit und gleichheit. Frankfurt am Main, V. Klostermann, 1973.

Zeitlin, I. M. Liberty, equality and revolution in Alexis de Tocqueville. Boston, Little, Brown, 1971.

Zetterbaum, M. Tocqueville and the problem of democracy. Stanford, Stanford Univ. Press, 1967.

JOHN STUART MILL

Aiken, Henry D. Mill and the justification of social freedom (In Friedrich, C. J., ed., Liberty, Nomos IV, New York, Atherton Press, 1962, 119-39).

Berlin, Isaiah. Two concepts of liberty. Oxford, Clarendon Press, 1958.

Bouton, C. W. John Stuart Mill: on liberty and history. 1965. 18 W. Polit. Q. 569-78.

Brown, D. G. Mill on liberty and morality. 1972. 81 Philos. Rev. 133-58.

Ebenstein, William.
John Stuart Mill: democrat, liberal, socialist? 1974. 39 Politico 194-209.
John Stuart Mill: political and economic liberty (In Friedrich, C. J., ed., Liberty, Nomos IV, New York, Atherton Press, 1962, 89-109).

Halliday, R. J.
John Stuart Mill. New York, Barnes & Noble/Harper, 1977.
John Stuart Mill's idea of politics. 1970. 18 Polit. Studies (Oxford) 461-77.

Himmelfarb, Gertrude. On liberty and liberalism: the case of John Stuart Mill. 1st ed. New York, Knopf; dist. by Random House. 1974.

Knight, Frank H. Some notes on political freedom and on a famous essay (In Friedrich, C. J., ed., Liberty, Nomos IV, New York, Atherton Press, 1962, 110-18).

Levi, A. W. The value of freedom: Mill's *Liberty* (1859-1959). Oct. 1959. 70 Ethics 37-46. Reply: H. A. Holloway; Jan. 1961. 71:130-32.

Lichtman, R. The surface and substance of Mill's defence of freedom. 1963. 30 Soc. Research 459-94.

Lindquist, Emory Kempton. John Stuart Mill's essay *On liberty:* a centennial review. Wichita, Univ. of Kansas, 1959.

McCloskey, Henry John. John Stuart Mill: a critical study. London, Macmillan, 1971.

Megill, A. D. J. S. Mill's religion of humanity and the second justification for the writing of *On liberty.* 1972. 34 J. Polit. 612-29.

Morris, C. On liberation and liberty: Marcuse's and Mill's essays compared. 1970. 118 U. Pa. L. Rev. 735-45.

Qualter, T. H. John Stuart Mill, disciple of Tocqueville. 1960. 13 W. Polit. Q. 880-89.

Radcliff. P., ed. Limits of liberty: studies of Mill's *On liberty*. Belmont, Calif., Wadsworth Pub., 1966.

Rees, J. C. A re-reading of Mill on liberty. 1960. 8 Polit. Studies (Oxford) 113-29.

Robson, John Mercel. The improvement of mankind; the social and political thought of John Stuart Mill. Toronto, Univ. of Toronto Press; London, Routledge & Kegan Paul. 1968.

Russell, Bertrand. John Stuart Mill (In British academy, London, Proceedings, 1955, v.4, 43-59).

Schneidermeyer, W. John Stuart Mill's principle of liberty and legislative reality. 1972. 20 J. Human Relations 147-55.

Spitz, David. Freedom and individuality: Mill's *Liberty* in retrospect (In Friedrich, C. J., ed. Liberty, Nomos IV, New York, Atherton Press, 1962, 176-226).

Stephen, James Fitzjames. Liberty, equality, fraternity. Ed. with an introd. and notes by R. J. White. Cambridge, Cambridge Univ. Press, 1967.

Ten, C. L. Mill and liberty. 1969. 30 J. Hist. of Ideas 47-68.

Wollheim, R. John Stuart Mill and the limits of state action. 1973. 40 Soc. Research 1-30.

BENEDETTO CROCE

Benedetti, Ulisse. Benedetto Croce e il fascismo. Roma, G. Volpe. 1967.

Bruno, Antonino.
  La crisi dell'idealismo nell'ultimo Croce. Bari, Laterza, 1964.
  Croce e le scienzà politico-sociali. 1. ed. Firenze, La Nuova Italia, 1975.

Capozzi, Gino. Individuo, società e stato nella dialettica della politica come forza. Napoli, Ediz. Scientifiche Italiano, 1974.

Clone, Edmondo. Bibliografia crociana. Roma, Bocca, 1956.

Colapietra, Raffaele. Benedetto Croce e la politica italiana. Santo Spirito/Bari, Ediz. del Centro Librario, 1969-70. 2v.

Corsi, Mario. Le origini del pensiero di Benedetto Croce. 1. ed. Firenze, La Nuova Italia, 1951.

De Feo, Italo. Croce: l'uomo e l'opera. 1. ed. Milano, A. Mondadori, 1975.

Ferola, V. Critica del Croce al concetto di coazione. 1960. 37 Riv. Internazionale Filosofia Diritto 150—

Iofrida, Vincenzo. La libertà come fondamento dello stato; saggio sulla filosofia dello spirito di Benedetto Croce. Varese, Istituto Edit. Cisalpino, 1959.

Lalla, M. di. Croce tra fascismo e antifascismo. 1972. 148 Nord e Sud 69-115.

Leoni, B. Benedetto Croce, pensatore politico (In Studi in memoria Gioele Solari. Torino, Ed. Ramella, 1954, 449-62).

Roggerone, G. Benedetto Croce e la fondazione del concetto di libertà. Milano, Marzorati, 1965.

Sartori. Giovanni.
Croce etico-politico e filòsofo della libertà. Firenze, Univ. degli Studi, 1956.
Stato e politica nel pensiero di Benedetto Croce. Napoli, Morano, 1966.

Mack Smith, Denis. Benedetto Croce: history and politics. 1973. 8 (1) J. Contemp. Hist. 41-61.

John Dewey

Boydston, Jo Ann and Poulos, Kathleen. Checklist of writings about John Dewey, 1887-1973. Carbondale, Southern Illinois Univ. Press, 1974.

Chimera, J. M. Some implications of Dewey's philosophy for American foreign policy. 1969. 6 (1) Int'l. Rev. Hist. & Pol. Sci. 15-27.

Dewey, John.
Freedom and culture. New York, Capricorn Books, 1963. (Reprint of 1939 ed.)
Individualism, old and new. New York, Capricorn Books, 1962. (Reprint of 1929/30 ed.)
Liberalism and social action. New York, Capricorn Books, 1963. (Reprint of 1935 ed.)

Geiger, George R. John Dewey in perspective. New York, Oxford Univ. Press, 1958.

Hook, Sidney.
John Dewey and the crisis of American liberalism. 1969. 29 Antioch Rev. 218-32.
John Dewey; philosopher of science and freedom; a symposium. New York, Barnes & Noble, 1967.

John Dewey and Arthur Bentley; a philosophical correspondence, 1932-1951. Selected and edited by Sidney Ratner and Jules Altman. New Brunswick, N.J., Rutgers Univ. Press, 1964.

Metz, J. G. Democracy and the scientific method in the philosophy of John Dewey. 1969. 31 Rev. Polit. 242-62.

Tarello, G. Norma e giuridificazione nella logica di Dewey. 1960. 37 Riv. Internazionale Filosofia Diritto 280—.

JACQUES MARITAIN

Cattaui de Menasce, G. Per una lettura del pensiero politici di Maritain. 1973. 29 Orientamenti Sociali 305-48.

Jung, Hwa Yol. The foundations of Jacques Maritain's political philosophy. Gainesville, Univ. of Florida Press, 1960.

Maritain, Jacques.
The concept of sovereignty. 1950. 44 Am. Pol. Sci. Rev. 343-57.
The meaning of human rights. Philadelphia. 1949. (Publication of Brandeis lawyers quarterly.)
Oeuvres 1912-1939; choix présentation et notes par Henry Bars. Bruxelles, Desclée, De Brouwer, 1975.
Principes d'une politique humaniste. New York, Editions de la Maison Française, 1944.
The social and political philosophy of Jacques Maritain; selected readings by Joseph W. Evans and Leo R. Ward. New York, Scribner's, 1955.

Mutel, A. Introduction à la philosophie politique de Jacques Maritain. 1972. 1 Annales Faculté Droit et Sciences Econ. de Lyon 105-80.

Rossetti, A. C. La filosofía política de Jacques Maritain. 1965. 29 (1-3) Bol. Facultad Derecho y Ciencias Sociales. 9-72.

Vaccarini, I. Attualità del pensiero storico-politico di Maritain. 1974. 25 Aggiornamenti Sociali 763-82.

JEAN-PAUL SARTRE

Audry, Colette. Sartre et la réalité humaine. Présentation, choix de texts . . . bibliographie. Paris, Seghers, 1966.

Danto, Arthur C. Jean-Paul Sartre. New York, Viking Press, 1975.

Hana, Ghanem Georges. Freiheit und person; eine auseinandersetzung mit der darstellung Jean-Paul Sartre. München, Beck, 1965.

Krosigk, Friedrich von. Philosophie und politische action bei Jean-Paul Sartre. München, Beck, 1969.

Sartre, Jean-Paul. Of human freedom. Ed. by Wade Baskin. New York, Philosophical Library, 1967.

Werner, E. De la violence au totalitarisme; essai sur la pensée de Camus et Sartre. Paris, Calmann-Lévy, 1972.

Wilcocks, Robert. Jean-Paul Sartre; a bibliography of international criticism. Pref. by Michel Contat and Michel Rybalka. Edmonton, Univ. of Alberta Press, 1975.

Historical Documents—National

THE MAGNA CHARTA (1215)

Adams, George Burton. The origin of the English constitution. New Haven, Yale Univ. Press, 1912. (Chap. V, Magna carta; chap. VI, The immediate results of magna carta.)

Blackstone, William. The great charter and charter of the forest, with other authentic instruments: to which is prefixed an Introductory discourse, containing the history of the charters (In Tracts, chiefly relating to the antiquities and laws of England, 3d ed., Oxford, Clarendon Press, 1771, beginning at p. 281.)

Dick Howard, A. E. Magna carta; text and commentary. Charlottesville, Pub. for the Magna Carta Commission by the Univ. Press of Virginia. 1964.

Goodhart, Arthur L. Law of the land. Charlottesville, Pub. for the Magna Carta Commission by the Univ. Press of Virginia. 1966.

The great charter; four essays on magna carta (by) Samuel E. Thorne and others. Introd. by Erwin N. Griswold. New York, Pantheon, 1965.

Holt, James Clarke.
  Magna carta. Cambridge, Cambridge Univ. Press, 1965.
  The making of magna carta. Charlottesville, Pub. for the Magna Carta Commission by the Univ. Press of Virginia. 1965.
  Rights and liberties in magna carta, album Helen Maud Cam (Louvain) I, 57-69, 1960.

Johnson, Samuel.
  A history and defence of magna charta. Shewing the manner of its being obtained from King John, with its preservation and final establishment in the succeeding reigns; with an introductory discourse, containing a short account of the rise and progress of national freedom, from the invasion of Caesar to the present times. Also the liberties which are confirmed by the bill of rights, &c. To which is added an essay on parliaments, describing their origin in England. . . . The 2d ed. London, J. Bell, 1792.
  Magna charta, with its history and defence . . . with the bill of rights, Scots claim of rights, habeas corpus act . . . with an essay on parliaments. . . . Edinburgh, J. Denoon and D. Clarke, 1794. (Habeas corpus act has separate paging.)

Magna carta and common law (In McIlwain, C. H., Constitutionalism and the changing world. New York, Macmillan; Cambridge, Cambridge Univ. Press. 1939, 127-77).

McKechnie, William Sharp. Magna carta; a commentary on the great charter of King John, with a historical introduction . . . 2d ed., rev. and in part rewritten. Glasgow, J. Maclehose & Sons, 1914. (Reprinted New York, B. Franklin, 1960.)

Meador, Daniel John. Habeas corpus and magna carta; dualism of power and liberty. Charlottesville, Pub. for the Magna Carta Commission by the Univ. Press of Virginia. 1966.

Malden, Henry Elliott, ed. Magna carta commemoration essays, with a pref. by the Rt. Hon. Viscount Bryce. London, Royal Historical Society, 1917.

Painter, Sidney. The reign of King John. Baltimore, Johns Hopkins Press, 1949.

Pallister, Anne. Magna carta: the heritage of liberty. Oxford, Clarendon Press, 1971.

Radin, Max. The myth of magna carta. 1947. 60 Harv. L. Rev. 1060-91.

Swindler, William Finley. Magna carta; legend and legacy. Indianapolis, Bobbs-Merrill, 1966.

Thompson, Faith.
  The first century of magna carta: why it persisted as a document. Minneapolis, Univ. of Minnesota, 1925. (Reprinted New York, Russell & Russell, 1967.)
  Magna carta; its role in the making of the English constitution, 1300-1629. Minneapolis, Univ. of Minnesota Press, 1948. (Reprinted New York, Octagon Books, 1972.)

THE ENGLISH BILL OF RIGHTS (1689)

Ashley, Maurice. Magna carta in the seventeenth century. Charlottesville, Pub. for the Magna Carta Commission by the Univ. Press of Virginia. 1965.

Bagehot, Walter. The English constitution, and other political essays. Rev. ed. New York; London, Appleton, 1911.

Courtney, Leonard H. C. The working constitution of the United Kingdom. London and Toronto, J. M. Dent, 1920.

Crawford, Clarence C. The suspension of the habeas corpus act and the revolution of 1689. 1915. 30 Eng. Hist. Rev. 613-30.

Pinkham, Lucile. William III and the respectable revolution. Cambridge, Harvard Univ. Press, 1954.

Pollock, Frederick. The history of English law as a branch of politics (In Jurisprudence and legal essays. New York, St. Martin's Press, 1961, 185-211).

Schwartz, Bernard. The roots of freedom; a constitutional history of England. New York, Hill & Wang, 1967.

Trevelyan, George Macaulay. The English revolution 1688-89. London, Butterworth, 1939.

Williams, E. Neville. The eighteenth-century constitution, 1688-1815, documents and commentary. Cambridge, The University Press, 1960. (Chap. I, The revolution.)

THE UNITED STATES DECLARATION OF INDEPENDENCE (1776)

Becker, Carl L. The declaration of independence, a study in the history of political ideas. New York, Harcourt, Brace, 1922.

Bonger, H. Lehre der menschenrechten: Thomas Jefferson. Arnhem, Van Loghum Slaterus, 1951.

Corn, Ira G., Jr. The story of the declaration of independence. Los Angeles, Calif., Corwin Books, 1977.

Friedenwald, Herbert. The declaration of independence, an interpretation and an analysis. London and New York, Macmillan, 1904.

Hawke, David. A transaction of free men; the birth and course of the declaration of independence. New York, Scribner's, 1964.

Malone, Dumas. The story of the declaration of independence. New York, Oxford Univ. Press, 1954.

Nicgorski, W. The significance of the non-Lockean heritage of the declaration of independence. 1976. 21 Am. J. Juris. 156-77.

Ramírez, M. A. Thomas Jefferson: la democracia como sucedáneo de la revolución (democracy as an outgrowth of revolution). 1966. 10 Rev. Ciencias Sociales (Puerto Rico) 451-69.

THE FRENCH DECLARATION OF THE RIGHTS OF MAN AND CITIZEN (1789)

Chantavoine, Henri. Les principes de 1789, la déclaration des droits, la déclaration des devoirs. Paris, Société Français d'Impr. et de Librairie, 1906.

Ferrier, Jean and Carré, Richard. La lutte pour la vie; note historique, texte intégral et commentaires sur la déclaration des droits de l'homme et du citoyen. Paris, J. Peyronnet, 1946.

Jellinek, Georg. The declaration of the rights of man and of citizens. Trans. by Max Farrand. Rev. ed. New York, H. Holt, 1901.

Vecchio, Giorgio del. La déclaration des droits de l'homme et du citoyen dans la révolution française. Traduit de l'italien par Antoinette Pellevant Gini. Rome, Foundation Européenne Dragan; Paris, Librairie Gén. de Droit et de Jurisprudence, 1968.

Walch, Emile. La déclaration des droits de l'homme et du citoyen et l'assemblée constituante. Travaux préparatoires. Paris, H. Jouve, 1903.

THE UNITED STATES CONSTITUTION (1789)

Bancroft, George. History of the constitution of the United States of America. 2d ed. New York, D. Appleton, 1882. 2v.

Chafee, Zechariah. How human rights got into the constitution. Boston, Boston Univ. Press, 1952. (Gaspar G. Bacon lecture, 1951)

Corwin, Edward S.
  The constitution and what it means today. Rev. by Harold W. Chase and Craig R. Ducat. 13th ed. Princeton, Princeton Univ. Press, 1973.
  The "higher law" background of American constitutional law. 1928/29. 42 Harv. L. Rev. 149-85, 365-409.

Dick Howard, A. E. The road from Runnymede: magna carta and constitutionalism in America. Charlottesville, Univ. Press of Virginia, 1968.

Farrand, Max. The framing of the constitution of the United States. New Haven, Yale Univ. Press, 1936.

Hazeltine, H. D. The influence of magna carta on American constitutional development. 1917. 17 Colum. L. Rev. 1-33.

Mason, Alpheus T. America's political heritage: revolution and free government—a bicentennial tribute. 1976. 91 Pol. Sci. Q. 193-217.

McDonald, Forrest. We the people; the economic origins of the constitution. Chicago, Univ. of Chicago Press, 1958.

Mitchell, Broadus and Mitchell, Louise Pearson. A biography of the constitution of the United States. New York, Oxford Univ. Press, 1964.

Pollak, Louis H. Law and liberty: the American constitution and the doctrine that all men are created equal. 1972. 2 Human Rights 1-26.

Rossiter, Clinton L. Alexander Hamilton and the constitution. New York, Harcourt, Brace & World, 1964.

Sources of our liberties. Documentary origins of individual liberties in the United States constitution and bill of rights. Ed. by Richard L. Perry, under general supervision of John C. Cooper. Chicago, American Bar Foundation, 1952. (See, especially, bibliography, 441-45.)

Story, Joseph. Commentaries on the constitution of the United States; . . . preliminary view of the constitutional history of the colonies before the adoption of the constitution. New introd. by Arthur E. Sutherland. New York, Da Capo Press, 1970. 3v.

THE FEDERALIST (1788)

Diamond, Martin. Democracy and the *Federalist:* a reconsideration of the framers' intent. 1959. 53 Am. Pol. Sci. Rev. 52-68.

Dietze, Gottfried. The *Federalist,* a classic on federalism and free government. Baltimore, Johns Hopkins Press, 1960.

Fairfield, R. P., ed. The *Federalist* papers; a collection of essays written in support of the constitution of the United States. From the original text of Alexander Hamilton, James Madison and John Jay. Garden City, N.Y., Anchor Books, 1961.

Kenyon, Cecilia M. Alexander Hamilton: Rousseau of the right. 1958. 73 Pol. Sci. Q. 161-78.

Mason, Alpheus T. The *Federalist*—a split personality. 1952. 57 Am. Hist. Rev.

Scanlan, J. P. The *Federalist* and human nature. 1959. 21 J. Polit. 657-77.

Smith, M. Reason, passion and political freedom in the *Federalist*. 1960. 22 J. Polit. 525-57.

Stockton, Constant Noble. Are there natural rights in the *Federalist?* 1971/72. 82 Ethics 72-82.

Wright, Benjamin Fletcher. The *Federalist* on the nature of political man. 1949. 59 (2) Ethics 1-31.

THE BILL OF RIGHTS AND SELECTED AMENDMENTS TO THE UNITED STATES CONSTITUTION

Brant, Irving. The bill of rights; its origin and meaning. Indianapolis, Bobbs-Merrill, 1965.

Dumbauld, Edward. The bill of rights and what it means today. Norman, Univ. of Oklahoma Press, 1957.

Drinker, Henry S. Some observations on the four freedoms of the first amendment: freedom of speech, freedom of the press, freedom of assembly and petition, freedom of religion. Boston, Boston Univ. Press, 1957. (Gaspar G. Bacon lecture)

The fourteenth amendment; centennial volume, edited by Bernard Schwartz. New York, New York Univ. Press, 1970.

Gillette, William. The right to vote: politics and the passage of the fifteenth amendment. Baltimore, Johns Hopkins Press, 1969.

Guthrie, William Dameron. Lectures on the fourteenth amendment to the constitution of the United States. New York, Da Capo Press, 1970. (Reprint of 1898 ed.)

Hudon, Edward G. Freedom of speech and press in America. Foreword by William O. Douglas. Washington, Public Affairs Press, 1963.

James, Joseph Bliss. The framing of the fourteenth amendment. Champaign-Urbana, Univ. of Illinois Press, 1956.

Levy, Leonard W. Legacy of suppression; freedom of speech and press in early American history. Cambridge, Mass., Belknap Press of Harvard Univ. Press, 1960.

Meyer, Howard N. The amendment that refused to die. 1st ed. Radnor, Pa., Chilton Books, 1973.

Miller, Helen D. H. The case for liberty. Chapel Hill, Univ. of North Carolina Press, 1965.

Paust, J. J. Human rights and the ninth amendment: a new form of guarantee. 1975. 60 Cornell L. Rev. 231-67.

Rutland, Robert A. The birth of the bill of rights, 1776-1791. Chapel Hill, Univ. of North Carolina Press, 1955.

Schwartz, Bernard, comp. The bill of rights; a documentary history. New York, Chelsea House, 1971. 2v.

Schwartz, Bernard. The great rights of mankind; a history of the American bill of rights. New York, Oxford Univ. Press, 1977.

Ten Broek, Jacobus. The antislavery origins of the fourteenth amendment. Berkeley, Univ. of California Press, 1951.

THE MONROE DOCTRINE (1823)

Donovan, F. Mr. Monroe's message; the story of the Monroe doctrine. New York, Dodd, Mead, 1963.

Dozer, Donald Marquand, ed. The Monroe doctrine; its modern significance. 1st ed. New York, Knopf, 1965.

Gilman, Daniel Colt. James Monroe. With a bibliography of writings pertinent to the Monroe doctrine, by John F. Jameson. Boston, Houghton Mifflin; New York, AMS Press. 1972. (Reprint of 1898 ed.)

May, Ernest R. The making of the Monroe doctrine. Cambridge, Mass., Belknap Press of Harvard Univ. Press, 1975.

Rappaport, Armin, ed. The Monroe doctrine. New York, Holt, Rinehart & Winston, 1964.

Robertson, William Spence.
  The Monroe doctrine abroad in 1823-24. 1912. 6 Am. Pol. Sci. Rev. 546-63.
  South America and the Monroe doctrine, 1824-1828. 1915. 30 Polit. Sci. Q. 82-105.

Ruiz Ruiz, Ramón. Doctrina de Monroe su génesis autes y después del congreso de Verona de 1822 y sus interpretaciones. León, Nicaragua, 1949.

Scudder, Evarts Eelye. The Monroe doctrine and world peace. Port Washington, N.Y., Kennikat Press, 1972.

Whitton, J. B. La doctrine de Monroe et la société des nations. 1927. Rev. Droit Int'l. et Législation Comparée 561-82.

Diplomacy and Human Rights—to 1918

TREATY OF PARIS (1856)

Gourdon, Edouard. Histoire du congrès de Paris . . . introd. par M. J. Cohen. Paris, Librairie Nouvelle, 1857.

Historii Parjiskogo mira 1856. Krasy Arkhiv 1936. S. 10ff.

Temperley, H. The treaty of Paris and its execution. 1932. 4 J. Modern Hist. 387—, 523—.

Three peace congresses of the nineteenth century, by C. D. Hazen, W. R. Thayer, R. H. Lord. Cambridge, Mass., Harvard Univ. Press, 1917. (Includes bibliographies)

TREATY OF BERLIN (1878)

Avril, Adolphe. Négociations relatives au traité de Berlin et aux arrangements qui ont suivi, 1875-1886 . . . Avec six croquis topographiques et le text du traité de 1878. Paris, E. Leroux, 1886.

Berner, Albert Friedrich. Die orientfrage. Beantwortet durch die verträge von 1856 und 1878. Mit den wichtigsten amtlichen urkunden. Zum handgebrauch. Berlin, Puttkammer & Mühlbrecht, 1878.

Bonghi, Ruggiero. Il congrèsso di Berlino e la crisi d'oriente; seguito dal testo completo dei protocolli della conferenza . . . dei trattati di s. Stefano e di Berlino e d'altri documenti, e corredato da due carte geografiche dei nuovi confini della Turchia e degli altri stati greco-slavi. Milano, Fratelli Treves, 1878.

Kohler, Max J. and Wolf, Simon. Jewish disabilities in the Balkan states; American contributions toward their removal with particular reference to the congress of Berlin. Baltimore, Pub. by the Lord Baltimore Press for the American Jewish Society. 1916. (pub. no. 24)

Maiwald, Serge. Der Berliner kongress, 1878, und das völkerrecht; die lösung des Balkanproblems im 19. jahrhundert, Stuttgart, Wissenschaftliche Verlagsgesellschaft, 1948.

Medlicott, W. N. The congress of Berlin and after; a diplomatic history of the near eastern settlement 1878-1880. London, Methuen, 1938.

Stern, Fritz. Gold and iron; Bismarck, Bleichröder and the building of the German empire. New York, Knopf, 1977. (Chap. 14, Rumania: the triumph of expediency)

Winckler, Martin. Bismarcks Rumänienpolitik und die durchführung des artikels 44 des Berliner vertrages, 1878-1880. München, 1951.

THE ARMENIAN QUESTION (1914-1918)

Lepsius, Johannes, ed. Deutschland und armenien 1914-1918. Potsdam, Der Templeverlag, 1919.

Toynbee, Arnold J., ed. The treatment of the Armenians in the Ottoman empire 1915-16: documents presented to Viscount Grey . . . secretary of state for foreign affairs, by Viscount Bryce, with a pref. by Lord Bryce. London, H.M.S.O., 1916. (Cmd. 8325)

WOODROW WILSON

Baker, Ray Stannard.
  Woodrow Wilson: life and letters. Vols. V-VIII (1914-1918). New
    York, Doubleday, 1935-39.
  Woodrow Wilson and the world settlement. New York, Doubleday,
    1922. 3v.
Carlisle, Charles H. Woodrow Wilson's panAmerican pact (1913-17).
  1949. So. Carolina Hist. Ass'n. Proc. 3-16, notes.
Blum, John Morton. Woodrow Wilson and the politics of morality. 1st
  ed. Boston, Little, Brown, 1956.
Grzybowski, Kazimierz. Woodrow Wilson on law, state and society.
  1962. 30 Geo. Wash. L. Rev. 808-52.
Jacobs, David. An American conscience; Woodrow Wilson's search for
  world peace. New York, Harper & Row, 1973.
Lansing, Robert. The peace negotiations, a personal narrative. Port
  Washington, N.Y., Kennikat Press, 1969.
Link, Arthur Stanley.
  Wilson. Princeton, Princeton Univ. Press, 1947-65. 5v. (See v.4 and
    5.)
  Wilson the diplomatist; a look at his major foreign policies. Balti-
    more, Johns Hopkins Press, 1957.
Pomerance, Michla. The United States and self-determination: per-
  spectives on the Wilsonian conception. 1976. 70 Am. J. Int'l. L.
  1-27.
President Wilson on the United States and Latin America; address
  . . . October 27, 1913. Boston, World Peace Foundation, 1913.
  (Pam. ser., v.III)

Human Rights Between the Two World Wars

THE LEAGUE OF NATIONS COVENANT (1919)

Auer, Pál. Plebiscites and the League of Nations covenant. 1921. 6
  Grotius Soc'y. 45-58.
Miller, David Hunter. The drafting of the covenant. New York and
  London, G. P. Putnam's, 1928. 2v.
Pollock, Frederick. The League of Nations. London, Stevens & Sons,
  1920.
Walter, Francis Paul. A history of the League of Nations. London and
  New York, Oxford Univ. Press, 1952. 2v.
Williams, John Fischer. Some aspects of the covenant of the League of
  Nations. London, Oxford Univ. Press, H. Milford, 1934.
Wilson, Florence. The origins of the League covenant: documentary

history of its drafting . . . introd. by P. J. Noel-Baker. London, L. and Virginia Woolf. 1928.

THE ATTEMPT TO PROTECT MINORITIES BY TREATY

Azcárate y Florez, Pablo de. The League of Nations and national minorities: an experiment. Trans. from the Spanish by Eileen Brooke. Washington, Carnegie Endowment for International Peace, 1945.

Balogh, Arthur von. L'action de la société des nations en matière de protection des minorités. Paris, Editions Internationales, 1937.

Bouffal, B. L'article 19 du pacte de la société des nations et le traité entre la Pologne et les principes puissances alliées et associées du 28 juin 1919 sur la protection des minorités de race, de religion et de langue. 1928. 9 Rev. Droit Int'l. et Législation Comparée 882-905.

Documents relating to the protection of minorities by the League of Nations. (Published in accordance with the council resolution of June 13, 1929) Geneva, 1929. (League of Nations. Official journal, spec. supp. 73)

Les droits des minorités nationales; rapport présenté par M. le baron Th. Adelswärd à la XXe conférence interparlementaire, Vienne 1922. 1923. 5 Société des Nations 694-715.

Dugdale, E. The working of the minority treaties. March 1926. 5 J. Brit. Inst. Int'l. Affairs 79-91.

Dupuis, C. L'envers de Trianon. Le conflit juridique roumano-hongrois. 1927. 99 Correspondant 526-41.

Feinberg, Nathan.
   La juridiction et la jurisprudence de la cour permanente de justice internationale en matière de mandat et de minorités (In Hague. Académie de droit international. Recueil des cours 1937, I, v.59, 587-708).
   La question des minorités à la conférence de la paix de 1919-1920 et l'action juive en faveur de la protection internationale des minorités. Paris, Conseil pour les Droits des Minorités Juives, 1929.

La France contre la révision du traité de Trianon. 1928. 10 Rev. des Balkans 303-35.

Haase, B. Die liquidation des vermögens der sogenannten geburtspolen gemäss art. 297 des vertrages von Versailles. 1926. 55 Juristische Wochenschrift 2809-2913.

Heyking, Al'fons A.
   The international protection of minorities—the Achilles' heel of the League of Nations (In Grotius society, Problems of peace and war. London, 1928, v.13, 31-49).

Quelques defectuosités dans la protection des minorités. 1923. 36 Rev. de Genève 766-76.

League of Nations. Council. Protection of linguistic, racial or religious minorities by the League of Nations. Resolutions and extracts . . . resolution and reports adopted by the assembly, relating to the procedures to be followed in questions concerning the protection of minorities. Geneva, 1929.

League of Nations. Secretariat. Minorities Section. Protection des minorités par la société des nations. Exposé historique et juridique par Helmer Rosting. Geneva, 1925.

Lowenfeld, Erwin. The protection of private property under the minorities protection treaties (In Grotius society, Problems of peace and war. London, 1931, v.16, 41-64).

Macartney, Carlile A.
National states and national minorities. London, Oxford Univ. Press, H. Milford, 1934.
A select list of references on minorities. 1930. 9 J. Royal Inst. Int'l. Aff. 819-25.

Nova, Rodolfo de. The international protection of national minorities and human rights. 1965. 11 How. L. J. 275-90.

Palmieri, A. La questione ebraica nella Polonia. 1922. 118 Vita Italiana 299-305.

Robinson, Jacob. From protection of minorities to promotion of human rights. 1948. Jewish Yb. Int'l. L. 115-51.

Robinson, Jacob and others. Were the minorities treaties a failure? New York, Institute of Jewish Affairs, 1943.

Rosting, Helmer. Protection of minorities by the League of Nations. 1923. 17 Am. J. Int'l. L. 641-60.

Sereni, Angelo Piero.
Il diritto internazionale delle minoranze. 1929. 21 Riv. Diritto Internazionale 461-500.
Il diritto internazionale delle minoranze—la garanzia internazionale delle norme per la protezione delle minoranze. 1930. 22 Riv. Diritto Internazionale 45-61.

Sottile, A. La limite de la compétence du conseil de la S.d.N. aux termes de l'art. 11 du pacte de la S.d.N. et le conflit roumano-hongrois au sujet des optants hongrois. 1927. 5 Rev. Droit Int'l. (Genève) 280-306.

Stone, Julius. International guaranties of minority rights; procedure of the council of the League of Nations in theory and practice. London, Oxford Univ. Press, H. Milford, 1932.

Stowell, Ellery C. Intervention in international law. Washington, D.C., John Byrne & Co, 1921.

United Nations. Secretary-General. Treaties and international instruments concerning the protection of minorities, 1919-1951. New York? 1951. (E/CN.4/sub.2/133)

United Nations. Sub-commission on Prevention of Discrimination and Protection of Minorities. The international protection of minorities under the League of Nations. Lake Success, 1947. (E/CN.4/sub.2/6)

Viefhaus, Erwin. Die minderheitenfrage und die entstehung der minderheitenschutzverträge auf der Pariser friedenskonferenz 1919; eine studie zur geschichte des nationalitätenproblems im 19. und 20. jahrhundert. Würzburg, Holzner, 1960.

Vishniak, Mark V. La protection des droits des minorités dans les traités internationaux de 1919-1920. Paris, 1920.

Woolsey, T. S. The rights of minorities under the treaty with Poland. 1920. 14 Am. J. Int'l. L. 392-96.

Human Rights—Post World War II Era

Selected National Documents

Italian Peace Treaty (1947)
Albrecht-Carrié, René. The Italian treaty. 1948. 257 Annals 76-86.

West German Basic Law (1949)
Brecht, Arnold. Re-establishing German government. 1950. 267 Annals 28-42.

Friedrich, Carl J. Rebuilding the German constitution, I. 1949. 43 Am. Pol. Sci. Rev. 461-82; pt. II, 704-20.

Germany (Territory under Allied occupation, 1945—U.S. zone). Office of Military Government. Civil administration division. Documents on the creation of the German federal constitution. Berlin, 1949.

Mason, John Brown. Federalism—the Bonn model (In Zurcher, A. J., ed., Constitutions and constitutional trends since World War II. New York, New York Univ. Press, 1951, 134-53).

Indian Constitution (1949)
Austin, Granville. The Indian constitution: cornerstone of a nation. Oxford, Clarendon Press, 1966.

Gajendragadkar, Pralhad Balacharya. The constitution of India; its philosophy and basic postulates. Nairobi, Pub. for University College by Oxford Univ. Press. 1969.

Gledhill, Alan. The republic of India: the development of its laws and constitution. London, Stevens, 1964.

Jennings, William Ivor. Some characteristics of the Indian constitution, being lectures given . . . under the Sir Alladi Krishnaswami Aiyar Shashtiabdapoorthi endowment. Madras; New York, Indian Branch, Oxford Univ. Press. 1953.

Krishnaswami Aiyar, Alladi. The constitution and fundamental rights. With a foreword by C. P. Ramaswamy Aiyar. Madras, Srinivasa Sastri Institute of Politics, 1955.

Kulshreshtha, V. D. Landmarks in Indian legal history and constitutional history. 2d ed. Lucknow, Eastern Book Co., 1968.

Narain, Brahmadeva. Constitutional restrictions, incorporating the relevant portions of the constitutions of America, Australia and Canada. 1st ed. Patna, International Book Co., 1953.

Pylee, M. V. India's constitution. London, Asia Pub. House, 1962.

Shukla, V. N. Commentaries on the constitution of India. Fwd. by M. H. Kidwai, 2d ed. Lucknow, Eastern Book Co., 1956.

Venkatarama Aiyar, T. L. The evolution of the Indian constitution. Bombay, Univ. of Bombay, 1970.

UNITED NATIONS

Charter (1945)

Bentwich, Norman and Martin, Andrew. A commentary on the charter of the United Nations, with an appendix on the developments of the charter between May 1949 and March 1951. London, Routledge & Kegan Paul, 1951.

Ermacora, Felix. Human rights and domestic jurisdiction; art. 2, sec. 7 of the United Nations charter (In Hague. Academy of international law. Recueil des cours II, 1968, v.124, 371-451).

Goodrich, Leland Matthew. Charter of the United Nations; commentary and documents, by Goodrich, Edvard Hambro and Anne Patricia Simons. 3d rev. ed. New York, Columbia Univ. Press, 1969.

Jenks, C. Wilfred. The world beyond the charter. London, Allen & Unwin, 1969.

Lauterpacht, Hersch. Human rights, the charter of the United Nations, and the international bill of the rights of man; preliminary report. Lake Success, 1948. (E/CN.4/89)

Newman, Frank C. Interpreting the human rights clauses of the UN charter. 1972. 5 Rev. Droits de l'Homme 283-91.

Schlüter, Bernard. The domestic status of the human rights clauses of the United Nations charter. 1973. 61 Calif. L. Rev. 110-64.

Self-executing treaties and the human rights provisions of the United Nations charter: a separation of powers problem. 1976. 25 Buffalo L. Rev. 773-86.

Sohn, Louis B. The human rights law of the charter. 1977. 12 Texas Int'l. L. J. 129-40.

United Nations. Carta de la naciones unidas y estatutos de la corte internacional de justicia. Con una breve introd. por Luis Antonio Eguiguren. Lima, Librería e Impr. Gil, 1968.

Protection of Minorities

Bagley, T. H. General principles and problems in the international protection of minorities: a political study. Geneva, 1950.

Branchu, Francoise. Le problème des minorités en droit international depuis la seconde guerre mondiale. Lyon, Bosc., 1959.

Bruegel, J. W. A neglected field, the protection of minorities. 1971. 4 Rev. Droits de l'Homme 413-42.

Claude, Inis L., Jr. National minorities: an international problem. Cambridge, Mass., Harvard Univ. Press, 1955.

Green, L. C. Protection of minorities in the League of Nations and the United Nations (In Gotlieb, A., ed., Human rights, federalism and minorities. Toronto, Canadian Inst. of International Affairs, 1970, 180-210).

Haksar, Urmila. Minority protection and international bill of human rights. Bombay, Allied Pub., 1974.

King, Robert R. Minorities under communism: nationalities as a source of tension among Balkan communist countries. Cambridge, Mass., Harvard Univ. Press, 1973.

Maver, B. La nazioni unite e la protezione delle minoranze. 1964. 31 Riv. Studi Politici Internazionali 536-64.

Tchirkovitch, S. La protection de l'individu et des minorités nationales d'après les traités diplomatiques du début du XVIIIème siecle à nos jours. Cours. Paris, 1948.

United Nations. Commission on Human Rights. Report of the twenty-third session of the subcom. on prevention of discrimination and protection of minorities to the commission on human rights. New York, 1970. IV. (E/CN.4/1040, E/CN.4/sub.2/316)

United Nations. Secretary-General.

Recommendations to governments concerning the application of special measures for the protection of minorities: study of the whole question, including definition of the term "minority" for the purpose of such recommendations. New York, 1953. (E/CN.4/sub.2/151)

Study of the legal validity of the undertakings concerning minorities. Lake Success, 1950. (E/CN.4/367)

Treaties and international instruments concerning the protection of minorities, 1919-1951. New York? 1951. (E/CN.4/sub.2/133)

Veiter, T. Commentary on the concept of "national minorities." 1974. 7 Rev. Droits de l'Homme 273-90.

Vukas, Budislav. General international law and the protection of minorities. 1975. 8 Rev. Droits de l'Homme 41-49.

Whitaker, Ben, ed. The fourth world: victims of group oppression; eight reports from the field work of the minority rights group. New York, Schocken Books, 1973.

The Universal Declaration of Human Rights (1948)

Asbeck, Frederick M. van. The universal declaration of human rights and its predecessors (1679-1948). Leiden, Brill, 1949.

Autour de la nouvelle déclaration des droits de l'homme; textes réunis par l'Unesco. Introd. de Jacques Maritain. Paris, Sagittaire, 1949.

Cassin, René.

La déclaration universelle et la mise en oeuvre des droits de l'homme (In Hague. Academy of international law. Recueil des cours II, 1951, v.79, 237-67).

Historique de la déclaration universelle de 1948 (In his La pensée et l'action. Boulogne-sur-Seine, Lalou, 1972, 103-18).

De la place fait aux devoirs de l'individu dans la déclaration universelle des droits de l'homme (In Modinos collection, 1968, 479, Paris, Pédone).

Clark, R. and Nevas, L. The first 25 years of the universal declaration of human rights, and the next. 1974. 48 Conn. B. J. 111-60.

Droits de l'homme 1968-1973. Numéro spécial consacré aux droits de l'homme, à l'occasion du vingt-cinquième anniversaire de la déclaration universelle des droits de l'homme. 1974. Annales de Droit 217.

Fisher, Dorothea Frances. A fair world for all; the meaning of the declaration of human rights; with a foreword by Eleanor Roosevelt. New York, Whittlesey House, 1952.

Malik, Charles Habib and Roosevelt, Eleanor R. The covenant on human rights. Lake Success, 1949. (Reprinted from UN bulletin, July 1, 1949.)

Marie, Jean-Bernard. Les pactes internationaux relatifs aux droits de l'homme confirment-ils inspiration de la déclaration universelle? 1970. 3 Rev. Droits de l'Homme 397-425.

Robinson, Nehemiah. Universal declaration of human rights; its origins, significance and interpretation. New York, Institute of Jewish Affairs, World Jewish Congress, 1950.

Schwelb, Egon. Human rights and the international community; the roots and growth of the universal declaration of human rights, 1948-1963. Chicago, Quadrangle Books, 1964.

Sohn, Louis B. The universal declaration of human rights. A common standard of achievement? The status of the universal declaration in international law. 1967. 8 (2) J. Int'l. Comm'n. of Jurists 17-26.

Sorensen, Max. Den internationale beskyttelse af menneskerettighederne. Kobenhavn, Munksgaard, 1967.

United Nations. Collation of the comments of governments on the draft international declaration on human rights and the question of implementation. Lake Success, 1948. (E/CN.4/85)

United Nations. Dep't. of Social Affairs. The impact of the universal declaration of human rights. Rev. ed. New York, 1953. (ST/SOA/5/Rev. 1)

Vegleris, Ph. Principe d'égalité dans la déclaration universelle et la convention européenne des droits de l'homme (In Ganshof van der Meersch collection, I, 565-88; Bruxelles, Bruylant).

Verdoodt, Albert. Naissance et significance de la déclaration universelle des droits de l'homme. Louvain, E. Warny, 1964.

Convention on the Prevention and Punishment of Genocide (1951)

Convention on the prevention and punishment of the crime of genocide, Paris, 9 December 1948. London, H.M.S.O. 1970. (Gt. Brit. Foreign and Commonwealth Off., treaty ser. no. 58, Cmnd. 4421)

Horowitz, Irving Louis. Genocide: state power and mass murder. 2d New Brunswick, N.J., Transaction Books, 1977.

Robinson, Nehemiah.
  The genocide convention; a commentary. New York, Institute of Jewish Affairs, World Jewish Congress, 1960.
  The genocide convention; its origins and interpretation. New York, Institute of Jewish Affairs, World Jewish Congress, 1949.

Graven, Jean. Les crimes contre l'humanité (In Hague. Academy of international law. Recueil des cours I, 1950, v.76, 433-522).

Levasseur, G. The prevention of genocide. 1967. 8 (2) J. Int'l. Comm'n. of Jurists 74-82.

The Rights of Women

Bokor-Szegš, H. L'effet exercé par le progrès social sur les traités internationaux assurant les droits des femmes. 1975. 18 Allam-és Jogtudomány 353-81.

Boly, F. La condition de la femme dans la communauté internationale. 1974. Mem. I.H.E.I.

Bruce, Margaret K. Work of the United Nations relating to the status of women. 1971. 4 Rev. Droits de l'Homme 365-412.

Commission to study the organization of peace. International protection of women's rights: preliminary report. New York, 1975.

Convention on Political Rights of Women. Political rights of women:

convention between the United States of America and other governments. New York, March 31, 1953. Washington, Gov't. Print. Off., 1976. (Eng., Chinese, French, Russian, Spanish)

Guggenheim, Malvina H. The implementation of human rights by the UN commission on the status of women: a brief comment. 1977. 12 Texas Int'l. L. J. 239-49.

Inter-American convention granting of political rights to women between the United States of America and other governments, signed at Bogotà, May 2, 1948. Washington, Gov't. Print. Off., 1976. (Eng., French, Portuguese, Spanish)

McDougal, Myres S., Lasswell, Harold D., and Chen, Lung-chu. Human rights for women and world public order: the outlawing of sex-based discrimination. 1975. 69 Am. J. Int'l. L. 497-533.

Organization of American States. General Legal Division. Inter-American conventions on women. Washington, 1972. (OEA/Ser.X/8— treaty ser. 38)

Shelton, Dinah L. Women and the right to education. 1975. 8 Rev. Droits de l'Homme 51-70.

Taubenfeld, R. F. and Taubenfeld, H. J. Achieving the human rights of women: the base line, the challenge, the search for a strategy. 1975. 4 Human Rights 125-69.

Tomsić, V. Ujedinjene nacije i položaj žena. 1976. 23 (1/2) Jugoslovenska Revija za Medunarodno Pravo 31-46. (summ. in Eng.)

United Nations. Commission on the Status of Women. International instruments relating to the status of women. Implementation of the declaration on the elimination of discrimination against women. Report of the secretary-general, July 28, 1976. New York, 1976. (E/CN.6/592)

United Nations. Dep't. of Economic and Social Affairs. The convention on the political rights of women; history and commentary. New York, 1955. (ST/SOA/27)

United Nations. Dep't. of Social Affairs. The road to equality; political rights of women. New York, 1953. (ST/SOA/13)

Women and the UN (special issue). 1975. 7 (1) UNITAR News 1-58.

Racial Discrimination

Bitker, Bruno V. The international treaty against racial discrimination. 1970. 53 Marquette L. Rev. 68-93.

Buergenthal, Thomas. Implementing the UN racial convention. 1977. 12 Texas Int'l. L. J. 187-221.

Cassese, A. Il sistema di garanzia della convenzione dell'ONU sulla discriminazione razziale (In Studi in memoria di Carlo Esposito, Padova, Cedam, 591-646).

Coleman, D. H. The problem of antisemitism under the international convention on the elimination of all forms of racial discrimination. 1969. 2 Rev. Droits de l'Homme 609-31.

Das, Kamleshwar. Measures of implementation of the international convention on the elimination of all forms of racial discrimination with special reference to the provisions concerning efforts from states parties to the convention. 1971. 4 Rev. Droits de l'Homme 213-62.

Declaration on elimination of racial discrimination [adopted by the UN general assembly, Nov. 20, 1963: includes text]. Jan. 1964. 11 U.N. Rev. 35-39.

Décennie de la lutte contre le racisme et la discrimination raciale, 1973-1983. Ottawa, Secrétariat d'Etat, 1975.

Elkind, J. B. Discrimination: a guide for the fact finder. International convention on the elimination of all forms of racial discrimination. 1971. 32 U. Pitt. L. Rev. 307-46.

Lerner, Natan.
Anti-semitism as racial and religious discrimination under United Nations conventions. 1971. 1 Israel Yb. on Human Rights 103-15.
The U.N. convention on the elimination of all forms of racial discrimination. Leyden, Sijthoff, 1970.

M'Baye, Kéba. Les réalités du monde noir et les droits de l'homme (summ. in Eng.). 1969. 2 Rev. Droits de l'Homme 383-92.

Moskowitz, Moses. The narrowing horizons of United Nations concern with racial discrimination. 1971. 4 Rev. Droits de l'Homme 278-92.

Paladin, L. Il divieto di discriminazione e la convenzione europa dei diritto dell'uomo. 1974. 57 Riv. Diritto Internazionale 446-53.

Petzold, H. Gegenwärtige wirkungsbereich der europäischen menschenrechtskonvention und ihrer zusatzprotikolle, der konvention zur beseitigung aller formen von rassendiskriminierung sowie der menschenrechtspakte der vereinten nationen. 1970. 30 Zeitschrift für Offentliches Recht 400-26.

Regout, A. Het implementatiestelsel van de conventie tot uitbanning van rassendiscriminatie. 1972. 26 Internationale Spectator 2038-61.

Reisman, W. M. Responses to crimes of discrimination and genocide: an appraisal of the convention on the elimination of racial discrimination. 1971. 1 Denver J. Int'l. L. & Polit. 29-64.

Santa Cruz, Hernán. Racial discrimination. Rev. and updated version, 1976. New York, United Nations, 1977.

Schachter, Oscar. How effective are measures against racial discrimination. 1971. 4 Rev. Droits de l'Homme 293-310.

Schreiber, Marc. L'année internationale de la lutte contre le racisme et la discrimination raciale. 1971. 4 Rev. Droits de l'Homme 311-40.

Schwelb, Egon. International convention on the elimination of all forms of racial discrimination. 1966. 15 Int'l. & Comp. L. Q. 996-1068.

Souliotis, Y. L'application des résolutions de l'O.N.U. relatives à la discrimination raciale par les institutions spécialisées. 1973. 6 Rev. Droits de l'Homme 303-28.

The United Nations and race: will United Nations law affect victims of racial discrimination and oppressors? [Panel: F. C. Newman, E. R. Richardson, R. Hauser, T. T. B. Koh, W. T. Coleman, Jr.] 1970. Am. Soc'y. Int'l. L. Proc. 106-30.

United Nations. Comm. on Human Rights. Subcom. on prevention of discrimination. Special study of racial discrimination in the political, economic, social and cultural spheres. June 24, 1969. New York, 1969. (E/CN.4/Sub.2/301)

International Covenant on Economic, Social and Cultural Rights (1966)

Bossuyt, M. La distinction juridique entre les droits civils et politiques et les droits économiques, sociaux et culturels. 1975. 8 Rev. Droits de l'Homme 783-820.

Ganji, Manouchehr. Question of the realization of the economic, social and cultural rights contained in the universal declaration of human rights and in the international covenant on economic, social and cultural rights in developing countries; the widening gap. . . . Rev. observations, conclusions and recommendations. New York, United Nations, 1974. (F/CN.4/1131)

Human rights questions (In United Nations yearbook. New York, Office of Public Information, 1966, 406-88).

Ramcharan, B. G. Implementation of the international covenant on economic, social and cultural rights. 1976. 23 Netherlands Int'l. L. Rev. 151-61.

Schwelb, Egon. Some aspects of the measures of implementation of the international covenant on economic, social and cultural rights. 1968. 1 Rev. Droits de l'Homme 363-77.

International Covenant on Civil and Political Rights (1966)

Carey, John. UN protection of civil and political rights. Syracuse, Syracuse Univ. Press, 1970.

Eissen, M.-A. The European convention on human rights and the United Nations covenant on civil and political rights: problems of coexistence. 1972. 22 Buffalo L. Rev. 181-218. [See also 30 Zeitschrift für Ausländisches Offentliches Recht 237-52 (1970).]

Entrée en vigueur du pacte international relatif aux droits civils et politiques, ainsi que du protocole facultatif se rapportant audit pacte. 1976. 9 Rev. Droits de l'Homme 131-90.

Human rights questions (In United Nations yearbook. New York, Office of Public Information, 1966, 406-88).

Meyer, Jan de. La convention européenne des droits de l'homme et le pacte international relatif aux droits civils et politiques. Luxembourg; Heule, Editions UGA. 1968.

Modinos, Polys. Coexistence de la convention européenne des droits de l'homme et du pacte des droits civils et politiques des nations unies. 1968. 1 Rev. Droits de l'Homme 41-69.

Robertson, A. H. United Nations covenant on civil and political rights and the European convention on human rights. 1968-69. 43 Brit. Yb. Int'l. L. 21-48.

Schwelb, Egon.
Civil and political rights; the international measures of implementation. 1968. 62 Am. J. Int'l. L. 827-68.

Entry into force of the international covenants on human rights and the optional protocol to the international covenant on civil and political rights. 1976. 70 Am. J. Int'l. L. 511-19.

The international measures of implementation of the international covenant on civil and political rights and of the optional protocol. 1977. 12 Texas J. Int'l. L. 141-86.

Nature of the obligations of the states parties to the international covenant on civil and political rights (In Cassin collection, 301, Paris, Pédone, 1969).

Zanghi, Claude. La liberté d'expression dans la convention européenne des droits de l'homme et dans le pacte des nations unies relatif aux droits civils et politiques (comparaison des dispositions respectives). 1970. Rev. Générale Droit Int'l. Public 573-89.

Proclamation of Teheran (1968)

Capotorti, F. La conferenza di Teheran sui diritti dell'uomo. 1968. 23 Comuniti Internazionali 609-29.

Cassese, A. Conferenza internazionale di Teheran sui diritti dell'uomo. 1968. 51 Riv. Diritto Internazionale 669—.

Cassin, René. La proclamation de Téhéran (mai 1968). 1968. 1 Rev. Droits de l'Homme 324-31. (French and English)

United Nations action in the field of human rights. New York, United Nations, 1974. (ST/HR/2) (Based on two studies submitted to the International Conference on Human Rights, Teheran, 1968.)

EUROPEAN CONVENTION ON HUMAN RIGHTS

Antonopoulos, Nicolas. La jurisprudence des organes de la convention européenne des droits de l'homme. Leyden, Sijthoff, 1967.

Barsotti, Roberto. Tendenze evolutive nell'interpretazione della convenzione europea dei diritto dell'uomo. 1976. 59 Riv. Diritto Internazionale 268-90.

Bobbio, Norberto. Il preambolo della convenzione europea dei diritto dell'uomo. 1974. 57 Riv. Diritto Internazionale 437-45.

Cassin, René, Modinos, Polys, and Vasak, Karel. 25ᵉ Anniversaire de la convention européenne des droits de l'homme, 4 novembre 1950-4 novembre 1975; l'europe et les droits de l'homme. 1975. 8 Rev. Droits de l'Homme (no. spécial) 687-770.

Castberg, Frede. The European convention on human rights. Ed. by Torkel Opsahl and Thomas Ouchterlony; trans. from the Norwegian by Gytte Borch. Leiden, Sijthoff; Dobbs Ferry, N.Y., Oceana Pub. 1974.

Les clauses facultatives de la convention européenne des droits de l'homme. Bari, Levante, 1974.

Condorelli, L. Diritti politici nella convenzione europea dei diritti dell'uomo. 1971. 54 Riv. Diritto Internazionale 189-225.

Council of Europe.
European convention on human rights; collected texts. 10 ed. Strasbourg, 1975. 1v. (English and French)
Rapports et documents relatifs à la convention européenne des droits de l'homme. Strasbourg. (irreg., also in English)
Comm. on Experts on Human Rights. Human rights; problems arising from the coexistence of the United Nations covenant on human rights and the European convention on human rights. Differences as regards the rights guaranteed. Strasbourg, 1970.
Directorate of Human Rights. European convention on human rights; national aspects. Strasbourg, 1975. (text partly in English and French)

Danelius, Hans. A survey of the jurisprudence concerning the rights protected by the European convention on human rights. 1975. 8 Rev. Droits de l'Homme 431-73.

Daubie, Christian. La convention européenne des droits de l'homme et la raison d'état. 1970. 3 Rev. Droits de l'Homme 247-74.

Denecke, Uwe. Die humanitäre intervention und ihr verhältnis zum rechtschutzsystem der europäischen menschenrechtskonvention. Ein beitrag zum stand der menschenrechte im völkerrecht und zur problematik der völkerrechtlichen intervention. Würzburg, 1972.

Draper, G. I. A. D. Implementation of the European convention on human rights, 1950. 1972. 2 Israel Yb. on Human Rights 121-41.

Le droit à l'éducation dans le monde actuel. Liège, Science et Lettres; Paris, Sirey. n.d.

European Commission on Human Rights. Les droits de l'homme et leurs limitations. Strasbourg, Conseil de l'Europe, 1974.

Expulsion and expatriation in international law; the right to leave, to stay, and to return (In Proceedings, American Society of International Law, 67th meeting, 1973. Washington, 1974, 122-40).

Fawcett, J. E. S.
The application of the European convention on human rights. Oxford, Clarendon Press, 1969.

The European convention on human rights: recent trends. 1971. 24 Current Leg. Prob. 246-56. (4th protocol)

Higgins, R. The human right of Soviet Jews to leave: violations and obstacles. 1974. 4 Israel Yb. on Human Rights 275-87.

Hoffmann-Remy, Ulrich. Die möglichkeiten der grundrechtseinschränkung nach den art. 8-11 abs. 2 der europäischen menschenrechtskonvention; dargestellt anhand von beispielfällen aus der rechtssprechung der konventionsorgane und nationaler gerichte. Berlin, Duncker und Humblot, 1976.

Human rights: the European convention and its national application (a collection of articles on the European convention on human rights, adopted by fifteen European states). 1970. 18 Am. J. Comp. L. 233-366.

Jacobs, Francis G. The European convention on human rights. Oxford, Clarendon Press, 1975.

Kiss, Alexandre C. La protection internationale du droit de l'enfant à l'éducation. 1973. 6 Rev. Droits de l'Homme 467-86.

Marin Lopez, A. Derechos del hombre en el consejo de europa: el cuarto y quinto protocolos al convenio europeo de 1950. 1968. 21 Rev. Española Derecho Internacional 483—.

McNulty, A. B. Note sur les résultats obtenus par la convention des droits de l'homme, 1953-1972. 1972. 50 Rev. Droit Int'l. Sciences Diplomatiques et Politiques 82-118.

Modinos, Polys.
La convention européenne des droits de l'homme; ses origines, ses objectifs, ses réalisations. 1975. 8 Rev. Droits de l'Homme (no. spécial) 689-716.

Perspectives d'avenir de la convention. 1975. 8 Rev. Droits de l'Homme (no. spécial) 737-52.

Monconduit, François. La commission européenne des droits de l'homme. Leyden, Sijthoff, 1965.

Nanda, Ved P. The right to travel: an international human right? 1971. 1 Denver J. Int'l. L. & Policy 109-22.

Nett, R. The civil right we are not ready for: the right of free movement of people on the face of the earth. 1971. 81 Ethics 212-27.

Robertson, A. H. Promotion of human rights by the council of Europe. 1975. 8 Rev. Droits de l'Homme 545-85.

Sand, M. La quatrième protocole additionnelle à la convention européenne des droits de l'homme. 1964. Ann. Français Droit Int'l. 569-75.

Schwelb, Egon. The protection of the rights of nations under the first protocol to the European convention on human rights. 1964. 13 Am. J. Comp. L. 518-51.

Sorensen, Max. Diritti iscritti nella convenzione dei diritti dell'uomo nel 1950 hanno lo stesso significato nel 1975? 1975. 15 Riv. Diritto Europeo 267-300.

Stoiber, Carlton R. The right to liberty: a comparison of the European convention on human rights with United States practice. 1976. 5 Human Rights 333-63.

Selective bibliography of publications concerning the European convention on human rights. 1974. 22 European Yb. 782-86.

Strasbourg. Université. Centre d'études internationales. Bibliographie concernant la convention européenne des droits de l'homme. 2 ed. Strasbourg, 1969.

Turack, Daniel C. Freedom of movement and the travel document. Winter 1973. 4 Calif. West. Int'l. L.J. 8-42.

Varela Feijóo, Jacobo. La protección de los derechos humanos; jurisprudencia de la comisión y tribunal europeo de derechos del hombre. Barcelona, Editorial Hispano Europea, 1972.

Vasak, Karel. La convention européenne des droits de l'homme. Paris, Librairie Gén. de Droit et de Jurisprudence, 1964.

Verdross, A. Place de la convention européenne des droits de l'homme dans le hiérarchie des normes juridiques. 1969. 13 Comunicazioni e Studi, Univ. di Milano 1-13.

Weil, Gordon Lee. The European convention on human rights: background, development and prospects. Dobbs Ferry, N.Y., Oceana Pub., 1963.

Wiebringhaus, H. Convention européenne des droits de l'homme et la charte sociale européenne. 1975. 8 Rev. Droits de l'Homme 527-44.

Williams, Anne M. The European convention on human rights: a new use? 1977. 12 Texas Int'l. L.J. 279-92.

Wright, John T. The European commission of human rights: an analysis and appraisal. 1977. 3 Brooklyn J. Int'l. L. 119-74.

HUMAN RIGHTS AND THE AMERICAS

American convention on human rights. Convención americana sobre derechos humanos: pacto de San José de Costa Rica. Washington, OAS, 1977. (Serie sobre tratados 36)

Buergenthal, Thomas.
  American convention on human rights: an illusion of progress (In Ganshof van der Meersch collection, I, 385, Bruxelles, Bruylant, 1972).
  The American convention on human rights; illusions and hopes. 1971. 21 Buffalo L. Rev. 121-36.
  The revised OAS charter and the protection of human rights. 1975. 69 Am. J. Int'l. L. 828-36.
Cabranes, José A. The protection of human rights by the organization of American states. 1968. 62 Am. J. Int'l. L. 889-908.
Camargo, Pedro Pablo.
  Convención americana sobre derechos humanos. 1970. 3 Bol. Mexicano Derecho Comparado 272—. [Also in English, 3 Rev. Droits de l'Homme 333-56 (1970).]
  La protección jurídica de los derechos humanos y de la democracia en América; los derechos humanos y el derecho internacional. Prólogo, Luis Becasens Siches. 1.ed. México, Editorial Excelsior, 1960.
  Proyecto de convención interamericana sobre protección de derechos humanos. México, Agencia Mexicana de Noticias, 1969.
Convención americana sobre derechos humanos. 1971. 11 Rev. Derecho Puertorriqueno 237—.
Darrigrande Silva, Jorge. Los derechos humanos en América; estudio comparado entre el derecho vigente en los estados americanos y la declaración americana de los derechos y deberes del hombre. Santiago, Editorial Jurídica de Chile, 1969.
Fontaine, P. M. Les projets de convention interaméricaine des droits de l'homme. Analyses juridiques et considérations politiques. 1969. 1 Rev. Belge Droit Int'l. 146-74.
Fox, Donald T.
  The American convention on human rights and prospects for United States ratification. 1973. 3 Human Rights 243-81.
  The protection of human rights in the Americas. 1968. 7 Colum. J. Transnat'l. L. 222-34.
García Bauer, C. La proyectada convención interamericana de derechos humanos (In Seminario internacional sobre los derechos del hombre, univ. nacional autónoma de México, 1968. Veinte años de evolución de los derechos humanos, México, 1974, 425-61).
Goldman, Robert K. The protection of human rights in the Americas: past, present and future. New York, New York Univ., Center for International Studies. 1972. (Policy papers, v. 5, no. 2.)
Inter-American Commission on Human Rights.
  Anotación sobre el proyecto de convención interamericana sobre

protección de derechos humanos. Washington, Union Panamericana, 1969. (OEA/ser.L/V/II, 19 doc. 53)

Comparative study of the international covenant on human rights together with the optional protocol to the international covenant on civil and political rights . . . the draft convention on human rights of the inter-American council of jurists . . . and the text of the amendments to the IACJ draft . . . adopted October 1966 and January 1967. Washington, Pan American Union, 1968. (OEA/ser.L/V/II.19, doc. 4)

The organization of American states and human rights, 1960-67. Washington, OAS, 1972. (Spanish and English)

International American Conference, 9th, Bogotà, 1948. American declaration of the rights and duties of man, adopted . . . 1948. Rev. Washington, Pan American Union, 1957.

Kutzner, G. Die Amerikanische menschenrechtskonvention von 22 November 1969. 1971. Jahrbuch für Internationales Rect 274-95.

Landry, Walter J. The ideals and potential of the American convention on human rights. 1974-75. 4 Human Rights 395-412.

Moreno Méndez, Adalberto. Las instituciones y las doctrinas americanas, garantía de la independencía de los estados. México, 1954.

Mower, A. Glenn, Jr. The American convention on human rights: will it be effective? 1972. 15 Orbis 1147-72.

Organization of American States. Eighth meeting of consultation of ministers of foreign affairs, Punta del Este, Uruguay, Jan. 22-31, 1962. Final act. Washington, Pan American Union. 1962. (OEA/Ser.C/II.8)

Organization of American States. Dep't. of Legal Affairs. American convention on human rights: "Pact of San José, Costa Rica," signed at the inter-American conference on human rights . . . Nov. 7-22, 1969. Washington, OAS, 1970. (OEA/Ser.A/16, English)

Organization of American States. General Secretariat. Handbook of rules pertaining to human rights. Washington, OAS, 1977.

Pan American Union. Human rights in the American states. Study prepared in accordance with resolution XXVII. 10th inter-American conference. Washington, 1960.

Plaza, L. Antecedentes de la declaración de los derechos del hombre. May 1969. 28 La Justicia (México) 57—.

Ronning, C. Neale. Human rights and humanitarian laws in the western hemisphere. 1971. 38 Social Research 320-36.

Schreiber, Anna P. The inter-American commission on human rights. Leiden, Sijthoff, 1970.

Tardu, M. E. The protocol to the United Nations covenant on civil and political rights and the inter-American system: a study of co-existing procedures. 1976. 70 Am. J. Int'l. L. 778-800.

Thomas, Ann Van Wynen and Thomas, A. J., Jr.
Human rights and the organization of American states. 1972. 12 Santa Clara Law. 319-76.
The inter-American commission of human rights. 1966. 20 Sw. L.J. 282-309.

Uribe Vargas, Diego. Los derechos humanos y el sistema interamericano. Madrid, Ediciones Cultura Hispánica, 1972.

Vasak, Karel.
La commission interaméricaine des droits de l'homme . . . avant-propos de René Cassin. Paris, R. Pichon et Durand-Auzias, 1968.
La protection internationale des droits de l'homme sur le continent américain. 1967. 17 Oesterreichische Zeitschrift Offentliches Recht 113-22.

Zanghi, Claude. La convenzione interamericana dei diritti dell'uomo. 1970. 25 Communità Internazionale 26-97.

ADDITIONAL MATERIALS

Chaldize, Valerii. *Glasnost and social and economic rights*. New York, Freedom House, 1988.

C.P.D.H. report on the situation of human rights in Nicaragua, October 1987. New York, Puebla Institute, 1987.

Gelatt, Timothy A. Human rights in Taiwan, 1986–1987. 1987. Asia Watch, 269.

Human rights in Panama. 1988. iii, 71 Americas Watch, 4.

Inter-American Commission on Human Rights. *Report on the situation of human rights in Paraguay*. General Secretariat, Organization of American States, 1987, vii, 121.

Livezey, Lowell W. U.S. religious organizations and the international human rights movement. February 1989. 9 Human Rights Law Journal, 14-81.

Mendez, Juan E. Truth and partial justice in Argentina. New York, Americas Watch Committee, 1987.

Morgenthau, Hans Joachim. Human rights and foreign policy. New York, Council on Religion and International Affairs, 1979.

Nicaragua, civil liberties, and the central peace plan. Washington, D.C., Puebla Institute, 1988.

The Reagan administration's record on human rights in 1986. Watch Committees (Americas Watch/ Asia Watch/ Helsinki Watch). 1987. Lawyers Committee for Human Rights, iii, 178.

Renamo: the Khmer Rouge of Africa: Mozambique, its killing field. Testimony of the United States Committee for Refugees before the House Subcommittee on Foreign Operations, 1989.

Rubin, Barry M. and Spiro, Elizabeth P., eds. Human rights and U.S. foreign policy. Boulder, Colo. Westview Press, 1979.

Rubin, Barry M. Modern dictators. New York, McGraw-Hill, 1987.

Selby, David. Human rights. Cambridge, Cambridge University Press, 1987.

Stanek, Edward. Human rights. Monticello, Ill., Vance Bibliographies, 1987.

"Tolerating abuses: violations of human rights in Peru. 1988. American Watch Report, 83.

United States Congress. Commission on Security and Cooperation and Europe. Implementation of the Helsinki accords. Washington, D.C., U.S. G.P.O., 1988, iii, 99.

United States Congress. House Committee on Foreign Affairs. Subcommittee on Human Rights and International Organizations. Recent developments in U.S. human rights policy. Washington, D.C., U.S. G.P.O., 1988, iii, 214.

The U.S. and international human rights. 1988. 9, no. Z-3 Human Rights Law Journal, 141-62.

Weschler, Joanna. The persecution of human rights monitors. New York, Human Rights Watch, 1987.

Whitman, Lois. State of flux. New York, Helsinki Watch Committee, 1987.

Zielonka, Jan. Toward a more effective policy for human rights in Eastern Europe. 1988. *Washington Quarterly*, 199-220.